TO DEFEAT THE FEW

OSPREY
PUBLISHING

DEDICATION

This book is dedicated to the life and the memory of

Annette M. 'Annie' Dildy – September 14, 1956 to June 21, 2018

The Light, Love, and Inspiration of My Life – DCD

DOUGLAS C. DILDY AND PAUL F. CRICKMORE

TO DEFEAT THE FEW

THE LUFTWAFFE'S CAMPAIGN TO DESTROY RAF FIGHTER COMMAND,

AUGUST–SEPTEMBER 1940

OSPREY PUBLISHING
Bloomsbury Publishing Plc
PO Box 883, Oxford, OX1 9PL, UK
1385 Broadway, 5th Floor, New York, NY 10018, USA
E-mail: info@ospreypublishing.com
www.ospreypublishing.com

OSPREY is a trademark of Osprey Publishing Ltd

First published in Great Britain in 2020

ISBN: HB 9781472839183; PB 9781472839190; eBook 9781472839176; ePDF 9781472839152; XML 9781472839169

20 21 22 23 24 10 9 8 7 6 5 4 3 2 1

Maps by bounford.com
Diagrams by Adam Tooby
Index by Angela Hall
Originated by PDQ Digital Media Solutions, Bungay, UK
Printed and bound in India by Replika Press Private Ltd.

Front cover: Dornier Do 17Zs from II./KG 3. (Author Collection)
Back cover: Number 85 Squadron Hurricanes. (AHB)
Title page: Four-ship formation from 6./JG 27. (Andy Saunders, colourized by Richard Molloy)

All images marked 'Author Collection' are from the collection of Douglas C. Dildy, with the exception of the image on p.138 (top), which is from the collection of Paul F. Crickmore.

Osprey Publishing supports the Woodland Trust, the UK's leading woodland conservation charity.

To find out more about our authors and books visit **www.ospreypublishing.com**. Here you will find extracts, author interviews, details of forthcoming events and the option to sign up for our newsletter.

CONTENTS

ACKNOWLEDGEMENTS

Eighty years on from that fateful summer of 1940, none but a handful of those brave young pilots remain with us; their memories and nightmares of the life-or-death battles they faced are now diminished with the passage of time. For our research, the authors of this book were therefore reliant on a variety of other sources. The plethora of books written on the subject was certainly one useful stream – as a review of endnotes and bibliography will testify. The quality and reliability of this source varied however, the work of some authors being particularly noteworthy. We'd therefore like to acknowledge the deep and detailed research conducted by Walter Ansel, Christer Bergström, Donald Caldwell, Peter Cornwell, Eddie Creek, Brian Cull, Chris Goss, F.H. Hinsley, E.R. Hooten, T.C.G. James, Eric Mombeek, Andy Saunders, Richard Smith, Douglas Stankey, Telford Taylor, John Vasco, and Henry de Zeng. Of particular note is the benchmark research that underpins books written by the late Dr Alfred Price and Kenneth Wakefield – both of them are true inspirations to anyone interested in reading about or researching the Battle of Britain.

Primary sources were vital and always preferable and for this we were dependent upon the thousands of official records and documents that were written at the time, or shortly thereafter. The majority of these now reside in archives both sides of the Atlantic. As these were essential in identifying and accessing material relevant to our study, we were hugely dependent on the help of some truly gifted and patient archivists. We'd therefore like to thank Sebastian Cox and Stuart Hadaway at the RAF Air Historical Branch, Nina Hadaway at the RAF Museum, Hendon, and Tammy Horton and Sylvester Jackson of the US Air Force Historical Research Agency, for their generous and diligent assistance in 'getting to the bottom' of numerous undiscovered/unreported aspects of – or previously erroneously reported 'facts' about – the Battle of Britain.

Illustrating events leading up to and including the tactical element of the battle required powerful, evocative photographs that would engage the reader and which, ideally, had been rarely seen before. In this endeavour we had the good fortune to work with the best photographic archivists specializing in the subject. We're therefore forever deeply indebted to Lee Barton at the RAF Air Historical Branch (AHB), Brett Stolle at the National Museum of the United States Air Force

(NMUSAF), and Gina McNeely, professional photographic researcher who obtained many relevant images from the US National Archives and Records Administration (NARA). Gratefully, we were also provided access to the abundant private image collections of Daniel Brackx, Chris Goss, Thomas Laemlein, Ryan Noppen, Jean-Louis Roba, Andy Saunders and Clive Ellis.

Controversially – particularly in the case of 'photographic purists' – we decided to supplement several original coloured photographs with digitally colourized images; working with some of the best in the business; we'd therefore like to salute the work of Richard Molloy, Adam Tooby and Gherman Mihaly.

Others who have generously given us their time and support are Phil Dawe and Ray Ballard, who provided us with fascinating and detailed tours of RAF Northolt's Sector Operations Room and No. 11 Group's Operations Room at RAF Uxbridge. Through these tours and subsequent discussions, we learned how the oft-described 'Dowding System' really worked. Darren Priday and John Warburton gave us a wonderful insight into their important work at the Michael Beetham Conservation Centre, RAF Cosford; while Jason Banner painstakingly searched through the memoirs of Air Marshal Tommy Elmhirst at the Winston Churchill Archive, Cambridge, and John Stubbington guided us through the intricacies of the RAF's wartime Intelligence Directorates. Over the many hundreds of hours it has taken to research and write this book, we've both been encouraged and supported by friends and family. In this regard we'd like to thank Neil and Pauline, Nic, Adam, Karen, Phil and Claire, and Janet Capobianco.

Our publishers – Osprey – have as usual, been perfect partners in our endeavour, but we'd particularly like to thank Marcus Cowper for his encouragement, patience, and support of this project – from its very inception – Laura Callaghan for all her diligent working during the editorial phase, and Paul E. Eden for his knowledgeable editorial expertise and, to all three for going that extra mile that makes this work the book that it has become.

But most important of all, we wish to thank our wives – Ali and Annie, for their love, unrelenting encouragement and ceaseless patience – thank you!

If we've forgotten anyone, please accept our apologies. Any oversight was entirely unintentional and an unfortunate consequence of the overwhelming volume of materials, time and effort that it took to create this entirely different account of the Battle of Britain.

FOREWORD

Legend has it that in July 1588, Sir Francis Drake, commander of the English fleet, finished his bowls game before preparing to engage a Spanish fleet intent on invasion. Through clever tactics, a helping of good fortune and in no small part thanks to King Philip II of Spain's choice of a commander with no naval experience to lead his forces, Drake routed the Armada.

A century later, the Glorious Revolution was more or less invasion by invitation; fewer than 20 years after that, England had become part of Great Britain. Some 252 years passed before an altogether more sinister force threatened the British Isles. With France secure, Nazi Germany massed forces ready for a cross-Channel invasion that might solve Adolf Hitler's 'English problem'.

That solution required air superiority, at least while the invasion force was afloat and vulnerable. Air superiority could only be achieved by neutralising Britain's air defences, spearheaded by Royal Air Force Fighter Command.

Sir Hugh Dowding, Air Officer Commanding Fighter Command, recognised the Nazi threat to Great Britain early, keeping fighter aircraft back from France, where he believed they would almost certainly be lost, in readiness for home defence. For too long his squadrons employed obsolete, inflexible tactics when the attack finally came, but 'his' system of early-warning radars and reporting ultimately gave them the edge. Further capitalizing on a helping of good fortune and in no small part thanks to Hitler's choice of a commander with no air campaigning experience to lead his forces, Dowding thwarted the Führer's invasion plans.

The story of this, the Battle of Britain, is well known through biography and autobiography, histories and popular accounts. Surely, nothing new could be written?

In fact, little of the story from the German perspective has been told in English, and still less at a strategic level. We are familiar with the tale of the heroic Few battling hordes of powerful, yet ineptly led foes, but less aware of the strategic aims and operational decisions driving the Luftwaffe's campaign.

Doug Dildy and Paul Crickmore have taken a strategic and operational look at the Battle, deep-diving into primary source material in German, UK and US archives. What they have discovered is that much of the accepted history is based on a 1943 RAF narrative. Its author acknowledged at the time that his supposition must be checked against German records when the opportunity arose. After 80 years, the authors have acted upon his recommendation.

The result is a retelling of the Battle of Britain. It reveals how the Luftwaffe's most capable leaders were hamstrung by delusional commanders and poor, self-serving intelligence. Well-known rivalries and mutual distrust between British commanders are also discussed, but in a depth that shows how vital, perhaps battle-winning intelligence was denied Dowding at his most desperate hour. There is also confirmation, as if it were needed, that the UK and much of the world owe whatever freedom they enjoy to the unimaginably courageous Few and the thousands of men and women who fought so hard to support them on the ground.

But who are these authors to rewrite a story we thought we knew? Doug Dildy is an American… perhaps not the most obvious of starting points. However, as a former fighter pilot and retired US Air Force colonel, he is an expert in air campaigning and brings a modern, trained eye to the Battle. He acknowledges the significance of the Dowding System as key to the RAF's success, but also recognises it as the first example of what today is described as an integrated air defence system. It obliged the Luftwaffe to mount the world's first campaign to counter enemy air defences, an effort that foundered since there was no precedent for neutralizing such a system.

Paul Crickmore is a lifelong lover of all things aircraft, with a particular penchant for the A-12 and SR-71 'Blackbirds' and several definitive books on the type to his name. A former air traffic controller, he brought his insight into RAF airpower to this volume and played an indispensable role in helping navigate the American through the intricacies of research at the UK's premier archives. It's rumoured that several dinners and glasses of wine were amiably consumed along the way.

To Defeat The Few is a masterful, scholarly view of a campaign that most aviation enthusiasts and students of air warfare believe they know well. It will therefore challenge perceptions as much as it entertains. It took a brave authoring duo to see it to its conclusion and it is a particular honour to be asked to write its foreword.

Paul E. Eden
Paul E. Eden is an aerospace writer and editor who writes for the Official RAF Annual Review and Salute publications and contributes regularly to specialist publications.

PROLOGUE

The bookshelves of aviation historians and Battle of Britain enthusiasts alike literally sag and groan under the immense weight of the 80 years' worth of books written about the epic aerial contest that has become known to all English-speaking peoples worldwide as 'the Battle of Britain'. Most are devoted to one particular aspect – or personality – involved in the Battle, but a score or so were intended to be all-encompassing histories of that, history's first-ever independent air campaign.

All of them have one distinct feature in common.

That is, they were all written at the 'tactical level' of warfare – they cover in depth and detail the unit-versus-unit clashes and tactics, seasoned with individual accounts of dramatic, frightening and heroic personal combat. They rarely give more than lip service to the strategic context of this historically seminal campaign and almost no consideration of the antagonists' operational aims, plans, and conduct of the campaign.

How is this book different?

To Defeat The Few is written at the operational level of warfare. That is the classification of military operations lying between unit-versus-unit tactical actions and the national strategic levels of armed conflict – commonly called 'campaigning'.

In writing at this level, our book describes the Luftwaffe's operational theories, doctrine, and philosophies (concepts of operations, or CONOPS, in modern parlance); the operational objectives chosen to attain Hitler's national strategic goals; its plans to achieve those military objectives, and their execution. From the German perspective, the Battle of Britain, *die Luftschlacht um England* (the Air Battle over England), was the Luftwaffe's attempt to destroy RAF Fighter Command, and thereby enable the Wehrmacht's planned cross-Channel invasion of Britain. For context, we will necessarily examine the German (meaning Hitler's) strategic aims and options as well as the ensuing tactical actions that ultimately decided the outcome of the campaign.

Because it is written at the operational level, our account tells the story of the Battle of Britain from the German perspective or point of view. The Luftwaffe initiated all combats against Fighter Command, implementing various and constantly changing plans and tactics as it attempted to achieve its operational objective, so it is proper to describe the campaign, and the many battles that compose it, from its point of view.

However, there are two things this book is not.

It is not in any way an apology, redemption, or glorification of the Nazis, their air force, or their ways and means of bringing death and destruction, hardship and deprivation to the British people.

Second and just as important, it also is not an attempt to diminish the significance of the contributions, the courage, or the sacrifice of 'The Few' – those 2,332 RAF Fighter Command fighter pilots (plus Defiant air gunners and Blenheim Mk IF and Beaufighter Mk IF aircrew) who flew and fought in that desperate struggle against the Luftwaffe in the summer and autumn of 1940.

In fact, the reverse is true.

It is fervently hoped that learning of and understanding the true nature of the vicious bombing campaign and violent air combats that the Luftwaffe imposed upon Fighter Command will increase readers' respect of and appreciation for those brave young men – and 'the Many' of both genders on the ground at various RAF stations – that fought against the Nazis' aerial onslaught; especially for those who died doing so.

To appreciate the Battle of Britain at the operational level of conflict as an independent air campaign conducted by the Luftwaffe, it is necessary to set aside the traditional 'British understanding' of how the four months of combat transpired. This understanding is based largely on the Air Historical Branch's (AHB's) 1943 *RAF Narrative, Volume 2, The Battle of Britain*, in which the author, T.C.G. James, sets out a provisional sequence of events, but notes the requirement to refine his work once access to German records became possible. That refinement seems never to have happened. Those four months are therefore typically described as unfolding through the 'five phases' of the Battle; we, instead, refer to an initial period and then the five 'stages' that German historians use to delineate *die Luftschlact um England*. These are:

The Contact Period: from the end of the French Campaign to 7 August 1940. This includes the Channel Battles period that began on 2 July when commander-in-chief of the Luftwaffe, Hermann Göring, ordered the start of the *Kanalkampf* (Channel battle) maritime air campaign over the English Channel, which is where we choose to start our account because of the operational objectives established and the commander's order to begin. This period roughly correlates to the rather arbitrary, as Air Officer Commanding-in-Chief RAF Fighter Command Air Chief Marshal Sir Hugh Dowding admitted, Battle of Britain Phase I: 10 July through 7 August.

The First Period, Stage 1: 8–23 August, consisting primarily of air attacks against a wide variety of airfields in southern England and naval bases on the Channel coast in preparation for Operation *Sealion* (*Seelöwe*), the amphibious invasion of Britain. Roughly conforms to the British Phase II: 8–18 August. We choose to begin our account of the Luftwaffe air campaign on 12 August because that is when the accomplishment of specific air campaign objectives were set to be attained and the commander said 'Go'.

First Period, Stage 2: 24 August to 6 September, consisting of concentrated air attacks on airfields, principally against No. 11 Group sector stations, to defeat Fighter

RAF vs Luftwaffe Timelines for the Battle of Britain

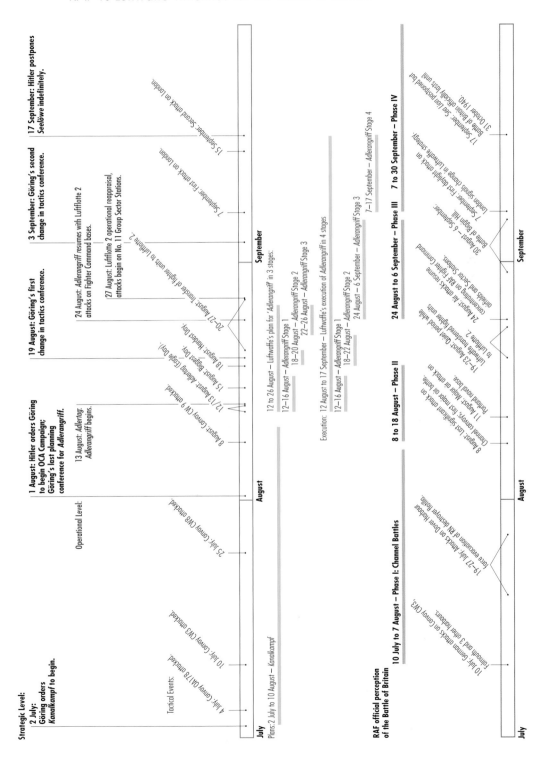

Command and establish air superiority over south-east England – the stated aim of the First Period. Correlates exactly with the British Phase III: 24 August to 6 September.

Second Period, Stage 1: 7 to 19 September, described erroneously by German historian Karl Klee, *The Battle of Britain, Decisive Battles of World War II: The German View* as 'the attack on Britain's economic potential' by initiating bombing against targets in and around London. Conforms roughly with the British Phase IV: 7 to 30 September when London was the principal target for daylight bombing attacks.

Second Period, Stage 2: 20 September to 13 November, which includes 'daylight fighter-bomber attacks and night-bombing raids, chiefly on London'. Correlates roughly with the British Phase V: 1 to 31 October, 'The Decline of the Battle'.

Second Period, Stage 3: 14 November to 21 May 1941, when the final bombing raids over Britain were flown. The Luftwaffe's bombers departed over the next few days for the Eastern Front, in preparation for the Russian campaign. This stage, generally referred to in British histories as the Night Blitz, or simply the Blitz, falls outside the scope of this book and will not be addressed.

With both sides' chronological arrangements known, we have taken a military perspective on the series of Luftwaffe operations, delineating them by the changes in campaign objectives and stratagems. German-language histories of the Battle of Britain typically regard the shift in attacks from RAF airfields to London to signify a different period because of the change in targets.[1] What these historians fail to consider is firstly that the objective of the air offensive had not changed – it remained the destruction of RAF Fighter Command, achieved through what in modern terms is an offensive counter-air (OCA) campaign. Secondly, as an independent campaign intended to defeat Fighter Command, it did not end until Hitler had eliminated the reason for it, when he postponed Operation *Seelöwe*, the cross-Channel invasion, on 17 September 1940.

Since this is an account of the Battle of Britain as an offensive counter-air campaign it is naturally told from the attackers' perspective, and relies primarily on German sources. Principally these are the largely untapped Luftwaffe post-war histories, known as the Karlsruhe Collection, on file at the US Air Force Historical Research Agency (HRA) at Maxwell AFB, Alabama, and the wartime Luftwaffe headquarters daily situation reports that also do not appear to have been referenced well in previous histories.

Likewise, we have relied upon the original draft, begun during the war, of the AHB's official history of The Battle of Britain[2] to provide Fighter Command's perspective. The damage caused by Luftwaffe attacks is drawn almost exclusively from the RAF stations' Operations Record Books (ORBs), augmented only as needed for critical salient facts not mentioned.

For our telling of this story on a day-by-day basis, the German records provided the targeting, timing, and weight of their attacks, the AHB history told us when and where the approaching raids were first detected by Fighter Command's coastal radars, and detailed the group commanders' and sector controllers' responses in deploying airborne fighter squadrons to meet the incoming attacks.

Unfortunately for modern-day historians, readers and students of military history, within the original AHB histories created for the Air Ministry and the material subsequently archived by the AHB, there is no record of the names of the sector controllers directing the tactical level of combat in the Battle. These men provided the interface between the ground-based command and control establishment (the 'Dowding System') and the airborne fighter squadrons; they were the men that placed the 'Few' in a position to engage the attacking enemy. Yet they appear to have been completely missed by British histories.

We have derived the descriptions of the combats that resulted from these engagements from those sources believed to be the most authentic and accurate, consistent with the context, timing, locations, and adversaries' accounts. The losses experienced by both sides in these vicious, intense and frenetic engagements are taken exclusively, except where errors have been discovered, from historian Peter Cornwell's outstanding tabulation of correlated 'victory claims' versus 'loss reports' that make up the most substantial and historically significant portion of *The Battle of Britain Then and Now* (Mk V edition, Battle of Britain International Ltd, 1989) edited by Winston G. Ramsey. We shall not indulge in mentioning or comparing 'kill claims' or 'victory credits' because they were, in wartime, quite naturally exaggerated and, being unverified, are therefore meaningless, except where claims motivated commanders' decisions during the course of the campaign.

Finally, in addition to addressing the Battle of Britain in terms of it being an independent offensive counter-air campaign presented at the operational level of warfare, it is also our aim to clarify the situation using a handful of modern military terms in describing various components and actions of the two air forces involved. Generally speaking, these are modern standard North Atlantic Treaty Organization (NATO) words, acronyms and abbreviations.

For example, we refer to RAF satellite airfields and Luftwaffe Feldflugplätze (field flying bases) as forward operating locations (FOLs) for both sides. Instead of 'patrol locations' or 'orbit points', we occasionally use the NATO standard combat air patrol (CAP). We also recognize that the 'Dowding System' was in reality the world's first integrated air defence system (IADS).

It is our goal to present the history of the Battle of Britain as the epic aerial campaign, a titanic struggle between the two most powerful air forces in the world at that time, that it was and, to ensure a quick and full understanding, to explain it as we do so. We learned an incredible amount about what occurred on both sides of the Channel and over it in our research and this is our opportunity to share what we've learned with you. We hope you are able to get as much out of this study as we have.

Paul F. Crickmore   Douglas C. Dildy
Worcestershire,   Albuquerque,
England, UK   New Mexico, USA

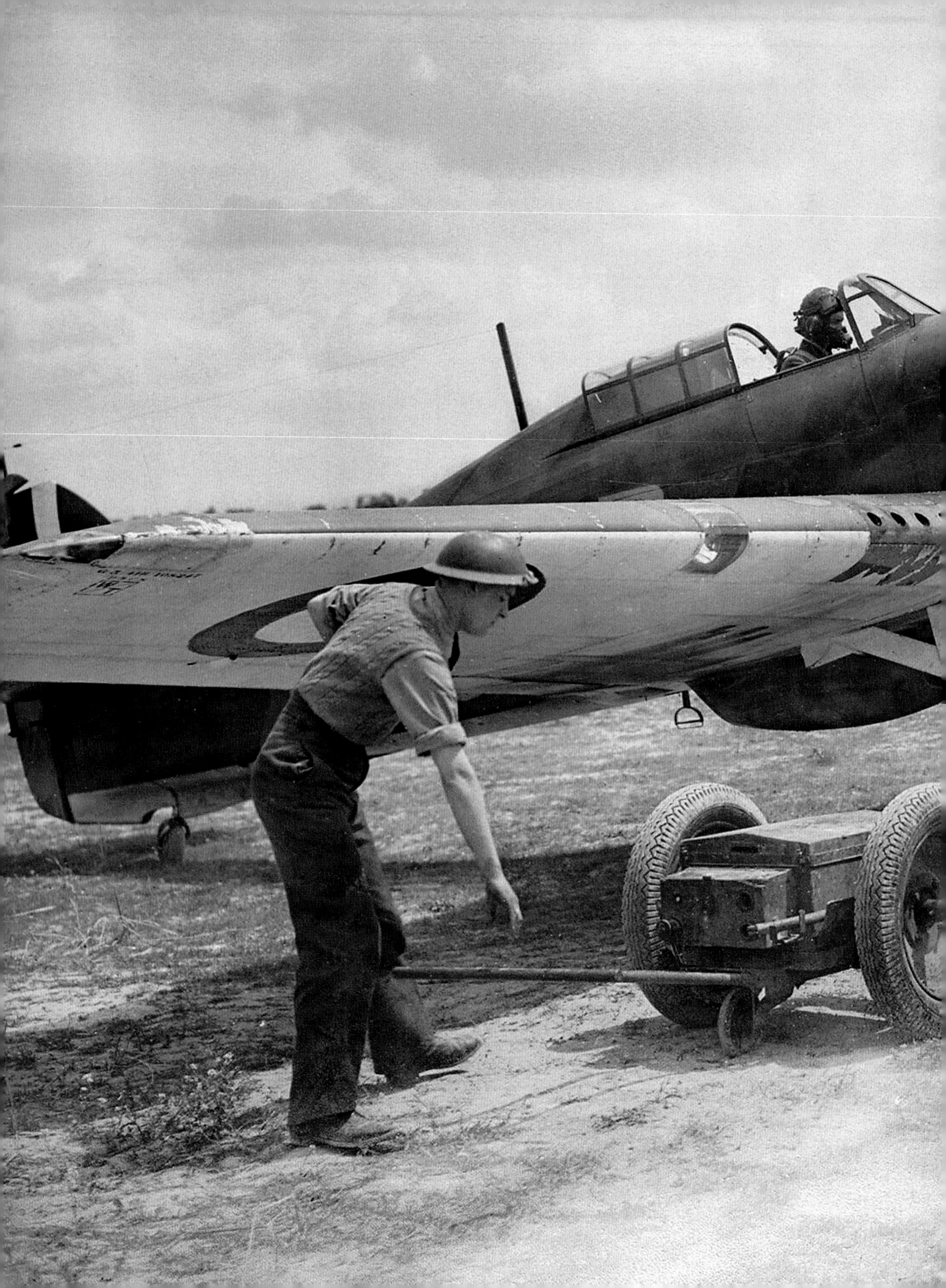

CHAPTER I

WESTFELDZUG
Why the Battle of Britain occurred

The purpose of this [Western] offensive will be to defeat as much as possible of the French Army and of the forces of the allies fighting on their side, and at the same time to win as much territory as possible in Holland, Belgium, and Northern France to serve as a base for the successful prosecution of the air and sea war against England.

Führer Directive Nr. 6 for the Conduct of the War, 9 October 1940[3]

'A gloriously sunny day with no low cloud but quite a lot of high wispy stuff,' wrote Flying Officer (Fg Off) Paul Richey in his autobiography, *Fighter Pilot: A Personal Record of the Campaign in France*, of 30 October 1939. 'I was on the airfield by my machine when we heard the noise of unfamiliar aircraft engines. After a lot of neck-craning and squinting we saw it – a Dornier 17 [reconnaissance aircraft] immediately above us at some 20,000 feet, travelling west and just visible in the thinner clouds. This was the first Hun we'd seen, and we were wildly excited. [Sergeant F.J.] Soper and I rushed off in pursuit, but of course had to watch our take-off and lost him… Up and up we climbed, turning gently from side to side and straining our eyes to find him. We didn't, and at 25,000 feet, with [gun]sights alight and gun-buttons on "Fire", we cursed like hell and came down.'

Richey and Soper were flying two of the three No. 1 Squadron Hurricanes scrambled from Étain-Rouvres airfield to intercept the Do 17P from 2.(F)/123 (second squadron, long-range [Fern] reconnaissance group 123). The third was flown by Pilot Officer (Plt Off) Peter Mould who 'had just finished refuelling after a patrol when the same Dornier went over. He took off without waiting for orders, pulled the plug (boost-override) and climbed up to 18,000 feet. He did an ordinary straight astern attack, firing one longish burst… The Hun caught fire immediately, went into a vertical spiral, and made a whopping hole in the French countryside: it exploded on striking the ground. There were no survivors.'[4]

Indeed, Staffelkapitän (squadron commander, often abbreviated to 'Staka') Hauptmann (Hptm, captain) Baldüin von Normann und Audenhove and his two-man crew were killed in the crash. Their Dornier was the first German aircraft shot down over France by a British fighter since 1918.

TO DEFEAT THE ALLIES – *WESTFELDZUG* BECOMES HITLER'S NUMBER 1 PRIORITY

The fierce aerial struggle we know today as the Battle of Britain was, in fact, both the goal and culmination of Adolf Hitler's *Westfeldzug* (Western Campaign), which began with the invasion of France and the Low Countries, launched on 10 May 1940. But that was not his original intent. Instead, he wanted to expand the German 'realm' (Reich) to the east.

PREVIOUS PAGES
One of Dowding's precious Hurricanes scrambles. This aircraft belonged to one of the four 12-aeroplane squadrons sent to France as part of the BEF's Air Component. (Author Collection, colourized by Richard Molloy)

The realization of Hitler's bellicose aims began with a series of successful *Blumenkriege* ('flower wars'): the occupation of the Rhineland in March 1936, annexation of Austria in April 1938, occupation of the Sudetenland in October 1938, occupation of the rest of Bohemia–Moravia and the annexation of Lithuania's Memel district in March 1939. These five bloodless victories progressively stunned the peaceful peoples and political leadership of Britain and France. In response, British Prime Minister Neville Chamberlain and French Premier Édouard Daladier offered no more than hollow rhetoric and worthless accords.

Adolf Hitler

The man whose name has come to epitomize the personification of evil in Western civilization was born on 20 April 1889 to an elderly Austrian customs inspector, Alois Hiedler (also spelt Hüttler, meaning 'one who lives in a hut') and his young third wife, living on the German–Austrian border at Braunau am Inn. With the simplified spelling, the future Nazi leader was christened Adolf Hitler and, after Alois's retirement, the family settled at Leonding, Austria, in 1898.

Adolf Hitler. (Author Collection)

Moving to Vienna at 18, Hitler grew to despise the weak and declining Habsburg Monarchy and Austria–Hungary's diversity of ethnic groups. Like many Christian Austrians of the day, he developed a growing fear and resentment of the flood of Eastern European Jews settling in the country. He therefore moved to Munich in May 1913, where he exulted in being united with the 'Fatherland'. At the outbreak of World War I, Hitler enlisted in the Royal Bavarian Army, serving as a regimental dispatch runner on the Western Front where he 'got an imprint of... land warfare through the division level in all grim detail. But there his picture stopped.'[5] Wounded by artillery shell splinters during the Battle of the Somme in 1916, he received the Eisernes Kreuz 1. Klasse (Iron Cross, First Class) as a gefreiter (lance corporal) on 4 August 1918.

Embittered by Germany's defeat, Hitler remained in the army and returned to Munich as a member of the Reichswehr reconnaissance command. During the German Revolution (an urban conflict between the right-wing Freikorps (nationalist militias) and left-wing Marxists in 1918–19) he was appointed as an intelligence agent assigned to infiltrate the subversive Deutsche Arbeiterpartei (DAP, German Workers' Party), but, liking the vitriolic nationalist, anti-Semitic, anti-Marxist rhetoric, he joined the party and soon became one of its most enthusiastic and strident spokesmen, quickly gaining notoriety for his rowdy polemic speeches against the Treaty of Versailles, rival politicians and, especially, Marxists and Jews.

Dynamic, charismatic, and manipulative, even mesmerizing, Hitler was also a ruthless political gangster. He murdered opposing leaders – even the DAP founders – and was awarded absolute powers as Nationalsozialistische DAP (National Socialist DAP, NSDAP, or 'Nazi') party chairman in July 1921. In November 1923,

Hitler attempted a coup to seize power during the so-called Beer Hall Putsch in Munich; he was imprisoned for treason in April 1924, but released in December.

The Nazis' popularity grew enormously during the 1920s and early 1930s, fuelled by increasing bitterness over the harsh and humiliating provisions imposed by the 'schändliches Diktat' ('disgraceful dictate', the Treaty of Versailles), rampant inflation, worsening food shortages, the impotence of the Weimar Republic government and mounting fears of Communist uprising in Germany's industrial cities.

While Hitler was in prison, 1.9 million NSDAP voters elected 32 members to Reichstag (Imperial Diet, or legislature) seats. A national referendum in 1929 recognized the NSDAP, giving it credibility, and Hitler's party obtained 107 seats in the next year's elections. Through vigorous campaigning, the terror tactics of the paramilitary Sturmabteilung (SA) and open street warfare against the Rotfrontkämpferbund (Red Front Fighting League, the German Communist Party's paramilitary organization) the NSDAP obtained 17.3 million votes in February 1933, securing 288 of 647 seats. This victory resulted in Hitler's appointment, as the leader of the largest party in the Reichstag, as Kanzler (Chancellor, equivalent to prime minister) by Germany's octogenarian President Paul von Hindenburg.

Employing an amendment to the Weimar Constitution permitting the Cabinet – led by the Chancellor – to enact laws without the involvement of the legislature (an amendment implemented ten times over the previous 14 years to overcome the government's powerlessness), Hitler crafted the '1933 Enabling Act' giving him complete political power for four years. With 109 Reichstag deputies banned, imprisoned, or in hiding, and SA stormtroopers roving the chambers inside and out, the law passed 444 to 94 and was signed by Hindenburg on 30 January 1933, establishing Hitler's government as a legal dictatorship. In Germany the move was known as Hitler's Machtergreifung (seizure of power).

Now Hitler repeated his earlier ruthless approach to politics, but with far more lethality. During the 'Night of the Long Knives' in summer 1934, he eliminated a potential challenge to his power from Ernst Röhm, head of the SA, the Nazi party's own paramilitary organization.

On 2 August 1934, Hindenburg died. The day prior, Hilter's Cabinet had enacted a law stating that upon the elderly president's death, his office would be abolished and its powers merged with those of the Chancellor, making Hitler head of state (and commander-in-chief of the armed forces) as well as head of government, changing the office title to Führer und Reichskanzler (leader and chancellor).

Dispelling any notion that the establishment of Hitler's totalitarian and autocratic regime lacked popularity, legitimacy, or the consent of the governed, in a national referendum on 19 August 1934, 88 per cent of the voting electorate approved the merger of the presidency and chancellorship – giving Adolf Hitler absolute power and supreme authority over all things for life.[6]

The two Allied democracies, political leadership and public sentiment alike, dreaded even the suggestion of repeating the horrendous carnage of World War I. Likewise, irrational horror spawned by the popularly sensationalized and grossly exaggerated effects of aerial bombing of cities meant that the two Allies had to buy time to build up their own air forces to prevent it. Buying time sacrificed other peoples' freedoms, at least until it came to the Poles.

Next in line, in the summer of 1939, Poland was overtly threatened by Nazi Germany and doomed if the worst should occur. On 25 August 1939, the governments of Britain and France therefore pledged that if Germany invaded it, they would declare war on Hitler's relentlessly belligerent Third Reich. Undeterred, Hitler launched *Fall Weiß* (*Case White*), the deployment order for the invasion of Poland, on 1 September. Three days later and for the second time in 25 years, Germany was engaged in an armed conflict with the two Western democracies.

Hitler's real aim in his unrelenting succession of territorial acquisitions, espoused in his polemic manifesto *Mein Kampf, Band 2* (*My Struggle, Volume 2*), and his bellicose rhetoric once in power, was the invasion of Soviet Russia and the elimination of Bolshevik communism as a threat to Nazi Germany. The associated benefit would be expansive increases in *Lebensraum* (living space or 'habitat') for Germany's steadily growing population, a concept that had additional emotional merit by fulfilling the country's historic longing for *Drang nach Osten* (drive towards the east) and its medieval precedent *Ostsiedlung* (colonization in the east).

It is also instructive to understand Hitler's attitude towards Great Britain – which he and most Germans of the time typically referred to as 'England' – and his modus operandi in dealing with other nations. *Mein Kampf* reveals both. Of the British he wrote: 'There is in Europe only one possible partner [in his quest for *Lebensraum*]: England. Only with England could one [meaning Germany] his back being covered, begin new Germanic expansion [eastward]… to win England's acquiescence… no sacrifice should [be] too great.'[7] Hitler's *Weltanschauung* (world view) was that the 'marriage' of the two greatest European powers – *Großbritannien* ruling the seas and Germanic hegemony on the Continent – would exterminate

ABOVE LEFT
At about 0130hrs on 30 September 1938, Neville Chamberlain, Édouard Daladier, Adolf Hitler and Benito Mussolini (left to right) signed the Munich Agreement. It permitted Germany to annex the Sudetenland. (NARA)

ABOVE
Neville Chamberlain returns from Munich, waving the Anglo-German Declaration, naively boasting that he'd secured a deal with Hitler that would provide 'peace for our time'. (© IWM D 2239)

On 3 October 1938, Hitler was driven triumphantly through an enthusiastic crowd in the city of Eger, Czechoslovakia, having reoccupied Sudetenland. (Bundesarchiv Bild 137-004055)

Bolshevism and create an unbeatable 'European Union'.

As a 'political gangster', Hitler rose to dominate the Nazi party, then became Germany's Chancellor, then *der Führer* (the Leader), and finally the supreme warlord of Central Europe, through his employment of a carefully balanced and judiciously applied combination of persuasion (euphemistically called 'courting' by the Germans) and coercion, sometimes punctuated with heavy-handed violence.

Very early in Hitler's '*tausendjähriges Reich*' ('thousand-year Reich') – actually only 12 – he actively 'courted' Britain, during which time the shining achievement was the Anglo-German Naval Agreement of June 1935. In this, Hitler obtained Britain's permission to ignore the naval provisions of the Treaty of Versailles and embark upon a massive capital ship construction programme, constrained only by the agreed 35:100 tonnage ratio compared with the Royal Navy (RN). Buoyed by this success and Britain's inaction over his reoccupation of the Rhineland in March 1936, at the 5 November 1937 Führer Conference he announced to his military chiefs his intention to 'use force in achieving his ends on the Continent, starting with Austria and Czechoslovakia. England, he averred, would not interfere.'[8]

Austria, also a Germanic nation, was annexed peacefully, Germany succeeding through overt threat of invasion.

Czechoslovakia, however, was regarded by most Germans as a bastard child of the '*Schanddiktat von Versailles*' (disgraceful or shameful Versailles dictate) and Hitler determined that it would have to be crushed, achieving his initial quest for *Lebensraum* at the expense of what he considered a nation that had no right to exist.

However, the Rhineland reoccupation was a clarion call to the British government and his annexation of Austria was an alarming harbinger of what was to come. Thus, the 'courtship' quickly cooled and, with the 30 September 1938 Munich Accord, it ended. Typically, Anglo-American historians assess Chamberlain's 'appeasement' at Munich as the first defeat of diplomacy in averting World War II.

But it is also instructive to realize that Hitler viewed the outcome – that he was allowed to annex the ethnically German Sudetenland, but could not crush Czechoslovakia as he wished – as a personal and political defeat. Following his return to Berlin, Walter Ansel, in *Hitler Confronts England,* reports: 'a chagrined Hitler sulked like a child… He had been robbed of a chance to smash the Czechs. Worst of all, the defeat, for so it counted, came of his own making; it was he who had weakened… On reflection, instead of a smashing victory, he had only a half-loaf deal with the interloping meddlers [primarily Chamberlain], and far worse, around about him, the German nation took an un-Nazi delight in the fact that violence had been averted.' Hitler blamed the British for his failure at Munich and vowed repeatedly, 'I don't give a damn if it takes ten years, I am going to beat them down!'[9]

Despite the lack of his (previously considered prerequisite) 'marriage' with Britain to give him a free hand to the east, Hitler continued to work his *Blumenkriege* in that direction, 'courting' Soviet Premier Josef Stalin. Through the Molotov–Ribbentrop Pact of 23 August 1939, Hitler adroitly avoided the Kaiser's most egregious strategic error of World War I – the ill-fated attempt to fight a two-front war – by, at least temporarily, neutralizing any threat from the Soviet Union (USSR). In addition to dividing Poland between them, the Pact included pledges of non-aggression between the two tyrannical dictatorships, giving Hitler time to prepare for his ultimate geopolitical goal: the invasion of Russia. Conveniently, it also proved an effective hedge against Stalin intervening in, or joining, a war in the West.

In fact, the chief reason for the Wehrmacht (German armed forces) leadership's continued support of their Führer was that he had effectively eliminated the threat of having to fight a two-front conflict. However, the Allies' seemingly hasty, imprudent and ineffective declaration of war now dictated that France and Britain must be eliminated from combat before it could be continued against Soviet Russia. Consequently, on 9 October 1939, even before the embers of a heavily bombed and burnt-out Warsaw had cooled, Hitler directed his military chiefs to begin planning *Fall Gelb* (*Case Yellow*), the deployment order for the invasion of France and the Low Countries. It was schemed as a pre-emptive offensive campaign 'on the northern flank of the Western front, through Luxembourg, Belgium and Holland.'[10]

It took just 18 days of blitzkrieg to fully implement *Case White*, the German invasion of Poland. Here Heinkel He 111s occupy a former Polish airfield. (NMUSAF)

Hitler takes the salute during a victory parade through Warsaw in October 1939. (Author Collection)

While France could be overrun by the Wehrmacht's revolutionary blitzkrieg (lightning war) mechanized air-land campaign, German army and navy studies conducted in November–December that year concluded that Germany's otherwise powerful war machine lacked the means to conduct a successful cross-Channel offensive against the British Isles. Consequently, the Oberkommando der Wehrmacht (OKW, High Command of the Armed Forces, Hitler's personal military staff[11]) strategic plan for defeating Britain lay in the hope of an effective U-boat blockade and a strategic air offensive against British ports, armaments industries, and oil refinery and storage facilities.

For its part, from its very beginnings the Luftwaffe – which began as a small office within the Weimar Republic's Truppenamt (Troop Bureau) supervising a handful of clandestine flying units and a training and testing establishment at Lipetsk, USSR – had embraced 'strategic air attack' as one of its three combat missions.[12] The first opportunity to plan for the employment of this 'strategic' capability was in August 1938, when Hitler began making his first bellicose moves to 'crush Czechoslovakia'. His deputy, Reichsluftminister (Reich Aviation Minister) and self-appointed commander-in-chief of the Luftwaffe, Hermann Göring, feared a strong British reaction, most notably by Royal Air Force Bomber Command. He therefore directed General der Flieger Hellmuth Felmy, commander of what would soon become Luftflotte 2 (Air Fleet 2), to provide an assessment of his command's counter-offensive potential.[13]

Felmy's *Planstudie 38* determined: 'A war of annihilation against England appears to be out of the question with the resources thus far available,' because most industrial targets lay beyond the range of his medium bombers, the meagre size of his bomber force was limited by the lack of modern airfields, and there were no escort fighters yet available. Felmy's conclusion was that 'the only solution… [is] to seize bases in the Low Countries [Holland and Belgium] before undertaking an air offensive against the British.'[14]

Following this recipe, the strategic aim of Hitler's *Westfeldzug* was to knock France out of the war by blitzkrieg and in the process to bring British targets into bomber range by acquiring airfields in northern France, Belgium and Holland, as well as obtaining U-boat bases that allowed easy access to throttle Britain's maritime lifeline across the Atlantic.[15] While the first would be a relatively fast and very decisive victory over the French, the second had the potential to be a long, drawn-out strategic strangulation.

THE PHONEY WAR BEGINS

A full year after Felmy's *Planstudie 38* and three days after Hitler invaded Poland, Britain and France began actively organizing their defences, planning on halting any Nazi invasion of Western Europe until a counter-offensive could be mounted in 1941 when their combined strengths, based on industrial production forecasts, would exceed Germany's. At the same time the two neutral nations – the Netherlands and Belgium – finally had to get serious about preparing their own defences. Unwilling to antagonize Hitler by entering any co-operative agreements with the two Allies, they clung desperately to the fantasy of maintaining their neutrality.

While France mobilized its sizeable and fairly modern army, on 9 September 1939 the British Army began shipping across the English Channel the first of ten infantry divisions that would form the fighting elements of the British Expeditionary Force (BEF).[16] To provide air support, the RAF established the BEF (Air Component), which eventually comprised four Bristol Blenheim reconnaissance/ bomber squadrons and six (later reduced to five) Westland Lysander army co-operation squadrons. These units and their airfields were to be protected from the Luftwaffe by what Major L.F. Ellis in the official *The War in France and Flanders 1939–1940*, called a 'token force' of four small, 12-aeroplane Hawker Hurricane Mk I squadrons deployed from RAF Fighter Command.[17]

The French Armée de l'Air (AdA, 'army of the air' or French air force) had a substantial fighter force totalling 490 single-engined and 67 twin-engined aircraft in 22 two-squadron *groupes de chasse*. These were an uneven assortment of aircraft ranging from obsolescent Morane-Saulnier MS.406s to modern but under-armed US-made Curtiss Hawk 75s. The AdA fighter force was primarily responsible for air defence along the German frontier and army front lines, and for protecting Paris. The French did not have a substantial bombing force. It had mostly been withdrawn to southern France and North Africa for conversion from decidedly obsolete multi-place aircraft to modern, fast, all-metal bombers, leaving only a handful of units in the northern and eastern zones of operation.

Although under-armed, the best Armée de l'Air fighter was the imported Curtiss Hawk H75-C1, 200 of which had been delivered before the Wehrmacht invaded France on 10 May 1940. The French did not use the 'Hawk' name. (Author Collection)

To compensate for the AdA's bomber deficiency, 226 Squadron was among ten RAF Fairey Battle units deployed to France as part of the AASF. Lumbering and under-armed, the Battles were slaughtered by Luftwaffe flak and fighters. (AHB)

To make up for this deficiency, the RAF deployed the whole of its No. 1 Group, ten squadrons of single-engined Fairey Battle light bombers, plus two squadrons of No. 2 Group's improved twin-engined Blenheim IV light bombers, to form the strategic Advanced Air Striking Force (AASF), based in the Champagne region east-north-east of Paris. To provide air defence for the AASF bases the new command received two BEF(AC) Hurricane squadrons (Nos 1 and 73). These were replaced by Nos 607 and 615 Sqns, Auxiliary Air Force, equipped with patently obsolete Gloster Gladiator biplanes, although they began upgrading in April 1940 when 16 more Hurricanes arrived. If and when the Germans attacked, arrangements were in place for four more Hurricane squadrons to provide rapid reinforcement. No squadrons flying the new, highly advanced (and operationally immature) Supermarine Spitfire squadrons could be spared.[18]

At that time the standard procedure was to mount standing patrols – combat air patrols, or CAPs in modern terms – over the airfields or other anticipated targets, or to patrol sectors along the front. Interception of incoming enemy raiders depended upon sighting the intruders then manoeuvring into position to attack.

To provide early warning of incoming raids, the British brought with them six 'sets' of the new high-technology electronic radio direction finding equipment, now known as radar. The first of these sets was mobile base unit (M.B.1), used for research and development by the Air Ministry Experimental Station (AMES) Bawdsey. It consisted of two collapsible 105ft towers, carried on trailers and erected on site with the transmitting aerials strung between them. Operating on 40–50MHz frequency, with 300kW power, it was erected at Calais, looking north to provide early warning of enemy aircraft approaching along the Belgian coast. It was tied into Fighter Command HQ's Filter Room at Bentley Priory to supplement the RAF's Chain Home (CH) early-warning radar network.

The other five were modified British Army gun-laying (G.L.1) sets, designated as G.M.s by the RAF. They had short, 70ft towers and lower power output, resulting in extremely limited range. Four of these were positioned in a widely scattered line from Boulogne to Le Cateau to provide warning for BEF(AC) units. The fifth was established at Bar-le-Duc, behind the Maginot Line west of Nancy, to warn AASF bases of incoming raids. Short, uneven ranges, numerous blind zones, and no means to distinguish friend from foe resulted in 'no useful information coming from [this system]' according to the Air Ministry's official history.

The five radar sites in the north reported to No. 5 Signals Wing's underground 'filter centre'. Purpose built at Arras, it was expected to sort through the units' radar plots and various air observer reports to alert the nearby BEF General Headquarters (GHQ) of incoming air raids. The Army's Wireless Intelligence Screen provided observer reports from 25 observation posts, each manned by two RAF wireless telegraphy (W/T) operators and four Army observers (and a driver), attached to various BEF field units and headquarters. Mirroring Fighter Command's Observer Corps back in Britain, it was chronically slowed because W/T transmitted in Morse code and each message had to be encrypted and encoded, and then decoded and deciphered on the receiving end. In the fast-paced campaign that was coming, there would be little time for all that.

Additionally, the RAF deployed a section from its Wireless Telegraphy Intercept Service, known as 'Y-Service', which 'listened' for telltale transmissions from enemy radio transmitters to gather signals intelligence. Headquartered at Fismes in the Marne region, the unit was networked with AASF HQ at Reims and the British Air Forces in France (BAFF) Rear Area HQ at Columbiers using the French civilian telephone system.

Listening primarily to the Luftwaffe medium frequency (MF) navigation beacons and, to a lesser degree, its MF and high frequency (HF) Morse and voice communications, the section was able to create a notional air order of battle (AOB) of Luftwaffe units facing Allied forces. The AASF 'Y' Section's diligent 'listening watch' revealed the Nazis' 9 April 1940 invasion of Denmark and Norway, as noted in the report *A.A.S.F. 'Y' Section, France – Sept 1939–June 1940*, 'four hours before the German Troops crossed the Danish border', but the Luftwaffe's heightened communications security precluded a repetition during the early morning hours of 10 May 1940.[19]

The first German aircraft shot down over France was a Dornier Do 17P of 2.(F)/123, brought down by a Hurricane of No. 1 Squadron flown by Plt Off Peter Mould. This example is a Do 17P of 3.(F)/123, flown by Fw Helmut Ackenhausen. (AHB donated by Ken Wakefield)

JG 3 was formed on 1 May 1939 in Bernburg/Saale. Here pilots, ground crew and Bf 109Es of Stab I./JG 3 await their call to arms during the Phoney War. When it came, I./JG 3 proved to be more than up to the task at hand, claiming a total of 179 Allied aircraft destroyed during the Battle of France. (Jean-Louis Roba)

FALL GELB – THE LUFTWAFFE'S DEPLOYMENT FOR *WESTFELDZUG*

As the BEF's first divisions and the RAF's first squadrons crossed the Channel to begin moving into position along the Belgian border near Lille (HQ at Arras), the Luftwaffe systematically destroyed the Polish air force, supported the blitzkrieg overrunning that doomed nation, and eventually bombed Warsaw into obliteration. Meanwhile, protecting Germany's North Sea coast, the Ruhr industrial basin, and Germany's Belgian, Dutch and French frontiers were 16 Jagdgruppen (fighter groups) equipped almost exclusively with the Messerschmitt Bf 109D and E, scattered from the North Sea coast to the Alps. For the time being, there were only seven Kampfgruppen (literally 'battle groups', meaning bomber groups) and a single Stukagruppe (Stuka group or dive-bomber group), ready in case the French mounted a meaningful counter-offensive to relieve the blitzkrieg's pressure on the Poles.

Beginning on 22 September 1939, with Poland prostrate from the Wehrmacht's onslaught, Göring's personal staff HQ, the Oberkommando der Luftwaffe (ObdL, High Command of the Air Force), began transferring units from east to west, assigning them to the two Luftflotten (air fleets) arrayed against Great Britain and France. During the seven months that followed, a period of quiescence known as the Phoney War, the Luftwaffe's striking force swelled to 40 Kampfgruppen comprising 877 Heinkel He 111, 448 Dornier Do 17Z and 268 Junkers Ju 88A twin-engined bombers, along with ten close air support groups containing 362 Junkers Ju 87B/R Stukas and 49 Henschel Hs 123 biplanes. To guard against the Allies initiating bombing operations against German cities and the strategically critical Ruhr industrial region, the Luftwaffe's defensive shield in the west grew to

34 fighter groups containing 1,102 single-engined Messerschmitt Bf 109 'frontal fighters' and 334 twin-engined Bf 110C and D escort fighters, so called Zerstörers (destroyers).[20]

To command this huge assortment of He 111H/P and Ju 88A medium bombers, Do 17Z light bombers, Ju 87B/R dive-bombers and Hs 123 ground-attack aircraft, seven Fliegerkorps (flying corps) were created. Additionally, three Jagdfliegerführer (JaFü, fighter commands) were also established, two for Luftflotten 2 and 3 to use in offensive operations and the other (JaFü Deutsche Bucht/German Bight, defending the North Sea coast) to control the vastly increasing numbers of Bf 109s and 110s.

Because the Luftwaffe was primarily an integral part of the Wehrmacht's revolutionary and powerfully aggressive blitzkrieg concept pairing close air support 'flying artillery' with fast-moving panzer (armoured) mechanized and motorized ground forces, there was no operations planning element on the ObdL staff. Instead, the various echelons were assigned to the respective army command level for planning and executing future offensive operations. For example, for *Fall Gelb*, Luftflotte 2 was attached to Heeresgruppe B (Army Group B), which was charged with penetrating deep into Belgium to draw the BEF and French mobile forces into battle there; Luftflotte 3 was

Gaining 14 victories with the Condor Legion during the Spanish Civil War, Werner 'Vati' Mölders was the first Luftwaffe fighter pilot to be awarded the Knight's Cross. He shot down 18 Allied aircraft before being shot down on 5 June 1940. Liberated after the fall of France, he was promoted to Major and given command of JG 51. (Author Collection)

attached to Heeresgruppe A. Within the former, VIII. Fliegerkorps, primarily composed of Stukas, Do 17Z light bombers, and Bf 109Es, was attached directly to Armeeoberkommando (AOK, numbered army) 6, which was the army chosen to penetrate into central Belgium.

Because of this close working relationship between the Luftwaffe operational commands and their commensurate army echelons, all operational planning – assigning various subordinate units to attack the targets that the army needed destroyed – was done at the Luftflotte and Fliegerkorps levels. The ObdL's role in offensive operations was limited to assigning units, supplying logistics, providing intelligence on targets and air defence, and nominating enemy air force targets, including airfields, depots, HQs and aviation industry facilities, for the Luftflotten's first attacks. According to Luftwaffe employment doctrine, this was 'planned in sudden swift action to destroy hostile air forces while still on the ground.'[21]

The resulting *Luftüberlegenheit* (air superiority) would then enable ground forces and subsequent aerial operations to be conducted without interference from the enemy's air arm. The best means of achieving this was by attacking the enemy's aircraft on their airfields, where they were most vulnerable, in the opening moments of the offensive and by conducting follow-up attacks against airbases and depots, and even enemy aviation industries (especially aeroengine manufacturers) that could provide replacements for losses sustained in the opening rounds.

Messerschmitt Bf 109E

The aeroplane upon which the Battle of Britain would ultimately turn was the Luftwaffe's Messerschmitt Bf 109E, or 'Emil'[22], day fighter, which gained its nickname from the word for 'E' in the German phonetic alphabet. Following the clandestinely developed Arado Ar 65/68 and Heinkel He 51 biplanes, Professor (actually Diplomingenieur, abbreviated Dipl.-Ing., for Diploma Engineer) Wilhelm Emil 'Willy' Messerschmitt's design took advantage of rapidly advancing aeroengine development, aerodynamic improvements in streamlining and aerofoil design, and all-metal construction techniques. This sleek, fast, monoplane was, according to the nascent Luftwaffe's developing doctrine, planned to be a tactical 'frontal' defensive fighter and strategic point-defence interceptor for protecting vital industrial and political centres within Germany.

Propelled by a powerful, low-drag, liquid-cooled inline engine, the Bf 109's lightweight all-metal construction and small fuel load made it a fast-climbing bomber interceptor, but limited its radius of action (or range) to only 200km (125 miles). However, this was adequate for its 'frontal fighter' role, providing air superiority over the army's front lines to a depth of approximately 50km (30 miles) into enemy territory. Inevitably sacrificing, to a degree, some of the manoeuvrability traditional to biplane fighters, the Bf 109's high performance meant that it could attack swiftly and disengage easily, at its pilot's discretion, obviating the need to outmanoeuvre an opponent in a dogfight.

While the initial Bf 109B, C and D production variants had employed the Junkers Jumo 210 engine, the initial production Bf 109E-1 used the excellent fuel-injected and supercharged 1,085hp Daimler-Benz DB 601A inverted V12 inline. The E-1 mounted four 7.92mm Rheinmetall MG 17 machine guns, later 'Emil' models carrying various combinations of MG 17s and 20mm cannon. To test the type's potential as a Jagdbomber (fighter-bomber, or Jabo), the E-1/B and E-4/B could carry a single 250kg (550lb) SC250 or four 50kg (110lb) SC50 bombs, their success resulting in the E-7, a dedicated Jabo variant that could also carry a 300-litre (66-Imp gal) jettisonable external fuel tank, or drop tank. The 'Emil' was equipped with the FuG 7 Funkgerät 7 (radio apparatus) HF voice radio employing 2.5–7.5MHz frequencies and effective to ranges of 48–56km (30–35 miles).

Messerschmitt Bf 109.
(Clive Ellis)

A section of 73 Squadron Hurricanes based at Rouvres, France, maintain the typically tight formation that would cost RAF pilots dearly at the hands of the more experienced Jagdwaffe pilots. (AHB)

FIRST ENCOUNTERS OF A LETHAL KIND

Until the Luftwaffe could launch its offensive counter-air campaign against the AdA, BEF(AC), and AASF, the German air force would have to meet its opponents in the air while flying aerial reconnaissance of Allied fortifications, rail networks, and airfields, while also trying to prevent enemy air arms from doing the same over Germany.

The Bf 109 'frontal fighters' proved particularly effective at intercepting intruding AdA and RAF reconnaissance aircraft, even without radar early warning, shooting down 22 French twin-engined aeroplanes (the Potez 637 for example) and 11 RAF Blenheims over Germany. Along the frontier, they destroyed ten French single-engined observation aircraft (mostly the Mureaux 115) and eight Battle light bombers. The Allies' fighters also intercepted intruding reconnaissance aircraft, albeit less effectively, shooting down 25 Dornier Do 17Ps and ten Heinkel He 111s, some 12 of these falling to Hurricanes (which lost four to defensive fire).

Because the RAF fighters were stationed well behind the French border with Germany and Luxembourg (protecting the AASF airfields) and that with Belgium (protecting the BEF airfields), patrolling Messerschmitts were usually challenged by French Moranes and Curtiss Hawks, which lost 34 fighters for 25 Bf 109s and three Bf 110s shot down; two others and a Bf 109E were shot down by rear gunners in reconnaissance aeroplanes.[23]

On a few notable occasions Nos 1 and 73 Squadrons patrolled the frontier and encountered Bf 109s, most frequently those flown by III./JG 53 (third group, Jagdgeschwader [fighter wing] 53), an experienced unit led by Spanish Civil War veteran and 16-victory ace Hptm Werner 'Vati' ('Daddy') Mölders. Their first

NEXT PAGES
A Ju 87B-1 of II./StG 77. This unit distinguished itself in every early, major Wehrmacht operation. In May and June 1940, it operated in the interdiction, close air support and anti-shipping roles, supporting Heeresgruppen A and B in the invasion of the Netherlands, Belgium and France. (Jean-Louis Roba)

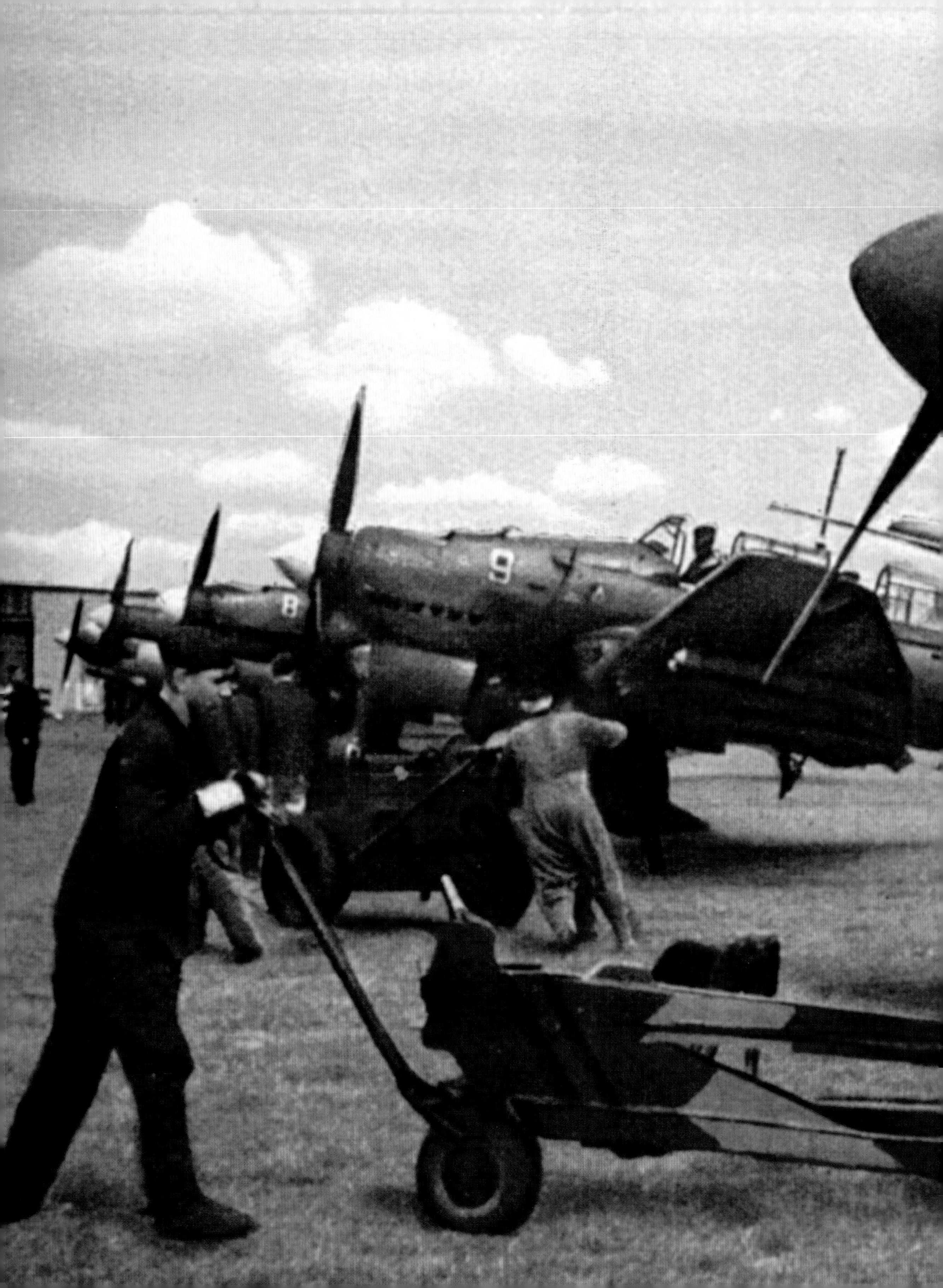
9
B

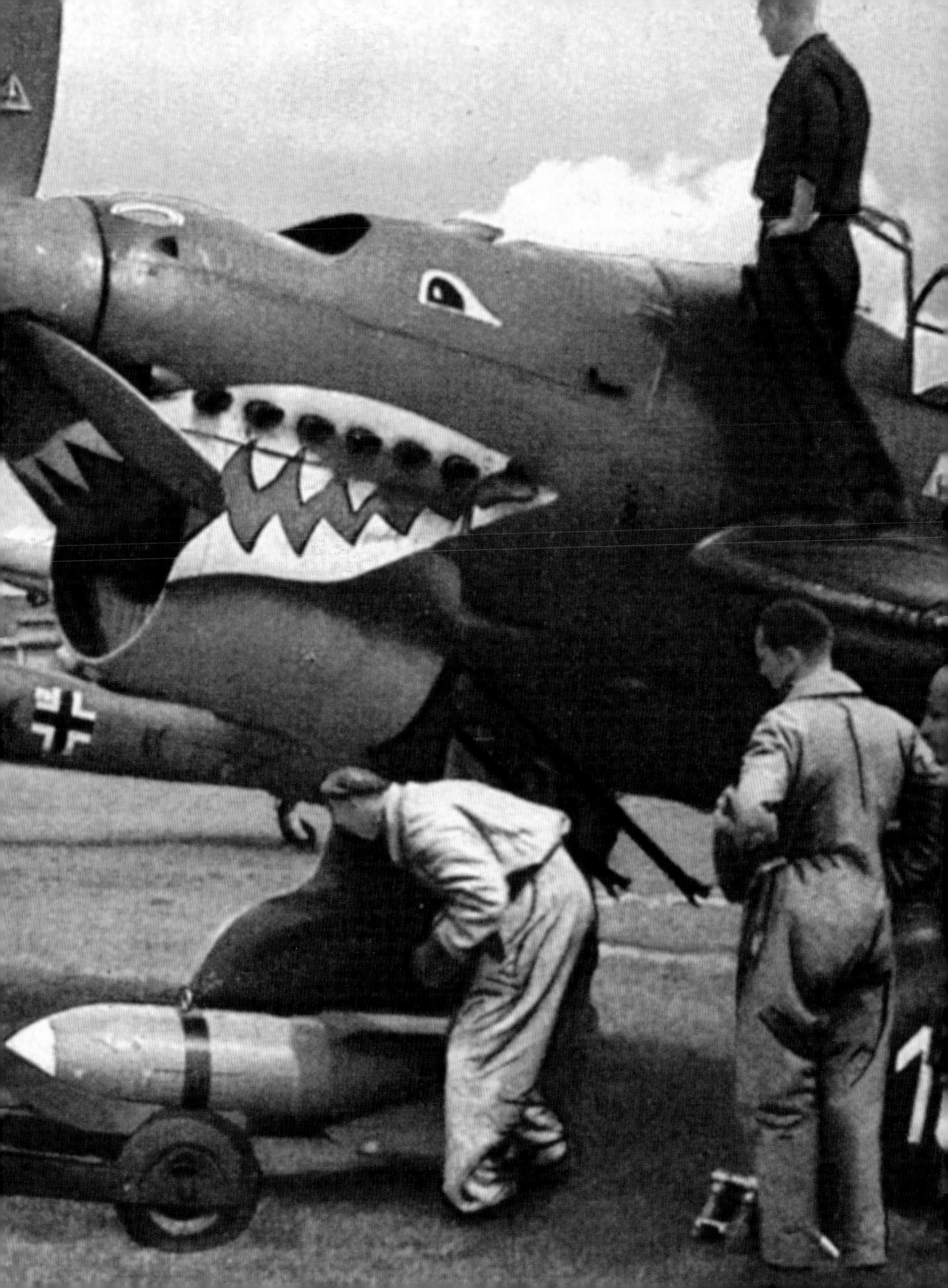

encounter did not go well for the young and inexperienced RAF fighter pilots. About 1430hrs on 22 December, three No. 73 Squadron Hurricanes patrolling north-east of Metz spotted two 1.(F)/123 Do 17Ps reconnoitring French defences west of Saarbrücken. Unseen, 11 III./JG 53 Bf 109Es, led by Mölders, were covering the Dorniers. As noted in Christopher Shores et al, *Fledgling Eagles: The Complete Account of Air Operations During the 'Phoney War' and Norwegian Campaign, 1940*, he later reported, 'Diving from great height to attack, I shot at the aircraft on the left. It began to "swim" immediately – I must have hit the pilot. The aircraft burned, and crashed close to a village [Homburg-Budange].' Shot through the head, Sergeant (Sgt) R.M. Perry had indeed been killed in the first fusillade of machine-gun bullets.

Mölders' wingman, Oberleutnant (Oblt) Hans von Hahn, shot down the second Hurricane. 'I remembered the orders of "Vati" Mölders to "go up to the enemy and sit up straight behind the gunsight". Then I pushed the gun button, the Hurricane went into a slight turn and just at that moment it was hit by a cannon shell under the cockpit. My burst must have hit the pilot. The Hurricane tipped over, a blast of flame, and like a fiery comet the aircraft crashed down.' Sgt J. Winn, also killed by the first burst of machine-gun fire, crashed near Altroff.[24]

During the Phoney War, Bf 109s flown by the combat-experienced Jagdwaffe (fighter force) pilots using their superior formations and fighting tactics, shot down nine Hurricanes for four losses, establishing the 'exchange ratio' that would prove disturbingly consistent in the coming battles. In the much rarer encounters with twin-engined Bf 110Cs, Hurricanes destroyed three for no losses.

The reasons for the unfavourable results of these initial lethal encounters are threefold: the Bf 109E was a superior fighter aircraft, its pilots were better trained and more experienced, and their four-aircraft formations and more fluid engaged tactics were far superior to Fighter Command's rigid, three-aeroplane formations and the restricted freedom of manoeuvre imposed by the RAF's outmoded, unrealistic and inflexible attack procedures.

The Hawker Hurricane had been designed as an air defence interceptor and bomber-destroyer. It was a transitional airframe, employing modern design elements in its retractable undercarriage, enclosed cockpit and eight-gun armament, but of heavy, mixed construction comprising thick wings and metal frame fuselage with fabric skinning, albeit pulled by a new, powerful, supercharged 12-cylinder inline engine. This gave it impressive climbing performance for reaching incoming bombers quickly, but relatively poor manoeuvring versus the lighter, more modern and similarly powered Bf 109E.

Hurricane pilots had also been training in bomber interceptions, rather than air-to-air combat, for months. Their formations and tactics were intended to give them the best chance of success in bringing their batteries of eight Browning .303in machine guns to bear against targets they expected to be defended by single dorsal or ventral 7.92mm weapons.

Hawker Hurricane Mk I

The rapidly advancing aviation technologies of the mid-1930s, spurred by the increasing payload, speed and range demands of the growing commercial airline industry, had finally produced bombers that were faster than opposing fighters, making them virtually immune to interception. To meet the threat posed by modern bombers, three things were needed: speed, heavy armament and the ability to locate and intercept the approaching aircraft.

Seeking fighters that possessed the first two of these requirements, in November 1934 the Air Ministry (AM) issued Specification F.5/34 for an Experimental High Speed Single Seat Fighter able to catch the fastest bomber and bring it down with a two-second burst of machine gun fire. The AM required the design to reach 275mph (443kph) at 15,000ft, be able to climb to 20,000ft in seven and a half minutes, and have a ceiling of 33,000ft. The aircraft was to mount eight 0.303in Browning machine guns, with 300 rounds per gun, aimed through a Barr & Stroud GM 2 fixed reflector gunsight and firing at 1,150 rounds per minute; a two-second burst ought to riddle the target with more than 300 rifle-calibre bullets.

No successful tender was made against F.5/34, but the specification was close to the Interceptor Monoplane private venture design that Sir Sydney Camm was developing at Hawker. The machine showed such promise that F.36/34 was written around it and the Hawker Hurricane developed from it. A robust, stable, retractable-gear monoplane, the Hurricane was built using outdated mixed construction methods, which made it relatively heavy but permitted high production rates for the expanding Fighter Command. The prototype's maiden flight was on 6 November 1935 and it was judged to possess remarkable manoeuvrability and docility. Powered by the new, supercharged 1,030hp Rolls-Royce Merlin II or III V12 liquid-cooled engine, the new fighter had a maximum speed of 320 or 325mph (515 or 525kph), depending on propeller type, at 18,500ft, a ceiling of 34,000ft and an operational range of 250 miles (400km).

Hurricane. (Author Collection, colourized by Adam Tooby)

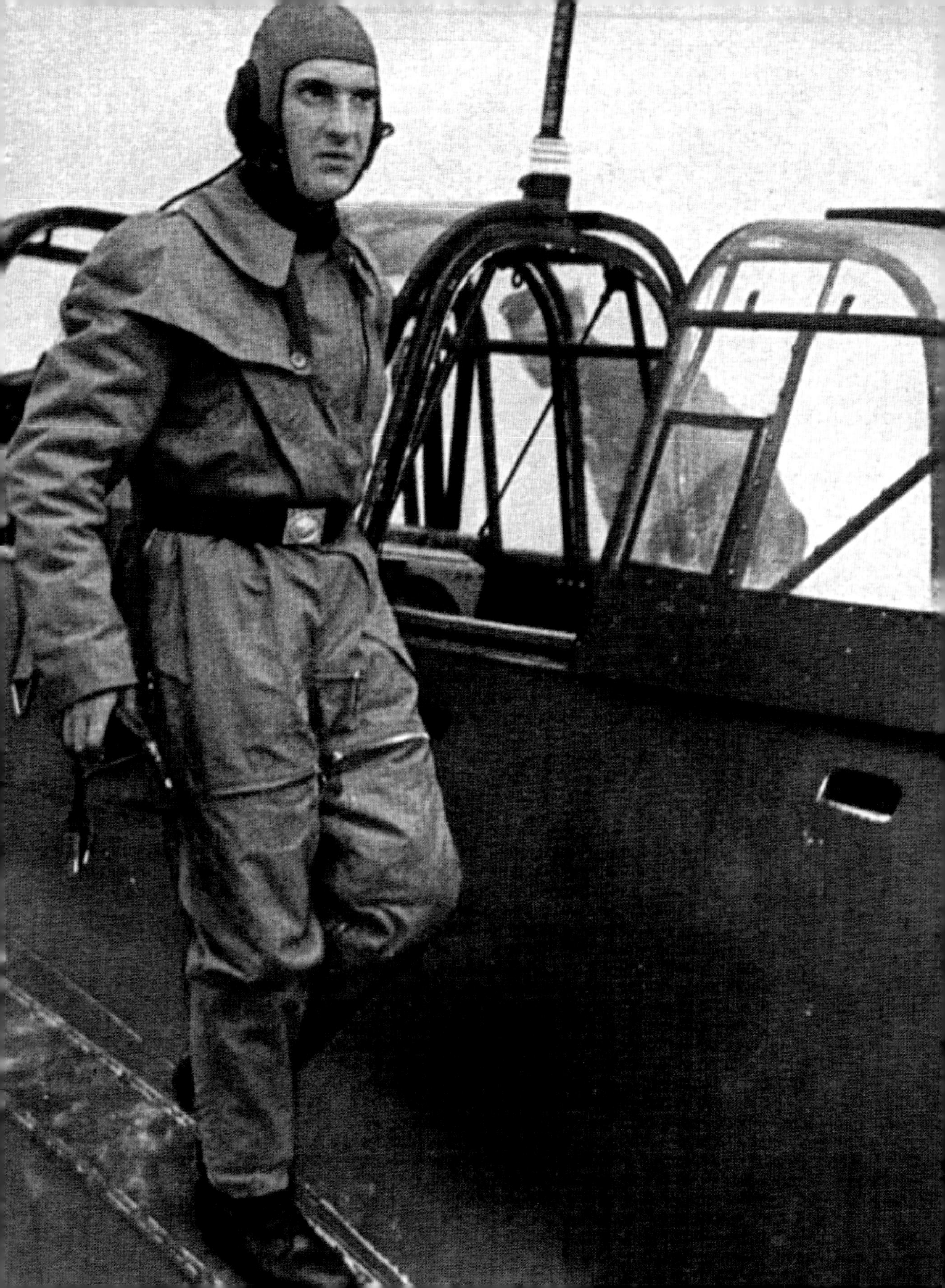

A legacy from World War I, their formations were based on tightly flown three-aircraft sections called 'vics' by the RAF and *patrouilles* (patrols) by the AdA. Their tactics were highly scripted Fighting Area Attacks, where a section deployed in line astern to serially attack a single bomber, or line abreast to attack two or three bombers in formation, or the much more complicated and almost impossible simultaneous attack against a single target from directly astern, rear quarter, and beam.[25]

Fighter-versus-fighter combat was never seriously contemplated because, flying from bases in Germany, Luftwaffe bombers approaching England would have outdistanced fighter escorts well before reaching the British coastline. James E. 'Johnny' Johnson, who joined the RAF and trained on fighters in 1939–40 and later, with 34 personal victories, became arguably the RAF's greatest ace and unit leader in air-to-air combat said, in his autobiography *Full Circle*: 'Fighter Command's tactical training was based on the theory that the air threat to Britain would be hordes of German bombers flying in close formation, and not escorted by fighters, since the Messerschmitt 109 could not reach our shores from airfields in Germany. Apparently those who assessed the nature of the threat did not take into account the possibility of more adjacent airfields becoming available to the Luftwaffe.'[26]

That of course was precisely the aim of *Westfeldzug*.

LEFT
This Ju 87 Stuka crewmember wears early smock-type flying overalls. The style of belt buckle indicates that he is an NCO. (Jean-Louis Roba)

ABOVE
Bf 109E 'Black 3' of 2./JG 2, and the Luftwaffe standard, on the eve of *Fall Gelb*. (Clive Ellis)

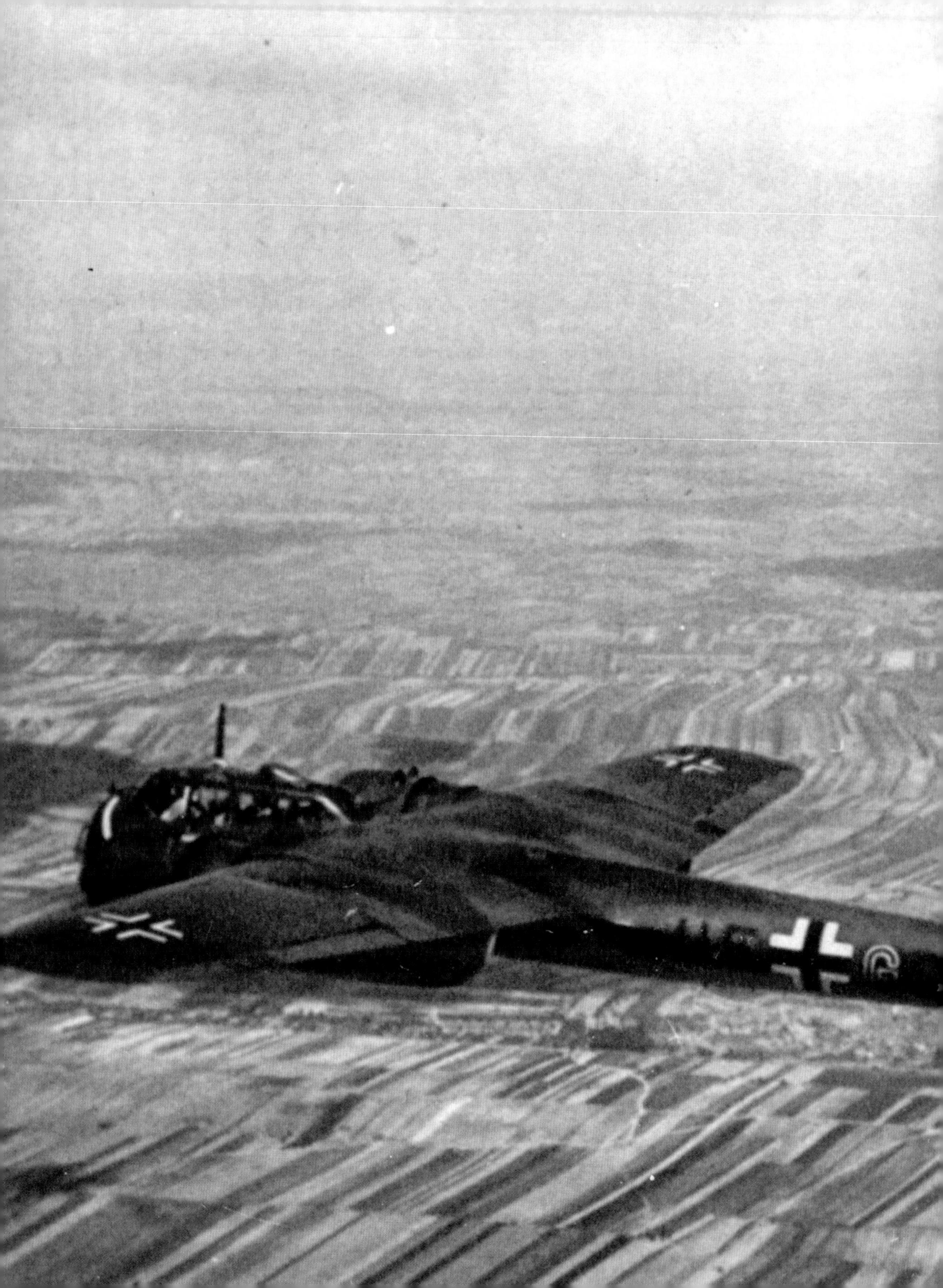

CHAPTER II

FALL GELB
Prologue to the Battle of Britain

Should the Army succeed in defeating the Anglo-French Armies in the field and in seizing and holding a sector of the coast of the Continent opposite England, the task of the Navy and Luftwaffe to carry the war to English industry becomes paramount.

Führer Directive Nr. 9, Instructions for Warfare against the Economy of the Enemy, 29 November 1939[1]

'The night of 10th May brought the decision,' 24-year-old Ju 88A pilot Leutnant (Lt, lieutenant) Werner Baumbach of 5./KG 30 (fifth squadron, Kampfgeschwader 30) wrote in his personal diary:

> The vital thing is to capture and hold certain key positions in Belgium and Holland until the army formations crossing the frontier can come up. The *coup* [*de main*] planned cannot succeed unless there is very accurate timing of the operations. Our job is to attack flak [anti-aircraft battery] positions in the Rotterdam–The Hague area. A pitch black night hides all preparations…
>
> Take-off is at 4.30am. We fly into thick mist and the contours of the Dutch landscape below us becomes vague. The engines hum their monotonous song and for a long moment we are all wrapped in our own thoughts. It is the rhythm of war, modern air war, which drones in our ears. We are abruptly brought back to reality. Our battle area has been reached. Salvoes of white puffs accumulate ahead of us… we must be close to our target. Ahead of me the leading aircraft is already diving. I soon recognize the exact position of the little target on the edge of the airfield; it is a flak battery firing from a farm. We must hit it if the landing of the parachute troops coming up behind is not to be endangered.
>
> I decide to come in from the west in a wide curve and make my attack from a low height. I do a steep glide, then dive. The target rushes up towards me and the farm in my sights gets bigger every second. I don't notice that my left thumb has pressed the little button on the stick. 'Bombs away, ' reports my gunner followed by his dry 'direct hit'.[2]

FALL GELB – NEUTRALIZING THE NEUTRAL NATIONS

PREVIOUS PAGES
Dornier Do 17Zs of II./KG 2 'Holzhammer' operating over the Netherlands in May 1940. (AHB donated by Ken Wakefield)

Along with Baumbach and his crew, by dawn on 10 May 1940, over 500 Luftwaffe bombers were airborne from their bases in Germany and winging their way towards a vast array of targets in Holland, Belgium and France. It initiated the largest offensive air operation yet in the history of modern warfare. Consistent with the Nazi air arm's employment doctrine, the primary target set that morning was the enemies' air forces – the plan was to destroy them on the ground before they had a chance to scramble airborne and mount an effective defence.

Of this vast aerial armada, approaching their targets in overwhelming waves, almost a quarter – 115 bombers – were intent on removing the kingdom of the Netherlands from the opposition's order of battle as quickly as possible. Escorted by around 40 Bf 110C long-range Zerstörers of I. and II./ZG 1, 90 Heinkel He 111 and Junkers Ju 88A bombers from KG 4 and KG 30, respectively, struck six Dutch airfields.

Shortly afterwards, Bf 109Es of JG 26 and JG 51 began continuous combat air patrols over Amsterdam and Rotterdam, shooting down 17 of the 48 Dutch defenders that scrambled that fateful morning. By the end of the day, the combination of bombing and air battles had destroyed half of the 124 operational aircraft with which the Militaire Luchtvaart (Military Aviation, the semi-autonomous air arm of the Dutch Army) started the day.[3]

Eliminated were two of the three squadrons of obsolete fixed-gear Fokker D.21 single-engined fighters and both squadrons flying the modern G.1 twin-engined 'heavy fighter', as well as the single squadron of new, but outmoded, US-built Douglas DB-8A/3N two-seat ground-attack aircraft pressed into the air defence

Pinpoint dive-bombing attacks by Ju 88 crews from KG 30 played a pivotal role in destroying the Dutch air force on the ground and suppressing Dutch Army AA batteries during the opening hours of *Fall Gelb* on 10 May 1940. (Jean-Louis Roba)

'Red 13', a Bf 109E of 2./JG 26, taxis out from the cover of trees for take-off. The 'Emils' were superior in performance to every Allied fighter type they encountered during the opening rounds of *Fall Gelb* – a fact painfully apparent in the resulting kill ratio. (Jean-Louis Roba)

role. The surviving ten D.21s and two G.1s, augmented by those later repaired, were gathered at a tiny camouflaged auxiliary field near Amsterdam and one surviving airbase (Bergen in North Holland) to carry on a sort of aerial guerrilla warfare for the next four days.

Behind the first wave – and 27 IV.(St)/LG 1 Ju 87B Stukas dive-bombing Dutch ground positions protecting the vital bridges spanning the Maas River at Moerdijk – came 400 Junkers Ju 52/3m trimotor transports, delivering five battalions of paratroopers and three regiments of air assault infantry under Unternehmen *F* (Operation *F*). Most of these landed at three airfields surrounding The Hague in an attempted *coup de main* against the Dutch royal family, government and military high command.

Effective anti-aircraft (AA) fire and artillery bombardment of the landing zones destroyed or disabled 232 transports and stiff resistance by local defence forces repulsed all attempts to enter the capital. Unternehmen *F* was a failure. But two other simultaneous airborne operations successfully seized bridges at Moerdijk and Rotterdam and held them against determined ground attacks and desultory Dutch air raids.

Following preparatory flak suppression raids, at 0630hrs on 10 May, over 190 Ju 52/3m transports began disgorging their paratroopers from 390ft altitude in an attempt to secure vital airfields and bridges. (Jean-Louis Roba)

Clearly the Luftwaffe's aim of establishing aerial supremacy over the Dutch nation was achieved. Subsequent offensive air operations effectively isolated the Netherlands, preventing any link with the French 7ᵉ Armée approaching from Antwerp and precluding any British seaborne assistance other than evacuating the Dutch royal family, cabinet and gold reserves. Except for sporadic engagements with surviving D.21s and G.1s, the Luftwaffe's dominance went virtually unchallenged until 13 May, when RAF Fighter Command dispatched six 264 Sqn Bolton Paul Defiant turret

The obsolete, fixed-gear, mixed-construction Fokker D.21 was exceptionally manoeuvrable, but no match for the modern, much faster Messerschmitts. Its pilots paid a high price for their courageous defence. (Author Collection)

fighters, escorted by an equal number of 66 Sqn Supermarine Spitfires. Spotting a formation of IV.(St)/LG 1 Stukas, the Spitfires left their charges to attack, shooting down three, but allowing escorting 5./JG 26 Bf 109Es to jump the Defiants and shoot down five in quick succession; three aircrew were captured, two killed and one missing.

By 14 May, the Netherlands had almost nothing left in the way of air defence. Even ammunition for its remaining AA guns was running low and it capitulated shortly after a devastating bombing raid against Rotterdam that killed 874 civilians, destroyed the homes of 85,000 residents and gutted the entire city centre. The terror-filled fears of many regarding the potential destructiveness of modern airpower were horrifically realized when viewing photographs of the city's fiery destruction.

The Belgian portion of *Westfeldzug*'s opening phase was much the same, only worse.

Having located most of the Aéronautique Militaire (AéM, the Belgian Army's air arm) 'campaign fields' through thorough aerial reconnaissance during the eight-month long Phoney War, Luftflotte 2 bombers (KG 27 and KG 77) and Stukas (II./StG 2), escorted by JG 1 and JG 27 Bf 109Es and ZG 26 Bf 110Cs, attacked 15 airfields throughout the day with devastating results. The Belgians' single Hurricane squadron was destroyed, along with one of the two flying obsolete Italian-made Fiat CR.42 Falco biplanes and a third equipped with abysmally ancient Fairey Fox two-seat 'reconnaissance-fighter' biplanes (the second of these was wisely reassigned to AéM's reconnaissance regiment).

Before dawn, the morning's fourth major airborne operation, a glider-borne assault by a reinforced paratrooper-engineer battalion, neutralized Fort Eben Emael and seized the three bridges spanning the Albert Canal west of Maastricht, only one of which was successfully 'blown' by the defenders.

Maastricht was the gateway for the Wehrmacht's panzers to drive onto the Belgian plain, but there were two major water obstacles to overcome: the Maas as it passes through the city and the almost parallel Albert Canal, just behind it. After taking Maastricht at noon, German 'pioneers' (combat engineers) replaced the

The 1e Jacht Vliegtuig Afdeling (1e JaVA, 1st Fighter Unit), stationed at De Kooy naval airfield, defended Den Helder, the Dutch Navy's main fleet base. In a low-level dogfight between nine D.21s and eight Bf 109s, the Dutch shot down two 'Emils', this one crash-landing on the airfield. (Author Collection)

The Wehrmacht's campaign in Holland ended as it began, with a devastating bombing attack by Heinkel He 111s. (Author Collection)

city's 'blown' bridges with three small pontoon bridges, allowing a motorized rifle brigade, an armoured car reconnaissance battalion and three batteries of half track-mounted flak guns to cross the river and, driving three miles to the west, relieve the paratroopers holding the two intact bridges spanning the Albert Canal. Meanwhile, the pioneers worked through the night to build a large pontoon bridge for heavy mechanized equipment and the next day 3. and 4. Panzer Divisions, comprising the XVI. Panzer Corps[4], began flowing through the city, crossing the canal, and deploying line-abreast to create an armoured wedge (a *Keil*) for their thrust into central Belgium.

Above all, the Belgians recognized the strategic imperative of destroying those bridges and on the second day of the campaign, launched their only modern bomber squadron, flying nine slow, under-armed Battles, in a raid to destroy them. Escorted by six AéM Gloster Gladiators, the raid was intercepted by 1./JG 27 Bf 109Es. Six Battles were shot down by fighters and flak, effectively destroying the unit. Four Gladiators were lost to 1./JG 1 Bf 109Es, and that afternoon the rest of the squadron was annihilated on the ground in a I./JG 1 strafing attack. The last surviving Belgian fighter squadron was withdrawn to the north-west with its CR.42s and ordered not to engage German fighters. Having lost 135 aircraft of an original 178 in the first two days of the campaign, the AéM was effectively eliminated from the contest, giving the Luftwaffe uncontested aerial supremacy over eastern Belgium.[5]

ASSAULTING THE ALLIES

While the Dutch and Belgians had excellent intelligence information indicating the coming hour of Hitler's *Westfeldzug* and were able to alert their frontier defences, disperse their air forces to auxiliary campaign fields and place their fighter aircrews at readiness, the two Allied powers were almost completely surprised by the Nazis' first attacks. Not only did they lack any strategic warning but there was no tactical heads up either. The RAF's deployed radar units gave no indication whatsoever that massive numbers of Luftwaffe bombers were penetrating French airspace.

Twenty-year-old Plt Off Peter Parrott, who survived World War II with six aerial victories, a DFC and Bar, and became one of the earliest jet test pilots, later reflected:

> Our [607 Sqn] Mess was in the village [Vitry-en-Artois] and our dispersal point on the airfield was about a half mile away. We were in the Mess having a cup of tea waiting for transport to pick us up. We heard it pull up and then the driver came running into the Mess (an unheard of breach of discipline!) shouting that German aeroplanes were flying over the field. We made all speed as we indeed saw several He 111s [II./KG 1] in ones and twos passing over in a north-easterly direction. Discipline again went by the board as we piled into our aircraft and took off individually.
>
> Take-off [was] to the east and I started to climb at full throttle in pursuit of two He 111s. It was a long stern chase and I was still out of range when I realized that we were nearing the Belgian border. We had been repeatedly warned not to go into Belgium because of the risk of internment should we be forced down. I therefore opened fire at long-range on the rearmost aircraft, and was rewarded with a return of tracer [fire] from the dorsal air gunner. Before I had finished my ammunition, the air gunner had stopped firing, but whether this was [from] a hit by me, or he was reloading his gun I shall never know. All I could claim was 'possibly damaged'. On the way back home I passed several Heinkels making their way home, but could do nothing about them, being out of ammunition.[6]

The Heinkels that Parrott and 607 Squadron scrambled to intercept were among the other half of the first day's first wave, sent to attack 47 airfields in France. Most of these were AdA bases but few suffered significant damage – altogether the French reported losing 60 aircraft in the opening attacks.[7] Three airfields used by BAFF units were also hit, resulting in the destruction of six Battle light bombers from 88 and 142 Sqns.

Luftwaffe bomber losses were notably higher than over Holland and Belgium. During the first day of combat, the two air fleets lost 64 bombers over France, mostly to intercepting AdA and RAF fighters scrambled to protect their airfields. By the time they reached these well-defended targets, most bomber formations

After fierce fighting, the 9. Panzer-Division finally crossed the Holland Deep and drove to Rotterdam to relieve Generalleutnant Kurt Student's exhausted air assault troops, who were holding the south side of the city. (Ryan Noppen)

had no fighter escort. All of the very numerous and very effective Bf 109Es were used as they were designed, establishing and maintaining air superiority over the front lines to a depth of 30 miles (50km). They effectively covered the two panzer divisions crossing the bridges in and near Maastricht and seven more[8], comprising the main armoured assault threading its way through the thickly forested Belgian Ardennes.

Of the long-range Bf 110C escort fighters, two Zerstörergeschwader (destroyer wings, ZG 1 and ZG 26) were actively engaged over Holland and Belgium, leaving only 103 Bf 110Cs (with II./ZG 76, I./ZG 52 and V.(Z)/LG 1) to escort the almost 300 bomber sorties that were flying deep into French territory, although many of these targets lay beyond even the Zerstörers' extended range. Consequently, most bomber formations were not escorted at all and the single 7.92mm MG 15 machine guns in the bombers' dorsal and ventral gun positions were inadequate to defend them against determined fighter attack. A total of 35 He 111s and 21 Do 17Zs was lost to Allied fighters on the first day of Luftwaffe attacks.

Like their AdA counterparts, the RAF Hurricane squadrons rose to defend their airfields and brought down 19 He 111s and ten Do 17Zs, although 'kill claims' were considerably higher, with 42 officially credited. Of course, there were no claims against German fighters the first day simply because they never came close enough to engage in combat. Patrolling overhead Wehrmacht panzer columns winding their way through the Ardennes, Bf 109Es shot down three AdA Potez 63.11 reconnaissance aircraft, but three returned to report the enormous numbers of mechanized vehicles clogging the narrow roads through Luxembourg. The AASF mounted two large attacks against them, with 48

Belgium's most modern fighter squadron, Escadrille 2/I/2, had eight serviceable Hawker Hurricanes at dawn on 10 May. That morning four were destroyed on the ground at Schaffen and another two at Evere. The remaining two suffered a similar fate at Beauvechain/La Bruyére the following day. (Author Collection)

unescorted Battles, 21 of which were shot down by fighters and the panzers' accompanying motorized flak batteries.

Meanwhile, the Hurricane squadrons lost eight aircraft shot down, all to bombers' defensive fire, but were reinforced by the arrival of three 16-aeroplane squadrons. Numbers 3 and 79 Squadrons joined the BEF(AC) from Croydon and Biggin Hill, respectively, and No. 501 Squadron arrived from RAF Tangmere to reinforce the AASF.

Next day, the Hurricane pilots got their first real taste of fighting one of their main adversaries, the Bf 110. Mid-afternoon a group of the much-vaunted Zerstörers from I./ZG 2 were escorting 30 III./KG 53 He 111Hs when 73 and 501 Sqns attacked, shooting down one bomber and two Messerschmitts. Later in the day, 15 I./ZG 76 Bf 110s, escorting 30 III./KG 76 Do 17Zs, were attacked by No. 1 Squadron, losing another two. An emerging feature of modern aerial combat, the problem of chronic overclaiming presented itself dramatically in these two battles when three squadrons of Hurricane pilots, pumped full of adrenalin from their first, fast and furious, kill-or-be-killed combats against enemy fighters, claimed 18 Bf 110s destroyed.[9] As will be seen, this problem plagued both sides' combat reporting and prevented accurate assessment of actual enemy losses.

Mercilessly, the Luftwaffe continued its anti-airfield missions on the second day, bombing 23 installations in France. In one spectacular early-morning low-level attack on Condé-Vraux airfield, south-east of Reims, No. 114 Squadron was wiped out on the ground. Six Blenheim IVs were destroyed and the unit's other five were damaged to the extent that they had to be abandoned when the airfield was evacuated three days later.

Meanwhile, the slaughter of Allied bombers and their crews continued unabated. Lacking self-sealing fuel tanks and armour protection for the pilots and crewmen, the RAF and AdA bombers were slow and very vulnerable targets. Without fighter escort, the stage was set for massacre: throughout 11 May, the Allied air forces launched several strikes against bridges and motorized columns in Belgium. The raids employed a mix of 44 Battle, Blenheim and LeO 451 light and medium bombers, all without fighter escort. Bf 109Es and flak shot down 13 of them. The next morning, nine unescorted 139 Sqn Blenheim IVs attempted to bomb German motorized columns between Maastricht and Tongeren. Defending fighters and flak destroyed eight of them, all lost without slowing the panzers' progress across the Belgian plain.

Belatedly realizing that the two bridges west of Maastricht were critical chokepoints – although well after the two panzer divisions were across them – the RAF launched a near-simultaneous double raid of Battles and Blenheims. Having delayed long enough for the Luftwaffe to ring the bridges with flak batteries and position I./JG 1 and I./JG 27 overhead, the doomed mission had all the makings of a classic military disaster requiring heroic sacrifice from its crews, who attacked in the near-certainty that they would not survive.

At last the AASF commanders had recognized that their exceedingly vulnerable light bombers required fighter protection, so the AASF strike, consisting of five 12 Sqn Battles, followed a sweep by eight 1 Sqn Hurricanes. The latter engaged the southern Bf 109E patrol of 2./JG 27, losing three aeroplanes to the Messerschmitts, which also shot down one bomber. The other four got through to the target, but were all shot down by flak. Negligible damage was done.

The 24 UK-based Blenheims of 15 and 107 Sqns were supposed to follow a sweep by two BEF(AC) fighter squadrons, 85 and 87 Sqns, but the fighters' timing and navigation were off, so the bombers went in with no protection. Eleven were shot out of the sky by Messerschmitts and flak. Number 85 Squadron failed to maintain mission discipline, its pilots allowing themselves to be lured from their sweep to engage passing German bombers, shooting down a pair of 2./KG 54 He 111s and a 1.(F)/121 reconnaissance Ju 88A. The 87 Squadron formation angled off south of course, winding up approaching Liège instead of Maastricht, where it was engaged by, among others, the Stabsschwarm (staff flight) of four fighters from JG 27, led by Hptm Adolf Galland, the group's operations officer.[10]

As Galland later related in his autobiography, *First and the Last*:

Some five miles west of Liège my flight companions and I dove from an altitude of about 12,000 feet on a flight of eight Hurricanes flying 3,000 feet below us. The Hurricanes had not yet spotted us. I was neither excited nor did I feel any hunting fever. 'Come on, defend yourself!' I thought as soon as I had one of the eight in my gunsight. I closed in more and more without being noticed. 'Someone ought to warn him!'

I gave him my first burst from a distance which, considering the situation, was still too great. I was dead on target. The poor devil at last noticed what it was all about. He took rather clumsy avoiding action which brought him into the fire of my wingman [Lt Gustav Rödel, who also claimed a kill]. The other seven Hurricanes made no effort to come to the aid of their comrade in distress, but

Flying the inadequate Fairey Battle, Escadrille 5/III/3 was Belgium's only modern bomber squadron. On the second day of the Nazi invasion, all nine of its Battles attacked three bridges spanning the Albert Canal. In the face of fierce fighter opposition and flak barrages, six were shot down. (Daniel Brackx)

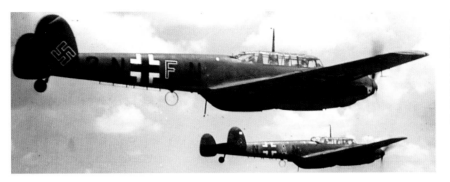

Luftflotte 3 employed more than 100 Messerschmitt Bf 110Cs during *Fall Gelb*. Here, two Zerstörers of ZG 76 are leading the formation. '2N+AN', in the background, was lost off Portland on 12 August 1940. (Andy Saunders)

made off in all directions. After a second attack, my opponent spun down in spirals minus his rudder. Parts of his wings came off. Another burst would have been a waste of ammunition…[11]

Galland's attack correlates best with the experience of Sgt Frank Howell. In Brian Cull and Bruce Lander's book *Twelve Days in May*, he recalled: 'They came from the sun with an altitude advantage and I never saw them. Suddenly there was a shattering noise and the cockpit was full of burnt cordite.' Howell later told a squadron mate that 'His starboard wing was shot off by a Me 109 and his aircraft went into a steep dive. He managed to bale out but… landed very heavily on his back.'[12]

Galland continued, 'I immediately went after another of the scattered Hurricanes. This one tried to escape by diving, but I was soon on his tail at a distance of 100 yards. [He] did a half-roll and disappeared through a hole in the clouds. I did not lose track of him and attacked again from very close quarters. The plane zoomed [up] for a second, stalled, and dove vertically into the ground from a height of only 1,500 feet.'[13] Galland's victim was Fg Off J.A. Campbell who was killed in the crash.

The drastic difference in combat experience between the two sets of participants in this combat is plainly and painfully obvious.

LUFTÜBERLEGENHEIT ACHIEVED

Air superiority (*Luftüberlegenheit*) is the ability to subdue enemy aerial opposition to the point where other friendly air and surface operations may be conducted at specific times and locations without significant enemy interference. Air supremacy is the opposition-smothering superiority that enables the conduct of friendly air and surface operations with impunity across the entire area of operations at any time or place.

Without question the Luftwaffe achieved air supremacy over the Netherlands during the first day of the offensive, and over eastern Belgium on the second. By the third day, as the panzers emerged from the Ardennes and approached Sedan and Monthermé, air superiority over the battlefronts in central Belgium and the French frontier was also achieved.

Attacking German motorized columns advancing through Luxembourg on the first day of the campaign, Battle P2200/GB-K of No. 105 Squadron, RAF, was shot down by flak and force-landed at Clémency, where its crew of three were captured. (Thomas Laemlein)

ABOVE
Unlike fellow Condor Legion veteran Werner 'Vati' Mölders, Adolf 'Dolfo' Galland initially specialized as a ground-attack pilot. Transferring to Bf 109s, he was the adjutant of JG 27 when he claimed his first aerial victories – two 87 Squadron, RAF Hurricanes – on 12 May. (Author Collection)

Initially, the Allied fighter units were able to maintain a daily average of 594 sorties, 434 by the AdA and 160 by the RAF. To help sustain the British contribution, No. 504 Squadron arrived from RAF Debden with 16 Hurricanes to reinforce the BEF(AC) on 12 May and, the following day, the first of 32 additional Hurricanes and pilots began arriving to bolster the other squadrons. However, this failed to make up for 41 lost to all causes thus far.[14]

Against the Allies' almost 600 sorties daily, the Jagdwaffe mounted an average of 1,500 sorties, an overwhelming numerical advantage covering the rapidly advancing armoured columns. These increasingly forced its opponents, when not escorting their own bombers' ground-attack missions, to defend the airspace over their own bases, railway stations (protecting the movement of army reinforcements) and other important rear area targets.

On 13 May, panzer general Heinz Guderian's three armoured divisions arrived at Sedan and began their two-day assault under a devastating Luftwaffe bombardment. Some 270 Stuka and 310 Do 17Z tactical bombing sorties paved

RIGHT
Number 85 Squadron Hurricanes. During the Battle of France, the unit suffered heavily, losing all but four of its aircraft in the 12 days between the start of the German offensive and its return to Britain. (AHB)

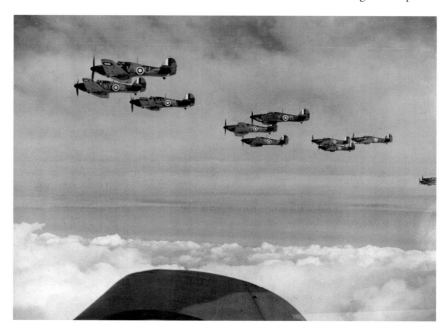

the way for pioneers and infantry to vault across the Meuse River, all without any interference from Allied fighters. The only loss was a single 3./StG 76 Ju 87B shot down by ground fire.

LEFT
On 12 May, five RAF Battles from 12 Squadron were sent to destroy the heavily defended bridge spanning the Albert Canal at Veldwezelt, one of two being used by German panzers to enter Belgium. All but one Battle was shot down. (Thomas Laemlein)

Overnight, Guderian's engineers constructed four pontoon bridges and, on the second day, these, along with the long motorized columns jamming the roads leading to them, became the primary targets for a series of spirited Allied aerial counter-attacks. Altogether, the AdA and RAF flew 124 bombing sorties, escorted by 63 fighters. However, over Sedan, the bridges and the grid-locked roads leading to them, defending Bf 109Es had a field day. Of 63 Battles and 36 Blenheims attacking, 47 were lost to enemy fighters, flak, and friendly fire, representing the highest single-day loss in the RAF's history.[15] None of the bridges was hit.

The Luftwaffe's air superiority could not have been more dramatically demonstrated than by this two-day long series of battles. On the first day the Jagdwaffe's dominance over the Sedan battlefields permitted unimpeded bombing operations enabling successful river crossings at several points. The second day, German air superiority prevented any effective interference by the enemy's repeated attempts to attack.

The next morning, 15 May, after destroying the two defending French infantry divisions (55ᵉ and 71ᵉ Division d'Infantrie) at Sedan, Guderian wheeled his panzers west and began a headlong drive towards the Channel coast. To neutralize

Commanded by Mölders during *Fall Gelb*, JG 53 'Pik As' ('Ace of Spades'), was at the forefront of the fighting. On 14 May the unit claimed 43 victories in one day. (Clive Ellis)

the Allied air forces' ability to interfere with his daring armoured thrust through northern France, the Luftwaffe mounted a renewed series of bomber attacks against airfields. The first wave started that morning by striking 16 AdA fields, reducing that day's French fighter missions to only 153 sorties.

MORE HURRICANES FOR FRANCE

This drastically crippling situation prompted French Premier Paul Reynaud to urge British Prime Minister Winston Churchill to provide additional RAF fighter reinforcements. Commandant Suprême des Armée Alliées (Supreme Commander of the Allied Armies) Général d'Armée Maurice Gamelin and Théâtre d'Opérations du Nord-Est (North-east Front Commander) Général d'Armée Alphonse-Joseph Georges – were convinced that the key to the panzer breakthroughs the previous day at Sedan, Monthermé and Dinant were the devastatingly accurate and frighteningly demoralizing Stuka bombardments, operating as they were in a near-totally permissive environment provided by the Jagdwaffe's complete air superiority. The AdA was operating at maximum capacity and had no residual 'surge' or reserve capability. To the French, the RAF appeared to have an abundance of fighters not yet committed to defeating the Germans.

Winston Churchill

Winston Churchill.
(Photo by Culture Club/
Getty Images)

The man whose name came to epitomize British resistance to Nazi oppression was born of mixed English and American parentage on 30 November 1874. A direct descendant of the Dukes of Marlborough, Winston Leonard Spencer-Churchill and his family moved among the highest levels of British aristocracy and the governing elite. Although fascinated by innovation and change, Churchill fervently believed in maintaining the social status quo and was a staunch Royalist and Imperialist.

In February 1895, he was commissioned as a second lieutenant in the 4th Queen's Own Hussars and saw action in India and during the Anglo-Sudan War and Second Boer War. During this time, he gained accreditation as a correspondent and began writing news articles and books sharing his observations and experiences.

Arriving back in Britain in 1900, Churchill was elected as a Conservative Member of Parliament (MP). Over the next four years, he increasingly voted against his own party, eventually defecting to the Liberal opposition. In the 1906 general election, he was elected a Liberal MP and, two years later, was appointed to the Cabinet as President of the Board of Trade, at just 33 years old.

After serving as Home Secretary in 1910, Churchill was appointed First Lord of the Admiralty by Prime Minister Herbert Asquith in 1911. During the following two years, he encouraged the Royal Navy to experiment with aircraft in offensive roles and increased spending on submarines. He also closely monitored the build-up of the German navy, vowing that Britain would build two new battleships for every new one launched by Germany.

After the outbreak of World War I in November 1914, Churchill became one of the five members of Asquith's War Council. There, he encouraged the development of the tank as a way of breaking the bloody stalemate on the Western Front. More controversially, he strongly advocated opening a second front in the Dardanelles; the result was a calamitous campaign that cost the lives of thousands of Allied troops and lost Churchill his job.

After World War I, Churchill returned to the Conservative Party as Chancellor of the Exchequer. In 1924, he announced that Britain was returning to the Gold Standard, a disastrous decision that ultimately led to the General Strike of 1926. When the Conservative government was defeated in 1929, he returned once again to his writing and did not become politically active again until the 1930s, when he was given confidential access to sensitive information concerning the military preparedness of other nations. This enabled him to argue effectively for the case of re-arming against Germany.

A fierce critic of Neville Chamberlain's appeasement of Adolf Hitler, he was again appointed First Lord of the Admiralty on the day that Britain declared war on Germany, 3 September 1939, making him a high-profile member of the War Cabinet. He was the chief architect of and advocate for British and French intervention in Norway following the German invasion of the country in April 1940. The defeat and evacuation of the Allied Expeditionary Force from Norway in early May resulted in a vote of no confidence against Chamberlain, leading to his resignation just hours before Hilter's blitzkrieg was unleashed on France and the Low Countries.

With Great Britain facing its greatest crisis of modern times, Conservative Party favourite, Foreign Minister Edward Wood, 1st Earl of Halifax, architect of Chamberlain's failed appeasement policy, declined to become prime minister, leaving Churchill as the country's last hope against Hitler. Halifax stated that he felt Churchill would be a more suitable war leader.

Churchill later wrote, 'I felt as if I were walking with destiny, and that all my past life had been but a preparation for this hour and for this trial...'[16]

Consequently, at 1745hrs on 14 May, Reynaud sent a telegram to Churchill saying, in part:

Having just left the War Cabinet, I am sending you in the name of the French Government the following statement: The situation is indeed very serious. The German Army has broken through our fortified lines south of Sedan. Between Sedan and Paris, there are no defences comparable with those in the line which we must restore at almost any cost... You were kind enough to send four squadrons [3, 79, 501 and 504] which is more than you promised, but if we are to win this battle, which might be decisive for the whole war, it is necessary to send at once, if possible today, ten more squadrons. Without such a contribution, we cannot be certain that we shall be able to stem the German advance.'[17]

At 0730hrs the next morning, a dejected and panicked Reynaud called Churchill to say: 'We have been defeated… We are beaten; we have lost the battle'. The British Prime Minister took the shocking news and Reynaud's request for ten more RAF fighter squadrons to his 1030hrs chiefs of staff meeting, a half hour before the morning's War Cabinet meeting.[18]

Resulting from discussions in the chiefs of staff meeting two days prior, ACM Sir Hugh Dowding was invited to the meeting. When asked to share his opinion, the staunchly conservative and pessimistic AOCinC Fighter Command stated 'if things go badly we will have to face an attack directed against this country… If more fighters are taken, however, they would not achieve decisive results in France, and [I] would be left too weak to carry on over here'. He was absolutely opposed to parting with a single Hurricane unless overruled by the War Cabinet.[19]

Half an hour later Dowding's negative appreciation was shared with the War Cabinet, his opinion initially being expressed by Chief of the Air Staff ACM Cyril Newall, saying, 'Additional fighters for France could only be found by withdrawing them from the active defence of this country' and he 'would not [emphasis in original], at this moment advise the despatch of any additional fighters to France'. When asked his opinion, Dowding again reportedly 'made strong representations against sending any fighters out of the country'. The War Cabinet agreed that 'no further fighter squadrons should for the present be sent to France.'[20]

Apparently 'for the present' meant only that day.

That evening Gamelin sent Newall another, similarly worded appeal for ten fighter squadrons. Newall presented the second appeal at the following morning's chiefs of staff meeting. Despite Dowding's caution the day prior, in his absence the military chiefs agreed that sending more fighters was 'the right thing to do'. Churchill prevaricated, saying on the one hand it was 'a very grave risk', but the French needed to be bolstered in light of the 'new and critical situation'. The question was, really, how many squadrons to send? After debating between sending four or sending six, the chiefs of staff decided to recommend deploying four squadrons, with two more held in readiness, to reinforce the RAF's ten tired and badly depleted (78 Hurricanes lost thus far) squadrons.[21]

The War Cabinet agreed with the decision.

That afternoon, Churchill flew to Paris to convene with Reynaud, the French War Cabinet and the Allied High Command. There, he continued to be bombarded with more of the same pleas. After earnestly discussing the rapidly worsening situation and debating the continuing French insistence on more RAF fighter squadrons, at 2100hrs Churchill cabled London calling for a late-night meeting of the War Cabinet to consider further action by the RAF. In addition to directing Bomber Command to strike heavily against 'the German masses crossing the

LEFT
The victim of RAF
Hurricanes, Heinkel
He 111P 'B3+BK' of 3./KG
54 made a forced landing
between Épinoy and Oisy-le-
Verger on 19 May.
(NMUSAF)

BELOW
The navigator/bomb-aimer
of a Heinkel He 111 checks
his position. (Jean-Louis
Roba)

Meuse and flowing into "the Bulge"... [and] whether we can give further and above four squadrons for which the French are very grateful... I personally feel that we should send the squadrons of fighters demanded (i.e. six more) to-morrow [sic]... to give the last chance to the French army to rally its bravery and strength.'[22]

At 2330hrs the War Cabinet cabled its agreement.

By the next morning (17 May) the situation in northern France had reached a crisis. Guderian was halfway to the Channel, the headlong dash precipitously reducing the number of airfields available to host Fighter Command's reinforcements. Therefore, Newell decided that in lieu of deployments, the six additional squadrons (actually three squadrons and six 'half-squadrons', or detachments) would fly from bases in England, land, refuel and rearm in France, and return to British bases overnight.

This worked for only three more days. On 20 May, with the rapidly advancing panzers threatening to overrun their main bases, the BEF's Air Component was ordered withdrawn from France. Next day the surviving 66 Hurricanes of its seven squadrons returned to Britain to begin rebuilding.

A total of 215 fighters had been lost in or over France, about half of them in combat. Of these, 77 were lost to the Jagdwaffe. In return, 35 Bf 109Es had been shot down by Hurricanes, resulting in a kill:loss ratio (or exchange rate) of 2.2 Hurricanes shot down for every Bf 109E lost, a ratio that statistically confirms the Messerschmitt's superiority to the Hawker design.[23]

But aeroplanes could be readily replaced. Far more disturbing was the loss of 56 pilots killed and 18 captured during the fighting in France, the equivalent of four fighter squadrons.[24]

Likewise, the AdA also withdrew Groupement de Chasse 25, its fighter defence in northern France, to bases south of the Somme. By agreement between the two Allies' air commanders, from this point forward, air cover for the BEF and the surviving elements of the French 1ère Armée, both of which by now were retreating towards Boulogne, Calais, and Dunkirk, would be provided by Fighter Command's No. 11 Group, operating from its airfields in south-east England.[25]

NEXT PAGES
Ground crew refuel a 501
Squadron Hurricane from a
fuel bowser at Bétheniville.
Joining the AASF in May,
the squadron took part in
the retreat across France to
Brittany, ending its time in
France at Dinard between
11 and 18 June, before
being withdrawn to Jersey
and then back to the south
of England. (AHB)

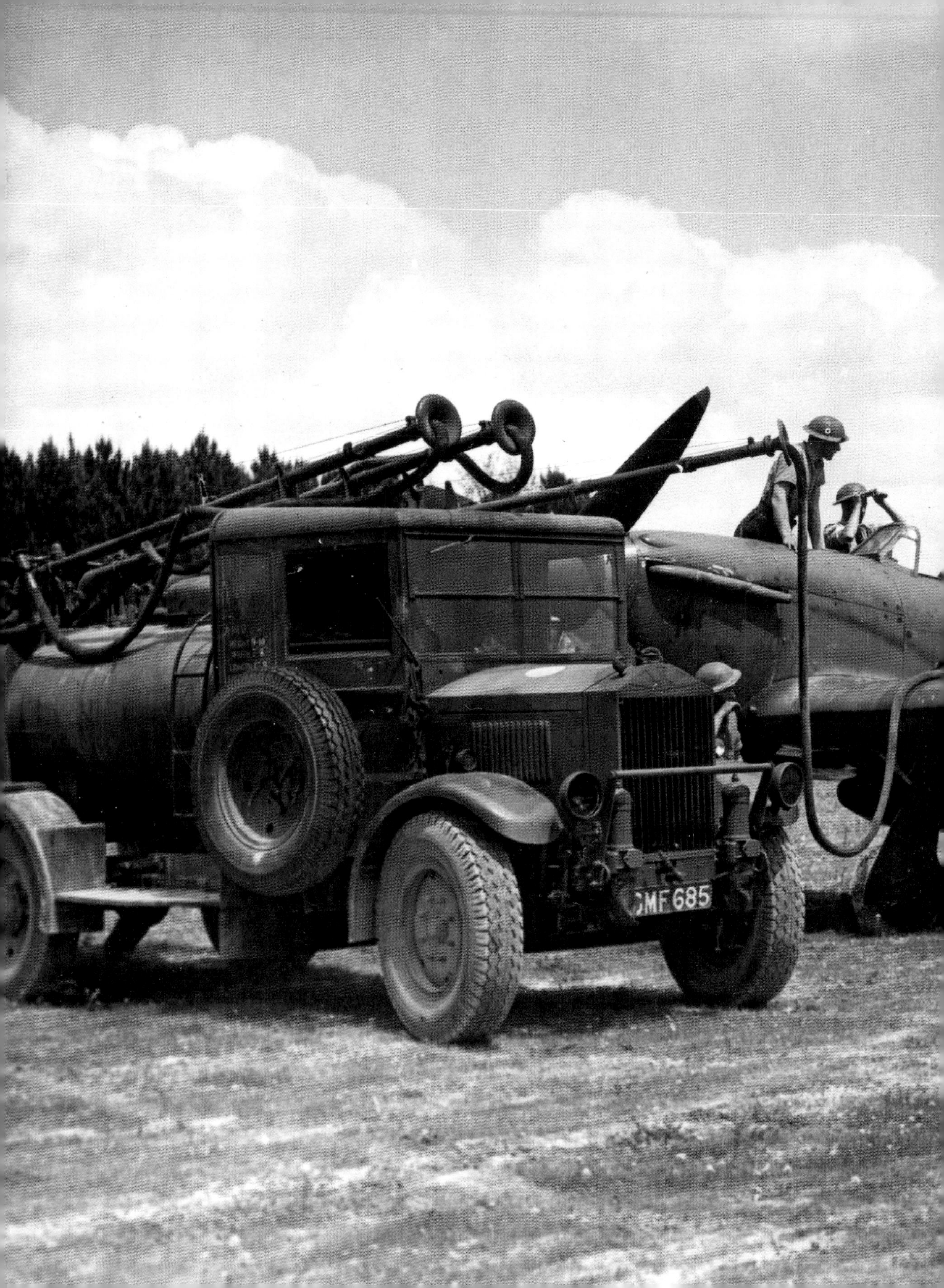
MF 685

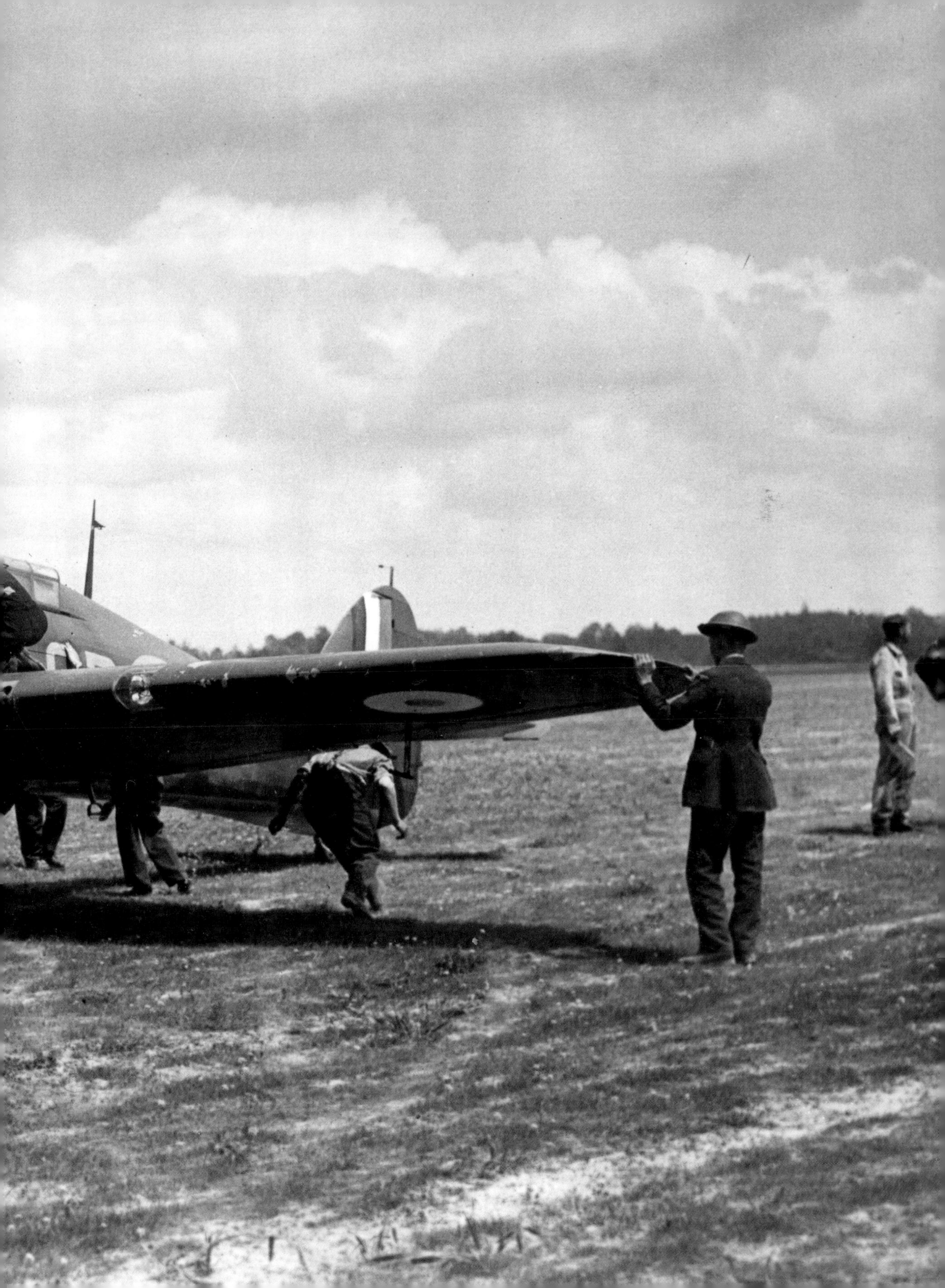

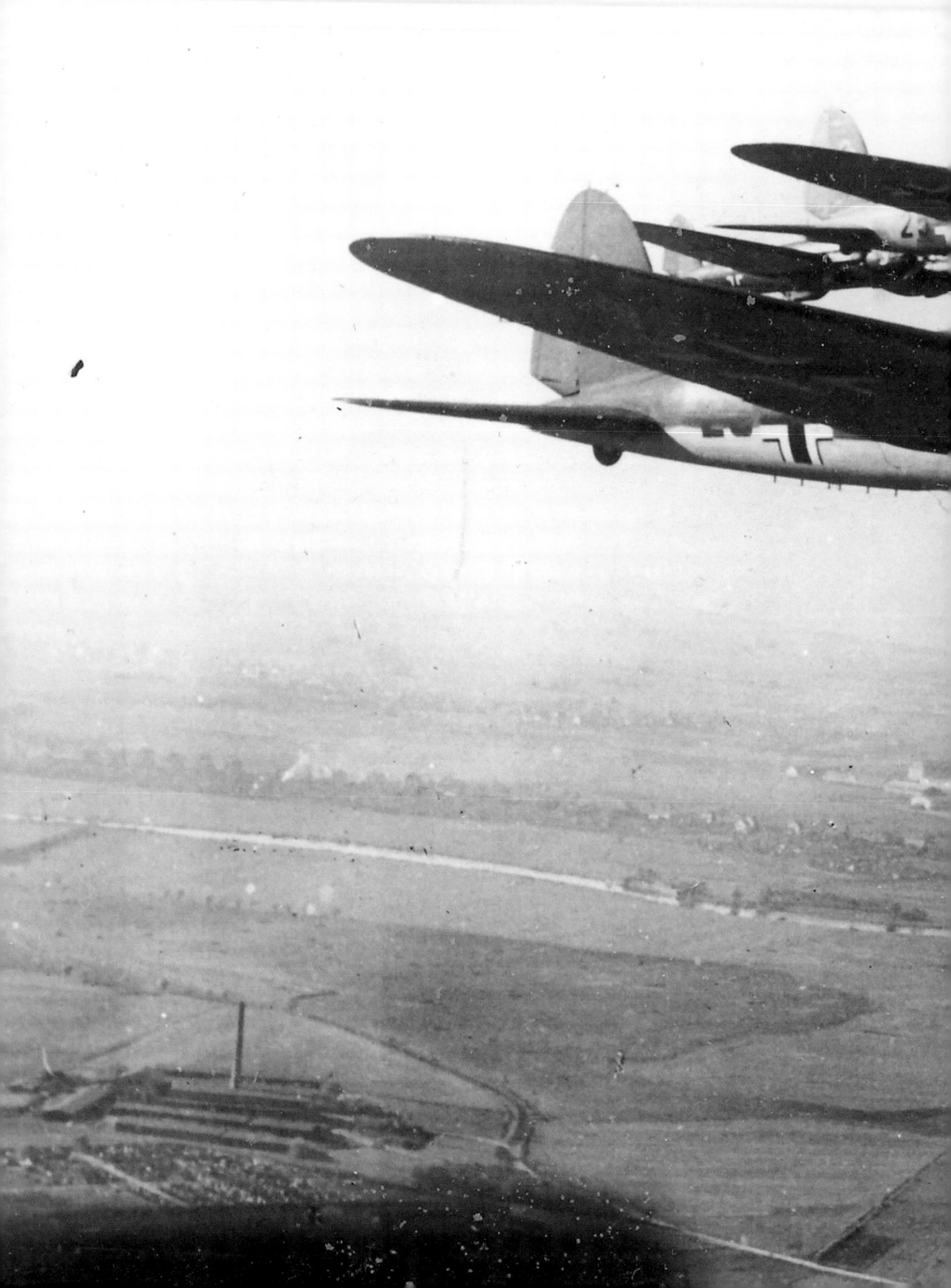

CHAPTER III

DUNKIRK

Triumph without victory

*The task of the Luftwaffe will be to break all enemy resistance on
the part of the surrounded* [British and French] *forces, to
prevent the escape of the English forces across the Channel, and to
protect the southern* [Somme River] *flank of Heeresgruppe A.*

Führer Directive Nr. 13 for the Conduct of the War, 24 May 1940[1]

'Stick to my tail, and for God's sake keep a look out behind.' Norman Franks' *Air
Battle Dunkirk* records these as the final words of advice from Flight Lieutenant (Flt
Lt) C.P. 'Paddy' Green, a 92 Squadron section leader, to his two wingmen, Pilot
Officers B.H.G. 'Pat' Learmond and A.C. 'Tony' Bartley, before they mounted their
Spitfires for a patrol over Dunkirk on 23 May 1940. That morning, one of 92
Squadron's flights had deployed forward from Northolt to Hornchurch and, joining
with a flight from 54 Squadron, took off around 0830hrs for what would become
the first encounter between RAF Spitfires and the Luftwaffe's Bf 109E.

Bartley later recounted:

'Look out, 109s!' someone yelled [on the radio] and almost simultaneously I saw
it. It was grey and evil-looking with its large black crosses, and I could see the
pilot crouched in his cockpit. So this was it… and as I started after him, I had
time to wonder if he felt as I did; if he loved to roll and loop in the towering
cumulus, and reach for the sun, high up and alone in the sky… He suddenly
turned a tight circle, but I turned tighter, and we both knew that the Spitfire
could outturn a Messerschmitt. He was looking back at me as I pressed the
trigger, and the tracer flickered over his wingtips.

Then I heard the bullets thudding into me as his compatriot flashed past. I'd
forgotten Paddy's warning to look behind. I was angry now, and I attacked again,
but Paddy suddenly appeared in front of me. He hit the 109 with his first burst
and an aileron flew off and fluttered earthwards like an autumn leaf. The aircraft
twisted in its agony, and spewed out its pilot. His face was white, and his blond
hair streamed grotesquely. He didn't pull his rip-cord. My petrol gauge was
showing next to zero, so I radioed Paddy I was going home. I saw the blazing
wreck of a Spitfire and I darted seawards over the swarming beaches. It was Pat
Learmond's – the squadron's first war casualty. [2]

PREVIOUS PAGES
On 27 May the Germans
once again unleashed their
panzers, while Heinkel
He 111s from KG 1 and
KG 4 pulverized Dunkirk's
harbour facilities, ending its
viability as an operating
seaport. (Jean-Louis Roba)

Number 92 Squadron reported encountering six Bf 109Es (I./JG 27) and claimed
all six shot down. Actually, two Messerschmitts were destroyed in this engagement,
both pilots baling out to become prisoners of war (POWs).[3]

However, in only two days of combat, 92 Squadron lost five Spitfires shot
down; two pilots were killed and three more captured, including their commander,
Squadron Leader (Sqn Ldr) Roger J. Bushell[4]; two other pilots were wounded and
seven fighters were damaged. Having claimed 30 Luftwaffe aircraft shot down

(Luftwaffe records verify the loss of one Do 17P, two Bf 109Es and three Bf 110s to 92 Sqn), on 25 May, the surviving Spitfires and pilots were withdrawn to Duxford, near Cambridge, to rebuild the squadron, temporarily under command of Flt Lt Robert 'Bob' R. Stanford Tuck.[5]

On 25 May, 19 Squadron moved from Duxford to Hornchurch. Over the next ten days, the squadron saw intense action while providing cover for Operation *Dynamo*. (Clive Ellis)

A NEW BATTLEGROUND – THE SKIES OVER THE FRENCH CHANNEL COAST

When the seven badly depleted BEF(AC) fighter units withdrew to England on 21 May, only 79 Sqn was fit for further fighting, leaving Fighter Command with 37 combat-ready single-engined fighter squadrons. Of these, eight Hurricane, seven Spitfire and one Defiant squadrons were under Air Vice-Marshal Keith Park's No. 11 Group, defending southern England, the part of Britain closest to the German forces rapidly approaching the Channel coast. Five of them, all flying Spitfires, were reserved for home defence; of 114 serviceable Spitfires, 137 Hurricanes and 18 Defiants, about 200 could be used on operations over France on any given day.[6]

At this point the Allied armies were attempting to defend a large boot-shaped area encompassing Dunkirk, Lille and Bruges, sealed by the panzers' arrival at the shores of the English Channel at Noyelles-sur-Mer, on the Somme Estuary near Abbeville, on 20 May. After a day of rest and reorganizing, Guderian was ordered to send 2. PzDiv north to besiege Boulogne and 1. PzDiv to invest Calais, then to advance eastwards towards Dunkirk, only to be stopped by Hitler's famous *Halt-Befehl* (halt order) on 24 May: 'By the Führer's orders… hold [along] the favourable defensive line Lens–Béthune–Aire–St Omer–Gravelines [along the canal

Guderian's hard-charging panzers arrived at the Channel coast on 20 May, trapping the BEF and French 1ère Armée in the Dunkirk–Lille Pocket. Two days later, 2. Panzer-Division invested Boulogne, its motorized infantry brigade dismounting to assault the city's defences. The British 20th Guards Brigade was evacuated that evening but the French 21e Division held out until 25 May. (NARA)

connecting Lens, Béthune, Aire, St Omer and Gravelines], and allow the enemy to attack it… The principal thing now is to husband the armoured formations for later and more important tasks.'[7]

Because Hitler wanted to preserve his victorious panzers for the *coup de grâce* against the French, once the Allies were surrounded in the 'Dunkirk–Lille Pocket' he hoped that they would try to break out to the south-west and attempt to rejoin the French armies south of the Somme, thereby destroying themselves in attacks against the panzers arrayed like so many steel casemates along the 'Canal Line' prescribed in the directive. According to Göring's boasts it would never come to that, because that same day he begged Hitler for a chance at glory, saying 'Mein Führer, leave the destruction of the enemy surrounded at Dunkirk to me and my Luftwaffe'. Before the day ended Hitler granted Göring's request in OKW War Directive No. 13, quoted above.[8]

Reichsmarschall Hermann Göring

On 26 February 1935, Adolf Hitler signed the secret decree authorizing the establishment of the Luftwaffe (formerly the Reichsluftwaffe) as Germany's third military service, separate and independent from, but equal with the Heer (army) and Kriegsmarine. The decree appointed Hermann Wilhelm Göring as commander-in-chief of the Luftwaffe. In his appointment, Hitler was ratifying the de facto command arrangements that had existed since 1933, when Nazi sympathizer Generalfeldmarschall Werner von Blomberg, the Wehrmacht commander-in-chief and Minister of Defence, moved supervision of Germany's rather disparate secret military aviation activities, at that time consolidated in the Luftschutz Amt (Air Defence Bureau), from the Reichswehr staff to Göring's Reichsluftfahrtministerium (RLM, Reich Aviation Ministry) on 15 May 1933.

Göring had been a fighter pilot during World War I. Born to a Bavarian foreign service officer and his peasant wife in 1893, he attended the Berlin Lichterfelde military academy and joined the Imperial German Army's Prince Wilhelm Regiment (112th Infantry) in 1912. Following a severe bout of rheumatism resulting from months of exposure in the dampness of trench warfare, in 1916 he arranged for his own transfer, through connections fostered with the royal family, to Feldflieger Abteilung 25 (FFA, Field Flying Unit 25), initially as an observer. Drawn to the glory of being a fighter pilot, he completed flight training and was eventually posted to Jagdstaffel (fighter squadron, commonly shortened to Jasta) 26, in February 1917.

Through the next year he became a successful fighter pilot and was made commander of Jasta 27, amassing 18 accredited victories. Afraid that the war would end before he reached 20, the number required to be considered for the coveted Pour le Mérite (the famous 'Blue Max'), he persuaded an influential friend to lobby for him and was awarded the prestigious decoration on 2 June 1918, although he eventually tallied 22 kills.

Reichsmarschall Hermann Göring. (Author Collection, colourized by Richard Molloy)

Adroit at leveraging connections, Göring was an inscrutable and sometimes ruthless political animal; when Baron von Richthofen's replacement was killed in July 1918 while test flying an experimental all-metal monoplane, Oberleutnant (Olt, 1st Lieutenant) Göring had himself appointed as the next – and last – commander of Jagdgeschwader Nr. 1, the famous 'Richthofen Flying Circus'. Inheriting the famous 'Rittmeisters Geschwaderstock' (literally 'the baron's wing stick', a knobby walking stick that served as the unit commander's baton), Göring was not appreciated by the unit, one member commenting: 'Richthofen flew and fought for the Kaiser and his Fatherland, not for decorations, but from a sense of duty. Göring fought until his ambition was satisfied. He had the Pour le Mérite and was commander of the most famous unit in the Fliegertruppen (flying troops)… then he led the Geschwader with the stick from the ground.'[9]

Marrying into money and Swedish nobility on 3 February 1922, after the war Göring did a little barnstorming before moving to Munich to study political science, where he soon met and became enthralled with Adolf Hitler, joining the NSDAP the next year. Göring came into his own as a Nazi politician, being elected to the Reichstag in 1928, and arranged to have himself appointed as Prussia's Minister of the Interior, the position from which he controlled the state police.

When Hitler came to power, he appointed Göring to his Cabinet as a minister without portfolio. Once Hitler had made him Reich Air Minister, he oversaw the development and expansion of the Luftwaffe, mostly as a basis for promoting his own power and influence. Prior to Hitler beginning World War II, Göring only exerted his command authority over personnel moves and aircraft production. He was no airpower expert. He had not flown an aircraft since 1922, had no knowledge of or experience in air campaigning, and left doctrine, technological development and combat operations to the professionals, at least until the wartime employment of 'his Luftwaffe' put his prestige at risk.[10]

Completely detached from the concerns of ongoing operations, Göring's vainglorious scheme failed to take into account the high losses sustained in the fortnight of intense, continuous and unrelenting aerial operations against determined AdA and RAF fighter defences. As of 25 May, 641 combat aircraft had been destroyed or badly damaged, 23 per cent of the Luftwaffe's starting inventory, and serviceability was down to 50 per cent due to battle damage and wear from incessant high-tempo operations. Even with timely replacements many Kampfgruppen were down to 15 serviceable aircraft, against a statutory strength of 30.[11]

Consequently, Göring did not have the support of his two Luftflotte leaders. Luftflotte 2, led by General der Flieger Albrecht 'Albert' Kesselring, was supporting Generaloberst Fedor von Bock's Heeresgruppe B, an all-infantry command advancing on a broad front against the eastern side of the Allied pocket. In his autobiography *The Memoirs of Field-Marshal Kesselring*, he stated that he believed, 'The job is completely beyond the strength of my depleted forces,' and that such 'an operation could hardly be carried out successfully by fresh forces. I expressed this view to Göring and told him it could not be done even with the support of VIII. Fliegerkorps… But Göring had pledged himself to the Führer to wipe out the English with his Luftwaffe. I pointed out that the modern Spitfires had recently appeared, making our air operations difficult and costly.'[12]

Kesselring's command comprised I. and IV. Fliegerkorps, consisting of 24 Kampfgruppen, all of which were still based in Germany except I. and III./KG 30, which had deployed to Amsterdam's Schiphol airport. Trained and experienced during the Norwegian campaign in the anti-shipping role, these two Ju 88A units were intended primarily for employment against the RN forces operating in the southern part of the North Sea and the eastern end of the English Channel.

Ju 88A '4U+AL' flown by Fw Ackenhausen of 3.(F)/123, was brought down near Abbeville during a reconnaissance sortie on 24 May. The unit was just transitioning from Do 17Ps to the Ju 88 and had only three at the time of the incident. (AHB donated by Ken Wakefield)

Luftflotte 3's General der Flieger Hugo Sperrle commanded II., V. and VIII. Fliegerkorps. Of these, Generalleutnant Robert Ritter von Greim's V. Fliegerkorps was responsible for guarding the left flank, Generaloberst Gerd von Rundstedt's Heeresgruppe A, protecting the overstretched invaders from Allied counter-attacks from south of the Somme River. Supporting Rundstedt's right flank operations against the Dunkirk–Lille Pocket, the nine Kampfgruppen of Generalleutnant Bruno Loerzer's II. Fliegerkorps were flying from their bases back in Germany. With some of these as far as 300 miles from Dunkirk, the units were operating at the limits of their range and could manage only one mission each day.

This left Generalmajor Wolfram von Richthofen's VIII. Fliegerkorps as the only air command capable of executing Göring's stated intention, but it too had problems. Richthofen's three Ju 87 Stukageschwader (Stuka wings), StGs 1, 2 and 77, tried to follow closely behind their armoured charges, but struggled to keep up. By this time, StG 1 had leapfrogged forward to Cambrai, 65 miles (105km) from Dunkirk, but StG 2 was still at Guise, near St Quentin, 40 miles farther back, while StG 77 remained at Rocroi, another 43 miles (70km) to the rear, operating at the very limits of its combat radius. Reported in Hans-Dieter Berenbrok's *Luftwaffe War Diaries*, Richthofen lamented, 'My Stukas are too far back, their approach flights too long. Consequently, I can use them twice a day at most, and am unable to focus them at one point of effort.[13]

Richthofen's comment reflects his frustration with the extraordinary demands being made on his command. For example, during the first two days' operations against Dunkirk, VIII. Fliegerkorps could not participate because it was heavily engaged against French forces at Boulogne, Lille, and Amiens, and the embattled French–British contingent defending Calais. Additionally, resupply to the Stuka units had slowed appreciably due to the rapid pace of advance. Vehicle columns were delayed behind marching infantry formations and the debilitating losses of 232 of 476 of the Luftwaffe's Ju 52/3m transports meant that the surviving airlift units could not carry enough fuel, bombs and ammunition to sustain the earlier high-tempo operations.[14]

Nevertheless, attempting to fulfil their leader's promises to their Führer, the two Luftflotten opened their campaign against Dunkirk on 25 May with I., II. and IV. Fliegerkorps conducting heavy bombing raids, knocking out all electrical power and water mains, destroying the main harbour entrance lock and wrecking all the massive cranes needed for loading and unloading ships. Catching a French re-supply convoy in the harbour, the raiders sank five of the 13 cargo ships at their moorings.[15]

Meanwhile, that morning the French defenders at Boulogne surrendered and the Allies defending Calais were overrun the next day, leaving Dunkirk as the only possible embarkation point for the British and French forces trapped within the pocket. Because Park's No. 11 Group was providing fighter cover over the British 30th Brigade, fighting for its life inside the ancient city walls of Calais, RAF fighters made little attempt to stop the incessant bombing of Dunkirk's port facilities.[16]

At 1530hrs on 26 May, OKH HQ ordered Rundstedt to resume his offensive with: 'A forward thrust from the west by panzer groups and infantry divisions in the direction[s] of Tournai, Cassel [and] Dunkirk.' Motorized infantry began their assaults against the Canal Line almost immediately, with the panzers joining in the next day. Supporting them, the Luftwaffe completed its destruction of Dunkirk as an operating seaport. Flying 225 bomber and 75 Stuka sorties and dropping over 350 tons of bombs, waves of KG 1 and 4 He 111s pulverized the city's harbour facilities, completely devastating the seven docking basins, five miles of quays and 115 acres of docks and warehouses. Attacks by KG 54 and StG 2 sank two French steamers, an auxiliary minesweeper and a small British coaster. Do 17Zs from KG 2 and 3 wrecked the railyards and set fire to the town and Saint-Pol oil refinery. By noon the port was completely blocked and the fires raged unchecked, killing 1,000 civilians. A huge pall of oily black smoke, rising 11,000ft into the air, provided a beacon for both raiders and defenders.[17]

Assuring Hitler that 'his Luftwaffe' had destroyed Dunkirk harbour, in his biography *Adolf Hitler*, John Toland notes that Göring crowed, 'Only fish bait will reach the other side [of the Channel]. I hope the Tommies are good swimmers.'[18]

Number 11 Group countered with 23 squadron-sized (typically 12 fighters each) patrols in 287 sorties, flying as far east as Ostend and south to Saint-Omer. They accounted for 15 bombers destroyed, but lost heavily to the bombers' defensive fire and escorting fighters. Battling 550 Messerschmitts operating in Gruppe strength (40 fighters) the badly outnumbered RAF squadrons lost fourteen Hurricanes and five Spitfires. Four Bf 109Es and five Bf 110Cs were destroyed.[19]

OPERATION *DYNAMO* BEGINS – EVACUATING THE BEF FROM FRANCE

The plan to rescue the BEF was developed quickly on an ad hoc basis by the Royal Navy's Dover Command, which then began organizing the increasing amounts of shipping provided and plotting their routes through the numerous minefields to the beachhead. With the destruction of Dunkirk's port, Captain William G. Tennant, Senior Naval Officer ashore, directed the first evacuation ships to three new embarkation

points: the beaches at Malo-les-Bains, an eastern suburb of Dunkirk (for III Corps), Bray-Dunes Plage (I Corps) and La Panne Bains, now De Panne (for II Corps), to its east. Operation *Dynamo* was ordered to commence at 1857hrs on Sunday, 26 May.

To prevent the Luftwaffe from interrupting this desperate process, the RAF was directed to provide continuous effective air cover over the port, beaches and ships. To do so, Park planned to provide alternating waves of Spitfires and Hurricanes beginning at dawn each day. Initially, these were to launch at 50-minute intervals (from 0430 until 1930hrs) to cover the French coast in squadron strength. Launching from Hornchurch, Gravesend, Hawkinge and Manston, up to 60 miles from Dunkirk, the fighters' flight time to reach the patrol area at a fuel-conserving cruise speed of 180mph, including 10 minutes to assemble the squadron formation once airborne, was 30 minutes.[20] This left 20 minutes of flying time for the actual patrol for Spitfires flying from Hornchurch and Gravesend, and 40 minutes for Hurricanes staging from Manston and Hawkinge, with 20 minutes of fuel for the return to base, and a 10-minute reserve. As a result, when one squadron had to begin its return flight, its replacement was just launching, leaving as much as 30 minutes when no British fighters were overhead the embattled city, beaches, or the Allies' defensive perimeter.

The high losses the previous day motivated Park immediately to change tactics: squadrons were combined (or 'paired') in order to meet the Messerschmitts on anything like equal terms. On 28 May, No. 11 Group launched 11 two-squadron patrols averaging 29 fighters each, for 321 sorties. But pairing the squadrons increased the gap between them departing and arriving in the patrol areas, since Park was effectively launching 11 larger formations of similar endurance, compared with 23 smaller formations: over the course of the day's 15 hours of flying operations, RAF fighters were overhead for only about 6 hours, with up to 90 minutes between appearances. Is it any surprise the BEF and Royal Navy began to ask: 'Where's the RAF?'[21]

Still outnumbered, although not as badly now that combined formations were being used, the Spitfire and Hurricane pilots had an additional disadvantage. They

ABOVE LEFT
The speed of the panzer thrust was such that the supporting Stuka units – StG 1, 2 and 77 – found it difficult to keep up and were often operating at the limit of their combat range. At an abandoned BEF(AC) airfield a wrecked RAF Hurricane provides evidence of the defeat, with a victorious Ju 87 parked in the background.
(Thomas Laemlein)

ABOVE
Disabled British anti-aircraft guns along the promenade at Bray-Dunes. (© IWM HU 2286)

were patrolling beyond the effective range of the new Chain Home early-warning radar system and No. 11 Group's sector stations' radio range. Thus, the relatively untested Spitfire and Hurricane pilots found themselves operating against the Luftwaffe's battle-hardened Jagdflieger in an aerial no man's land.[22]

Supermarine Spitfire Mk I

The second design spawned by Air Ministry specification F.5/34 was another private venture. Sir Reginald Mitchell's high-speed seaplanes had won the Schneider Trophy outright for Great Britain and he applied many of the aerodynamic and power concepts of his racers to a sleek, fast, all-metal fighter design. Ironically, Mitchell had designed a disappointing monoplane against the earlier F.7/30 specification, which called for an advanced monoplane fighter but proved too demanding for contemporary technology.

He set out to design an all-new machine informed by the Schneider designs, the Type 300 showing such promise that the Air Ministry drew up F.37/34 around it. The resulting Supermarine Spitfire was an elegant design featuring a thin, graceful and efficient elliptical wing. Powered by the same 1,030hp Rolls-Royce Merlin II/III as the initial Hurricanes, it offered higher performance, but its modern, more complex stressed-skin, all-metal semi-monocoque structure required skilled labour, greater effort and took 2.5 times longer to construct.

The Spitfire initially struggled with a series of technical problems, not least with its guns, when the outermost weapon, being so far from the aircraft's centreline, was prone to misalignment as the thin wing flexed and twisted under high-g loading in a turning fight, resulting in 25 per cent of the ammunition being fired falling outside the harmonized target area. There were also issues with icing and jamming, while the aircraft's narrow-track retractable landing gear gave it tricky ground-handling characteristics.

Nonetheless, the Spitfire was a speedy interceptor capable of 355mph (571kph) at 19,000ft – slightly faster than the Bf 109E – and boasted a ceiling of 34,000ft. It could turn more tightly than the 465lb-heavier Hurricane at 300mph (483kph) and 10,000ft altitude, under which conditions it had virtually identical turning performance to the Bf 109E. As speed diminished in a turning fight, the Spitfire's lower wing loading gave it an increasing advantage until the Messerschmitt's leading-edge slats deployed (at about 150mph, depending on g), which then gave the advantage to the Bf 109. The Messerschmitt also had the advantage in negative-g flight, where its fuel-injection system ensured even fuel flow, while the Spitfire's gravity carburettor did not.

For receiving radio vectors from sector stations and for intra-flight communications, the Mark I, in common with the Hurricane, was initially equipped with the single-channel HF TR9 radio-telephony (R/T) set, which had its operating frequency set ('crystalized') on the ground; it had an air-to-air range of five miles and an air-to-ground range of 35 miles (56km). Because of the TR9's severely limited range,

Fighter Command established mobile HF relay stations at 30–40 mile (48–64km) intervals ahead of (towards the threat) its sector stations and ordered the development of longer-ranged, multi-channel VHF radios.

Conversion to the vastly superior (100/140-mile, 161/225km range) TR1133 four-channel VHF radio was under way by May 1940, but the immediate need for standardized radio sets among Fighter Command squadrons resulted in Dowding ordering the eight VHF-equipped fighter squadrons to be retrofitted with the TR9D. The conversion to TR1133 was re-initiated in August, but did not progress quickly enough for Fighter Command to take advantage of the superiority of VHF over HF.

Spitfire. (Clive Ellis)

Considering the destruction of Dunkirk's port facilities complete, on the 28th, Luftflotte 2 turned its attention to other, smaller seaports inside the Allied pocket – Ostend, Nieuport and Zeebrugge, Belgium – while Luftflotte 3 continued pounding the French 1ère Armée's large troop concentrations around Lille. Having eliminated the enemy's opportunity to escape, or at least believing they had, from this point on the Luftwaffe leaders expected to be able to bomb the cornered Allied troops into submission just as they had the luckless Poles the previous September.

Only 75 bombing sorties were therefore flown against Dunkirk, the largest raid arriving at 1000hrs and comprising KG 77 Dorniers heavily protected by Bf 109Es. From JG 3, 26, 51 and 54, the 'Emils' were numerous and effective. Only two Dorniers were lost to RAF fighters (although 23 victories were claimed), while in this and other sporadic clashes during the day three Spitfires, three Defiants and eight Hurricanes were shot down for the loss of only two Bf 109Es.[23]

Continuing heavy losses prompted yet another change in tactics. The following day, No. 11 Group began simultaneously launching up to four squadrons in two

INSET
Dunkirk harbour as it appeared when the Royal Navy arrived. The Saint-Pol oil refinery burns fiercely in the background as a paddle-wheel minesweeper steams into the harbour and HMS *Vanquisher* (foreground), positions to follow. The east mole is to the left, with one vessel docked, and the west mole with its lighthouse is to the right. (AHB)

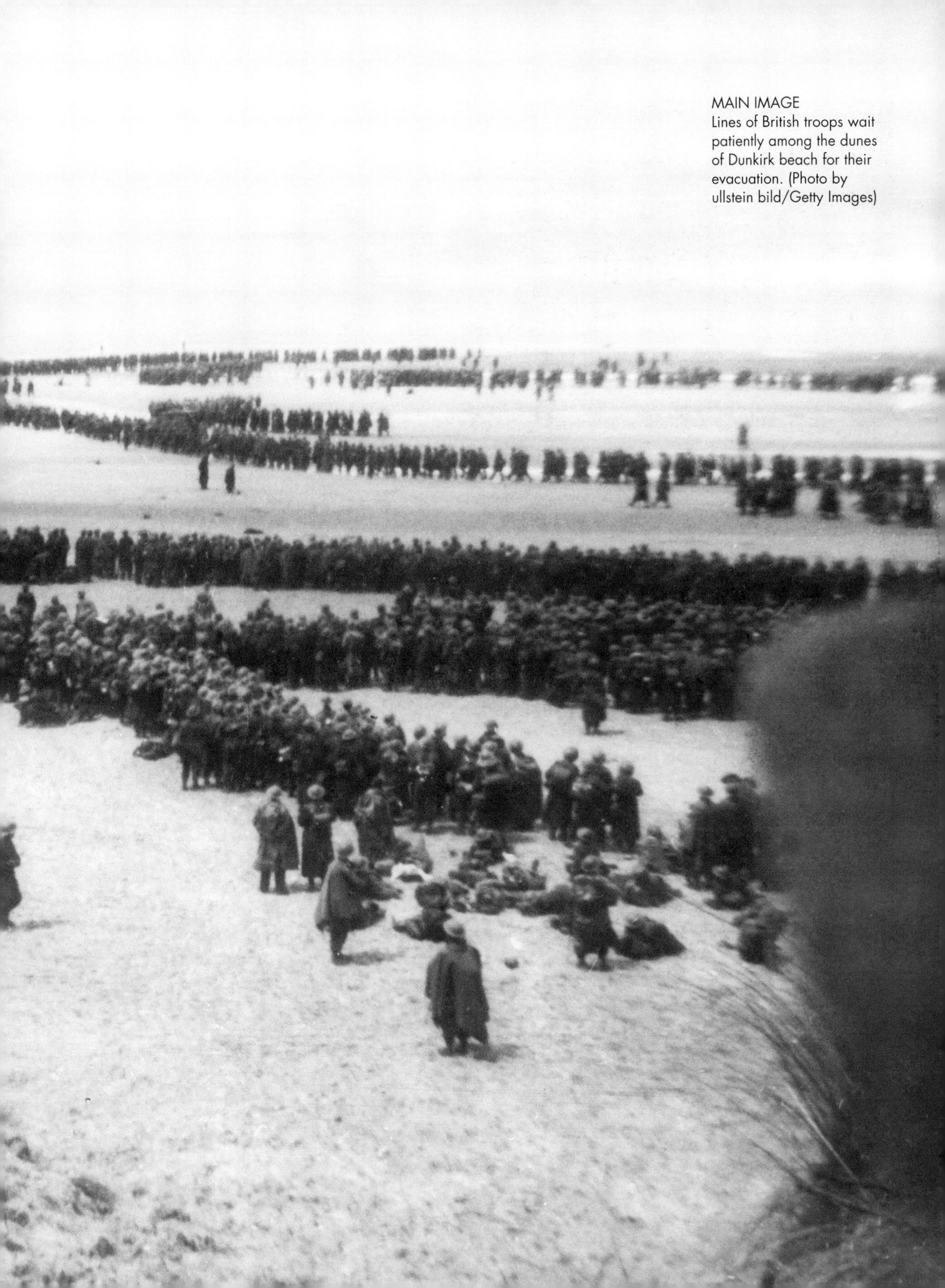

MAIN IMAGE
Lines of British troops wait patiently among the dunes of Dunkirk beach for their evacuation. (Photo by ullstein bild/Getty Images)

concurrent two-squadron efforts, averaging two 30-aircraft patrols (for 275 sorties in nine missions) in the operational area. This new grouping lengthened the gaps in fighter coverage even more, resulting in up to three hours between appearances.

Taking advantage of these three-hour breaks, the Germans hit Dunkirk with five massive raids, twice attacking virtually unopposed. In 175 bombing sorties, the Luftwaffe lost four 1./KG 1 He 111s and four II./LG 1 Ju 88s, while escorting Bf 109Es shot down seven Spitfires from 41, 64, and 610 Sqns, and seven 151, 229, and 241 Sqn Hurricanes for the loss of six aircraft from I./JG 3 and I./JG 27, plus one Bf 110C.

Having brought the retreat of the French 4ᵉ and 5ᵉ Corps to a standstill – they surrendered at Lille on 1 June – Richthofen's VIII. Fliegerkorps shifted its attention to the French 16ᵉ Corps and the BEF trapped at Dunkirk. Operating with near impunity, 235 Stukas attacked the many merchant vessels and their warship escorts off Dunkirk. At 1500hrs the first raid –180 Ju 87s – arrived overhead. Number 56 Squadron alone intercepted them, losing two Hurricanes to their rear gunners without shooting down any of the attackers. Dive-bombing Ju 88s from I./KG 30 and II./LG 1 followed up 30 minutes later. Another 55 Ju 87s arrived between 1930 and 1955hrs to complete the maelstrom of destruction. Four StG 2 and 77 Stukas were lost, some of them to ships' AA fire.

Targeting the many stationary vessels embarking troops from the harbour's 4,200ft-long (1.3km) eastern jetty and standing just offshore, this devastating series of attacks sank one destroyer and damaged eight others so badly they were withdrawn for repairs. Off Bray-Dunes, the stern of the 1,105-ton escort sloop HMS *Bideford* was blown off and it was beached to prevent sinking. Off La Panne, two ancient wooden paddlewheel minesweepers, a pair of small trawlers and six large personnel ships were sunk. The largest was the 6,787-ton Glasgow merchantman SS *Clan MacAlister*, which was hit repeatedly and, burning fiercely, sank in shallow water. Stukas also sank four French steamers and three Belgian tugboats in the harbour.[24]

Bad weather closed in the next day, providing both sides with a reprieve from the exhausting pace of operations. Low thick clouds and fog cloaked the entire coast with ceilings of 300ft and tops at 3,000ft, completely precluding bombing operations.[25]

Dowding took advantage of the brief lull to reinforce No. 11 Group, bringing 43 Squadron from Wick to Tangmere to replace 601 Squadron, which moved west to just-opened Middle Wallop, and ordering 66 Squadron from Coltishall to Gravesend for one day, relieving 610 Squadron, which returned to Biggin Hill. Next day, 72 Squadron was also sent to Gravesend, from Acklington, with 66 Squadron moving to Martlesham Heath. Number 266 Squadron joined 66 Squadron from Wittering on 2 June.[26]

'THOUSANDS OF THE ENEMY GET AWAY TO ENGLAND RIGHT UNDER OUR VERY NOSES...'[27]

By Friday 31 May, 126,606 Allied soldiers had been ferried to safety, leaving some 92,000 British and 160,000 French troops cornered within and defiantly defending

The Messerschmitt Bf 109E 'Emil' dominated the air battles fought over Dunkirk. Seen here is a Bf 109E-1 of 2./JG 2 'Richthofen'. (Clive Ellis)

Seven hospital ships, three of them making the trip to Dunkirk twice, brought 2,284 wounded troops back to Britain. (Media Drum World)

the Dunkirk perimeter. That morning, the invaders initiated a co-ordinated series of assaults to break through the Allied defences.

Once the thick morning haze gave way to fair, though cloudy skies, the Luftwaffe returned, targeting the British troop concentrations on and near the beaches rather than bombing ships offshore. Three large waves, totalling 195 bomber sorties, protected by 260 Messerschmitts were challenged by 289 RAF fighters flying in eight three- to-four-squadron missions. Some of these patrols were present when the raids arrived, at 1415, 1700 and 1900hrs but, outnumbered by fighter escorts, they failed to impede the attacks significantly, shooting down only six KG 4 and 27 and LG 1 bombers and four escorting III./JG 26 Bf 109Es. Return fire and Messerschmitts destroyed six Spitfires, eight Hurricanes and five Defiants, the highest daily loss during *Dynamo*.[28]

On 1 June, finally realizing that the prey was escaping and his boasts would likely backfire, Göring, who had been touring Dutch cities confiscating loot for his personal collections, rushed back to work in an attempt to re-energize his commanders and reverse the Luftwaffe's impending failure to fulfil his promises.[29]

The Luftwaffe therefore struck ferociously and with renewed intensity, attacking with 160 bomber and 325 Stuka sorties, the largest numbers used during the battle and marking its climax. Arriving in five major raids, the enemy was met by the RAF's typical defensive response: 267 fighter sorties were flown in eight missions. Again though, there were long periods with little cover, and even when the RAF was present the 420 Bf 109Es and 110 Bf 110s successfully protected their charges. Only two bombers, from 1./KG 4 and 4./KG 76, and two I. (Stuka)/ Trägergruppe (carrier group) 186 Stukas were lost to RAF fighters, while six Hurricanes and ten Spitfires were shot down. The Luftwaffe lost seven Bf 109Es and three Bf 110Cs.

Diving out of clear blue skies, the heavy air assaults wreaked havoc upon the evacuation fleet. Attacks began at 0515hrs, when a formation of 40 StG 1 Stukas arrived before 11 Group's 'dawn patrol' and attacked ships offshore. At 0720hrs an even larger raid followed, comprising Ju 87s from StG 2 and 77 and LG 1 Ju 88s; it went unopposed.

The primary target, off Bray-Dunes, was the 1,400-ton destroyer HMS *Keith*, flagship of Rear Admiral William F. Wake-Walker, the on-scene commander for *Dynamo*. Down to only 30 rounds of AA ammunition, it was soon defenceless, overwhelmed and bombed by all three waves, finally capsizing and sinking. The destroyers *Basilisk* and *Havant* were also hit; the former subsequently sank and the latter had to be scuttled. The modern minesweeper *Skipjack* was hit by five bombs and exploded, sinking immediately. The large Admiralty tug *St Abbs*, having just rescued many of the *Keith*'s survivors, was blown out of the water by a single bomb from a Ju 88A.

At 1000hrs the carnage continued as KG 76 Dorniers and KG 4 Heinkels rained sticks of bombs on the huge collection of vessels. The tiny gunboat *Mosquito* was hit, set on fire, abandoned and scuttled after it flooded while under tow back to England. The 4,240-ton steamer *Prague*, returning with 3,000 French troops aboard, was badly damaged but made it back to British waters to beach on Sandwich Flats.

Hurricanes from 43, 145, 245 and 609 Sqn were overhead at midday when the Stukas returned, but escorting II./JG 26 Bf 109Es kept them at bay, shooting down five for the loss of two. The Ju 87s sank the 1,356-ton French destroyer *Foudroyant* with three direct hits. The old 3,454-ton steamer *Scotia* was also hit by three bombs and sank quickly.[30]

Hauptman Helmut Mahlke, Staka of 2. Staffel (Stuka)/Trägergruppe (carrier group) 186, the dive-bomber unit organized and trained for anti-ship operations from Germany's never-finished aircraft carrier *Graf Zeppelin*, was a three-mission veteran of the day's attacks against shipping off Dunkirk's beaches. Subordinated to StG 1, I.(St)/TrGr 186 had supported the panzers' penetrations at Sedan, pounding French fortifications, artillery and fieldworks. Moving to Guise, it had been part of Richthofen's 'flying artillery' supporting Guderian's decisive dash to the Channel.

In his autobiography, *Memoirs of a Stuka Pilot*, Mahlke recalled:

> By this time the British were sending every vessel – naval, merchant or civilian which was capable of carrying troops – across the Channel in a desperate attempt to evacuate their expeditionary corps from Dunkirk. And on this particular day we were ordered to attack this shipping off Dunkirk's beaches. In the harbour itself a number of ships were lying half-submerged on the bottom. Along the beaches the British had driven long lines of vehicles into the water, presumably to act as makeshift boarding stages. I led my staffel down against a fair-sized steamer that was getting under way just offshore. We scored several hits amidships and near the stern of the vessel. [It was probably HMS *Skipjack*, which reported being attacked by '10 aircraft' and taking hits from five bombs at 0845hrs, sinking with the loss of 19 crewmen and 275 troops.] There were some heavy

TOP RIGHT
A heavily loaded drifter
makes 'best speed' for
England as Dunkirk
continues to burn in the
background. These 'little
ships' returned 28,708 men
home and provided the
crucial link in ferrying wet,
weary troops from the
beaches out to the larger
vessels waiting farther
offshore. (© IWM HU
2108)

BELOW RIGHT
A target-rich environment:
dozens of 'little ships' and
their RN escorts wait
offshore at La Panne as an
RAF Coastal Command
Hudson keeps a watchful
eye. Dawning bright and
clear, 1 June brought
perfect weather for Stuka
attacks. One destroyer
heads outbound while a
minesweeper, destroyer and
large tug, none of which
survived the morning, steam
towards the crowd of
schuyts, trawlers and drifters
nearer the shoreline. (AHB)

bursts of flak to port… then more flak to starboard – this time pearls of little red 'mice' chasing each other through the air, indicating tracer fire. We hurriedly jinked away – turning sometimes gently, sometimes sharply – until we were safely out of range.

Two hours later, we were taking to the air again. Same situation, same orders… For this mission we split up into separate Ketten [three-aircraft bombing formations] and were searching for fresh targets a little further out to sea… Not far away a small transport of scarcely 2,000 tons [most likely the paddlewheel minesweeper *Brighton Queen*, sunk at 1035hrs with 700 French Moroccan troops aboard] was fleeing northwards at top speed. It wasn't long before I had it in my bombsight. We were already at a fairly low altitude, but with just enough height left to carry out an attack. Release bomb – recover – observe the results: I had missed completely but my wingmen more than made up for it with two direct hits on the vessel's afterdeck. The ship's sternpost disappeared beneath the waves as it slowly began to sink.

Another two hours and we were taking off again and heading for Dunkirk and the British evacuation shipping for a third time. Close inshore, all we could see were stranded and half sunken vessels and floating wreckage. Further out to sea, about ten kilometres from the coast, there was still a whole flotilla of little ships of every kind: coastal steamers, sailing boats, tugs towing barges and much more… Not far away I caught sight of a small ship that had been hidden by cloud up until that moment… [I] Put her nose down – attack! My bomb hit the water immediately ahead of the ship's bow. As we started to climb away we kept our eyes glued to the vessel. Unable to take avoiding action in time, it was steaming straight through the widening circle of ripples that marked the spot where the bomb had disappeared into the water. At that moment there was a mighty explosion immediately under the middle of the ship. It seemed to lift right out of the water and bits of wreckage were hurled a good 50 metres into the air. A fascinating sight – but a horrible one!

Mahlke's target this time was undoubtedly one of four 300-ton French minesweeping trawlers returning to Dunkirk for more troops. Nine Ju 87s attacked them just north of Gravelines (west of Dunkirk), at 1330hrs. The official Royal Navy History of Operation *Dynamo* records that *Denis Papin* was 'blown out of the water by a direct hit' that killed the entire crew. *Vénus* was also hit, and sank in four minutes, followed by *Moussaillon*.

Pulling out of their dives, Mahlke said his Stukas were attacked by Spitfires:[31]

'Fighter to port,' [gunner/radio operator Fritz] Baudisch's voice sounded in the earphones. The Spitfire was curving in for a stern attack. I reefed my machine around in an effort to meet it. But the distance between us was far too small. Both still banking vertically, we flashed past each other no more than 20 metres apart. He turned in for another attack. Again I dragged the Ju 87 around onto a collision course. Again we shot past each other with only metres to spare.

A second Spitfire was closing in fast from the other side and already getting dangerously close. No time to turn in towards this one. I hauled back hard and sharp on the stick and the fine white strands of his machine-gun fire passed beneath us… The enemy fighters made several more passes, but each time I was able to face them almost head-on. A Spitfire raced past me one last time before they broke away. They must have been running short of fuel and needed to get home. Then I noticed that one of the pair had curved in on my tail again and was slowly drawing level with me off to my right. He was presumably out of ammunition, for he showed no evil intent. He must also have realized that he had nothing to fear from Fritz [whose gun had jammed during the initial attack] in the rear cockpit… When we were almost wingtip-to-wingtip, he looked across at us and raised his hand to his flying helmet in salute! Then he banked away in a graceful arc and was quickly lost to sight.[32]

Although some 64,429 Allied troops were evacuated on 1 June, the cost was severe. Some 17 ships, including four destroyers, were sunk and another eight badly damaged. Quite obviously, RAF Fighter Command could not prevent determined Luftwaffe attacks from causing crippling losses, losses so severe that in the evening, Vice-Admiral Bertram Ramsay, directing *Dynamo* as head of Dover Command, ordered all ships to withdraw from Dunkirk before sunrise. From this point on the evacuation would continue only at night, and even then, lasted only two more nights.[33]

'TOWN AND COAST IN OUR HANDS – FRENCH AND BRITISH GONE'[34]

It was just as well as far as the British were concerned. After evacuating 189,441 Tommies and 94,785 French soldiers, including those delivered directly to French ports, only 7,208 British remained ashore, along with about 87,000 French. One more night's effort got all the Tommies home, and over two nights, as many Frenchmen as possible (46,792 as it turned out) were to be saved.

Next morning, 2 June, the Luftwaffe's first raid arrived at 0800hrs. It comprised KG 54 Heinkels and StG 2 Stukas, which found no ships to bomb, plus fighter escort. Including the protection of four Gruppen – JG 26 plus I./JG 27 – of Bf 109Es and one of II./ZG 26 Bf 110Cs the 120 German aircraft were met by the

Operation *Dynamo* provided RAF Spitfires with the first opportunity to test their mettle against what would become their principal adversary in the Battle of Britain to come – the Bf 109E. When *Dynamo* ended on 4 June, the RAF had lost 20 Spitfires, 30 Hurricanes and six Defiants, in exchange for 26 'Emils'. (AHB)

RAF's 32, 66, 92, 266 and 611 Sqns and a fierce air battle ensued. The Messerschmitts again prevailed, shooting down five Spitfires and one Hurricane for the loss of a single 3./JG 27 Bf 109E. Back in action after a week's rest, 92 Squadron destroyed six bombers for no loss. Number 611 Squadron accounted for the single Ju 87B (from 1./StG 2) shot down, but was mauled by Messerschmitts, losing two Spitfires shot down, their pilots killed in action and six damaged, their pilots unhurt.[35]

This was the last major air battle of Operation *Dynamo.*

The French defenders continued their courageous stand for two more days, the RN returned at night to embark their ally's soldiers, and the RAF flew two morning patrols and two more at dusk each day. Meanwhile, the Luftwaffe stood down most of its units to prepare for Unternehmen *Paula,* a massive afternoon offensive that pitched 640 bombers, escorted by 460 Messerschmitts, against AdA bases and French aviation industry targets around Paris, in the textbook opening move of the sequel offensive, *Fall Rot* (*Case Red*), the final conquest of France.

During *Dynamo,* Park's No. 11 Group was credited with destroying 258 German aircraft. A close examination of Luftwaffe loss reports and unit operational records reveals that in reality, only 45 bombers and 36 fighters were lost to British

Throughout May and June, the Third Reich's *Propagandakompanien* (PK) were kept extremely busy. Here personnel are working at Bray-Dunes, the designated assembly point for I Corps, British Army, gathering images of POWs and abandoned Allied hardware to illustrate the French defeat and the effectiveness of blitzkrieg. (Photo by: SeM/Universal Images Group via Getty Images)

fighters over Dunkirk. Additionally, four Stukas and two Ju 88As are known to have fallen to ships' AA fire. In return, Park's No. 11 Group lost 84 fighters (of 106 overall) and 63 pilots (killed or captured) to Messerschmitts and bombers' defensive fire, thus losing more than one fighter for every enemy aircraft downed.[36] Park's high losses to bombers' defensive fire were primarily due to the location of the aircraft's oil system header tank in front of the engine, making the aeroplane particularly vulnerable to well-aimed return fire. While the Spitfire was a superb fighter, on a par with the Bf 109E, its high losses in aerial combat were due to the RAF's obsolete formations and tactics.

In *Air Battle Dunkirk*, Franks reports that in the judgement of Sqn Ldr John M. Thompson, commanding 111 ('Treble One') Squadron:

We had not at that stage of the war, in my opinion, developed an effective method of flying our aircraft in a suitable battle formation that would allow us to attack quickly and together and which would also provide us with the all-round cover needed, particularly behind. We were still flying our

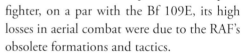

aircraft in Vics of three, not too close, but on reflection, not open enough. This meant that we were not manoeuvrable enough and, in the face of German fighters, this was a serious handicap.

In view of the intensity of operations, it was not possible to develop and work up a suitable formation until the battle was over. We had to make do with what we had. I always felt, even in the Battle of Britain, that our formations were not entirely suitable for the task in hand. It was a part of our pre-war training which was neglected, or shall I say, was perhaps not given enough thought. It was not until 1942 that [we] flew what we called 'finger 4' formations. This was the best to be developed and which was to be the basic battle formation of the day fighter throughout the rest of the war.[37]

While official resistance and bureaucratic inertia prevented revision of Fighter Command's 'neglected' pre-war formations and tactics, a few squadrons – notably 72 and 74 – adopted four-ship formations. The inability of the hidebound command to adapt during combat subsequently cost the young lives of many more of the 'Few' than need to have been sacrificed and very nearly cost the RAF its victory in the upcoming Battle of Britain.

Traditionally, Dunkirk is considered as the Luftwaffe's first major setback of the war. While this is true, it is not because RAF Fighter Command dominated the skies over Dunkirk or achieved any measure of air superiority; clearly it did not. It is because the Luftwaffe failed to attain the aims of its commander to destroy the BEF and French defenders and prevent their escape by sea. Attacking substantially on only three of *Dynamo*'s nine days, it quite obviously failed despite all the death and destruction it caused. Given the numbers of ships sunk on those three days, one can only wonder whether success would have resulted from attacking over six to eight days (30 May was 'weathered out') instead of only three.

The RN's evacuation delivered 196,649 British and 141,577 French troops to British ports. Another 27,949 French troops were ferried to French ports aboard French ships. While this constituted a great triumph, Churchill was quick to remind the hugely relieved British people and Parliament: 'We must be very careful not to assign to this deliverance the attributes of victory. Wars are not won by evacuations.'[38]

Over the beaches, the Luftwaffe had lost 42 bombers and 36 fighters to RAF fighters; in addition, four Stukas and two Ju 88s fell to ships' anti-aircraft fire. The remains of a Ju 88A of 6./LG 1, shot down by two Hurricanes of 151 Squadron, RAF on 29 May, rests on the beach at Nieuwpoort, Belgium a few months after the battle. (Jean-Louis Roba)

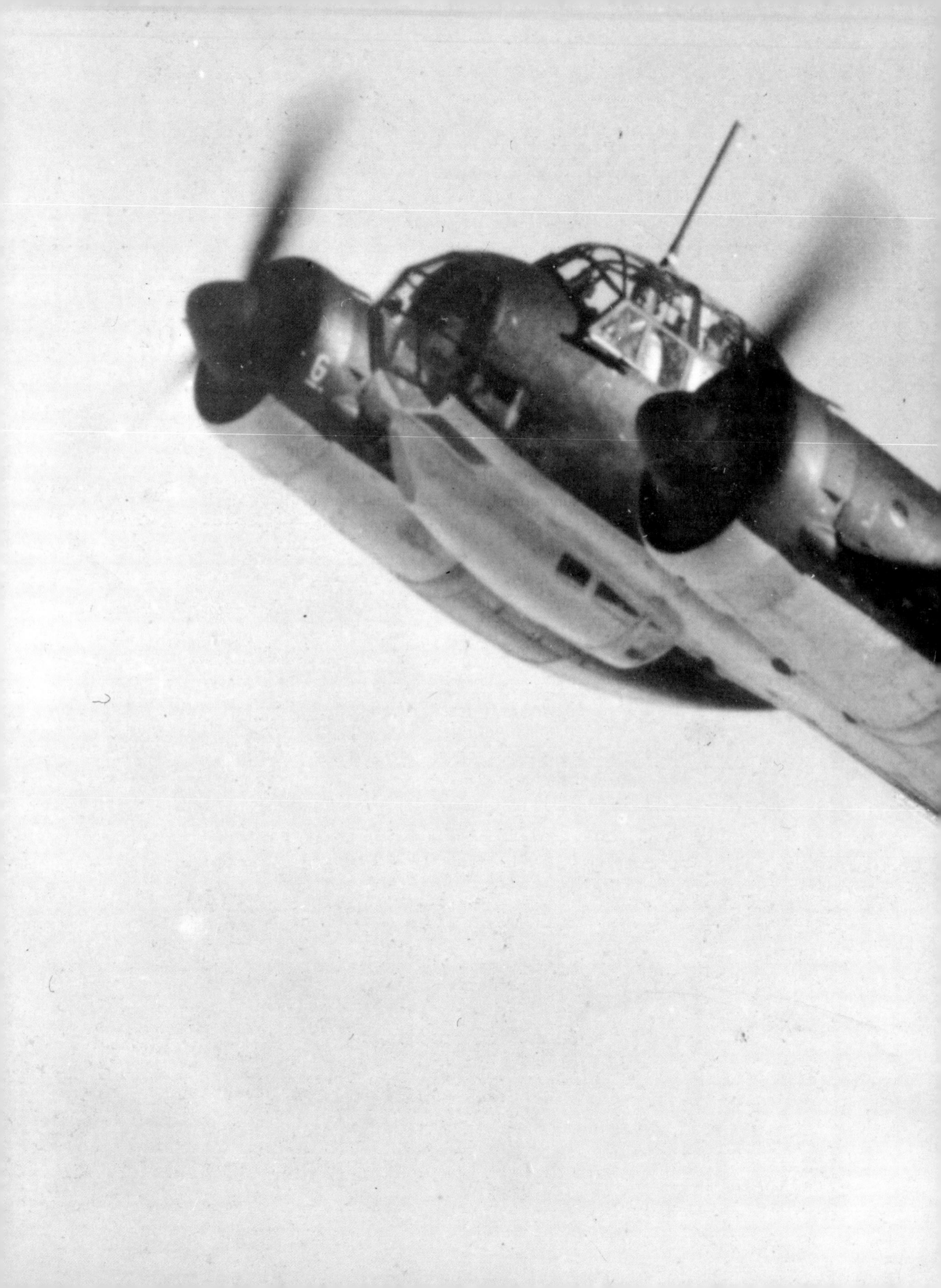

CHAPTER IV

'WAS NUN?'

Hitler's strategic options, July 1940

*To all intents and purposes, the war is won; all we have to do is
figure out how we are going to win it.*

Generalmajor Alfred Jodl, OKW Chief of Operations Staff, in a
Memorandum to the Wehrmacht's three armed services, 30 June 1940[1]

Among the ways 'we are going to win it', according to General Jodl, was that the
British would very soon be seeking a peaceful settlement to the conflict. Should
that not be forthcoming, he considered either a direct assault or an indirect
approach would ultimately achieve the victory in the 'war [that] is [already] won'.

For his own assessment of the risks involved and the chances of success of a
direct assault of the British Isles, Jodl pulled from the OKW archives a conceptual
campaign study called *Nordwest*. Except for off-hand remarks and a few speculative
discussions, little attention had been given to the possibility that it might take an
invasion to remove Britain from Hitler's War. After all, wasn't one of the purposes
of *Westfeldzug* to position U-boats and the Luftwaffe to conduct a siege or blockade,
so-called *Handelskrieg* or 'merchant shipping war', to force Britain to surrender?
Sieges take a long time, abundant resources and enormous patience, and Jodl,
considering that these might not be sufficiently available, took time to review
Studie Nordwest (actually two independent studies from the army and navy filed in
the same dossier) before adding 'invasion' to his list of possible courses of action
for the Führer to decide upon.

Studie Nordwest had as its genesis the concern of Großadmiral (Grand Admiral)
Erich Raeder, the Commander-in-Chief of the Kriegsmarine (war navy), that if
Westfeldzug proved successful, the Führer might be tempted to embark upon a
potentially disastrous cross-Channel amphibious operation rather than wait for
the blockade to become effective. Following a meeting with Hitler on 14 November
1939 that discussed occupying Dutch, Belgian and French Channel ports as the
desired aim of *Fall Gelb*, the next day Raeder instructed his Seekriegsleitung (SKL;
literally Maritime Warfare Directorate, but more appropriately Naval War Staff,
the operations branch of Oberkommando der Marine or OKM) Chief-of-Staff for
Operations, Konteradmiral (KAdm or 'rear admiral') Otto Schniewind, to examine
'the possibility of [conducting] troop landings in England should the future
progress of the war cause the problem to arise.'

In just five days Korvettenkapitän (corvette captain) Hans-Jürgen Reinicke,
the OKM Operations Branch officer assigned the responsibility for evaluating
the possibility of conducting an amphibious operation for the invasion of
Britain, produced the 12-page *Studie Rot* (Study Red), a pessimistic appraisal
that emphasized the imposing difficulties of executing an opposed landing on
British shores. Due to RAF aerial reconnaissance, surprise would be impossible,
and British mines, submarines, and airpower – to say nothing of the RN's
mighty Home Fleet – made the proposition a non-starter unless four criteria
were fulfilled:

PREVIOUS PAGES
Ju 88. (NMUSAF)

- British naval forces eliminated or sealed off from the approach and landing areas
- RAF airpower neutralized
- All RN naval power in the 'coastal zone' [including the Channel and all forces based along Britain's east coast up to, but not including, the Home Fleet anchorages in Scotland and Scapa Flow] destroyed
- Any underwater threat – mines and submarines – to the landing fleet neutralized

Simultaneously, Schniewind worked with the OKW to construct Führer Directive (FD) Nr. 9, which added substance to FD Nr. 6 by specifying the sort of air and naval operations required to successfully conduct a maritime and aerial blockade of Britain. It was duly issued under Hitler's signature on 29 November.

To ensure the Führer's adoption of Raeder's *Handelskrieg* strategy, *Studie Rot* – which argued against an invasion attempt – was submitted to the OKW two days later. Dutifully, Jodl requested the OKH and ObdL review the navy's invasion study. Prepared by Major Helmuth Stieff, OKH's response was entitled *Studie Nordwest*. In it, Stieff concluded that a landing was risky but feasible provided the navy fulfilled six tasks: closing the Dover Straits, neutralizing British naval power, clearing mines, assembling transport vessels, providing special landing craft and supporting the landings with naval gunfire. Having eliminated the possibility of actually conducting such an unthinkable adventure by assigning the navy preconditions that could not be met, Stieff then whimsically elaborated how landing 3–4 infantry divisions – supported by an airborne landing – on East Anglian shores could, after landing two panzer and one motorized divisions in the second wave, advance upon and capture London.[2]

Göring's response was an even more succinct dismissal of the preposterous idea. Disdaining both the navy and the notion of invasion, he had a minor staff officer send OKW a one-page denunciation saying 'a combined operation having the objective of landing in England must be rejected. It could only be the final act of an already victorious war against England as otherwise the preconditions for success of a combined operation would not be met.'

Mid-December, ObdL's letter, Stieff's *Studie Nordwest*, and Reinicke's *Studie Rot* were all shelved together in the OKW archives without ever having been seen by Hitler.[3]

Five months later the speed at which blitzkrieg scythed through Western Europe staggered both the victims and victors alike. But before he could resume pursuing his primary aim – eliminating Bolshevik Communism as 'a threat to Germany', Hitler needed to solve the 'English problem' (as he called it). While FD

DER FÜHRER UND DER OBERBEFEHLSHABER DER KRIEGSMARINE. Großadmiral Dr. h. c. RAEDER

Commander-in-Chief of the Kriegsmarine, Großadmiral Erich Raeder (right), planned a ten-year warship construction programme that would, by 1948, result in Germany's navy becoming as powerful as the RN. However, with Hitler initiating the war in 1939, parity was never achieved. (Author Collection)

Nr. 9 provided the most viable long-term approach, in reality the Führer was uncertain how next to proceed. What he needed was a plan that would ensure the intransigent British became willing to negotiate an end to the conflict.

To begin the discovery process, Jodl reviewed *Studie Nordwest* and, on 30 June 1940, he drafted a comprehensive six-page thought-piece – entitled 'The Continuation of the War against England' – that concisely yet accurately outlined Germany's six strategic options:

- Diplomacy: Negotiate a peaceful settlement with Great Britain
- *Handelskrieg*: Throttle Britain's economy by sinking merchant shipping and bombing commercial ports and other critical facilities
- Direct assault: Launch a cross-Channel invasion of Britain
- Indirect approach: Conduct military operations against Gibraltar, Malta and Suez, Britain's Mediterranean possessions, to close the shortest supply route from the Middle and Far East
- Switch to a defensive strategy: Ignore Great Britain and fortify Germany's position in occupied Europe. Demobilize part of the army, strengthen the German economy and wait for the enemy to make mistakes
- Terror bombing: Break the British civilian population's will to continue the war through indiscriminate bombing of all major cities[4]

DIPLOMACY – AN OLIVE BRANCH HELD IN A MAILED FIST

A negotiated peace with Great Britain was certainly Hitler's preferred option to end the war. Although this may have stood a chance of success with Britain's appeasers (Chamberlain, Halifax and the like), it was a non-starter with Winston Churchill. As unlikely as it initially seemed, Churchill and Halifax (seen here), were able to build a working relationship. (Photo by ullstein bild/ullstein bild via Getty Images)

Unrecognized by British historians, although Churchill certainly saw it for what it was, Hitler's first conciliatory overture was made at Compiègne on 22 June, when his armistice terms were read to the French delegates and broadcast across Europe by Goebbels' propaganda network. 'It takes one to know one' and American historian Walter Ansel, a US Navy officer of German heritage, correctly identified that the first proffered olive branch was issued when Hitler 'magnanimously' permitted the prostrate French government to keep its navy. 'The French fleet shall be collected in ports… demobilized and disarmed… The German government solemnly declare that they have no intention of using the French fleet for their own purposes during the war.'[5] Hitler had effectively promised he would not use French ships against the Royal Navy.

Flushed with victory over the French, Hitler's approach towards Britain returned to his previous pattern of courting and coercion. The first courtship had ended at Munich late in 1938, when Hitler believed that Chamberlain had thwarted his intention to 'crush' Czechoslovakia, permitting him only to have the ethnically German Sudetenland. Coercion and intimidation followed in increasing doses, resulting in Hitler

KAPITÄNLEUTNANT PRIEN KEHRT MIT SEINEM U-BOOT VON SCAPA FLOW ZURÜCK

Handelskrieg (blockade/ trade war), represented a very real chance of bringing Britain to its knees. It was dependent upon importing arms and raw materials for waging war, and an effective U-boat campaign and the bombing of commercial ports could have throttled Britain's economy – but it needed time. (Author Collection)

taking the rest of Czechoslovakia in March 1939, as soon as he was sure that Britain would do no more than protest. When coercion didn't work and Britain and France declared war at the outset of *Fall Weiß*, Hitler was incensed. But, in true bullying gangster style, once he had given Britain a 'sharp punch on the nose' in northern France, he decided to resume the courting of his, as he saw it, mortally weakened foe.

Unlike his *Niederschlagen* ('beat to pieces') approach in dealing with inferior Continental neighbours, Hitler's cherished impression of Britain as an equal power and, potentially, a viable partner, caused him to seek *Friedensbereitschaft* (a readiness for peace). To quote Ansel's *Hitler Confronts England*, '*Friedensbereitschaft* implied something political, something short of surrender for Britain. It carried a sense of dealing and negotiating, a willingness to talk after a spate of not too desperate fighting. In other words, German measures against Britain wound around a central theme of a deal rather than a conquest.' Hitler's assurance that Britain would continue to rule the seas was to be part of his 'deal'.

Otto Meissner (Chief of the Presidential Chancellery, the highest administrative post in Hitler's regime), recorded in his diary that at the end of June, Hitler told him that he would, 'in a Reichstag speech make an offer of a covenanted peace with precise detailed proposals which would accordingly set forth the basis for a peace treaty; he hoped that the English people themselves, if their government still resisted, would concur with his proposal and thereby exert pressure on the warmonger-led [read: Churchill] cabinet.'

Totally lacking any education, training, or experience as an actor on the world stage, the urban political gangster had absolutely no idea how completely his name had become synonymous with 'evil' in the English language. 'He had no

The Focke-Wulf Fw 200 Condor was modified from an airliner design. Although possessing the long range necessary to pursue a maritime air strike campaign, the type was unreliable and structurally unsound, and too few in number to make a significant contribution. (Author Collection)

comprehension of the loathing and disgust his name called forth, especially among Englishmen,' Ansel notes.

If the British leadership ever realized Hitler's solemn declaration that the French fleet would not be used by Germany 'for their own purposes during the war'[6] was meant as an assurance that he had no hostile intentions towards Britain, there was no formal acknowledgement of it. Instead, ignoring his pledge, on 3 July the RN virtually destroyed the French main battle fleet at Mers-el-Kébir, Algeria, and peacefully neutralized the cruiser squadron at Alexandria, Egypt. At great cost in French lives and causing almost irreconcilable damage to post-war Anglo-French relations, Churchill's government sent the strongest possible rebuff to der Führer.

This shocking episode shook Hitler's self-confidence to its very core.

The next day, Churchill put the punctuation mark on the British response to Hitler's implied offer, saying in Parliament, 'Any idea of [negotiation] should be completely swept away by the drastic and grievous action we have felt ourselves compelled to take… We shall on the contrary prosecute the war with utmost vigour.' Not much ambiguity there.

Three days later, Hitler's reaction was effectively captured by Italian Foreign Minister Count Galeazzo Ciano, who had gone to Berlin to hear the much-heralded 'Reichstag speech' – only to learn that it was being postponed. Following a personal meeting with Hitler, he recorded, 'He is rather inclined to continue the struggle and to unleash a storm of wrath and steel upon the English. But the final decision has not been reached, and it is for this reason he is delaying his speech, of which, as he himself puts it, he wants to weigh every word.'[7]

The Wagnerian tragedy culminated at the Kroll Opera House on 19 July, when Hitler gave his long awaited, two-hour long 'Last Appeal to Reason' speech before the Reichstag. It is singularly noteworthy that it included absolutely no 'precise detailed proposals' whatsoever. Instead, he said: 'In this hour I feel it to be my duty before my conscience to appeal once more to reason and common sense in Great Britain… I consider myself in a position to make this appeal since I am not the vanquished, begging favours, but the victor speaking in the name of reason. I can see no reason why this war must go on. I am grieved to think of the sacrifices which it will claim… Possibly, Mr Churchill will again brush aside this statement of mine by saying that it is merely born of doubt in our final victory. In that case, I shall have relieved my conscience in regard to the things to come.'[8]

It was an absolution, not a peace proposal.

The imaginary courtship had ended once again. Coercion, in the most powerful ways available to him, took over as der Führer's guiding principle.

ABOVE
The Germans placed great faith in the hoped-for effectiveness of mine warfare in imposing a blockade against Britain. The Luftwaffe established 9. Fliegerdivision as a dedicated command for sowing air-dropped mines in the approaches to British ports. This He 111 is carrying two 500kg LMA parachute-delivered magnetic mines. The weapon housed a 300kg (660lb) explosive charge. (Chris Goss)

LEFT
Luftminen (LMs, air-delivered mines) on their trolleys. (Chris Goss)

AIR AND SEA BLOCKADE – A POTENTIALLY EFFECTIVE LONG-TERM SOLUTION

Hitler's stated intentions, formalized in Führer Directive Nr. 9, were to conquer France and use captured ports and airfields along France's coastline to subdue Britain by U-boat blockade and aerial bombardment, a viable long-term solution to the geographic impasse imposed by the English Channel. On 14 June, he had reaffirmed the *Handelskrieg* strategy by directing 'industrial resources to be switched to the navy for U-boat production and to the Luftwaffe for the Ju 88 twin-engined dive-bomber programme, so these services might continue the war of siege against Britain.'[9]

Yet the task was immense and the maritime option unviable for the time being. Since signing the Anglo-German Naval Agreement in June 1935, the Kriegsmarine had concentrated on an ambitious and exceedingly expensive and time-consuming capital ship construction programme. Of its 58-strong submarine fleet when Hitler invaded Poland therefore, only 27 were operational ocean-going boats, the remainder comprising training and coastal vessels. Encouraged by the fairly effective, although not decisive U-boat campaign during World War I, however, Germany's inferiority to the RN in capital ships quickly caused Raeder to rethink and realign his navy's priorities, resulting in a programme that focused on building increased numbers of much cheaper and more speedily produced submarines. But it took time to shift the steel supply and skilled workers to U-boat production, so the pre-war pace of two per month continued until the summer of 1940. Additionally, the U-boat crew training programme took nine months to complete, graduating *untersee* sailors at about the same rate.

What became known as the Battle of the Atlantic therefore began slowly, albeit with a few spectacular strikes against RN units, specifically the sinking of the battleship HMS *Royal Oak* in Scapa Flow and of the aircraft carrier HMS *Courageous,* while on an ill-advised coastal anti-submarine patrol. Initial results were certainly encouraging. Using all means available, including surface raiders, from the outset of the war the Kriegsmarine had, by the end of June 1940, accounted for 469 merchant ships sunk (totalling 1.67 million gross registered tons (grt, informally 'tons')). However, 25 U-boats had been lost. Because U-boat construction and crew training lagged so significantly, in June the Kriegsmarine still had only 32 ocean-going U-boats available, limiting operations to a maximum of 22 at sea at any one time.[10]

Until construction and training outpaced losses by a wide margin, Raeder had little hope of mounting an effective, economy-strangling submarine blockade until 1942, when more than 100 U-boats would be available for *Handelskrieg* operations.

Generalfeldmarschall Albert Kesselring

Son of a Bavarian primary school teacher, in July 1904 Albrecht (later Albert) Konrad Kesselring joined the army as an aspirant officer candidate (cadet) at age 19. After attending the Munich Kriegsschule the following year, he rejoined his unit, Bayerische Fussartillerie-Regiment Nr. 2 (2nd Bavarian Foot Artillery Regiment) and was commissioned as a Leutnant on 8 March 1906. Two years later he attended the 18-month Artillerie und Ingenieurschule (Artillery and Engineer School) and in June 1912 trained as an artillery balloon observer. At the start of World War I he was the battalion commander's adjutant and proved so adept at handling administrative and operational matters that he moved steadily upwards. After graduating from the Kriegsakademie (War Academy) as a general staff officer, he finished the war on the staff of the III. Königlichen Bayerischen Armee Korps (Royal Bavarian Army Corps).

Generalfeldmarschall Albert Kesselring.
(Author Collection)

Following the war, he commanded an artillery battery, then a battalion, before settling into the staff as a colonel in 1933. An able administrator and capable commander, Kesselring impressed his superiors as an expert in efficiency; consequently, in October 1933, he was one of the talented officers transferred to the clandestine Reichsluftwaffe, becoming the chief of administration. Aged 48, he learned to fly and, as Göring grew the power and prestige of the new Luftwaffe, was promoted to Generalleutnant in April 1936. With the death three months later of Generalleutnant Walther Wever, Luftwaffe chief of staff, Göring promoted Kesselring to be the chief of the Luftkommandoamt (Air Command Bureau, essentially the Luftwaffe chief of staff).

A stocky, balding man whose pleasant disposition exuded a cheerful confidence, Kesselring worked diligently to organize a new military service that seemed to be expanding out of control, but he soon found himself embroiled in the power politics of Göring's realm, especially when attempting to deal with his deputy, the ruthlessly ambitious Erhard Milch, who wanted the job for himself. The political intrigues of the job soon found Kesselring looking to return to the field and after only nine months in office, he was promoted to General der Flieger and made commander of Luftkreiskommando III (Regional Air Command), which later became Luftwaffengruppenkommando 1 and, in April 1939, Luftflotte 1 (Air Fleet 1). Kesselring led this command in the conquest of Poland that September.[11]

When General der Flieger Hellmuth Felmy was sacked following the embarrassing Mechelin Incident, during which a courier aircraft mistakenly landed in Belgium with the Luftwaffe's paratrooper plans for *Fall Gelb*, Kesselring was given command of Luftflotte 2 and, once again, led his forces effectively and with distinction, this time in the conquest of Holland and Belgium, contributing to the ultimate success of Hitler's *Westfeldzug*.

When Stalin announced his intention to take two provinces from Romania, Hitler saw him as an even greater threat and decided that his 'English problem' needed resolution sooner rather than later, a decision that might require an amphibious assault directly across the English Channel. In preparation for such an operation the navy converted more than 1,000 Rhine river barges into makeshift landing craft called 'Prahme', many of which were unpowered. Towed by tugboats, this unpowered Prahm was engaged in landing exercises in coastal waters. (Author Collection)

The Luftwaffe was far better prepared to participate in an air/undersea blockade of the British Isles and, a fortnight into *Fall Gelb*, it had already begun a limited maritime air campaign attempting to close British ports to arriving merchant shipping. On 24 May, just as the battle for and evacuation from Dunkirk was about to begin, FD Nr. 13 authorized the Luftwaffe to begin attacking 'the English homeland… in accordance with Directive Nr. 9 and further orders issued by the OKW.' Führer Directive Nr. 9 ordered 'Attacks on the principal ports by mining and blocking the sea lanes leading to them, and by the destruction of important installations and locks, attacks on English merchant shipping and on enemy warships protecting it', along with three other lesser aims. London, Liverpool, and Manchester were specified as the primary targets.[12]

At the outset of *Fall Gelb* two Luftwaffe commands were dedicated to anti-ship operations: 9. Fliegerdivision and X. Fliegerkorps.[13] The latter was the Luftwaffe's primary maritime strike command, but it was in Norway supporting ongoing operations against the British–French–Polish expeditionary force at Narvik, so it was out of play for the time being. Generalmajor Joachim Coeler's 9. Fliegerdivision began the campaign with the three dozen He 111Hs of Kampfgruppe 126 (KGr 126) and three Küstenfliegerstaffeln (Coastal Aviation Squadrons) flying 34 He 115B and C twin-engined torpedo-bomber floatplanes.

Coeler's units had operated against Britain, in a rather desultory fashion, since 18 November 1939, sowing anti-shipping mines in the Thames and Humber estuaries and off Harwich. In the following five months 205 sorties were flown, sowing a total of 262 500kg (1,102lb) Luftminen A (LMA) and 1,000kg (2,205lb) Luftminen B (LMB) mines. During this time, these sank seven ships totalling 14,564grt – not a decisive contribution to 'strangling England' with a blockade.[14]

Once *Fall Gelb* was successfully completed, to enlarge the forces executing Führer Directive Nr. 13 on 30 May KG 4 was reassigned to 9. Fliegerdivision, while the rest of the Luftwaffe flew in support of *Fall Rot*. After flying a spate of Staffel-strength night-bombing attacks against various RAF airfields during the first week of June, each of the Geschwader's component groups rotated back to Germany for two weeks of minelaying training.[15]

Squadron-strength raids – averaging about 50 sorties each night – resumed on 17/18 June and continued almost every night until the end of July. By the end of June, KG 27, 51, and 55 had joined in the nightly attacks but the inadequacies of the Heinkels' chronically inaccurate bomb-aiming equipment were exacerbated by the nocturnal operations, and the aircraft generally spread their bombloads broadly across empty fields around their targets.[16]

Additionally, I./KG 40, equipped with the new four-motor Fw 200C-1 Condor long-range maritime reconnaissance aircraft, was assigned to 9. Fliegerdivision and had begun nocturnal minelaying operations from Oldenburg/Marx in mid-June. Never fielding more than about nine aircraft, with rarely more than half serviceable at any time, the unit transferred to Brest, France, on 12 July to conduct 12 minelaying missions in the Bristol Channel, off Merseyside and in the Firth of Clyde, while KGr 126 and KG 4 He 111s spread mines off the mouths of English Channel ports. After losing two Condors in these operations, the unit's mission was changed back to long-range maritime reconnaissance, ranging out over the eastern Atlantic, beyond the reach of RAF fighters, looking for convoys for U-boats to attack.[17]

Overall, the results of the Luftwaffe's initial blockade operations were consistent with Generalleutnant Hans Geisler's May 1939 prediction in Luftflotte 2's report *Planstudie 1939* that 'the Luftwaffe could only inflict significant damage upon Great Britain with a *protracted* air campaign over a period of two years.'[18] If successful, from both the Kriegsmarine and Luftwaffe perspectives, the *Handelskrieg* strategy could not achieve Britain's surrender until 1942.

Hitler could not wait that long.

Junkers Ju 88A

Unlike the Dornier Do 17 and Heinkel He 111, which had their origins in commercial designs, the Junkers Ju 88A was a purpose-designed medium bomber incorporating respectable dive-bombing capabilities. The Ju 88's lineage can be traced back to the RLM's 1934 specification for a new multipurpose combat aircraft called the Kampfzerstörer (battle destroyer). The specification was cancelled a year later in favour of a Schnellbomber (fast bomber) requirement for an aircraft whose performance would not be compromised by any need for suitability in other roles.

The Schnellbomber's specification called for a three-seat aircraft capable of carrying 800kg (1,764lb) of bombs at a maximum speed of 500kph (311mph), faster than any operational fighter in service at the time. Consequently, its defensive armament was just one MG 15 machine gun in the dorsal position. However, the inherent inaccuracies of the Zeiss Lotfernrohr 3 ('vertical telescope', or Lotfe 3) bombsight led Ernst Udet, the new Generalluftzeugmeister (Luftwaffe Director-General of Equipment), to insist that dive-bombing capability be included in the design, resulting in a protracted development and test programme, and a much heavier and slower aircraft.

Incorporating the latest advances in aerodynamic design and metal stressed-skin construction, and employing the most powerful aeroengines available the Ju 88's designers, W.H. Evers and A. Gassner, created a robust mid-wing cantilever monoplane, initially powered by two Daimler-Benz DB 600Aa 12-cylinder, liquid-cooled engines producing 1,000hp each for take-off.

The early-production Ju 88A employed a pair of 1,200hp Junkers Jumo 211B V12 engines, making it capable of carrying up to 2,400kg (5,290lb) of bombs some 1,260km (782 miles), for an effective combat radius of 580km (360 miles). But its increased weight decreased maximum speed to less than 450kph (280mph), requiring an increased defensive armament and a dedicated gunner. Operationally, it was faster than the He 111 but shorter ranged and typically carried a smaller bombload, but when used in dive-bombing attacks it was far more accurate.

The tightly cowled Jumos, running directly behind annular radiators, suffered chronic overheating problems in the initial A-1 variant and inflight fires were frequent, reducing the reliability and serviceability of the type during the summer of 1940. The He 111 and older, smaller Do 17Z therefore bore the brunt of operations during the early stages of the Battle of Britain. Following heavy losses of the Heinkel and Dornier to RAF interceptors in August and the first half of September, however, the Ju 88A's higher speed saw it relied upon for daylight bombing missions during the latter portion of the campaign.

Ju 88. (NMUSAF)

DIRECT ASSAULT – CROSS-CHANNEL INVASION

The previous December's shelving of *Studie Rot* and *Studie Nordwest* should have ended all consideration of this 'irresponsible' (Raeder's word) idea. However, after the French signed the Armistice Agreement at Compiègne, Hitler began to seriously contemplate a speedier solution to his 'English problem'.

The chief motivator for this pivot from his pledge to pursue the *Handelskrieg* strategy had nothing to do with the British and everything to do with the Russians.

During *Fall Rot*, Stalin's forces occupied Estonia, Latvia and Lithuania, as permitted by the amended and renewed (28 September 1939 and 10 January 1940) German–Soviet Non-Aggression Pact, and began incorporating them into the USSR. The process was completed on 11 August with the expulsion of German diplomatic legations and consulates.

At first this aggrandizement was not alarming – but the day after the Armistice was signed, the Foreign Minister, Vyacheslav Molotov, informed German Ambassador Friedrich Werner Graf von der Schulenburg that Stalin intended to take – by force if necessary – Bessarabia and Bucovina from Romania, an independent nation 'under German protection'. Hitler was greatly disturbed by this sudden imperious and opportunist expansionism, but nevertheless convinced Romania's King Carol that ceding the two provinces was in his and Germany's best interests. In fact, Germany had no forces in the country at the time and Romania's military was too weak to resist, so neither could do anything to stop a Soviet occupation, which occurred on 28 June.[19]

Subsequently, Hitler became increasingly worried that Stalin's 'no respect' boldness, identifying him as a duplicitous, dangerous and unpredictable foe, might represent a rising threat from the East. Thinking that the USSR would have to be dealt with sooner rather than later, Hitler began wanting the 'English problem' solved speedily and on 25 June instructed OKW chief Generaloberst Wilhelm Keitel to have his staff conduct preliminary studies on the feasibility of an amphibious assault against Britain. Despite the OKH and OKM's negative appraisals six months prior, a favourable assessment was forthcoming, prompting Hitler to order Keitel to issue an initiating directive on 2 July.

It read, 'The Führer and Supreme Commander has decided that a landing in England is possible, provided air superiority can be attained and certain other necessary conditions fulfilled. The date of commencement is still uncertain. All preparations are to be begun immediately.' The directive ordered the three armed services provide Keitel's staff with conceptual proposals, including force requirements and timing estimates.[20]

Kesselring (right) and Sperrle (left), commanders of Luftflotte 2 and Luftflotte 3, respectively, were ultimately responsible for the implementation and continued evolution of plans to win air superiority over the south of England. (AHB)

Another option for resolving the 'English problem' was to initiate operations on peripheral fronts, such actions perhaps involving closing the Straits of Gibraltar, forcing Britain's 'imperial lifeline' to go around Africa and exposing merchant shipping bringing resources from the Middle East, India and Asia to U-boats in the Atlantic. Closing Gibraltar would require the assistance of Spain's Generalissimo Franco (at right), seen here meeting with Generalmajor von Richthofen (left), commander of the Luftwaffe's Condor Legion during the Spanish Civil War. (AHB)

Ten days later, Keitel's initial planning directive was followed by an OKW memorandum – authored by Jodl – that incorporated Hitler's own thoughts on the subject as well as those developed by his staff. Intended to provide a broad basis for aligning more detailed planning by OKH and OKW, it proposed that the invasion be treated as 'a mighty river crossing' on a wide front, and tentatively named it Unternehmen *Löwe* (Operation *Lion*).

The very next day (13 July) Generaloberst Walther von Brauchitsch, army commander-in-chief (CinC), and his chief of staff, General der Artillerie Franz Halder, met with Hitler and briefed the OKH's concept of operations. He reported that assuming the navy could get the troops across the Channel and the Luftwaffe could protect the beachheads from RAF attacks, then the Army chiefs were reasonably confident of success. Hitler was pleased and approved Halder's recommendations 'as the basis for practical preparations [and ordered] the immediate start of invasion preparations.'[21]

On 16 July, three days after Brauchitsch and Halder's briefing and three days prior to Hitler's lamentably lame 'Appeal to Reason' speech, OKW issued his FD Nr. 16, stating 'Since England, in spite of her hopeless military situation shows no signs of being ready to come to an understanding, I have decided to prepare a landing operation against England and, if necessary, carry it out.'[22] The operation was christened Unternehmen *Seelöwe* (Operation *Sealion*) and all preparations were to be completed by 15 August.

INDIRECT APPROACH – OPEN OPERATIONS ON PERIPHERAL FRONTS

While Hitler was eager to have his military and naval staffs begin detailed planning and preparations for a massive cross-Channel amphibious operation, he was by no means confident of its prospects for success. The penalties for failure of such a grandiose enterprise made it a daunting proposition: should the assault be interdicted en route across the Channel or even repulsed on British shores, materiel and manpower losses would have been substantial but not debilitating. However, the political penalties, especially the encouraging effect it might have on Stalin, were more than Hitler could bear to contemplate. So, the prospects for *Seelöwe's* success had to be assured before he would order its attempt. Consequently, he and the OKW had to seek out other ways to reduce Britain without risk of grand failure.

Geographically, Hitler's war had already expanded immensely when, on 10 June, his Italian ally Mussolini had joined in, attacking France through the Maritime Alps, bombing Malta and organizing a major offensive from Libya to capture the Suez Canal. Britain's shortest 'lifeline' from her primary imperial possessions – India, Iraq, Iran, the Middle and Far East, supplying oil, rubber, and other resources essential for modern war – lay through the Mediterranean via the Suez Canal and Straits of Gibraltar. Mussolini might, or might not, be able to capture and close the former but, especially following the Nazis' decisive support of Caudillo (Dictator) Francisco Franco in the Spanish Civil War, the more certain opportunity to seal off this route lay in controlling Gibraltar.

Consequently, on 13 July Hitler stated that he wished 'to draw Spain into the game in order to build up a front [against Britain] from North Cape [top of Norway] to Morocco [opposite Gibraltar]'. That same day he wrote to 'Il Duce', declining Mussolini's offer of 10 Italian divisions and 30 air force squadrons to join in *Seelöwe*, but instead stressed that, considering 'the strategic breadth of the conflict with England[,] an Italian invasion of Egypt would be a fine idea.'

Mussolini responded four days later stating that he 'hoped to attack Egypt at the time of the German assault on England.'[23]

With this assurance, on 22 July OKW sent the head of its foreign intelligence division (Amt Ausland/Abwehr, the Bureau [for] Foreign Affairs/Defence, known as the 'Abwehr'), Admiral Wilhelm Canaris to Madrid to begin discussions with Franco and his War Minister, General Juan Vigón, and reconnoitre the approaches to Gibraltar. He returned to inform Keitel that Franco was reluctant to enter the war for a host of reasons, but if his co-operation could be obtained an attack force of two infantry regiments and three combat engineer battalions, supported by one Jagd and two Stukageschwader, could seize Gibraltar in a co-ordinated air-ground assault.

On 8 August, a week before the preparations for *Seelöwe* were due to be completed, Franco informed the German ambassador in Madrid of his 'toll charges' to allow Wehrmacht forces to transit Spain to position themselves for the assault. The principal one was that 'German forces must first land on the British mainland in a full-scale invasion'.

Thus what was supposed to be an alternative (or parallel) strategy of indirect approach at both ends of the Mediterranean became contingent upon the successful launching of the direct assault option: *Seelöwe*.

SWITCH TO A DEFENSIVE STRATEGY –
A POLITICALLY UNACCEPTABLE NOTION

One of the most appealing options, especially to the German people and their civilian administration, lay in recognizing that the Channel imposed just as much of an obstacle to the British return to the Continent as it did to the proposed Operation *Seelöwe*. Switching to a defensive posture behind this great barrier would permit the demobilization of 25 per cent of the army, permitting approximately 250,000 men to return to the industrial and agricultural work forces, just in time for harvest.

Even before *Fall Rot* was successfully concluded, on 14 June Hitler directed, upon final victory, that the army reduce from 167 to 120 divisions. As Halder wrote in his diary, 'Since the final collapse of the enemy is now imminent, the Army will have fulfilled its mission, and accordingly… [can] comfortably start on preparations for its projected peacetime organization. Luftwaffe and Kriegsmarine

Another possible solution to the 'English problem' was to break the civilian population's will to continue the war through the indiscriminate bombing of all major cities. By early 1940, the Nazi war machine had already demonstrated this at Warsaw and Rotterdam. These are the ruins of Rotterdam. (NARA)

alone [will] be carrying on the war against England.'[24]

But *not* threatening Britain, except through a distant air and sea blockade, was not in Hitler's nature, nor was it to his political advantage. In fact, the consequences of 'not doing anything' against Britain were almost as grave as failing in an attempt to do something (*Seelöwe*, for example). It constituted de facto recognition that the British had indeed bested him, final victory had actually eluded him, and, when he inevitably turned against Stalin's Russia, a capable and growing foe would remain at his rear.[25]

Something had to be done – but it had to be something that did not carry with it grave risks of and consequences for grand failure.

TERROR BOMBING – HITLER'S TRUMP CARD

The German bombing campaign fought during World War I primarily against England caused widespread alarm throughout its civilian population. The 78 raids, conducted during 1915–18 by airships and multi-engined, heavier-than-air night-bombers, killed almost 1,400 and injured 3,330. As tragic as such statistics were, they led to an overestimation of both the material and psychological effects that the bombing of cities could cause. After the war, Italian army artillery general Giulio Douhet, author of *The Command of the Air* (1921, heavily revised in 1928), theorized that a future war would be won entirely by airpower and he identified five basic target categories: industry, transport infrastructure, communications, government and 'the will of the people' (terror bombing).

Douhet's sensational 'what if' books (1928–30)[26] stirred the popular imagination because they promised a way of avoiding the carnage and slaughter that defined World War I by 'carrying the war to the people'. In the 1920s defending air forces could not prevent bombing strikes against large targets such as cities – as Stanley Baldwin said in November 1932 in a speech before Parliament entitled 'A Fear for the Future', 'the bomber will always get through'.[27] Consequently, civilians could now expect to be subjected to the carnage and slaughter that previously occurred only on the front lines. Lurid pulp fiction of the era escalated this fear to a dread and, in the event of actual war, national leaders anticipated unbridled terror and panic.

Ever sensitive to their populace's feelings and morale, politicians everywhere, even totalitarian, were afraid that, if unleashed, Douhet's prognostications might become reality. Consequently, from the very beginning of World War II national leaders on both sides were steadfastly reluctant to be the first to employ bombers against enemy civilians for fear of retaliation in kind. Therefore, most of them, including Churchill and Hitler, initially withheld their use of airpower against enemy cities because it provided a deterrent to the enemy's use against their own populations.

Likewise, Göring, being more of a politician than anything else, also had an exaggerated opinion of the validity of Douhet's theories. But his understanding of airpower was so shallow, and his natural penchant for bullying his adversaries so dominant, that he eagerly embraced Douhet's naively optimistic predictions and advocated city bombing to terrorize the civilian populace into submission.[28]

His generals, however, had much less faith in Douhet's unproven theories of breaking civilian morale through terror bombing and instead advocated strategic attacks on British industrial targets and ports. In fact, in May 1939, when ObdL staff reviewed Luftflotte 2's unpromising *Planstudie 39* (a repeat of *Planstudie 38*, resulting from a five-day staff 'map exercise'), they commented, 'furthermore, terror attacks on London as the stronghold of the enemy defence would hardly have a catastrophic effect or contribute significantly to a war decision. They would only strengthen the British will to resist.'[29]

Fearing the opposite effect on his own people, Hitler, even when issuing his guidance 'For the Conduct of Air and Sea Warfare against England' (FD Nr. 17, 1 August 1940), continued to hold this option in abeyance stating, 'I reserve for myself the right to decide on terror attacks as measures of reprisal.'[30]

SUMMARY

Hitler's 'Appeal to Reason' speech was intended for the ears (and minds) of the British people and their representatives in Parliament. The reaction of the British press, representing to Hitler the mood of the populace, was both prompt and hostile. On 20 July, the Führer told Ciano: 'the reaction of the English press to yesterday's speech has been such to allow no prospect [of peace].'

Hitler's diplomacy, if one can call it that, had failed utterly. An inactive defensive strategy was a non-starter, the ongoing *Handelskrieg* campaign would take two years too long, the indirect approach in the Mediterranean had become linked to the successful initiation of the direct assault (*Seelöwe*), and terror bombing was effectively deterred by RAF Bomber Command's perceived capabilities. This left the cross-Channel invasion as his only viable option. As the record from Hitler's 21 July meeting with Raeder attests, 'preparations for a decision by arms must be completed as quickly as possible, [the Führer] will not let the military-political initiative pass out of his hands.'[31]

So *Seelöwe* it would be.

Attaining the critical and essential prerequisite for the invasion – securing air superiority over the Channel and southern England – was fully and solely the responsibility of Göring's Luftwaffe.

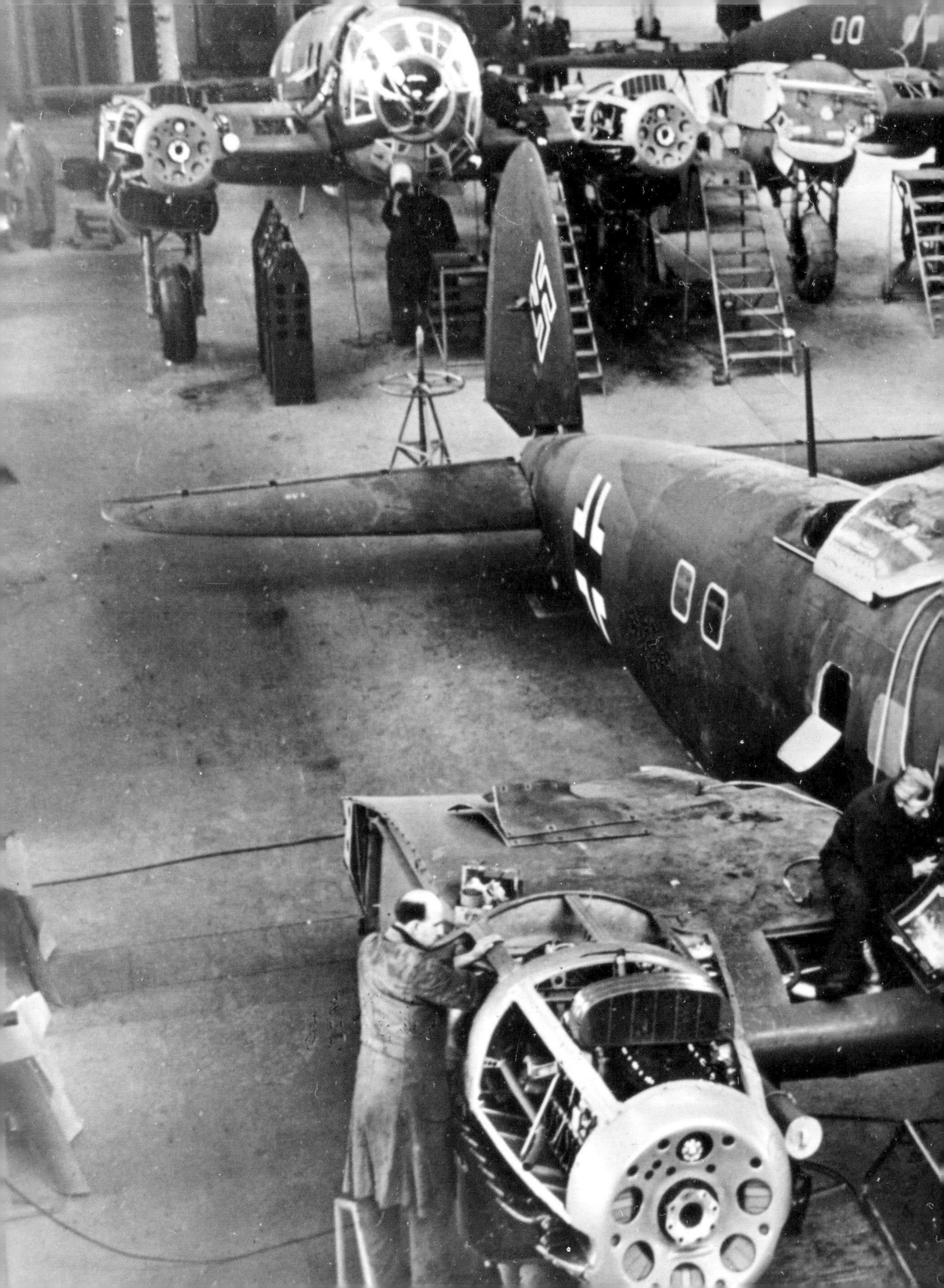

CHAPTER V

THE LUFTWAFFE'S CAPABILITIES

Germany's only real means to defeat Great Britain

And now, gentlemen, the Führer has ordered me to crush
Britain with my Luftwaffe. By means of hard blows
I plan to have this enemy, who has already suffered a
decisive moral defeat, down on his knees in the nearest
future, so that an occupation of the island by our troops can
proceed without any risk!

Hermann Göring, meeting with Luftflotte commanders,
The Hague, 1 August 1940[1]

The Wehrmacht's shockingly fast conquest of France and the ejection of the BEF from the European Continent, accomplished through the unflagging support of the most powerful, efficient and successful tactical air force the world had ever seen, had taken only six weeks. Göring's Luftwaffe was organized, trained and equipped for exactly the kind of campaign it had just won. But with the conquest of France, Hitler's *Westfeldzug* was only half complete. From the beaches at Dunkirk to the harbour at Cherbourg, and especially from the grey cliffs of Cap Gris-Nez near Calais, Wehrmacht and Luftwaffe officers alike wondered if they could eliminate Great Britain from Hitler's war.

As has been said many times before, the Luftwaffe was no strategic air force. Under its first chief of staff, Generalleutnant Walther Wever, who was killed in an aircraft accident in June 1936, it had attempted to fulfil that tenet of its initial theoretical doctrine[2] with the design and development of a four-engine Großnachtbomber (large night-bomber) aircraft. Flown in autumn 1936, the Do 19 and Ju 89 prototypes, optimistically called 'Ural bombers', were expected to carry 1,600kg (3,527lb) of bombs for 2,000km (1,243 miles). Lacking superchargers for improved performance, especially at higher altitudes, the two designs were woefully underpowered. While they had great range, they could not carry the bombload of an He 111 or match its speed.[3]

Consequently, with the April 1937 arrival of the 1,060km (660-mile) range – with a 2,000kg (4,410lb) bombload – He 111, in April 1937, the Luftwaffe's new chief of staff, Kesselring (replacing Wever), decided that Germany could not afford to spend twice the resources – twice as many engines, double the fuel consumption, and 2.5 times the aluminium – for roughly the same bombload, so he accepted the shorter-ranged medium bomber to fulfil both strategic and tactical bombing roles, at least as far as 500km (300 miles) beyond Germany's borders or the battlefront. Kesselring had the full agreement of Göring, who is often quoted as having said, 'The Führer will never ask me how big our bombers are, but how many we have.'[4]

Heinkel He 111H/P

Banned from operating an air force by the 1919 Treaty of Versailles, the Luftwaffe sponsored a number of designs as commercial aircraft which had obvious military potential. In the case of the Heinkel He 111, collaboration between the newly created Luftfahrtkommissariat's Technical Department and Deutsche Luft Hansa (DLH), Germany's national airline, resulted in a basic specification for a high-speed airliner, optimized for development into a bomber, being issued early in 1934.

Designed by Siegfried and Walter Günter, the He 111 was a conventional twin-engined low-wing monoplane of metal stressed-skin construction, with a semi-monocoque fuselage mated to a thick, broad, semi-elliptical wing. The large wing provided generous fuel tankage and stable flying characteristics, making it a superb bombing platform within the limitations of the inherently inaccurate Lotfernrohr 7 bombsight. Additionally, its defensive armament was inadequate, consisting of two flexible 7.92mm Rheinmetall MG 15 machine guns in the rear-facing dorsal and ventral positions and a third in the extensively glazed nose.

The He 111 could carry a maximum internal bombload of 4,410lb (2,000kg), comprising eight 250kg (550lb) SC250 HE bombs carried nose-up in eight vertical chutes, or four 50kg (110lb) SC50s in each chute, or 16 BSK 36 incendiary canisters (each containing 36 1kg/2.2lb incendiary bomblets). With this bombload, the Heinkel had an effective combat radius of 482km (300 miles).

In order to maximize production, the aircraft was built as the He 111P, powered by two Daimler-Benz DB 601A-1 engines rated at 1,100hp for take-off, and He 111H, which had a pair of Junkers Jumo 211D-1 engines rated at 1,200hp for take-off. In 1940 the RLM discontinued production of the P-series in favour of the H versions, primarily because the P-models' Daimler-Benz engines were needed for Messerschmitt Bf 109E and Bf 110C/D fighter production.

In July 1940, the He 111H/P was the Luftwaffe's standard medium bomber, equipping almost half of the 33 Kampfgruppen stationed in Holland, Belgium and northern France for the air assault on Britain.

Heinkel He 111. (AHB donated by Ken Wakefield)

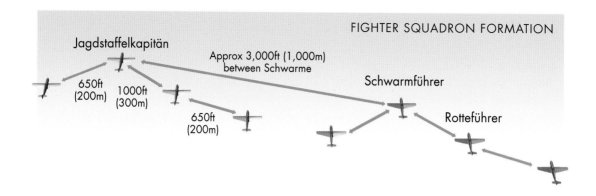

FIGHTER SQUADRON FORMATION

Jagdstaffelkapitän

Approx 3,000ft (1,000m)
between Schwarme

Schwarmführer

650ft
(200m)

1000ft
(300m)

650ft
(200m)

Rotteführer

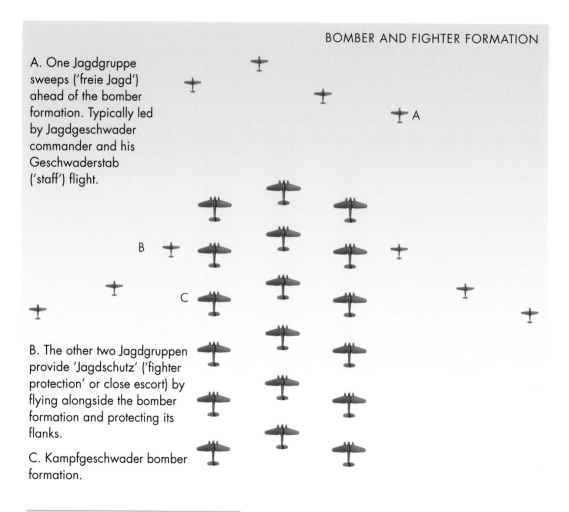

BOMBER AND FIGHTER FORMATION

A. One Jagdgruppe sweeps ('freie Jagd') ahead of the bomber formation. Typically led by Jagdgeschwader commander and his Geschwaderstab ('staff') flight.

A

B

C

B. The other two Jagdgruppen provide 'Jagdschutz' ('fighter protection' or close escort) by flying alongside the bomber formation and protecting its flanks.

C. Kampfgeschwader bomber formation.

KEY

Each Bf 109 symbol represents one 'Schwarm' (four-aeroplane) formation and each He 111 symbol represents one 'Kette' (three-aeroplane) formation.

OPPOSITE • LUFTWAFFE COMBAT FORMATIONS

The standard Luftwaffe fighter formation was a four-aeroplane Schwarm (flight) comprising two Rotten (pairs) operating as one flight. The two wingmen (on the flanks) flew approximately 200m alongside and slightly aft of their Rotteführer (two-ship leader) with the second Rotteführer flying 300m alongside and aft of the Schwarmführer (four-ship leader). In both pairs the leaders could engage enemy aircraft, co-ordinating their attacks via radio, while each Katschmarek (wingman) protected his leader's tail. Either Rotteführer could take the Schwarmführer role, but it typically fell to the more experienced man.

Typically, a Jagdstaffel operated nine primary aircraft plus as many as three held in reserve and would launch two Schwärme. Because both the Schwarmführer and Rotteführer were permitted to attack enemy aeroplanes, two Schwärme had four 'shooters', the same number as a typical RAF fighter squadron flying in its outdated three-aeroplane 'vic' formation. Occasionally, a Jagdstaffel would be augmented by the Jagdgruppe Stabsschwarm (staff flight), resulting in an offensive formation with six 'shooters', outnumbering an equivalent RAF fighter squadron 1.5 to 1.

Unit nomenclature reflected the Staffel, Gruppe and Geschwader organization. Staffeln, typically three to a Gruppe, took Arabic numerals; Gruppe, typically three to a Geschwader, took Roman numerals. Staffeln within a Gruppe were numbered sequentially, thus I. Gruppe comprised 1, 2 and 3 Staffeln, and II. Gruppe, 4, 5 and 6 Staffeln. It follows that I./JG 2 denotes the first Gruppe of Jagdgeschwader 2, comprising 1, 2 and 3 Staffeln. Similarly, 5./JG 2 denotes the fifth Staffel of JG 2, being the second Staffel of II. Gruppe.

As it turned out, long range and four motors were superfluous anyway. Like the He 111, neither of the two Ural bombers' defensive armaments could protect them from determined fighter attack and, for survival against enemy interceptors, they would have to be escorted by fighters during the necessity of daylight missions. With the failure of the Bf 110 Zerstörer to fulfil its intended role of bomber escort, four-engined 'strategic bombers' would have been limited to the 125-mile (200km) combat radius of the Bf 109E.

So, Kesselring's economic decision proved correct.

In executing the *Handelskrieg* strategy, bombing ports along England's southern shores and shipping in the Channel would be conducted within the limited range of the Bf 109E, while longer-ranged maritime strikes against ships well out to sea had little to fear from Fighter or Coastal Command's Blenheim IF/IVF twin-engined fighters. Likewise, night-bombing attacks against ports beyond the escort range of the 'Emil' – including Bristol, Liverpool and Glasgow – had nothing at all to fear from Fighter Command's at that time pathetically ineffective night-fighter capabilities.

The idea of supporting the cross-Channel invasion really was viewed by senior Luftwaffe officers and their army counterparts as little more than a gigantic overnight 'river-crossing on a broad front'.[5] The Luftwaffe's doctrine of knocking out the enemy air force as its first priority, as well as covering the army's crossing of the Channel and supporting the pioneers and infantry fighting their way ashore on the other side, was conceptually identical to its *Fall Gelb* attacks on the first day

The Bf 110 proved unsuccessful as an escort fighter and as production continued it was pressed into other roles, including photo-reconnaissance, especially since the slower Do 17P/Z was experiencing heavy losses on missions over Britain, but even the faster Messerschmitt was not immune to interception. Bf 110C '5F+CM' of 4.(F)/14 (an army co-operation unit) was shot down on 21 July by three 238 Squadron Hurricanes while on a low-altitude coastal defences reconnaissance sortie. The pilot, Olt Friedrich-Karl Runde, crash-landed near Chichester where he and his radio operator were captured. Restored to flying condition at Farnborough (as seen here), the aeroplane was used by the RAF for evaluation purposes. (Clive Ellis)

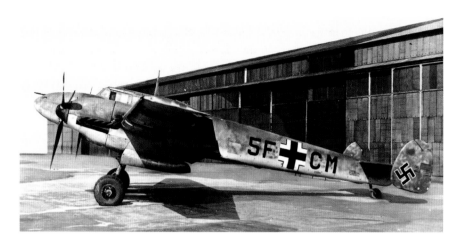

against AdA and BAFF bases in France and the subsequent very successful support of the panzers vaulting across the Meuse four days later. Because cross-Channel operations would be conducted within the Bf 109E's operational range, the concept of operations, roles and missions of Kesselring's and Sperrle's two Luftflotten remained unchanged.

What *was* different this time was that if Hitler went forward with *Seelöwe*, the Luftwaffe would have to launch an effective offensive counter-air campaign against the toughest opponent it had yet encountered. Possessing an air force qualitatively and quantitatively more robust than any other European air arms it had faced previously, it was estimated that it would take several days, perhaps even two weeks, to beat down the British air defences sufficiently to enable the navy to carry the army across the Channel without interference from the RAF.

Unlike previous campaigns, during which the initial attacks on enemy airpower occurred concurrently with the army's first assaults against the enemy frontiers, in this case the Luftwaffe would be required to conduct an air campaign independent of the army for weeks on end, until all preparations, materiel and training, were completed by the other two services and the combination of favourable tides and moonlight for a nocturnal Channel crossing occurred. Conducting an air campaign independent of the army was something that the Luftwaffe had never done before, nor was there any guidance in its doctrine manual, *Luftwaffe Dienstvorschrift 16: Luftkriegführung* (*Luftwaffe Service Regulation 16: Air War Guidance*, or LDv 16).

Nor was it organized to do so.

OBDL HQ'S ROLE IN PLANNING AN INDEPENDENT AIR CAMPAIGN

Despite its impressive might and proven prowess, one of the Luftwaffe's most serious deficiencies was its lack of a proper general staff. An outgrowth and redesignation of the RLM's early (1933–35) Luftkommandoamt (Air Command Office), the ObdL was established and organized 'to serve as the operations staff of… Commander in Chief of the Luftwaffe' much like the OKW was Hitler's personal military staff. It was not, despite many uninformed claims otherwise, a true 'General Staff' or 'High Command' such as the OKH or the navy's OKM.[6]

ObdL's six Abteilungen (branches) were organized into two Amtsgruppen (departments), with the RLM communications staff, ostensibly assigned to the ministry's Staatssekretär der Luftfahrt (State Secretary for Aviation, Göring's deputy minister) Erhard Milch, forming a seventh, all answering to Göring's chief of staff Generalmajor Hans Jeschonnek, a 41-year-old Hitler-worshipping prodigy who was promoted to General der Flieger on 19 July 1940, skipping the rank of Generalleutnant.

ObdL's two departments were the Operations Staff, under Generalmajor Otto Hoffmann von Waldau, and the three logistics branches under the Generalquartiermeister (Quartermaster General), Generalmajor Hans-Georg von Seidel. All communications-related services were under the independent Chief of Signals, Generalmajor Wolfgang Martini.[7]

None of these was responsible for planning combat operations.

As described in the opening chapter, combat operations were planned by the Luftflotten and Fliegerkorps HQs working closely and directly with their associated Heeresgruppe and Armeeoberkommando HQs, respectively. The army commands, implementing OKH's offensive plans, provided operational direction and dictated priorities to their attached Luftwaffe echelons, which would, in turn, assign target groups and apportion missions, thus directing their assigned Kampf- and Stukageschwader to attack the targets intended to meet the army's desired objectives.

Waldau's Operations Staff, comprising Operations (1. Abteilung), Training (3. Abteilung), and Fremde Luftwaffen (Foreign Air Forces, more commonly known as 'Intelligence', 5. Abteilung), assigned and transferred units to the Luftflotten and Fliegerkorps, determined operational objectives and priorities for offensive counter-air phases of combined-arms campaigns, and disseminated suggested target lists and intelligence information. The Operations Branch comprised Gruppen (groups of offices), such as 'Flying Forces', 'Flak', etc., composed of various offices (Referat, or substaffs) for current operations, training requirements, technical requirements, etc.

In its one contribution to Luftflotte campaign planning, the 'current operations' office periodically produced target lists compiled by researching intelligence files and reconnaissance photos. Usually appended to Göring's orders or directives, ObdL's target lists were a catalogue of enemy installations that, if destroyed, were expected to contribute significantly to achieving the operation's stated aims and objectives; it was up to the field commands (air fleet commanders and staffs) to make the targeting choices from this list.

Seidel's logistics department consisted of Mobilization Planning (2. Abteilung), Quartermaster (more commonly 'Supply', 4. Abteilung), and Armaments (6. Abteilung). Following the victory over France, 2. Abteilung was consumed

with the tasks of locating suitable airfields in the newly occupied territories closest to Britain and preparing them to receive the vast armada of Luftwaffe flying units, ordering the shipment and stockpiling of fuel, ordnance (bombs, aerial mines and incendiary canisters), ammunition and other supplies necessary to sustain a major air campaign. In addition to supplying these, 4. Abteilung was also attempting to replace the 1,401 aircraft[8] lost in the first two phases (*Fall Gelb* and *Fall Rot*) of Hitler's *Westfeldzug*.

Martini's Nachrichtendienst (Signals Service, the ObdL staff element of which was 7. Abteilung) was one of the four departments that, following the 1 February 1939 reorganization, remained directly assigned to the RLM and administered by Milch.[9] However, for operational matters, Martini reported to Göring, through Jeschonnek. This was deemed acceptable because, as described by Generalleutnant Andreas Nielsen and recorded in 'The German Air Force General Staff', USAF Historical Study No. 173, Martini was considered 'an officer who placed the good of the cause above his own person and continued to co-operate in the closest possible way with the General Staff.'

Managing a large, industrious and ever-expanding organization, the Signals Service HQ staff was responsible for electronic systems development, installation and maintenance of all communications and ground-based air navigation equipment, and for effective communications networks and activities at and between all Luftwaffe units, bases, and HQs. In the summer of 1940, its main field elements were busy laying landlines between the latter two, tying them into large, complex switchboards, and setting up 11 new Luftaufsicht (Air Safety Service, the organization that provided Luftwaffe air traffic control [ATC] services) facilities

and 38 navigation beacons at newly acquired bases and airfields. Additionally, Martini's Funkhorchdienst (radio monitoring service) units deployed along the occupied coasts to start eavesdropping on RAF radio communications to learn as much as they could about their next adversary.

INTELLIGENCE – WHAT YOU KNOW DETERMINES WHAT YOU THINK YOU CAN DO

Beginning 1 April 1939, the ObdL's Chief of Intelligence was Oberstleutnant (Obstlt; promoted to Oberst 18 July 1940) Josef Schmid, a young, ambitious non-flying officer who was a close associate of Göring's. Immediately after taking office, Schmid went to work creating three intelligence assessments: *Studie Blau* (blue: Britain), *Studie Grün* (green: Poland) and *Studie Rot* (red: France), the most important of which was the first.

Göring had ordered *Studie Blau* in November 1938, when Hitler railed at 'being beaten' by Chamberlain at Munich and vowed to 'punish the English' as a result. The initiative lacked energy or progress under Oberst Hilmer Freiherr von Bülow, a 56-year-old reservist. Göring sent him to be the Luftattaché (air attaché) in Rome and appointed the ambitious 38-year-old Schmid to head 5. Abteilung instead[10]. It was the new Intelligence chief's first opportunity to impress his patron. Meeting twice a week, for 4–5 hours each time, for more than a month, a carefully chosen committee considered information from a diverse variety of sources.

Appointed by Göring, the permanent members of the study group included his chief of staff, Jeschonnek, RLM Deputy Erhard Milch, who had undertaken a fact-finding and 'goodwill' trip to Britain 18 months prior and Generalluftzeugmeister (Director-General of Equipment) Ernst Udet, who brought technological experts from his Technisches Amt (T-Amt, Technical Department). From the private sector Schmid invited notable civilian scientists, prominent economists, geopolitics professors and industrialists to participate. Information considered included that acquired by Generalleutnant Rudolf Wenninger, Luftwaffe air attaché in London since April 1936 (and until 3 September 1939), Admiral Canaris's Abwehr espionage network, Martini's Funkhorchdienst (which had compiled a fairly accurate air order of battle by 'listening' to RAF radio traffic), translated British news media articles exploited by the ObdL Pressegruppe (Press Group) and imagery gathered by Oberst Theodor Rowehl's clandestine photo-reconnaissance unit using camera-equipped He 111C 'mailplanes' flying Luft Hansa 'route proving trials'.

From the assorted lectures, discussions and interrogations, Schmid created a coherent and surprisingly accurate 94-page intelligence assessment. In his preliminary report, published on 2 May 1939 and sent to Göring and three Luftflotte commanders (Luftflottenchefs), Schmid concluded: 'The weakest points in the overall British economy are its dependences on imports from abroad and on sea routes. This gives special importance to the sensitivity of Britain as a whole,

because of her geographical position, and of British naval and mercantile ports to air attack. The inescapable condition for air warfare against Britain is the neutralization of her Air Force and Navy.'[11]

Additionally, Schmid prophetically warned that RAF fighter strength was projected to match the Jagdwaffe by 1941, but that 'British defences [at that stage were] inadequate to defend anything more than the general areas around London. This would leave the rest of England open to attack.'

After considering the Luftflotte commanders' feedback and Operations Staff comments, on 9 July 1939 Jeschonnek issued instructions, including the potential target list and a prospective RAF Luftkriegsgliederung (Air Order of Battle) provided by *Studie Blau*, to Felmy's Luftflotte 2 chief of staff to begin developing an air attack plan against British war industries and supply centres once closer bases, or longer-ranged bombers, were acquired.[12]

Studie Blau became the ObdL's primary information source for the forthcoming campaign, no matter which options Hitler pursued, because Luftwaffe intelligence functions changed dramatically once war was initiated. Before hostilities started, the Luftwaffe's primary sources of information on enemy air forces and aviation industries relied on translations of foreign news media and reports from the Abwehr and Luftattachés.

These sources ceased once combat began.

Translated and exploited open-source enemy news media information was originally the purview of the RLM's Pressegruppe. Initially part of the its Zentrale Abteilung (Central [administrative] Branch), with initiation of *Studie Blau* it was transferred to Schmid's 5. Abteilung and contributed significantly to the basis of the study and its report. According to Generalleutnant Andreas Nielsen, noted in 'The Collection and Evaluation of Intelligence for the German Air Force High Command', USAF Historical Study No. 171, the primary supplier of 'foreign

newspapers, illustrated journals, industrial catalogues, and other military important writings' was the Nazi Party's Sicherheitsdienst (SD, Political Security Service). Obsessed with ensuring the security of the Nazi regime, Reinhard Heydrich's SD was never concerned about meeting the Luftwaffe's intelligence needs; these materials were 'delivered at irregular intervals and selected unsystematically so that intelligence exploitation was impossible'. This source practically evaporated with the start of the war and Schmid's press group turned to producing Luftwaffe propaganda and censoring German media publications to ensure nothing of intelligence value would be available to the enemy.

Göring, Hitler and 'Beppo' Schmid confer over a map, discussing possible Luftwaffe options. The fact that Göring is in his 'sky blue' uniform and brandishing his Reichsmarschall baton tells us that the photo was taken after 19 July 1940. (AHB)

An alternative source of foreign publications was, of course, the air attachés 'but [they] encountered considerable difficulties in obtaining the necessary foreign [currency] exchange'. In any event, with the onset or anticipation of hostilities, air attachés were recalled or expelled, just as Wenninger had been, eliminating that source as well.

Accepting that most pre-war agents would be liquidated (arrested or killed), Abwehr operations shifted from intelligence collection to conducting sabotage and, at Hitler's insistence, active counter-intelligence operations, eliminating the last external source of foreign intelligence information. Even interrogation of captured enemy aviators was an Abwehr counter-intelligence function, with the information gleaned being passed not to ObdL, but to a Luftwaffe intelligence officer at the local military district level. The official history confirms 'The Luftwaffe headquarters and staffs had <u>no</u> [emphasis in original] intelligence collecting agencies of their own.'[13]

Within the Luftwaffe, the principal sources of information were high-altitude reconnaissance photos from Rowehl's Berlin-based Aufklärungsgruppe ObdL (reconnaissance group ObdL, a four-squadron expansion of his pre-war clandestine unit), Martini's Funkhorchdienst, and reports and imagery 'upchannelled' from Luftflotte HQ Intelligence Sections. From these sources, occasionally Schmid's 5. Abteilung would be required to produce 'an air estimate of the situation from the sum total of information collected by the field headquarters'.

One example is the 1 January 1940 *Gliederung der Britischen Fliegertruppe (Heimat)* (*Structure of the British Air Force (Homeland)*) in which Schmid's branch updated, primarily through inputs from Martini's Funkhorchdienst, their original 1 June 1939 RAF AOB and issued it to the field headquarters as a replacement for the original Appendix 3 to *Studie Blau*. When compared with the actual RAF AOB of that time, the document proves remarkably accurate regarding No. 11 Group bases and units. However, relying on Wenninger's outdated information concerning Fighter Command's future expansion plans, the rest of the document is understandably fallacious.[14]

Comparison of Luftwaffe Intelligence RAF AOB and
Actual RAF AOB, 1 January 1940

RAF AOB COMPOSED BY OBDL INTELLIGENCE	ACTUAL RAF AOB
NO. 11 GROUP UXBRIDGE	NO. 11 GROUP UXBRIDGE
Tangmere 1 Sqn (Hurricanes) 43 Sqn (Hurricanes)	Tangmere 1 Sqn (Hurricanes) 43 Sqn (Hurricanes) 601 Sqn (Blenheims) 605 Sqn (Hurricanes)
Kenley 3 Sqn (Hurricanes) 17 Sqn (Hurricanes) 615 Sqn (Hurricanes)	Kenley 3 Sqn (Hurricanes)
	Croydon 615 Sqn (BEF Nov 1939 to Apr 1940)
Biggin Hill 32 Sqn (Hurricanes) 70 Sqn (Hurricanes)	Biggin Hill 32 Sqn (Hurricanes)
Hawkinge 25 Sqn (Hurricanes)	
Hornchurch 54 Sqn (Hurricanes) 65 Sqn (Hurricanes) 74 Sqn (Spitfires)	Hornchurch 54 Sqn (Hurricanes) 74 Sqn (Spitfires) 611 Sqn (Spitfires)
	Manston 79 Sqn (Hurricanes) 600 Sqn (Blenheim IFs)
	Rochford 611 Sqn (Spitfires)
North Weald 56 Sqn (Hurricanes) 151 Sqn (Hurricanes)	North Weald 56 Sqn (Hurricanes) 151 Sqn (Hurricanes) 604 Sqn (Blenheim IFs)
Debden 29 Sqn (Blenheims) 85 Sqn (Hurricanes) 87 Sqn (Hurricanes)	Debden 17 Sqn (Hurricanes) 29 Sqn (Blenheim IFs) 85 Sqn (BEF July 1939 to May 1940) 87 Sqn (BEF Sept 1939 to May 1940)
Northolt 111 Sqn (Hurricanes) (not until May 1940 – before that in Drem & Wick, Scotland)	Northolt 65 Sqn (Spitfires) 25 Sqn (Blenheim IFs)
Hendon 192 Sqn (Spitfires) 600 Sqn (Blenheims) 601 Sqn (Blenheims) 604 Sqn (Blenheims)	
Total: 21 squadrons	**Total**: 21 squadrons

Comparison of Luftwaffe Intelligence RAF AOB and
Actual RAF AOB, 1 January 1940

RAF AOB COMPOSED BY OBDL INTELLIGENCE	ACTUAL RAF AOB
NO. 12 GROUP HUCKNALL	NO. 12 GROUP HUCKNALL
Duxford 19 Sqn (Spitfires) 66 Sqn (Spitfires)	Duxford 19 Sqn (Spitfires) 66 Sqn (Spitfires)
Wittering 23 Sqn (Blenheim IFs) 213 Sqn (Hurricanes)	Wittering 23 Sqn (Blenheims) 213 Sqn (Hurricanes)
Digby 46 Sqn (Hurricanes)	Digby 46 Sqn (Hurricanes)
Castle Bromwich 605 Sqn (Hurricanes) 606 Sqn (Hurricanes)	Castle Bromwich Manufacturing plant only
Unknown 121 Sqn (Spitfires) 122 Sqn (Spitfires) 124 Sqn (Spitfires) 128 Sqn (Spitfires) 130 Sqn (Spitfires) 134 Sqn (Spitfires) 136 Sqn (Spitfires) 168 Sqn (Spitfires) 187 Sqn (Spitfires) 191 Sqn (Spitfires)	RAF status 121 Sqn formed 14 May 41 (Eagle Squadron) 122 Sqn formed 1 May 41 (Spitfires) 124 Sqn formed 10 May 41 (Spitfires) 128 Sqn formed Oct 41 (Hurricanes) 130 Sqn formed Jun 41 (Spitfires) 134 Sqn formed Sep 41 (Hurricanes) 136 Sqn formed Aug 41 (Hurricanes) 168 Sqn formed Jun 42 (Tomahawks) 187 Sqn formed Feb 45 (Halifax Transport Command) 191 Sqn formed May 43 (Catalina Maritime recon.)

Complete with this updated AOB and a revised target list, Schmid produced an amended *Studie Blau* six and a half months later, on 16 July 1940. While still promoting the *Handelskrieg* strategy presented in the original, Schmid had no external sources to provide any new or current information making the 'new' edition lamentably inadequate as an accurate intelligence assessment because it relied on data that was more than a year old and merely extrapolated over time. In other words, it was largely guesswork.[15]

With the cessation of virtually every external source of information, Schmid's primary tasks actually changed from intelligence 'evaluation and interpretation' (assessment) to providing Göring and Jeschonnek's ObdL staff with 'the daily estimate of the situation [*Lagebericht*, 'management report' or, in modern military terms, 'situation report']. This estimate was a synthesis of the daily situation reports of subordinate Air Force headquarters, army and navy agencies, and of the reports and messages originating from other intelligence sources, above all from radio interception.'[16]

FUNKHORCHDIENST – THE LUFTWAFFE'S 'RADIO INTERCEPT SERVICE'

Through Martini's Funkhorchdienst, Schmid and the Luftwaffe leadership were aware of the RAF's new early-warning radar network, but at the time no one recognized its capabilities or potential, and Schmid did not mention it in either version of *Studie Blau*. In fact, Martini and his staff had been aware of the Chain Home radar system for two years.

In May 1934, Martini established within his RLM Signals Division[17] an office (Referat IIIC) for the interception of enemy radio communications, deciphering and evaluating them, and the dissemination of intelligence derived from them. Field units, disguised as 'Weather Report Receiving Stations', were established along Germany's borders and coastlines and from 21 September 1936 they began recording the location of foreign transmitters (through direction-finding [DF] triangulation) and message content, feeding this 'raw' information to a *Chiffrierstelle* (Cryptographic Centre, or 'Cypher Site') at Potsdam for processing (plotting locations), deciphering and interpretation.

According to the official history, 'Following the developments of foreign policy in 1938 and the establishment of the Protectorate of Bohemia and Moravia on 15 March 1939 [Hitler's occupation of the rest of Czechoslovakia] the tendency of future military–political developments appeared to indicate that Britain must also be counted as a future enemy in the event of war.'[18]

Upon mobilization a central control station was established in each Luftflotte region of operations, with that in Kesselring's command responsible for monitoring Great Britain through two fixed intercept sites at Telgte, near Münster, and Husum-Milstedt, and two mobile companies. These facilities 'monitored communications traffic in general and air communications in particular in adjacent countries; [determined] the foreign air forces' ground organization, tactics, command, reporting, navigation systems, operating procedures, radio frequencies… [and] exploited foreign radio traffic for navigation by own bomber forces.'[19] But they did not report to Kesselring. Instead, they sent their raw intercepts to the Cryptographic Centre at Potsdam.

Martini's Funkhorchdienst was particularly interested in locating radio transmitters in Britain since, being much farther away than Germany's Continental neighbours, it was anticipated that RAF and civil air navigation beacons and BBC broadcast stations could be used to guide Luftwaffe bombers across the sea and into the interior of the country. Because the greater distance precluded comprehensive coverage of radio beacons and stations located in Britain's interior, Martini petitioned Göring to use one of the nation's two surviving dirigibles, *LZ 127* and *LZ 130*, both named *Graf Zeppelin*. Approved, 'The Radio Intercept Service of the German Air Force', Vol. 2, USAF Historical Study No. 191 quotes Colonel Kurt Gottschling as noting: 'Two cruises were carried out by Zeppelin [*LZ 127*] in 1938, with radio intercept personnel aboard, along

The Luftwaffe used the two surviving Zeppelin passenger-dirigibles – *LZ 127* and *LZ 130*, both named *Graf Zeppelin* – to search for RAF navigation beacons and BBC radio station transmitters in 1938 and 1939. (Author Collection)

the eastern coast of Britain to detect frequencies not hitherto recorded.'[20]

Although commonly thought to have been sorties specifically intended to investigate the RAF's Chain Home radar network, they were not. However, the coastal radar transmitters were included in the Funkhorchdienst's resulting list of British radio stations, prompting another, but unproductive, electronic intelligence flight using *LZ 130* carrying '28 radio-listening and radiolocation personnel' and a special 'radio-measuring "spy basket"' the following year.

ABOVE
The Ju 88 was the Luftwaffe's most versatile bomber, able to deliver bombs during medium-altitude level attacks in Gruppe strength against large-area targets, or to hit smaller targets in dive-bombing attacks. This dual capability provided significant flexibility for Luftflotte and Fliegerkorps mission planners. (AHB)

Martini intended his radio intercept service to be 'an intelligence organ serving the Commander-in-Chief of the Air Force' by providing 'operational intelligence to gain an insight into the areas of strategic concentration of foreign air powers, their ground organization, their strengths and their targets to attack.'[21]

The rest of the ObdL staff did not necessarily agree.

Funkhorchdienst was considered 'almost a private sphere of General Martini', the official history of ObdL Intelligence reports. He issued the field units their mission assignments without input from Schmid's 5. Abteilung and his Cryptographic Centre evaluated and interpreted the decoded British messages in a vacuum, with no awareness of other intelligence information. While the resulting 'intelligence' was transmitted to 5. Abteilung for dissemination to Luftflotten and lower echelon HQs, it was frequently erroneous, completely out of context and conflicted with information ObdL Intelligence office was disseminating.

In modern parlance, this is known as an 'intelligence fusion failure', where

LEFT
KGr 100, here on a low-altitude maritime armed-reconnaissance mission, was a specialist in using X-Gerät (X-apparatus), advanced radio navigation-bombing equipment for 'blind' weapons delivery at night or in bad weather. Due to the highly classified nature of its equipment, roles and procedures, mission tasking was transmitted to the KGr 100 staff by the most secure communications means available – Enigma. The Luftwaffe was unaware that the British routinely intercepted these messages. (AHB donated by Ken Wakefield)

intelligence derived from different sources has been combined without correlation or correction, thus creating a misleading or inaccurate 'product'.

According to the official history, 'The radio intercept service could only supplement or confirm the other sources of information; for this reason, the assignment of missions and the direct evaluation of results should have been the responsibility of the agency in charge of the overall intelligence situation. This was not the Chief of the Signal Communications System, but the 5. Abteilung of the ObdL staff…'[22]

THE MISSION PLANNING PROCESSES

Finally, before describing Luftwaffe combat operations against Britain in the summer of 1940, it is important to understand the Luftflotte mission planning process. Offensive operations operated on a 48-hour cycle that began at dawn on 'Day 1' with the launching of systematic photo-reconnaissance missions (which had their own 24-hour operations cycle). Typically, these sorties returned prior to noon, and the aircrew would report their observations while the photographic films were being developed, after which the images would be passed to the HQ planning staffs.[23]

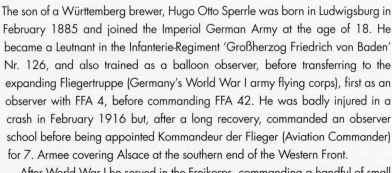

Generalfeldmarschall Hugo Otto Sperrle

Generalfeldmarschall Hugo Sperrle. (Author Collection)

The son of a Württemberg brewer, Hugo Otto Sperrle was born in Ludwigsburg in February 1885 and joined the Imperial German Army at the age of 18. He became a Leutnant in the Infanterie-Regiment 'Großherzog Friedrich von Baden' Nr. 126, and also trained as a balloon observer, before transferring to the expanding Fliegertruppe (Germany's World War I army flying corps), first as an observer with FFA 4, before commanding FFA 42. He was badly injured in a crash in February 1916 but, after a long recovery, commanded an observer school before being appointed Kommandeur der Flieger (Aviation Commander) for 7. Armee covering Alsace at the southern end of the Western Front.

After World War I he served in the Freikorps, commanding a handful of small government mail/army courier units operating as Deutsche Luftreederei (German Air Shipping Company). During the mid-1920s he commanded the observation school at the clandestine training centre at Lipetsk, USSR, before being appointed to the Reichswehr's 'Air Operations Desk' in 1927. During the Nazis' rampant expansion of Germany's secret air force between 1933 and 1935, he was chosen to lead the new Luftwaffe's first tactical command, Fliegerdivision 1 (Flying Division 1), which was established at Berlin in April 1934.

Two years later, Sperrle was commander of Condor Legion, the Luftwaffe expeditionary air corps supporting Generalissimo Francisco Franco during the

Spanish Civil War. Returning to Germany, in April 1938 Sperrle was given command of Luftwaffengruppenkommando 3 (later redesignated Luftflotte 3), based in Munich. Within a year, his command participated in the annexation of the Sudetenland and the subjugation of Czechoslovakia with impressive airpower demonstrations. Although drawn down to a minimum deterrent force facing France during Hitler's invasion of Poland, afterwards Luftflotte 3 swelled to 588 bombers, 103 Stukas, and 509 fighters for Hitler's *Westfeldzug*. Following that very successful campaign, on 19 July 1940, Sperrle was one of 12 generals promoted to the rank of Generalfeldmarschall by Adolf Hitler.[24]

A big 'bear of a man' who squinted through a monocle, Sperrle was described by Hitler as one of his 'two most brutal-looking generals' and was sent on several 'diplomatic' missions where an intimidating appearance might prove helpful. Widely known for his coarse wit and gross table manners, Sperrle was the most experienced air campaigner in the Luftwaffe and the only high-ranking field commander with any understanding of airpower and its application.

Using Göring's directives and Jeschonnek's supplementing instructions as their guidance, the HQ mission planners would select targets within their area of operations from ObdL's current target list and, after reviewing target particulars and anticipated enemy defences, determine which type of unit (Stuka, He 111, Do 17Z, or Ju 88A) would be best suited for the attack, establish timing requirements (with feints on the flanks and fighter sweeps of the ingress routes) and co-ordinate that timing with the neighbouring Luftflotte.

Then, later that afternoon the command's chief of staff would assign the next day's missions to their subordinate Fliegerkorps, depending on the type of aircraft, attack profile (dive-bombing, medium-level or low-level bombing) and ordnance best suited to destroy the selected targets. The Fliegerkorps operations planners would assign the mission to a selected Kampf- or Stukageschwader's staff, co-ordinate with the Luftflotte's JaFü staff for Jagdschutz (close fighter escort), and plan the flight profile for the mission, mapping out routes and altitudes to minimize exposure to enemy air defences and deconflict locations and timings with other raids in the area. KG and StG staffs would do the detailed mission planning by examining the target dossier folders, preparing briefing map-boards and printing target area photographs for navigators/bomb aimers (in the Luftwaffe these tasks were combined in the Beobachter (observer) aircrew position) to use during briefings and in flight.

The next morning, while Day 2's photo-reconnaissance missions were under way, the KG and StG mission commanders would brief their constituent Gruppe and Staffel commanders on the mission details, beginning with take-off times and rendezvous procedures to form the 'strike package' formations and get their fighter escort on station. If the weather was favourable, the first missions would typically launch before noon, about the time the morning's reconnaissance missions would be returning to begin the next cycle of mission planning.

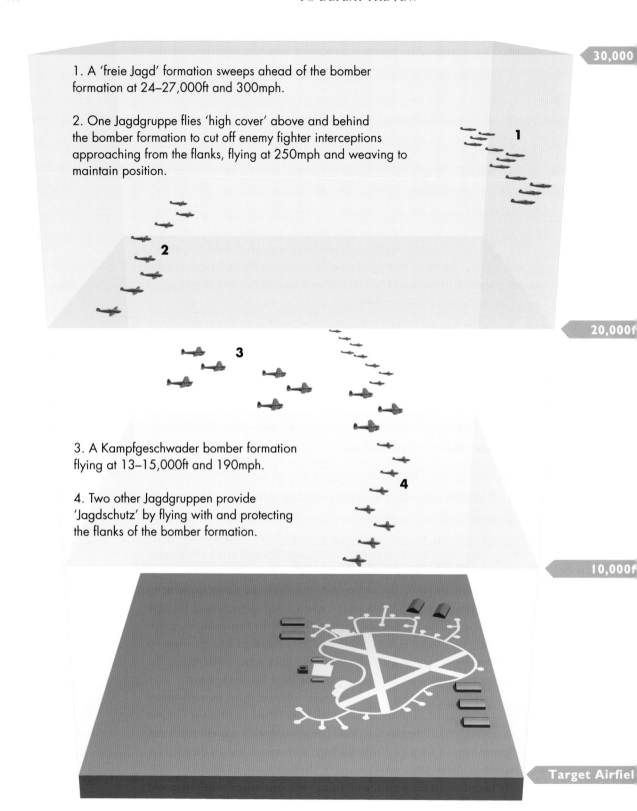

1. A 'freie Jagd' formation sweeps ahead of the bomber formation at 24–27,000ft and 300mph.

2. One Jagdgruppe flies 'high cover' above and behind the bomber formation to cut off enemy fighter interceptions approaching from the flanks, flying at 250mph and weaving to maintain position.

3. A Kampfgeschwader bomber formation flying at 13–15,000ft and 190mph.

4. Two other Jagdgruppen provide 'Jagdschutz' by flying with and protecting the flanks of the bomber formation.

30,000

20,000f

10,000f

Target Airfiel

OPPOSITE • LUFTWAFFE OFFENSIVE COUNTER-AIR MISSION COMPOSITION

Initially, Luftwaffe doctrine called for every bomber wing (each comprising three Kampfgruppen, typically launching 18 bombers each) to be escorted by a single Jagdgeschwader of around 72 Bf 109Es. In this case, one of the fighter wing's Jagdgruppe (between 24 and 30 fighters) would range ahead of the combined bomber-fighter formation on a 'freie Jagd' ('free hunt') fighter sweep, with the wing's other two Jagdgruppen positioned on the bomber formation's flanks, providing Jagdschutz (close escort).

The sweeping Jagdgruppe would fly above 20,000ft altitude at the Bf 109E's normal engagement speed of 300mph (480kph) and have complete freedom to engage any enemy interceptors they spotted. The close escort Jagdgruppen were tied to the bombers, flying slightly above them and on their flanks, and, since they flew at 190mph (305kph), having to keep pace with them. They were typically not permitted to engage enemy interceptors unless they, or their charges, were threatened with attack.

Later during the campaign, there was a change in heavy escort tactics. The 'freie Jagd' sweep was undertaken by a large formation from one Jagdgeschwader while the escorting wing's third Jagdgruppe provided high cover. This Jagdgruppe normally maintained close to fighting airspeed (approximately 250mph/400 kph) and flew a weaving pattern above and behind the trailing bombers. Upon sighting approaching enemy interceptors this formation moved to the threatened flank and dived to engage before the attackers reached the bombers, allowing the flank escorts to accelerate and position themselves to defend the bomber formation.

Frequently, when missions were postponed or cancelled for the day, the planning results would stay in place, permitting the mission to be flown on the next, or a subsequent day. Once a target was selected for attack, it was rarely cancelled altogether. Unlike the army's daily target selection, which was on occasion overtaken by events when the targets were overrun by hard-charging panzers, the ObdL's offensive counter-air targets would be there the next day and still need to be attacked if the Luftwaffe was ever to beat down RAF Fighter Command to the point where a cross-Channel amphibious operation could be undertaken.

Lacking a command-level planning staff, the Luftwaffe's air campaign planning process devolved to Luftflotte and Fliegerkorps HQs using Göring's directives and ObdL target lists as guidance. Communications between the two echelons and the Kampf- and Stukageschwader staffs were usually conducted over secure teletype landlines, with urgent information relayed by phone. Ironically, landline communication was more secure than Enigma radio traffic. (NARA)

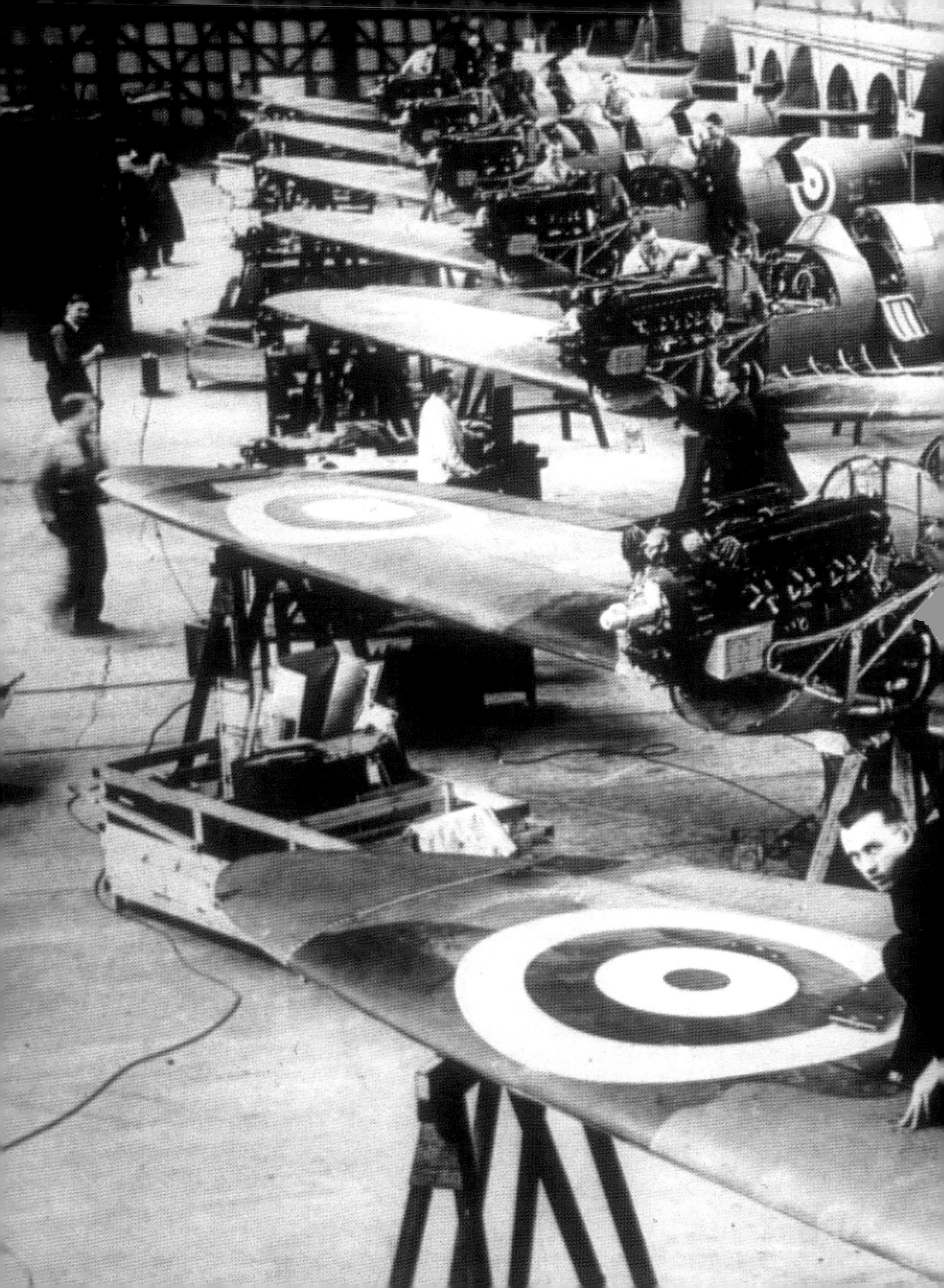

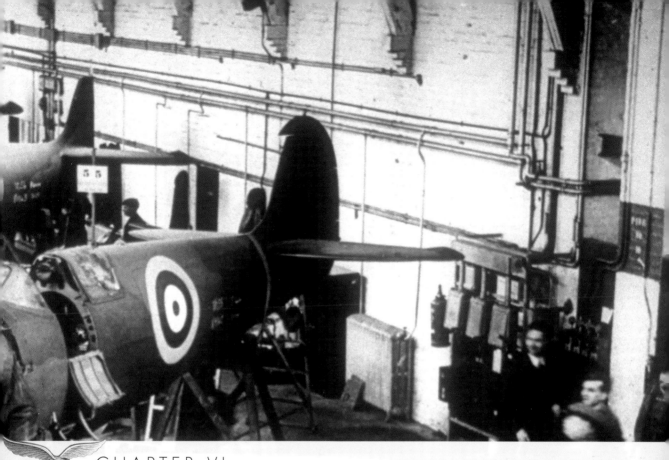

CHAPTER VI

THE LUFTWAFFE'S OPPONENT

RAF Fighter Command

The best defence for the country is the fear of the fighter. If we were strong in fighters we should probably never be attacked in force. If we are moderately strong we shall probably be attacked and the attacks will be brought to a standstill… If we are weak in fighter strength, the attacks will not be brought to a standstill and the productive capacity of the country will be virtually destroyed.

ACM Sir Hugh Dowding, AOCinC, Fighter Command[1]

In June 1940, when Hitler's panzers arrived at the French shore of the English Channel, the Luftwaffe faced the most sophisticated and effective air defence network in the world. History's first ever integrated air defence system (IADS) consisted of six major components supported by two other organizations supplying intelligence and information to what became colloquially known as 'Dowding's System'.

Three of the components and one supporting organization detected and tracked incoming enemy aircraft; three other components controlled the response of RAF interceptors, enabling them to be directed to the location of the enemy intruders and attack them. A noteworthy and much discussed additional organization system supplied useful strategic intelligence to the Air Ministry. While Hurricane and Spitfire interceptors were the combat core – and the largest, most glamourous and famous ('the Few') component – of the defences facing the Luftwaffe, they were supplemented by AA artillery and balloon barrages as active and passive 'point defence' measures, respectively, at vital targets within the UK.

The six components were networked into a command and control system that was designed to enable defending fighters to intercept the raiders, engage and destroy them, and limit the damage their bombing could do.

First, the RAF's Wireless Telegraphy Intercept Service (Y-Service) detected the radio emissions indicating the Luftwaffe was preparing to launch aircraft from airfields in Holland, Belgium and northern France. Then the earliest effective form of air defence radar network, known as Chain Home (CH), along Britain's coasts provided advance warning that aircraft were airborne and approaching from across the Channel or North Sea. Second, because the crude (by later standards) coastal CH radars could not see behind them over land, when clear weather allowed, an expansive network of visual observation posts tracked and reported the flights of intruders as they continued towards their targets.

PREVIOUS PAGES
Spitfire manufacturing began at Supermarine's facility in Woolston, Southampton, a fact well known by Luftwaffe intelligence, making it a prime target. Production was therefore dispersed across other locations, including a major factory built at Castle Bromwich, a suburb of Birmingham, in the West Midlands. After chronic start-up issues, the plant's first Spitfire was completed on 6 June 1940. (Photo by Keystone/Getty Images)

Air Chief Marshal Sir Hugh C.T. Dowding

Responsible for the air defence of Great Britain, 58-year-old Air Chief Marshal Sir Hugh Caswall Tremenheere Dowding faced Göring's Luftwaffe in 1940. Son of a Scottish schoolmaster, Dowding was born on 24 April 1882 in Moffat, Dumfriesshire. Educated at Winchester College and the Royal Military Academy, he was posted to the Royal Garrison Artillery (RGA), serving in Gibraltar, Ceylon (now Sri Lanka), Hong Kong, India, and on the Isle of Wight. New technologies intrigued him; while posted on the Isle of Wight he attended the Vickers School of Flying, was awarded his aviator's certificate in December 1913, and he graduated from the army's Central Flying School the following year. Although he returned to the RGA on the Isle of Wight, when World War I erupted he was immediately called to the Royal Flying Corps (RFC) as a reconnaissance pilot.

Initially posted to No. 7, then No. 6 Squadrons, flying Farman MF.7s, MF.11s and HF.20s, and Royal Aircraft Factory B.E.2s and B.E.8s, Dowding's senior rank quickly saw him posted as a staff officer to RFC HQ, which soon formed a detachment pioneering the use of radio for reconnaissance missions. His success in this rapidly developing field resulted in his posting to command the Wireless Experimental Establishment at Brooklands in March 1915. He returned to the front to command No. 16 Squadron, primarily operating B.E.2cs, four months later. Although noted for being an efficient leader, he was considered too reserved and aloof from his juniors by squadron members, resulting in the nickname 'Stuffy'.

Nevertheless, Dowding's leadership potential was recognized and further advancement followed. After commanding the 7th and 9th Wings, he was promoted to brigadier-general to command the Southern Training Brigade in the summer of 1917. Following the Armistice, he was rewarded with a permanent commission as a group captain in the RAF, commanding No. 16 Group and then No. 1 Group. Following service as chief staff officer at Inland Area HQ at Uxbridge and for RAF Iraq Command, in May 1926 he was appointed director of training at the Air Ministry and, after being promoted to AVM in 1929, became AOC Fighting Area, ADGB. Later he joined the Air Council as Air Member for Supply and Research, where he encouraged the aero industry to develop the monoplane as the basis for an eight-gun interceptor. By the time Fighter Command was formed on 14 July 1936 and its HQ established at Bentley Priory, a large, old Gothic house near Stanmore on the north-west edge of London, the sum of Dowding's natural talents and military experience made him the single most qualified officer to lead it into the coming conflict.[2]

ACM Hugh Dowding. (Author Collection, colourized by Richard Molloy)

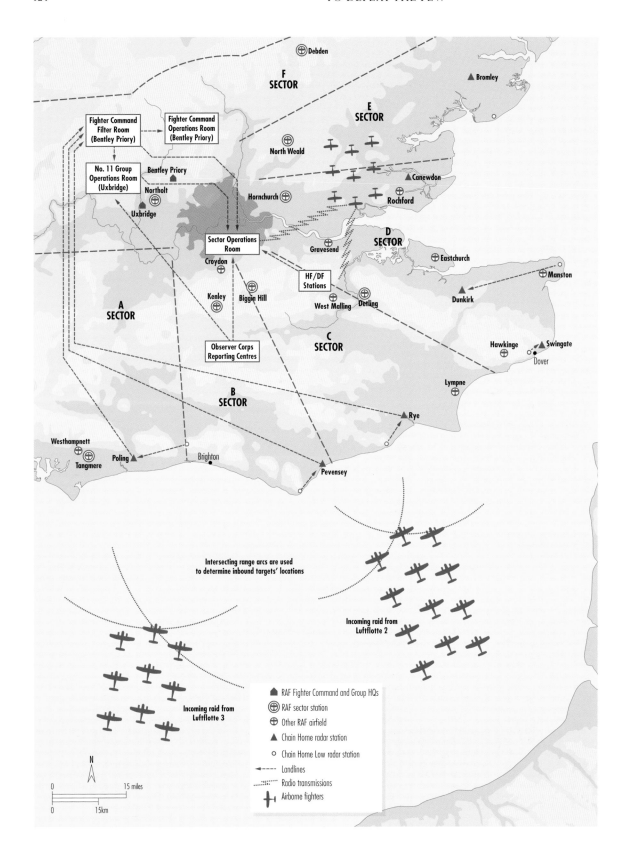

Fighter Command Filter Room (Bentley Priory)

Fighter Command Operations Room (Bentley Priory)

No. 11 Group Operations Room (Uxbridge)

Bentley Priory

Northolt

Uxbridge

Sector Operations Room

Croydon

HF/DF Stations

Kenley

Biggin Hill

West Malling

Detling

Observer Corps Reporting Centres

Debden

Bromley

F SECTOR

E SECTOR

North Weald

Canewdon

Hornchurch

Rochford

D SECTOR

Gravesend

Eastchurch

Manston

Dunkirk

A SECTOR

C SECTOR

Hawkinge

Swingate

Dover

B SECTOR

Lympne

Westhampnett

Poling

Brighton

Rye

Tangmere

Pevensey

Intersecting range arcs are used to determine inbound targets' locations

Incoming raid from Luftflotte 2

Incoming raid from Luftflotte 3

N

0   15 miles

0   15km

▲ RAF Fighter Command and Group HQs

⊕ RAF sector station

⊕ Other RAF airfield

▲ Chain Home radar station

○ Chain Home Low radar station

- - - Landlines

······· Radio transmissions

Airborne fighters

RAF INTEGRATED AIR DEFENCE SYSTEM DIAGRAM

Fighter Command's radar, command and control and interceptor/AA artillery interface system was history's first integrated air defence system. Incoming raids were detected by long-range Chain Home early-warning radars, their locations and tracks being determined by intersecting range arcs from neighbouring radar stations. This information was passed to Fighter Command HQ Filter Room. Fighter Command HQ was responsible for notifying Group HQs, sounding air raid alarms, and shutting down BBC transmitters to eliminate them as possible navigational aids for the attackers. Group HQ scrambled interceptors, directed them to patrol areas, assigned each incoming raid to a sector controller for interception and alerted the appropriate AA batteries. Knowing the location and direction of the incoming raid (from Chain Home and Observer Corps reports) and the position (via HF/DF), sector controllers used radio to vector their assigned fighter squadrons to engage the attackers.

Preliminary Y-Service signals intelligence, CH radar information and visual tracking of enemy aircraft were fed into Fighter Command HQ, where they were 'filtered' to eliminate redundant and erroneous information. As the third component, the HQ Filter Room reported 'raids inbound' information to the Command's Operations Room (Ops Room). From there Dowding or his 'Duty Air Commodore' assigned the raid to one of his three (later four) constituent groups to meet the incoming raiders with intercepting fighters, alerted AA Command, activated the civilian Air Raid Precaution (ARP) network for the threatened area, and shut down BBC broadcasting stations so that they could not be used as homing beacons by Luftwaffe bombers.

Ground crew roll out 65 Squadron Spitfire Mk Is in readiness for the day's flying. The type's early camouflage scheme included a characteristic half white, half black underside. (NARA, colourized by Richard Molloy)

Inside the concrete Receiver Room of an AMES Type 1 Chain Home radar station. To the left is one of the two RF7 receivers, and to the right the Mark 3 communications console. All coastal radar stations communicated position and height information via a direct telephone line to the Filter Room at Fighter Command HQ. (AHB)

At the group level, the commanders would launch fighter squadrons from their airfields (at the outset of the campaign, No. 11 Group had 21 squadrons based on seven sector stations and 14 forward operating locations [FOLs]), assign the raid to one of his sector controllers for the tactical direction of the air battle, and inform the AA defences within his area of operations, or, in modern terms, area of responsibility (AOR), to minimize fighter losses due to 'friendly fire'.

The sector controllers kept track of their assigned fighters through an independent position reporting system called High Frequency Direction Finding (HF/DF or 'Huff Duff'). The positions of both the raid, supplied by the Fighter Command Filter Room, and their airborne fighter squadrons were displayed on a large map table that resembled a huge game board, providing a visual representation of the relative positions of the raiders and interceptors.

Calculating geometric 'cut-off' headings, the sector controller would direct the movement of airborne fighter units by radio, a process known as 'vectoring', to an intercept point (IP). The fighter unit commander would lead his formation to the IP where, upon arrival, he would begin a racetrack-shaped orbit (similar to the modern combat air patrol) perpendicular to the inbound heading of the raiders. From there, the leader would look out to the side from his cockpit, searching the sky for the inbound raiders and, on seeing them, call 'Tally-ho!', letting his wingmen and the Controller know that he had spotted his targets. He then led the formation in to attack.[3]

Once the engagement began, it was a combination of advantageous positioning, the relative strengths of the opposing forces, performance of the different aircraft types, manoeuvring and shooting skills of the pilots, co-ordinated engaged tactics, and individual courage and discipline that determined the outcome of each battle.

The stages and processes from Y-Service's first detection of Luftwaffe radio emissions to the engagement of the enemy are described below.

11 Group Sector Details – September 1940

SECTOR	STATION	CALLSIGN	SENIOR FIGHTER CONTROLLER
Sector A	Tangmere	Shortjack Control	Sqn Ldr David Lloyd
Sector B	Kenley	Sapper Control	Sqn Ldr Anthony Norman
Sector C	Biggin Hill	Tophat Control	Sqn Ldr John Worrall
Sector D	Hornchurch	Lumba Control	Fg Off Ronald Adam
Sector E	North Weald	Cowslip Control	Sqn Ldr John Cherry
Sector F	Debden	Garter Control	Wg Cdr Laurence Fuller-Good
Sector Z	Northolt	(Unknown)	Gp Capt Stanley Vincent

Y-SERVICE AND R/T EXPLOITATION

For navigation assistance, German bomber crews used a nationwide network of medium-frequency radio beacons transmitting in the 176–580KHz range. Each Luftwaffe airbase had its own discrete beacon for airborne crews to 'home' onto for return to base. Following the fall of Norway, Denmark, Holland, Belgium and France, the beacon network was expanded to include coastal locations within the occupied countries, permitting aircraft to return safely from long and potentially disorientating flights over the sea, beyond sight of land. Through DF triangulation, by June 1940, the RAF's Y-Service had correctly located the position of all 38 navigation beacons and 11 Luftaufsicht ATC radio transmitters scattered from Norway to Bordeaux. Despite daily changes to beacon communications frequencies and callsigns, the Luftwaffe's use of correlated unit designations and radio identifier codes resulted in the Y-Service soon establishing an accurate air order of battle for German bomber, reconnaissance and transport units.

Prior to launching a mission, each airfield involved would activate its radio beacon, thus alerting Y-Service to expect aircraft to take off from that location. Additionally, while the aircrew were being briefed on the day's mission, as part of readying their aircraft for the mission, ground crews would calibrate each aircraft's onboard HF wireless telegraphy Morse code transmitters, which were used to communicate with the base and ATC stations during the sortie. These calibration checks generally confirmed that a mission would soon be launched by that unit.

NEXT PAGES
The interior of the Receiver Block of an AMES Type 2 Chain Home Low station. To the right are the two plan position indicators and range consoles and at the centre, the air plotting board. Since the radar type was capable of monitoring the movements of low-flying aircraft and shipping, these stations were staffed by RAF and RN personnel. (AHB)

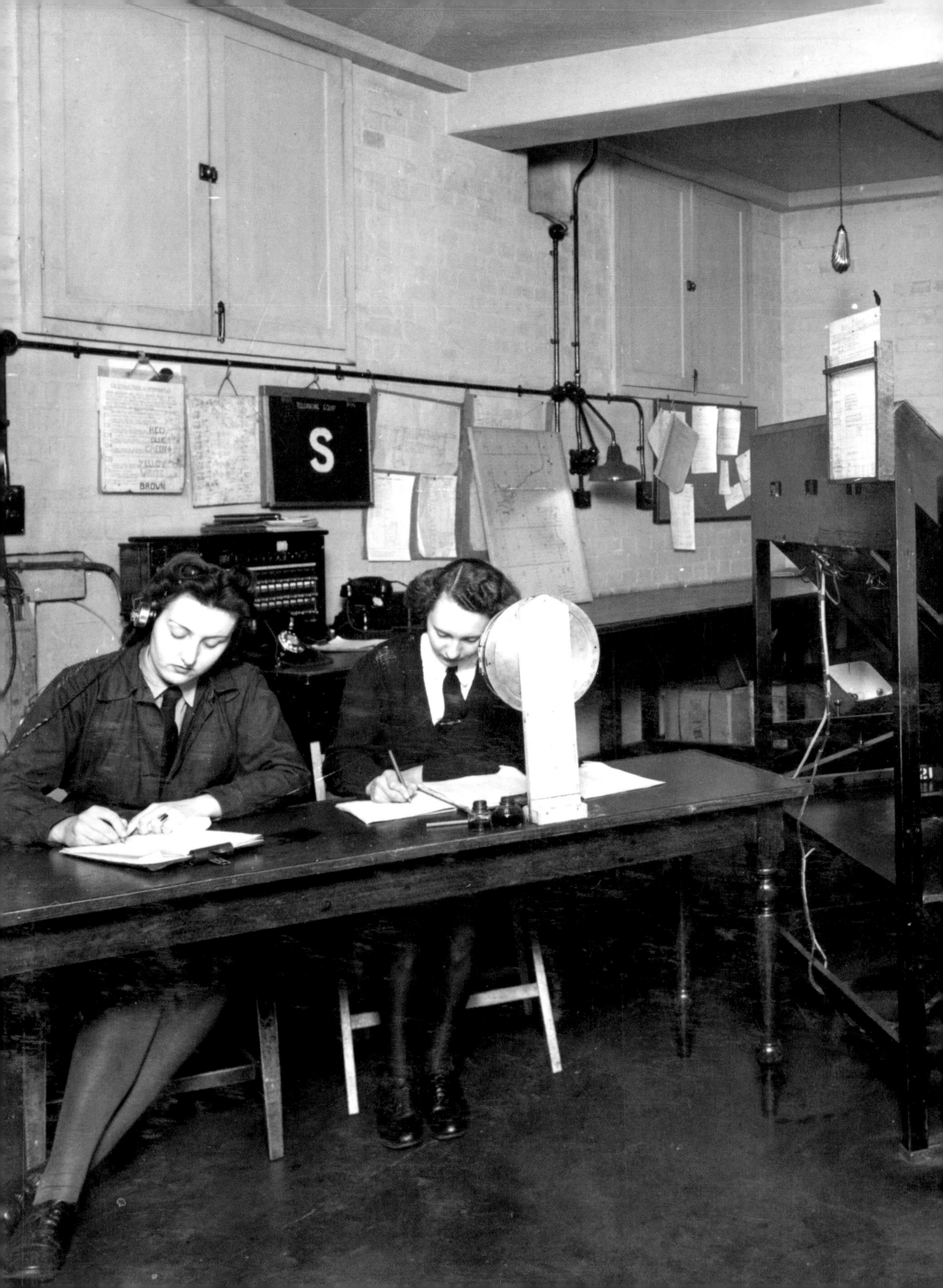
RED
BLUE
GREEN
YELLOW
WHITE
BROWN
S

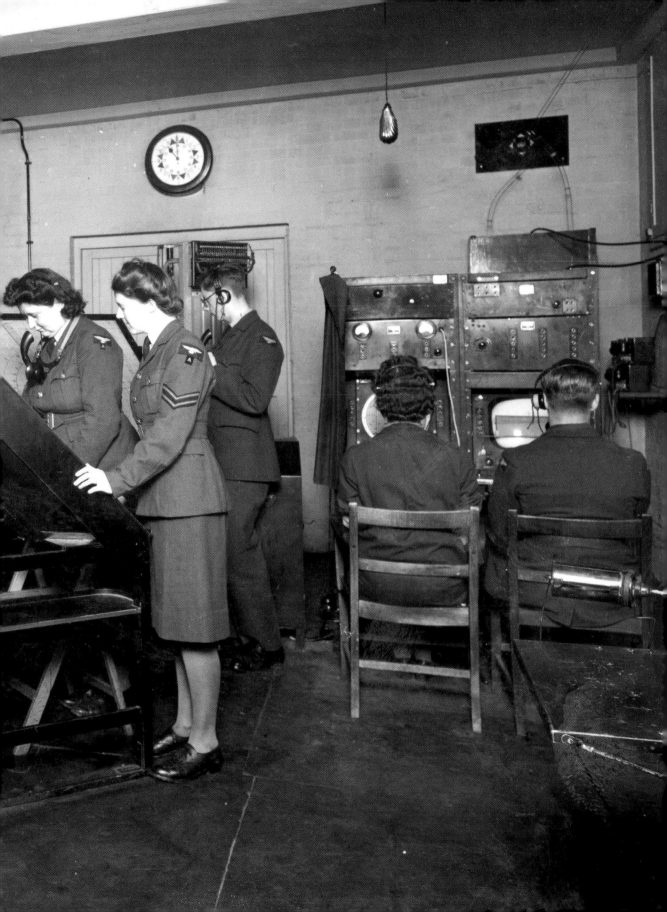

For security in HF W/T air-to-ground/ground-to-air tactical communications, German bomber and long-range reconnaissance crews used 'low-grade' codes[4] and ciphers. From before the war began, radio listening posts scattered along the coast passed Luftwaffe low-grade tactical wireless traffic to Y-Service's Central Intercept Station (CIS) at RAF Cheadle, Staffordshire, where it was decoded and deciphered by RAF intelligence officers, augmented by a small team of cryptologists from the highly classified Government Code and Cypher School (GC&CS, primarily responsible for deciphering high-grade Enigma intercepts at Bletchley Park). By late 1940, CIS at RAF Cheadle had broken 75 air-to-ground codes and 18 airfield serviceability codes, and two systems used for enciphering map references.

As the German bombers took off from their bases, Y-Service DF stations triangulated and plotted the sources of Luftaufsicht ATC transmissions reporting aircraft airborne, resulting in confirmation that a raid had been launched from that location. By correlating the activation of MF navigation beacons and pre-mission HF radio checks with the locations of the 'aircraft airborne' announcements by ATC, and, knowing the Luftwaffe AOB, F.H. Hinsley writes in *British Intelligence in the Second World War, Volume 1* that Cheadle was often able to identify the bomber units involved in any developing raid 'very soon after the start of each operation' and report this information to Fighter Command HQ Filter Room.

While Luftwaffe bomber, reconnaissance and transport aircraft used slow and ponderous Morse code W/T communications, German fighters used faster and immediately understandable voice radios or radio-telephony (R/T) on HF frequencies. To listen in on Jagdwaffe and Zerstörer air-to-air/air-to-ground communications, early in 1940 the Air Ministry established a small experimental signals unit at RAF Hawkinge, on England's south-east coast, just west of Dover. During June and July, the unit expanded rapidly with several fluent German-speaking members of the Women's Auxiliary Air Force (WAAF) being recruited to eavesdrop on fighter R/T transmissions. The WAAFs recorded the transmitter's details and message content in German, added the English translation, and messages of immediate tactical use were passed by telephone to No. 11 Group Ops Room at RAF Uxbridge.

During this time, to increase R/T interception coverage, three more coastal intercept stations (called 'Home Defence Units' as a deception measure) were established at Gorleston in Norfolk, Beachy Head in East Sussex, and Strete in Devon, extending Y-Service voice intercept from Denmark to Brittany. This wide and rapid expansion resulted in the establishment of the RAF's main R/T communications intelligence site at RAF West Kingsdown, on the North Downs. While not as operationally significant as Cheadle's pre-raid information, R/T exploitation contributed to Fighter Command's awareness of the ongoing air battles and was especially useful in alerting No. 11 Group and its sector controllers when German fighters were beginning their return to base.

THE CHAIN HOME EARLY-WARNING RADAR NETWORK

One of the chief advantages that the RAF's IADS had over all other air defence organizations of the day was its ability through the development and deployment of a comprehensive early-warning radar screen to detect incoming attacks before they reached Britain's shores. The developmental history of Fighter Command's Chain Home radar and its integrated network has received detailed coverage in many previous histories of the Battle of Britain; this volume will instead focus upon its use within the context of Fighter Command's IADS.

The primitive Air Ministry Experimental Station (AMES) Type 1 early-warning radar aerial transmitter array broadcast a 100-degree-wide swath of RF (radio frequency) energy, similar to a floodlight but outside the visual spectrum, in a single cardinal direction (south for those sites on the south coast, east for those located on the east coast) out to approximately 100–120 miles (160–190km) at 20,000ft, depending on atmospheric conditions. The reflected RF energy was received by a separate array of aerial wires strung at angles to the transmitter's broadcast direction in the hope of determining the direction of the radar return, the azimuth and distance providing the location of the reflecting aircraft or target. Try as they might, the radar operators found that the crude 'radiogoniometer' technique was too vague and ambiguous for operational use, so overlapping 'range

WAAF plotters at work in the underground Operations Room at Fighter Command HQ. In the Filter Room next door, the Filter Officer deduced accurate raid information from data provided by radar stations and informed a 'teller', who communicated this by telephone simultaneously to the General Situation Map (GSM) table plotter and the plotters at the relevant Group Ops Room. Raid-position information displayed on the GSM Table in the Fighter Command HQ Ops Room enabled the Duty Air Commodore to make critical decisions concerning the deployment of fighter squadrons and to activate air raid alerts. (AHB)

cuts' from neighbouring radar sites were typically used to determine the location of the target – this correlation became a 'radar plot' and a series of 'plots' of the same target resulted in a 'track'.

RAF AMES Type 1 Chain Home and AMES Type 2 Chain Home Low Radars

Chain Home. (AHB)

Officially named Radio Direction Finding (RDF) to disguise the fact that it could not determine a target's azimuth (the target's direction – or bearing – from the radar station), the RAF's early-warning radar network was composed of essentially range-only radars that broadcast a fixed 'floodlight' of radio frequency (RF) energy in a horizontal 100-degree swath, with the reflected RF energy received by a separate set of fixed aerials. The three sets of transmitting aerials (wires) were strung between four 350ft-tall(106m) steel towers in what were sometimes called 'curtain arrays'. Except at the Dunkirk RDF Station near Canterbury and the coastal CH station at Rye, the towers were arranged in a cardinal direction. The early sites, built on England's east coast, 'looked' east; later installations, on the south coast, looked south. Initially the system operated on 22.7–29.7MHz megahertz frequency with an original power output of 450kW (kilowatts), increasing to 750kW by July 1940.

The receiving aerials were strung between four 250ft (76m) wooden towers arranged to optimize reception in an attempt to determine azimuth by the relative strength of the radar returns. This very primitive concept, invented by Bellini-Tosi in 1907, proved to have little operational utility. With practice it was soon discovered that the target's location was best determined by triangulation using the intersecting range arcs of the radar returns from two adjacent radar sites.

The limitations of the AMES Type 1 radar resulted in the RAF recognizing the need for a short-range, low-altitude 'gap filler' to augment the long-range Chain Home sites. Fortunately, the Admiralty had developed its own radar for coastal defence against surface warships and low-flying aircraft. This was accepted by the RAF as the AMES Type 2 Chain Home Low (CHL) radar system.

Lower-powered at 150kW and with an effective range of only 30–35 miles (48–56km), the 200MHz Type 2 was more advanced than the RAF radar, using a narrower 'spotlight' beam 20 degrees wide that could be rotated manually, enabling more accurate determination of a target's azimuth. However, the Chain Home Low stations were more quickly saturated by the returns from large raids than the Chain Home stations,

Chain Home Low. (AHB)

and azimuth ambiguities could be resolved only if no more than two tracks were received simultaneously.

Initially mounted atop turntables on separate gantries, the transmitting and receiving aerials could be turned to sweep back and forth through 180 degrees. Hand-operated, the aerial turning gear proved troublesome, however, especially in windy conditions when it could be difficult to control. Besides which, during periods of intense activity, even the slowest rate of sweep often overwhelmed the cathode ray tube and there was nothing to be gained by rotating the aerial.

Despite its limitations, it was an expedient supplement to the more primitive AMES Type 1, with one or two Chain Home Low sites 'tied' to each of the Chain Home stations by telephone for reporting radar contacts upstream to Fighter Command HQ's Filter Room, thus ensuring a more comprehensive early-warning network.[5]

The radar operator watched the radar returns on a large cathode ray tube (CRT) oscilloscope where the site's reflected energy was displayed as a 'blip' in the line along a range scale. The blip moved down the range scale as the target approached the radar site, with the distance being recorded by a 'plotter' who sat near the operator and relayed the range information to Fighter Command HQ Filter Room. With practice, this two-person team could track up to 12 targets at a time, recording and relaying the updated information about each target every two minutes. However, if targets headed perpendicular to the station, the range information at first decreased before increasing once again as the aircraft passed abeam the radar; this resulted in the blip momentarily merging with others at the same range, causing mounting confusion as the blips passed each other on the oscilloscope's range line.[6]

THE OBSERVER CORPS

Due to several technological limitations, CH radars could not track targets overland behind them and this work was done instead by the civilian Observer Corps. Originally created during World War I to track German airship and night-bomber raids, the organization was developed by Major General E.B. Ashmore into a reliable and responsive reporting system using volunteer 'special constables' and a dedicated telephone network that reported, along with searchlight and AA units, to an Operations Centre at his HQ.

Resurrected in 1925 as part of the Air Defence of Great Britain (ADGB) and expanded to include 100 observation posts reporting to four group HQs, four years later the organization became part of the RAF and provided the foundation of Dowding's IADS when Fighter Command was established in May 1936. Commanded by Air Commodore Alfred D. Warrington-Morris, the network began at the coast with small, three-to-five-man observer posts spread every six to ten miles, with more arrayed in depth at about the same distance so that their fields of view overlapped. They were connected by telephone to a group HQ, which reported 'observer plots' to the sector station within its area.[7] In south-east England, Park's sector controllers received up-to-the-minute raid tracking information from the Observer Corps' Nos 1 (Maidstone), 2 (Horsham), 3 (Winchester), 4 (Oxford), 17 (Watford), 18 (Colchester) and 19 (Bromley) Groups.

While Chain Home and Chain Home Low provided early warning of approaching raids, once the enemy had penetrated the British coast, visual reporting by the Observer Corps was the only way of tracking the formations. (AHB)

The posts reported numbers ('strength' in tens) and types of aircraft (Heinkels, Dorniers, Stukas, etc), position, heading and height. As Andy Saunders reported in his *Battle of Britain RAF Operations Manual*, 'The importance of information gleaned by the Observer Corps and its value to Fighter Controllers during the Battle of Britain cannot be overestimated. Its volunteer observers worked around the clock, 7 days a week, 365 days a year, to keep this vital flow of crucial information feeding into the command and control system.'[8]

COMMAND AND CONTROL – FIGHTER COMMAND AND GROUP OPS ROOMS

The Chain Home radar sites and Observer Corps Group HQs were connected to Fighter Command HQ Filter Room by a vast network of telephone lines, converging like a giant spider web into the underground command bunker located at Bentley Priory, Fighter Command HQ. Here the constantly changing information was assessed and collated to quickly identify and eliminate erroneous information and correlate redundant reports into single plots. Once a raid was determined and designated, its location, direction, strength and height was passed by a 'teller' to the Command Ops Room next door, where WAAF plotters positioned wooden markers on an expansive General Situation Map (GSM). These markers represented the locations of friendly fighters and enemy formations, like chess pieces on a chessboard. From his position in the elevated gallery, Dowding's Duty Air Commodore[9] was presented with a constantly updated overview of the operational situation across the entire country, enabling him to allocate specific incoming raids to the appropriate Group and call upon reinforcements, if he considered it necessary, from a neighbouring Group.

At the similarly constructed Group Ops Rooms, the GSM depicted each Group's AOR, along with a significant overlap into the adjacent Group's area. The tellers' phone line at Fighter Command Filter Room was also connected to the Group Ops Room, enabling information to be passed in parallel. This ensured that the Group's GSM was updated simultaneously, allowing the Group Commander and his Senior Fighter Controller to watch the tactical situation develop without relay delays as the enemy formations continued towards their targets. On the wall beyond the GSM, horse-race-like 'tote boards' provided up-to-the-minute state-of-readiness information for each squadron, by sector, under the Group's command, and a system of lights on the board illuminated to indicate whether a squadron/flight/section was at readiness, airborne, had sighted the enemy or was engaged.

Typically, the Group commander launched (scrambled) the number of squadrons he felt were needed for the developing situation and his senior fighter controller directed each of them to a specified patrol line, or to intercept an approaching raid, passing them to the sector controller for tactical control of the intercept.[10]

More than 1,000 Observer Corps posts fed position, heading, altitude and estimated strength information on enemy formations to one of 32 reporting centres. These centres collated the information and passed it to the Filter Room at Fighter Command HQ, where it was integrated into the air defence system. (Author Collection)

Group Captain Baron Willoughby de Broke

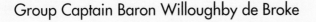

The Luftwaffe slang for British fighters was 'Lords' and little did they know that the man co-ordinating No. 11 Group's fighter defence was, actually, a lord. When John Henry Peyto Verney, son of Richard Verney, was born on 21 May 1896, he automatically became the 20th Baron Willoughby de Broke. Educated at Eton and the Royal Military College, Sandhurst, Willoughby de Broke joined the 17th Lancers, where he served as a lieutenant. He was awarded the Military Cross in 1918.

Following the Armistice, he became aide-de-camp to the Governor of Bombay, Sir George Lloyd, from 1919 to 1922, after which he served as adjutant of the Warwickshire Yeomanry from 1925 to 1929. He retired from the 17/21st Lancers, with the rank of captain, in 1929. Very much part of the British social class referred to as the 'landed gentry', Willoughby de Broke served as Master and Joint Master of the Warwickshire Foxhounds from 1929 to 1935, and Vice Lieutenant (1938–39) and Lord Lieutenant of Warwickshire (1939–67).

On 4 October 1933, he married Rachel Wrey, daughter of Sir Robert Bourchier Sherard Wrey, the 11th Baronet of Tavistock. Both keen aviators, they had an aeroplane and owned and operated their own airfield at Kineton, Warwickshire.

As a squadron leader in 605 (County of Warwick) Squadron, Auxiliary Air Force, Willoughby de Broke served as its commander from 1936 to 1939. In January 1939 the squadron converted from the Hawker Hind light bomber to become a fighter squadron, initially equipped with the obsolete Gloster Gladiator, before receiving its first Hurricanes a few weeks before the outbreak of World War II.

Subsequently promoted to group captain, he became Park's senior fighter controller at No. 11 Group, orchestrating the dynamic fighter defence of south-east England. As such his opponent was Oberst Paul Deichmann, Kesselring's chief of staff, who was designing the daily attacks that attempted to defeat Fighter Command and establish Luftwaffe air superiority over south-east England.

Willoughby de Broke's direction of No. 11 Group's air defence was so effective that he was mentioned in dispatches during the Battle of Britain.

Group Captain Willoughby de Broke in 1943. He was a wing commander during the Battle of Britain. (AHB)

In No. 11 Group, Park's senior fighter controller was Wing Commander (Wg Cdr) John Verney, Baron Willoughby de Broke, who described his role: 'The Group controller's job was like a glorified game of chess, only infinitely more exciting and responsible as so much was at stake. The Germans would frequently put up spoof raids with the deliberate intention of foxing our controllers, so that squadrons were ordered to patrol lines only to find that the plots had faded away as the enemy aircraft dispersed back to their bases in northern France. Our squadrons would then have to land and refuel and, sensing this, the Germans would follow their spoof raid pretty quickly with a genuine one, which necessitated putting up fresh squadrons to meet it while the others were refuelling.'[11]

RAF Integrated Air Defence System, with units assigned, as of 12 August 1940

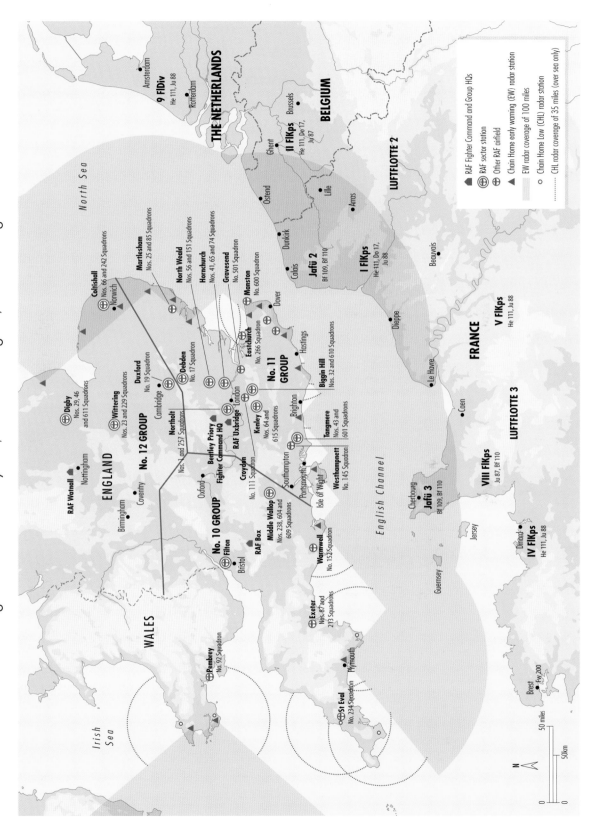

THE SECTOR OPERATIONS ROOM

Each Sector's Ops Room was a scaled-down version of the Group Ops Room, surrounding a GSM identical to the Group's, with the sector's 'tote boards' on the wall beyond the map table. The Sector Ops Room GSM was updated with information about hostile radar tracks by a multi-phone (one line to each sector in the group) amplifier located at the Group Ops Room that connected the same Filter Room teller to the Sector Ops Room plotters.[12]

During the initial stages of the campaign each sector could typically be assigned up to four fighter squadrons. Two were usually based at the sector station, with dispersed earthen berm revetments protecting the aircraft and an 'alert shack' with a dedicated telephone hotline to the Ops Room. Each sector also had at least one,

and usually a second 'satellite airfield', typically capable of supporting one fighter squadron. Occasionally a third squadron would be based at the sector station, but in any event, due to communications limitations, a sector could only control a maximum of four squadrons individually. Towards the end of the campaign this limitation was overcome by pairing two or more squadrons together into 'wings'.

The communications limitations were because each sector had a dedicated radio frequency and the squadrons based in that sector had their aircraft's TR9D radios tuned (set by ground-installed crystals) to that frequency. So, if all four squadrons were airborne and talking on their radios, the sector controller would soon be overwhelmed with 'chatter'. As the air battle developed into intense, dynamic, desperate, individual kill-or-be-killed combats, confusion, sometimes even chaos, inevitably ensued.

This limitation did not prevent a sector controller from vectoring his interceptors against a raid in an adjacent sector, but airborne unit leaders could not switch channels to the other sector's frequency for further instructions in the engagement. The success of these 'cross-boundary' interceptions was restricted to the TR9D's 30–40-mile (50–65km) range from the sector's furthest mobile HF radio relay station.[13]

HUFF DUFF AND 'PIP-SQUEAK'

A second limitation was imposed by the HF/DF system each sector used to keep track of its four airborne squadrons.

To direct a successful interception, the sector controller had to know the precise location of his own interceptor units as well as the position and direction of the enemy formation. Within each sector were around three HF/DF Fixer Stations. Arranged in a triangle and located about 30 miles (48km) from each other, they triangulated an airborne radio transmitter – called Pip-Squeak – usually mounted

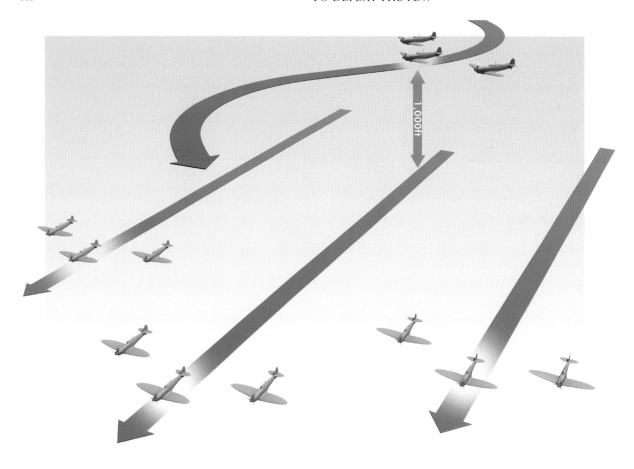

1,000ft

ABOVE • RAF FIGHTER FORMATIONS

An RAF fighter squadron of August–September 1940 typically comprised 16 aeroplanes and 22 pilots, with the requirement to have 12 serviceable every day for combat operations. Consequently, if sufficient serviceable aeroplanes and pilots were available, every squadron was expected to launch a 12-aeroplane formation composed of four three-aeroplane sections.

By August 1940, learning from the savage lessons of the French campaign and the early clashes with Bf 109Es over the Channel, instead of the rigid Fighting Area Attacks formations of sections in line astern prescribed in the 1938 *RAF Manual of Air Tactics*, squadrons generally flew as three three-aeroplane sections, each arranged in a V-shaped 'vic', with the three 'vics' arranged in a 'V of Vs' formation.

The 'V of Vs' formation inherently lacked visual look-out for attackers because the leader's wingmen and the section leaders had to watch their squadron leader to avoid mid-air collisions, leaving only the squadron leader to search the sky for enemy aircraft. It was hoped that the fourth section, weaving above and behind the main formation, would provide sufficient coverage of the squadron's vulnerable 'six o'clock' position.

However, with the three 'vics' cruising at reduced speeds so that the weavers could fly the longer serpentine flightpath required for them to keep station, the whole force was at a tactical disadvantage against Bf 109s using high-speed 'slashing' attacks. The weavers were at a particular disadvantage in constantly offering their own 'six o'clock' first to one side, then the other. High losses among the weavers resulted in the practice being discontinued.

in the unit leader's and another (alternate leader's) aircraft.

The aircraft's TR9D radio was modified to transmit on a second pre-set HF frequency through Pip-Squeak, via a piece of apparatus called the Master Contactor. Each of the Sector's four squadrons was assigned a separate 14-second 'quarter-minute' transmission time, synchronized with the Sector's HF/DF receivers and deconflicted with the Sector's other three squadrons, so that every minute each squadron transmitted a 14-second 1MHz 'whistle' (or 'squeak') to the three Huff Duff stations.[14]

The receiver stations triangulated each Pip-Squeak transmission once every minute and plotted their locations on the Fixer Table, then relayed the fixed position to the Sector Ops Room via a dedicated landline, where it was placed on the controller's GSM. This information was then fed back up the system to both the Group and Command Ops Rooms.[15] In this way, the sector and group controllers and Fighter Command's Duty Air Commodore were provided with a constantly updated position for each sector's four airborne squadrons.

BOMBERS

GESCHWADER	MARKING	LOCATION	EQUIPMENT	ESTABLISHMENT
K.G.1.(Hindenburg)	V4			
I/K.G.1.		ROSIERES EN SANTERRE	He.111	39
II/K.G.1.		ROSIERES EN SANTERRE	He.111	39
III/K.G.1.		GIESSEN	He.111	39
K.G.2.	U5			
I/K.G.2.		SAINT LEGER, Area	Do.17	39
II/K.G.2.		SAINT LEGER	Do.17	39
III/K.G.2.		CAMBRAI NIERGNIES	Do.17	39
K.G.3.	5K			
I/K.G.3.		ANTWERP DEURNE	Do.17	39
II/K.G.3.		ANTWERP DEURNE	Do.17	39
III/K.G.3.		SAINT TROND BRUSTEM	Do.17	39
K.G.4.(General Wever)	5J			
I/K.G.4.		SOESTERBERG	He.111	39
II/K.G.4.		ARDORF (WITTMUNDHAFEN)	He.111	39
III/K.G.4.		AMSTERDAM SCHIPOL	Ju.88	39
K.G.26.	1H			
I/K.G.26		DENMARK-NORWAY	He.111	39
II/K.G.26		LUBECK	He.111	39
III/K.G.26		DENMARK-NORWAY	He.111	39

FIGHTER COMMAND'S ENGAGED TACTICS

Typically, in the summer of 1940 an RAF fighter squadron was composed of 16 aircraft, 12 of which could be called upon for operations, while the remaining four were undergoing maintenance or repair. Tactically the squadron was made up of two flights of six aircraft as 'A' and 'B' Flights, each comprising two sections of three, identified over the radio by a colour code: Red, Yellow, Blue and Green Sections. Each section consisted of a section leader and two wingmen, identified numerically. For example, Blue Section Leader was identified as Blue 1, the wingman on his right, Blue 2 and on his left, Blue 3.

The problem came in maintaining 12 aircraft in a tight formation with only the lead pilot free to search for the enemy, the remaining 11 having to concentrate on maintaining station to avoid mid-air collisions. Once the enemy had been spotted, the formation leader called 'Tally-Ho' and ordered the scripted Fighter Area Attack he thought appropriate for the situation.

Pre-war Fighter Area Attacks envisaged a three-aeroplane section attacking up to three unescorted bombers and had absolutely no practical utility in fighter-versus-fighter combat. Additionally, the principal drawback of the three-aeroplane 'vic' formations, after the abysmally poor defensive visual lookout, was that only the section leaders were 'shooters'. The two wingmen's jobs were to protect their section leader.[16]

One of 19 pages of the Luftwaffe air order of battle report, as compiled by DDI3 for 1 August 1940. While demonstrating an impressive level of detail, it also reveals a monumental error when estimating the size of the Luftwaffe's bomber force. An RAF squadron consisted of 12 aircraft, but a Luftwaffe bomber Staffel of nine, leading to a 23 per cent over-estimation in Gruppe strength. (Churchill Archive Centre ELMT 2/1)

RIGHT
Lacking collaborating or confirming evidence, as well as basing its estimate of Luftwaffe bomber strength on RAF unit sizes, Air Intelligence added 194 aircraft labelled 'unidentified', producing an overall estimate of 2,000 enemy bombers – there were actually 1,260. The wildly over-estimated numbers of transport aircraft and parachutists was of less immediate consequence to Fighter Command. (Churchill Archive Centre ELMT 2/1)

FAR RIGHT
Another important source of intelligence came from POWs. Wing Commander S. Denys Felkin headed AI1(k), responsible for interrogating Luftwaffe captives. Innovative methods were used, including the use of hidden microphones in cells and recreational areas, and German 'stooges', which often led prisoners to provide previously unknown information. (Author Collection)

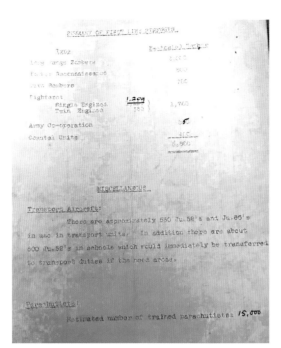

Therefore, a squadron of 12 fighters had only four shooters, the combat equivalent of the Luftwaffe's eight-aeroplane Jagdstaffel. When the Jagdgruppe's Stabsschwarm joined the two Jagdstaffel Schwärme, especially for fighter sweeps, the dozen 'Emils' outgunned the British 12-aeroplane squadron six to four. Interestingly, being outnumbered 1.5 to 1 was a number remarkably close to the Jagdwaffe's kill ratio of Bf 109Es over RAF Hurricanes and Spitfires (1.77:1) over the course of the coming campaign.

INTELLIGENCE

Supporting the six components of the British IADS, the Dowding System benefited from two organizations. Y-Service provided advanced warning of Luftwaffe operations by the interception, decoding and deciphering of low-grade tactical message traffic, while the other should be considered in the context of more general and strategic 'intelligence'.

Within the Air Ministry a dedicated Air Intelligence (AI) Branch had been created, which by 1940 had expanded to 240 officers. During the summer of 1940, the Directorate of Intelligence (DI) was supported by an assistant director (ADI) and three deputy directors (DDIs), each deputy directorate being subdivided into a number of sections or offices.

A key question facing Fighter Command in the summer of 1940 was just how big were the combined air fleets of Luftflotte 2, 3, and 5. The establishment of an accurate AOB was therefore crucial and one of DDI3's most urgent tasks, requiring access to the most sensitive intelligence-gathering tools available.

RAF Air Intelligence Organization

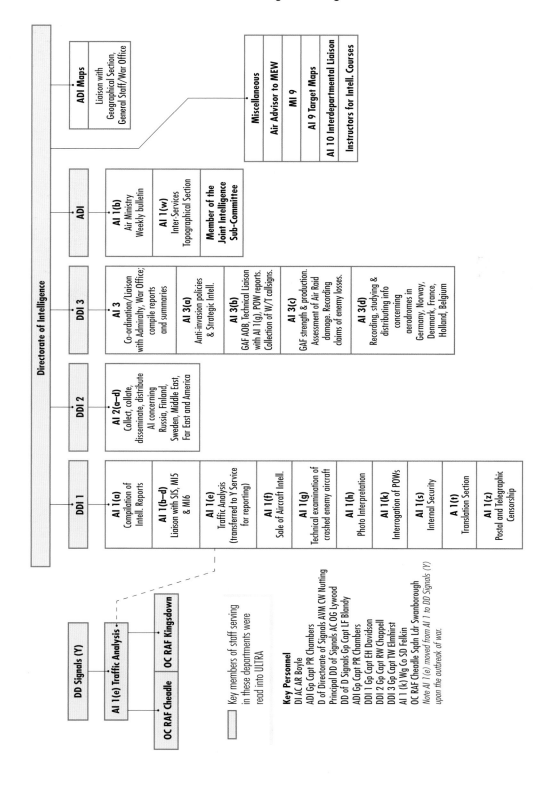

Directorate of Intelligence

ADI Maps
- Liaison with Geographical Section, General Staff/War Office

Miscellaneous
- Air Advisor to MEW
- MI 9
- AI 9 Target Maps
- AI 10 Interdepartmental Liaison
- Instructors for Intell. Courses

ADI
- AI 1(b) — Air Ministry Weekly bulletin
- AI 1(w) — Inter-Services Topographical Section
- **Member of the Joint Intelligence Sub-Committee**

DDI 3
- AI 3 — Co-ordination/Liaison with Admiralty, War Office; compile reports and summaries
- AI 3(a) — Anti-invasion policies & Strategic Intell.
- AI 3(b) — GAF AOB, Technical Liaison with AI 1(g), POW reports. Collection of W/T callsigns.
- AI 3(c) — GAF strength & production. Assessment of Air Raid damage. Recording claims of enemy losses.
- AI 3(d) — Recording, studying & distributing info concerning aerodromes in Germany, Norway, Denmark, France, Holland, Belgium

DDI 2
- AI 2(a–d) — Collect, collate, disseminate, distribute AI concerning Russia, Finland, Sweden, Middle East, Far East and America

DDI 1
- AI 1(a) — Compilation of Intell. Reports
- AI 1(b–d) — Liaison with SIS, MI5 & MI6
- AI 1(e) — Traffic Analysis (transferred to Y Service for reporting)
- AI 1(f) — Sale of Aircraft Intell.
- AI 1(g) — Technical examination of crashed enemy aircraft
- AI 1(h) — Photo Interpretation
- AI 1(k) — Interrogation of POWs
- AI 1(s) — Internal Security
- A 1(t) — Translation Section
- AI 1(z) — Postal and Telegraphic Censorship

DD Signals (Y)

AI 1(e) Traffic Analysis

OC RAF Cheadle

OC RAF Kingsdown

Key members of staff serving in these departments were read into ULTRA

Key Personnel
DI AC AR Boyle
ADI Gp Capt PR Chambers
D of Directorate of Signals AVM CW Nutting
Principal DD of Signals AC OG Lywood
DD of D Signals Gp Capt LF Blandy
ADI Gp Capt PR Chambers
DDI 1 Gp Capt EH Davidson
DDI 2 Gp Capt RW Chappell
DDI 3 Gp Capt TW Elmhirst
AI 1 (k) Wg Co SD Felkin
OC RAF Cheadle Sqdn Ldr Swanborough
Note AI 1(e) moved from AI 1 to DD Signals (Y) upon the outbreak of war.

ULTRA

The Germans believed that their sophisticated and complex multi-service Enigma message encryption device permitted communications in codes that were unbreakable. Used primarily by the high command to communicate sensitive information to senior field commanders, Enigma revolutionized secure battlefield communications. Resembling an oversized portable typewriter, the machine was a battery-powered, electro-mechanical device, enabling the creation of a highly complex, ciphered message that had one hundred and fifty million, million, million different possible message settings.

Breaking the Enigma ciphers was the challenge presented to a hand-picked group of geniuses later known as cryptologists but initially called 'Computors', recruited by the GC&CS and located at Bletchley Park for just that purpose. Overseen by the Foreign Office's head of the Secret Intelligence Service (later and better known as MI6) the cryptanalysts housed in 'Hut 3' at Bletchley Park translated high-grade Luftwaffe Enigma messages that had been deciphered by the cryptologists in 'Hut 6', providing the resulting intelligence to the Air Ministry's AI1(e) Traffic Analysis office for dissemination to those officers given clearance into the ULTRA signals intelligence programme.

Originally referred to as 'JQ Information', the high-grade intelligence gleaned from Enigma was so vital to the British war effort that its security classification went beyond Top Secret. To conceal its origin during the early war years, terms such as, 'Information from a most reliable source…' or 'It is reliably reported that…', were used, thus giving the impression that the information had come from a well-placed spy. To lend further credence to this subterfuge, some of the decrypts were attributed to 'BONIFACE'. However, eventually the classification ULTRA became standardized.[17]

Luftflotte 5, headquartered at Stavanger, Norway, had under its command KG 30, equipped with two Gruppen of Ju 88s, and KG 26, with two Gruppen of He 111s. Here, mechanics cover the Jumo 211 engines of a KG 26 aircraft after a mission. Note the unit's emblem, a sitting black lion, located below the cockpit. (Jean-Louis Roba)

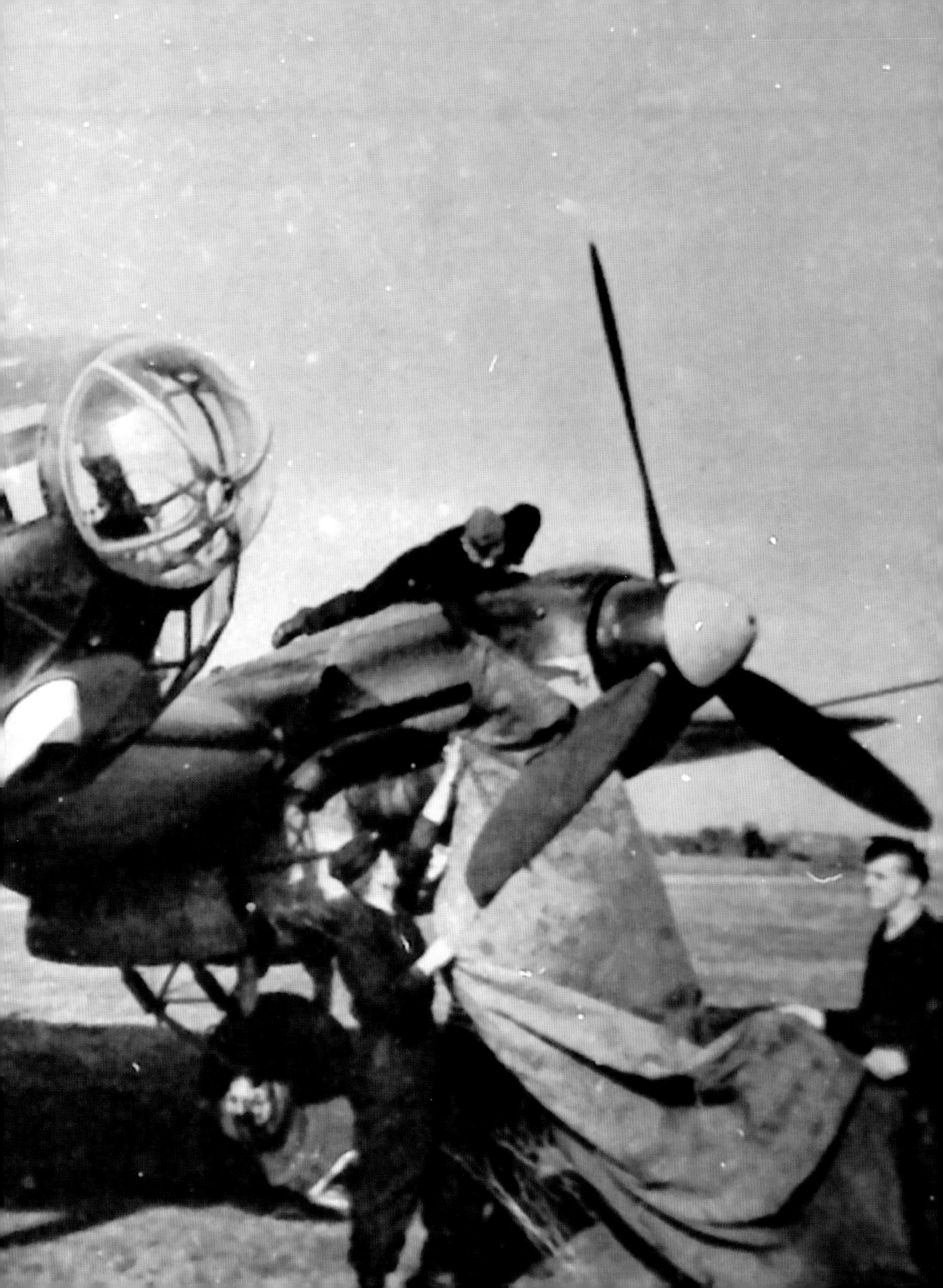

GB *1212* bc
Geheim

Queensferry (Firth of Forth)
Hilfsstützpunkt Port Edgar

Karte 1:100 000
Blatt
Sch. 27

1:63 360
Blatt
Sch. 68

Kriegsaufnahme:
597 R 54

Länge (westl. Greenw.): 3° 23' 20' Breite: 56° 0' 0'
Mißweisung -13° 24' (Mitte 1939) Zielhöhe über N.N: 50m

Nachträge:
2.10.39.

500 0 500 1000 m

Maßstab etwa 1: **15 000**   (⊢1cm⊣ 150 m)

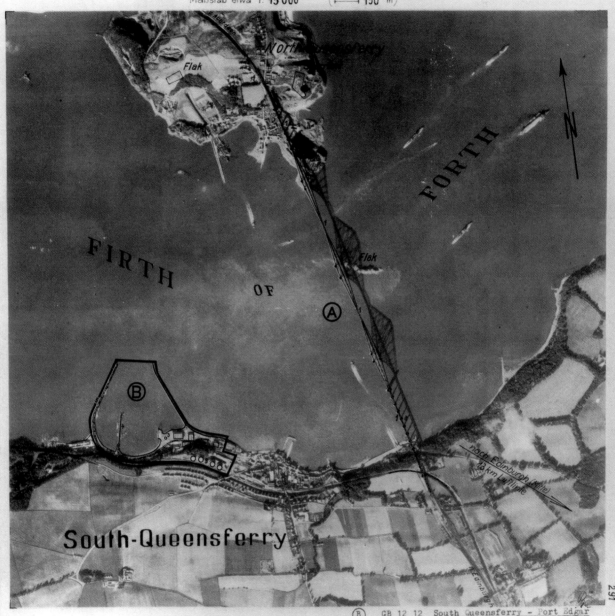

291

B GB 12 12 South Queensferry - Port Edgar
(Hilfsstützpunkt)

Ⓐ   GB 41 6   Eisenbahnbrücke über den Firth of Forth

1) 2 Stahlbrückenbogen auf 3 Hauptpfeilern, in je 4
    massiven Fundamentblöcken verankert
1a) 2 Viadukte mit 17 Steinpfeilern
    Brückengesamtlänge etwa 2 500 m, Breite etwa 8m

2) 5 Depothallen   etwa 6 000 qm
3) 6 Tanks: 4 große ∅ etwa 35m, 2 kleine ∅ ca 5m
                                                          etwa 4 200 qm
4) Ölpier mit Gleisanschluß
5) Kai mit Entladekränen
6) Verwaltungsgebäude
    bebaute Fläche (Schwerpunkte) etwa 10 200 qm

Gleisanschluß vorhanden

Distribution of ULTRA information was highly restricted, and included only those involved in formulating strategy and policy – Churchill, a few senior members of government, Foreign Office officials and appropriate members of the three armed services. Within the Air Ministry in 1940, 58 people were cleared to receive ULTRA (including some 25 junior officers required to maintain a 24-hour watch of at least six officers to ensure its proper distribution). Of this number, only 11 were aware of its true origin. Since Fighter Command's AOCinC, ACM Dowding, wasn't directly involved in the long-term formulation of strategy, there is no record that he was 'read-in' to ULTRA until mid-October 1940, just days before his 'retirement'.

A BRITISH FUSION FAILURE

The Air Ministry hadn't expected the Luftwaffe also to use high-grade cyphers for operational traffic. Consequently, it made no arrangements for the Air Intelligence Branch to participate in operational intelligence, beyond supplying Cheadle with details about the Luftwaffe's AOB, or for the cryptologists at Bletchley Park to pass high-grade intelligence that they had decrypted to Cheadle or the operational commands. Consequently, when ULTRA began to produce operational/tactical intelligence, it was distributed to AI3(b), the Air Intelligence Branch section that dealt with the Luftwaffe's AOB. But this section, unlike Cheadle, wasn't organized or staffed for the exploitation of operational intelligence.

The result was another intelligence fusion failure. Tactical information obtained from high-grade sources wasn't correlated with tactical information secured from low-grade sources, leading to repeated gaps in information. The situation was identified by the Air Section in Hut 3 (AI4(f)), which championed fusing the two intelligence strands together. However, much to their discredit, some senior, influential members within the Air Ministry initially resisted the move, and the situation wasn't resolved until a root-and-branch restructure of Air Intelligence during the winter of 1940/41.[18]

AN INAUSPICIOUS START

To cover the approach to the Firth of Forth's important RN bases, CH stations were sited at Douglas Wood, Drone Hill and, later, Anstruther. Drone Hill became operational on 7 April 1939 and six months later, at 0920hrs on 16 October, the station detected two intruders heading inbound from the North Sea. Fighter Command HQ was alerted and No. 13 Group's sector station at RAF Turnhouse scrambled Blue Section of 602 Squadron. Its targets were two He 111s, from KG 26, on an armed reconnaissance mission. Despite being

This image of HMS *Edinburgh*, *Southampton* and *Mohawk* immediately after KG 30's attack on 16 October was taken by Lt Rolf Niehoff from an He 111 of Stab/KG 26. Luftwaffe ordnance designed for use in the maritime strike role incorporated dye, enabling crews and post-strike analysis to determine the accuracy of an attack. (AHB)

intercepted, both intruders returned to Westerland, reporting favourable weather conditions in the area and that they had observed the battlecruiser HMS *Hood* (actually the very similar HMS *Repulse*) inside the Firth. That such a 'juicy' target was not moored at a dock was highly significant, since at that time Hitler imposed highly restricted rules of engagement (ROE) on the Luftwaffe. These rules prohibited attacks on targets that could cause death or injury to civilians.

With Hitler's ROE having been met, X. Fliegerkorps ordered an immediate strike against one of the RN's prize warships. Twelve Ju 88As from I./KG 30 took off from Greifswald at 1155hrs and headed north-west across the North Sea. RAF Cheadle had decoded sufficient Luftwaffe message traffic about the raid to warn

Fighter Command that an attack on the warships in the Firth of Forth was imminent. However, Fighter Command policy at the time was to not accept uncorroborated signals intelligence warnings.

By this time, however, Drone Hill CH station was off air due to a technical fault, so the attackers arrived undetected and struck three RN warships in the Firth before any air raid sirens could be sounded. Fortunately, *Repulse* had put into Rosyth naval dockyard and was, in accordance with Hitler's ROE, no longer an authorized target. Instead the Ju 88As attacked two Town-class light cruisers, HMS *Edinburgh* and *Southampton*, and the Tribal-class destroyer *Mohawk*. Although no ships were sunk, *Mohawk* was peppered with shrapnel and had 13 ratings and two officers killed. Spitfires from 602 and 603 Squadrons intercepted the raiders during egress and shot down two, which crashed into the sea, while a third was destroyed and its crew killed during an attempted forced landing after having limped back to the Netherlands.

Dowding later explained to the Air Ministry that he was aware of enemy activity in the area and that patrols were investigating, but his first knowledge of the raid came from the Admiralty. He judged that no good purpose would be served by issuing an air raid alert at that late stage. The significance and potential of intelligence provided by Cheadle was a lesson not lost on Fighter Command.[19]

The mistakes made by Fighter Command on 16 October were not repeated on the 28th, when a KG 26 raid was intercepted by 602 and 603 Squadron Spitfires. Heinkel He 111 '1H+JA', flown by Unteroffizier (Uffz) Kurt Lehmkuhl, was shot down by Flt Lt Archie McKellar and became the first enemy aircraft to crash on British soil during World War II. Lehmkuhl, his observer and aircraft commander, Lt Rolf Niehoff, were captured, but the two gunners were killed in the attack. Personnel from AI1(g) were responsible for the technical examination of crashed enemy aircraft. (Clive Ellis)

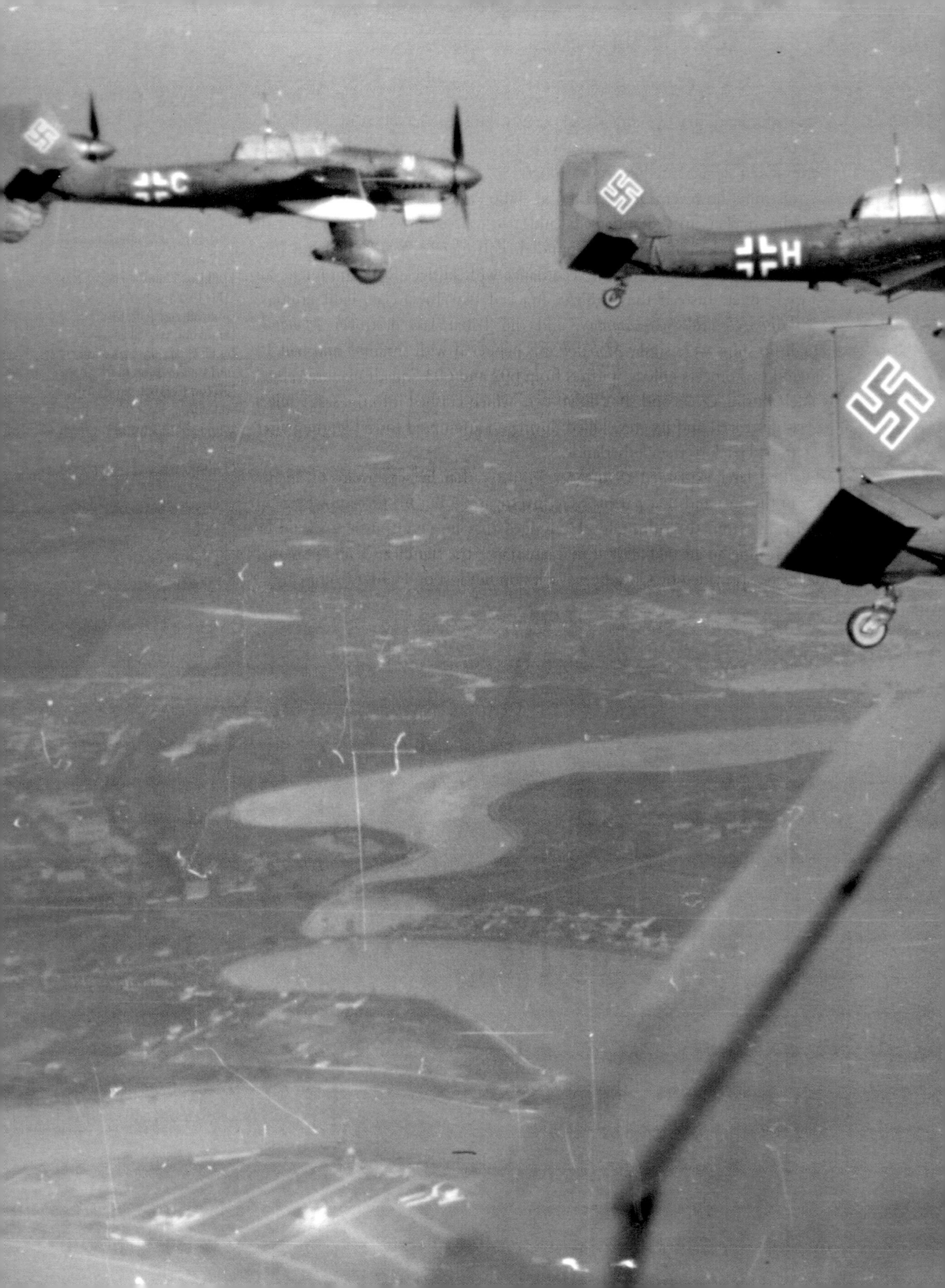

CHAPTER VII

KANALKAMPF (CHANNEL BATTLE)
The Luftwaffe's maritime air campaign

*The Luftwaffe is authorized to attack the English homeland in the fullest manner, as soon as sufficient forces are available... in accordance with the principles laid down in Directive Nr. 9. The struggle against the English homeland will continue after the commencement of land operations [*Fall Rot*, the final conquest of France, slated to begin on 5 June 1940].*

Führer Directive Nr. 13 for the Conduct of the War, 24 May 1940[1]

'The attack came from right overhead. The plane seemed to start at about 3,000 feet and dived almost vertically, and from photographs shown to me I think I can almost certainly identify the machine as a Junkers 87,' recalled the master of the 10,058-ton liner SS *Aeneas*, the first victim of the Luftwaffe maritime air campaign intended to close the English Channel and British Channel ports to merchant shipping, in Brian Cull's *Battle for the Channel*.

Captain David Evans continued, 'The first bomb dropped [hit] the port side and made a hole about 6 inches [15cm] in diameter amidships, but dropped back into the sea [before it exploded]. The explosion shook the vessel considerably and set her on fire. The second bomb fell abaft the funnel. She took a list of about 25 degrees to starboard. He dropped another bomb about 100 yards away on the starboard beam.'[2]

The largest of 14 ships comprising convoy OA177 (the code meaning 'Outbound from the Thames' convoy number 177; OB was 'Outbound from Liverpool'), *Aeneas* was attacked 30 miles south of Plymouth by a Kette of Stukas from I./StG 2 and hit by two 250kg (5510lb) SC250 bombs, the first passing through the port side and the other exploding deep within the ship, blowing out the starboard side. The blast killed almost all of the engineers and stokers in the engine room, along with eight other crewmen. The first attack of *Kanalkampf* also damaged the 3,178-ton steamer *Baron Ruthven*, killing two, including the captain.

KANALKAMPF BEGINS THE *HANDELSKRIEG* CAMPAIGN

To implement Hitler's Directive Nr. 13, on 30 June Göring determined that 'sufficient forces [were] available' and ordered the campaign to begin 'By attacking the enemy air force, its ground organization, and its own industry to provide the necessary conditions for a satisfactory overall war against enemy imports, provisions, and defence economy... [and by] attacking importing harbours and their installations, importing transports and warships, destroy the English system of replenishment. Both tasks must be carried out separately, but must be [done] in co-ordination with one another.'[3]

PREVIOUS PAGES
Four Stukagruppen, including III./StG 2, were in action on 8 August. (Chris Goss)

Bf 110C-1s of Stab III./ZG 76 (formerly Stab II./ZG 1) on patrol over the Channel. Note the unit's early emblem of three small wasps above the clouds on the nose. (Andy Saunders)

Beginning on 22 June, ObdL began directing the movement of Luftflotte 2 and 3 units northwards to take their positions along the French Channel coast and to airfields in Belgium and Holland. This enormous migration of aircraft, personnel and ground equipment took a fortnight to accomplish, especially bearing in mind Göring's instructions in his ObdL Directive of 30 June 1940 to establish 'adequate anti-aircraft and fighter defences, adequate provisioning [fuel, ammunition, and supply stocks], and absolutely trouble-free chain of command [meaning an effective communications network]' before the 'planned offensive can be put in motion.'

Also during the next few weeks, the high losses experienced in *Fall Gelb* and *Fall Rot* were made good. During the intense six-week *Westfeldzug*, the two Luftflotten had lost 477 of their 1,120 twin-engined bombers; by 20 July, their frontline strength was back up to 1,131 bombers (with another 129 in Norway). Meanwhile, most of the approximately 1,833 Luftwaffe personnel shot down and captured in the French campaign were released and returned to their units, undergoing refresher training to resume their roles as qualified aircrew. Additionally, freshly minted flying personnel arrived from their training programmes to replace the 1,092 aircrew killed in the French campaign, along with those of the 1,395 wounded who were now fit enough to fly again.[4]

On 2 July, on the new front's left flank off Cherbourg, in Sperrle's Luftflotte 3, Göring ordered Richthofen's VIII. Fliegerkorps to begin attacking 'Channel sea traffic'. The command's nine Stukagruppen had rushed to the French Channel coast and were given priority in supply of bombs, ammunition, and fuel; they were ready to begin the fight the next day.[5]

Carrying a varied cargo that included raw rubber, SS *Aeneas* was attacked and struck by two bombs on 2 July. It sank two days later. (Author Collection)

The campaign's first great success occurred only two days in.

Convoy OA178, 14 heavily laden merchantmen bound for North America, departed the Port of London on 3 July and passed safely through the Dover Straits that night. The next morning a 1.(F)/123 reconnaissance Ju 88A discovered the vessels strung out midway between Torquay and Cherbourg. Navigation and station-keeping were both poor and Fighter Command provided no air cover; Dowding viewed the protection of convoys 'to be a matter for the Navy'[6]. In fact, the convoy's only escort was the 940-ton corvette HMS *Clarkia*, whose pitifully inadequate AA battery comprised two pairs of machine guns.

Having just arrived at airfields near Caen and Laon, Major Oskar Dinort's StG 2 had enough bombs on hand to mount an immediate strike, the targets being only 55 miles (90km) north-west of Cherbourg. Two dozen I./StG 2 Stukas, escorted by Bf 109Es from I./JG 1, pounced upon the hapless merchantmen. The 4,952-ton *Dallas City* was quickly hit, caught fire and wallowed out of control, colliding with the 4,674-ton *Flimstone*. The two ships were locked together for 15 minutes before *Flimstone* could extricate itself, leaving the blazing *Dallas City* to sink. Following it to the bottom were the Dutch steamers *Britsum* (5,255grt) and *Deucalion* (1,796grt) and the Estonian *Kolga* (3,526grt). Another eight freighters and tankers were damaged in the savage Stuka attack.

Meanwhile, Portland harbour, where the convoy attempted to take sanctuary, had been assaulted by 26 III./StG 51 Stukas, escorted by Bf 110s from V.(Z)/LG 1. Three more British steamers (16,000grt) were damaged, a 55-ton tug blown out of the water, and HMS *Foylebank*, a nine-year-old merchant ship (ex-MV *Andrew Weir*; 5,582grt) converted to an 'AA auxiliary', was set ablaze and sunk. Mounting four twin high-angle 4in gun turrets, two quad 2-pounder 'pom-poms' and several 0.5in machine guns, the vessel was overwhelmed in the furious dive-bombing attack. Hit by 22 bombs, it suffered 176 (of 298) crewmen killed, including

RIGHT
On 1 July, He 111s of III./KG 27 conducted an attack against the newly completed airfield at Warmwell. (AHB donated by Ken Wakefield)

Leading Seaman John F 'Jack' Mantle, who was posthumously awarded the VC for his 'great courage [which] bore him up to the end of the fight when he fell by the [starboard 'pom pom'] gun he had so valiantly served'.[7]

The victorious Luftwaffe units lost one Stuka to *Foylebank*'s 4-inch AA guns but 'the first RAF fighters to arrive on the scene were too late to engage the attacking force'. According to Hptm Horst Liensberger, leading the Zerstörer escorts, 'Over the English harbour, and out to sea, the RAF fighters

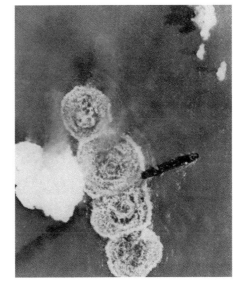

didn't come to meet us. We can only think that they could see our force was too strong for them, and they just stayed away. Our Stukas did their work, and we merely circled above and watched the whole performance. It was all too easy. They were even late and ineffective in getting their flak guns working!'[8]

That evening, adding insult to injury, OA178 was attacked by 1. Schnellbootflotilla (1. S-Flotilla, equipped with Schnellboote [S-boats], fast boats, which were powerful motor torpedo boats, known as E-boats, for 'enemy boats', by the British). The Kriegsmarine attackers sank one 4,343-ton freighter, killing 16 sailors, and damaged a tanker and another freighter, killing four more.[9]

Upon hearing the news, Churchill was livid, demanding that Fighter Command 'do much more to protect Channel shipping'. Dowding had to be ordered to provide 'a standing patrol [of] six fighters. These were [to be] reinforced as soon as a German formation was reported approaching.'[10] To provide the directed air cover, Dowding instructed Park to deploy 65 Squadron forward to Manston and 79 Squadron to Hawkinge (from Hornchurch and Biggin Hill, respectively), both on the south-east coast, and transferred 238 and 501 Squadrons from

Middle Wallop to the newly completed Warmwell airfield on the south-west coast near Weymouth.[11]

Having no confidence in Fighter Command because of its embittering experience off Dunkirk, the Admiralty's solution was to re-route Atlantic convoys around the north of Scotland, avoiding the dangers of steaming through the English Channel.

With dive-brakes extended and its load of four SC50 and one SC250 bombs released, this Ju 87 is about to be recovered from its dive by the Askania automatic pull-out device. (Author Collection)

Dornier Do 17Zs from KG 2 'Holzhammer' took part in the first large aerial engagement over the English Channel, on 10 July 1940, when they attacked convoy 'Bread', sinking two ships and a 700-ton sloop. They also damaged four RAF fighters with their effective defensive fire. (AHB)

Upon learning this, the Kriegsmarine's SKL noted that the London convoys' vastly extended route to join ships departing from Glasgow, Liverpool, and Bristol increased their exposure to U-boat attacks. 'The complete re-routing of British supply traffic to the northern route… results in an extremely strong concentration of enemy supply traffic in the area west of the Hebrides and the North Channel which will be very favourable to submarine operations.'[12]

ATTACKING CHANNEL CONVOYS – 10–24 JULY

The following week was filled with increasing numbers of reconnaissance missions, desultory attacks against British aviation industry targets, night-time 'nuisance' raids, and occasional strikes against south coast ports and shipping in the Channel, few of which proved very accurate or damaging. Interceptions were few, primarily because the small formations of one to three aircraft employed failed to show up on radar until very short range and disappeared quickly as they crossed the shoreline because the Observer Corps network in the south-west was not yet organized. Most intruders were not spotted, tracked or reported. ObdL's daily situation reports list the loss of only 11 bomber and reconnaissance aircraft during this seven-day period.[13]

Six larger raids, three each on convoys and RN bases, flown by 15–20 bombers and escorted by similar-sized fighter formations, appeared on radar at much longer range because their larger formations reflected commensurately more RF energy, allowing Park to launch quicker and stronger responses. Successful intercepts resulted in whirling dogfights between opposing fighters, generally overhead the Channel convoys. In these engagements 15 RAF fighters were shot down and 12 pilots killed. The Luftwaffe lost six Bf 109Es and two Bf 110s in return, although five times that number were claimed.[14]

With London's ocean convoys taking circuitous routing around the north of Scotland, Channel shipping was reduced to daily convoys of small ships carrying coal from Welsh mines to the extensive industrial and commercial enterprises concentrated in the Empire's capital. Electrical power stations, factories, railway locomotives and outbound steamships between them required approximately 7,000 tons of coal per day, provided by mines in Wales, Northumberland and Yorkshire. For shipments coming from Wales, it was a 400-mile (650 km) trek through the 'Narrow Sea', as the Royal Navy traditionally described the English Channel, which funnelled from 110 miles (180km) wide at the west end to 60 (95 km) between Cherbourg and Isle of Wight, and only 22 miles (35 km) at the Dover Straits. These convoys were designated 'CE' for 'Convoy East', meaning 'eastward', for those headed for London and 'CW' for those returning (normally in ballast rather than loaded with goods). Fighter Command HQ assigned a codename for co-ordinating fighter cover to each convoy.[15]

Across the Channel, on the right flank (Pas de Calais area) Kesselring formed a task force composed of Oberst Johannes Fink's KG 2 Do 17Zs and two Stukagruppen (II./StG 1, just transferred from VIII. Fliegerkorps, and IV.(St)/LG 1), and Oberst Theo Osterkamp's JG 51 Bf 109Es. Appointed to lead this dedicated maritime strike force, Fink was named Luftflotte 2's Kanalkampfführer (Channel Battle Leader).

On 10 July, CW3, codenamed 'Bread', comprising 25 small steamers covered by six 32 Squadron Hurricanes, rounded North Foreland bound for the Dover Straits and was duly discovered by a Do 17Z 'scout' from Fink's KG 2. A strike was quickly organized, with I. and III./KG 2 launching 27 Dorniers from two airfields near Cambrai, joined by I./JG 3 and III./JG 51 Bf 109Es. One Staffel from each Jagdgruppe formed up on the bombers' flanks for close escort and the other two climbed 3,000 to 6,000ft above to provide top cover. A formation of III./ZG 26 Zerstörers swept ahead on a convergent course to try and attract the enemy's attention, the entire force totalling about 70 aircraft.[16]

At 1320hrs, the Swingate CH Station near Dover detected the formation gathering over Calais and alerted Fighter Command HQ, which naturally assigned the interception to No. 11 Group. Park scrambled Hurricanes from 56 and 111 Squadrons, and Spitfires from 64 and 74 Squadrons, for 32 fighters in total, to intercept the raiders.[17]

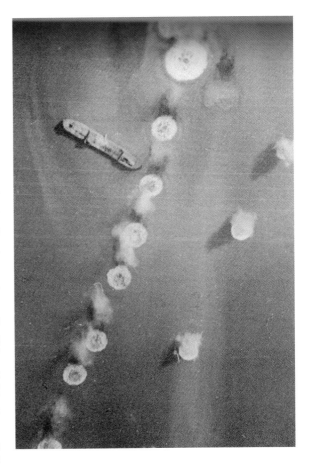

Dornier Do 17Zs typically carried ten small SC50 bombs, resulting in a string of splashes and very few hits. The small explosive charge meant that little damage was done even when hits were scored. (Chris Goss)

Air Vice-Marshal Keith Park

Confronting Kesselring's powerful Luftflotte 2 was Keith Rodney Park, the son of a geologist from Scotland, born in Thames, New Zealand, in June 1892. Educated at King's College, Auckland and then Otago Boys' High School, Dunedin, he joined the army as a Territorial soldier in the New Zealand Field Artillery, before opting to go to sea as a steamship purser, where he earned his family nickname 'Skipper'.

At the outbreak of World War I, Park re-joined his artillery battalion, where, as an NCO in April 1915, he participated in the landings at Gallipoli. In recognition of his achievements in trench warfare he was commissioned as a second lieutenant three months later. Having transferred to the British Army Royal Horse Artillery, he was shipped to France in January 1916 and participated in the Battle of the Somme, learning from personal experience the value of aerial reconnaissance, especially the manner in which German aircraft were able to spot Allied artillery for counter-battery fire. In one of these barrages, on 21 October 1916, he was seriously wounded by a German shell and evacuated to England.

AVM Keith Park. (Author Collection, colourized by Richard Molloy)

Medically 'unfit for active service' in the army, after recovering from his wounds he joined the RFC that December. Once qualified as a pilot, he gained further experience as an instructor before joining No. 48 Squadron in France in July 1917, flying the Bristol F.2B Fighter. Successful from the very start, he was promoted rapidly and, as a major, was given command of 48 Squadron in April 1918.

Park was considered a tough but fair leader and combat commander, and an excellent pilot and aerial tactician who understood the technical aspects of air warfare. By the Armistice, he was officially credited with five enemy aircraft destroyed and 14 more falling 'out of control' – he'd been shot down twice.

After the war, Park was awarded a permanent commission as a captain, which became a flight lieutenant when the new RAF officer ranks were introduced in 1919. He served as a flight commander on 25 Squadron in 1919–20, before commanding the RAF School of Technical Training. He later commanded a number of RAF stations and, in 1937, attended the Imperial Defence College before being promoted to air commodore and appointed Dowding's Senior Air Staff Officer (SASO) the following year. Promoted to the rank of air vice-marshal, Park took command of No. 11 Group in April 1940, his thorough knowledge of air defence operations at the highest levels prompting his appointment ahead of more senior officers.

Tall, lean, and modest, Park earned a deserved reputation as a shrewd tactician with an astute grasp of strategic issues and, flying a personalized Hawker Hurricane around his fighter airfields during the Battle of Britain, he was a very popular hands-on, inspirational leader.[18]

Twenty minutes later, Hptm Johannes 'Hannes' Trautloft, leading III./JG 51 out ahead of the bombers, spotted the 32 Squadron Hurricanes ahead and below and was stalking them, manoeuvring his formation into a favourable position to attack, when, one after another, the four scrambled squadrons arrived. 'Suddenly the sky was full of British fighters,' he wrote afterwards, 'Today we were going to be in for a tough time.'

Number 111 Squadron charged headlong into the 'waves of enemy bombers approaching from France' and, already under attack by 7./JG 51's Oblt Walter Oesau (a 15-victory ace at this point), Fg Off Tom Higgs crashed his Hurricane head on into a 3./KG 2 Do 17Z, destroying both. Higgs was killed; two German crewmen parachuted to become POWs and two others were missing in action.

The rash attack failed to deter the bombers, as one of the formation leaders, Obstlt Werner Kreipe, Kommandeur of III./KG 2, reported. 'The Channel was bathed in brilliant sunshine. A light haze hung over the English coast, and there, far below us, was the convoy like so many toy ships with wispy wakes fanning out behind. As soon as we were observed, the ships dispersed, the merchantmen manoeuvring violently and the escorting warships moving out at full speed. Flak shells peppered the sky. We made our first bomb run, and fountains leapt up around the ships. By now the fighter squadrons of the RAF had joined in, and the sky was a twisting, turning mêlée of fighters.'[19]

After unloading their bombs, the Dorniers immediately turned for home, diving to accelerate away from the British fighters tied up by their escorts. The bombing from 4,000ft against the ships spread 150 small bombs liberally among the convoy, but hit only one, sinking the 466grt Dutch *Bill S.*

Overclaiming, a problem that began in France and went viral over Dunkirk, resumed with this encounter. Major Johann Schalk's Zerstörers claimed 14 'English fighters' downed and Trautloft's Jagdgruppe claimed seven Spitfires. In fact, only four Hurricanes and three Spitfires were damaged in air-to-air combat. RAF claims of shooting down three Do 17Zs, six Bf 110s and a Bf 109E inflated the actual loss of two Dorniers and three Bf 110Cs destroyed and two Bf 109Es damaged.[20]

ABOVE
Hannes Trautloft secured five victories serving with the Condor Legion in Spain and another with 2./JG 77 during the Polish campaign. By the end of the Battle of France he had been promoted to Hauptmann, commanded I./JG 20 (which became III./JG 54), and increased his score to 11 victories. On 25 August 1940, he became Kommodore of JG 54. (Author Collection)

BELOW LEFT
On 11 July, Bf 110s from ZG 76 escorted Ju 87s from III./StG 2 against Portland. Damaged by Hurricanes from 238 Squadron, Bf 110C-4 '2N+EP' of 9./ZG 76 was shot down at 1210hrs near Lulworth. Two pilots were credited for its demise, Sqn Ldr John Dewar of 87 Squadron and Fg Off H. Riddle of 601 Squadron. The Zerstörer crew, Oblt Kadow and Gefreiter (Gefr) Scholz, were captured, their aircraft becoming the first example of its type to be recovered intact. During the same action, Oblt Hans-Joachim Göring, Göring's nephew, flying with the same unit, was shot down and killed. (Clive Ellis)

Three Bf 109E-3s of II./JG 2 low over the Channel. The pale blue sides of the fuselage and tail had been given a mottled overspray to reduce their conspicuity over the sea, as operations moved against Britain. (Jean-Louis Roba)

That same day, Hptm Bernd von Brauchitsch's newly arrived III./LG 1 began operating in earnest, sending singletons or pairs of Ju 88As to attack harbours at Plymouth, Cardiff, Looe and Falmouth. At the last of these, two Junkers arrived overhead only two minutes after 'Air Raid Warning RED' (an RAF public announcement for 'Air Raid, Your Location, Imminent') had been announced and, with no RAF fighters anywhere nearby, delivered a devastating attack. The British tanker SS *Tascalusa* (6,499grt) erupted into a raging inferno and sank at its pier; the Greek SS *Marie Chandris* (5,840grt), packed with bales of cotton, was also set alight and burnt into a charred hulk; a Dutch salvage tug was damaged so badly it later sank.[21]

During the next two weeks sporadic but relatively heavy individual unit attacks on Channel convoys, Portland, Portsmouth and Dover continued but, with the exception of bombing against Dover, were largely unsuccessful. During these 14 days, Luftwaffe attacks sank eight vessels totalling 12,975 tons.

EXTENDING FIGHTER COMMAND'S IADS TO THE SOUTH-WEST

Except for reconnaissance flights, Sperrle's operations on the battlefront's left flank went largely unchallenged because the air defence network for south-west England was just being established. During May and June six new radar stations were constructed along the coast west of Southampton, all networked to a temporary Filter Room established at Coastal Command's No. 15 Group HQ at Plymouth. It began functioning on 23 June, feeding information to Fighter Command HQ and No. 11 Group, but the expansive breadth of the battlespace along the south coast, the great distances involved, and the inherent time delays all argued for the establishment of a separate command.

Built atop a disused quarry converted into an Army Central Ammunition Depot near Bath, No. 10 Group HQ was established under AVM Sir C.J. Quintin Brand, KBE, DSO, MC, DFC, and, after six months of construction, became operational on 13 July. However, fighter control could not be exercised until the construction of two sector stations – Middle Wallop and Colerne – was completed. The Observer Corps network also had to be built from scratch, with the area's group HQ at Exeter beginning operations on 17 July.

At the outset of the war the sole fighter defence in this expansive area was 501 Squadron, based at Filton for the protection of the Bristol Aeroplane Company factory. It was sent to France 'when the balloon went up' and was replaced by 236 Sqn's Blenheim IFs, transferred from Coastal Command. Following the fall of France and the arrival of Luftwaffe units in Brittany and Normandy, the air defence of south-west England became a serious concern and three squadrons each of Hurricanes (87, 213 and 238) and Spitfires (92, 234 and 609) were transferred to newly built RAF Middle Wallop and airfields at Pembrey in Wales, Exeter and St Eval.

The newly established 238 Squadron arrived at Middle Wallop on 2 June, followed by 609 Squadron on 6 July, at which time the former was transferred to Y Sector's FOL at Warmwell. Fifteen days later, Fighter Command's newest sector station was passed to No. 10 Group. Brand's HQ Filter Room (initially RAF Box, near Colerne, later RAF Rudloe Manor) became operational on 24 July, but was unable to assume control of all its outlying fighter stations until the second week in August, just in time for the Luftwaffe's offensive counter-air campaign.[22]

A Bf 110 of II./ZG 76 over the Channel Islands. (Clive Ellis)

At 0845hrs on 19 July, 141 Squadron was ordered to move its Defiants forward from West Malling to Hawkinge. Four hours later, nine were attacked from below and astern by Bf 109s from II./JG 2. A rout ensued and within 15 minutes, six were destroyed and a seventh badly damaged. (Author Collection, colourized by Adam Tooby)

DEFEATING THE DEFIANTS – 19 JULY

During the reshuffle to improve the air defence of south-west England, on 11 July, No. 141 Squadron, flying the new Bolton-Paul Defiant turret fighter, was rotated down from Turnhouse, near Edinburgh, to Biggin Hill's new FOL at West Malling. As the Channel battles began escalating, Sqn Ldr William Richardson's unit was ordered forward to C Sector's other FOL at Hawkinge, near Folkestone, also the temporary home of 111 Squadron (from Croydon).

Junkers Ju 87 dive-bomber

To reduce exposure to enemy AA fire, the Luftwaffe's He 111s and Do 17Zs typically bombed from around 13,000ft. However, from this altitude the Lotfernrohr 3 bombsight did not permit accurate bombing. In fact, during tests in 1937, bomb aimers were able to place only two per cent of their bombs within a 200m (660ft) radius around the target; RAF Bomber Command faced similar challenges with British technology. The lack of accuracy inherent in medium-altitude level deliveries led directly to the Luftwaffe's obsession with dive-bombing, especially for pinpoint attacks against small targets such as bunkers, bridges, artillery emplacements, field HQs and communications sites.

After Udet's investigations with his own Curtiss Hawk and following successful trials with the He 50 first-generation biplane dive-bomber, the Luftwaffe ordered the large, robust Ju 87 'Stuka' (short for Sturzkampfflugzeug or 'dive-bombing aeroplane') as its primary tactical support aircraft. Designed by Hermann Pohlmann, the first Stuka prototype was built by AB Flygindustri (sv) in Sweden and secretly brought to Germany in late 1934, making its maiden flight in September the following year.

A typical Stuka dive-bombing profile involved approaching the target at 15,000ft, the pilot locating his aimpoint through a bombsight window in the cockpit floor and then rolling the aircraft over onto its back to begin the dive. The Ju 87B dived at between 60 and 90 degrees, although usually at 75–80 degrees, its underwing dive-brakes deploying to hold a constant speed of 350–370mph (565–595kph), which increased the accuracy of the aircraft's aim. The pilot released the bomb at a minimum height of 1,500ft (460m) and initiated the automatic 6g pull-out mechanism by depressing a button on the control column. Once the nose was above the horizon the dive-brakes were retracted, the throttle opened, and the propeller set to climb, at which point the pilot resumed normal flight, climbing away from enemy ground fire.

Like several of its early Luftwaffe contemporaries, the Ju 87 made its combat debut in 1937 with the Condor Legion, during the Spanish Civil War. Although gaining a fearful reputation with ground troops and civilians alike, the Stuka was, in reality, terminally slow due to its heavy weight and fixed undercarriage, making it very vulnerable to fighter attack. Poorly defended by a single aft-facing flexible MG 15, the type required a permissive environment – air superiority – so that it could do its job without prohibitive losses.

The Ju 87 Stuka. (Jean-Louis Roba)

Just after noon on 19 July, Swingate radar station detected a formation gathering over the Pas de Calais and Park ordered Hawkinge's two units airborne; 111 Squadron took off at 1220hrs, with nine Defiants following 10 minutes after. Park's Senior Fighter Controller, Wg Cdr Willoughby de Broke, directed 'Treble One' towards Deal at 10,000ft, telling 'Wagon Leader' (Sqn Ldr John Thompson) to expect enemy bombers, and 'Plater Leader' (Richardson) to patrol 20 miles (32km) south of Folkestone at 5,000ft. If no enemy were encountered, they were to sweep towards Cap Gris-Nez.

The two squadron leaders checked in with 'Tophat Control' where Biggin Hill Station Commander Wg Cdr Richard Grice was, at this time, also the C Sector

Fighter Controller. Even though, geographically, Hawkinge lay within D Sector's AOR, since the airfield was a C Sector FOL, Tophat Control issued intercept vectors and other instructions to its squadrons deployed there.

As the Hawkinge units launched, a dozen Bf 110C/D fighter-bombers of the newly arrived Erprobungsgruppe (ErprGr; Trials Group) 210[23] attacked RN vessels in Dover harbour, with top cover provided by 20 Bf 109Es of Trautloft's III./JG 51.

Noted in Cull's *Battle for the Channel*, Trautloft later related:

Visibility was so good that one could see any aircraft taking off from the airfields near the coast. Suddenly Lt Wehnelt reported 'Down below to the right, several aircraft just crossing the English coast. I looked towards the spot and located the aircraft, counting three, six, nine of them. They seemed to have only just taken off. They climbed rapidly and made a large turn towards the middle of the Channel coming straight at us. They hadn't spotted us yet, and we headed towards them out of the sun.

When I was only 800m [2,600ft] or so above their formation I noticed the aircraft had turrets behind the cockpits… 'Defiants' suddenly went through my head – heavily armed two-seaters whose back gunner had four heavy machine guns with enormous firepower. The enemy formation was still flying tightly together, as if on exercise, when it suddenly turned back… After checking once more for signs of Hurricanes or Spitfires, I gave the order to attack [and] peeled over and dived towards the rearmost Defiant, with my wingmen Wehnelt, Kath and Pichon following right behind. Slightly further behind the three staffeln followed suit. I aimed for the right-hand Defiant.

Suddenly all hell broke loose. The Englishmen had seen us. Defensive fire from a number of turrets flew towards me, fireworks all over the place. I could see the bullets passing by on either side and felt hits on my machine, but pressed home my attack. The first volley was too high, but the second was right in the middle of the fuselage and parts of the Defiant broke loose and flashed past me. I saw a thin smoke trail appear below the fuselage and suddenly the aircraft exploded in a huge ball of flames, which fell towards the sea. I'd gained speed in my dive and used it to curve into the attack again to the right… By this time all my pilots were attacking, and then suddenly my engine vibrated and began to run unevenly. I could smell burning oil in the cockpit and my coolant temperature indicated 120° with oil temperature also rising steadily. I felt uneasy – I didn't want to have to bail out in the middle of the Channel.

On the receiving end of this overwhelming attack, Richardson later reported, 'The squadron was attacked out of the sun by about 20–25 Me 109s. I immediately turned to port completing a steep turn of 360°. This proved ineffective as my aircraft was attacked from below and on the outside [of the turn]. I then carried out S-turns, always turning towards the attack; this proved effective. After five minutes "Red 2" and myself were the only two Defiants left, so I decided to break off the combat and return to base.'

Number 141 Squadron lost six Defiants shot down and a seventh so badly damaged its turret-gunner baled out. Four pilots and six gunners were killed in the massacre. Their aircraft badly damaged, Trautloft and one of his wingmen were able to crash-land back in France, both Messerschmitts being written off as 'damaged beyond repair'. Number 111 tried to intervene and save the luckless Defiants, but arrived too late; it was able only to chase the victorious 'Emils' back to France (but claimed three shot down anyway).[24]

Another convoy is subjected to an attack on 14 July. (AHB)

Finally recognizing that, like the Stuka, the Defiant was unsuited for combat in anything but a permissive (air superiority attained) environment, three days later 141 Squadron was withdrawn to 13 Group at Prestwick, where there was little likelihood of encountering Luftwaffe bombers, much less their predatory fighters.

CONVOY ATTACKS RESUME – 25 JULY 1940

Through 11 to 24 July, much of the required refresher and tactical training had been accomplished, especially familiarizing Jagdwaffe pilots with escort timing, station-keeping procedures and mission co-ordination (there was no common radio frequency to use for re-planning once airborne). The system of rendezvousing and flying fast fighters together with the plodding, fixed-gear Stukas had also been practised enough to have become reasonably proficient. These training missions, giving the appearance of feints and attempts to probe Fighter Command defences or to draw British fighters out over the Channel, became increasingly common as additional units settled into their new bases, returned to their statutory strengths, and resumed combat operations. The large numbers of Bf 109E and Bf 110C/D units coming online allowed the two Luftflotten to mount strong defensive fighter patrols along the French channel shores, from Calais to Cherbourg, from 1130 to 2000hrs daily.[25]

Increased proficiency permitted the first major operation to be flown on 25 July. The *RAF Narrative, Volume II, The Battle of Britain* records it as a 'fine day with haze in the Straits of Dover', and the 21 coasters of convoy CW8, escorted by a pair of armed trawlers, were passing through the straits from 1200 to 1800hrs. Seeing the large convoy crawling at 6kt only 20 miles (32km) off Cap Gris-Nez, Luftflotte 2 mounted a series of four attacks from 1130 to 1840hrs, each comprising a Gruppe of Ju 87s or the new Bf 110C/D Jabos closely escorted by Zerstörers, with one or two Jagdgruppen sweeping ahead, crossing the water at wave-top

Bf 110C-4 'A2+AL' of
6./ZG 2 flown by Hptm
Heinlein, Staffelkapitän,
along the cliffs of Cape
Antifer, near Étretat.
(Jean-Louis Roba)

height and therefore unseen beneath CH radar coverage. This new tactic was
designed to ensure maximum fighter protection when the Stukas were most
vulnerable, as they pulled out of their dives.

The first three attacks (at 1150, 1450 and 1630hrs) each got through the three
or four scrambled British fighter squadrons without serious interference as the
Bf 109Es popped up from sea level to intercept the approaching defenders, tying
them up while the Stukas dived from high above and escaped unscathed. These
swirling dogfights resulted in five Spitfires from 54, 64, and 610 Sqns being shot
down in exchange for two Bf 109Es, one each from 9./JG 26 and 5./JG 51. During
the final raid, around 1840hrs, 54 and 610 Squadrons were finally able to get at
the attackers, shooting down two II./StG 1 Stukas plus four escorts (from the
newly arrived III./JG 52) for the loss of a single 54 Sqn Spitfire.

Stukas from I. and II./StG 1 and IV.(St)/LG 1, and the Bf 110 Jabos from ErprGr
210, sank five small coasters totalling 5,107 tons and damaged five more, one of
them so badly it had to be beached.[26] Two destroyers, HMS *Boreas* and *Brilliant*, sent
out from Dover to try and ward off the incessant attacks, were also hit, badly
damaged, and had to be towed back into harbour. That evening Kriegsmarine
S-booten sank three more of the convoy's small ships, totalling 2,480 tons.[27]

Although the tonnage sunk was modest, the impact of the Luftwaffe's very
effective demonstration was not lost on the Royal Navy or Churchill. The next
day, he wrote to the Admiralty, 'It is evident that the precautions taken for the

safety of this convoy were utterly ineffectual, and that both in its composition and escort it was unsuited to the task prescribed. I must consider this one of the most lamentable episodes of the naval war so far.'[28]

Dutifully the Admiralty 'closed the Straits' during daytime. No merchant traffic was permitted to sail through the east end of the Channel in daylight until more effective air defence measures were instituted.[29] Luftflotte 2 had partially achieved one of the stated aims of *Kanalkampf*.

JG 26's first Battle of Britain mission was on 24 July, escorting KG 2 Do 17Zs attacking a convoy in the Thames Estuary. Led by Major Gotthard Handrick in this Bf 109E, the unit engaged Spitfires from 54 and 65 Squadrons, losing two aircraft shot down for one pilot killed and the other captured. Leading III. Gruppe, Hptm Adolf Galland and his wingman shot down two 54 Sqn Spitfires north of Margate. (Author Collection)

ATTACKING DOVER – 19–27 JULY

Erprobungsgruppe 210's morning attack on 19 July against the RN's Dover base hit only an armed trawler, but initiated a series of attacks that sought to drive the Dover Local Defence Flotilla out of its Channel base. The Jabos returned that afternoon with more success, hitting the 5,581-ton Royal Fleet Auxiliary *War Sepoy* in the engine room and setting the cargo-tanker afire. They also damaged two destroyers and two other vessels.[30]

Next day, 2./ErprGr 210 attacked Dover at 1310–1340hrs, diving from 8,000ft to release bombs at 2,000ft. It failed to score any hits, but was not intercepted. With II./JG 51 escorting at 10–15,000ft, it returned at 1740hrs, along with II./StG 1, to attack a convoy off Dover, the combined attack sinking the 860grt collier SS *Pulborough* and damaging the destroyer HMS *Brazen* so badly it sank the following day. Number 32 Squadron Hurricanes intercepted and claimed one Bf 110D shot down; it landed in France damaged but repairable. The escorts jumped the interceptors, shooting down two Hurricanes (one pilot missing in action) for no losses.[31]

Following several days of bad weather, on 27 July the Jabos returned to Dover in full cry. Their first attack, at 1430hrs, was ineffectual, but the second sank the 2,012-ton destroyer flotilla leader HMS *Codrington*, and badly damaged the 11,500-ton depot ship *Sandhurst* (to which *Codrington* was moored) and destroyer *Walpole*. Number 501 Squadron attempted to intercept but lost a Hurricane to a 3./ErprGr 210 Bf 109E-4/B Jabo flown by Lt Horst Marx.

Meanwhile, along the Sussex coast KG 53 He 111s sank the destroyer *Wren* and damaged *Montrose* as they provided AA escort to minesweepers clearing the entrance to Harwich of the increasing numbers of German mines, sown by 9. Fliegerdivision, S-boats and U-boats. Two days later, III./StG 2 sank the destroyer HMS *Delight* 15 miles (25km) off Portland. The loss of four destroyers – the warship type that would be the RN's primary defence against any cross-Channel amphibious operation – ably demonstrated the Luftwaffe's effectiveness in countering the Royal Navy's superiority in the 'Narrow Sea'.

Coupled with the RAF Photographic Reconnaissance Unit's (PRU's) discovery that the Wehrmacht was assembling long-range artillery near Calais, the Admiralty ordered the abandonment of Dover as a base, withdrawing survivors of the Dover Local Defence Flotilla to Sheerness. Of seven destroyers assigned on 1 July, only HMS *Vivacious* was seaworthy and it, along with the crippled *Walpole* and damaged *Brilliant* (towed by the Admiralty salvage tug *Lady Brassey*), evacuated their base that evening.[32]

By forcing the RN destroyers to withdraw from Dover, the Luftwaffe achieved another important operational objective in the *Kanalkampf* maritime air campaign, better enabling the proposed Unternehmen *Seelöwe* by compelling intercepting RN destroyers to undertake a longer route to intercept cross-Channel movements, thus imposing a time delay to their response and exposing them to the Stukas' and Jabos' effective anti-shipping strikes during daylight and S-boat and U-boat attacks at night.

THE CHANNEL IS CLOSED – UNTIL FURTHER NOTICE

The 'more effective air defence measures' ordered by the War Cabinet were 'barrages' of balloons tethered above or around targets to foil or discourage low-altitude and dive-bombing attacks. Filled with 20,000cuft (566,300 litres) of hydrogen, the Mk VII kite balloon (KB) 'gas bags' were tethered at the end of 5,000ft (1,500m) cables moored to fixed positions, heavy lorries and barges anchored in rivers and estuaries. By the end of July some 1,466 barrage balloons were deployed in 52 squadrons consisting of varying numbers of flights of eight or nine balloons each, protecting major cities, ports and industrial centres. One of the newest balloon barrage units was 961 Squadron at Dover, deploying 16 'gas bags', half moored ashore, the rest floating over the harbour from waterborne moorings, in the hope of discouraging dive-bombing attacks sufficiently for the RN destroyer flotilla to return. It became operational on 31 July.[33]

Additionally, 952 Squadron at Sheerness naval base, located in the Thames Estuary, added a flight of eight balloons for convoy escort (known as the Maritime Balloon Barrage Flotilla, MBBF). Tethered to motorized fishing boats known as 'drifters', this small flotilla, led by the 451-ton former Belgian pilot cutter HMS *Astral*, was embedded in the convoy formation and would accompany it from Sheerness to the Isle of Wight, a full day's passage.[34]

With this new protection in place, on 7 August the Admiralty gathered two dozen coasters and colliers at Southend-on-Sea, deep in the Thames Estuary, forming CW9, codename 'Peewit', as the first Channel West(bound) convoy in two weeks. That morning, Luftflotte 2's morning reconnaissance flight, a Do 17Z from Stab/KG 2, was flying from off Dungeness, north-east around the Kent coast to North Foreland. After checking the entrance of the Thames Estuary, the Dornier turned north to reconnoitre up the coast of Essex and Suffolk. Weather inhibited visual reconnaissance; visibility was limited to between two and five miles (3–8km) beneath an 'overhead fog' at 2,000ft, so the crew failed to spot the convoy. The cloud deck thickened to the east, blanketing north-eastern France, Belgium and Holland, precluding any Luftflotte 2 strikes that morning.

On 24 July, only one of 2./KG 2's Do 17Zs was damaged by RAF interceptors. Here, KG 2's Oblt Gerherd Plöhn enjoys a brief quiet moment and a cigarette at his Cambrai base. (AHB donated by Ken Wakefield)

Later that day, CW9 steamed in two long parallel columns, rounding North Foreland and filing past Dover unmolested at 1430hrs. The escorts consisted of the destroyers HMS *Bulldog* and *Fernie*, four anti-submarine (A/S) trawlers and six MBBF vessels, one at each end of the columns and one abeam each flank.[35]

That night 1. S-Flotilla attacked the convoy off Beachy Head and Newhaven. Surprise was complete, the four S-boats sinking two freighters and causing evasive action in the darkness that caused a collision, sinking a third; 11 sailors were killed. The chaos and confusion created by the repeated nocturnal attacks resulted in the convoy becoming so completely disorganized that, by dawn, it was scattered across 50 square miles (130 sqm km) of open water. The morning's reconnaissance, a Do 17P from 4.(F)/14, an army co-operation/reconnaissance unit attached to Heeresgruppe B HQ, located the widely dispersed ships off Selsey Bill at 0620hrs, a task assisted by the six barrage balloons floating serenely above the thin, wispy layer of cloud.[36]

A Stuka attack was ordered, some 57 Ju 87s taking off between 0825 and 0830hrs carrying 285 bombs totalling 32.4 tons of high explosives (HE), escorted by 'Emils' from I. and III./JG 27. The Stukas and their escorts formed into two attack groups. The first, III./StG 1 (formerly I.(St)/TrGr 186), flying from Cherbourg towards the Isle of Wight, was detected by the Ventnor radar station at 0840. The second, I./StG 1, was detected halfway to Selsey Bill 15 minutes later. RAF fighter cover comprised six 145 Sqn Hurricanes that had just taken off from Westhampnett.

Now about two hours behind schedule, the widely spread vessels of CW9 were still partially obscured by cloud, but a small group of six freighters steaming together from St Helen's Road (Solent's eastern approaches) to join CW9 off St Catherine's Point was spotted easily and Hptm Mahlke's III./StG 1 Stukas circled round to position themselves for an attack from the west-north-west.[37]

Recorded in Andy Saunders' *Convoy Peewit: Blitzkrieg from the Air and Sea 8 August 1940*, one survivor recounted:

> We were six ships sailing to meet a westbound convoy off the Isle of Wight… [and] were subject to the most awful and frightening attack by Junkers dive-bombers. The attack came out of broken cloud and without warning when the German planes fell upon us. First, there was the screech of the diving aeroplanes and a sound like sirens wailing over the roaring engines. Then when the bombs dropped they made a shrieking whistle. We must have had at least 50 dive down onto us in little over five or six minutes. One after the other they came. It was just a hell of noise… The shock waves hit you again and again and literally winded you, great plumes of water hit you, and the smell hit you, too.[38]

Mahlke also recalled the attack: 'The convoy was spotted some ten nautical miles to the south-west of the Isle of Wight. I decided that we would attack in Ketten. The wind was steady. The targets were fixed firmly in our sights during the dive and bombing results were consequently very good. Several direct hits had been scored on a number of ships, which were seen to be sinking. Others had been severely damaged by our bombs.'[39] The attack had been devastating, sinking the steamers SS *Ajax* and *Coquetdale* (totalling 2,539grt) and damaging the other four so badly they all limped back into St Helen's Road, with four dead.

A propaganda image of an attack on a British warship 12 miles (20km) south of Portland. (Chris Goss)

Arriving about the same time, Sqn Ldr John Peel, 145 Squadron's 'Patin Leader', 'Received warning of enemy aircraft approaching from SW and climbed into the sun at 16,000ft. Saw large formation of Ju 87s approaching from SW in formation with Me 109s stepped up to rear at 12,000ft. Approached unobserved from sea and went into attack on rear Ju 87s with Yellow Section before enemy fighters could intercept.' Eight Stukas were claimed shot down; only two 9./StG 1 aircraft were actually lost with all four crewmen missing as well as two other pilots and one radio operator/gunner wounded. Number 145 Squadron lost two Hurricanes to escorting I./JG 27 'Emils', both pilots missing in action, while three JG 27 Bf 109Es failed to return, with two pilots killed.[40]

As the last Stukas began egressing at low altitude over the water, SS *Empire Crusader* (the convoy commodore's ship), the first two MBBF ships, and a few CW9 coasters were spotted emerging from beneath the thin scattered cloud deck, so a second strike was ordered. Some 49 I. and III./StG 2 Stukas, loaded with 245 bombs (27.75 tons), began taking off at 1145hrs, escorted again by I. and III./JG 27 to form one large formation. The '100-plus' raid was detected by Ventnor radar station 20 miles (30km) north of Cherbourg headed directly towards Convoy Peewit.

Sweeping ahead of the strike force were 16 Zerstörers of Liensberger's V.(Z)/LG 1, flying towards Beachy Head as a feint. It worked. Number 145 Squadron was airborne once again and 'Shortjack Control' (at this stage Middle Wallop Station Commander Wg Cdr Jack Boret was also A Sector Fighter Controller) vectored 'Patin Leader' to intercept.

This 152 Squadron Spitfire force-landed on 8 August after engaging Bf 109s from II./JG 53. Its pilot, Sgt D.N. Robinson, escaped unhurt. (Andy Saunders)

As Liensberger recorded, 'We swept between the opposing RAF fighters, once above and once below. Suddenly there was hell to pay. They came at us in force, from above and below… They were all around us, brown and camouflaged. Then there were the phosphorus stripes of the [tracer] bullets going by. That was really a dogfight! I hit two of them, but what happened to them I don't know.' None of the intercepting Hurricanes was lost; 14.(Z)/LG 1 lost one Bf 110C, its crew killed; three more returned damaged but repairable.[41]

Meanwhile, patrolling overhead the widely scattered ships, now slowly re-forming into their two columns as they progressed westwards, were six 609 Sqn Spitfires. Quickly realizing that these would not be enough, Park scrambled six 601 Sqn Hurricanes from Tangmere at 1155hrs to patrol overhead their airfield (in case the raiders were headed there) at 20,000ft and launched three more squadrons (30 Hurricanes) between 1209 and 1215hrs.[42]

The second dive-bombing attack of the day began with a Schwarm of 9./JG 27 Messerschmitts sweeping in at low altitude to shoot down the balloon barrage. That towed by HMS *Borealis* fell flaming into the sea a mile astern of its ship. The balloon gone, the MBBF ship quickly became one of the initial targets and was wrecked with the first attack. The 1,042grt *Empire Crusader* was hit twice, capsized and sank, and the Norwegian SS *Tres* (946grt) was so badly damaged it sank after being towed to St Helen's Road. Two other smaller ships were also damaged.

Only 609 Squadron intercepted the raiders. It attacked, but failed to shoot any down.

Overhead, 24 Hurricanes from 238 and 257 Sqns arrived but, before they could attack the Stukas, they were immediately engaged by Hptm Joachim Schlichting's III./JG 27, losing five Hurricanes shot down, all five pilots being killed or missing. Schlichting lost one Bf 109E, pilot missing in action.[43]

By the time the final attack on CW9 was launched at 1530–1620hrs, most of the convoy's survivors were headed into the shelter of Weymouth Bay and

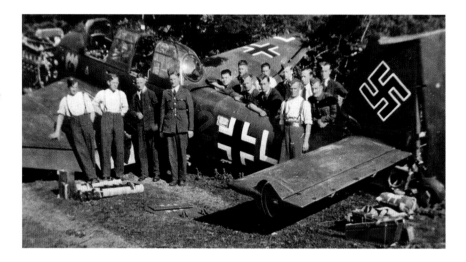

Ju 87B 'S2+LM' of 4./StG 77 was shot down on 8 August by Plt Off Parrott of 145 Squadron, while attacking convoy 'Peewit'. The aircraft force-landed at St Lawrence, Isle of Wight, at 1740hrs. The pilot, Uffz Pittroff, was captured, but the gunner, Uffz Schubert, had been killed during the battle. (Andy Saunders, colourized by Richard Molloy)

Yarmouth Roads (the Solent's western approaches). All that remained at sea was the crippled *Borealis*, under tow by two MBBF ships (all the balloons had been shot down in the midday attack), under the 'protection' of two A/S yachts and the convoy's four A/S trawlers.

A total of 82 Stukas were launched (from III./StG 1. I./StG 3 and II./StG 77), lugging 328 bombs to drop on the nine small RN vessels. They sent HMS *Borealis* to the bottom and damaged six of the small vessels attending to it.

While lacking as a decisive finale to the afternoon's action, the raid, escorted by II./JG 27 and II./JG 53, spawned the largest air battle of the day. Park scrambled 152 and 238 Sqns to cover 'Peewit' as it straggled into Weymouth Bay and 43 and 145 Sqns to patrol over the RN ships. The resulting wide-ranging, dynamic and confusing battle defies coherent description, but the results are telling. Four Stukas from I./StG 3 and II./StG 77 were shot down, as well as six Bf 109Es (four pilots rescued, two missing in action). Number 43 Squadron lost two Hurricanes, 145 lost three and 152 Squadron lost one Spitfire; all five Hurricane pilots were killed.[44]

For the Luftwaffe it was a disappointing end to an otherwise victorious day. Nevertheless, the loss of seven merchant ships (6,114grt) with another seven badly damaged, totalling 14 of 24 vessels (58 per cent) lost or damaged, resulted in the Channel being closed until further notice. In fact, it was not until three weeks later – 30 August, while the Luftwaffe was fully engaged in its offensive counter-air campaign to destroy RAF Fighter Command – that the next CW convoy sailed from Southend.[45] In this sense, *Kanalkampf* had finally and fully accomplished its primary operational aim.

In the words of Oberst Walter Gaul, Luftwaffe liaison officer to Raeder's staff, 'All in all, these bombing operations made an effective contribution to the naval [blockade] objective, namely the stoppage of supplies to Britain, and was a promising opening to the coming siege of Britain. On 13 August, attacks on shipping were relegated to secondary importance. Most of the available bomber forces were briefed for bombing attacks on land targets.'[46]

STRATEGIC ASSESSMENT

While, in five weeks of sporadic efforts, *Kanalkampf* had indeed achieved its operational aims, contrary to Gaul's assessment it did not portend well for a sustained *Handelskrieg* blockade/siege strategy. During this localized maritime air campaign, the Luftwaffe sank a total of 34 British and Allied merchant ships totalling 77,450grt, as well as four RN destroyers, four naval auxiliaries and five armed trawlers, by air attack alone.[47] Additionally, German mines sown by aircraft, S-boats, U-boats and destroyers/torpedo boats sank another nine ships totalling 31,135grt, plus five minesweeping trawlers, mostly in the English Channel. Furthermore, S-boat attacks sank one large and seven small ships, totalling 10,112grt. Total British shipping losses during the maritime campaign came to 51 ships and 118,697grt.[48]

On the face of it, these figures seem impressive. However, they actually represent only a small fraction of the sea traffic transiting the 'Narrow Sea'. On average, each week there was almost a million tons of shipping in the Channel for a daily average of 103 vessels of all sizes.[49] In a month of battle, the Luftwaffe flew four major attacks against convoys (OA178, CW3, CW8 and CW9), or about one every week. While these were individually devastating, sinking an average of five ships totalling (on average) about 10,000 tons, compared with the above figures they can hardly be considered decisive.

This, of course, emphasizes the point that a *Handelskrieg* strategy was truly a long-term approach and, as both Raeder and Geisler predicted, the siege or blockade strategy, even including mines and S-boats, could hardly provide the outcome Hitler desired until 1942. If he wanted his 'English problem' solved in 1940, he would have to resort to invading the British Isles before the approach of winter.

Throughout the Battle of Britain, a trace was meticulously recorded from the radar plot delineating the track of every Luftwaffe raid. This is a copy of one of the very few that survive. (Author Collection)

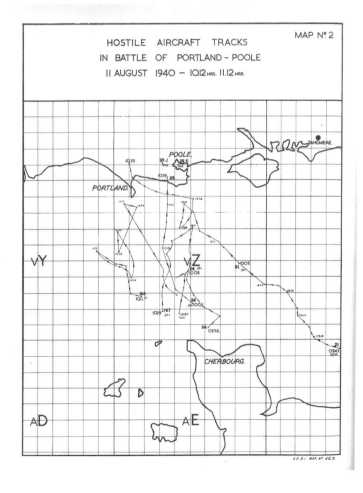

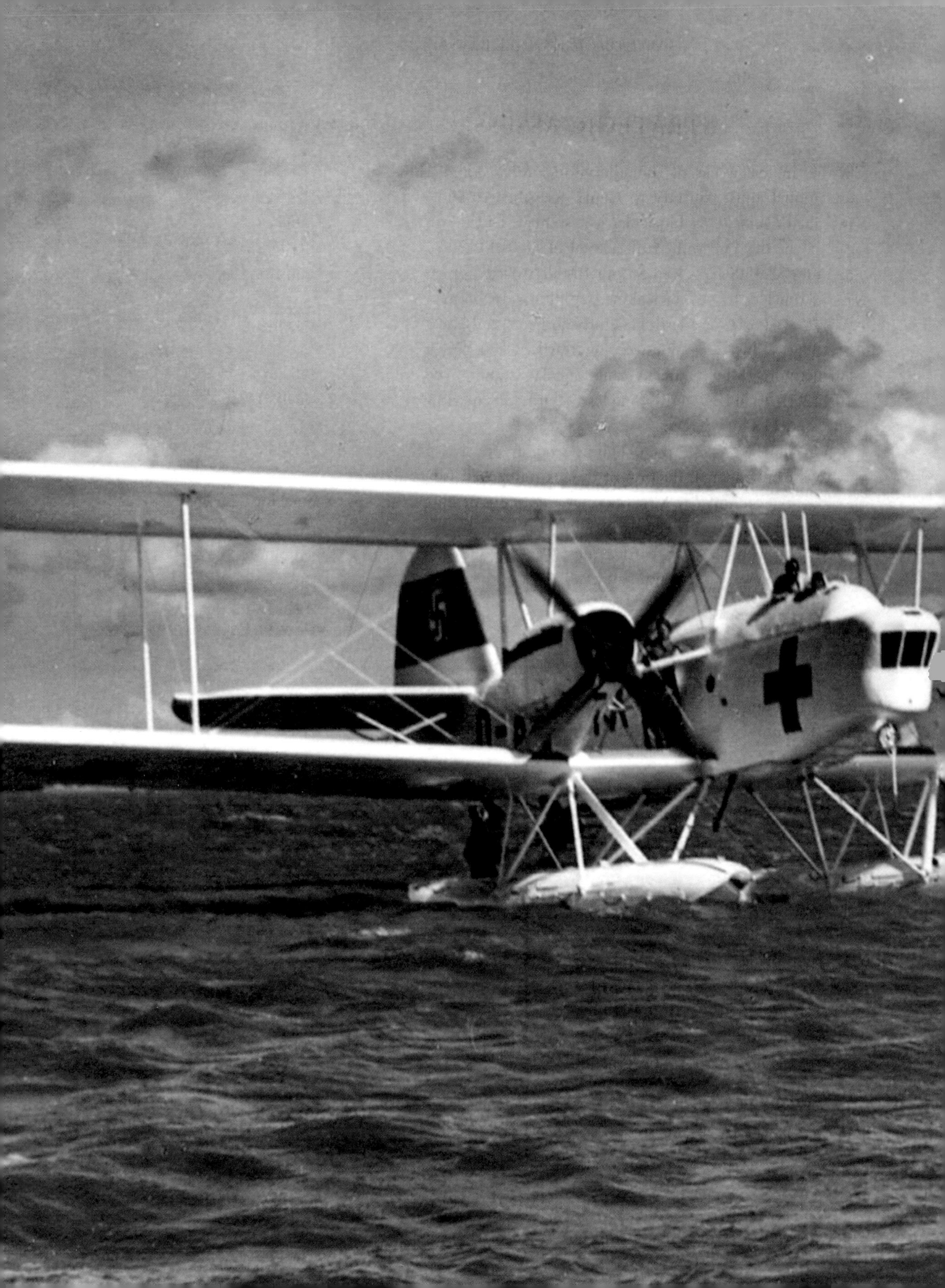

CHAPTER VIII

SEELÖWE (SEALION)
Hitler's plan to invade Britain

The aim of [Operation *Sealion*] *will be to eliminate the English homeland as a base for the prosecution of the war against Germany and, if necessary, to occupy it completely.*

Führer Directive Nr. 16, 'On preparations for a landing operation against England', 16 July, 1940[1]

PLANNING OPERATION *SEELÖWE*

Midway through *Kanalkampf*, Hitler's famous 'Führer Directive Nr. 16' ordered the initiation of planning and preparations for Unternehmen *Seelöwe* (Operation *Sealion*). Parroting Halder's OKH proposed concept of operations, as presented to Hitler three days prior, Jodl's OKW directive postulated: 'The landing will be in the form of a surprise crossing on a wide front from about Ramsgate to the area west of the Isle of Wight. Units of the Luftwaffe will act as artillery, and the units of the Kriegsmarine as pioneers [combat engineers].'

In this initiating directive, Hitler appointed himself 'overriding' CinC, with each service CinC commanding his respective arm's participation in this historically unprecedented and unbelievably massive undertaking. He ordered the OKH, OKM, and ObdL chiefs to position their HQs within 30 miles (50km) of his own at Ziegenberg Castle, codenamed '*Adlerhorst*', or 'Eagle's Nest'; some 22 miles (35km) north of Frankfurt-am-Main – and that the operations staffs from OKH and OKM (SKL) 'should be placed together at [nearby] Giessen' (Kransberg Castle, ObdL operations HQ).[2]

For *Seelöwe*, the Luftwaffe's mission assignments were straightforward. The Luftwaffe was to reduce the RAF so that it was 'unable to deliver any significant attack against the German crossing' (establish air superiority), to 'destroy coastal fortresses [and] break the first resistance of enemy land forces' (provide close air support), 'destroy important transport highways by which enemy reserves might be brought up' (interdiction), and 'attack approaching naval forces as far as possible from our embarkation points' (maritime strike).[3]

For the army's part, in an inexcusable breech of military protocol and incredible lapse in joint-service co-ordination, except for a brief discussion with now Vizeadmiral (Vice-Admiral) Schniewind (SKL chief of staff) on 1 July, neither Halder nor Jodl (author of FD Nr. 16) had bothered to check with OKM to determine the extent of the navy's capability to transport army forces across the Channel. Consequently, the resulting OKW directive blindly and stupidly ordered the overly ambitious landing of the army's 'first wave' – 260,000 men and 30,000 vehicles – on an extraordinarily broad 250-mile-wide (400km) front.

Directed 'to provide and safeguard the invasion fleet [and] provide adequate protection on both flanks during the entire Channel crossing', Raeder and his SKL

staff were appalled by the enormity of the army's requirements and the immense responsibility they entailed. Even if the needed 'lift' (river barges modified into amphibious assault craft) could be acquired, with only the heavy cruiser *Admiral Hipper*, three light cruisers, ten destroyers, and 32 U-boats operational, the Kriegsmarine could hardly be expected to protect the crossing from being ravaged by the RN's Home Fleet, which had eight battleships, 21 cruisers and 50 destroyers available.

On the day of Hitler's infamous 'Appeal to Reason' speech, Raeder complained to OKW (via memo): 'the task allotted to the Kriegsmarine in *Seelöwe* is all out of proportion to the navy's strength… [and] causes the OKM staff to see exceptional difficulties that cannot be assessed individually until a detailed examination of the transport problem has been made.'

Equipped with Ju 88s, 3.(F)/123 was based at Brest-Guipavas airport from July 1940. (Chris Goss, colourized by Richard Molloy)

The friendship between Hitler and Göring is readily apparent as the two confer in one of the luxurious railway carriages that were part of Hitler's personal train. It comprised a restaurant car, two passenger carriages, five sleeping carriages and two carriages for luggage. (Author Collection)

The S-boat, known to the Allies as the E-boat, was a fast, highly manoeuvrable torpedo boat. Powered by three 2,000hp Daimler-Benz MB 501, 20-cylinder diesel engines, they were capable of a top speed of 40kt and had a range of 800nm (1,500km). Armed with two 21-inch torpedo tubes and four torpedoes, a 40mm Bofors anti-aircraft cannon amidships and a 20mm anti-aircraft cannon in a single or double mounting aft, they were the scourge of British coastal merchant shipping. (Author Collection)

Before this study could be completed, on 21 July, spurred by the British press's rejection of his 'appeal' and motivated by Stalin's worrisome initiatives in the East, Hitler convened the first top-level military conference in Berlin to discuss the matter. Raeder, Brauchitsch, and Jeschonnek represented their three services. Following a long, rambling prologue that reviewed 'England's hopeless situation', the dim prospects of either the 'indirect approach' (primarily via Spain) and the *Handelskrieg* strategy to produce timely results, Hitler stated that while 'invasion is to be taken only if no other means is left to come to terms with Britain, Britain must be reduced by the middle of September' and 'If it is not certain that preparations can be completed by the beginning of September, other plans must be considered.'

The ensuing discussion created more questions than it answered, especially for Raeder, so Hitler scheduled a second high-level joint service conference, this one

The airscrew-driven Prahm was among the more innovative proposals for carrying assault troops across the Channel. (Author Collection)

The Kriegsmarine's Plan for Operation *Sealion*

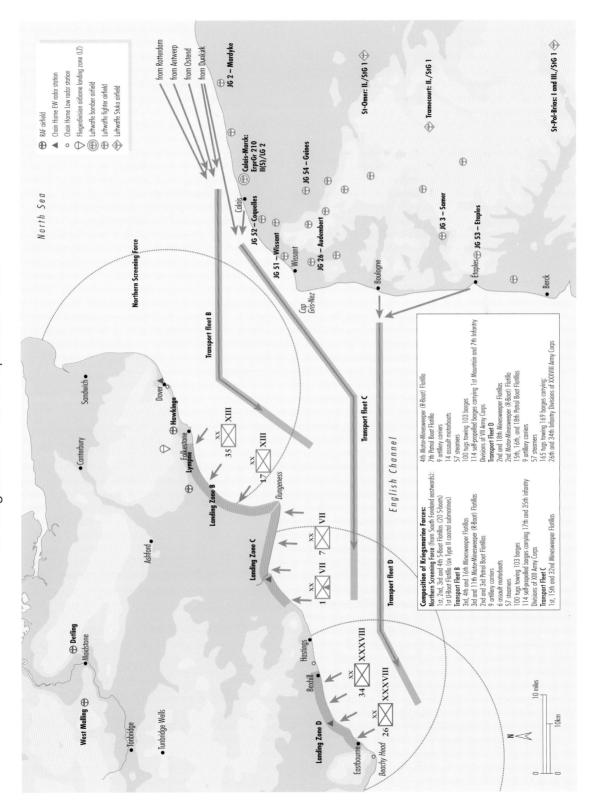

Composition of Kriegsmarine Forces:

Northern Screening Force (from South Foreland eastwards):
1st, 2nd, 3rd and 4th S-Boat Flotillas (20 S-boats)
1st U-Boat Flotilla (six Type II coastal submarines)

Transport Fleet B
3rd, 4th and 16th Minesweeper Flotillas
3rd and 11th Motor-Minesweeper (R-Boat) Flotillas
2nd and 3rd Patrol Boat Flotillas
9 artillery carriers
6 assault motorboats
57 steamers
100 tugs towing 103 barges
114 self-propelled barges carrying 17th and 35th Infantry
Divisions of XIII Army Corps

Transport Fleet C
1st, 15th and 32nd Minesweeper Flotillas

4th Motor-Minesweeper (R-Boat) Flotilla
7th Patrol Boat Flotilla
9 artillery carriers
14 assault motorboats
57 steamers
100 tugs towing 103 barges
114 self-propelled barges carrying 1st Mountain and 7th Infantry
Divisions of VII Army Corps

Transport Fleet D
2nd and 18th Minesweeper Flotillas
2nd Motor-Minesweeper (R-Boat) Flotilla
15th, 16th, and 18th Patrol Boat Flotillas
9 artillery carriers
57 steamers
165 tugs towing 169 barges carrying:
26th and 34th Infantry Divisions of XXXVIII Army Corps

to be held on 31 July at his Berghof retreat, near Berchtesgaden in the Bavarian Alps. Five days after the Berlin conference, Hitler departed for the Berghof to spend three days arbitrating the Romanian–Hungarian–Bulgarian territorial dispute stemming from the recent Russian occupation of Bessarabia and Bucovina and to review military intelligence on the Soviet Union.[4]

Meanwhile, on 28 July, Raeder informed OKH that the Kriegsmarine would be unable to conduct an amphibious cross-Channel operation on the scale that Brauchitsch and Halder envisaged. Instead, SKL proposed a narrow-front approach across the Straits of Dover, relying on minefields to protect the flanks, battleship-calibre guns mounted for coastal artillery support and the Luftwaffe's guarantee of uncontested German air superiority to prevent any RN or RAF interference. This option meant it would take ten days to get the army's first wave forces onto British soil.

Three days later, Raeder, Brauchitsch, Halder, Jodl and his boss, Generalfeldmarschall Wilhelm Keitel, head of the OKW, met with Hitler at the Berghof; the Luftwaffe was not represented. Raeder confirmed the collection of suitable river barges was in full swing but that these could not be modified and positioned before early September. Therefore, 15 September was the earliest date that could be fixed for the crossing, and he recommended that the operation be postponed until May 1941. Hitler courteously considered the admiral's suggestion, but concluded, 'We have the impression that the British are crumbling and that the effects will soon begin to tell, we shall proceed to the attack'.

Amazingly, the vast difference between the army's enormous requirements and the navy's limited means was not resolved. Raeder also lobbied to have the army drop the far western landing (three divisions of Army Group B's II Corps landing in Lyme Bay) as physically impossible and recommended 'confining the assault to a single area in the Straits of Dover'. Hitler accepted the admiral's recommendations without discussing or acting upon them.

The two services would have to work it out.

True to his bullying gangster nature, Hitler preferred the intimidating appearance of continuing preparations for invasion to the actual planning to execute one. He directed that 'the preparations continue with target date September 15', but put off deciding whether or not to launch the invasion, pending the results of a major Luftwaffe assault on Britain's air defences, and ordered Keitel to instruct Göring to get on with it, resulting in the 31 July OKW directive to ObdL.

The next day Keitel issued an OKW directive to the other two services instructing OKH and OKM. '(1) Preparations for "Seelöwe" are to be continued and completed… by 15 September, (2) The Führer will decide whether the invasion will take place this year or not… depend[ing] on the outcome of the air offensive… [and] (4) Preparations are to be continued for the attack on a broad basis as originally planned.'[5]

Simultaneously OKW issued, under Hitler's signature, FD Nr. 17, 'for the Conduct of Air and Naval Warfare against England'. 'In order to establish the necessary conditions for the final conquest of England' the Luftwaffe was ordered to 'overpower the English air force… in the shortest possible time [and] may begin on or after 5 August. The exact time is to be decided by the Luftwaffe after completion of preparations and in the light of the weather.'[6]

PLANNING UNTERNEHMEN *ADLER*

Because the Luftwaffe lacked the means, guidance and experience for planning an air campaign independent of the army, planning what would become known as Unternehmen *Adler* (Operation *Eagle*) began with a sporadic series of high-level conferences and correspondence soliciting ideas on how to orchestrate an independent air campaign against Britain. At ObdL HQ, upon receiving the Luftflotte's recommended concept of operations and courses of action, it was Waldau's responsibility to synthesize the different suggestions into a cogent and coherent strategy.

This iterative process began on 18 July, two days after FD Nr. 16 was received, when Göring convened a meeting of his ObdL staff to discuss the responsibilities and priorities assigned in Hitler's directive and consider the offensive operations that could be anticipated. Each department affected by the proposed cross-Channel invasion prepared and presented various papers covering their respective areas of expertise.

Of the four responsibilities assigned in FD Nr. 16, the most urgent and important to the staff, including Jeschonnek and Waldau, was the elimination of the RN's capability to interfere with the cross-Channel movement of the invasion fleet. Air superiority, apparently based upon the previous unbroken string of successes, was taken for granted. Consequently, *Kanalkampf* needed to be continued with the intent to drive RN destroyer flotillas from their Channel bases at Dover (which occurred on 29 July), Portland and Portsmouth.

Docked airscrew-propelled Prahme. (Author Collection)

Combat operations were to be continued also to train new and returning aircrews and to develop and practise close co-ordination between bomber and Bf 109E fighter units. The disturbing inadequacy of the Bf 110C/D Zerstörer to fulfil this role meant that the Bf 109E 'frontal fighter' units had to learn to do so and they required practice to become proficient in this new mission.

Additionally, Göring ordered the expansion of the Luftwaffe's effective air-sea rescue service (Seenotdienst; literally Sea Emergency Service) to cover the breadth and depth of the Channel. Addressing the British Air Ministry's announcement (Bulletin 1254) four days prior that RAF fighters would not honour the Geneva Convention protections normally accorded to unarmed ambulance aircraft bearing the International Red Cross markings, he also authorized the arming of the service's He 59 twin-engined air ambulance floatplanes so they could defend themselves against fighter attack.

Three days later, following the 19 July Nazi 'victory rally' and 'promotion fest' before the Reichstag at Berlin's Kroll Opera House (which included Hitler's 'Appeal to Reason' speech) and an opulent follow-on Luftwaffe celebration at Göring's elaborate and luxurious Carinhall hunting lodge, the Luftwaffe CinC convened a Besprechung (top-level commanders' conference) to discuss how to implement preparations for a landing operation against England. In addition to his two western Luftflottenchefs, Kesselring and Sperrle, the gathering also included Luftflotte 5's Generaloberst Hans-Jürgen Stumpff. [7]

Oberst Josef 'Beppo' Schmid

Oberst Josef 'Beppo' Schmid. (Author Collection)

Son of a brick company owner, Joseph 'Beppo' ('Boy') Schmid, was born in Göggingen, near Augsburg, in September 1901. Too young to serve in World War I, at age 18 he joined Freikorps Epp, a right-wing paramilitary organization that was fighting the Red Ruhr Army (a communist party) in the streets of Munich in 1919–20. Joining the Reichswehr as a Fahnenjunker (officer cadet) the following year, he was assigned to 19. Bayerische Infanterie-Regiment (19th Bavarian Infantry Regiment) and attended the infantry school at Munich.

During this time Schmid became an ardent young Nazi. In November 1923 he was one of the 2,000 that accompanied Hitler in the 'Beer Hall Putsch', after which he received the Blood Order of the NSDAP, an award revered among Nazis. Graduating as a Leutnant at the end of 1924, he was assigned to the 21. Bayerische Infanterie-Regiment at Nuremburg soon after. After nine years' experience in various arms (mortar, machine gun and infantry), he was selected to attend General Staff training at the Berlin Kriegsakademie (War Academy).

An average officer with Nazi connections, when Hitler ordered the wholesale expansion of the newly created Wehrmacht and formal establishment of the Luftwaffe in 1935, Schmid volunteered for transfer to the latter because of – with Göring as its chief – its strong Party affiliations. Despite the fact he knew nothing about air warfare, he was assigned to the Operations Department where he worked – and was promoted – for four years. There Schmid became a fawning admirer and convivial sycophant of Göring and, in April 1939, he was rewarded by being appointed ObdL's Chief of Intellligence, and was promoted to Oberst on 22 September 1939, becoming the third-ranking General Staff Officer (Führungsstab Ic) in the ObdL HQ.

In the German military, intelligence work was traditionally disdained and typically less-capable officers, or reservists, were employed in this essential, but under-valued capacity. However, Schmid quickly impressed his boss with three glowingly optimistic and generally accurate intelligence assessments of Poland, France and Great Britain. Like so many Nazi sycophants, Schmid was dedicated to ensuring that his boss heard what he wanted to hear, rather than being bothered by uncomfortable military facts and figures. As a result, his later wartime intelligence reports were far from objective or realistic, with dire consequences for the Luftwaffe in the upcoming campaign.[8]

After Schmid's introductory operational assessment and intelligence briefing, Göring emphasized that the Luftflotten staffs should concentrate their planning on attacking RN warships and naval bases, but that docks in southern English ports should be spared for use by arriving army forces. However, the field commanders' primary concern, based on the recent heavy losses experienced over France, Belgium, and Holland, and especially over Dunkirk, was the anticipated losses of large numbers of Stukas and bombers to RAF fighters. Göring's suggestion that 'fighter cover should try to drive off the English forces before the arrival of the massed bombers' did nothing to dissuade the Luftflottenchefs from their strongly held convictions.

The resulting consensus was that attacking RN units and bases should be secondary to and subsequent to the attainment of *Luftüberlegenheit* (air superiority). Kesselring and Sperrle departed with instructions to submit their staffs' and their subordinate Fliegerkorps' assessments and recommendation for initial operations within a week.[9]

Landing exercises for 17th Division during the summer of 1940. (Author Collection)

The first large-scale landing exercise gets under way. (Author Collection)

To oversee this process, Göring positioned his ObdL forward element HQ (codenamed 'Robinson'), housed in an armoured train, on a secluded siding at Boissière-le-Déluge, near Beauville, about 50 miles (80km) north of Paris. 'Robinson' consisted of Waldau's Operations Staff, Martini's Signals Staff, part of Schmid's Intelligence Branch and the Chief of Training, General der Flieger Bernard Kühl. For close co-ordination, Göring parked his lavishly appointed personal train (codenamed 'Asia') alongside and, having left Jeschonnek at the rear echelon HQ (codenamed 'Kurfürst', 'Elector') to field the Führer's questions, he actively participated in the frequent conferences, discussions and staff meetings. However, he was unavailable for the ensuing *Seelöwe* discussions.[10]

The chiefs of staff of Luftflotte 2 in Brussels and Luftflotte 3 in Paris tasked their subordinate Fliegerkorps Stabs (staffs) to provide their proposed concept of operations and *Beurteilung* (commander's assessment) for review, comment and inclusion in their consolidated operations proposals to ObdL.

These were received on or about 24 July.

From Luftflotte 3, only Generalmajor Wolfram Freiherr von Richthofen's VIII. Fliegerkorps response survives and it only recommended the use of his command's Stukas against 'RAF ground installations' (airfields, aircraft depots and known HQs). While there is otherwise little of value in this document, it does imply that, in Sperrle's command, it was anticipated that the destruction of the RAF would come through bombing of airfields and other ground installations.

From Kesselring's Luftflotte 2, details are known regarding I. and II. Fliegerkorps' responses. Generaloberst Ulrich Grauert's I. Fliegerkorps (chief of staff Oberst Walter Boenicke) recommended: 1) 'achieve air superiority by destroying the RAF sources of strength, especially the aircraft motor industry', 2) 'protect the Army's passage across the Channel by striking the British fleet and the RAF, and ground support for the Army once it was landed', 3) 'blockade England by rendering harbours unusable', and 4) 'consider... ruthless terror attacks as reprisals against large cities'.

A German low-level oblique reconnaissance image of Seaford (AHB)

Boenicke did not believe air superiority could be attained 'by attacking the RAF's bases and ground organization, but must be accomplished in the air.' He recommended daily two-wave assaults, 'the first by forces only large enough to bring up English fighters and get them engaged, and the second by "*Masse der Jagdkräfte*" ['masses of fighter arm aircraft'].'

In (now) General der Flieger Bruno Loerzer's II. Fliegerkorps response, chief of staff Obstlt (promoted to Oberst 1 August 1940) Paul Deichmann emphasized that London should be the primary target. His theory was: 'Attacking London would bring up the English fighters in defence of the city, and thus enable the Jagdwaffe to so reduce Fighter Command that thereafter German bombers could sweep inland unchecked.'[11] Notably, in both I. and II. Fliegerkorps' concepts, the 'reduction' of Fighter Command was expected to occur in fighter-versus-fighter combat, in an airborne battle of attrition.

To these documents, the two Luftflottenchefs (actually their chiefs of staff) appended their own comments and recommendations and forwarded them to ObdL, which was to distil them into a coherent set of priorities standardized between the two Luftflotten, determine overall objectives and recommend targets. At Boissière-le-Déluge, Göring, Jeschonnek and 'Robinson' considered the various commands' vastly disparate inputs and sent their feedback to the Luftflotte staffs on 29 July, with orders to return their synthesized concept of operations recommendations in three days.

Hitler did not give Göring that kind of time. On 31 July, the day he met with the OKW, OKH and OKW chiefs at Berghof, Jodl sent a 'bullet' to 'Robinson'

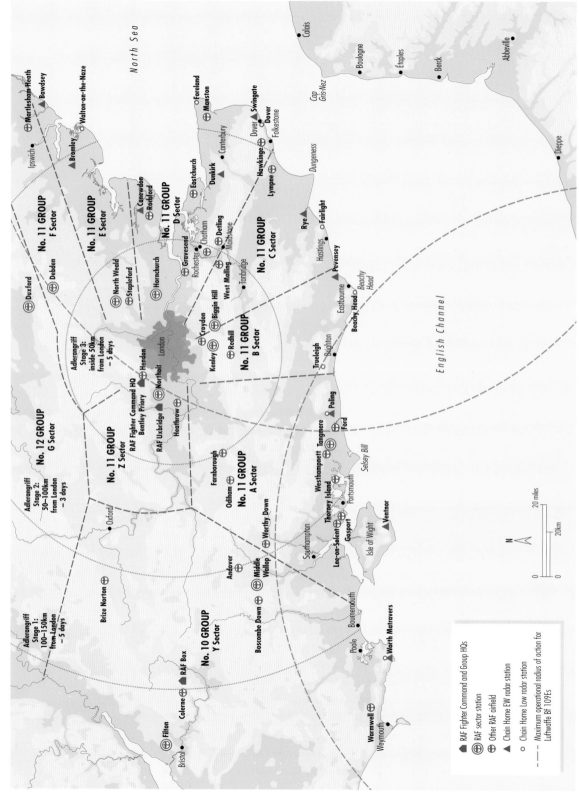

The Luftwaffe's 'roll back' Offensive Counter-air Campaign Plan

stating, 'The Führer has ordered that the preparations for the Luftwaffe's great attack against England should immediately and with great dispatch be completed, so that it can be commenced within 12 hours after the Führer so orders.'[12]

Not waiting for the written responses, Göring scheduled another top-level Besprechung for 1 August, to be held at the Wehrmacht occupation HQ in The Hague, to finalize the Luftwaffe's plan for opening the air attack on Britain. By the time the conference convened, ObdL had received FD Nr. 17, reflecting the agreements and decisions made at the Berghof meeting on 31 July. In it, Hitler ordered: 1) 'attacks are to be directed primarily against [RAF] flying units, their ground installations, and their supply organizations, but also against the aircraft industry, including that manufacturing anti-aircraft equipment' and 2) 'After achieving temporary or local air superiority the air war is to be continued against ports, in particular against stores of food, and also against stores of provisions in the interior of the country.' The Luftwaffe's 'marching orders' were clear: destroy the RAF to enable the success of Operation *Seelöwe*, then resume the *Handelskrieg* strategy.

But the question still remained: 'how?'

In the ensuing discussion, both Sperrle and Kesselring[13] expressed strong reservations about launching bomber attacks before the British fighter force had been destroyed. Quoting Osterkamp in *The Breaking Wave*, Telford Taylor notes that both agreed that they needed to 'first destroy, with continuous night-bomber attacks, the ground organization and airfields, etc., of the fighters, as well as the fighter-producing industry centres. Only after the British fighter force has been decisively weakened should mass [day-bomber] attacks on the fighter fields around London take place.'

Göring vehemently disagreed, declaring these objections 'ridiculous', and adding that 'Jagdgeschwader 51 [commanded by Osterkamp, who was present, representing the Jagdwaffe], which is alone at the Channel has downed over 150 planes [during *Kanalkampf*]. That is enough of a weakening. And besides, considering the number of bombers of both Luftflotten, the few British fighters [remaining] will be of no consequence!'

Both Sperrle and Kesselring were overruled and, the 'matter of orders and directives for the execution of the plan was taken up… The destruction in the air and on land was to be carried out in three stages. During the first five days in a semi-circle starting in the west and proceeding south then east, within a radius of 150 to 100 kilometres [93–62 miles] south of London; in the next three days within 50 to 100 kilometres [30–62 miles]; and during the last five days within the 50-kilometre [30-mile] circle around London.'[14] Between each of these three stages one day would be reserved to review the results of the preceding stage and plan the next stage of the assault, for 15 days total.

Four of the five Fliegerkorps composing the two Luftflotten would be dedicated to this daylight bombing campaign and its strategy of 'rolling back' enemy air defences. London, of course, would be the primary objective of the planned invasion, and so it was with the Luftwaffe. ObdL's 15-day *Adlerangriff* (Eagle

A German high-altitude reconnaissance image of Dover. (AHB)

Attack – Göring referred to 'his Luftwaffe' as 'my eagles') plan was designed to 'roll back' the RAF to the outskirts of London.

General der Flieger Robert Ritter von Greim's V. Fliegerkorps was initially directed to undertake a night-bombing campaign against Bomber Command airfields, aircraft and aeroengine manufacturing plants, depots and supply centres. Greim's efforts would be augmented by Generalmajor Joachim Coeler's 9. Fliegerdivision, flying night-bombing missions in addition to its usual coastal minelaying operations.

For daylight operations, by choosing such a geographically based roll-back strategy it is readily apparent that the Luftwaffe's leadership viewed their challenge from a ground-based, almost 'army', perspective. That was because, with the notable exception of Sperrle, almost all the men making up the service's executive leadership were, like Kesselring and IV. Fliegerkorps commander General der

Flieger Kurt Pflugbeil, transferred into the Luftwaffe from the army or, like I. Fliegerkorps commander Grauert, had served in the Reichswehr (in his case as an artillery officer) following World War I, or had not continued their military careers after the first war. Göring had been a World War I fighter ace who had spent the inter-war years as a Nazi politician, while the three other Fliegerkorps commanders had also been World War I aces, who had spent the inter-war years in other pursuits.[15]

One of the few early Spitfires made available for high-altitude reconnaissance. A series of experiments determined the most effective camouflage colour for these operations and this one, PR.Mk IB, was painted overall light blue. It was flown by the Photographic Development Unit at Heston, Middlesex. (Author Collection)

Experienced only at the tactical level and never trained or educated as military professionals at the operational or strategic levels of conflict, the Luftwaffe's leadership were almost without exception unequipped to address the problem from an airpower perspective.

The first stage of the roll-back strategy was intended to oust RAF Fighter Command from FOLs along the coast, as well as any other RAF, naval, or civilian airfields that might be useable as ad hoc fighter bases beyond 100km (62 miles) from London. The Luftflotte planners did not distinguish between fighter and other airfields because, from their own experience, they were well aware that a fighter squadron could operate from any suitable landing ground given appropriate support. Thus all of the airfields along the southern coast and in south-east England would have to be rendered inoperative, and these were prioritized on a geographical rather than command-association basis.[16]

OPERATIONAL OBJECTIVES OF OPERATION *EAGLE*

On 2 August 1940, 'Robinson' issued Göring's 'Preparations and Directives for Unternehmen Adler'.[17] Its stated objectives were:

- Neutralization of RAF Fighter Command forces through aerial combat and bombing airfields to attain air superiority over southern England
- Destruction of other RAF Bomber and Coastal Command units that could interfere with a cross-Channel operation
- If 'particularly favourable' naval targets presented themselves, the destruction of RN units in ports and at sea along the England southern coast, and
- Harassing (night) attacks against ports, communications, aircraft and aeroengine factories, RAF depots and bomber airfields.

To this directive was appended an expansive target list provided by Schmid's

A high-flying RAF PR Spitfire photographed these invasion barges in a Channel port. (Crown Copyright courtesy of the Medmenham Collection)

intelligence studies; it included RAF units and airfields of all kinds, and factories producing aircraft, components and armaments. For the third objective, the appendix included RN ships and installations, and for the fourth, a long list of ports and harbours that constituted blockade targets.

The next day another priority target was added by Generalmajor Martini. During the previous six weeks, his Funkhorchdienst had been monitoring the continuous electronic emissions emanating from the mysterious towers that dotted the English coastline. By listening to RAF voice radio frequencies, they had become aware that German aircraft were being detected at great distances and Fighter Command interceptors were being directed by radio from certain airfields using information derived from these coastline installations. Martini urged Jeschonnek to have the first attacks of *Adlerangriff* knock out the *Funkstationen mit Sonderanlagen* (radio stations with special installations).

On 3 August, the day after Göring's directive was distributed to the Luftflotte and Fliegerkorps HQs, Jeschonnek supplemented his boss's orders with 'tactical instructions' transmitted via telephone to the two Luftflotte HQs. In these, along

The Luftwaffe's Deployment for Operation *Adlerangriff*

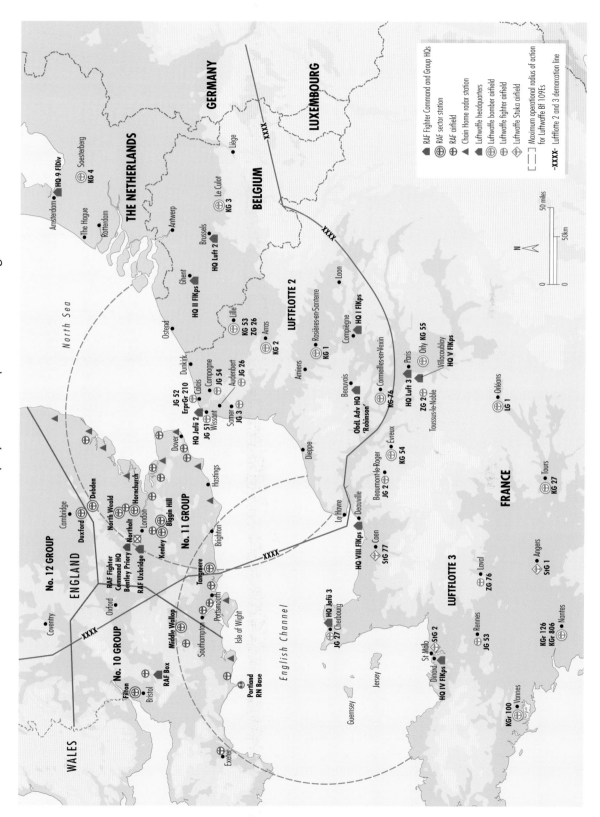

Legend:

- RAF Fighter Command and Group HQs
- RAF sector station
- RAF airfield
- Chain Home radar station
- Luftwaffe headquarters
- Luftwaffe bomber airfield
- Luftwaffe fighter airfield
- Luftwaffe Stuka airfield
- Maximum operational radius of action for Luftwaffe Bf 109Es
- -XXXX- Luftflotte 2 and 3 demarcation line

50 miles
50 km

GERMANY

LUXEMBOURG

THE NETHERLANDS

Soesterberg
KG 4
HQ 9 FlDiv
Amsterdam
The Hague
Rotterdam
Antwerp
Liège

BELGIUM

Le Culot
KG 3
Brussels
HQ Luft 2
Ghent
HQ II FlKps
Ostend

LUFTFLOTTE 2

Loon
Rosières-en-Santerre
KG 1
Compiègne
HQ I FlKps
Lille
KG 53
ZG 26
Arras
KG 2
Amiens
Beauvais
Corneilles-en-Vexin
KG 76
Dunkirk
Campagne
JG 54
Calais
JG 52
ErprGr 210
Audembert
JG 26
HQ Jafü 2
JG 51
Wissant
Somme
JG 3
Orly KG 55
HQ V FlKps
Villacoublay
Paris
HQ Luft 3
ZG 2
Toussus-le-Noble
Orléans
LG 1

North Sea

Dover
Hastings
Dieppe
Évreux
KG 54
Beaumont-le-Roger
JG 2

FRANCE

Tours
KG 27

No. 12 GROUP
ENGLAND

Cambridge
Duxford
Debden
North Weald
Hornchurch
Kenley
Biggin Hill
Northolt
London
RAF Fighter Command HQ
Bentley Priory
RAF Uxbridge

No. 11 GROUP

Brighton
Le Havre
Deauville
Caen
StG 77
HQ VIII FlKps

Oberd Adv HQ
'Robinson'

Coventry
Oxford
Middle Wallop

No. 10 GROUP

Southampton
Portsmouth
Isle of Wight
Tangmere

Laval
ZG 76

LUFTFLOTTE 3

WALES

Filton
Bristol
RAF Box

Portland
RN Base

Exeter

English Channel

Guernsey
Jersey

St Malo
StG 2
Dinard
HQ IV FlKps

Rennes
JG 53

Angers
StG 1

Nantes
KGr 126
KGr 806

Vannes
KGr 100

Cherbourg
JG 27
HQ Jafü 3

LUFTFLOTTE 3

Invasion barges at Dunkirk, imaged by an RAF Spitfire flying at high altitude. (Crown Copyright courtesy of the Medmenham Collection)

with admonishments to the JaFü commanders to have their fighters 'stick close to the bombers' and 'break off the engagements [with RAF fighters] soon enough to avoid running out of fuel', he instructed Sperrle and Kesselring's chiefs of staff to be sure to have 'special aircraft [Bf 109 and 110 fighter-bombers, and Ju 87 and 88 dive-bombers] of the first wave… attack the English radio stations'.[18]

Thus, the Luftwaffe would open *Adlerangriff* with a series of attacks that established the pattern of offensive air operations against viable IADS – first attempt to blind the enemy IADS by destroying its early-warning radar network.

It took five days of conferences with fighter and bomber Gruppenkommandeure (group commanders) and map exercises with pilots and aircrew to familiarize all involved with the plan of attack. Göring hosted a final Besprechung at Carinhall, on 6 August, to ensure all preparations were complete. The opening attack, called *Adlertag* (Eagle Day), was set for the morrow, but the weather turned bad over England for the following five days.[19]

At 1330hrs on 12 August, following initial attacks on four Chain Home radar sites that morning and at midday, an Enigma message informed Fliegerkorps, JaFü and Kampfgeschwader HQs (using city codenames) that *Adlertag* would be launched shortly. Intercepted by Y-Service and decrypted by GC&CS at Bletchley Park's Hut 6, then passed to AI1(e) by Hut 3, it read:

[Subject] ADLER
[To] FREIBURG, BRUSSELS, KARLSRUHE, HAMBURG, DARMSTADT, LEIPZIG
[Text] Final decision follows by telephone
(Signed) Luftflotte 2, Führungsabteilung 1A [Luftflotte 2 chief of staff]
[Message No.] Nr. 2180–40.
Geheim Kommandosache [Secret Command Matter]

Hut 3 advised, 'Source has no further information about the meaning of this document, but thinks it is an important operational matter, and conjectures that the [city] names may be code-names. The document bore no address, but there are indications that it may have been intended for Fliegerkorps 1 (and perhaps for 3 and 2 also).'

A second intercepted message passed by Hut 3 on the same day read: 'It is now confirmed by the same originator that operation ADLER is ordered for 13/8, and that places called FREIBURG, BRUSSELS, KARLSRUHE, HAMBURG, DARMSTADT and LEIPZIG are concerned in it.'[20]

It would soon become apparent to the code-breakers that 'ADLER' was in fact the codename that signalled the launch of *Adlertag* and the initiation of *Adlerangriff*, Göring's all-out attack on Fighter Command. There is no indication that Fighter Command ever received this notification.

SEELÖWE PLANNING CONTINUED

While Göring, ObdL staff, and Luftflotte 2 and 3 commanders and staffs were trying to determine the scope, aims and plans for an independent offensive counter-air campaign to destroy RAF Fighter Command, the OKH, OKM and OKW staffs continued the frustrating and contentious discussions of their mutually exclusive requirements, limiting factors and operations plans to actually invade Britain if Hitler so ordered.

Halder's concept of operations, as ordered in Keitel's OKW directive, was for the main assault to take place at three *Landungsräume* (landing zones, or LZs) from Folkestone to Beachy Head, with smaller forces coming ashore near Deal and Brighton to guard the flanks. A secondary landing in Lyme Bay was intended to draw off British forces responding to the main attack. If the British army's response was chiefly against the main assault, this was to become the primary thrust, taking London from the west. Raeder contended that, due to the Kriegsmarine's limited capabilities, the navy could provide landings on beaches only between North Foreland and Eastbourne.

Following nearly a fortnight of unproductive debates and arguments, and after meeting separately with the two service chiefs and their principal subordinates, Hitler finally decided between the two services' positions. In the resulting OKW directive (16 August), the secondary landing at Lyme Bay was cancelled, and the landing at Deal (Landungsraum A) was postponed until sufficient shipping returned to Channel ports after delivering the initial assault wave. This would consist of nine infantry divisions, aided by the Luftwaffe's 7. Fliegerdivision (paratroopers) landing north and north-west of Folkestone. To deliver them, the naval transport operation would run continuously for four days and nights.

These forces were expected to establish a beachhead 12–20 miles (20–30km) deep, capture Brighton and Dover, and hold against British counter-attacks for 7–10 days until the second wave – the so-called 'breakthrough force' of nine motorized and panzer divisions – could be loaded and landed.

In the final Transport Plan of 14 September, these forces were to be landed at four Landungsräume: B and C, west of Folkestone to Cliffs End, east of Hastings; D, from Bexhill (west of Hastings) to Eastbourne; and E, the left flank guard force landing east of Brighton. These were the beaches that the Jagdwaffe would have to protect from RAF bomber attacks and where Richthofen's VIII. Fliegerkorps Stukas and Loerzer's I. and II. Fliegerkorps Jabos and Dorniers would need to

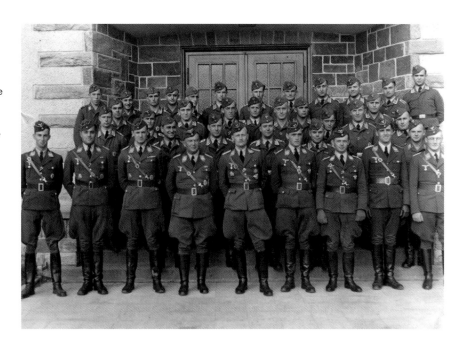

The flight crews of 3. (F)/123 and their Ju 88s were kept extremely busy throughout the summer of 1940. From left to right, the personnel are: (front row) Oblt Komter, Oblt Forster, Oblt Kirch, Hptm Manzerd, Hptm Liebe Piederid, Oblt Beisiegel, Oblt Heide, unknown, unknown; (second row) Oberfeldwebel (OFw) Schmitt, Feldwebel (Fw) Hopf, OFw Ziegenbalg, OFw Heisterberg, Fw Herbst, Fw Duckgeischel, Fw Riehle, Uffz Leisner; (third row) OFw Brehm, Lt Kobold, unknown, unknown, Fw Kunz; (back row) unknown, OFw Hering, OFw Tehfel, OFw Eigner, Fw Bemer and Lt Heuger. (AHB donated by Ken Wakefield)

provide close air support and battlefield interdiction. Sperrle's IV. and V. Fliegerkorps would interdict British Army lines of communications (routes for reinforcements and supplies) by bombing bridges, railways, and other transport targets north and west of London. [21]

Dornier Do 17Z

In 1932, the Heereswaffenamt (the Reichswehr's 'army weapons office'), which controlled development of all German commercial and secret military aircraft, issued a specification for a high-speed mailplane and six-passenger executive transport for Deutsche Luft Hansa (DLH), the German national airline, and a light freight transport for Deutsche Reichsbahn-Gesellschaft, the German national railway.

Design work began in August and on 23 March the following year, in one of his first official acts, Göring's deputy, Erhard Milch, the former director of DLH, authorized the construction of prototypes. Because of his World War I and previous DLH experience, Milch was well aware that the Dornier Do 17 mailplane had potential as a high-speed light bomber and, in the prototype contract, specified that 'even the civil version should be capable of rapid conversion to a military role'.

The aircraft was of all-metal, semi-monocoque, stressed-skin structure, with twin engines mounted on a broad, thick wing faired into a small-diameter, circular-cross-section fuselage mounting a 'twin tail'. The machine's slim fuselage earned it the nickname *Fliegender Bleistift* (flying pencil). As a bomber, the aircraft handled well at low level and was popular with its crews.

The first bomber version, the Do 17E, was powered by a pair of 750hp BMW VI inline engines, enabling it to haul a three-man crew and 500kg (1,100lb) bombload at 355kph (220mph), a speed comparable to that of contemporary British and French fighters. The ultimate version of the original design, designated Do 17Z, carried a crew of four in a redesigned forward fuselage and was powered by upgraded 1,000hp Bramo Fafnir 323P nine-cylinder air-cooled radial engines, enabling it to carry 2,205lb (1,000kg) of bombs.

Specializing in low-altitude level bombing for greater accuracy against smaller targets, the Do 17Z was primarily used for relatively short-ranged battlefield interdiction and airfield attacks. Like all Luftwaffe bombers of the period, its defensive armament was inadequate, consisting of four 7.92mm MG 15 machine guns, two firing forward, one from the cockpit and another from the glazed nose, and two more firing aft, one above and the other below the fuselage.

While accurate in its low-level attacks, especially with SC50 bombs, the Do 17Z's small bombload and slow speed relative to the Hurricane and Spitfire rendered it obsolete. By July 1940, Dornier-equipped units were undergoing re-equipment with the new Ju 88A, a process that might have happened sooner had the Junkers design not suffered engine overheating problems.

Do 17s. (Author Collection)

The initial assault wave would consist of 250 assault motorboats, 1,130 barges, 390 tugs and 165 small transports divided into four Transportflotten (transport fleets). From Rotterdam, Antwerp, Ostend, Dunkirk and Calais Transportflotten B and C would carry four divisions of Generaloberst Ernst Busch's 16. AOK[22] to assault the two beaches from Folkestone to Cliffs End. Transportflotte D would carry two divisions of Generaloberst Adolf Strauss's 9. AOK from Boulogne and Étaples to land from Bexhill to Eastbourne. The left flank guard, three more of Strauss's divisions[23], would be transported by Transportflotte E in two waves, one directly across the Channel from Le Havre and, later, the other from Boulogne.

The west flank of this gigantic cross-Channel movement was to be protected from RN surface attacks by ten destroyers, 24 torpedo boats (a legacy warship class

Aufklärungsräume der 2.(F)/123 – Einsatz England

This chart, belonging to 2.(F)/123 based at Cherbourg-West, shows its area of responsibility from 3 July to 3 August 1940. (AHB donated by Ken Wakefield)

similar in size and armament to RN sloops and US Navy destroyer-escorts) and 15 U-boats[24], under the Kriegsmarine's Flottenchef (CinC Fleet) Admiral Günther Lütjens. Crossing the eastern entrance to the Channel, Transportflotten B and C would be guarded by four S-boat flotillas (totalling 20 vessels) and six coastal U-boats[25], as well as, during daylight, being supported by Kesselring's Stukas and Jabos when maritime strike missions were needed.

To distract the overwhelmingly powerful RN Home Fleet from interfering, all of Raeder's three light cruisers would be escorting Unternehmen *Herbstreise* (Operation *Autumn Journey*), four empty ocean liners and 11 transport steamers heading across the North Sea towards the British coast between Newcastle and

Aberdeen, while the heavy cruiser *Admiral Hipper* attempted a breakout into the North Atlantic, passing between Iceland and the Faroes.[26]

The overnight voyage across the Channel required moonlight for navigation and formation station-keeping, and high tide had to occur just before dawn for the initial assault landings to beach as close as possible to British defensive positions, limiting exposure to enemy fire while advancing to assault those positions. These essential requirements created a full moon/high tide window of opportunity for *S-Tag* (*Sealion*

The RAF lacked a proper air-sea rescue service. Launches intended to ferry seaplane crews and equipment to and from their aircraft were pressed into service, in an attempt to plug a yawning gap in Britain's wartime provision. Otherwise, downed pilots relied on civilian lifeboats and other vessels for rescue, and many perished. (AHB)

Day – similar to the Allies' D-Day four years later) to be from 21 to 27 September, with departure from the ports beginning the evening prior. To start the lengthy and arduous process of loading the larger vessels with stores, horses and vehicles, the decision for *Seelöwe zu starten* (*Sealion* to launch) was needed ten days in advance or 'S-minus-10'. The OKW's 3 September directive established S-Tag as 21 September, which required Hitler's decision on 11 September.[27]

The Luftwaffe had five weeks (7 August to 11 September) to defeat Fighter Command and complete its preparations for supporting *Seelöwe*. It would be much more difficult than Göring ever imagined.

LUFTWAFFE AERIAL RECONNAISSANCE PROGRAMME – SPLIT PRIORITIES

During these five weeks, another of the Luftwaffe's responsibilities was to reconnoitre the landing beaches, defensive fighting positions, coastal fortifications, troop concentrations and lines of communication. But Jeschonnek's ObdL staff, the source of targeting information for the Luftflotte planners, also realized its knowledge of RAF installations in southern England was insufficient and ordered a systematic photo-reconnaissance effort beginning 27 June, to be conducted concurrently with the tactical reconnaissance for the army's landings.

The resulting problem was that the Luftwaffe's limited reconnoitring capabilities, 18 Aufklärungsstaffeln, including three ostensibly assigned to army HQs for tactical reconnaissance, were split between two 'number one' priorities. On the one hand, to permit Generalfeldmarschall Gerd von Rundstedt's Army Group A to prepare for its *Seelöwe* landings and initial combat on British soil, considerable effort had to be dedicated to photographing beach defences, inland defensive lines and potential British army movement and reinforcement routes – a primary task devolving from FD Nr. 16. On the other hand, both Luftflotten's planners needed current aerial photography of RAF ground installations to prioritize and plan the attacks that were intended to enable *Seelöwe* to succeed.

Accomplishing both these tasks might have been possible had it not been for the effectiveness of Fighter Command's IADS. Intercepted by radio-directed fighters vectored against radar-detected and Observer Corps-tracked reconnaissance overflights, during July and the first week of August, the Aufklärungsgruppen lost 27 poorly armed reconnaissance aircraft; the Kampfgeschwader units augmenting them lost another 23, sometimes even when escorted by as much as a Jagdgruppe of fighters.[28]

Y-Service was listening in during one of these tragic episodes…

In her autobiography *The Enemy is Listening: The Story of the Y Service*, Aileen Clayton, among the first six WAAFs recruited into the RAF Y-Service at Hawkinge, recalled the fate of one such regular reconnaissance flight early in her distinguished career:

> One of the aircraft engaged on 'The Milk Train' [RAF slang for the Luftwaffe's daily morning reconnaissance missions] had become quite a friend of ours, and we quite looked forward to him 'coming on the air' to give his reports. His callsign, I remember, was 'Amsel Eins'. He assumed that we were listening, and he would chatter away at us in English. 'I know, you English listening station, can you hear me?' he would cheerfully declare. 'Would you like me to drop a bomb on you? Listen – whee! – boomp!' and he would chuckle into his microphone.

Then one day, he was shot down by a flight of Spitfires:

> He was unable to get out and we listened to him as he screamed and screamed for his mother and cursed the Führer. I found myself praying, 'Get out, bale out. Oh, please dear God, get him out.' But it was no use, he could not make it. We heard him the whole way down until he fell below range. I went outside and was sick.[29]

The ability of hastily converted Rhine barges to take on the challenging sea conditions of the English Channel to enable the successful prosecution of Operation *Sealion* was, at best, questionable. (Bundesarchiv Bild 101II-MN-1369-10A)

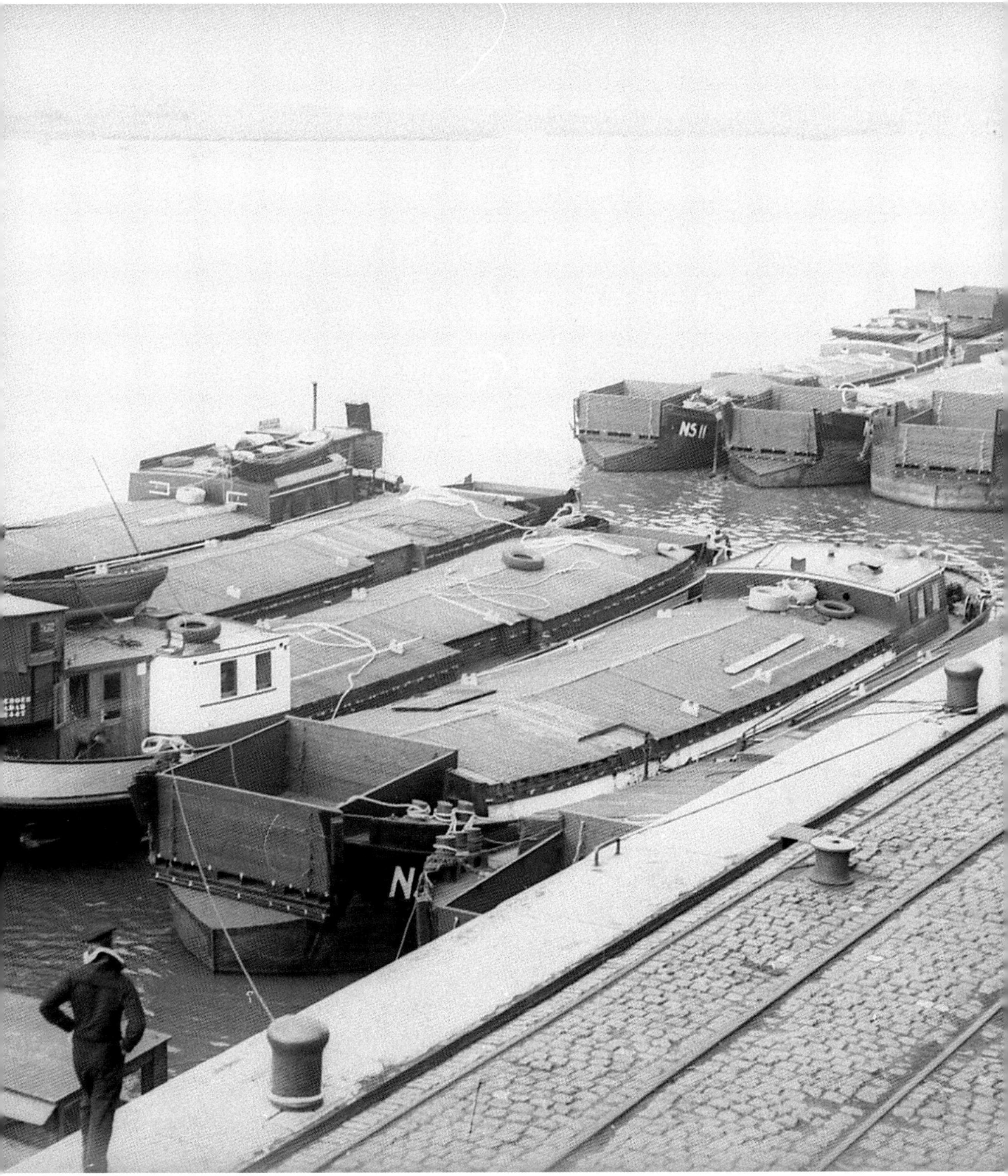
NS 11
N

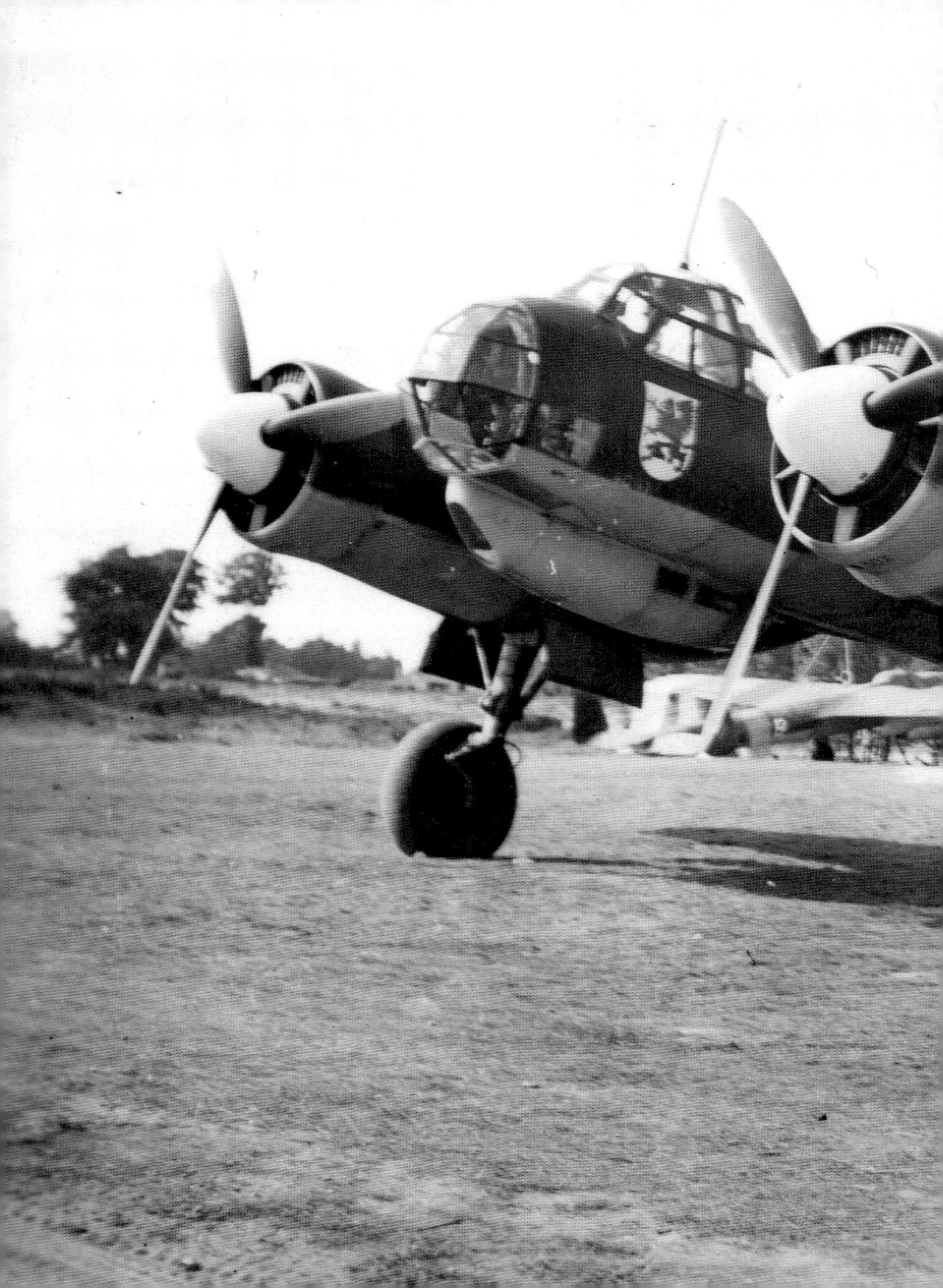

ADLERANGRIFF STAGE 1
12–16 August 1940

In order to establish the necessary conditions for the final conquest of England… I therefore order the Luftwaffe to overpower the English air force with all the forces at its command, in the shortest possible time.

Führer Directive Nr. 17, 'For the conduct of air and sea warfare against England', 1 August 1940[1]

FIRST STRIKES ON CHAIN HOME EARLY-WARNING RADARS – 12 AUGUST

The morning of 12 August broke clear, but hazy over the Dover Straits. As the sun climbed into the sky it began burning off the haze; by 0900hrs it was turning 'fine and sunny' over the English Channel coast.

More than an hour and a half earlier the Rye CH Station detected a raid of 'six plus' approaching from Cap Gris-Nez and Park scrambled a dozen Biggin Hill Spitfires from 610 Squadron. Led by eight-victory ace Sqn Ldr John Ellis, they took off from their FOL at Hawkinge at 0731hrs and climbed rapidly to 10,000ft to intercept.

The 'six-plus raid' proved to be nine Do 17Zs from Major Martin Gutzmann's I./KG 2 at 14,000ft and escorted by a dozen II./JG 52 Bf 109Es 2,000ft above, all headed for Lympne airfield, located near the coast just west of Folkestone. A former Fleet Air Arm (FAA) and RAF army co-operation base, Lympne was now used as an FOL for No. 11 Group's C Sector (Biggin Hill). The raid was intended to keep any Lympne-based interceptors, of which there was none at the time, from interfering with Kesselring's initial strikes farther west against No. 11 Group's two south-facing CH radar stations between Dungeness and Beachy Head.

As the interceptors climbed towards their targets, the 'Emils' dived on Ellis's Spitfires, shooting down two and tying the rest up, allowing Gutzmann's Dorniers to bomb Lympne unopposed at 0800hrs. The Dorniers rained 90 50kg (110lb) SC50 bombs upon the airfield, with two-thirds of the bombs falling on hangars and quarters.[2]

An hour later, Hptm Walter Rubensdörffer led 14 bomb-laden ErprGr 210 Bf 110s and eight Bf 109 Jabos westwards from Calais at 18,000ft in the first-ever attack on enemy air defences other than aircraft or their bases; it was the beginning of the modern suppression of enemy air defences (SEAD) mission. Taking off from Calais-Marck at 0815hrs, Rubensdörffer cleared Cap Gris-Nez headed almost due west towards Eastbourne, joined en route by his III./JG 54 Bf 109E escorts. The joint formation flew across the sea perpendicular to the radar broadcast swath from the Rye CH station and, due to the system's inherent lack of azimuth tracking capability, the confusing range information generated by the formation

PREVIOUS PAGES
Part of IV Fliegerkorps, I. and II./LG 1 were based at Orléans/Bricy and commanded by Hptm Kern and Major Debratz, respectively. This aircraft was from II./LG 1. (Chris Goss)

The preliminary assaults for *Adlertag* on 12 August began with a morning 'freie Jagd' sweep by Bf 109Es from II./JG 52 to clear the way for the day's first attack on Lympne. Number 610 Sqn was vectored to intercept and engaged 5. Staffel, shooting down three 'Emils'. Spitfires 'DW-H' and 'DW-K' were shot down; both pilots survived, one with severe burns. (Clive Ellis)

passing abeam the station caused the Fighter Command HQ Filter Room to label the contact as an 'X raid' (doubtful origin, possibly friendly aircraft). No interceptions were ordered. In any event, around the time the first bombs were falling on Pevensey CH station the only unit airborne, 501 Squadron from Gravesend, had completed its patrol over Hawkinge and begun landing there at 0935hrs.

Passing abeam Dover, Rubensdörffer peeled off Oblt Otto Hintze's 3. Staffel's eight Bf 109E-4/B Jabos, half of which were lugging 250kg (550lb) SC250s, to attack the Swingate CH radar site, but they failed to cause any damage. Once beyond Dungeness, Rubensdörffer split his Jabogruppe into two formations, Oblt Martin Lutz's 1. Staffel hitting the Pevensey radar site at 0932hrs with eight SC500 bombs, cutting the electricity supply and taking it offline for most of the day. Oblt Wilhelm Rössiger's 2. Staffel continued westbound and, at 0945hrs, dropped six SC500s on the CH station at Rye, none of which did significant damage.[3]

Three hours later, hoping to take advantage of the reduced early-warning coverage and following a 'freie Jagd' sweep feinting past Dungeness and Hastings, at 1235hrs two 'strike packages' and their covering fighters rendezvoused over Cap Gris-Nez and headed directly towards Manston, a D Sector FOL being used by Hornchurch's 65 Squadron. These formations were detected by the Swingate CH radar and Willoughby de Broke quickly scrambled Sqn Ldr H.C. Sawyer and his dozen Spitfires, as well as ordering airborne Sqn Ldr G.A.L. 'Minnie' Manton's 56 Squadron Hurricanes from Rochford, D Sector's other FOL, to patrol their airfield; he sent Ellis's 610 Squadron from Biggin Hill to patrol the line from Hawkinge to Canterbury at 20,000ft. None of these was launched in time.

Only 15 minutes later, Rubensdörffer's ErprGr 210, with 14 Bf 110s and seven Bf 109Es, made a stunning low-level surprise attack. The exposed airfield, perched atop the cliffs overlooking the sea, had almost no warning at all. Number 65 Squadron's Spitfires were 'all lined up,' according to Lutz in *Luftwaffe War Diaries*:

After it was badly damaged by fighters over Hastings on *Adlertag*, Uffz Leo Zaunbrecher crash-landed his 2./JG 52 Bf 109E-1, 'Red 14', in a wheat field near Lewes. He was captured, but two of his squadron mates were killed in the same action. (Clive Ellis)

OPPOSITE
This enlarged portion of a Luftwaffe high-altitude reconnaissance image shows Swingate radar station. Note the ground shadows of the four tall transmission antennas (left), and the smaller receiving antennas (right). The image has been annotated by photo interpreters: *Landungshindernisse* are landing obstacles preventing assault gliders from landing close to the facility. The umbrella-like annotations indicate the location of shelters. The triangles indicate the positions of pillboxes and the series of crosses, barbed-wire entanglements placed around them. (AHB)

'Our bombs fell right among them.' According to Manston's Operations Record Book (ORB): 'Two hangars were damaged and the [station's] maintenance workshops were destroyed.' The Jabos were followed immediately by 25 Dorniers (reportedly from KG 3) dropping 500 SC50s fairly accurately from 14,000ft; 'The aerodrome was pitted with approximately 100 craters [20 per cent hits] and rendered temporarily unserviceable.'

From the air it looked as if the airfield was a write-off, and *Luftwaffe War Diaries* notes Rubensdörffer reporting, 'Direct hits by 12 SC500 and four Flam C250 [250kg oil-filled incendiary bombs] on hangars and billets. Four SC500 among fighters taking off. Result: four Hurricanes [*sic*] and five other aircraft destroyed on ground.' Actually, one 600 Squadron Blenheim IF was destroyed and a 65 Squadron Spitfire damaged, but the airfield was left non-operational for 12 hours and 'Lumba Control' (Sector D Controller, at this time under the direction of Hornchurch Station Commander, Wg Cdr Cecil Bouchier) directed airborne fighters to land at airfields farther inland. The raiders and their escorts egressed back to France without loss.[4]

Having received Göring's 'Go' order to execute *Adlertag* on the morrow, that afternoon Loerzer's II. Fliegerkorps launched the day's major strike against No. 11 Group's coastal FOLs, with Fink's KG 2 and ErprGr 210 attacking two airfields and a fourth radar site near-simultaneously. The raiders and their escorting fighters, Major Martin Mettig's JG 54, showed up on radar as four formations totalling 150 aircraft forming up over Pas de Calais between 1645 and 1722hrs. 'Anxious to avoid a repetition of the attack on Manston earlier in the day,' says the *RAF Narrative*, 'as soon as the first of these forces were detected, the No. 11 Group Controller took immediate action to protect the airfields in the south-east.' Willoughby de Broke launched 32, 54, 56, 65, and 501 Sqns, totalling 53 interceptors.

Escorted by III./JG 54, the leading formation of approximately 24 II./KG 2

Do 17Zs, led by Fink's Stabskette (staff flight), flew north-north-west from Calais to cross the shoreline near North Foreland at 1733hrs and turned west to drop 24 tons of SC50s and three Flam C250s on Bekesbourne Aerodrome at Canterbury. This historic airfield had been activated as an RAF site in May 1940 for 2 and 13 Squadrons' Westland Lysanders returning from France. The Lysanders were withdrawn farther north on 8 June and the airfield was abandoned and obstructed by strakes to prevent its use as an LZ by Luftwaffe paratroopers, assault gliders and troop transports. Nevertheless, to Luftflotte 2 planners, it was a potential fighter FOL and had to be rendered unusable.

ABOVE
The four masts supporting the transmission array (left), and the four receiving antennas (centre), of the Swingate (Dover) Chain Home station, with its barrage balloon screen. (NARA)

Crossing the coast near Dover at 1730hrs, 14 III./KG 2 Dorniers attacked Hawkinge 10–15 minutes later, delivering 280 SC50s, followed by ErprGr 210 dropping 16 SC500s and eight Flam C250 incendiaries. The landing grounds were cratered by 28 bombs, one hangar was destroyed and another badly damaged, along with two Spitfires inside. The airfield's large maintenance workshops and

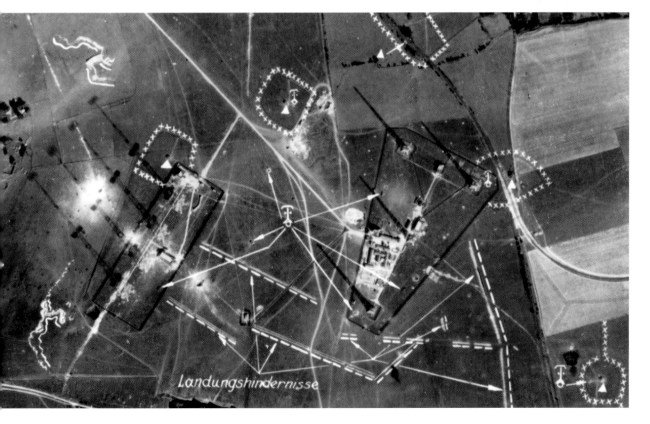

Landungshindernisse

equipment stores buildings, and all that was in them, were also destroyed. Five personnel were killed. Although enough clear space was available to land damaged fighters, as an operational base Hawkinge was not fully active again until 0900hrs the next morning.

Using the Bekesbourne and Hawkinge raids as cover, Rössiger's 2./ErprGr 210 attacked the north-east-facing Dunkirk CH radar station near Canterbury with five SC500s and a single Flam C250 incendiary, destroying two huts, but failed to disrupt the station's reporting. About the same time, at least three Jabos (possibly Rubensdörffer's Stabskette) attacked the Swingate radar site, dropping three SC250s that smashed huts inside the compound and slightly damaged the aerial masts, but failed to topple them.

At 1800hrs Lympne was hit again, 21 I./KG 2 Dorniers dropping 420 SC50s that ploughed up the airfield's landing grounds with around 200 hits, rendering it non-operational for the rest of the day, killing one serviceman and injuring two others. Using the Lympne raid as cover, in a follow-up attack on the Rye CH station, at 1750hrs, 14 bombers (reportedly Ju 88s of II./KG 76) delivered 28 SC250s, 20 of which were reported to have landed within the site. This time the attack destroyed all the huts except the transmitting (T), receiving (R), and watch office blocks. Although badly damaged, 'the essential equipment was working by the following day'.[5]

Despite the large numbers of interceptors engaging these raids and claims of two enemy shot down, the escorting 'Emils' intervened and effectively shielded their charges. KG 2 suffered no losses but near Margate and Manston, two escorting III./JG 54 Bf 109Es were lost. The interceptors lost two Hurricanes (from 32 and 56 Sqns) with one pilot badly burned.[6]

In the west, Sperrle's major strike drove deeper, using a heavy attack against Portland to mask a knockout blow to the Ventnor radar station. Initially steering almost directly for Brighton, Oberst Dr Johann-Volkmar Fisser initially led his 78 Ju 88s, from KG 51 and 54, northwards across the Channel; they were escorted by 120 ZG 2 and 76 Bf 110s and 24 II./JG 53 Bf 109Es. Outflanking the broadcast swath of the Ventnor station, once the huge formation approached the coast, it turned west, crossing in front of the Poling radar station and, having thrown off the initial interceptors' vectors with the feint towards Brighton, headed into the Solent Estuary. As it passed unseen behind Ventnor's coverage, Poling's lack of azimuth capability and the confusing approaching-then-receding range information baffled the 'track-tellers' resulting in heavy, unopposed attacks that devastated Portsmouth's city centre, railway station, fuel storage tanks, docks and naval base, killing 96 people.

Finally alerted by Observer Corps coastal posts on the Isle of Wight, Brand scrambled four squadrons and Park two more, totalling 48 Hurricanes from 43, 145, 213, and 257 Sqns, and a dozen Spitfires from 266 Sqn, while the Portsmouth AA batteries shot down two Junkers. The interceptors began arriving as the remaining 61 bombers started egressing the battered target.[7]

Fifteen of the Ju 88s – Fisser's Stabskette and II./KG 51 – had previously turned south from over the Solent and struck the Ventnor radar station from behind. The raid was witnessed by one of the station's personnel who published (anonymously) the following account in the *R.D.F. Bulletin*, a semi-official monthly newsletter produced by the RAF's No. 60 Group:

The attack, which occurred at noon on the 12th August was not unexpected [because] we had a warning from the [Fighter Command HQ] Filter Room that Dover, Rye and Pevensey had all been bombed that morning... After the main raid had passed overhead, the [civilian maintenance engineer] reported the first bombs falling on Portsmouth and, at about 1205, he heard an unfamiliar sound and without waiting to identify its source tactfully descended from the roof. As he reached ground level the sound identified itself as the roar of dive-bombers and as the whistle of bombs was by then mingled with it, he [ran to] the doorway of R[eceiver] block as the first bombs landed in the compound.

The first bomb to fall bounced the clock off the wall into the middle of the R-hut, the second caused large pieces of the roof to fall in and the fusillade thereafter caused the [plotting] table to run smartly about the room followed by those trying to shelter beneath it. Plotting from the R-hut had been abandoned [because the power supply] mains had failed completely, the receiver was off and the block in complete darkness. There was no point in further commentary from the R-hut as the inmates were simply waiting for the noise to finish and spent their time in silent prayer...

When the noise of the aircraft had died down, and this took some time because the Portsmouth raiders were coming back over the site, the various bodies [began] emerging from their holes. The three Bofors guns which had been furiously engaging the Huns were now silent and the only sound was a steady crackling and sizzling and this was found to be coming from the Army guard quarters, the N.A.A.F.I. and the Officers' Mess, all of which were ablaze. Two motor transports, a Dennis 3-tonner and a Fordson 15cwt were both standing upside down and burning, their wheels were spinning slowly with the tyres on fire giving a very beautiful but expensive Catherine Wheel effect. The staff carried out an inspection of the site and found the following: the wardens' quarters practically demolished with a large crater some ten feet in front of the building; the newly built W.A.A.F. rest room blown in two by the blast, all Army accommodation and the N.A.A.F.I completely burnt out, the water tower wrecked, and the T[ransmitter] block was straddled by delayed action [D-A] bombs.

At about 1500 the first of the D-A bombs exploded outside the compound; thence at roughly three hour intervals some twenty of them went off. At 1800 one, which was embedded in the blast wall of the T-block, exploded. It severed the main incoming cable, wrecked the substation end of the building, blew all the panels out of line and wrecked the [telephone] switchboard.[8]

Ventnor radar station was offline for three days. In the interim, an obsolete M.B.1 mobile radar set was erected on site, with the wire aerial array strung from the receiver towers and transmitter moved into the T-hut, 'and the channel was serviceable within the hour'. While this arrangement had no reception capability, it did fool Martini's Funkhorchdienst that the CH radar remained on the air.

Arriving too late to stop the bombers, the RAF interceptors initially engaged the Bf 110s circling high overhead the Solent, shooting down five, the 213 Squadron Hurricanes diving down to chase the fleeing bombers at low level, while two additional Spitfire squadrons, 152 and 609, arrived to join the pursuit, chasing the enemy well out to sea. They shot down eight bombers before two Gruppen of Bf 109Es from I. and III./JG 53 swept across the Channel to stop the massacre, shooting down two Hurricanes and a pair of Spitfires for one loss, that of III./JG 53 commander Hptm 'Harro' Harder.

In *Luftwaffe Fighters & Bombers: The Battle of Britain*, Chris Goss records how Fisser's pilot, Oblt Werner Luederitz, recalled the raid:

We rendezvoused over Le Havre at 5,000m [16,000ft] altitude and headed for England. After overflying the western half of the Isle of Wight, we turned and split up – Geschwader Kette and II. Gruppe towards Ventnor from the north, while I. and III. Gruppen turned towards Portsmouth. We came down at a 70-degree angle in a loose formation from 4,000m [13,000ft], released the bombs at 1,200m [4,000ft] and intended to climb from 800m [2,500ft] to transit level and fly home. However, the port engine quickly lost power and stopped – during our dive we had taken a lot of flak and shrapnel had hit the port engine and interrupted the fuel supply. We remained far behind the formation, which was climbing, and I took the necessary steps for asymmetric flight

The Ju 88 effectively merged the bombing payload of a twin-engined bomber with the accuracy of a dive-bomber. This aircraft is loaded with four SC250 bombs. (AHB)

One of the many hundreds of clandestine pre-war images taken by Luft Hansa aircraft as they conducted a systematic aerial survey of Britain during 'route proving flights'. This one, taken on 12 April 1939, five months before the outbreak of war, was subsequently incorporated into a target folder. (The National Archives)

(feathering the propeller, trimming and dumping all unnecessary fuel and equipment, except for parachutes and machine guns). We found ourselves alone over the Isle of Wight at about 1,000m flying south and still trying to gain height. There was no sign of our escort – they were in dogfights further north.

Shortly after crossing the coast, we were attacked by three Hurricanes [actually believed to be Spitfires from 152 Squadron], one after another from behind. We could see the bullets hitting our control surfaces – a few shots went through the cockpit without doing any great damage. However, our impaired flying performance was further affected by damage to the flying controls. The Hurricanes were, of course, much faster and on each attack let off a short burst. Our aircraft was fitted with side machine guns in the cockpit so that we were able to fire at the departing fighters, which exposed their undersides. I do not know if we had any success. As a result of evasive manoeuvres, we had lost height very quickly and were, after five or six attacks, about 50m above sea level and expected to ditch. However, as we had been told that coastal waters around the United

Kingdom had been mined in expectation of an invasion, we turned towards land. After further attacks while we were very low, I put the aircraft down wheels up. We crashed through hedges and the aircraft burst into flames.[9]

Fisser was killed in the crash, but Luederitz and two other crewmen, badly burned, survived to become POWs.

For the two Luftflotten, the day's efforts had been promising: 300 bomber and dive-bomber sorties knocked out three coastal airfields and one radar station, and had caused significant damage and civilian casualties to Portsmouth. In addition to the five Bf 110s and ten Ju 88As lost on the Portsmouth raid, the day's combats cost the Luftwaffe two more bombers (an He 111 from III./KG 55 and a Ju 88A from I./LG 1), one Jabo Bf 110 damaged beyond repair and nine Bf 109Es (plus a tenth returning damaged beyond repair).

ADLERTAG – 13 AUGUST

Scheduled to begin with the first formations of both Luftflotten simultaneously crossing the English coastline at 0630hrs, *Adlertag* dawned with a cold wet fog smothering most of Kesselring's airfields and a low, grey cloud deck stretching across the Channel to blanket southern England – the high-pressure zone that provided clear skies on the 12th had dissipated overnight. Göring postponed 'Zero-hour' until 1300hrs. However, the first formations, including Fink's KG 2, launching from near Arras and Cambrai between 0450 and 0510hrs, were already airborne when the order was sent and, as invariably happens to some participants in a large, complex military operation, they did not get the word.

Specifically, Gutzmann's I./KG 2, planning to attack the Sheerness naval base, received the recall order and returned to Épinoy. However, Fink's Stabskette, leading the combined II. and III. Gruppen to bomb Eastchurch airfield, near

Ju 88A-1 '9K+EL' of 3./KG 51 was one of ten Ju 88s from KG 51 that were shot down during a raid on Portsmouth and the Ventnor radar station on 12 August. Of its four crew, only Gefr Fleischmann managed to bale out. (Clive Ellis)

Sheerness, had already reeled in their long wire HF antenna and failed to get the message. Joining Fink's 55 Do 17Zs over Pas de Calais was a formation of ZG 26 Zerstörers, KG 2's assigned escorts. But instead of taking station on the bombers' flanks, the Bf 110s began flying across their noses, diving in front of them, then zooming up to repeat the manoeuvre. In *Luftwaffe War Diaries*, Berenbrok notes that thinking the escorting fighter pilots were 'just showing off', Fink continued doggedly, not realizing that these 'odd antics' were meant to signal him that the mission had been scrubbed for the morning.

As amusing as this comic pantomime may seem, it aptly demonstrates the inability of the Luftwaffe to properly co-ordinate in the air between bomber units, which used HF W/T, and their escorting fighters, which were on HF R/T.

Consequently, when the Bf 110s turned back to their base, the Dorniers continued towards the target alone. Descending beneath the cloud deck and most of the radar coverage, the Luftwaffe's low-flying experts were spotted as they crossed the coast, but their low altitude and the adverse weather foiled effective Observer Corps tracking. Alerted late, Willoughby de Broke scrambled five squadrons, which climbed above the clouds. Only 74 Squadron successfully intercepted, engaging the last of the attackers as they emerged from cloud to begin their bombing runs. Some 53 Dorniers struck the target in two large waves.

Dropping 480 SC50 bombs, three Flam C250s and three D-A SC250s from only 1,500ft altitude, the surprise attack wrecked the barracks, killing 16 and injuring 48, damaged every hangar and destroyed all 266 Squadron's ammunition, and a Spitfire, as well as five 53 Sqn, Coastal Command Blenheim IV patrol bombers deployed from Detling. It is worth noting that KG 2's attack on Eastchurch and I. Gruppe's planned strike on the nearby Sheerness naval base were planned in preparation for Operation *Seelöwe*, rather than against Fighter Command. Eastchurch was home to No. 22 Group, a Coastal Command anti-shipping strike force positioned to oppose the anticipated invasion. Number 266 Sqn, deployed from Tangmere, was also in residence to provide fighter escort.[10]

During the bombers' egress, the pursuing Spitfires of 74 Sqn and Hurricanes of 111 and 151 Sqns shot down five Dorniers.[11]

There is no indication in surviving Luftwaffe records that Sperrle's Luftflotte 3 received Göring's postponement order. If it did, the order was ignored. Taking off from Évreux between 0500 and 0520hrs, 20 I./KG 54 Ju 88As were followed 5 to 15 minutes later by another 18, from II./KG 54 out of St André-de-l'Eure, the two formations joining up before heading north, intending to bomb the airfield at Farnborough and Odiham army co-operation airfield. As they winged past Cherbourg, they were joined by their escorts and passed 87 bomb-laden StG 77 Stukas struggling for altitude as they headed for Portland naval base. Ahead of the two large, broadly spread formations flew a phalanx of 173 Bf 109Es from JGs 2, 27 and 53, with 60 ZG 2 and V.(Z)/LG 1 Bf 110s taking station with the bomber formations as high cover and close escorts.

The alert was raised by Y-Service radio intercepts and the new, smaller (two-

Portsmouth in the grip of a bombing raid. (Jean-Louis Roba)

mast) CH station at Worth Matravers. Although it had a reduced detection range compared to the standard AMES 1 radar, it gave Brand sufficient warning to scramble 238 Sqn from Middle Wallop and 152 Sqn from Warmwell, augmented by Willoughby de Broke's timely launching of 43 and 601 Sqns from Tangmere. As the dive-bombers approached the coast, Major Clemens Graf von Schönborn found the clouds closing up beneath them, completely blanketing Portland, so he turned his Stukas for home before the interceptors arrived.

The Ju 88As continued northwards, Obstlt Otto Höhne hoping for breaks in the undercast, but he too had to abort, although not before the defenders arrived. Number 238 Squadron engaged a formation of 28 escorting Bf 110s from I./ZG 2, which immediately went into the type's typical Abwehrkreis (defensive circle) and successfully fended off their attackers before returning to base with two aircraft damaged and three aircrew wounded. Numbers 43 and 601 Squadrons' Hurricanes intercepted the KG 54 formation over the coast at 0630hrs, shooting down four Ju 88As in rapid succession. Sweeping ahead of the KG 54 formation, I./JG 2 was also engaged by 43 Squadron, losing one Bf 109E that crash-landed near Shoreham airfield and another that crash-landed on the French coast.[12]

As the frustrated survivors of Sperrle's abortive first effort licked their wounds back at base, Luftflotte 3's afternoon strikes began taking off, hoping that the weather over southern England had broken up enough for them to hit their targets. From Orléans-Bricy and Châteaudun, south of Paris, Oberst Alfred Bülowius led

58 Ju 88As, comprising all three LG 1 Kampfgruppen, northwards to bomb the airfields at Boscombe Down, Worthy Down and Andover.[13] Staging through FOLs on the Cotentin Peninsula, south of Cherbourg, 52 Stukas from StG 1 and StG 2 took off to attack Warmwell and Yeovil.

As a diversion, at midday Liensberger led 23 V.(Z)/LG 1 Bf 110s to a point overhead Portland where they were to draw No. 10 Group's interceptors to the south-west before the two formations of attackers crossed the coast. By that time, Berenbrok records, it was hoped, 'these squadrons would have reached the end of their fuel, and would be helpless. Then, after they had landed to re-arm and re-fuel, was just the right moment to bomb them and their bases.'

The plan, on the one hand, worked too well. Intercepted by 152, 213, and 601 Sqns, Liensberger lost five Zerstörers with two more crash-landing in France damaged beyond repair.[14] One Hurricane was shot down and two more damaged before the RAF squadrons recovered to Exeter, Tangmere and Warmwell. On the other hand, the plan failed completely because none of these bases was targeted in the follow-on attack.

The raid, coming three hours later, was another weather-plagued fiasco. Alerted by four radar plots approaching from Jersey, Brand launched five squadrons, and 'Starlight Control' (Middle Wallop Sector Controller, Station Commander Wg Cdr David Roberts) positioned them over Weymouth (609 Sqn from Warmwell), the Isle of Wight (601 Sqn from Tangmere) and the coast in between (152, 213 and 238

Airborne early on the morning of *Adlertag* from Beaumont-le-Roger, Oblt Paul Temme, Gruppe Adjutant of I./JG 2, was part of a fighter sweep providing cover for a scheduled raid by KG 54 on Odiham and Farnborough. The raid was cancelled on account of the weather. Temme's Bf 109E-1 was nonetheless engaged and shot down by a Hurricane flown by Sgt J.P. Mills of 43 Squadron. It crash-landed at 0710hrs in a wheat field just south of Shoreham airfield and Temme was taken prisoner. Note the camouflaged hangars and control tower in the background. (Clive Ellis)

During the late afternoon of 14 August, three small formations of He 111s from III./KG 27 penetrated 10 Group's fighter screen undetected and attacked fighter maintenance units at Colerne in North Wiltshire and Sealand in Cheshire, where they inflicted minor damage. This image, showing AA fire in the area between Bristol and Cardiff, was taken by Oblt Walter Schalles during the raid. (AHB donated by Ken Wakefield)

Sqns). These last were engaged by the pre-strike fighter sweep and Stuka escorts (I. and II./JG 53 and ZG 76), leaving 609 Squadron Spitfires to pounce upon II./StG 2's Stuka formation, which very quickly lost six aircraft shot down with nine aircrew killed, one captured and two rescued by S-boat. Both Stuka targets were obscured by cloud cover at 3,000ft, causing the survivors to turn back and bomb Portland – now in the clear – instead.

Hauptmann Wilhelm Kern, flying with I./LG 1, was so discouraged by the expansive undercast, he diverted to bomb Southampton. The sudden late change in direction foiled Brand's interceptors resulting in heavy damage and high civilian casualties in the city's port and residential areas. The II./LG 1 attack on Royal Naval Air Station (RNAS) Worthy Down was abandoned, but a dozen III./LG 1 Junkers found Andover, claiming hits 'on groups of tents and sheds along the [airfield] edge', according to the daily ObdL situation report. A dozen bombs fell within the airfield boundary, demolishing the station HQ and officer's quarters, damaging one aircraft and killing two personnel. Penetrating deepest into No. 10 Group's airspace, this formation suffered the worst, losing two Ju 88As to 43 and 257 Squadrons.[15]

In the east, half of Kesselring's afternoon Stuka strikes suffered the same frustrating experience. Hauptmann Anton Keil, leading I. and II./StG 1, could not find Rochester airfield due to cloud cover and the 46 Ju 87s dumped their bombs ineffectively upon Ashford, Canterbury, Ramsgate and Lympne instead.

But at 1716hrs Hptm Bernd von Brauchitsch's 40 IV.(St)/LG 1 Stukas struck Detling in a devastating attack, hitting three mess halls and killing 67 persons, including the station commander, destroying the operations block, cratering the tarmac taxiways and hardstands, and destroying 22 Coastal Command aircraft. Despite the shock and extensive damage, Detling was fully operational again by noon the next day. The Stukas suffered no loss because a well-timed 'freie Jagd' sweep by I. and III./ZG 26 effectively tied up 56 Squadron at the cost of four Zerstörers for four Hurricanes shot down, before JG 26's 'Emils' arrived to extricate them.[16]

Overall, on *Adlertag* the Luftwaffe had launched 1,484 sorties, the vast majority being ineffective due to weather. But it accomplished very little for its high losses, suffering 42 aircraft lost with 89 pilots and aircrew killed or captured, for seven per cent of the striking force. Of the 13 airfields targeted on 12–13 August, the Luftflotte intelligence officers erroneously reported attacking nine, Berenbrok's *Luftwaffe War Diaries* recording, 'five of them to such good purpose that they can be considered to have been put out of action.' In addition to the three coastal FOLs, Eastchurch and Detling were indeed badly hit, so much so that Park was forced to withdraw 32 Squadron to Biggin Hill and 266 Squadron to Hornchurch. While 24 RAF aircraft were destroyed in the two days of airfield attacks, only one was a day fighter, to which can be added 13 lost in aerial combat, with three pilots killed and two more severely burned.[17]

Following *Adlertag's* disappointing debut, the next day's persistent cloudy skies continued to throttle Luftwaffe operations, with only 91 bomber and 398 fighter sorties flown. Kesselring's main effort involved 80 Stukas from II./StG 1 and IV.(St)/ LG 1, escorted by Major Gotthard Handrick's JG 26. The cloud cover foiled the planned airfield attacks, but Willoughby de Broke's response – 32, 65, 610 and 615 Sqns, launching 42 interceptors – resulted in a huge whirling dogfight overhead Dover.

With this distraction, at 1300hrs ErprGr 210 came out of the clouds to successfully strike Manston once again, 22 Bf 110s and six Bf 109E Jabos destroying two hangars and three 600 Sqn Blenheim IFs, damaging two other hangars and causing 16 casualties. The airfield was non-operational for the next 48 hours. Two 2. Staffel Jabos were shot down by ground fire and crashed on the airfield; only one crewman survived.

Later in the day Luftflotte 2 bombers attacked eight airfields in small raids that did little damage. Similarly, Luftflotte 3 mounted nine small raids that approached England's south-west coast simultaneously, line abreast, in a 100-mile-wide (160km) front, dispersing Brand's interceptors and limiting their effectiveness. Oberst Alois Stoeckl's KG 55 Stabskette bombed 609 Squadron's hangars and offices at Middle Wallop, causing considerable damage and destroying three Blenheim IFs and 'several Spitfires', according to the station ORB, but two of the scrambling Spitfires shot down the Geschwaderkommodore's aircraft, killing him and the chief of staff of Luftgau VIII (the administrative and logistics district HQ attached to V. Fliegerkorps), Oberst Walter Frank. Other small formations bombed Sealand airfield and the new station at Colerne, both home to Hurricane maintenance units, but negligible damage was done.[18]

In the first three days of *Adlerangriff* Fighter Command lost 36 Spitfires and Hurricanes in aerial combat while the Jagdwaffe lost 26 'Emils'. Two of Park's squadrons were virtually spent as combat-capable units. After losing four Spitfires and two pilots during *Kanalkampf*, in three days of combat 74 Squadron had lost another four fighters and two more pilots. It was withdrawn north to Wittering (No. 12 Group) to regroup, being replaced at Hornchurch by 266 Squadron (withdrawn from Eastchurch).

Number 145 Squadron had suffered even worse. Between 8 and 12 August, the unit had lost ten Hurricanes with nine pilots missing in action and one killed. Thoroughly decimated and demoralized, the unit was withdrawn to Drem (No. 13 Group) to completely rebuild, being replaced at Westhampnett by 602 Squadron (from Drem).[19]

According to one survivor, Plt Off James E. Storrar, the extreme losses were because Fighter Command still had not adapted its peacetime 'air display' formations and completely inappropriate anti-bomber attack tactics to the dynamic and dangerous environment of modern air-to-air combat. In Franks' *Air Battle Dunkirk*, Storrar shared: 'At that stage we were [still flying] in Vics, and if anyone yelled, "109s!" there were 12 Hurricanes travelling in opposite directions as fast as possible or looking around rapidly. We kept by the book in Vics, right through the Battle of Britain and in August, 145 Squadron was virtually destroyed and had to be reformed at Drem.'[20]

A KG 26 crew relax by their aircraft. Primarily a maritime strike unit, KG 26 was a component of Luftflotte 5, based at Stavanger, Norway. It was called into battle on 15 August, when the Luftwaffe completed its largest number of sorties of the entire campaign. Tasked to strike Bomber Command airfields in the north of England, the unit lost two of its number to AA and six to RAF fighters. (AHB donated by J. F. Rowling)

THE BIGGEST DAY – 15 AUGUST

The bad weather that precluded most missions over England on 14 August was forecast to remain the following day, so Göring convened another Besprechung at Carinhall to carry out a post-mortem on the disappointments of *Adlertag*. Despite the departures of Kesselring, Sperrle and their Fliegerkorps commanders, plans were in place to renew bombing operations following the *Adlertag* pattern, but this time they would include Generaloberst Hans-Jürgen Stumpff's Scandinavia-based Luftflotte 5. After three days of combat over the south of England, Waldau and his ObdL Operations Staff expected Dowding to reinforce Park and Brand's commands with units from the northern groups, leaving the Midlands open to unopposed attacks. There is no evidence that Luftwaffe Intelligence had any indication that this anticipated move had been accomplished, basing Luftflotte 5's missions solely on supposition.

Generaloberst Hans-Jürgen Stumpff

Generaloberst Hans-Jürgen Stumpff. (Author Collection)

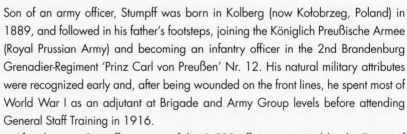

Son of an army officer, Stumpff was born in Kolberg (now Kołobrzeg, Poland) in 1889, and followed in his father's footsteps, joining the Königlich Preußische Armee (Royal Prussian Army) and becoming an infantry officer in the 2nd Brandenburg Grenadier-Regiment 'Prinz Carl von Preußen' Nr. 12. His natural military attributes were recognized early and, after being wounded on the front lines, he spent most of World War I as an adjutant at Brigade and Army Group levels before attending General Staff Training in 1916.

After the war, Stumpff was one of the 1,500 officers permitted by the Treaty of Versailles to become members of the Weimar Republic's Reichswehr, where he held a series of adjutant positions before, in 1929, being assigned to the Heerespersonalamt (Army Personnel Office). There he became more involved in personnel issues associated with building the expanding Reichsluftwaffe, his decisions determining who would have the critical positions when the Luftwaffe emerged from its secret beginnings. His success resulted in his own transfer, in September 1933, to the air arm as the RLM's Chief of Personnel.

His skills at personnel management resulted in promotion to Generalmajor in April 1936 and, 14 months later, his appointment to replace Kesselring as Göring's ObdL chief of staff. In April 1936 he was promoted to Generalleutnant, promotion to General der Flieger following in November 1938. However, he was unable to tolerate or accommodate the ambitious and arrogant Staatssekretär der Luftfahrt (State Secretary for Aviation, Göring's deputy for running the RLM) Erhard Milch's intrusive involvement in Luftwaffe affairs, and sought reassignment. On 1 February 1939, he was appointed Inspekteur der Flakartillerie (Inspector of Flak Artillery) and replaced as ObdL chief of staff by Jeschonnek, which ostensibly made Stumpff the Luftwaffe's Chief of Air Defences.

In January 1940 he was named commander of Luftflotte 1, facing the Russians from Berlin while the rest of the Luftwaffe prepared for *Westfeldzug*, when Kesselring was sent to replace Felmy as the commander of Luftflotte 2. The day *Fall Gelb* began, after the civilian technocrat Milch persuaded Göring to allow him command of Luftflotte 5 for 28 days, Stumpff was appointed to lead the new command and successfully concluded the Norwegian Campaign that June.

It was from the northern flank of Nazi-occupied Europe that Generaloberst (he was promoted on 1 July 1940) Stumpff's Luftflotte 5, which was primarily an anti-shipping command to deter the Royal Navy's Home Fleet from operating in the North Sea, conducted desultory night-bombing against targets in Scotland and northern England before the Battle of Britain began.

While Göring was berating his commanders for their units' poor performance in the *Adlertag* operations, surprisingly, the weather began clearing rapidly and, in the absence of his commander, II. Fliegerkorps chief of staff Oberst Paul Deichmann ordered the planned attacks to be launched. As well as conform to the planned concept of operations of starting with small raids to get the defender's fighters airborne, II. Fliegerkorps' first wave, repeating attacks on Hawkinge and Lympne, was intended to draw Fighter Command's attention away from Luftflotte 5's more northerly operations, so Stumpff's KG 26 He 111s and KG 30 Ju 88s were ordered off as well.[21]

Half an hour after the departure of 17 Küstenfliegergruppe 506 He 115 floatplanes flying a feint towards Dundee, the Aalborg- and Stavanger-based bombers took off around 1030hrs for their 450-mile (650km), two-and-a-half-hour flight to bomb RAF bomber bases at Linton-on-Ouse, Dishforth and Driffield, home of No. 4 Group's six squadrons of Armstrong Whitworth Whitley twin-engined medium bombers. Once Stumpff's bombers were airborne, from airfields around Pas de Calais Loerzer's two Stukagruppen launched and formed a wide line-abreast formation, with their escorting Jagdgeschwader (JG 51) sweeping ahead and flying top cover.

When the large, wide, ill-defined radar echo was received by the Rye and Swingate CH stations at 1100hrs, 'Tophat Control' (Biggin Hill Sector Controller, who at that time was Station Commander Gp Capt Richard Grice) established a two-squadron patrol (54 and 501 Sqns) inland from the coast, on the line between Ashford and Dover, with three other squadrons patrolling a line farther inland, while Grice waited for the broad radar return to resolve into individual raids. This indecision resulted in the 16 Stukas of IV.(St)/LG 1 arriving overhead Hawkinge unmolested; they tipped over into their dives as the first British interceptors arrived. Two Ju 87s were shot down during egress but intervening Bf 109s prevented further losses, shooting down two 501 Sqn Hurricanes. The bombs demolished one hangar and the end of a barrack block, and severed power cables to the Rye and Swingate CH radars, knocking them off-line for the rest of the day. Similarly, attacks on Lympne were executed without interference. Some 26 II./StG 1 Ju 87s pounded the airfield, its devastation preventing operations for the next two days.[22]

Flying in from the north-east, Luftflotte 5's simultaneous two-pronged attacks were intended to neutralize Bomber Command's capability to interfere with the anticipated cross-Channel invasion of England by hitting all three of No. 4 Group's Whitley bases. However, the hoped-for movement of RAF fighter units to the south, or even the distraction of II. Fliegerkorps' Stuka raids on the coastal airfields, had not happened and Stumpff's two bomber formations were savaged by Saul's and Leigh-Mallory's interceptors.

From Stavanger came 63 He 111s from I. and III./KG 26, escorted by 21 I./ZG 76 Bf 110D-1/R1s, which approached the Northumberland coast at noon. The escorts, flying a parallel course up-sun from the two Kampfgruppen, were operating beyond their normal range, facilitated by carrying non-jettisonable plywood-encased ventral fuel tanks. Called *Dackelbäuche* (Dachshund bellies), these ungainly 1,050-litre (231-Imp gal) tanks extended the type's operating radius beyond 800 miles (1,300km), but at the expense of leaving the rear gunner behind on account of the extra weight and making the already poorly manoeuvring Zerstörer much more of a target than a fighter.

Anstruther CH radar detected the raid at 1205hrs, quickly passing the alert to

A Bf 110D with the *Dackelbauch* non-jettisonable external fuel tank fitted to the underside of the forward fuselage. (Author Collection)

Kampfgeschwader 30 originally included an organic Zerstörerstaffel (Z./KG 30) equipped with Ju 88Cs. Increasing RAF Bomber Command raids on the Ruhr prompted the organization of the Luftwaffe's first Nachtjagdgeschwader (NJG 1) in June, however, and Z./KG 30's aircrew were transferred back to Germany. The unit's 13 Ju 88Cs were distributed among the KG 30 squadrons. On 15 August, seven of these, along with two Ju 88A bombers, were lost to 73 Sqn Hurricanes. (AHB)

No. 13 Group HQ at Blakelaw. Air Vice-Marshal Saul's Senior Fighter Controller aggressively launched all available fighters to meet the incoming bombers. Intercepted over the sea by 11 72 Sqn Spitfires, the escorts immediately entered their usual Abwehrkreis but quickly lost seven shot down, including the Gruppenkommandeur, Hptm Werner Restemeyer. Immediately afterwards, 18 Hurricanes from 79 and 605 Sqns attacked the Heinkels, scattering them. Some bombed their secondary targets, Newcastle-upon-Tyne and Sunderland, at 1300–1305hrs, and 13 No. 41 Sqn Spitfires intercepted them during egress. In all, Obstlt Karl Freiherr von Wechmar's KG 26 lost eight He 111s; a 605 Sqn Hurricane was so badly damaged by return fire it crash-landed. No damage was done to the intended targets, Linton-on-Ouse and Dishforth.

Air Vice-Marshal Richard Saul

Born in April 1891 in Dublin, Ireland, Richard Ernest Saul joined the Royal Army Service Corps as a second lieutenant in November 1914. Promoted to captain in August 1915, he transferred to the embryonic RFC, becoming an observer with 16 Squadron, locating artillery targets and taking aerial photographs from Royal Aircraft Factory B.E.2 and B.E.8 biplanes. By August 1916, Saul had decided to train as a pilot and by the end of 1917, as a major, he was commanding No. 4 Squadron, RFC, flying R.E.8s on strafing missions over the Western Front.

Awarded the Distinguished Flying Cross for his wartime exploits, Saul was granted a permanent commission in the RAF and appointed Officer Commanding (OC) 12 Squadron, flying Bristol F.2Bs in Germany as part of the short-lived forces of occupation. In the 1920s he held a number of posts, including Staff Officer at HQ Iraq Command; OC, 2 Squadron at Manston; and Commandant at the School of Army Co-operation. In 1933 he attended a flying boat course at RAF Calshot before being appointed as OC 203 Squadron, flying the Short Rangoon from Basra.

In 1938, Saul was named the Senior Air Staff Officer (SASO) of Bomber Command's No. 2 Group. Promoted to the rank of air vice-marshal in July 1939, he was appointed OC No. 13 (Fighter) Group where he played an important role in organizing Fighter Command into an effective fighting force. The group was responsible for the aircraft and sector stations defending the north of England, Northern Ireland and Scotland, including the Home Fleet's strategically important naval base at Scapa Flow in the Orkneys.

Number 13 Group also provided an essential recovery and recuperation facility for exhausted pilots from the south and Saul took pride in the quality of pilots he transferred back to the squadrons defending London and the South East. At the height of the conflict, during the first few days of September 1940, Air Vice-Marshal Keith Park of No. 11 (Fighter) Group, compared the pilots transferred by Richard Saul with those supplied by Leigh-Mallory's No. 12 (Fighter) Group. Saul's transferees had brought down 43 enemy aircraft for the loss of just two pilots. In contrast, Leigh-Mallory's pilots had claimed only 17 kills and lost 13 of their own.

AVM Richard Saul. (AHB)

As the bombs were falling upon Newcastle and Sunderland, No. 12 Group's Staxton Wold CH radar reported a second raid inbound, apparently aimed at Church Fenton. This formation consisted of 27 Ju 88A bombers and 13 Ju 88C Zerstörers formerly belonging to Z/KG 30, a dedicated 'heavy-fighter' squadron organic to the 'Adler Kampfgeschwader' (Eagle Bomber Wing).

Leigh-Mallory's Senior Fighter Controller had a much more tentative response to the incoming raid, establishing a 'base combat air patrol' over Church Fenton, ordering 264 Sqn Defiants to cover a 28-ship convoy steaming out of Hull, and sending 18 fighters from 73 and 616 Sqns to intercept the incoming bombers. As a result, Obstlt Walter Loebel's Ju 88As were able to pound Driffield, wrecking

ABOVE LEFT
The 15 August attack on Driffield by 30 Ju 88s from KG 30 supported the planned German invasion, as part of an effort to destroy as many bombers as possible. Ten Whitleys were destroyed and six damaged in the day's largest single blow against the RAF. (Clive Ellis)

ABOVE
Driffield. (Clive Ellis)

LEFT
Driffield. (Clive Ellis)

four hangars, destroying ten Whitleys and badly damaging six more (from 77 and 102 Sqns). Two I./KG 30 bombers were lost in the attack, but five Zerstörers were shot down and two more so badly damaged they crashed/crash-landed during their return flight.[23]

Out of three targets only one had been effectively bombed, but at enormous cost: almost 20 per cent of the attacking force. This resounding defeat deterred Luftflotte 5 from participating in any further daylight bombing missions in the campaign. It also proved beyond doubt that the Luftwaffe's bombers had to be escorted by Bf 109Es if they were to survive.

Meanwhile, back along the Channel coast, Luftflotte 2's main effort for the day was a massive strike by 88 Do 17Zs, every serviceable KG 3 'Blitz Kampfgeschwader' (Lightning Bomber Wing) aircraft, which took off from their Belgian airfields at 1350–1406hrs. As they passed over Pas de Calais, they were detected as a large, broad radar return by the south-east coast CH stations, but as the escorting 130 Bf 109s from JGs 51, 52, and 54 climbed into the electronic swath in front of the bombers, their larger, broader formation effectively screened the Dorniers, leading to a confused radar picture in the Bentley Priory Filter Room. While the escorts climbed slowly through the bombers' altitudes to take station as high cover, 60 JG 26 Bf 109s approached the coast at lower level and high speed, making landfall either side of Dover on a large 'freie Jagd' sweep, while ErprGr 210 used the massive formation to mask its own mission to attack Martlesham Heath airfield, near Ipswich, on the Suffolk coast.

Three airborne patrols, of 24 Hurricanes and 12 Spitfires, were vectored against the approaching phalanx of raiders and four more squadrons scrambled. The escorts proved almost impenetrable and, as Oberst Wolfgang von Chamier-Glisczinski's raiders reached Faversham, they split, I. and II. Gruppen attacking Rochester and III. Gruppe hitting Eastchurch. Some 300 bombs rained down on Rochester and the co-located Short Brothers aircraft factory. The same target had been hit two nights before, destroying five new Stirling four-engined bombers, and this new attack caused further damage, destroying the stockpile of components, thus reducing deliveries and delaying the start of Stirling operational missions until February 1941.

Meanwhile, ErprGr 210's 16 Bf 110 and eight Bf 109 Jabos skirted the Kent coastline at low level and crossed the Thames Estuary at its widest point, heading across the water towards Harwich, providing only occasional, spurious returns to the east coast CH radars. Number 17 Squadron was launched from Martlesham Heath but the intermittent radar contacts resulted in it stooging about some 20 miles (32 km) offshore, searching vainly for the raid when it suddenly showed up

LEFT
The damage suffered by Croydon at the hands of ErprGr 210 was substantial, and a large number of civilians were killed and wounded. (Clive Ellis)

on the Walton-on-the-Naze CHL radar only 18 miles, or four minutes, prior to landfall. The Jabos swept in unopposed, attacking viciously, destroying one aircraft, severely damaging two hangars, and wrecking the station workshops and No. 25 Squadron's equipment store. The devastated base was out of action for 48 hours.

'Cowslip Control' (North Weald Senior Fighter Controller Sqn Ldr John Cherry) then vectored in 'Acorn Leader', Sqn Ldr David Pemberton leading nine 1 Squadron Hurricanes from Northolt, while No. 12 Group sent a dozen 19 Sqn Spitfires from Fowlmere, but only the Hurricanes arrived in time. The Bf 109E-4s, having dropped their bombs, pulled up to engage the arriving Hawkers, shooting down three for no loss.[24]

Luftflotte 2's final operation of the day was set up by Luftflotte 3's attacks against No. 10 Group bases. Sperrle hoped to draw Park's fighters to the south-west, allowing Kesselring's bombers to hit his airfields while returning interceptors were refuelling.

BELOW
Staffelkapitän Lt Horst Marx was flying Bf 109E-4 '3+' of 3./ErprGr 210 when Plt Off A.R.H. Barton, flying a 32 Squadron Hurricane, shot him down as he attempted to protect Rubensdörffer's Stabskette, all aircraft of which were lost during the Croydon raid. Marx baled out and was captured. (Clive Ellis)

Taking off from their bases south of Paris at 1515–1545hrs, Bülowius' LG 1 attempted once again to strike Andover (I./LG 1) and RNAS Worthy Down (Stab and II./LG 1) with 27 Ju 88As, escorted by 40 II./ZG 76 and II./ZG 2 Bf 110s. Intercepted over the coast at 1715hrs, the Junkers forced their way through defending Hurricanes from 43, 249, and 601 Sqns, and 609 Sqn Spitfires, and then split. Half mistakenly bombed Middle Wallop instead of Andover, six miles away, while the others hit Worthy Down and

On 15 August, a Bf 109E flown by the III. Gruppe Technical Officer of JG 53, Oblt Georg Claus, intercepted a Spitfire Mk I. He forced it to land at his Cherbourg base, where it was captured. (Jean Louis Roba)

Odiham. Bombing from level flight at medium altitude, accuracy was generally lacking and losses were heavy, with five Ju 88As from 4./LG 1 falling to 601 Sqn Hurricanes and two more failing to return.

Launching at 1600hrs, Bülowius' formation was followed by 47 Stukas from I./StG 1 and II./StG 2, heavily escorted by 60 JG 27 and JG 53 Bf 109s and 20 V.[Z]/LG 1 Bf 110s, all winging towards Warmwell when they were detected at 1700hrs by the degraded CH radars along the south-west coast. Brand scrambled two Hurricane squadrons (87 and 213) from Exeter and 14 Spitfires from 234 Sqn at St Eval. The Spitfires engaged the escorting Bf 109s while the Hurricanes went after the Stukas and Zerstörers but, outnumbered four to one, they were quickly overwhelmed and four Spitfires were shot down. Faced with determined opposition from the harrying Hurricanes, the Stukas turned back and bombed Portland instead.[25]

Trying to exploit Park's supposedly disrupted fighter defence, Luftflotte 2 launched Staffel-strength formations of KG 1 He 111s and KG 2 Do 17s, escorted by four Jagdgruppen. The sector station at Biggin Hill was targeted and Hawkinge hit again, and the radar stations at Dover (Swingate), Rye – both already non-operational due to the morning strike on Hawkinge – and Foreness were also attacked. But the results from these raids were disappointing. The Dorniers hit West Malling, a new base not yet fully operational, instead of Biggin Hill, and little damage was done to the radar stations.

Under the cover of these scattered raids, Rubensdörffer's ErprGr 210 approached London intending to attack the Kenley sector station from the north. Instead, his 15 Bf 110s and eight Bf 109s struck London's Croydon airport – the FOL for 111 Squadron – hitting the terminal, hangars and armoury, and killing six servicemen. Just outside the airfield, several aircraft engine, radio and parts manufacturers and two aircraft overhaul facilities were also destroyed, resulting in

62 civilians killed and 187 injured. The airfield was completely devastated; 111 Squadron was directed to land at Hawkinge and could not return for 48 hours. The cost was high, however. Number 111 Squadron had scrambled just before the raiders struck and intercepted immediately, shooting down six Bf 110s, including Rubensdörffer and his entire Stabskette, and one Bf 109E-4, almost a third of the attacking force.[26]

Despite this sharp defeat, in the south, Luftflotten 2 and 3 enjoyed considerable success in the 1,950 sorties (801 bomber, dive-bomber and reconnaissance sorties and 1,149 fighter sorties) they flew on 15 August; it was the largest number flown in the entire Battle of Britain. But the cost continued to be high. In addition to the seven Jabos, the two Luftflotten lost 12 Zerstörers, 11 bombers, seven Stukas and four Bf 109s over southern England (ten per cent of the strike forces). Stumpff's dramatic losses, ten bombers (11 per cent of the bombing force) and 14 Zerstörers (Bf 110Ds and Ju 88Cs) in 124 sorties, tipped the 'score sheet' in Dowding's favour, making the day appear victorious for the defenders.[27]

On the ground, especially at the devastated RAF airfields, the situation seemed less sanguine. Two of Luftflotte 5's three attacks had been dispersed by defending fighters and, in the south, four others either failed to find their target, bombed a different airfield by mistake, or had been turned away by interceptors. Nonetheless, of the 14 airfields targeted, half had been struck effectively, three of them being so badly battered they were non-operational for the next two days. In fact, even after Lympne had been repaired, Dowding judged it 'fit only for emergency use until spring of 1941', closing it for further fighter operations.[28]

Wounded and with his Spitfire, N3277/AZ-H, damaged in combat, Plt Off R. Hardy of 234 Squadron was forced to land at Cherbourg. Repainted in German markings, his Spitfire was sent to Germany and tested extensively by the Erprobungsstelle (Evaluation Station) at Rechlin. (Jean-Louis Roba)

From the defending units, 22 Hurricanes and Spitfires had been destroyed, 18 of them by Bf 109s, with the loss of 15 pilots captured, killed, or severely injured. The Jagdwaffe's 'Emils' dominated the many swirling aerial combats, winning the developing battle of attrition with a 4.5-to-1 victory-to-loss ratio (kill ratio) over Dowding's defending interceptors.

Remarkably, Jagdwaffe pilots claimed to shoot down 70 RAF fighters, including 46 Spitfires. Actually Fighter Command lost seven Spitfires and 11 Hurricanes in combat with ten pilots missing – having gone down at sea – one killed and four wounded, three of them badly burned. Another 12 aircraft, including four Hurricanes, were claimed destroyed by bombing attacks.

THE NEXT DAY – 16 AUGUST

Luftwaffe operations on 16 August continued in the same pattern as before, Kesselring launching what the *RAF Narrative* describes as three 'small raids' at around 1030hrs to prompt Willoughby de Broke to scramble his defenders, following with a much larger strike 90 minutes later to catch the interceptors back at their bases refuelling and rearming. De Broke regarded the first three formations as feints and his sector controllers countered with only a few three-aeroplane formations of their own, none of which completed successful intercepts. One of the feints flew unmolested all the way to West Malling, III./KG 2 pulverizing the airfield with 80 bombs, killing two personnel, cratering the landing grounds, and wrecking a hangar and most of the facility's wooden structures.[29] It was out of action for two days.

At 1145hrs the south-eastern CH radars reported enemy raids totalling approximately 300 aircraft approaching from Pas de Calais. Ahead of the main

The third substantial raid of 16 August split into four, the largest element, consisting of 54 Stukas, making for Tangmere where it inflicted severe damage before being intercepted by Hurricanes from 1, 43 and 601 Squadrons. (Clive Ellis)

LEFT
The highly successful raid on Tangmere hit all its hangars, the workshop and station stores, destroying seven Hurricanes and several Spitfires that were undergoing maintenance, and damaged the RAF's first Beaufighter night fighter. (Clive Ellis)

body, one Gruppe of 24 II./KG 2 Do 17Zs crossed Kent and turned to follow the south bank of the Thames Estuary westbound, apparently headed for Hornchurch sector station, hoping to draw Park's fighters northwards and away from the main attack. 'Lumba Control' at Hornchurch only 'paired' 54 Sqn against the raid, 'Rabbit Leader', Sqn Ldr James Leathart, intercepting the formation with nine Spitfires. Their spirited attacks broke up the raiders' formation and, despite the fact no Dorniers were shot down, the scattered elements failed to locate their target due to cloud moving in from the north.

Meanwhile, a larger force of about 100 bombers from II./KG 1, I./KG 2, III./KG 53 and III./KG 76 crossed the coast near Dover

ABOVE
When Ventnor's Chain Home radar was knocked out by Stukas a Remote Reserve radar unit was deployed at nearby Bembridge. Its erroneous information proved more confusing than helpful. (AHB)

and were met by 51 interceptors from 32, 64, 65, 111 and 266 Sqns. At 1218–1222hrs, 111 Sqn Hurricanes attacked a I./KG 2 Dornier formation head-on, shooting down three for the loss of two; one collided with its target and the other was shot down by escorting Bf 109s and its pilot badly burned. The escorts successfully shielded their remaining charges as the four other squadrons attempted intercepts, II./JG 26 shooting down four 266 Sqn Spitfires for the loss of Gruppenkommandeur and seven-kill ace Hptm Karl Ebbighausen.

However, the bombers found their targets – Duxford, Debden, Hornchurch and North Weald – obscured by cloud, so they dispersed to bomb targets of opportunity. Various railway stations, Tilbury Docks, Gravesend and Harwell airfields, and Farnborough were attacked.[30]

In the now-familiar 'one-two-punch' pattern, Sperrle's main attack crossed the Channel at 1230–1250hrs with four formations totalling 104 Ju 87s flying convergent courses towards the Isle of Wight. They advanced behind a broad wave of 214 much faster Bf 109Es from JG 2, 27 and 53, while 54 ZG 2 and V.(Z)/LG

Ju 87B-2 'T6+HL' of 3./StG 2 was one of nine Stukas shot down during or shortly after the attack on Tangmere. Both crew from this aircraft were captured. (Clive Ellis)

1 Zerstörers weaved high above to provide close escort. It was the largest Stuka strike of the campaign. To meet this massive attack Brand launched 152, 213, 234 and 249 Sqns, and Park scrambled 1, 43, 601, and 602 Sqns.

The four formations of raiders merged over the Isle of Wight and then immediately split into four divergent attack groups. Forty-six of StG 2's Stukas pushed directly to Tangmere before tipping over into their dives, with Park's three Hurricane squadrons arriving only after they pulled out of their near-vertical attacks. According to the station ORB: 'The following buildings were destroyed: All Hangars, Workshops, Stores, Sick Quarters, Y[-Service] Hut and Officers Mess. The following services were temporarily [*sic*] out of action: Tannoy Broadcasting System, all lighting, power, water and sanitation.'

Five of the Fighter Interception Unit's seven Blenheims were destroyed and the rest, as well as a newly arrived Beaufighter Mk IF, were damaged. A 602 Sqn Spitfire and seven Hurricanes under repair in the hangars were destroyed or eventually written off as damaged beyond repair. Casualties included 14 servicemen and six civilians killed, and 41 injured.

The ORB continued: 'The discipline at this Station during, and after the attack, was exceptionally good. The depressing situation was dealt with in an orderly manner and it is considered that the traditions of the R.A.F. were upheld by all Ranks.' Amazingly, despite the extensive damage and considerable cratering of its landing grounds, Tangmere was never non-operational for more than an hour.

Number 43 Squadron's Hurricanes, still climbing through lower altitudes after take-off, were perfectly positioned to attack the Ju 87s as they pulled out of their diving attacks on Tangmere, quickly shooting down seven I. and III./StG 2 aircraft around 1305hrs. Two more Stukas were lost to the base AA gunners and 602 Squadron Spitfires.

Meanwhile, eight StG 1 Stukas hit the Ventnor CH radar station with 22 bombs, knocking it out for another seven days. This time: 'One bomb fell near the R-tower carrying the M.B.1 transmitting array and completely finished off the

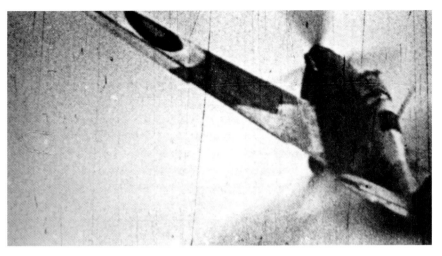

Just after midday on 16 August, newly deployed 249 Squadron was scrambled from Boscombe Down and caught sight of a raid developing over Gosport. The pilots of Red Section, Flt Lt James Nicolson (lead), Sqn Ldr Eric King and Plt Off M.A. King, were detached to attack ZG 2 Bf 110s. They were bounced by a Staffel of Bf 109s and all three Hurricanes were hit. Squadron Leader King managed to disengage and recover his damaged aircraft back to Boscombe. Pilot Officer King baled out of his flaming Hurricane, as did Nicolson, having pursed 'his' Bf 110 for a few extra seconds. Nicolson was awarded the Victoria Cross for his part in the engagement, but always struggled to understand why he had been singled out for the award. (Chris Goss)

T-hut, another bomb fell near [another] one of the R-towers and wrecked R-hut as well… [Repairing the extensive damage] was no job for the station staff, so Ventnor passed out completely from that day and did not take the air again until two months later, when all the technical damage had been repaired. The damaged administration building and the M.T. [motor transport – the wreckage of destroyed vehicles] and so on were left lying about to fool the enemy into thinking that the station had been abandoned. This appeared to work for although the odd Hun stooged over the station now and then it never came in for another official beat-up.'[31]

With the site wrecked for the foreseeable future, Ventnor's Remote Reserve (stand-by mobile) radar, an AMES Type 9(T) 40–50MHz/300kW mobile unit, was deployed onto its 105ft (32m) tower close to Bembridge, but its erroneous information proved more confusing than helpful.

Another 28 Stukas, from III./StG 1, struck the RNAS Lee-on-Solent, destroying three hangars and six aircraft, killing 14 people and injuring five more. Although intercepted by 213 Sqn Hurricanes it suffered no losses, while the escorting Bf 109s shot down a Hurricane, killing the pilot.

Additionally, 22 I./StG 3 Ju 87s struck Gosport, a Coastal Command base housing the RAF's Torpedo Development Unit, 'causing considerable damage to station buildings and hangars' according to the station ORB and killing four servicemen; 234 Squadron was vectored to intercept, but failed to find the raiders. Number 249 Squadron attempted to engage the escorting Zerstörers but was bounced by Bf 109s, which shot down two of the Hurricanes. Flight Lieutenant James Nicolson, baling out of one of them, was awarded Fighter Command's only Victoria Cross and perhaps justifiably struggled to understand why he had been singled out for recognition among so many worthy candidates.[32]

In synchronized raids later that day, Luftflotten 2 and 3 attempted pincer attacks on airfields near London. The former sent II./KG 76 across Kent behind a strong 'freie Jagd' sweep by ZG 26 Bf 110s, then turned west to fly down the

ABOVE
Mistaken for Luftwaffe
aircrew while suspended
helplessly beneath their
parachutes, both Plt Off
M.A. King and Flt Lt James
Nicolson were fired upon,
on the orders of a British
Army officer. King's
parachute canopy collapsed
and the young pilot plunged
to his death. Nicolson, in
great pain from burns
sustained during the fight
and subsequently wounded
by shotgun pellets, was
eventually rushed to
hospital, where he made a
full recovery. He later
received Fighter Command's
first and only Victoria Cross
of World War II. (AHB)

Thames Estuary, intending to hit Biggin Hill from the north. At about 1715hrs the bombers were intercepted by 56, 501, and 610 Sqns, which failed to score but lost two to the escorts. The raiders once again found their objective obscured by cloud and split into small formations to bomb targets of opportunity during the flights home. Meanwhile, the Zerstörers were intercepted off Harwich by 19 Squadron, which used its new cannon-armed Spitfire Mk IBs to shoot down three of the heavy fighters without loss. Finally, after completing their initial sweep over the Thames Estuary, eight Bf 109s from I./JG 52 turned south, then east, and viciously strafed Manston, destroying three 600 Sqn Blenheim IFs and a Spitfire during their return to base.

Luftflotte 3's attack, comprising He 111s from I. and II./KG 27 and II. and III./KG 55, escorted by JG 53 and III./ZG 76, attempted to outflank Brand's No. 10 Group defences and crossed the Sussex coast near Brighton just after 1700hrs. It was intent on bombing the Fairey Aviation Company factory at the Great West Aerodrome (on the site of today's London Heathrow Airport), RAF Benson (home to the Fairey Battle operational conversion unit), and minor airfields west of London. The manoeuvre failed and the tightly bunched formations were soon intercepted by 1, 32, 64, 601 and 615 Sqns, while 234 and 602 Sqns engaged a 'freie Jagd' sweep over the Isle of Wight. The Spitfires shot down three Bf 109s from I. and II./JG 53 and two III./ZG 76 Bf 110s, for the loss of two 234 Sqn aircraft.

The result was a classic large-scale air battle in which four Heinkels were shot down and a fifth damaged beyond repair between 1720 and 1740hrs. In his combat report, 602 Sqn pilot Flt Lt Robert Boyd wrote: 'Sighted enemy aircraft approx. 1,000ft above and coming towards us. "Blue 1" did climbing turn and delivered beam attack, followed by "Blue 2" who stopped one motor. Successive attacks were delivered by Section until [the enemy aircraft] crashed in waste ground approximately four miles north of Worthing.' For the first time on a major scale, the raids were broken up without bombing their targets. A 64 Sqn Spitfire was lost to escorting fighters.

RIGHT
Number 19 Squadron
intercepted ZG 26's Bf 110s
off Harwich while they were
providing flank cover for
KG 76's Ju 88s. Flying
Spitfires equipped with
20mm cannon, 19 Sqn
dispatched three of the
Zerstörers without loss.
(NMUSAF, colourized by
Richard Molloy)

While most of the raiders turned back, a pair of 3./KG 27 He 111s continued, descending below an expansive undercast, looking for targets of opportunity. Arriving in the landing circuit at Brize Norton airfield (and mistaking it for RAF Benson), they lowered their undercarriages to fool the local AA gunners and safely approached the field without being fired upon. Suddenly they raised their wheels and, accelerating at full power, dumped 32 bombs into the base's hangars. The resulting explosions and conflagration destroyed 11 Hurricanes under repair by No. 6 Maintenance Unit and 35 Airspeed Oxford twin-engined training aircraft belonging to No. 2 Service Flying School.[33]

For the second day in a row, the two Luftflotten had launched more than 1,715 sorties against airfield targets in southern England. Of the dozen airfields targeted, weather thwarted attacks on the five sector stations fairly close to London but, farther afield, Tangmere was badly hit, but still operating, and four other airfields were damaged, one of them badly.

Some 20 day fighters and eight Blenheim IFs had been destroyed on the ground and another 19 Hurricanes and Spitfires lost in aerial combat, 13 of them to Bf 109Es. The British fighters shot down 15 'Emils', making the day's exchange rate, for a change, almost even. In addition, 11 bombers had been lost to Dowding's interceptors. The Luftwaffe's success on 16 August was modest and the costs were increasing; most disturbing was the day's loss of nine Stukas and eight Zerstörers.

At 1655hrs on 16 August, while returning from the aborted strike on the Fairey Aviation Company factory at Great West aerodrome, 7./KG 55 He 111P 'G1+FR' was attacked by Spitfires of Blue Section, 602 Squadron, based at Westhampnett, near Chichester. Badly damaged, the aircraft crash-landed near Worthing. Bordmechaniker Uffz Weber and Gefr Moorfeld were killed during the attack; the pilot, Lt Rudolf Theobald, Uffz Hornbostel and Gefr Glaser were all captured. (Clive Ellis)

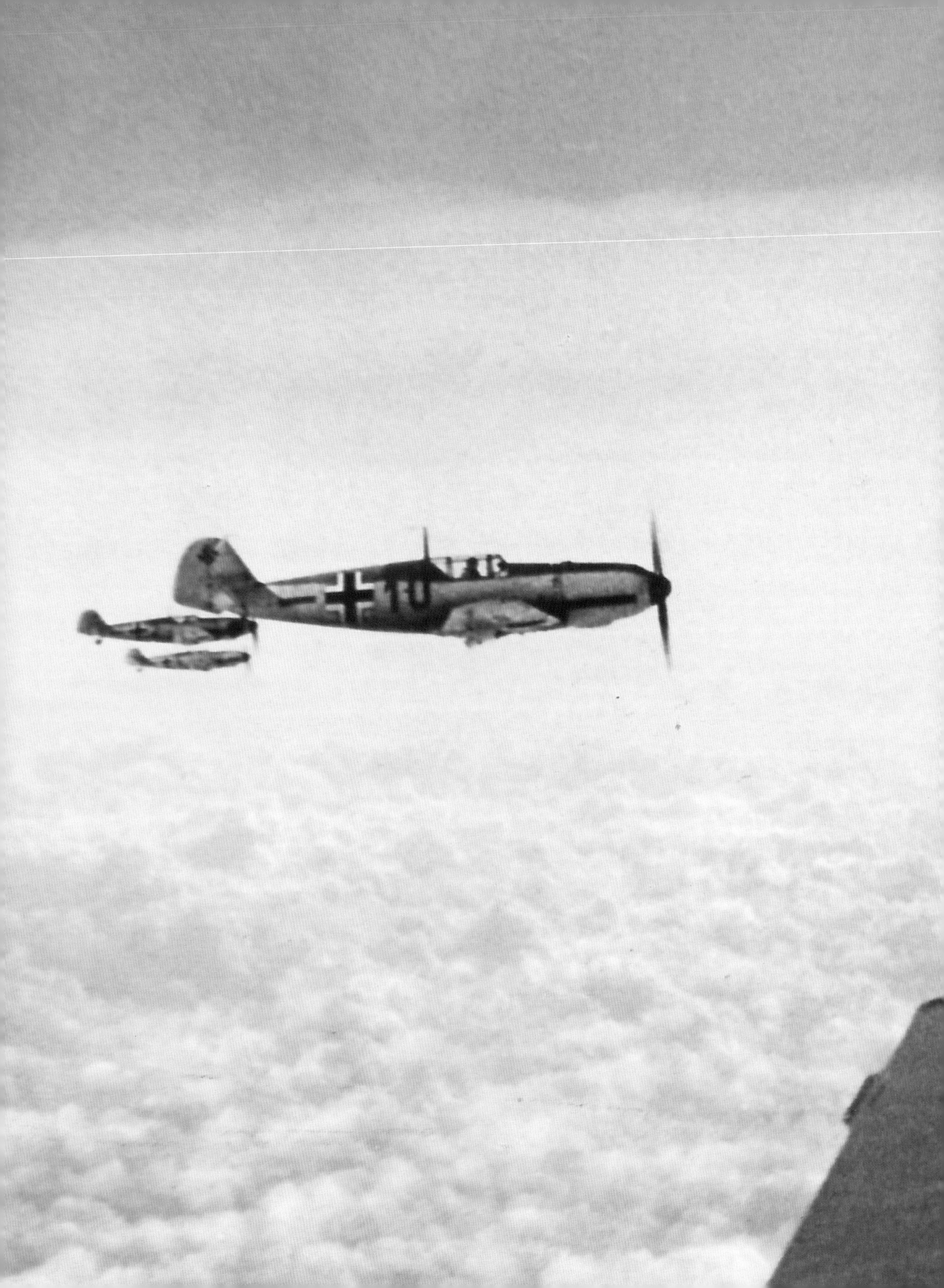

CHAPTER X

ADLERANGRIFF STAGE 2
17–19 August 1940

No plan of operations extends with any certainty beyond the first contact with the main hostile force. [Often summarized as 'No plan survives (or ever survives) first contact with the enemy'.]

Feldmarschall Helmuth Karl Bernhard Graf von Moltke, Chief of Staff of the Prussian General Staff, published in *Über Strategie* (On Strategy) 1871[1]

PLANNING STAGE 2: 17 AUGUST

After two days at full cry, despite the fine weather Luftflotten 2 and 3 stood down from daylight combat missions, flying only 65 day reconnaissance and night-bombing sorties with negligible results and no combat losses to either side.[2] Most British histories seem perplexed by the fact that on what the *RAF Narrative* describes as a 'perfectly fine day', the Luftwaffe flew no daylight bombing sorties, but German sources make it clear that this day was used by both Luftflotte staffs and their assigned Fliegerkorps commands to assess the campaign's first stage and begin planning its second.

Adlerangriff's first stage was planned to be five days of heavy attacks against airfield targets 'in a semi-circle… within a radius of 150 to 100 kilometres [93–62 miles] south of London'.[3] These attacks were delivered from 12 through 16 August. Overall the results, as evidenced by post-strike reconnaissance photographs, seemed favourable. In the prescribed 'outer ring' of coastal airfields, Luftflotte 2 had eliminated Bekesbourne (notwithstanding the fact it had already been abandoned) and Lympne as usable FOLs, and reduced Hawkinge and Manston to a marginal operating capability. Also near the coast, in Luftflotte 3's AOR Tangmere had been badly battered. Additionally, the 'middle ring' (100 to 50km, or 62–30 miles) airfields of Detling, Eastchurch and West Malling were also heavily damaged. Modest attacks against two 'inner ring' (inside 50km, or 30 miles) airfields – Biggin Hill and Kenley – had been attempted but Croydon and West Malling were hit instead.

Consequently, on 17 August, Kesselring's operations staff and his two Fliegerkorps' planners determined that it was now time to begin planning missions concentrated against Park's sector stations at Kenley (B), Biggin Hill (C), Hornchurch (D) and North Weald (E). The first two would be struck the next morning, the second pair in the afternoon. Martini's Funkhorchdienst had determined that these, the RAF's main fighter bases guarding the east-through-south approaches to London, were providing directions to airborne fighter units to intercept bombing raids. Even more important, Kenley and Biggin Hill's Sectors covered the invasion force's primary LZs (Landungsräume B, C, and D) in south-east England from Eastbourne to Folkestone.

To the west, Luftflotte 3 had been conducting a simultaneous, though separate and somewhat different, campaign striking equally at *Seelöwe*-preparation targets

Falling within Luftflotte 3's area of responsibility, Tangmere, an important Sector Operations Station, took a thorough battering, as witnessed from this high-altitude Luftwaffe reconnaissance image. (Clive Ellis)

and various airfields. Of the latter, Sperrle's staff considered A Sector's Tangmere 'virtually destroyed', a vital target because its 'command post' was known to have been issuing intercept instructions to 'the Lords' (Luftwaffe pilot slang for RAF fighter pilots) to co-ordinate the defence of Portsmouth and Portland harbours and nearby Einsatzhafen (auxiliary operational airfields) that had no direct ties to Fighter Command.

The other active sector station in Sperrle's AOR, Middle Wallop, had been attacked twice, but not seriously damaged. Only two coastal airfields, Gosport and Lee-on-Solent, had been hit, while attacks deeper inland against Andover, Boscombe Down, Worthy Down and Odiham had all gone awry, mainly due to weather. The one attack attempted against Warmwell, Middle Wallop's FOL near Portland naval base, had been aborted due to strong fighter opposition.

Even with Tangmere considered knocked out, Luftflotte 3 still had work to do to reduce Dowding's ability to use the several coastal airfields in Portsmouth's vicinity against *Seelöwe's* planned westernmost Channel crossing and the

beachhead to be established near Brighton (Landungsraum E). So, while Kesselring's staff planned major strikes against Park's four primary sector stations, Sperrle's command planned to pound three airfields near Portsmouth and Warmwell, close to Portland naval base.

Following the Luftwaffe's prescription for its 48-hour planning cycle, the 17th was needed to co-ordinate targets and timing between the two Luftflotte staffs and for the Fliegerkorps' staffs to finalize their individual attacks, publish the mission orders and distribute them to the subordinate commands. Upon receipt, the Kampfgeschwader and Gruppestabs then developed the individual mission 'strike plans' and briefed the unit aircrew slated to fly the missions the next day.

It became known among British historians as the 'the Hardest Day'.

THE HARDEST DAY – 18 AUGUST[4]

After a day of planning, co-ordinating and briefing, Luftflotten 2 and 3 returned to the battle with renewed vigour. Following the usual early-morning weather and operational reconnaissance, and after a delay caused by 8/10ths cloud at 6,500–10,000ft over northern France, Luftflotte 2 launched its first effort shortly after midday.

To attack Kenley and Biggin Hill, Generaloberst Ulrich Grauert's I. Fliegerkorps organized two packages of bombers, one each from KG 1 and KG 76, each consisting of three parts. Behind a 'freie Jagd' sweep of 60 III./JG 3 and III./JG 26 Bf 109Es, a dozen Ju 88As from II./KG 76 would lead a strike on Kenley by dive-bombing the sector station's hangars and buildings. They were to be followed by 27 Do 17Zs from I. and III./KG 76 bombing the landing grounds from medium altitude, with nine Dorniers from 9./KG 76 providing a precision follow-up low-level attack to destroy hangars and buildings that survived the first two waves. Major Friedrich Möricke led the Ju 88As, escorted by 20 III./JG 51 Bf 109Es, while Major Theodor Schweitzer was supposed to follow with the Do 17Zs, protected by 40 'Emils' from I. and II./JG 51 and 20 ZG 26 Zerstörers.

A Do17Z of 9./KG 76, a unit that was in action on 18 August, 'the Hardest Day', based at Cormeilles-en-Vexin. The heraldry of the unit's emblem depicts three runes on a red and white shield, symbolizing Tyr, the god of war in Germanic mythology. (Clive Ellis)

Five minutes behind KG 76 was the second package: 60 He 111s of Oberst Karl Angerstein's KG 1 flying in three Gruppe-strength waves, escorted by 40 JG 54 Bf 109Es, heading at medium altitude for Biggin Hill. The whole operation was covered by 60 JG 52 'Emils' and 40 Zerstörers from ZG 26, primarily for egress support.

Far beneath the large wide-ranging fighter sweep, at very low level, unescorted, unhindered by clouds and unseen by radar, the nine Do 17Zs of Hptm Joachim Roth's 9. Staffel raced across the chilly Channel waters in a wide 'vic' formation, making landfall near Beachy Head, where the Observer Corps stations alerted Park's HQ and began reporting their progress following the Brighton–London railway line leading past Kenley.

Meanwhile, over the Pas-de-Calais, KG 76's 39 medium-level bombers climbed through the broken cloud deck, the five squadron-sized formations emerging ragged and disorganized. Schweitzer orbited once to re-form his strike group then headed north-west, attempting to catch the faster Ju 88As; Möricke actually took longer to re-form his two-squadron formation and ended up following the Dorniers instead of being ahead of them. The three groups of raiders therefore advanced steadily across the Channel in reverse order from that planned.

The mid-level bomber formations were first detected by the Swingate CH radar at 1227hrs as two contacts, a large one estimated at '100+' aircraft (KG 1 and escorts) appeared to be headed north from Calais and a smaller

Dornier Do 17Zs perfecting the art of low-level flying, which reduced the range at which they could be detected by radar, decreasing the defenders' chances of an early, successful intercept. (AHB donated by Ken Wakefield)

one of '24+' (KG 76) arrowed almost due west from overhead Boulogne. Willoughby de Broke read the latter as a feint and concentrated his defence against the larger group, positioning 24 Hurricanes and 17 Spitfires from 54, 56, 65 and 501 Sqns to patrol the Canterbury–Margate line at 20,000ft, blocking the route to port facilities along the Thames Estuary and airfields north of it. He scrambled a further 27 Hurricanes and 23 Spitfires from 32, 64, 610 and 615 Sqns to patrol over the two southern sector stations and held six more squadrons at readiness (to be airborne in five minutes).[5]

KG 1 made landfall at South Foreland, between Dover and Deal, at 1249 and turned almost due west behind the large 'freie Jagd' sweep. Far to the west and one minute later, KG 76 went 'feet dry' at Beachy Head, turning north towards Tonbridge. The two formations were making a classic military pincer attack on the two closely adjacent sector stations.

A thick haze layer above 4,000ft and 'considerable cloud at about 5,000ft' prevented the Observer Corps from accurately tracking the two formations and

TOP RIGHT
Rolf von Pebal, a photographer from the Propagandakompanien, took a series of images recording the 18 August low-level raid by 9./KG 76 Do17s against Kenley. Here, people are running for cover in Cyprus Road, Burgess Hill. (Clive Ellis)

BOTTOM RIGHT
Low over Kenley, Rolf von Pebal photographed a 64 Squadron Spitfire in a revetment on the northern edge of the airfield. (Clive Ellis)

they successfully outflanked the patrol line to the south while III./JG 26 engaged the southernmost interceptor squadron (501 Sqn), shooting down four without loss. Meanwhile, Adolf Galland and Werner Mölders were meeting Göring at Carinhall, where they were awarded the rare 'Pilot's and Observer's Badge in Gold with Diamonds' to honour their exceptional achievements. As a result, III./JG 26's 'freie Jagd' sweep was led by 9. Staffelkapitän Oblt Gerhard Schöpfel.

Crossing the coast, at 1255hrs Schöpfel spotted a dozen Hurricanes ahead of and below him, flying in textbook Fighter Command formation, circling above Canterbury, and clawing for altitude. Manoeuvring his formation up-sun, as soon as the Hurricanes turned away Schöpfel and his wingman dived into the 'blind zone' behind their rearmost 'vic' as it weaved back and forth 'covering' the rest of the squadron. In less than a minute, he shot down all three Hurricanes, wounding their pilots; in the next minute he attacked the rest of the squadron, shooting down a fourth and killing Plt Off J.W. Bland. Schöpfel broke off only when his windscreen was smeared with oil from Bland's mortally stricken Hurricane.[6]

Meanwhile, from Beachy Head Schweitzer's Dorniers flew north at 10–12,000ft with their escorting fighters, weaving to stay behind them, at 26–30,000ft. 'Sapper Control' (B Sector Controller, Sqn Ldr Anthony Norman) vectored 'Panta Leader', Sqn Ldr J.R. Kayll's 615 Squadron, one of Kenley's two base CAP units, south-east to intercept them. Kayll's dozen Hurricanes clashed with the raiders over Tonbridge at 1300hrs but caused no losses. In turn, they were quickly engaged by escorting JG 51 'Emils', which shot down four, with one pilot killed in action and three wounded, for no losses.

At 1310hrs the nine Dorniers of Roth's 9. Staffel roared in at low level to hit three of Kenley's hangars and scatter the rest of their 70 SC50 bombs across the airfield. The station's fully alerted AA defences filled the air with 'ack-ack' and parachute and cable rockets. Four of the speeding light bombers were shot down (all claimed by 32, 111, and 615 Sqns) and two more badly damaged; of the 40 aircrew, 16, including all the unit's officers, were killed, wounded, or captured.

Schweitzer's medium-level Dorniers arrived 12 minutes later. Eight Spitfires attacked them head on over the target, disrupting some of the formations. The Do 17Zs unloaded 21 tons of HE bombs on and around the airfield, hitting several buildings and cratering the landing grounds. Several Do 17Zs, their bombing runs upset by 64 Squadron's daring head-on attacks, jinked out of the way and one Kette dropped 19 of its 36 bombs on Croydon airfield 3 miles (5km) to the north-west, doing little damage.

The smoke and debris thrown into the air dissuaded Möricke's Ju 88As from dive-bombing so they struck West Malling instead, dropping over 13.2 tons of bombs and claiming 'eight direct hits on hangars which burned with thick smoke. Four single-engined aircraft observed to be on fire,' according to ObdL's 19 August situation report. In fact, three 26 Sqn Lysanders were destroyed in the attack. According to the *RAF Narrative*, 'Repair work at the airfield was further retarded as a result of this attack and it was not serviceable again until 20 August.'

Do 17Z-2 'F1+DT' was one of four 9./KG 76 raiders shot down during the attack on Kenley; five more took varying degrees of damage. This aircraft crashed at Leaves Green, near Biggin Hill, at 1330hrs and burned out. Its four crew were captured. (Clive Ellis)

Despite the costly errors in executing the complicated attack, Kenley was devastated. Three of the base's four hangars were gutted, one of them housing the station's MT vehicles, which were all destroyed. The Station HQ was also wrecked and the telephone system knocked out. Two messes, a barracks and the sick quarters were damaged. Ten Hurricanes (six from 615 Sqn) and two Blenheims were destroyed or written off and the station ORB reported 12 personnel killed. Two dozen delayed action bombs were scattered about the base, although half were 'rendered ineffective [through] prompt attention'.

Exploding bombs severed underground cables, cutting communications with No. 11 Group HQ and all other outside agencies. The *RAF Narrative* records: 'The effect on communications was such that the sector operations room had to be closed down and the emergency one brought into use.' It took 60 hours to fully restore B Sector operations. Consequently, 615 Squadron's survivors were sent to Croydon. During egress, three base CAP squadrons (32, 64, and 615 Sqns) shot down two Do 17Zs and two Ju 88As of the 39 level bombers.

At 1327hrs, the three waves of Angerstein's He 111Hs attacked Biggin Hill, where most of the 93.7 tons of bombs fell in woods east of the airfield. The *RAF Narrative* says, 'No buildings were hit and the landing grounds were only lightly cratered'. The fourth base CAP squadron (610 Sqn) attempted to intercept the Heinkels and 'fought a running fight with the escorts but found great difficulty getting through to the bomber formation'; only one 2./KG 1 Heinkel was lost on the mission.[7]

Among others, Oblt Wolfgang Ewald was leading 16 Bf 109Es from I./JG 52 across Kent to cover the egress of the two Kampfgeschwader. During their own return to base, they spotted 266 Squadron's 11 Spitfires landing at Manston.

Seeing the British fighters taxi into a neat row for refuelling, Ewald left ten 'Emils' 'upstairs' as high cover and dived down with six to start strafing them. Two Spitfires caught fire immediately and Manston's ORB records another six 'severely damaged', virtually destroying the squadron for the time being.

As Luftflotte 2's bombs were falling on Kenley and around Biggin Hill, from their FOLs around Cherbourg the first of 109 Ju 87s began taking off for their primary mission of the day. All three Stukagruppen from StG 77 and I./StG 3 launched at 1330hrs, escorted by 157 JG 27 and I./JG 53 Bf 109s, following a 'freie Jagd' sweep of 55 Bf 109s from JG 2. Each Stukagruppe was assigned a separate target from the Coastal Command bases at Thorney Island and Gosport, RNAS Ford and the Poling CH station.

With Ventnor off the air, Poling was the only CH radar still operating between Bournemouth and Eastbourne; its destruction would limit Park's A and B Sectors to the two 35-mile (55km) range CHL radars flanking Poling. The station's CH radar detected the first echoes of the huge strike force at 1359hrs, about 20 miles (32km) north of Cherbourg, just as the four Jagdgruppen joined in their escort positions. Brand and Park each scrambled three squadrons, totalling 45 Spitfires and 23 Hurricanes, and, from Thorney Island, Coastal Command's 235 Squadron launched a flight of Blenheim IVF twin-engined fighters. Most of these took off too late and none of the Stuka attacks was prevented.

Air Vice-Marshal Sir Quintin Brand

A South African from Beaconsfield (now part of Kimberley, Northern Cape), Christopher Joseph Quintin Brand, nicknamed 'Flossie', was born in 1893, the son of a detective with the Johannesburg police. He joined the South African (Union) Defence Force at age 20, and two years later travelled to England, where he transferred to the RFC. Completing flight training, Brand was awarded his Royal Aero Club Certificate in March 1916 and was posted to No. 1 Squadron, flying Nieuport 17 scouts. Credited with seven victories and awarded the Military Cross, he was posted back to England to help counter German Zeppelin/Gotha night-bombing attacks.

In February 1918, Brand was promoted to major and appointed to command 112 Squadron, a home defence night-fighting squadron flying modified Sopwith Camels from Throwley, Kent. He achieved his first 'night-fighter' success, shooting down a Gotha bomber over Faversham, on 19 May. Shortly thereafter he returned to France, this time to command 151 Squadron, another night-fighter unit, combating German night raids over the Western Front; he was credited with four more nocturnal victories. By the time the guns fell silent on 11 November 1918, Brand had been credited with 12 kills, five of them at night, and had been awarded the DSO and DFC.

In 1920, Lt Col Pierre van Ryneveld and Brand participated in a challenge set by

AVM Quintin Brand. (Ed Swindell, colourized by Richard Molloy)

The Times newspaper in an attempt to become the first aviators to fly from London to Cape Town, South Africa. Three aircraft and several days later, the pair arrived at their destination and, although not winning the £10,000 prize, each was given £5,000 by the South African government and appointed 'Knight Commander of the British Empire, in recognition of their valuable services rendered to Aviation'.

Five years later, Brand was posted to the RAE at Farnborough, where he served as a Senior/Principal Technical Officer. In 1927 he was sent to Abu Qir (Aboukir), Egypt, as senior engineering officer, and served as Director-General of Aviation in Egypt from 1932 to 1936. Returning to Britain he became the RAF's Director of Repair and Maintenance and was promoted to air commodore two years later. On 1 January 1940, Brand was appointed as the Director of Maintenance and Design.

With his combat experience as a World War I night-fighter pilot, Brand was arguably the most qualified air defence expert available to command the newly established No. 10 Fighter Group. Although his command initially comprised only three sectors and eight squadrons, he proved very responsive to providing AVM Park with fighters when needed and actively supported him in advocating the employment of small, rapidly deployed groups of fighters to intercept Luftwaffe raiders.

Led by Major Helmut Bode, III./StG 77 Gruppenkommandeur, at 1420hrs the huge formation of Stukas approached Selsey Bill and split, two Stukagruppen heading off to the west while Bode continued north-east to RNAS Ford and Poling with the other two.

Attacked by II./StG 77's 28 Stukas, Ford was devastated. The fuel dump was set alight and two aircraft hangars, the MT hangar, stores and several buildings were wrecked. Twelve 829 NAS biplane torpedo bombers[8], readied for operations against the *Seelöwe* invasion fleet, were destroyed and 26 other aircraft damaged; 28 personnel were killed and 75 injured. The base was so badly devastated the RN evacuated its flying units and it was not returned to service until it was handed over to the RAF the next month to become a night-fighter station.

Flying a little farther east, Bode's III./StG 77 struck Poling radar station, 31 Stukas placing about 90 bombs around the receiver section, damaging the R-hut and watch office. One bomb took the top off a receiver mast, knocking down the aerial array. 'Emergency [radar] equipment was installed but it could no longer give comprehensive and reliable information of enemy movements' and, according to Fighter Command Signals branch, the site was 'out of action for the remainder of the month'. As the 59 Stukas attempted to escape, they were finally intercepted. A dozen 602 Squadron Spitfires shot down four and two

Smoke and debris left in the air over Croydon after KG 76's attack compelled II. Gruppe Ju 88s to divert their attacks to West Malling. Serving with 92 Squadron at the time, Flt Lt R.R. Stanford Tuck shot down one of the two 5./KG 76 Ju 88s lost there, while he was visiting 11 Group from Pembrey. (AHB)

more were lost in crash-landings back in France.

Meanwhile, to the west, having hit Gosport two days prior, Hptm Walter Siegel's 22 I./StG 3 Ju 87Bs returned, dive-bombing at 1430hrs to wreck two hangars and five buildings, and damage another ten, including the Station HQ, operations room and torpedo workshop. Five aircraft, including two torpedo bombers, were destroyed and two more badly damaged. Siegel's I./JG 27 escorts were engaged by 11 Spitfires from 234 Sqn and lost two 'Emils' shot down, but all the Stukas 'passed on [by, to bomb Gosport] without being interfered with'.

At 1430hrs on 18 August, 109 Ju 87s from StG 77 and I./StG 3 attacked the airfields of Ford, Gosport and Thorney Island, and the radar station at Poling. A thick pall of smoke hangs over Ford airfield as a result of the devastating attack. (Clive Ellis)

Not so lucky were the 28 Stukas of Hptm Herbert Meisel's I./StG 77, which were intercepted by 19 Hurricanes from 43 and 601 Sqns as they manoeuvred into line-astern formation to begin their dives on Thorney Island airfield. One Ju 87B was shot down straight away, but the others caused significant damage – two hangars and several buildings were wrecked, and three aircraft destroyed. The fighters resumed their attacks as the Stukas pulled out of their dives; another ten were shot down and two more crash-landed in France. Total losses were 28 aircrew, including Gruppenkommandeur Meisel, killed, captured, or wounded.[9]

For Luftflotte 2's late afternoon raid, Loerzer's II. Fliegerkorps planned to hit the sector stations at Hornchurch and North Weald with 58 KG 2 Dorniers and 51 KG 53 Heinkels, respectively, escorted by 140 Bf 109s and 110s as elements of JG 3, 26, 51 and 54, and ZG 26. The two formations, separated by 15 minutes, gathered their escorts over the Pas-de-Calais and headed north past Dover before turning inland. They were first detected at about 1700hrs and Willoughby de Broke positioned 33 Hurricanes and 11 Spitfires from 32, 54, 56 and 501 Sqns on the Canterbury–Margate patrol line; Park launched 49 Hurricanes from 46, 85, 151 and 257 Sqns to fly base patrols and called two more squadrons to readiness; a total of 143 interceptors was eventually launched, including those from six squadrons held in reserve.

The raiders found their targets blanketed by thick cloud at 5,000–10,000ft and turned back to bomb their secondary targets, the army barracks at Shoeburyness and the Royal Marine barracks at Deal. The abort spoilt intercepts against the Dorniers, but 56, 85 and 151 Squadrons caught the Heinkels during egress and shot down one from II. Gruppestab, killing Gruppekommandeur Major Reinhold Tamm and his five crewmen, and three others from III./KG 53.[10]

Overall, the two Luftflotten flew approximately 300 daytime bombing sorties, escorted by 360 Messerschmitts. Fighter Command had countered with 886 interceptor sorties, less than half of which (403) engaged the raiders, their escorts or fighter sweeps. Those that did destroyed 14 bombers, 19 Stukas, 15 Zerstörers and 18 Bf 109s – a total of 66 warplanes. However, the Luftflotten's aggressive airfield attacks destroyed 19 RAF aircraft, including ten Hurricanes and 12 RN torpedo bombers on the ground, while 34 Spitfires and Hurricanes were shot down in aerial combat. (Jagdwaffe and Zerstörer pilots claimed 68 Spitfires and 56 Hurricanes shot down.)[11]

Both Luftflotten were prepared to continue their onslaught for the next two days when a halt was called. Since the Luftwaffe used a 48-hour planning cycle, Kesselring's staff had planned to reattempt the attacks against Hornchurch and North Weald that had been aborted due to weather. Sperrle's command, having 'virtually destroyed' Tangmere two days prior, decided it was now time to do the same to Y Sector's coastal FOL – Warmwell.[12]

However, alarmed by 'his' Luftwaffe's grievous losses in the initial stage of *Adlerangriff*, Göring called for another conference at Carinhall. On 19 August, operations were therefore greatly reduced while Kesselring, Sperrle and their Fliegerkorps commanders journeyed to Berlin for the Reichsmarshall's next Besprechung.[13]

GÖRING'S SECOND CONFERENCE – THE CAMPAIGN'S FIRST 'MID-COURSE CORRECTION'

In preparation for Göring's next commanders' conference at Carinhall, Schmid used the daily situation reports from Luftflotten 2 and 3's intelligence sections to compose an assessment that glowingly trumpeted the Luftwaffe's successful accomplishment of *Adlerangriff*'s Stage 1. Since the operation's primary goal was the destruction of RAF forces on the ground through repeated bombing attacks, he dutifully reported that 'eight major air bases… [have been] virtually destroyed'.

During the previous week's combats (12–18 August), Göring's two Luftflotten had launched bombing missions against some 50 RAF and FAA airfields, 11 of which were aborted due to bad weather and four more, against Benson, Heathrow, Dishforth and Linton-on-Ouse, disrupted by timely fighter interceptions.

Nevertheless, Luftwaffe attacks had resulted in Ford and Lympne being so badly damaged that they were abandoned as operating bases, while Hawkinge, Manston and West Malling had been severely damaged, drastically limiting sustained operations. Two of Park's sector stations – Kenley and Tangmere – were considered among those 'virtually destroyed'. Additionally, four other airfields in No. 11 Group's AOR – Croydon, Detling, Eastchurch and Martlesham Heath – were under repair for significant damage. Another ten airfields had been hit and suffered substantial, but not debilitating damage and ten more had been attacked in small Störangriffe (nuisance or harassment raids).

The Luftflotten's photographic reconnaissance seemed to confirm that thus far *Adlerangriff* had successfully 'rolled back' Dowding's defences to within 30 miles

Results of *Adlerangriff* Stage 1, showing airfields attacked 12–18 August 1940

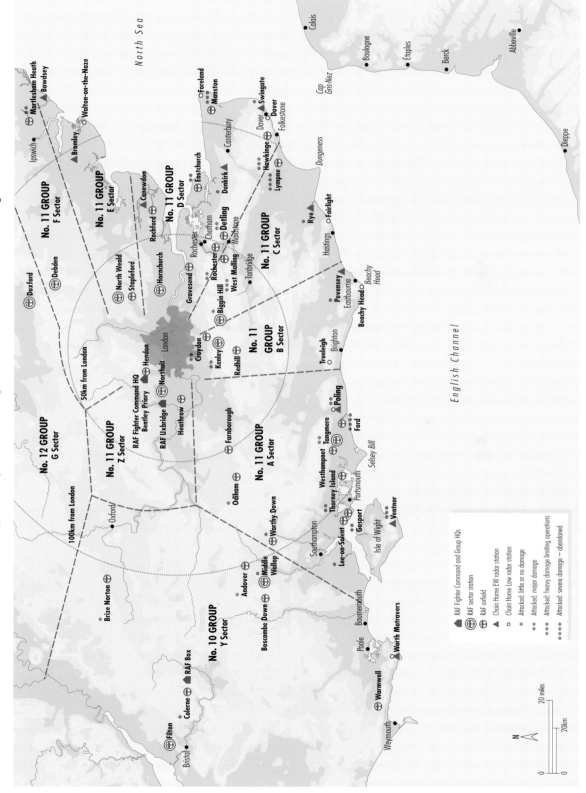

North Sea

Calais
Boulogne
Étaples
Berck
Abbeville
Cap Gris-Nez
Dieppe

Marlesham Heath
Bawdsey
Walton-on-the-Naze
Ipswich
Bromley
Canewdon
Duxford
Debden
Rochford
North Weald
Stapleford
Hornchurch
Gravesend
Biggin Hill
Foreland
Manston
Canterbury
Dover
Swingate
Dover
Folkestone
Eastchurch
Dunkirk
Detling
Chatham
Rochester
West Malling
Maidstone
Tonbridge
Hawkinge
Lympne
Rye
Fairlight
Dungeness
Hastings
Pevensey
Eastbourne
Beachy Head
Brighton
Trueleigh
Croydon
Kenley
Redhill
London
Hendon
Northolt
RAF Fighter Command HQ Bentley Priory
RAF Uxbridge
Heathrow
Farnborough
Poling
Ford
Westhampnet
Tangmere
Thorney Island
Portsmouth
Selsey Bill
Gosport
Ventnor
Isle of Wight
Lee-on-Solent
Southampton
Odiham
Worthy Down
Oxford
Middle Wallop
Andover
Bournemouth
Poole
Worth Matravers
Boscombe Down
Brize Norton
RAF Box
Colerne
Warmwell
Filton
Bristol
Weymouth

No. 11 GROUP F Sector
No. 11 GROUP E Sector
No. 11 GROUP D Sector
No. 11 GROUP C Sector
No. 11 GROUP B Sector
No. 11 GROUP A Sector
No. 11 GROUP Z Sector
No. 12 GROUP G Sector
No. 10 GROUP Y Sector

50km from London
100km from London

English Channel

Legend
▲ RAF Fighter Command and Group HQs
⊕ RAF sector station
⊕ RAF airfield
○ Chain Home EW radar station
○ Chain Home Low radar station
• Attacked: little or no damage
•• Attacked: major damage
••• Attacked: heavy damage limiting operations
•••• Attacked: severe damage – abandoned

N

20 miles
20km

The Poling radar station suffered a vicious attack by 31 Stukas of III./StG77, concentrating primarily on the receiving antenna array seen to the right of the taller transmitter towers. A bomb knocked the top from one of the receiver masts, knocking down the aerial array. A week's work was required to restore full operation. (AHB)

(50km) of London, forced the withdrawal of fighters from the coastal FOLs, except Manston, and the abandonment of Ford and, to a lesser degree, reductions in the numbers of RAF/FAA aircraft at the airfields around Portsmouth and Southampton. Using this evidence, Schmid briefed that 'the bulk of Fighter Command has withdrawn to the capital's [London's] environs.'

Coincidentally, Martini's Funkhorchdienst had pinpointed six locations, all on airfields within 30 miles (50km) of London, from which RAF fighter squadrons were being directed to intercept incoming raids. In light of the difficulty bringing down the coastal radar towers, he recommended these be targeted instead. If the efficacy of Dowding's picket line of early-warning radars could not be significantly reduced in coverage area, then the sectors' means to use the information they provided should be interrupted, thus reducing their ability to vector defending fighters to intercept the attacking bomber formations. Additionally, Waldau recommended more and heavier defensive patrols over the Channel and fighter sweeps inland to saturate the Chain Home radars and 'shield' the inbound bomber formations before they attempted to penetrate the radar screen en route to their targets.

From the Luftflotte situation reports, Schmid tallied the numbers of RAF fighters claimed destroyed by Jagdwaffe and Zerstörer pilots, and made an assessment of Fighter Command's strength at this stage of the campaign. In seven days of sustained combat the two Luftflotten had claimed 424 Spitfires and Hurricanes shot down and another 24 (of 101 aircraft total claimed) destroyed on the ground. Using this and previous data, Schmid assessed that the RAF had lost 561 fighters, including 12 Defiants, destroyed since 1 July, the day before increased operations (*Kanalkampf*) began.[14] Additionally he generously estimated 196 'minimum addition[al] losses due to other causes'.

By subtracting this overestimate from his initial tabulation and adding back his underestimated Spitfire and Hurricane production of 270–300 replacements delivered, he derived a deceptively optimistic estimate that Dowding had only 430 day fighters remaining, of which approximately 330 were thought to be in southern England. Some 127 Bf 109Es had been lost over the same period for a perceived exchange ratio of 4.5:1, encouraging increased fighter-versus-fighter combat as a prescription for further success.[15]

But this perceived success in 'rolling back' Fighter Command from its forward bases near the coast and the Jagdwaffe's very favourable perceived exchange ratio had been achieved at unacceptably high, and disturbing, costs. During the nearly week-long offensive thus far, the Luftwaffe had lost 297 aircraft on combat operations, up drastically from the 204 losses sustained during the preceding six weeks (2 July through 11 August, a weekly average of 34). The Luftwaffe was Göring's primary power base and the source of his prestige and position within the leadership of the Third Reich; ever the politician, win or lose, he could not afford to see it heavily eroded in accomplishing its mission, so the theme of the Besprechung was to reduce the unacceptably high loss rates as much as possible.

Some 127 light and medium bombers (12.7 per cent of those serviceable on 13 August) and 52 Stukas (16.7 per cent of strength) had been lost to interceptors and ground-based defences. While bomber losses had been readily replaced with new aircraft, combat damage had reduced serviceability to 70 per cent. Far more critical were aircrew losses, including 172 officers, among them two KG

Delivered earlier on 18 August (note the squadron code letters have yet to be applied), Spitfire X4111, flown by Flt Lt J.D. Urie of 602 Squadron, stationed at Westhampnett, received severe battle damage during the battles over Ford and was written off that same afternoon – note the ripples along the skin of the upper fuselage indicating that the aircraft's back has been broken. Despite being wounded in both legs, Urie managed to land back at base. (Andy Saunders, colourized by Richard Molloy)

The last significant Stuka raids against British targets took place on 16 and 18 August. Göring subsequently withdrew the type to bases in the Pas-de-Calais, saving it for close air support sorties during Operation *Sealion*. (AHB)

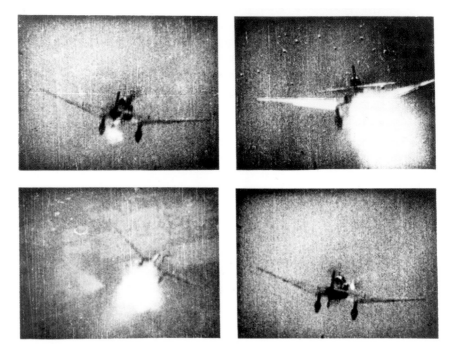

Kommodoren, two Fliegerkorps chiefs of staff and seven Gruppenkommandeure. This haemorrhaging of personnel had to be stopped if the Luftwaffe was to survive its anticipated victory.

Also, the Stuka force had to be preserved for its primary role – providing close air support for the Wehrmacht's upcoming cross-Channel offensive. In any event, the Ju 87's limited range and critical need for a permissive operating environment (secured through local air supremacy) precluded its participation in missions that penetrated any deeper into fighter-contested airspace. Attempting to reserve them for *Seelöwe*, at his 19 August commanders' conference, Göring directed: 'Until the enemy fighter force has been broken, Stuka units are only to be used when circumstances are particularly favourable'. To facilitate this decision, on 29 August ObdL transferred Richthofen's VIII. Fliegerkorps to Luftflotte 2.

The withdrawal of the Stukas was balanced somewhat by the arrival of II. (Schlacht)/LG 2 by the end of the month (officially 4 September, although operational missions were flown as early as 31 August). It had just completed a four-week conversion from the Henschel Hs 123 assault biplane to the new Bf 109E-7 Jabo. This unit's arrival doubled Kesselring's fighter-bomber force.

Finally, there was the unsatisfactory situation with the Bf 110 Zerstörer. With an alarming 53 aircraft or 20.15 per cent of strength lost, it was now obvious that the type was unsuited for its intended role. Nonetheless, Göring directed: 'Twin-engined fighters are to be employed where the range of single-engined fighters is insufficient, or where they can facilitate the breaking-off from combat of single-engine formations.'

Messerschmitt Bf 110 'heavy fighter'

Encouraged by Göring, in 1934 the RLM Technical Office issued a request for a new long-range, multi-role combat aircraft known as the Kampfzerstörer (battle destroyer). The specification called for a twin-engined, three-seat, all-metal monoplane equipped with cannon and a bomb bay. Of the original seven companies invited to submit designs, only Bayerische Flugzeugwerke (BFW, led by Wilhelm Emil 'Willy' Messerschmitt), Focke-Wulf and Henschel responded. Realizing that the Kampfzerstörer specification would result in an aircraft incapable of excelling at any one task, Messerschmitt's design emphasized the long-range 'heavy fighter' aspects of the requirement and, as a result, was initially rejected.

But Ernst Udet, a man of considerable influence, was impressed and convinced the RLM to include BFW in the request for each of the three companies to build a prototype. The Messerschmitt design was assigned the designation Bf 110.

In the spring of 1935, interest in a multi-purpose Kampfzerstörer waned and the specification was cancelled, Bf 110 development continuing to create a Zerstörer to fulfil the Luftwaffe's need for a long-range bomber escort fighter. A slim, fast, twin-engined two-seater, the Zerstörer mounted a nose battery of two 20mm cannon and four 7.92mm machine guns, and was intended to range ahead of the bombers to sweep away enemy interceptors. It was not yet appreciated that the Bf 110's adversaries, typically small, light, single-engined interceptors, would have a decisive manoeuvring advantage once combat was joined.

Bf 110 heavy fighter. (Clive Ellis)

The doctrinal requirement for fighter escorts was so well accepted that the Luftwaffe's initial procurement and force structure plans intended for half of the Jagdwaffe to be heavy fighters. However, the Bf 110's development lagged while the Bf 109 was quickly improved through four iterations, resulting in the superb Bf 109E 'Emil'. When Hitler began World War II by invading Poland, seven of ten Zerstörergruppen (destroyer groups) in the Luftwaffe's order of battle were actually equipped with the Bf 109D as interim equipment.

The good news in all this for the Germans was that the Jagdwaffe remained healthy, with 65 'Emils' (7 per cent of the force) lost during Stage 1 for 114 RAF interceptors shot down during this week-long period. It amounted to a 1.75:1 kill ratio, with losses rapidly replaced and 85 per cent serviceability in frontline units.

Göring's strategy review with Sperrle and Kesselring and their Fliegerkorps commanders centred on two issues: first, how to finally destroy or defeat Dowding's Fighter Command and, second, how to do so without sustaining prohibitively high bomber losses. Taking the second item first, the field commanders agreed

Ju 87B-1 'T6+KL' of 3./StG 2 was shot down by 601 Squadron's American volunteer pilot, Flt Lt C.R. Davis. The mortally wounded Stuka crew force landed at South Mundham, where pilot OFw W. Witt and Bordfunker Fw H. Rocktäschel succumbed shortly afterwards. (Clive Ellis)

that bomber formations larger than Gruppe strength could not be adequately protected, so, instead of Stage 1's Kampfgeschwader-strength raids, each comprising two or three Gruppen, smaller Gruppe-size bomber formations, each of two or three squadrons, should be used. Göring agreed, emphasizing that 'bombers were to be used only in sufficient numbers to draw up British fighters.'

The resulting concept of operations emphasized the dual and synergistic effects of bombing Fighter Command's primary bases, which were mainly in the south-east, 'behind' the planned invasion beaches. Bombing would destroy Dowding's forces on the ground at these stations, while attacks on the main bases (sector stations) should force Park to defend them, thus engaging his Hurricanes and Spitfires in a battle of attrition that the consistently victorious Jagdwaffe seemed sure to win. To facilitate this, Göring directed that, for daylight missions, British fighter bases were to be targeted to 'force them into battle by directing bomber attacks against [those] targets within range of our fighters'.

The bomber formations, even if reduced in size, should continue to have close escort consisting of three Jagdgruppen, but beyond that requirement, Göring stressed that the maximum number of fighters should be sent on 'freie Jagd' missions, saying: 'Only part of the fighters are to be employed as direct escorts to our bombers. The aim must be to employ the strongest possible fighter forces on free-hunt operations in which they can indirectly protect the bombers, and at the same time come to grips under favourable conditions with enemy fighters.'

Twice as many fighters would therefore be needed to escort and sweep for bomber formations than had been used during Stage 1. The only way to double the size of Jagdwaffe operations was to concentrate all available Bf 109E units within one of the two Luftflotten and have that command take the fight to the enemy. Therefore, the conferees decided to shift all of Sperrle's single-engined fighters to Kesselring's command, thereby confronting Park with an overwhelming strength of 849 'Emils' versus the believed 330 Hurricanes and Spitfires stationed in south-east England (actually 357 at the end of the day on 18 August).

German army officers were taught that, historically, at least a 3:1 numerical superiority is required to ensure an attacker's victory on the battlefield. Being a former army officer transferred to the Luftwaffe during the new service's great expansion in the mid-1930s, Kesselring was pleased that his fighter forces would now have almost the prescribed force ratio to ensure victory.[16]

Therefore, immediately following the conference, Jeschonnek set in motion the staff planning and deployment orders that transferred all Luftflotte 3's 'Emils' to Luftflotte 2, beginning with the arrival of Stab and III./JG 53 on 23–24 August. In addition to receiving JG 2, 27 and JG 53 from Sperrle, JaFü 2 was also reinforced with I./JG 77 from Norway (Luftflotte 5), adding an additional 40 'Emils' to its strength.

With practically all the Luftwaffe's Jagdwaffe units in the Pas-de-Calais area, the 'Emil's' short range limited daylight operations to attacks against Park's No. 11 Group, focusing the campaign on a relatively narrow 165-mile-wide (265km) front, instead of the previous 280-mile (450km) front against Nos 10 and 11 Groups. This was acceptable because it was Park's command that provided fighter coverage for all the anticipated invasion beaches, so concentrated attacks were required to destroy it, or at least force Dowding to withdraw it behind London and the River Thames.

Again, thinking like a ground-based military commander, Kesselring saw the sense in this geographical shift in strategy.

This decision also meant that Sperrle's command would only have the benefit of using the unsuitable Bf 110 for fighter escort. Therefore unable to continue daylight bombing, Luftflotte 3 was re-roled into night operations. To facilitate this, KGr 100, specializing in radio-directed bombing, was transferred to Sperrle on 17 August, joined by I. Fliegerkorps at the end of the month. Following an abortive daylight attack on Portsmouth on 26 August, Luftflotte 3 began a concerted night-bombing offensive against Bomber Command bases, major ports, industrial areas and other strategic targets.

With the decisions made in this conference, the strategic complexion of the Battle of Britain shifted significantly. Instead of continuing to batter various elements of Britain's defences and infrastructure across a wide front in preparation for *Seelöwe*, *Adlerangriff*'s new Stage 2 would concentrate on defeating Park's No. 11 Group, enabling the cross-Channel operation to proceed under the prerequisite of air superiority, at least over the Channel and the planned beachhead areas.

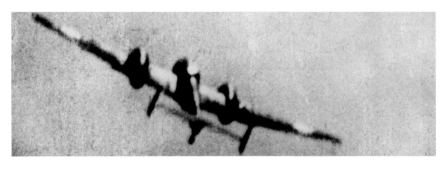

A Bf 110 seen through a gun camera. (AHB)

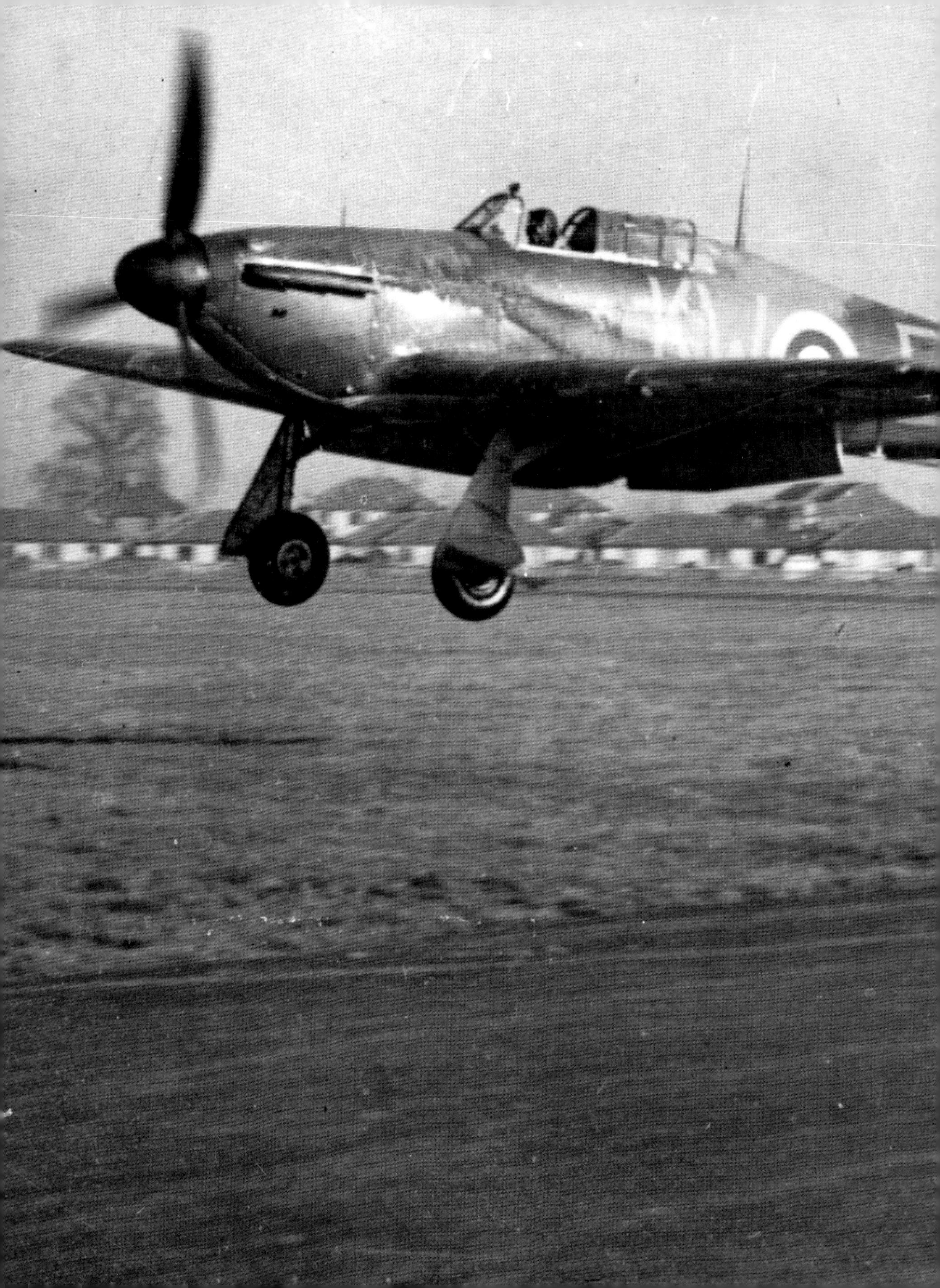

CHAPTER XI

ADLERANGRIFF STAGE 3

24 August to 6 September 1940

We have reached the decisive period in the air war against England. The vital task is to turn all means at our disposal to the defeat of the enemy air force. Our first aim is the destruction of enemy fighters. If they no longer take to the air, we shall attack them on the ground, or force them into battle by directing our bombers against targets within range of our fighters.

Hermann Göring, meeting with Luftwaffe commanders and ObdL staff officers, Carinhall, 19 August 1940[1]

ADLERANGRIFF RESUMES – 24 AUGUST

The movement of nine Jagdgruppen required several days[2] of planning and preparation. Kesselring's logistics and signals staffs had to locate two new airfields east of Calais, four south of Cap Gris-Nez and two near Guines, make billeting and maintenance arrangements, stock them with fuel and ammunition, and establish operational communications connectivity with Generalmajor Kurt-Bertram von Döring's JaFü 2 HQ at Wissant. Additionally, an ad hoc JaFü 1 was established at Wissant, under Generalmajor Theo Osterkamp, for administrative control of the arriving fighter units, most of his small staff transferring from Oberst Werner Junck's JaFü 3 HQ at Cherbourg.[3]

All this, plus four days of bad weather, delayed renewed operations until 24 August. Kesselring planned to restart *Adlerangriff* where he'd left off – attempting to bomb Hornchurch and North Weald, a dual-mission attack that had been weather-aborted on 18 August. On the western flank, Sperrle continued his own campaign, once again attacking Portsmouth and still attempting to drive the RN from its main mid-Channel base.

In the intervening days of light activity, all of Dowding's radars except Poling had been repaired and were back on line, although Ventnor's 'Reserve Remote' was operating in an unreliable, degraded mode. Lympne remained an 'emergency landing ground' only, but Hawkinge had been returned to service, although the *RAF Narrative* says it was 'operating at a much reduced capability.'

Meanwhile, Dowding adjusted his fighter force, replacing the 'spent' 64 Squadron with the 'fresh' 616 Squadron at Kenley on 19 August. Two days later, Dowding also withdrew 266 Squadron to No. 12 Group. It had suffered horrendous attrition, with six pilots killed, including its commanding officer, 11 Spitfires destroyed and six more under repair at Manston.

The only replacement unit immediately available was 264 Squadron, based at Kirton-on-Lindsey in No. 12 Group, and, much to his regret, as he later acknowledged, Dowding ordered the unit's Defiants to Hornchurch. Unlike the

PREVIOUS PAGES
Two Hurricanes from 615 Squadron clear the fence to land at Northolt. The squadron was based at Kenley from May, before being withdrawn from the front line by Park on 29 August, and sent to Prestwick to rest. (AHB)

new and untried 141 Squadron, this unit was combat experienced and overshadowing 264 Sqn's previous heavy losses was the allure of success established over Dunkirk because of the exaggerated overclaiming by the squadron's turret-gunners.

At the tactical level, on 19 August Park issued his 'No. 11 Group Instructions to Controllers No. 4', recognizing that: 'The German Air Force has begun a new phase in air attacks, which have been switched from coastal shipping and ports to inland objectives... concentrated against aerodromes, and especially fighter aerodromes on the coast and inland.'

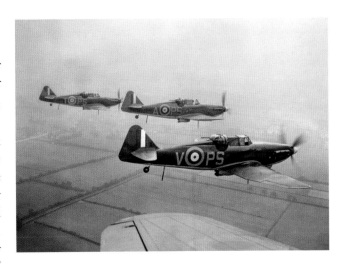

A four-day lull in fighting came to an end on 24 August when the Luftwaffe began *Adlerangriff* Stage 3. The Defiant's decimation continued when 264 Sqn was deployed forward to Manston. The folly of the decision became obvious at 1315hrs, when four were shot down and two more badly damaged in a collision while scrambling. (Author Collection, colourized by Richard Molloy)

Concerned about the serious losses of pilots – and the lack of an effective ASR organization, his first instruction was to withdraw the forward defence to 'within gliding distance of the coast. During the next two or three weeks, we cannot afford to lose pilots through forced landings in the sea; avoid sending fighters out over the sea to chase reconnaissance aircraft or small formations of enemy fighters.'

Recognizing that the key to eventual victory was to minimize losses in fighter-versus-fighter combat and maximize attrition of the Luftwaffe bomber force, he directed: 'Against mass attacks coming inland, despatch a minimum number of squadrons to engage enemy fighters. Our main object is to engage enemy bombers... If heavy attacks have crossed the coast and are proceeding towards aerodromes, put a Squadron to patrol under clouds over each Sector aerodrome.'[4]

Because base combat air patrols maintained a defensive position awaiting the arrival of the enemy raiders they were not vectored and, therefore, did not use Pip-Squeak unless directed to do so by the sector controller. This allowed each Sector to employ four vectored squadrons with the base CAPs providing additional units as 'goalies' to defend their aerodromes, expanding each Sector's defensive response to six or more squadrons.

On 24 August, Luftflotte 2 resumed the campaign with approximately 150 bomber and 700 fighter sorties. Many of the latter were in large formations of Bf 109Es and Zerstörers flying along the English coast, about 20 miles (30km) offshore, and feinting inland, attempting to draw Park's fighter squadrons into combat over the Channel while simultaneously screening the bombers forming up over the Pas-de-Calais from the coastal early-warning radar.

Under cover of these screens and feints and behind two mid-morning 'freie Jagd' sweeps came a series of three Gruppe-strength airfield bombing raids, all penetrating Park's D Sector, about an hour apart. In the first two, an estimated 30 Ju 88As dropped 36.8 tons of bombs on the abandoned Bekesbourne Aerodrome at 1035hrs, followed by 20 He 111s dumping 13 tons onto Ramsgate's airfield at

Mid-afternoon on 24 August, Luftflotte 2 launched its second major airfield attack of the day. It comprised two strike packages and the escorts tied up the RAF interceptors while the bombers inflicted minimum damage on Hornchurch because of intense AA fire, but pounded North Weald. Luftflotte 2 lost ten bombers and 15 Bf 109s, Fw Bischoff of I/JG 52 having to force land at Westgate at 1545hrs, following an engine failure over the Thames Estuary. (Clive Ellis)

1135; a quarter of the estimated 210 bombs fell on the town's small civil airfield, most of the rest causing extensive damage to the town.

The first raid was intercepted by 501 Squadron. The *RAF Narrative* reports: 'The German fighters effectively protected their charges. No sooner had the squadron commenced to attack the rearmost section of the bombers when it was itself attacked from each flank.'

The second formation was accompanied on both flanks by Bf 109Es, engaged on one side by 151 Squadron and on the other by 610 Squadron. Each of the three British units engaged lost one fighter (two Hurricanes and one Spitfire) with one pilot killed and the other two injured. Two of II./JG 51's 'Emils' were shot down and a third damaged beyond repair; one pilot was rescued, another captured.

The third attack was flown by 20 Ju 88As from II./KG 76, heavily escorted by 66 III./JG 3 and III./JG 26 Bf 109Es, headed for Manston. Number 501 Squadron was back on station, but too far from the enemy to intercept before the attack was carried out. A dozen Defiants, ordered forward from Hornchurch after the two morning attacks, had just arrived, nine of them landing to refuel while one section patrolled over the base. Major Friedrich Möricke's Junkers dive-bombed the hapless airfield between 1240 and 1245, delivering 13.25 tons of bombs with devastating precision.[5]

Flying Officer William Fraser reported: 'This was the worst attack yet and seven men were killed, the landing ground being covered with craters. Unexploded bombs were everywhere, buildings and aircraft were burning fiercely, communications had been cut and the station was completely isolated.' Hangars and buildings on the north-west corner were pounded, completely destroying the living quarters, and an ammunition dump was hit, resulting in 'large-scale' secondary explosions.[6]

Number 264 Squadron's Defiants scrambled and chased the egressing Ju 88As as they pulled out of their dives and began accelerating out over the sea. The

Defiants closed on the fleeing Junkers and shot down four, including Gruppenkommandeur Möricke's, before III./JG 3 'Emils' and return fire from the Ju 88As shot down four of the turret fighters, including that of the unit commander, Sqn Ldr Philip A. Hunter, and badly damaged a fifth. The surviving Defiants returned to Hornchurch.

Because 264 Squadron's Defiants had been observed taking off in response to KG 76's diving attack, another of ErprGr 210's sudden, dramatic low-level attacks, using a dozen Jabos, was ordered, arriving at 1539hrs to batter the devastated airfield again. This was the last straw. Afterwards, Dowding ordered 600 Squadron withdrawn to Hornchurch and had the coastal airfield evacuated of all personnel except ground defence units and aircraft servicing technicians; he designated the wrecked airfield as another 'emergency landing ground'.

Kesselring's second wave launched mid-afternoon with two strike packages totalling 46 of Oberst Erich Stahl's II. and III./KG 53 He 111s flying across the Thames Estuary at 13,000ft and 15,000ft to attack Hornchurch and North Weald. Hornchurch's 'Lumba Control' vectored 54, 111, 151 and 615 Sqns to intercept and Park called Leigh-Mallory at No. 12 Group to request coverage for the two bases. The latter's units failed to arrive and left the bases exposed.

The first package, Major Edler von Braun's III. Gruppe, escorted by JG 52 Bf 109Es, crossed the Thames Estuary near Shoeburyness, arriving over Hornchurch at approximately 1530hrs, where intense AA fire disrupted its bomb runs. Just six bombs (of 24.35 tons of HE and 16 BSK 36 incendiary canisters dropped) fell within the airfield boundary, cratering only the perimeter taxi track. Number 264 Squadron scrambled again; two of its six remaining Defiants were damaged in a take-off collision. Sections from 151, 610 and 615 Squadrons intercepted the raiders during egress, shooting down five Heinkels (four from 9. Staffel) and losing one 610 Sqn Spitfire to the escorts.

Braun's Hornchurch raid was intended to tie up Park's interceptors and was followed 20 minutes later by a similar-sized formation from Obstlt Erich Kaufmann's II./KG 53, which flew a roughly parallel course offset to the north-

At 1540hrs on 24 August, a raid launched by Luftflotte 3, comprising 50 Ju 88s from LG 1, escorted by a similar number of Bf 110s, was detected by Ventnor radar. The intercepting fighters were erroneously kept low by the Tangmere and Middle Wallop Sector Controllers. As a result, more than 200 SC250 bombs rained down on the Portsmouth naval base in less than four minutes, causing extensive damage. Spitfire L1082, flown by American volunteer Plt Off Andy Mamedoff of 609 Sqn at Warmwell, was damaged and force landed at 1650hrs, having been involved in a fight with the Bf 110 escort from ZG 2. (Clive Ellis)

east, headed for North Weald. The station ORB reports that above a cloud deck at 15,000ft, II. Gruppe was flying 'in very close formation of sections of three in line astern. Waves of Me 110s [ZG 26] were stepped up above the bombers which were [also] encircled by other Me 110s at the same level, traveling at about 200mph.'

This was the plot that 'Lumba Control' was vectoring his fighters against. Numbers 54, 615 and 151 Squadrons all sighted the bombers and their escorts as they ingressed, but 54 was engaging JG 52 and none was

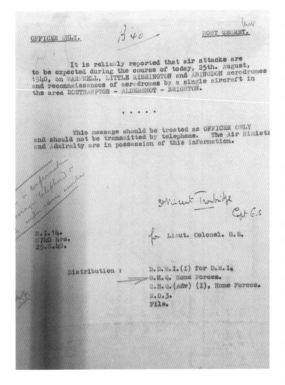

Generated at 0740hrs on
25 August, this signal was
sent to General
Headquarters Home Forces,
warning of air raids on
three specific airfields later
that day. This intelligence
was a direct result of
GC&CS at Bletchley Park
having broken the Red key,
used by the Luftwaffe to
pass and receive highly
sensitive message traffic via
a complex cypher machine
known as Enigma. The
deciphered material was
given the codename ULTRA,
which was among Britain's
most closely guarded
secrets. For obvious security
reasons, its distribution was
extremely limited and the
phrase, 'It is reliably
reported that...' was a
coded term used to indicate
its origins to those 'in the
know'. (The National
Archives)

able to intercept. 'Treble One' Squadron engaged but 'were unable to press home their attacks owing to the interference of the enemy fighters,' the *RAF Narrative* reports. One 8./ZG 26 Zerstörer was damaged, with a crewman wounded, in the high-altitude swirling dogfight.

Unopposed, Kaufmann's Heinkels pounded North Weald with 24.3 tons of bombs and 32 incendiary canisters that virtually destroyed the station's electrical powerhouse, wrecked the officer and airmen's married quarters, and damaged the water (fire-fighting) supply and gas mains. 'A number of delay-action bombs dropped; some exploding the following day. Nine servicemen were killed and 10 wounded, the killed and majority of wounded were in a shelter which suffered a direct hit.'[7]

Stahl's ingress tactics had worked like a charm. None of II./KG 53's Heinkels was lost. Escort was by Bf 110 because North Weald lay beyond the 'Emil's' combat radius; it is therefore remarkable that no Zerstörers were lost either. Overall, Luftflotte 2 lost five KG 53 He 111Hs and five KG 76 Ju 88As, and 15 Bf 109Es. Number 11 Group lost eight Hurricanes, five Spitfires and four Defiants.[8]

In the west, Sperrle's single operation was once again flown against Portsmouth, targeting the Royal Dockyards and harbour docks. Bülowius' LG 1 launched 46 Ju 88As, each loaded with four SC250 bombs, from Orléans-Bricy and Châteaudun and, passing Cherbourg, they were joined by 'Emils' from JGs 2 and 53, and ZG 2's Zerstörers.

Due to difficulty calibrating its new receivers, Ventnor's 'Remote Reserve' radar was still having serious problems determining accurate range information and at 1615hrs, with the attackers about 20 miles (30km) south-east of the Isle of Wight, the limitations of radar technology confused the situation as the primary echo dissolved into seven smaller returns. By this time Brand and Park had launched 17, 43, 234 and 609 Sqns, with 234 and 609 Sqns ordered to patrol Portsmouth and the Isle of Wight.

Ingressing at 16,000ft, the raiders passed 6,000ft above 609 Squadron's Spitfires as they crossed the Isle of Wight and arrived overhead the target area completely unimpeded. Beginning at 1625hrs, 184 bombs rained down on Portsmouth in just four minutes, an estimated 35 falling upon the dockyards, badly damaging RN facilities, causing more than 50 casualties and setting alight the warships' fuel oil storage, which burned for a day and a half. Others impacted the north and south districts of the city, killing 104 civilians and injuring 237.[9]

None of Bülowius' bombers was lost but the late intercept by 234 Squadron's

Spitfires shot down two escorts, one each from 6./JG 2 and 5./ZG 2. The failed defence cost a single 234 Sqn Spitfire.

THE WARMWELL RAID – 25 AUGUST

Next day Sperrle was finally able to launch his postponed attack on Warmwell.

Planned on or before 19 August, an ULTRA intercept in the early hours of 20 August resulted in a Most Secret message from the War Office's MI8 to, among others, Air Ministry's AI1(e), reporting: 'From a reliable source [codeword indicating ULTRA intelligence], information has been received of an impending attack on WARMWELL this morning. Aircraft to be ready to leave at 0700 hours.'

Due to decisions made at Göring's conference at Carinhall on the 19th, the raid was postponed, but mentioned again in message traffic during the early morning hours of the 22nd, and once again the next morning. Finally, after yet another postponement, MI8 stated: 'It is reliably reported that air attacks are to be expected during the course of today, 25th August 1940, on WARMWELL, LITTLE RISSINGTON and ABINGDON aerodromes.' While AI1(e) was informed of the 'impending attack', there is no evidence in the UK National Archives, RAF Historical Branch records, or other British archival sources that this, or any other ULTRA intelligence, at this stage of the war, was ever passed directly to Fighter Command HQ.

On the 25th, Luftflotten 2 and 3 launched 480 fighter sorties 'employed in cooperation with 250 bombers', according to ObdL's daily situation report, the 'bomber formations in some strength, heavily escorted by single-engined and twin-engined fighters, attacked Warmwell airfield… As a result of this attack and another on the area east of London, air battles of considerable proportions developed, and these proved to be successful for our formations.'[10]

The Warmwell attack was flown by II./KG 51 and II./KG 54, taking off from Paris-Orly and St André-de-L'Eure around 1530hrs. Consisting of about 30 Ju 88As each, the two groups rendezvoused into a lead-trail formation five minutes

During the Warmwell raid on 25 August, Staffelkapitän Hptm Hans-Karl Mayer of JG 53 dived his Bf 109E to the rescue of the Bf 110 escort that was being attacked by 213 and 87 Squadron Hurricanes. (Clive Ellis)

apart and, passing Cherbourg, I. and II./ZG 2, III./ZG 76, and V.(Z)/LG 1, totalling 103 Bf 110s, joined them as they headed north-west across the Channel. Top cover was provided by I. and II./JG 53 and III./JG 2 was to cover their egress.

The raid was detected at 'unusually long range' off St Malo by the CH station at Worth Matravers (now improved to the normal AMES 1 detection range). At 1640hrs, Brand's chief fighter controller, Wg Cdr David Roberts at Middle Wallop, placed base combat air patrols over his Y Sector Station (234 and 609 Sqns) and Warmwell (213 Sqn), positioned Warmwell's 152 Squadron over Portland and vectored 87 and 602 Sqns to intercept.

Passing Portland between 1722 and 1724hrs, the first group's escorting Zerstörers (I./ZG 2 at between 15,000 and 20,000ft) were engaged by 213 Squadron with 87 Squadron arriving shortly thereafter. According to the latter's squadron intelligence report, '"B" Flight went for the Ju 88s and the Me 110s went for "B" Flight. "A" Flight then attacked the Me 110s. Our pilots noticed that some of the Me 110s discharged red Verey lights [flares], presumably to call down

RIGHT
On 26 August, Kesselring launched 40 Do 17s from KG 2 and KG 3, escorted by 80 Bf 110s and 40 Bf 109s, against the airfields at Debden and Hornchurch. The raid failed to cause significant damage and the escort failed to provide adequate cover. As a result, eight Dorniers were shot down. This is '5K+FA' from 7./KG 3, which lost three aircraft. (Clive Ellis)

BELOW
The stepped-up Staffel formation provided the Do 17 with optimum mutual, defensive fire coverage, but proved of little benefit on 26 August. (Jean-Louis Roba)

the high escort of Me 109s. The latter did in fact come down and join in the fighting while the bombers continued to press on inland to their objective which proved to be the fighter station at Warmwell.'[11]

Leading the counter-attack was 14-kill ace 1. Staffelkapitän Hptm Hans-Karl Mayer, whose combat report stated, 'The Staffel engaged a Staffel of Hurricanes that was attempting to get at the Ju 88s. I got on the tail of a Hurricane that was shooting at a Ju 88 from a great distance. It then broke off and dived away north-west towards the coast. I dived after it and shot the machine down in flames from a range of 50 metres. Another burst of machine-gun fire from just ten metres away, the pilot baled out. Machine and pilot fell into the water 500 metres off the coast.'[12] Even parachuting so close to shore, Plt Off JAL Philippart, a Belgian volunteer, did not survive the encounter and was drowned; JG 53 lost four Bf 109Es in the fighter-versus-fighter free-for-all.

Meanwhile, the defenders shot down two Junkers and four Zerstörers as Major Friedrich Winkler's II./KG 51 arrived over the target. Immediately thereafter, 609 Squadron intercepted Obstlt Rudolf Köster's II./KG 54, which was approaching from the east, but 'all combats were with Me 110s' according to the *RAF Narrative*, three more of which were shot down; two others returned to France damaged beyond repair.

The two Heinkel formations released 37 tons of high explosives at 1725–1730hrs. About 30 bombs impacted on the airfield, destroying the sick quarters, damaging two hangars, cratering the landing grounds and severing telephone and teleprinter lines. Nine bombs were delayed-action, exploding at various intervals, the last at 0640hrs on the 27th. There were no casualties but 'communications were disorganized until midday on the 26th'. The failed defence cost three Hurricanes and four Spitfires shot down, and five pilots killed.[13]

As the bombers egressed, flying from Tangmere, 17 Squadron attacked the melee of Bf 110s and 109s, losing another two Hurricanes and one pilot, their commander, Sqn Ldr Cedric W. Williams. Arriving to provide egress coverage, III./JG 2 lost two Bf 109Es, both pilots being rescued by a Seenotdienst He 59.[14]

As for the role of ULTRA in the Battle of Britain, Wg Cdr Roberts's response to the 'anticipated attack' was entirely typical of Fighter Command intercept practices and showed no evidence of prior knowledge or prescient intelligence. Of six squadrons airborne and available, only half were paired against the raiders. The raid was not disrupted. Warmwell was non-operational for the next 18 hours and only two bombers were shot down. The implication is that if Fighter Command had been informed that Warmwell was the primary target that day, then Dowding and his subordinate commanders made no effort to act upon that knowledge. Either at the Air Ministry's AI1(e) desk, or somewhere between it and No. 10 Group HQ, the flow of information from ULTRA halted and its intelligence was not made available to Brand's command. Using this convincing example, it is quite evident that ULTRA did not play the key part in the Battle of Britain that some histories have imagined.

The air battle east of London occurred between 1900 and 1930hrs, as No. 11 Group squadrons tangled with I./JG 54 Bf 109Es escorting a Do 17Z formation that apparently weather-aborted the attack on its assigned target. One 'Emil' was lost in exchange for two 32 Sqn Hurricanes and three Spitfires from 610 and 616 Sqns shot down; three RAF pilots were killed.

Next day, Sperrle launched Luftflotte 3's last major daylight attack of the campaign, an intended *coup de grâce* against Portsmouth harbour following the successful strike two days earlier. With significant damage already done, this was to be a final attempt to neutralize the RN's anti-*Sealion* capabilities before the concentrated night-bombing campaign was begun. Some 48 He 111H/Ps of Obstlt Hans Korte's[15] KG 55 took off from Dreux (I. Gruppe) and Chartres (II. Gruppe) carrying almost 67 tons of HE bombs intended for dropping on two large warship basins (No. 2 for cruisers and destroyers, and No. 3 for battleships) and five dry docks within the Royal Dockyards. No major warships were in port, but several RN destroyers damaged during Dunkirk operations and *Kanalkampf* were undergoing repair and could be further savaged, and repair facilities and capabilities destroyed, with one last successful strike. It was far easier to hit a small, fast, nimble destroyer while it was moored dockside or immobilized in a dry dock than it was under way at sea.

As Korte's two large formations winged past Cherbourg, they were joined by four groups totalling 107 escort fighters, a Zerstörergruppe flying a 'freie Jagd' sweep on a parallel course offset to the west and protecting the western flank of the bombers from interception by Warmwell's 152 Squadron. At 1600hrs, Ventnor's radar, showing marked improvement, detected the strike package 60 miles (95km) south of Portsmouth, initially angling towards Selsey Bill at 15,000ft with two formations of Bf 109Es (I. and II./JG 53) and the Zerstörergruppe 'freie Jagd' offset to the west. Jagdgeschwader 53's I. Gruppe tied up 245 Squadron's Hurricanes over the Isle of Wight, and II. Gruppe was attacked by 234 and 609 Squadrons' Spitfires over Swanage. Outnumbered, once again things did not go well for JG 53's pilots; they were able to damage two Spitfires, but lost three Bf 109Es shot down, with one pilot killed and two rescued.[16]

Greim's mission planners had not expected a strong reaction from the east. Anticipating that Kesselring's heavy 1500–1530hrs raid on Debden (No. 11

TOP LEFT
Do 17Z-3 'U5+GK' of
2./KG 2 was attacked by
fighters on 26 August over
Hornchurch and badly
damaged. The aircraft
crashed near Eastchurch at
1540hrs. Major Gutzmann,
the Gruppenkommandeur,
Uffz Buhr and Uffz
Schmolzer were taken
POW, while Oblt Hertel
was killed. (Clive Ellis)

LEFT
Another victim of the
fighting on 26 August,
Do 17Z-3 'U5+' from
7./KG 2 was shot down by
Hurricanes from 1 (RCAF)
Sqn at 1540hrs near
Whepstead, Suffolk, having
previously attacked Debden.
All four crewmembers, Uffz
Knorky, Uffz Schaffer, Uffz
Simon and Gefr Schadt
were taken prisoner,
although only the
Bordschütze, Schadt,
escaped injury. (Clive Ellis)

Group's F Sector Station on the far eastern edge of the battlespace) had drawn all Park's fighters in that direction, they made no provision for fighter protection on the main force's right flank. The two formations were therefore successfully and successively intercepted by 43 and 602 Squadrons from Park's A Sector (Tangmere and Westhampnett), and B Sector's 615 Squadron Hurricanes from Kenley.

Squadron Leader John 'Tubby' Badger's 43 Squadron Hurricanes attacked head on, followed two minutes later by Sqn Ldr AVR 'Sandy' Johnstone's 602 Sqn Spitfires, diving from 2,000ft above and up-sun of the bombers. With the first attacks, the bomber leaders fired Verey lights – there were still no bomber-fighter radio communications – to signal the top cover at 20,000ft to engage the attackers. Several Heinkels jettisoned their bombloads on and near Hayling Island. As the I./JG 2 'Emils' swooped down upon the interceptors, Korte's bombers approached Portsmouth at 1630hrs, just as 615 Squadron's Hurricanes hit them. The timely interceptions disrupted KG 55's bomb deliveries. Most of the weapons hit Fort Cumberland or fell harmlessly in Langston Harbour.[17]

Sperrle's last daytime attack in support of *Seelöwe* was definitely a defeat. The intended target had not been bombed, and four He 111Ps and seven 'Emils' were lost. Four Hurricanes and one Spitfire were shot down, with four pilots wounded and a fifth severely burned.

THE DEBDEN RAID – 26 AUGUST

Meanwhile, Kesselring continued his attempts to degrade Park's sector stations. After III./KG 53's inaccurate and ineffective high-level He 111H attack on Hornchurch on 24 August, Kesselring's new chief of staff, Oberst Paul Deichmann (appointed the previous day) ordered another attempt, assigning the task to his former command, Loerzer's II. Fliegerkorps, which tasked the mission to Fink's KG 2, the low-flying airfield-attack experts.

Oberst Paul Deichmann

Oberst Paul Deichmann. (Bundesarchiv Bild 183-R63015)

After Göring, Oberst (Obst) Paul Deichmann had the greatest influence over the Luftwaffe's conduct of the Battle of Britain, first as chief of staff for II. Fliegerkorps then, beginning in August 1940, as Kesselring's chief of staff. Deichmann, a career military officer who serving in both the infantry and air force, was born in Fulda in August 1898. After joining the Imperial German Army as an 18-year-old cadet with the 86th Regiment of Fusiliers, he was transferred the following year to the Luftstreitkräfte and, after pilot, radio-operator and artillery observer training, assigned to FFA 8 in February 1918.

Deichmann remained with the post-war air service until it was disbanded in accordance with the Treaty of Versailles, and he was transferred to the ground forces in May 1920. Retained by the Reichswehr, administratively assigned to Infanterie-Regiment 3, he served with various clandestine flying units and attended secret flight training at Lipetsk, USSR, in 1928. After attending the Berlin Technische Universität and General Staff Training, he was appointed an 'officer for special duties' in the RLM's Luftkommandoamt (forerunner of the ObdL Command Staff) in April 1934. After gaining command experience leading the clandestine KG 753 (operating Do 23 bombers from Gotha), he returned to the RLM as Chief of the Command Staff from October 1936, working under Kesselring.

Returning to the field in October 1937, Deichmann commanded II./KG 253, flying the badly flawed diesel-powered Ju 86 twin-engined bomber at Erfurt, leading his unit through conversion to the much better, but still operationally limited, He 111J. A decisive commander, demanding leader and diligent, far-sighted staff officer, he was promoted to Oberstleutnant in January 1939 and the next month appointed to be chief of ObdL's 2. Abteilung (Mobilization Planning) as the Luftwaffe prepared for war. His staff's meticulous preparations assisted in making the Polish campaign a quick one and helped enable the Luftwaffe's stunning success in *Fall Gelb*.

Rewarded for his excellent work, Deichmann was appointed chief of staff for General Bruno Loerzer's II. Fliegerkorps in June 1940, and promoted to Oberst. An ardent bomber advocate, he also had great respect and deep affinity for his aircrews and, knowing they were particular vulnerable to enemy fighter attack, constantly pushed for more Jagdschutz by the escorting Bf 109Es. Believing the exaggerated kill claims of the Jagdwaffe commanders, he was convinced that victory over Britain lay in a battle of attrition between the two fighter forces and advocated attacking London in order to ensure that Fighter Command came up to fight.

Appointed as Kesselring's chief of staff three weeks after his promotion, Deichmann was finally positioned to implement his convictions and, from that day on, was instrumental in orchestrating Luftflotte 2's campaign to defeat RAF Fighter Command.[18]

This major effort followed a smaller operation that took place from 1130 to 1230hrs, diversionary attack by I./KG 3 near Folkestone that was intended to open the way for a III./KG 3 attack on West Malling. The first wave, a 'freie Jagd' sweep by JG 3 detected by Rye radar station at 1135hrs near Cap Gris-Nez and reported as '30+', was headed due north, followed four minutes later by a '9+' group of bombers (I./KG 3) and their '20+' covering fighters (II./JG 51). Obstlt Rudolf Gabelmann's dozen Dorniers passed Dover to the east, turning inland south of Deal.

To meet them, between 1139–1145hrs Park scrambled five squadrons and Biggin Hill's 'Tophat Control' vectored 'Radpoe Leader', Sqn Ldr Marcus Robinson and his 616 Squadron, to intercept, but the raiders turned south and dove towards the coast, accelerating as they went. Approaching the shoreline, the Do 17Zs unloaded 12.67 tons of bombs meant for the small Sandgate auxiliary airfield (now a parade ground) near the army's Shorncliffe Redoubt. The bombardment failed to hit anything of military significance and Gabelmann's Dorniers headed back across the Channel at top speed.

The dozen 616 Sqn Spitfires were unable to catch the egressing bombers and turned back to the north, only to find around 50 Bf 109s, Hptm Günther 'Franzl' Lützow's[19] JG 3, ahead and high above them. Robinson attempted to climb the squadron to get up-sun of the 'Emils' but Lützow saw them and sent Hptm Walter Kienitz's III. Gruppe down to attack. These were soon joined by about 30 II./JG 51 Bf 109s and, badly outnumbered, very quickly seven Spitfires were shot down, two pilots killed and another four injured.

At around 1600hrs on 26 August, 50 He 111s from KG 55, escorted by 107 Bf 109s and 110s, attempted to attack Portsmouth. The bombers were repulsed before reaching their target and four were shot down. An He 59 seaplane of Seenotflugkommando 2, sent to search for downed crews, was shot down by five Spitfires of 602 Squadron. It was the last major daylight raid launched by Luftflotte 3 for about three weeks. These He 111s were with 9./KG 55. 'G1+LT' was lost on take-off on 8 December 1940. Note the additional nose-mounted and forward firing gondola machine guns. (AHB donated by Ken Wakefield)

The mission's second wave – a dozen Do 17Zs from III./KG 3 flying at 13,000ft – turned inland north of Deal and headed north-west towards Herne Bay. Hauptmann Erich Rathmann's Dorniers were spotted by the Defiant crews of Sqn Ldr Desmond Garvin's 264 Squadron, sent from Hornchurch to patrol over Dover. It took ten minutes for the seven slow, heavy fighters to close on the bombers, but they finally began moving in to begin their complicated 'cross-over attacks' at 1210hrs. They claimed six shot down before Lützow's I. and II./JG 3 jumped them. Three more Defiants were shot down, 15-victory ace Lützow being credited with two of them.

Boulton Paul Defiant

In April 1935, the Air Ministry released Specification F.9/35, which required a two-seat day and night 'turret fighter' capable of 290mph at 15,000ft. The aircraft was to be of modern monoplane design, concentrating its armament within a power-operated turret and having sufficient fuel capacity to allow it to perform standing patrols. Specifically, the powered turret was to provide a 360-degree upper hemisphere field of fire and be able to engage enemy bombers from below.

Boulton Paul, having been working on turret technology for some time, responded with a design that was similar in appearance, size and powerplant to the Hawker Hurricane, but much heavier owing to its one-ton turret and two-man crew. Mounting four guns, the turret was based on a design by French company Société d'Applications des Machines Motrices, which had been licensed by Boulton Paul for use in its earlier Sidestrand bomber, and eventually installed in the follow-on Overstrand and Blackburn Roc naval reconnaissance fighter.

Sadly, the misguided concept behind the Defiant (and Roc) ignored the realities of combat. The Defiant was primarily intended to be flown alongside opposing bombers and 'exchange broadsides' as if it were a 'flying frigate' engaging enemy 'ships of the line', as in Nelson's day. Heavy and manoeuvring sluggishly, it proved easy prey for Messerschmitts; on 13 May 1940, 264 Squadron lost five out of six Defiants in rapid succession attempting to attack escorted 12.(St)/LG 1 Stukas over Holland, but the disaster was masked by wildly exaggerated turret-gunner kill claims.

Defiant. (Author Collection, colourized by Adam Tooby)

From 10 to 31 May, Defiant gunners claimed 65 Luftwaffe aircraft shot down; German records reveal only eight actually lost to Defiants. Even on the one occasion that the Defiant was able to use its intended tactic against Heinkel bombers from II./KG 27 over Dunkirk on 31 May, three were lost and only two bombers shot down. During the Battle of Britain, the two Defiant-equipped squadrons were presented with two more opportunities to engage the enemy, both times with tragic results.

A Schwarm of Bf 109Es from 9./JG 2 'Richthofen', on a 'freie Jagd' fighter sweep over the English Channel. (Clive Ellis)

Rathmann's West Malling raid was repulsed by the Defiants' timely intercept. The Dorniers turned back to the east and attempted to dump their bombs on Manston. At 1230hrs they actually dropped 36 SC50s on Broadstairs, where, the *RAF Narrative* says, most fell 'on the foreshore', and others on a small village near Ramsgate. Three Do 17Zs were lost in the aborted raid, one ditching on Goodwin Sands, another crashing into the sea off Foreness and the last ditching in the Channel.

Arriving to cover the attackers' egress, I./JG 52 engaged the just-arriving 610 Squadron, shooting down three Spitfires for the loss of one Bf 109E. Number 56 Squadron chased the withdrawing II./JG 3, shooting down three more 'Emils' for the loss of two Hurricanes.[20]

Loerzer's second attack force, comprising I. and III./KG 2, launched from Épinoy and Cambrai around 1400hrs and rendezvoused with their escorts over the Pas-de-Calais. Major Adolf Fuchs' III. Gruppe led the mission, covered by I. and II./ZG 26's Zerstörers, with Major Martin Gutzmann's I. Gruppe following, escorted by Trautloft's I. and II./JG 54. The large formation (Swingate Chain Home station reported it as '60+') went 'feet wet' off Calais at 1450hrs with two more smaller echoes ('20+' I./JG 52 Bf 109Es and '12+' III./ZG 26 Bf 110s) advancing on the main formation's flanks.

By this time, the initial ambiguous returns received by Swingate radar had resolved and Park scrambled five squadrons. Of these, Willoughby de Broke directed 65 and 615 Squadrons to intercept and placed 1 (Royal Canadian Air Force), 85 and 501 Sqns on patrol over North Weald, Hawkinge and Maidstone (to cover West Malling). Between 1500 and 1502hrs, Park ordered 56 and 111 Sqns off and requested that Leigh-Mallory cover Debden and North Weald. Number 12 Group scrambled 19 and 310 (Czech) Squadrons from Duxford, the first taking off at 1510hrs.

At the same time, after passing to the east of Dover, Fuchs turned north-west, arrowing his large formation across the north-east corner of Kent between

Canterbury and Margate as 615 Squadron's nine Hurricanes surprised I./JG 52 over Whitstable, shooting down four Bf 109Es for the loss of three, and stripping them away from the package's western flank. As the bombers began crossing the mouth of the Thames Estuary, Gutzmann turned his part of the formation left, flying up the Thames towards Hornchurch, while Fuchs led his group diagonally across the water to Foulness Island.

From its patrol overhead Maidstone, 'Lumba Control' vectored 'Hydro Leader', Sqn Ldr Peter Townsend and his veteran 85 Squadron, to intercept Gutzmann's 15 Dorniers. One I. Gruppe pilot recalled:

> I catch sight of a large British fighter formation that flies past us on the right side. 'Haven't they seen us?' I think. But in the same moment they turn and attack us diagonally from the front, and pass through our formation, shooting wildly. The whole thing is over in seconds, but two Do 17s from the leading Kette go down with engines on fire. Suddenly our own aircraft is hit. I feel a burning pain in the left thigh. Shortly afterwards there is a muffled bang – and then we have no oxygen. The oxygen tank has burst. Luckily the fighters have ceased their attacks, so we can go lower where we don't need the oxygen masks.[21]

Ground crew bombing-up an He 111 of KG 26. The He 111's bomb bay carried its weapons nose up, in vertical compartments. They adopted a nose-down position upon release as they cleared the aircraft. (Author Collection)

Townsend's nine Hurricanes shredded Gutzmann's formation, his Stabskette turning away. Others continued and were attacked by nine 65 Sqn Spitfires as they approached Hornchurch. By this time Trautloft's 'Emils' had turned for home, their red 'fuel low' lights flickering on, and the bomber crews lost their nerve.

Nursing a battle-damaged aircraft back over the cold waters of the Channel was a dreaded ordeal that became familiar to many Luftwaffe crews. This Ju 88 was landing with the right engine shut down and the propeller feathered. (NMUSAF)

Some released their bombs early, hitting Hornchurch village and cutting the railway line to Elm Bank. Others turned away, descending for best speed, jettisoning their loads on or around their alternative targets – Detling, Eastchurch and West Malling – but without damage. The attack was repulsed with the loss of two bombers. Of these, one force-landed at Rochford, where its crew was captured. Gutzmann's bomber crash-landed south of Eastchurch with one dead aboard; Gutzmann and two crewmen became POWs.

As Fuchs' 21 Dorniers continued north-west, passing between Chelmsford and Colchester, Debden's 'Garter Control' attempted to vector three squadrons to intercept. While 56 and 111 Squadrons both sighted the bombers, neither was able to intercept. Scrambled at 1510hrs from Duxford, only nine miles (15km) north of Debden, 19 Squadron also failed to engage the Dorniers. The unit climbed its Spitfires above the 5,000–7,000ft broken cloud layer while, approaching the target from the south-east, Fuchs led his bombers down beneath them. As the Dorniers emerged beneath the clouds, the local Observer Corps post spotted them but reported they were headed east, completely throwing off the intercept attempts of 19 Squadron and others.

Breaking out of the clouds over Braintree and seeing Park's F Sector Station directly in front of him, Fuchs led a textbook airfield attack. At 1519hrs the 21 bombers began scattering over 13 tons of HE bombs and 600 incendiaries across Debden. An estimated 100 bombs impacted the airfield, scoring direct hits on four buildings, the MT yard and aircraft equipment section, damaging electrical and water mains, destroying one 257 Squadron Hurricane and killing five personnel. Despite the damage, the base was never non-operational and 111 Squadron landed 22 minutes later.[22]

More squadrons were vectored to attempt to cut off the raider's egress. These included 1 (RCAF), 85 and 310 (Czech). Initially directed to patrol over North Weald, 'Calla Leader', Sqn Ldr George Blackwood and his Czech 310 Squadron, was first to spot the raiders. Thrown into combat from their primary training duties, the Czech pilots flew with only TR9D HF radios for intra-flight communication, while Blackwood had TR1133 VHF to communicate with 'Garter Control'. This, as the *RAF Narrative* records, made it 'impossible to issue any order to the other pilots [and the Czech] pilots were unaware of any signals from the ground'. Sighting the Zerstörers first, the aggressive Czechs climbed to attack them and did not see the bombers passing below. In the ensuing high-altitude swirling dogfight, one fighter from each side was shot down.[23]

Meanwhile, Blackwood attacked the Dorniers and was shot down by their dorsal defensive fire. The other two squadrons lost one Hurricane each. Three of Fuchs' Do 17Zs and three Zerstörers were shot down.

The deepest penetration into No. 11 Group's AOR thus far, the Debden raid was a qualified success. While significant damage was done, none of it prevented the sector station from doing its job of co-ordinating No. 11 Group's air defence.

ANOTHER STAND-DOWN, ANOTHER RE-APPRAISAL – 27 AUGUST

After three days of moderately intense operations, on 27 August, Luftflotte 2 once again stood down for conferences, briefings, updated intelligence assessments and an operations re-appraisal. Most significant was a meeting hosted by Döring at his Wissant HQ. Kesselring, his chief of staff, Deichmann, and Loerzer were in attendance, ostensibly to welcome JaFü 2's three newly arrived Geschwaderkommodoren – Obstlt Harry von Bülow-Bothkamp (JG 2), Oberst Max Ibel (JG 27) and Obstln Hans-Jürgen von Cramon-Taubadel (JG 53) – and discuss integrating their units into Luftflotte 2's operations.

However, Deichmann, an ardent bomber advocate and veteran commander, seized the opportunity to address the Kampfflieger's complaints of a lack of fighter protection being provided by the Jagdwaffe. In the face of the RAF's continued determined interceptions, especially its tactical evolution towards employing unnerving head-on attacks, Loerzer's bomber crews had begun to do just that: lose their nerve. His Kampfgeschwader Kommodoren, echoing the vehement sentiment of their bomber crews, now demanded that the fighter escorts fly within visual range of the bombers, increasing the bomber crews' sense of security. Deichmann wanted changes made before resuming the costly airfield attack operations.

Supporting their bomber crewmen, Kesselring and Loerzer accused the Jagdgeschwader Kommodoren of being overly interested in accumulating aerial victories and awards at the expense of exposing the bombers to enemy attacks. The very newest of the fighter commanders, JG 3's Lützow countered with a vociferous defence, arguing that his fighters required speed and space to combat the fast, more agile Spitfires. The discussion ended with a compromise. More fighters would be ordered to fly close and at the same speed as the bombers, while the rest would fly ahead of the main bomber force, approximately 1,000–2,000m (3,300 to 6,600ft) above, clearing the airspace of enemy fighters in the direction the bomber force was flying.[24]

Ground crew rearm and refuel a 19 Squadron Spitfire I between sorties at its Fowlmere, Cambridgeshire base. Fowlmere was a satellite for Duxford. (NMUSAF, colourized by Richard Molloy)

Dowding took advantage of the day's reprieve to further adjust his fighter deployments. Since *Adlertag*, 32 Squadron had lost 14 Hurricanes and had only eight pilots fit for combat; 65 Squadron was down to nine Spitfires and a dozen pilots.

Dowding therefore sent what little was left of 32 Squadron north to Acklington (No. 13 Gp) to rebuild, its commander, Sqn Ldr John Worrall, staying behind to take over as C Sector Fighter Controller ('Tophat Control'). Next day, 79 Squadron was sent from Acklington to replace 32 Sqn at Biggin Hill. Number 65 Squadron was transferred to Church Fenton (also No. 13 Gp) to rebuild, 603 Squadron, another 13 Gp unit, replacing it at Hornchurch from Turnhouse.

At the tactical level, Park issued two more 'Instructions to Controllers' on 26 and 27 August. The first added information to the sector controller's knowledge of individual enemy raids by stating: 'formation leaders are to report approximate strength of enemy bombers and fighters, their height, course, and approximate position immediately on sighting the enemy… These reports should enable us to engage the enemy on more equal terms.' The next day, his instruction added detail, and registered a complaint against Leigh-Mallory's 12 Group, regarding Controllers' use of reinforcing squadrons, saying 'their obvious task is to patrol aerodromes or other inland objectives to engage enemy formations that break through our fighter patrols that normally engage well forward of our Sector aerodromes.'[25]

Since the reinforcing squadrons' radios were not tuned to the same frequencies as 11 Group's Sectors, they could not be vectored to intercept incoming raiders, but could only orbit at their directed patrol positions and await the arrival of the enemy. The most vocal and favoured commander of Leigh-Mallory's reinforcing squadrons, Sqn Ldr Douglas Bader, Officer Commanding (OC) 242 Squadron, did not see his role in the same light and frequently never went to his assigned patrol point but instead went looking for approaching German formations without any information about their location, altitude, or direction of flight.

BATTLE RESUMES AGAIN – 28 AND 29 AUGUST

Even though they did not comply with Göring's 19 August orders to maximize the numbers of 'freie Jagd' sorties, during the morning of 28 August, Kesselring put the new escort/sweep arrangements into effect with two strikes against No. 11 Group's middle ring of 'auxiliary fighter airfields', Eastchurch and Rochford. Originally planned for the previous day, these two missions, flown by Oberst Wolfgang von Chamier-Gliczinski's KG 3, totalled 50 of the 60 Luftflotte bomber/reconnaissance sorties flown that day; the remainder were weather and photo-reconnaissance missions.

The day's two bombing missions were protected by about half of the 576 fighter sorties flown that day. At Deichmann's insistence the rest were used for a massive three-and-a-half-hour series of 'freie Jagd' sweeps late in the afternoon.

The morning strike against Eastchurch, a Coastal Command base now temporarily housing Bomber Command's 12 Squadron, on anti-invasion alert, was flown by Gabelmann's I./KG 3, its 23 Do 17Zs carrying 19.35 tons of bombs. Park launched five squadrons. Four intercepted, but the formation was well protected by Galland's JG 26 and Mölders' JG 51.

Dropping from 16,000ft at 0850hrs, the bombers pummelled Eastchurch. The ObdL situation report notes a 'large number of hits on living quarters were observed' but no casualties were caused. Two Fairey Battles were completely destroyed and three damaged, and the landing grounds were churned up by numerous craters and seeded with several delayed-action bombs. The airfield was serviceable for restricted day flying only.

At midday the second raid, flown by Hptm Otto Pilger's II./KG 3, gathered its escorts over the Pas-de-Calais, headed north across the eastern mouth of the Channel and at 1235hrs cut across North Foreland to fly up the south shore of the Thames Estuary. At the Isle of Sheppey, Pilger turned his 27 Do 17Zs north, crossed the Estuary at Southend and bombed Rochford, Hornchurch's FOL.

Dropping 23.4 tons of bombs from 18,000ft, at 1250hrs the raiders pounded the airfield. Some 60 HE bombs impacted inside the perimeter, half of them leaving craters in the landing grounds, the others knocking out electrical power, telephone communications and water mains. Others set buildings ablaze and blocked the railway line.[26]

Between 1530 and 1900hrs, JaFü 2 launched numerous fighter sweeps across Kent, employing five Zerstörergruppen (60 Bf 110s) and eight Jagdgruppen (240 Bf 109Es), many of them as local area familiarization flights for the units just

A 64 Squadron pilot scrambles to his waiting Spitfire at Kenley. Ground crew have started the engine and positioned the parachute pack by the aircraft's tail ready for collection. (Author Collection)

arrived from Luftflotte 3. Over the course of three hours, Park responded with seven squadrons, resulting in several high-altitude combats between 18,000 and 25,000ft.

At the end of the day, Döring reported that his pilots had shot down 16 Hurricanes, 14 Spitfires and four Defiants, for the loss of a dozen 'Emils' – a very favourable 2.8:1 exchange ratio. In fact, six Hurricanes, five Spitfires and three Defiants had been lost in combat, two of them to Do 17Z rear gunners. Actual Jagdwaffe losses were 15 'Emils' – making for an unfavourable exchange ratio 0.8:1, masked by exaggerated overclaiming – and three Do 17Zs lost in the two airfield attacks.[27]

Three of Park's losses were of the hopeless Defiant. In five days, 264 Squadron had lost ten aircraft destroyed and ten crewmen killed. Dowding finally, and wisely, withdrew the decimated unit from daylight operations permanently, sending the remnants of the squadron north to No. 12 Group's Kirton-in-Lindsey that evening to rebuild and train exclusively as a night-fighter unit. It was replaced at Hornchurch the next day by 222 Squadron, drawn from the same station.

Illustrating the decisive numerical superiority possible with the transfer of all available Jagdwaffe units to Kesselring's command, the next day, in a hopeful *alles freie Jagd* (all free hunting) stratagem, 'approximately 700 single-engined and twin-engined fighters were employed together with 20 bombers'. The bombers were merely decoys (Lockvögel); no daylight raids were flown, the ObdL situation report describing the fighters as being 'employed primarily on freelance operations over England during which enemy fighter defences proved to be very evasive'.

Having learned from combating the three-and-a-half hours of fighter sweeps the day prior, Park's controllers held back airborne squadrons unless they determined that the target formation was of bombers, rather than a fighter sweep. This frustrated Kesselring. In his autobiography he expressed the opinion: 'After costly initial engagements the English fighters kept out of the way of the [numerically] superior German forces. By the employment of small bomber units to bait the English fighters we managed to bring them up again until even this chance of a battle became so rare that no decision could be forced as they were expressly ordered to avoid any engagement. Our difficulty was not to bring down enemy fighters… but to get the enemy to fight.'[28]

Since No. 11 Group's controllers judiciously and obstinately avoided fighter-versus-fighter engagements, the results of the full day of fighter sweeps were hugely disappointing. Only 16 Spitfires and three Hurricanes were claimed, for the loss of seven Bf 109Es. Actual losses were four Spitfires and six Hurricanes to eight 'Emils', six of the latter from Lützow's JG 3.[29] Air superiority could not be won this way.

With the failure of his short-lived '*alles freie Jagd*' stratagem, and with the need for the achievement of aerial superiority over south-east England beginning to grow more urgent with each passing day, Deichmann had no choice but to organize a resumption of the offensive counter-air bombing campaign. With the successful

Major Günther Lützow became Geschwaderkommodore of JG 3 on 21 August 1940. After scoring 15 victories during the Battle of Britain, he was awarded the Ritterkreuz (Knight's Cross), on 18 September 1940. (Author Collection)

The view forward from the cockpit of an He 111 also conveys the vulnerability of the crew, with just Plexiglass between them and volleys of .303 machine-gun rounds fired from RAF fighters. (Author Collection)

attack against Rochford on the 28th, all of Park's 'middle ring' of airfields had been struck, fulfilling the objectives of *Adlerangriff's* original Stage 2.

It was time to move on to Stage 3, the destruction of No. 11 Group airfields within 30 miles (50km) of London. These were the four primary sector stations, Kenley (B), Biggin Hill (C), Hornchurch (D) and North Weald (E), plus Biggin Hill's FOL, Gravesend. With a decreasing number of days before Hitler would have to make a decision to launch or postpone *Seelöwe*, the immediate question was which of these should II. Fliegerkorps concentrate on?

Since joining the RLM in 1934, Deichmann had specialized in bombers, but for 12 years between 1916 and 1928, he had been a Prussian infantry officer and viewed the problem from an army perspective. For him, it was a simple map exercise. Two of the three primary invasion landing areas (Landungsräume B and C), forming a 45-mile (56km) front stretching on either side of Dungeness from near Hastings to near Folkestone, lay in the region known to be under Biggin Hill's 'Tophat Control'.

Since Schmid's assessment of Fighter Command's integrated air defence system was that: 'The Command at high level is inflexible in its organization… as formations are rigidly attached to their home bases [sector stations]',[30] it was assumed that if Biggin Hill was destroyed there would be little or no means of fighter control overhead the two beachheads astride Dungeness and all the way north-east to London. If nearby (to the west) Kenley actually had overlap and was able to exert some control over C Sector's airspace, then it, naturally, would also have to be neutralized. The fact that Landungsräum C, from Eastbourne to Bexhill, also lay in its sector made it the obvious second priority after Biggin Hill.

Kesselring believed: 'In order to carry out an invasion, it was necessary to stun the island defences by sharp hammer-blows.' To deliver such blows, Deichmann planned to resume the offensive with a record number of sorties – 1,345 – and new tactics. Instead of sending two or three Gruppe-size formations of bombers together in tightly spaced packages, Luftflotte 2 would launch almost continuous streams of smaller-sized raids at 20- or 30-minute intervals across a three- to four-hour period. The intent was to saturate No. 11 Group's command and control capability over time rather than attempt to overwhelm it all at once.

Additionally, Deichmann saw no need to attack the coastal Chain Home/Chain Home Low radar sites. He reserved that for the afternoon of 'S-minus-1', planning to knock them out immediately prior to the army's Channel crossing. He noted: 'since the object of *Adlerangriff* was to destroy Fighter Command, it was better that the British should be warned of an approaching attack, so that their fighters would come up and offer combat in which they would be destroyed in the air.'[31]

ADLERANGRIFF STAGE 3, THE BATTLE OF BIGGIN HILL BEGINS – 30 AUGUST

Luftflotte 2 hit Biggin Hill twice during the first day, 30 August.

Following two fighter feints that swept across the Dover Straits at 0800hrs (two groups) and 0915hrs (three groups) and then returned to patrol off the Pas-de-Calais, the morning's main strike force of two packages was detected at 1030hrs with a large force of '50+' forming over Tramecourt, south-east of Boulogne, and three smaller groups of '20+' each, between Cap Gris-Nez and Calais.

The *RAF Narrative* reports that the first package comprised 27 He 111Hs from II./KG 1, led by Gruppenkommandeur Hptm Heinz Fischer and escorted by a similar number of II./ZG 76 Bf 110s . Fischer led his formation directly across the Channel, crossing the coast at Dungeness at 1103hrs and turning towards Tonbridge. The second package, a reported[32] 12–18 Do 17Zs of a unit not satisfactorily determined, flanked by two 'freie Jagd' sweeps by II./JG 54 and V.(Z)/LG 1, flew a parallel course, in echelon to the right/north, going 'feet dry' near Folkestone about 12 minutes later, headed towards Redhill.

Fischer's target was Farnborough, west of London, but initially he steered his formation towards Kenley, where Deichmann hoped he would attract Park's responding interceptors and draw them away to the west so that the following Dorniers could strike Biggin Hill unopposed. The plan worked well, in fact too well for Fischer's unfortunate formation.

Park responded by launching 1, 56, 79, 85, 151, 253, 501, 603 and 610 Sqns and requested that No. 12 Group cover Biggin Hill – Leigh-Mallory sent 19 Sqn from Duxford. Willoughby de Broke deployed two of his units to patrol Dover, positioned two more over Canterbury and Maidstone, and sent others to patrol over Kenley, Biggin Hill and Hawkinge. Vectored by the new C Sector controller, Sqn Ldr John Worrall, 'Hydro Leader', Sqn Ldr Peter Townsend, 85 Sqn, spotted the Heinkels west of Ashford at 16,000ft 'with numerous escorting fighters still higher [and he] led his formation inland until he could carry out a head-on attack

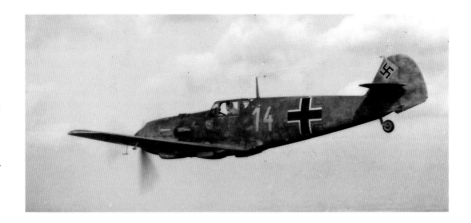

The Luftwaffe's all-out assault on Park's sector stations began on 30 August and lasted eight days. Biggin Hill was hit twice on day one. In the thick of it, JG 2 conducted a second 'freie Jagd' sweep during the afternoon and lost three 'Emils' to RAF interceptors. Bf 109E-4 'Yellow 14' of 3./JG 2 was flown by Lt Franz Fiby. (Chris Goss, colourized by Richard Molloy)

on the bombers from out of the sun.'

As Townsend was positioning his 11 Hurricanes for the attack, he provided a running commentary on the raiders' progress, reporting approximate strength, height, course and approximate position, as Park had instructed. Because cloud cover over Kent precluded effective Observer Corps reporting, this information proved vital and Willoughby de Broke quickly recognized the threat approaching his two southern sector stations. He recalled 253 Squadron from over Maidstone to patrol over Kenley. Receiving them, B Sector controller ('Sapper Control'), Sqn Ldr Anthony Norman, vectored 'Viceroy Leader', Sqn Ldr Harold Starr, south to intercept as well, but over Redhill they were attacked by Hptm Erich Groth's II./ZG 26, which shot down four Hurricanes (but claimed 18) between 1115 and 1120hrs, killing two pilots and wounding another, without loss.

Biggin Hill was subjected to an all-out bombardment and was attacked 11 times in eight days, after which time there was little left to bomb. At the left of the photograph, the airfield is pock-marked with bomb craters. (Jean-Louis Roba)

As they turned west over Tonbridge, the raiders were spotted by 79 Sqn, patrolling over Biggin Hill and, moving ahead of the bombers, Sqn Ldr J. 'Jim' Hervey Heyworth delivered a fierce head-on attack. A Hurricane and Heinkel collided over Reigate at 1112hrs. Soon, 79 and 85 Squadrons were joined by 501 and 610 Sqns, hastily withdrawn from over Hawkinge and Dover and, with their escorts stripped away, Fischer's Heinkels were very soon in desperate trouble.

Attacked by 45 fighters from three Hurricane and one Spitfire squadron, the formation was completely shattered, most of the bombers turning south and dumping seven tons of bombs on an 'industrial facility [and a] railway junction', according to the ObdL situation report, between Leatherhead and Dorking. Others continued westbound and reported dropping 2.5 tons of bombs on Aldershot Barracks. Five Heinkels, four from 5. Staffel (flying 10. (Ergänzungs) Staffel (replacement training squadron) aircraft), were shot down.

This costly failure nonetheless opened the door for the follow-up strike against Biggin Hill, but that was nearly foiled by the low scattered-to-broken cloud deck at 6,000–8,000ft. The Dorniers' flanking 'freie Jagd' sweeps tied up 151 and 603 Sqns, but most of the raiders overflew their target and, between 1130 and 1142hrs some dropped their bombs (5.8 tons) on Bromley railway station and urban areas in south London just east of Croydon.

Apparently the formation leader realized his navigator's error and reversed course, and, at noon, from 15,000ft, several Dorniers released ten tons of bombs over Biggin Hill which, according to the station ORB, 'did damage to the aerodrome surface and material damage to Biggin Hill village and Keston. The aerodrome surface was not rendered unfit for flying and aircraft still continued to operate.' The raiders returned to France, chased – but not caught – by 616 Squadron.

At 1456hrs, Observer Corps posts reported two 'freie Jagd' missions sweeping inland all the way to Redhill before retiring via Beachy Head. Four minutes later, nine Jabos (likely eight Bf 109E-7s of the just arrived II.(Schl)/LG 2 on a practice mission led by an ErprGr 210 Bf 110D) dropped nine SC250 bombs on Lympne, damaging its one remaining hangar and, from its ORB, killing six civilians 'by direct hit on air raid shelter'.

Kesselring's major effort of the day followed 40 minutes later. The deepest daylight penetration into British airspace made during the war, the Observer Corps reported three enemy formations crossing the Kent coast near Dover, headed north-north-west. The strike package was led by Obstlt Erich Kaufmann and consisted of an estimated 25–30 He 111s from I. and II./KG 53 (using aircraft from all three Gruppen), escorted by II./ZG 2, II./ZG 26, and II./ZG 76, briefed to bomb the Vauxhall Motors works and airfield at Luton, and the Handley Page factory at Radlett, both north-west of London.

Only 222 Sqn was airborne when the raid was first reported crossing the coast and, at 1550hrs, Park began scrambling 151, 501, 603, and 616 Sqns while Kaufmann's Heinkels and escorting Zerstörers continued northwards across Kent.

Left to right, Sergeant Joan Mortimer, Flight Officer Elspeth Green and Sergeant Helen Turner were stationed at Biggin Hill during the 30 August raid. Green continued sending vital teleprinter messages to 11 Group, despite being knocked to the ground when the Operations Room took a direct hit. Turner similarly continued to work on the telephone switchboard, even as the building was hit repeatedly, both women only leaving the building after fire broke out and they were ordered to abandon their posts. Mortimer also continued to relay messages throughout the raid, then rushed outside to mark the position of unexploded bombs with red flags, despite some exploding nearby. All three were awarded the Military Medal for their bravery and fortitude. (AHB)

Just after 1600, 'Kotel Leader', Sqn Ldr John Hill and his 222 Sqn, engaged the composite force over Canterbury. The unit lost two Spitfires to II./ZG 2 without getting to the bombers.

Clouds overhead permitted only sporadic and sketchy Observer Corps reports; raid plotting at Uxbridge was therefore confused and, correspondingly, Willoughby de Broke's defence was hastily organized and clumsy. When Kaufmann's formation was reported heading across the Thames Estuary from Eastchurch towards Southend-on-Sea, it appeared that Park's northern sector stations were threatened, so three more squadrons, plus two from No. 12 Group, were scrambled to intercept.

Still unopposed – the escorts repulsed an intercept over the Estuary by 151 Squadron (for the loss of one Hurricane) – Kaufmann's bomber formation flew all the way to North Weald, where Christer Bergström's *The Battle of Britain: An Epic Conflict Revisited* reveals that a 56 Squadron mechanic recalled, 'We nervously watched as it sailed majestically over the station, at great height, without dropping a bomb!'

Still in perfect formation, the raiders flew another 25 miles (40km), deep into Bedfordshire, and at 1645hrs dropped 194 bombs (23.5 tons) on the Vauxhall Motors works, believed to be involved in aeroengine manufacture, Luton's civilian airfield and the city. Vauxhall's experimental building was heavily damaged and 39 employees were killed; 20 more civilians were killed in the city and 141 injured.

Turning for home, Kaufmann's He 111Hs and the few II./ZG 76 Zerstörers remaining with them rather than tangling with 222 Sqn, found themselves cornered by six RAF fighter squadrons; they had to fight their way back across Hertfordshire and Essex to get home. According to OFw Alfred Sticht, Beobachter (observer) aboard the 1. Staffelkapitän's aircraft: 'Several He 111s limped back out over the Thames Estuary with severe damage, but despite the long return flight

Crews from 6./KG 53 relax at their base, Lille-Nord. He 111 'A1+JP', in the background, was severely damaged during an attack on Radlett on 30 August and crashed at Manston at 1635hrs during the return flight. Two of the crew were killed, the remaining three captured. (Clive Ellis)

and repeated British fighter attacks, the number of aircraft lost during the Luton mission [was] limited… At St Omer the "Haifisch Zerstörer" [II./ZG 76] wave[d] their wings in a farewell to us. Via radio we thank[ed] them for the excellent fighter escort. Without them it would have been really bad for us.'

Six He 111Hs and three Bf 110s were lost on the mission.

As the Heinkels were fighting their way home, Kesselring's next wave was reported as 20 Do 17Zs at 18,000ft accompanied by 'a similar number of escorts behind them at the same height, with a further fighter force some 2,000ft above'. They were first observed ten miles (15km) east of Dungeness, headed north. They crossed the coast at Folkstone and flew directly across Kent to Chatham, their escorts fending off 43 Squadron and a flight from 'Treble Two'. The other ten squadrons launched against the Luton raid, having exhausted their fuel, were landing to refuel and rearm, the attackers' planned timing working perfectly.

Reaching Chatham at about 1730hrs, the bombers turned south-west and ten minutes later dropped 8.8 tons of bombs on Detling; between 40 and 50 weapons impacted on the airfield. The bombers were unopposed. The landing grounds were cratered, electricity supply cables cut and an oil storage tank set ablaze. One person was killed, a second mortally injured and a Blenheim damaged. The base was non-operational until 0900hrs the next morning; the raiders returned to base without loss.

As these aircraft returned to France, the next wave was already inbound, crossing the coast near Dover at 1745 and heading north-north-west across Kent following the route used by previous packages. This time it was the indomitable ErprGr 210, now commanded by Hptm Hans von Boltenstern, with ten Bf 110Ds leading a half-dozen Bf 109E-7 Jabos from II.(Schl)/LG 2 on their very first operational mission. Major Hannes Trautloft's entire JG 54 was flying high cover escort for the fast fighter-bombers.

Willoughby de Broke ordered 501 Sqn to patrol over Hawkinge and 616 Sqn over Kenley, while Worrall vectored 'Kotel Leader' to intercept and scrambled 79 Squadron to patrol over Biggin Hill. Number 222 Squadron was spotted climbing in line astern formation and 7./JG 54 attacked it from out of the sun, shooting down three Spitfires and scattering the rest.

Meanwhile, over the Isle of Sheppey von Boltenstern's Jabos turned west, arrowing straight for Biggin Hill, which they attacked at 1800hrs. They came in fast and low, dropping 16 SC250 and SC500 bombs on hangars, buildings and other structures. One hangar, and a 32 Sqn Hurricane inside, was destroyed, as were the MT pool, station workshops, armoury, and stores; Sergeant's Mess and WAAF quarters; and NAAFI and cookhouse. Telephone/telegraph lines and the electricity, gas and water mains were all cut, and 39 personnel were killed, another 26 wounded. Worrall's 'Tophat Control' went off the air, but Norman (Kenley's 'Sapper Control') took over until power and communications could be restored. Once again the attackers escaped without loss.[33]

Following the morning's aborted mission against Farnborough, it became a day of encouraging successes. In addition to the escort missions mentioned, JaFü 2 flew enough 'freie Jagd' sweeps and feints to amass a record 1,265 fighter sorties, providing smothering fighter cover all across Kent. They were almost wholly responsible for shooting down the 12 Hurricanes and nine Spitfires lost that day (with seven pilots killed, four wounded), for the loss of 12 'Emils' and six Zerstörers, not a particularly favourable exchange rate.[34]

While, Luftflotte 2 had lost 11 bombers in 80 sorties (a 13.75 per cent loss rate) these were all on the long-range missions beyond the Jagdwaffe's ability to escort. Deichmann's operations planning, sequencing the missions so closely that Park had little time to organize an effective defence for the next wave, was notably successful, but was aided immeasurably by clouds precluding effective Observer Corps tracking.

BATTLE OF BIGGIN HILL CONTINUES –
31 AUGUST TO 6 SEPTEMBER

Following the obligatory fighter sweep early the next morning – Park's controllers largely ignored it – at about 0800hrs some 200 bombers and fighters were detected by the Dunkirk (Canterbury) and Canewdon CH radars approaching via the Thames Estuary. Park scrambled 13 squadrons to intercept two Gruppe-strength formations, each heavily escorted by Bf 110s.

Bf 109Es of JG 2 'Richthofen' at their Beaumont-le-Roger base. The aircraft in the foreground with the impressive kill score belongs to Helmut Wick of I./JG 2. It has the Gruppenkommandeur's chevron, but still carries the 3. Staffel badge. (NMUSAF)

TOP LEFT
At 1300hrs on 31 August, Do 17Zs from KG 2 and KG 3, escorted by Bf 109s, attacked Biggin Hill, Hornchurch and Croydon. Shortly after leaving Hornchurch, '5K+LM' from 4./KG 3 was attacked by fighters and damaged by AA fire. The crew, all wounded, crash-landed at Sandwich Flats at 1420hrs. (Clive Ellis)

BELOW LEFT
The crew of '5K+LM', OFw Lange, Uffz Krostopotsch, Fw Berndt and Fw Wuensch were captured. On the left, Lange, the pilot, and either Berndt or Wuensch, are escorted into captivity. (Clive Ellis)

Obstlt Paul Weitkus led 19 Do 17Zs from II./KG 2, escorted by II./ZG 76, all the way across Essex, carrying 19.3 tons of HE and 15 incendiary canisters to bomb Duxford airfield. Although they were not intercepted before arriving in the target's vicinity at 0835hrs, the formation failed to locate the airfield and meandered for 15 minutes, scattering ordnance in the fields south of Cambridge and without causing damage.

Behind them, Fuchs led 14 III./KG 2 Dorniers escorted by III./ZG 26, against Debden at 0838hrs with 13.9 tons of bombs and a dozen RSK 36 canisters. About 100 bombs and incendiaries fell within the aerodrome, hitting a hangar, the barracks, MT garage, Sergeants' Mess, Sick Quarters and NAAFI. Two personnel were killed and 12 injured. The station ORB reports: 'The operational side of the Station functioned throughout and there was no failure of lighting or communications in the Operations Room.'

Although heavily engaged by fighters during their egress, only one II./KG 2 Do 17Z was lost, with two from III./KG 2 damaged; Fuchs was wounded.

At 1001hrs a smaller 2./KG 76 force – six Lockvögel, escorted by the whole of JG 54 – attacked Eastchurch airfield, doing 'some damage to aerodrome surface which still remain[ed] serviceable for aircraft. Railway track immediately outside the camp received two direct hits. 1 airman slightly wounded.'

Headed for Croydon, a dozen II./KG 76 Ju 88As crossed the coast near Folkstone at 1238hrs, following four minutes behind a 'freie Jagd' sweep by Galland's III./JG 26, with the Geschwader's other two Gruppen providing Jagdschutz close escort. Diving from 15,000ft at 1255hrs, the bombers delivered 14 tons of SC50, SC250 and SC500 bombs, causing only minor damage to various airfield facilities, although the nearby Rollason aircraft works was severely damaged.

Continuing Deichmann's stratagem of sending streams of smaller-sized raids at half-hour intervals, the next raid, by II./KG 3, crossed the coast at Dover and steered towards the Thames Estuary at Sheppey. It was intercepted by 151, 501, 310 and 601 Squadrons as it approached Hornchurch and three of the four British squadrons were engaging when the Bf 109Es, low on fuel, turned for home.

The interceptors continued engaging the fighters as they egressed and the bombers, although harried by 310 (Czech) Squadron, dropped nine tons of SC50s, of which about 100 hit the aerodrome. The Hornchurch ORB reports: 'The only vital damage was to the power cable, which was cut. Emergency power equipment was brought into operation until repair was effected. Three men were killed and 11 wounded. 54 Squadron [Spitfires] attempted to take off during the attack and ran through the bombs. Three aircraft were destroyed, one being blown from the middle of the landing field to outside the boundary, but all three pilots miraculously

Based in the Pas-de-Calais, this Bf 109E-4 of 9./JG 26, flown by Oblt Fronhoefer, was damaged in combat with Plt Off C. Gray of 54 Squadron, based at Hornchurch, on 31 August. The 'Emils' were supporting the Do 17s of III./KG 76, which were tasked to attack Biggin Hill. Fronhoefer crash-landed his aircraft at 1845hrs near Ulcombe. Note the gothic 'S' of JG 26 and the 'Hollenhund' (Hellhound) insignia of 9 Staffel. (Andy Saunders, colourized by Richard Molloy)

escaped with only slight injuries.' Three Do 17Zs were lost in the attack.

Hornchurch and Biggin Hill were attacked in the late afternoon. Shortly after 1800hrs, the Hornchurch attackers (unit unknown, but reported in the *RAF Narrative* to have been Do 17Zs) dropped 16.5 tons of bombs and 20 RSK 36 canisters – 'about 80% of the bombs fell on the taxying area', the ObdL situation report says. This is confirmed by the Station ORB, which reported: 'The line of bombs fell towards the edge of the aerodrome. Two Spitfires parked near the edge were written off, and one airman killed… apart from damage to dispersal pens, the perimeter track, and the aerodrome surface, the aerodrome remained serviceable.'

Biggin Hill is believed to have been struck by I. and III./KG 76, with one Gruppe bombing the North Camp and the other the South Camp, both from 'high level'. Of 27 tons of bombs, approximately 100 impacted the airfield. The station ORB records that they caused 'extensive damage to buildings [and] Hangars in the South Camp… In the North Camp, the [large] Triple Bay Hangar was damaged, the Operations Block received a direct hit and was burnt [out], the Officers Married Quarters were all severely damaged by blast. The temporary lash-up of telephone lines and power cables made after the previous evening's raid was completely destroyed.'

Once again contact with Uxbridge was cut off, forcing 'Sapper Control' (Kenley) to take over control of C Sector. With its building destroyed, the Sector Ops Room was moved to a vacant shop in the Pantiles, a village half a mile south of the airfield. General Post Office (GPO) technicians worked through the night tying into the nearby main telephone/telegraph lines, building a switchboard and reconstructing the Sector Ops Room in a very confined space. Although contact with Uxbridge was re-established within three hours, even limited fighter control capability was not restored until the next morning. 'As a centre for control of squadrons operating within the sector the efficiency of the station was much affected.'

Park reported to Fighter Command: 'Only one squadron could operate from there, and the remaining two squadrons had to be placed under the control of adjacent sectors for over a week.' Number 72 Squadron, which lost a Spitfire destroyed in the attack, was transferred to Croydon the next morning, where it was assigned to B Sector – it would not return to Biggin Hill until 13 September. Number 501 Squadron, stationed at the Gravesend FOL, was reassigned to D Sector until 10 September, when it was transferred to Kenley. With only five serviceable Hurricanes remaining, 79 Squadron became a 'local base defence flight'.

Of the day's 1,450 sorties – a new record for Luftflotte 2 – only 150 were by bombers. These were protected by 1,300 fighter sorties, which limited actual RAF victories, in spite of much higher claims, to only eight bombers, while 25 Hurricanes and eight Spitfires were shot down in exchange for 19 Bf 109s and six Zerstörers shot down. Additionally, seven Fighter Command bases, four of them sector stations, had been bombed, one of them twice, destroying seven Spitfires on

Fighter Command suffered its highest losses of the Battle on 31 August. Thirty-nine of its fighters were shot down, ten pilots killed, 21 wounded (ten of whom were burned) and eight escaped unhurt. (NARA)

This Spitfire, belonging to 222 Squadron, was blasted onto its back during one of two raids on Hornchurch on 31 August. (AHB)

At 1400hrs on 1 September, Bf 110C-1 'L1+OH' of 14(Z)./LG1 was damaged by fighters. The pilot, OFw Rudolf Kobert, performed a controlled belly landing near Bilsington. He and his Bordfunker, Fw Werner Meinig, were captured. (Clive Ellis)

the ground. Another record was also set. At 39, Fighter Command suffered its highest daily loss of the campaign.[35]

It looked like the Luftwaffe had finally got it right.

The 110 bomber and 530 fighter sorties flown on 1 September included another, but very small, attack on Biggin Hill, a Staffel-size strike on Kenley (which missed), and token one-or-two aeroplane harassment raids on Abingdon, Hawkinge, Lympne and Detling.

The attacks on Kenley and Biggin Hill were two parts of the same operation. Fifteen Do 17Zs from KG 76 crossed the coast at Dungeness at 1340hrs and ten minutes later approached the two bases, masked by several simultaneous 'freie Jagd' sweeps. Park's controllers, believing them all to be fighter formations, refused combat, allowing the bombers to strike their targets unopposed. Approaching the targets, one Kette attacked Biggin Hill from 15,000ft, while the rest of the formation attempted to attack Kenley, but most of its bombs fell on the nearby Guards Depot at Caterham.

Even as small as it was, accurately dropping only three tons of bombs the raid on Biggin Hill almost completed the base's destruction. 'Bombs fell amongst the Camp buildings without doing much further damage, but shaking buildings and making them unsafe… All main services and communications were destroyed,' the station ORB notes. The landing grounds were practically unusable, only one hangar was left standing, virtually all buildings were uninhabitable, and all communications in and off the base were again severed, forcing many of the station's sections to move into nearby Keston village.[36]

Three 79 Squadron Hurricanes, the 'local base defence flight', was scrambled and had barely left the airfield when the first bombs fell. Engaged by the escorting Messerschmitts, two were shot down, with both pilots survived wounded and burned, and the third crashed upon landing.[37]

Three days later, during which no further raids occurred and repairs had restored the runway and were beginning to make the base inhabitable once again, Gp Capt Grice became concerned that the remaining hangar might entice the Luftwaffe to return and attack Biggin Hill again. Taking off in a Miles Magister to see what it looked like from the air, he quickly recognized that the large hangar, standing amid heaps of rubble, stood out invitingly and, upon landing, ordered it demolished; it was useless anyway.

At 1800hrs, explosive charges levelled the structure.[38]

Nevertheless, Kesselring's raiders returned at 1000hrs on 6 September, dropping 22.8 tons of bombs. This raid was to clear the way for the next day's major attack on London and, having battered Biggin Hill into reduced operations, Deichmann wanted to hit it again to ensure any repairs made in the previous five days were countered with further damage. The station ORB reports, 'Damage was done to some [fighter] Dispersal Points and the aerodrome surface, but most of the bombs overshot the aerodrome and fell on the Westerham Road and again destroyed telephone lines.'[39] The battered sector station could still operate only one squadron at a time.

During these five days, Kenley, Hornchurch, North Weald, Gravesend, Eastchurch and Detling were all attacked again, exerting continuing pressure and creating cumulative damage on the main Fighter Command bases in south-east England.[40] Kenley was so badly battered that the B Sector Ops Room had to be moved into an empty butcher's shop in Caterham, where it was tied into nearby GPO telephone lines.

With the relentlessly mounting damage and destruction, to say nothing of the increasing chronic fatigue experienced by his fighter pilots, Park was beginning to become concerned about his Group's ability to continue to mount an effective defence. He wrote: 'There was a critical period between 28 August and 5 September when the damage to sector stations and our ground organization was having a serious effect on the fighting efficiency of the fighter squadrons.'[41]

At this point Dowding came to the conclusion that, should the beating continue, he 'had no alternative but to withdraw 11 Group from south-east England altogether'.[42]

Had he done so, he might have given Göring the victory.

On 3 September, 54 Do 17s from KG 2, escorted by 80 Bf 110s from ZG 2 and ZG 26 (seen here), were sent to attack North Weald. Despite being heavily engaged by Hurricanes from six squadrons and Spitfires from 19 and 603 Squadrons, the Zerstörers protected their charges well and only one Dornier fell. Five RAF fighters were shot down for the loss of seven Bf 110s. Eight cannon-armed Spitfires from 19 Squadron downed two of the escorts, before six were forced to withdraw due to gun stoppages. Despite more than 200 bombs falling on the airfield, it remained open. (AHB donated by Ken Wakefield)

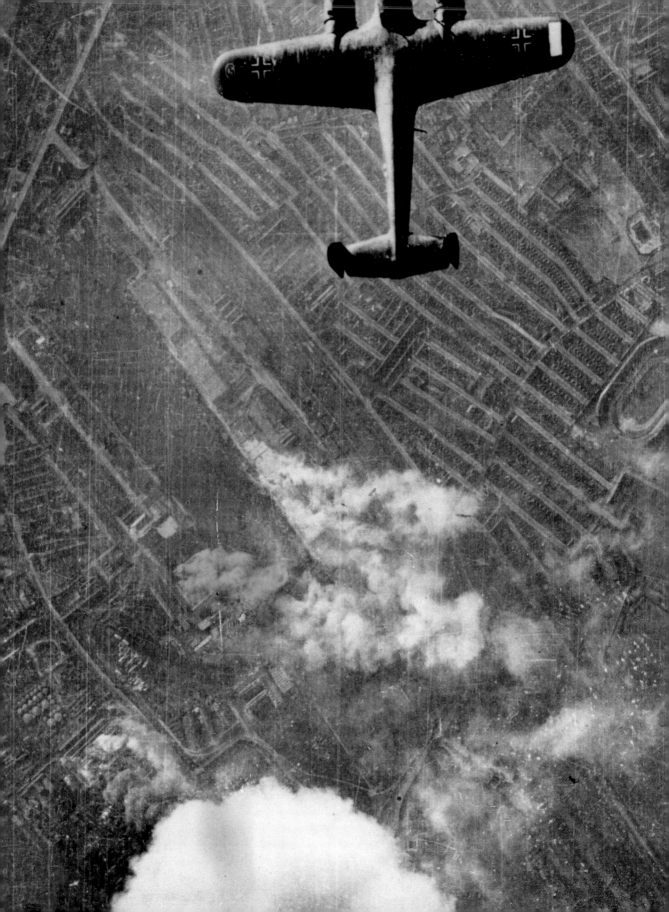

CHAPTER XII

ADLERANGRIFF STAGE 4
7–17 September 1940

We have no chance of destroying the English fighters on the ground. We must force their last reserves... into combat in the air.

Hermann Göring, meeting with Luftflotte commanders,
The Hague, 3 September 1940[1]

LONDON BECOMES THE TARGET

Begun on the night of 24/25 August, the Luftwaffe's increased night-bombing effort had an inauspicious beginning.

That night, 15 He 111Hs from KG 1 were dispatched to bomb a variety of targets that included the Hawker Aircraft factory at Kingston-on-Thames and the Pobjoy Airmotors and Aircraft facility at Rochester airfield (the former manufacturing Hurricanes and the latter Spitfire airframes), and the oil storage installation at Thameshaven. Crossing the coast between Beachy Head and Dungeness, the streams of individual bombers were blown off course by unusually strong easterly winds at altitude. The ObdL situation report records that the largest contingent, after 'the first aircraft identified the target through a gap in the clouds [below] and attacked it', dumped 8.65 tons of HE bombs and five RSK 36 incendiary canisters 'in open fields [in Surrey, south-west of Kingston] and no damage was done'.

Three Heinkels targeted Rochester with 2.3 tons of HE and five canisters. Two bomber crews reported that they 'identified the target and attacked it' at 2340hrs, but apparently these bombs fell well to the west, upon Millwall (near Canary Wharf docks), in Finsbury and the Islington Borough, causing a fire near central London that required 200 pumping engines. This agrees with the third bomber's crew report, 'observed violent explosions and large fires.'

Crossing the coast at Dungeness at 0030hrs, a fourth Heinkel arrived over the Thames at Tilbury, well west of Thameshaven, and turned west, exactly the wrong direction. From 0050hrs to 0110hrs it flew over the East End of London, liberally scattering two tons of HE bombs and two RSK 36s – with 'large fires observed' – in the Stepney, Bethnal Green, East Ham and Leyton districts, according to the *RAF Narrative*. Nine civilians were killed in these attacks.[2]

Churchill immediately authorized a retaliatory strike by Bomber Command. That night 81 twin-engined medium bombers comprising Handley Page Hampdens from 49 and 50 Sqns, and Vickers Wellingtons from 99 and 149 Sqns, were sent to bomb Berlin's Tempelhof airport and the large Siemens factory complex. But the persistent high winds aloft also conspired against this initial attack. Only ten bombers reached Berlin's outskirts and these unloaded their bombs on the city's municipal farms near Rosenthal. Six Hampdens were lost,

PREVIOUS PAGES
Two Do 17s from KG 3 over West Ham, during the attack on Woolwich Arsenal in the initial phase of the 7 September London raids. (AHB)

Assigned to Fliegerkorps IV, within Luftflotte 3, KGr 100 was a specialist pathfinder unit based at Vannes, in the Brest Peninsula. On the evening of 28 August, eight of the unit's He 111s used their X-Gerät navigation equipment and incendiary bombs to accurately mark the important Atlantic convoy port of Liverpool. This enabled a main force of more than 150 aircraft to inflict extensive damage on the city. Heinkel '6N+FK' was with 2./KGr 100. (Chris Goss)

three of them ditching in the North Sea due to fuel exhaustion from battling the high winds.

Marginally more successful strikes followed on 28/29 and 29/30 August.

Following the third raid on Berlin, Hitler authorized Göring to launch 'reprisal attacks with strong forces against London', provided they would not be Terrorangriff (terror attacks) against residential areas. Almost immediately, ObdL relayed the news to the Luftflotte commanders along with Göring's instructions to convene another Besprechung, at The Hague on 3 September, to plan the forthcoming attacks. Codenaming the new target as 'Loge' (in German; in English it was Loki, the ancient Norse giant god of fire) Göring saw this as an opportunity to win – and end – the conflict by forcing British capitulation while still pursuing the operational aim of attaining air superiority over south-east England through increased fighter-versus-fighter combat.

With the decision date for *Seelöwe* uncomfortably close, every evening Göring pored over Luftflotte 2's situation reports to see how the battle for Luftüberlegenheit (air superiority) was going. To Göring it was encouraging reading. But his understanding of military aviation and airpower, other than his belief in Douhet's terror-bombing theories, was gained from his experience as a World War I fighter pilot, flying defensive patrols over the front lines; he knew nothing about offensive operations or air campaigning. This limited experience convinced him that the only true measure of success in 'his Luftwaffe's' offensive counter-air campaign was the 'kill scores' of his Jagdwaffe and Zerstörer pilots. So, he was very pleased that from 24 August to 2 September, JaFü 2 reported that his Jagdgeschwader had destroyed 340 Spitfires, 193 Hurricanes, eight Defiants and 31 unknown aircraft in the air, for the loss of only 107 Bf 109Es and 30 Bf 110s.[3]

Additionally, the bombing of No. 11 Group airfields had resulted in claims for 44 RAF aircraft (types unknown) destroyed; 23 of these were at Hornchurch,

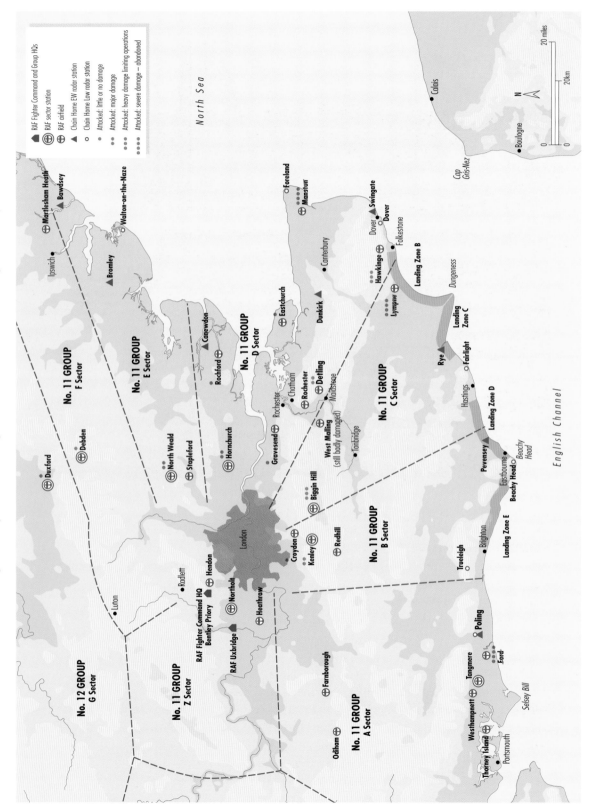

Results of *Adlerangriff* Stage 3, showing airfields attacked 18 August–6 September 1940

Croydon and Eastchurch, and were presumed to be fighters. The bomber claims seemed to be confirmed by ObdL and the Luftflotten's own post-strike photo-reconnaissance. Their diligent, though sometimes sketchy, morning photo-reconnaissance pictures showed the RAF bases' landing grounds pocked with scores of craters, although there were disappointingly few telltale scorch marks signifying burnt aircraft wreckage. So why continue to bomb them when 13 times as many enemy aircraft were being downed in air-to-air combat?

To the uninitiated, the greatest payoff (almost 5 to 1) seemed to be in aerial combat, not in bombing airfields.

The Luftflotten had also reported losing a total of 54 bombers in the airfield attacks, night-bombing, and reconnaissance missions, the vast majority of these being lost to RAF fighters during daylight bombing operations. Little more could be done to lessen losses, which amounted to around five per day for the ten-day period, but if this loss rate was 'the cost of doing business', it seemed a better 'investment' to expend them in attacking targets of much greater strategic significance, such as London, for psychological and propaganda reasons, and its

Reinforced and Reorganized Luftwaffe Deployments for *Adlerangriff* Stage 4

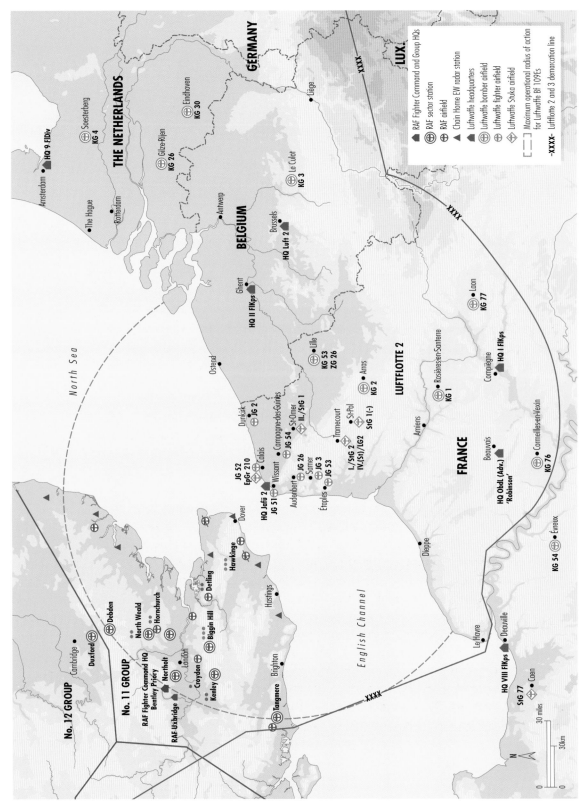

Legend:
- RAF Fighter Command and Group HQs
- RAF sector station
- RAF airfield
- Chain Home EW radar station
- Luftwaffe headquarters
- Luftwaffe bomber airfield
- Luftwaffe fighter airfield
- Luftwaffe Stuka airfield
- Maximum operational radius of action for Luftwaffe Bf 109Es
- **XXXX** Luftflotte 2 and 3 demarcation line

GERMANY

LUX.

THE NETHERLANDS

HQ 9.FlDiv
Amsterdam
The Hague
Rotterdam
Soesterberg
KG 4
Gilze-Rijen
KG 26
Eindhoven
KG 30
Le Culot
KG 3
Liège

BELGIUM

Antwerp
Brussels
HQ Luft 2
Ghent
HQ II Flkps

Loon
KG 77
HQ I Flkps
Compiègne
Rosières-en-Santerre
KG 1

LUFTFLOTTE 2

Lille
KG 53
ZG 26
Arras
KG 2
St-Pol
StG 1(-)
Framecourt

Amiens

Ostend

North Sea

Dunkirk
JG 2
Compagne-des-Guines
St-Omer
II./StG 1
JG 54
I./StG 2
IV.(St)/LG2
JG 52
EpGr 210
Calais
Wissant
JG 26
Samer
JG 3
JG 53
Étaples
JG 51
Audembert
HQ Jafü 2

FRANCE

Beauvais
HQ ObdL (Adv.)
'Robinson'
Corneilles-en-Vexin
KG 76

Dieppe

Évreux
KG 54

English Channel

Le Havre
Deauville
HQ VIII Flkps
Caen
StG 77

No. 12 GROUP

Cambridge
Duxford
Debden

No. 11 GROUP

North Weald
Hornchurch
London
Northolt
RAF Fighter Command HQ
Bentley Priory
RAF Uxbridge
Croydon
Kenley
Biggin Hill
Detling
Hawkinge
Dover
Hastings
Brighton
Tangmere

N

30 miles
30km

port facilities, resuming the *Handelskrieg* campaign.

And now Hitler had given Göring permission to do just that.

Göring had always wanted to bomb London and here was his opportunity. He'd made up his mind and ordered the 3 September Besprechung the same day Hitler's permission was granted.

In fact, to maximize the combat forces available to Kesselring, he ordered Stumpff to transfer his Luftflotte 5 bomber units to Luftflotte 2, to be assigned to Generaloberst Ulrich Grauert's I. Fliegerkorps. It was primarily conducting night-bombing under Sperrle's direction, but properly positioned to participate in Loerzer's daylight operations. Obstlt Karl Freiherr von Wechmar's KG 26 arrived at Gilze-Rijen, Holland, on 1 September with 57 He 111Hs and Obstlt Herbert Reickhoff's KG 30 landed at Eindhoven with 41 Ju 88As the next day. Additionally, two Gruppen of Obstlt Johann Raithel's KG 77 completed training and moved to Laon-Athies a week later, with the third following on 16 September. This fresh unit added 99 Ju 88As to Grauert's command.[4]

Now Kesselring, who frequently protested about having too few bombers to do the job, could not complain about lack of available aircraft.

While Kesselring's bases in Holland, Belgium and north-eastern France swelled with arriving bombers, during the next three days Schmid prepared another of his periodic assessments of the RAF. Counting on the accuracy of the Luftflotte situation reports, at the end of August Schmid had cheerfully assessed: 'In the battle for air superiority the RAF since August 8th has lost 1,115 fighters… [Additionally] Eighteen aerodromes [have been] destroyed and another 26 damaged. Ten per cent of the ground organization, offering facilities for fighter-plane repairs, has been destroyed… [But] Of the British planes reported shot down by us, a great number can be quickly repaired.'[5]

It seemed like 'mission accomplished'.

However, considering Fighter Command's continued and surprisingly active defence, Schmid was subsequently compelled to revise his RAF strength estimates upwards. In the above assessment he'd estimated that Fighter Command had only 100 Spitfires and Hurricanes remaining. However, the nearly week-long hiatus between 18 and 24 August while Jagdwaffe units were being moved around and bad weather struck, allowed him to suggest that this recess had permitted British aircraft production to make good Fighter Command losses. In his second increase in as many weeks, Schmid estimated Fighter Command strength on 1 September to be '600 fighter planes, of which 420 were [stationed in south-east England], and a reserve of 100 in the factories [awaiting delivery]'.[6]

The Besprechung began with Göring announcing the Führer's permission to bomb London and his intention to do so.[7] The only question, according to German historian Hans-Dieter Berenbrok, was: 'Could such an attack be launched without undue risk to the bomber force?' Kesselring, it is reported, believed it could.

Sperrle disagreed. He believed the current offensive counter-air campaign

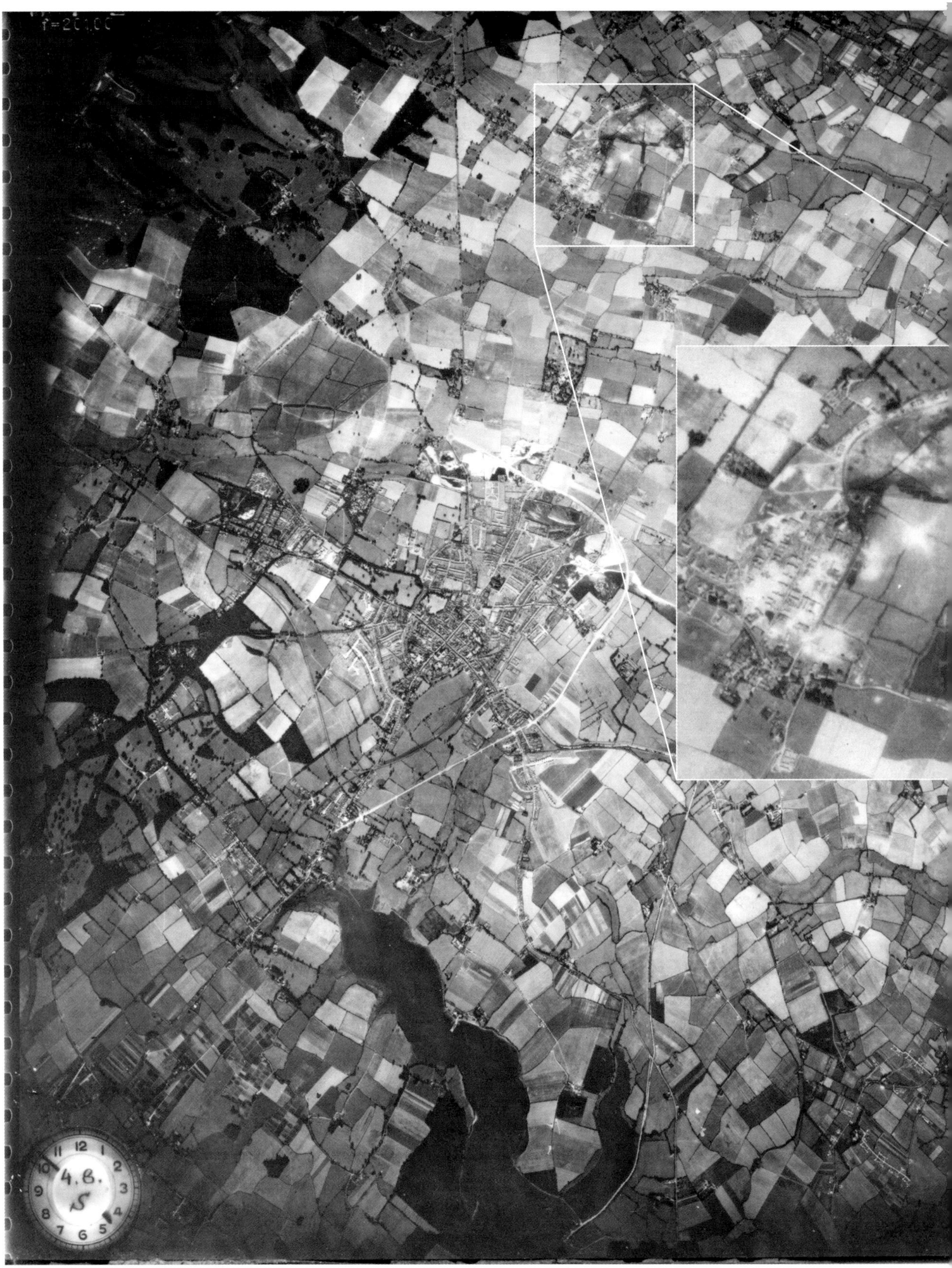
4.B.
S

should be continued because significant damage was obviously being done to the RAF's ground organization.

A career military aviator, Sperrle had been a World War I army observation pilot, commander and staff officer; the first commander of the reborn Luftwaffe's very first Fliegerdivision; the first operational commander of the Condor Legion in Spain; and become an even more experienced air campaigner in France. He seriously doubted the veracity of the Jagdwaffe's victory claims and scoffed at Schmid's assessments. He estimated that the RAF had 1,000 fighters available.

In any event, for *Seelöwe* to proceed and succeed, it was imperative that the RAF fighter units be driven out of their bases in southern England, regardless of how many aircraft there were.

Kesselring, a former army administrative officer who obtained his pilot rating so that he would have credibility with the aircrew he commanded, disagreed. He is reported to have stated: 'They [fighter bases] are expendable: if too badly damaged the fighter squadrons [can] withdraw to other bases behind London and these, being beyond [our] fighter range, would be safe from [our] bombers.' In fact, he reportedly said that he was 'surprised that the English had not made this move much earlier to save them from such horrendous losses'. He opined that it

LEFT
This high-altitude, high-resolution Luftwaffe image of Tangmere is typical of those used in the essential task of assessing the effectiveness of the bombing campaign. (Clive Ellis)

ABOVE
On 7 September, Ju 88 A '4U+BL' of 3.(F)/123, based at Buc, near Paris, was shot down by Sgt L.S. Pilkington of 7 OTU, during a reconnaissance sortie to photograph Liverpool. The aircraft crashed near Machynllech, Wales. The pilot, Lt Erich Böhle, and his crew were all injured, but survived the ordeal and became POWs. (Clive Ellis)

had not occurred because Fighter Command needed to be seen 'holding the line [and] setting an example for the people'.[8]

Now, he reasoned, it was quite possible that if the bombing continued, the forward units would be withdrawn and then return at the first indication that *Seelöwe* was under way.

Sperrle's response to this is unknown, but being an experienced campaigner, he was aware that continuing to bomb the sector stations, even if they were vacant of aircraft, would prevent the fighter squadrons from returning and thereby reduce Dowding's ability to cover the invasion beaches. Denied No. 11 Group airfields south of London, Park's fighters would have to fly greater distances to get to the combat zone. It would be like Dunkirk all over again, where No. 11 Group fighters spent 30 minutes going to and fro and only 20 minutes on station covering the beaches.

Additionally, despite being assigned 30 aviation industry targets by ObdL on 1 September as part of the continuing offensive counter-air campaign, Sperrle also knew that his three Fliegerkorps of night-bombers could easily reach the five sector stations north of London – Hornchurch, Northolt, North Weald, Debden and Duxford – and bomb them nightly and with impunity, since Fighter Command's night-fighter capability was so limited. 'So let them withdraw north of the Thames, we'll bomb them there.'

But Göring's mind was made up. He saw personal glory in his favoured option.

The responsible commander, Kesselring supported his chief.

And Deichmann, Kesselring's chief of staff, was getting what he had wanted from the very beginning, when he drew up II. Fliegerkorps' proposed concept of operations back in July. It would be an attack on London, the centre of the British Empire, under the guise of a strategic strike against port facilities but for the purpose of increasing the attrition of Fighter Command.

Ironically, it was Sperrle that delivered the first blow. On the night of 6/7 September he sent 25 bombers to drop 26.9 tons of HE and 50 RSK 36 canisters on the East End docks.[9] He was mentioned by name in the Wehrmacht press release about the first attacks on London: 'Despite particularly unfavourable weather conditions, strong associations [units] of Generalfeldmarschall Sperrle successfully attacked important destinations [targets] in and around London during the course of the day.'

THE FIRST DAYLIGHT BOMBING ATTACK ON LONDON – 7 SEPTEMBER

With great fanfare, Göring arrived at Cap Blanc-Nez, near Wissant, to watch 'his Luftwaffe' stream overhead towards London as he announced to the German people via a Nazi Propaganda Ministry radio correspondent that he had 'taken over personal command of the Luftwaffe in its war against England'. His bombastic pronouncement indicates that to him at least, the first major attack on the British capital was more about its propaganda value than its importance as a tactical operation.[10]

From: G.O.C. I Air Corps   Corps HQ 6.9.40

Ia Br.B.Nr. 10285 g.Kdos. N.f.K.

1. In the evening of 7.9. Luftflotte 2 will conduct major strike against target Loge.

To this end the following units will operate in succession:

For the Initial Attack: at 18.00 one KG of II Air Corps

For the Main Attack: at 18.40 II Air Corps

                         at 18.45 I Air Corps, reinforced by KG 30

2. Disposition of I Air Corps Units:

KG 30 (plus II/KG 76): on right

KG 1 central

KG 76 (less II/KG 76): on left

For target see general Appendix.

3. Fighter Cover

    (a)   Purpose of Initial Attack is to force English fighters into the air so that they will have reached end of endurance at time of Main Attack.

    (b)   Fighter escort will be provided by JafÜ 2 in the proportion of one fighter Geschwader for each bomber Geschwader.

    (c)   ZG 76 (for this operation under I Air Corps command) will as from 18.40 clear the air of enemy fighters over I Air Corps targets, thereby covering attack and retreat of bomber formations.

    (d)   JafÜ 2 guarantees two Fighter Geschwader to cover I and II Air Corps.

4. Execution

(a)   Rendezvous :

To be made with Fighter Escort before crossing coast. Bombers will proceed in direct flight.

(b)   Courses :

KG 30: St. Omer—just south of Cap Gris Nez—railway fork north of Sevenoaks—target.

KG 1 : St. Pol—mouth of la Slack River—Riverhead—target.

KG 76: Hedin—north perimeter of Boulogne—Westerham—target.

(c)   Fighter escort :

JG 26 for KG 30

JG 54 for KG 1

JG 27 for KG 76

In view of the fact that the fighters will be operating at the limit of their endurance, it is essential that direct courses be flown and the attack completed in minimum time.

(d)   Flying altitudes after RV with fighters :

KG 30: 4,500m - 5,000m.

KG 1 : 5,500m - 6,000m.

KG 76 : 4,500m - 5,000m.

To stagger heights as above will provide maximum concentration of attacking force. On return flight some loss of altitude is permissible, in order to cross English coast at approximately 4,000m.

(e)   The intention is to complete the operation by a single attack. In the event of units failing to arrive directly over target, other suitable objectives in Loge may be bombed from altitude of approach.

(f)   Return flight :

After releasing bombs formations will turn to starboard. KG 76 will do so with care after first establishing that starboard units have already attacked. Return course will then be Maidstone—Dymchurch —escort fighter bases.

(g)   Bomb-loads :

He 111 and Ju 88 : No SC 50 bombs

20 per cent incendiaries

30 per cent delayed-action bombs of 2-4 hours and 10-14 hours (the latter without concussion fuses)

Do 17: 25 per cent disintegrating containers with BI EL

and no SD 50. Load only to be limited by security of aircraft against enemy flak. Fuel sufficient for completion of operation and marginal safety to be carried only.

5. To achieve the necessary maximum effect it is essential that units fly as a highly concentrated force—during approach, attack and especially on return. The main objective of the operation is to prove that the Luftwaffe can achieve this.

6. I Air Corps Operational Order No. 10285/40 is hereby superseded. By order of the G.O.C.

(signed) Grauert.

Facsimile of I. Fliegerkorps Operations Orders for the first attack on London, 7 September. 'Loge' was the Luftwaffe codeword for London. (Author Collection)

This maximum effort totalled 320 bombers, accompanied by 642 fighters, attacking targets in and around London's East End docks. Deichmann planned for the largest single raid launched to date to comprise one large Geschwader-strength formation and, following 40 minutes later, two huge formations bombing the same target area five minutes apart. The II. Fliegerkorps operations order for the initial attack, flown by KG 3, notes that it was intended 'to force English fighters into the air so that they will have reached the end of [their] endurance at time of Main Attack'. The 'main attack' would consist of Loerzer's KG 53 Heinkels and KG 2 Dorniers bombing in tandem from the Thames Estuary, followed by the whole of Grauert's I. Fliegerkorps, attacking from the south-east.

For the initial attack and first wave of the main attack, Loerzer's II. Fliegerkorps would use all of its 142 serviceable Do 17Zs and 33 He 111Hs, supported by JG 2, 3, 51 and 52 flying 'freie Jagd' sweeps ahead and Jagdschutz close escort, and ZG 2 providing flank sweep to the north. The second wave comprised I. Fliegerkorps' three Kampfgeschwader, KG 1 (He 111H), 30 (Ju 88A) and 76 (Do 17Z), flying all 137 of its serviceable bombers and augmented by eight KG 26 He 111Hs, advancing behind a 'freie Jagd' sweep of ZG 76 Zerstörers and escorted by JG 26, 27 and 54.

The Luftwaffe had never flown bomber formations of this size before. During Stage 1, when attacks were made in Kampfgeschwader strength, the units flew as three Gruppen in trail or with two alongside a central leading column, creating a long 'vic'. When raids were reduced to Gruppe strength during Stages 2 and 3, two groups would frequently be paired to hit targets close to one another, such as Kenley–Biggin Hill or Hornchurch–North Weald. In these cases, the two Gruppen would fly in trail until approaching the targets and then split, or in parallel for near-simultaneous times over target.

But London, a vital, large target, required Fliegerkorps-strength formations. Called 'Valhallas' by the Luftwaffe, they were something altogether new for the planning staffs and airborne mission leaders. Planning began the day after Göring's Besprechung and was briefed to the KG commanders and Kampfgruppe leaders the following morning, but unfavourable weather precluded launching the massive strike. Instead, attacks were flown against Detling on 5 September, and Biggin Hill, Kenley and Rochester on the 6th, while Sperrle's night-bombing of the London, Silvertown and Rotherhithe docks went ahead as scheduled.

Between 1555 and 1615hrs, the Swingate and Rye radars detected three groups of contacts, each estimated at '15+' strength. One was first detected 'behind Cap Gris-Nez', another ten miles (15km) west of Dunkirk (France) headed towards the Thames Estuary, and the third was east of Boulogne, headed west. These were 'freie Jagd' sweeps attempting to lure Park's fighters to the south coast between Beachy Head and Folkestone.

Park was absent from his Uxbridge HQ this particular afternoon, in conference with Dowding, AVM Douglas Evill (Dowding's senior air staff officer, then the RAF equivalent of a chief of staff), and AVM Sholto Douglas, Deputy Chief of the

On 7 September, Göring travelled to Kesselring's advanced HQ, known as *Heiliger Berg* (Holy Mountain), a bombproof bunker on Cap Blanc-Nez to watch at first hand what he boasted would be the 'beginning of the end' of Dowding's Fighter Command. Here Göring is talking to II. Fliegerkorps commander Bruno Loerzer, a World War I flying comrade. (NARA)

Air Staff, at Bentley Priory. Willoughby de Broke was therefore in charge. At 1615hrs he launched five squadrons, directing them to patrol Maidstone (249 Sqn), Canterbury (504 Sqn) and Thameshaven (253 Sqn), while the 'Northolt Wing' of 1 and 303 (Polish) Squadrons was retained near London at 20,000ft as an airborne reserve, ready to react to the attackers' approach.

At 1620hrs the Swingate CH radar station reported a force of '20+' off Dunkirk – 'it came straight across the north[east]ern entrance to the Straits of Dover' – and CHL stations detected three more contacts as '6+' 15 miles (25km) east of Beachy Head, off Hastings, 'an even smaller force just south of Dover', and the third, of '20+', ten miles south-east of Dungeness, all headed inland.

About 1637hrs the pre-strike fighter sweeps began crossing the southern shores.

The Observer Corps No. 1 Group (Maidstone) coastal stations reported '20+' crossing the shoreline at Folkestone, '50+' coasting in near Hythe, and a force 'of unknown size… crossing the coast at New Romney… on a north-westerly course'. Willoughby de Broke responded by scrambling four more squadrons, one to patrol Beachy Head (43 Sqn), another to join 249 Sqn over Maidstone (111 Sqn), and base CAPs for Biggin Hill (79 Sqn) and Gravesend (501 Sqn); all of them were airborne by 1640hrs. At that time, Oberst Chamier-Gliczinski's KG 3, escorted by Mölders' JG 51, crossed the coast between Dover and Deal, headed west-north-west. The strike package was accompanied by ZG 2's Zerstörers, sweeping a parallel course offset to the north to fend off any interceptors attacking from that direction.

With bombers definitely inbound, Willoughby de Broke ordered 66 Sqn into the air to patrol over Kenley, 603 Sqn over Hornchurch and requested, through Fighter Command HQ, No. 12 Group to 'help in protecting the airfields north of the Thames'. Leigh-Mallory launched 19, 242, and 310 (Czech) Sqns from Duxford – the 'Duxford Wing' – initially with orders to patrol over North Weald. All five squadrons were airborne by 1650hrs. Ten minutes later a flight from 72 Sqn was scrambled to patrol the Thames Estuary, 1 (RCAF) Sqn to patrol over Croydon and 46 Sqn over North Weald, completing the defensive deployments facing the raiders.

At 1700hrs, Chamier-Gliczinski's 72 Do 17Zs flew past Faversham headed towards Rochester, where they were reported as '80 bombers in three formations of equal strength escorted by fighters', continuing on a 'westerly course… up the River Thames'. Willougby de Broke scrambled 73 Squadron from Debden with instructions to intercept and 'Lumba Control', the Hornchurch sector controller, vectored 249 and 501 Squadrons, and the 'Northolt Wing', to do so as well.

Before 'Ganer Leader', Sqn Ldr John Grandy (later Marshal of the RAF), could comply, 249 Squadron was 'bounced' by III./JG 51's pre-strike sweep over Maidstone. It quickly lost two Hurricanes destroyed (one pilot killed, another wounded) and a third damaged, in exchange for one 9./JG 51 'Emil' (pilot captured) and another ditched on return to base (pilot rescued). Fighting their way northwards, Grandy's squadron intercepted the bombers (incorrectly identified as 'He 111s') near Faversham, where it lost another Hurricane to the Dorniers' defensive fire. A fourth was shot down by AA fire.

Meanwhile, 'Tennis Leader', Fg Off Jimmy Elsdon, quoted in Tom Docherty's *Swift to Battle: No 72 Fighter Squadron RAF in Action, Volume I 1937–1942*, spotted 'a formation of enemy bombers escorted by Me 109s… proceeding toward London.'

The second wave of bombers comprised all 137 serviceable bombers from I. Fliegerkorps, supplemented by eight He 111s from KG 26. Flying at 20,000ft, this KG 1 He 111 was en route to bomb its target at Silvertown or Millwall. (AHB)

Elsdon added:

I saw no other fighter squadrons in the vicinity so I decided to lead the squadron [*sic*, actually a flight – seven Spitfires] into the leading sections of bombers, which were flying in section line astern, stepped up, in an attempt to break up the formation. I put the squadron into echelon starboard and led the attack onto the port quarter of the bombers, each machine in my squadron taking the port bomber in the first five sections, and two remaining rear guard. [The escorts intervened and] I shot down an Me 109 which formed the leading section but was hit in the knee and shoulder and forced to retire before I could see any further result of the attack.[11]

Elsdon belly-landed his damaged fighter at Biggin Hill, feeling faint from loss of blood.

About the same time, 'Hula Leader', Sqn Ldr J.W.C. 'Hank' More commanding 73 Squadron, intercepted the ZG 2 flank guard over the Estuary and was tied up by the Zerstörers, losing a Hurricane shot down, pilot killed, and another damaged, while the Dorniers continued to their target.

Records indicate the interceptions by the other three squadrons began about the time of bomb release over the Woolwich Arsenal, at 1715hrs. The Arsenal, Harland and Wolff's steelworks (building Matilda tanks and artillery components), and Siemens' large factory (making electrical cables and components) 'were all hit and heavily damaged'. A Do 17Z from KG 3's Stabstaffel was shot down by AA fire over the target with the loss of all aboard.

For egress, Chamier-Gliczinski initially turned his large formation to the right, where the 'Northolt Wing' intercepted '40 Do 215s [*sic*] flying northwards', with 1 Squadron engaging the escorts, while the Poles attacked the bombers. Number 603 Squadron arrived from Hornchurch as the Dorniers turned east, allowing 'the whole squadron to dive on them [from the rear] in line abreast from out of the sun'. Despite impressive claims, KG 3 experienced no further losses, but three Dorniers returned to their Belgian bases damaged and with five wounded aboard.

The 'Duxford Wing' headed south as individual squadrons and Sqn Ldr Douglas Bader, leading 242 Sqn, sighted '70–90 aircraft at 20,000ft' east of North Weald at 1725hrs and found them 'flying in tight box formation with Me 110s circling around and Me 109s 5,000ft above... Consequently, the majority of combats were with escorting fighters.' Numbers 19 and 310 Squadrons engaged the Zerstörers while Bader's unit shot down a 1./JG 27 Bf 109E but lost one Hurricane destroyed (pilot missing in action) and three damaged, including Bader's, in return.

By this time the Bf 110 was regarded as 'easy meat' and ZG 2 attracted 1, 73, 242, 249 and 504 Squadrons, which engaged between 1710 and 1730, shooting down five Bf 110s, with two more crashing or ditching during their return to base.[12]

The main attack on the capital on 7 September involved KG 53's Heinkels and KG 2's Dorniers. Here a Kette of Do 17Zs from KG 2 is raiding Beckton Gas Works. (The National Archives)

As the Dorniers' egress continued, 73, 253 and 504 Squadrons joined the chase and reported engaging the formation, but without success. The combats against Loerzer's initial attack cost the 12 defending squadrons seven Hurricanes and four pilots killed, plus three wounded.[13]

As KG 3's bombs were falling, Rye radar detected three '20+' forces crossing the Straits of Dover and, at 1718hrs, as the pre-strike sweep for Grauert's 'Valhalla' crossed the coast between Hythe and Dover, a force of '50+' was detected behind Cap Gris-Nez, apparently headed across the Channel towards Folkestone behind the three 'freie Jagd' formations.

From overhead Saint-Pol, the leading, central column of Grauert's I. Fliegerkorps 'Valhalla', Oberst Karl Angerstein's KG 1 (with 59 He 111Hs), flew at 19,685ft to Ambleteuse, a small coastal town halfway between Boulogne and Cap Gris-Nez, with Reickhoff's KG 30 (26 Ju 88As plus 21 more of II./KG 76) joining in echelon on the right side and the rest of Frölich's KG 76 (39 Do 17Zs) taking station on the left. It was a long, tightly packed formation with about three miles between columns. Oberst Max Ibel's JG 27 protected the left flank and covered the Dorniers, Galland's JG 26 guarded the right flank and the Ju 88As, and Trautloft's JG 54 escorted the Heinkels and provided top cover; ZG 76's Zerstörers swept ahead to 'clear the air of enemy fighters over I. Fliegerkorps targets, thereby covering the attack and retreat of the bomber formations'.

By the time this formation was detected, KG 3 had turned around from its earlier attack and was 'dragging' 12 intercepting squadrons eastwards, back towards the Estuary. But seven more units were airborne to meet this huge new threat – A Sector's 43 and 602 Squadrons were patrolling the coast from Beachy Head to Folkestone, 111 Squadron over Maidstone, 257 Squadron (scrambled from Martlesham Heath) was over Chelmsford, 609 Squadron (from No. 10 Group) over the large Brooklands industrial complex, and four squadrons were patrolling over Croydon, Kenley, Biggin Hill, and North Weald – Nos 1 (RCAF), 46, 66 and 79, respectively.

At 1730hrs 'Villa Leader', Sqn Ldr A.V.R. 'Sandy' Johnstone, spotted Frölich's Dorniers (reporting them as '28 Do 17s at 18,000ft') flying north-west and, over Biggin Hill, led his 602 Squadron to attack 'the rear section of the enemy formation but before our squadron could break away they were attacked by German fighters'. Johnstone shot down a 1./JG 77 'Emil' and its pilot was captured. Another ditched in the Channel (pilot rescued) on the way home, but two Spitfires and their pilots were lost.

From over Folkestone, Sqn Ldr Caesar Barrand Hull gallantly led 43 Squadron to attack the 'Valhalla's' right flank, sending one section up to fend off the hosts of Messerschmitts while he attacked the '20 Do 215s' (actually 21 Ju 88As from II./KG 76) with his other six Hurricanes. The overwhelming strength of Galland's JG 26 dictated the unequal combat and three Hurricanes were shot down; Hull was one of two pilots killed.

Ahead of Grauet's 'Valhalla', ZG 76 swept deep into Kent and to the southern suburbs of London, establishing a vast Abwehrkreis (defensive circle) over Croydon and effectively pinning 1 (RCAF) Squadron to its base patrol.

From the coast to the target area, Grauert's 'Valhalla' passed through C Sector's airspace without being engaged by any of the other squadrons airborne south-east of London. The *RAF Narrative* attributes this to poor performance by the Observer Corps, saying, 'The tracking of enemy forces, despite the clear weather, left much to be desired. Throughout the operation enemy tracks were disappearing and reappearing with disconcerting frequency [much to the frustration of] those who were controlling the defence at the time.'

A contributing factor may have also been that C Sector's emergency operations room, located in a vacated shop in the tiny village of the Pantiles, proved unsuitable for adequately controlling airborne fighters. There is no record in the *RAF Narrative* of any vectoring by 'Tophat', or even 'Sapper', Control, meaning all airborne squadrons merely patrolled static positions waiting for the bombers to pass within visual range, just as 43 and 601 Squadrons had done nearer the coast. At this time there was no active defence being directed from the ground, just a passive defence that succeeded only if the 'Valhalla' was seen flying by on its way to its target, but this did not happen.

Meanwhile, the second 'Valhalla' – Loerzer's 103-bomber II. Fliegerkorps formation – led by Oberst Erich Stahl's KG 53 with Fink's KG 2 following, apparently remained undetected. There is no record of radar contacts that correspond to the formation's flight path from Cap Blanc-Nez to Deal around 1725hrs. Instead, the *RAF Narrative* relates, 'It must be understood that it was extremely difficult for the controllers on the ground to appreciate the position clearly. The Germans went to considerable lengths to conceal both the direction of their attack for as long as possible, and which formations would execute it.'[14]

The 33 Heinkels and 70 Dorniers[15], and their escorting Bf 109Es, made landfall near Deal and were tracked by the Observer Corps as they 'advanced up the Estuary'. They were spotted by 257 Squadron, which reported them as '40–50 bombers… with Me 109s circling round them, at 18,000–20,000 feet', and Sqn Ldr Hill Harkness led his Hurricanes south across the river to intercept between Sheppey and Rochester at about 1730hrs. One section was able to get in a head-on attack against the left-hand Staffel of Heinkels, 'but with little effect. Most combats, in fact, were with the German fighters [I./JG 52 and I.(J)/LG 2] and went against 257 Squadron.' One 9./KG 53 bomber was lost in the intercept, but two Hurricanes were shot down for the loss of one 'Emil'.

At 1730hrs on 7 September, Plt Off O.V. Hanbury of 602 Squadron engaged a Do 17 over south London. His Spitfire (N3228) was damaged by return fire, forcing him to return to Westhampnett. Twenty days later the aircraft was sent to 9 MU for repairs and, on 13 October, was issued to 72 Squadron, only to be returned to 9 MU five days later. N3228 then served with a succession of OTUs until being Struck Off Charge on 18 November 1943, following an accident with 57 OTU. This ability of Fighter Command to quickly repair battle-damaged aircraft at RAF MUs and within the Civilian Repair Organization (CRO) provided an important advantage over the Luftwaffe. (Clive Ellis)

Ten minutes later, Stahl's formation was attacked by 'A Flight' of 46 Squadron, which was passing overhead Thameshaven, chasing Chamier-Gliczinski's egressing Dorniers. 'Angel Leader', Flt Lt A.C. Ribagliati, flying an experimental cannon-armed Hurricane, spotted the inbound II. Fliegerkorps formation and turned south to intercept. Ribagliati led his flight in a slashing starboard beam attack on II./KG 53, which was targeting the expansive Thameshaven oil storage facilities, at 1740hrs.

'Flight Lieutenant Ribagliati (four-cannon Hurricane) aimed for the leader of the second vic of bombers. He opened fire at 300 yards, closing to 100 yards when the cannons ceased firing [jammed]. No return fire was encountered from the bombers. Total rounds fired 130.' Three Heinkels returned to Lille-Nord with battle damage and three wounded.

Finally, at 1750hrs, from overhead Brooklands at 10,000ft, 609 Squadron 'saw a large formation over London surrounded by AA fire' and charged north-east to engage as it headed back down the Thames Estuary. One 4./KG 2 Do 17Z had been lost to fighters over London during the bomb run.

It is evident that for the main attack Willoughby de Broke's defence had broken down, largely due to the poor performance of early-warning radar and Observer Corps reporting. With a dozen squadrons chasing homeward-bound KG 3 eastwards, then hurrying back to base to refuel and rearm, the two much larger strike packages were engaged by only five squadrons and ineffectively so, allowing the bombers to arrive en masse over their targets largely unmolested. Deichmann's plan of attack had worked as designed.

From 1745 to1810hrs, the remainder of more than 350 tons of bombs dropped that day, including more than 100 of the new 1,800kg SC1800 'Satan' bombs, as well as 366 incendiary canisters, rained down upon the Silvertown and Millwall docks; the oil tanks at Purfleet, Grays, Thurrock and Thameshaven; and warehouses, granaries, and the residential areas of Barking, Rotherhithe, Limehouse and other districts. The large gasworks at Beckton erupted in flames and the West Ham power station was wrecked.[16]

The retiring bombers and fighters – the latter very low on fuel – were harried by Hurricanes and Spitfires, four belatedly scrambled squadrons joining the action. A post-strike sweep by I./JG 51 arrived at 1745hrs but could not fend off the host of pursuers, losing three Bf 109Es shot down with two pilots captured and one missing in action. The interceptors also shot down six more 'Emils', two each from JG 2, 3 and 26. Additionally, two KG 1 Heinkels were so badly damaged they crashed upon return to France and a I./KG 53 He 111H and a Stab/KG 76 Do 17Z were shot down while venturing over Essex and Kent on weather and post-strike reconnaissance missions.

Overall the day had been a surprisingly easy, but not decisive, victory for the Luftwaffe. Visually impressive, psychologically shocking and materially destructive, though not strategically significant, the devastation of the Port of London was carried out at the cost of only seven of 320 bombers. The many fighter battles had cost 16 Hurricanes and six Spitfires shot down at the expense of 15 Bf 109Es and seven Bf 110s, for an even exchange rate.[17]

Göring was extremely pleased with the Jagdwaffe's claim of destroying 93 British interceptors, an inflation of 4.2 times the actual losses incurred. But it seems the Luftwaffe commander-in-chief relished the wanton destruction of London and its suburbs even more. It had killed 448 civilians and injured 1,337. He gleefully reported: 'London is in flames… [and] for the first time [the Luftwaffe has] delivered a stroke right into the enemy's heart.'

The unprecedented daylight attack was followed by 170 Luftflotte 3[18] night-bombers, supplemented by 77 from Luftflotte 2. They delivered another 369 tons of HE and 440 incendiary canisters between 2010hrs and 0430hrs the following morning.

The docklands area of East London, burning after the Luftwaffe's first massed raid against the city on 7 September. (NARA)

According to ObdL's daily report:

> Target approach was facilitated by a fire-glow which was visible from a considerable distance (up to 200km [125 miles]). Elements of Luftflotte 2 made their attack with the same centre of main effort as during the day (Silvertown docks), while those of Luftflotte 3 concentrated on targets on both sides of the Thames between Vauxhall Bridge and Putney Bridge. In both target areas existing fires were extended and further large-scale conflagrations caused. In addition, six major conflagrations and a large number of similar fires were to be seen in the central London area. Owing to the weakness and inadequate cooperation between its various elements, night defence was practically ineffective – just as had been the case during the day.[19]

The inferno ravaged the eastern suburbs of the city for the next three days.

THE INTERIM – 8 THROUGH 14 SEPTEMBER

True to his bullying nature as a political gangster, as soon as he had dealt Britain a serious blow, Adolf Hitler once again offered to negotiate an end to the conflict. On the evening of 7 September, he had his personal envoy to Sweden, Dr Ludwig Weißauer,[20] contact a Swedish intermediary, Professor/Judge Birger Ekeberg, President of the Svea Court of Appeal, to arrange a meeting with the British Ambassador, Victor Mallet.

The message Weißauer passed was Hitler's surreptitious invitation for peace talks. Right out of Hitler's imaginary understanding of national destiny and European power relationships, it included his belief that 'for the white race there

During an assault against London on 9 September, Ju 88A-1 '4D+AD' of Stab III./KG 30 was shot down by Hurricanes of 253 Squadron, based at Kenley. The pilot, Gruppenkommandeur Major Hackbarth (Generalfeldmarschall Albert Kesselring's son-in-law), made a forced landing on the foreshore of Pagham Harbour. (Clive Ellis)

must be two great economic units – Germany, the Continental unit, and the British Empire and America'. Without responding, Mallet forwarded the message to the Foreign Office and Churchill's Cabinet.[21]

Meanwhile, Wehrmacht and Kriegsmarine preparations for *Seelöwe* were considered complete, needing only the order to begin minelaying operations and loading the larger transport ships. For a landing on England's southern shores on 21 September, the decision to go ahead was needed by the 11th, now only four days away.

While Hitler awaited a response from Churchill's government, unfavourable weather over the next three days largely discouraged Luftwaffe attacks. On the 8th, three of the five Kampfgruppen weather-aborted their missions, but two (36 Do 17Zs from II. and III./KG 2) dropped 33 tons of bombs and 48 incendiaries in the vicinity of 'railway communications' (alternate targets to the 'Thames Docks') in the areas of Dartford, West Malling, Wrotham and Sevenoaks.

Next day, some 94 bombers from KG 1, 30 and 53 attempted to deliver 115.5 tons of HE and 18 incendiary canisters on London, but: 'Weather conditions were unfavourable, particularly for the escort. German formation encountered fairly strong fighter defence (Spitfires) south of London. In the rest of the operational area only slight fighter defence was observed, and – as at London – this was aggressive and skilful.' This resulted in the first wave 'dumping' 50 bombs on Canterbury (an alternative target) at 1715hrs, the second wave bombing West Ham at 1738hrs and the third, the main attack, ineffectively scattering its bombloads through eight boroughs in the southern suburbs and four more in central London between 1745 and 1800hrs.

Willoughby de Broke's orchestration of No. 11 Group's defence was effective. Eleven of 21 airborne squadrons intercepted bomber formations in the Canterbury, Mayfield and south-west London areas. At the end of the day, ObdL informed OKW that two He 111s from KGs 1 and 53 and five KG 30 Ju 88As, as well as 17 fighters, had been lost to the 'strong… aggressive and skilful' defence. Some 39 Spitfires and Hurricanes were claimed shot down – half of the previously claimed exchange ratio of 4.5:1, indicating that RAF Fighter Command was 'not yet defeated'.[22]

Following this disappointing result, and to permit time for a British response to his 'peace talks' proposal, Hitler postponed *Seelöwe* to 14 September.[23]

Bad weather throttled Kesselring's operations the following day, with only five bombers conducting sporadic individual and inconsequential raids on the East End docks, Croydon suburb and fuel storage in north-east London. Intercepts were few and only one III./KG 76 Do 17Z was lost.[24]

With better weather, fully fledged operations resumed on the 11th, Martini's Funkhorchdienst providing electronic jamming against four CH radars for Grauert's I. Fliegerkorps strike. Noise jamming is typically a contest between the power of the jammers versus the strength of the target's radar return. As three formations rendezvoused over Calais at 1500–1520hrs, they were detectable but

indiscernible until they approached to a range at which the electronic echo 'burned through' the interference.

This range proved sufficient for Willoughby de Broke to organize his defences. He initially sent 41, 92, 253, 501 and 603 Sqns to patrol Maidstone, a central location astride the direct route from Cap Gris-Nez to London's East End docks.

Grauert's raiders approached in two parallel packages. The northern force comprised approximately 48 He 111Hs from I. and II./KG 1, followed by '100+' escorting fighters, crossing the coast near South Foreland at 1535hrs. Composed of I. and II./KG 26 Heinkels, the equally sized southern force coasted in between Folkestone and Dover ten minutes later.

Angerstein's KG 1 formation was intercepted sequentially by four squadrons early on. Then, between Maidstone and south-east London, they were attacked by three more plus Leigh-Mallory's 'Duxford Wing', comprising a composite 19/266 Sqn, alongside 74 and 611 Sqns, all flying Spitfires and led by Sqn Ldr Brian 'Sandy' Lane, OC 19 Sqn. The escorting Messerschmitts engaged the interceptors, permitting KG 1 to drop its half of the 92.3 tons of bombs and 70 incendiary canisters on the East End docks, 'as well as among railway installations south of the Commercial Docks', Woolwich Arsenal, Barking power station, Beckton gasworks and Port Victoria fuel storage depot, between 1610 and 1630hrs.

Three more squadrons joined in the chase during the bombers' egress, two of them engaging the retiring Zerstörers. Angerstein lost three Heinkels (the 'Duxford Wing' claimed 19 kills) and six ZG 26 Bf 110s failed to return.

Of the five squadrons not paired against KG 1, only two – 229 and 303 (Polish) Sqns comprising the 'Northolt Wing' – were vectored to intercept Wechmar's KG 26 as it approached London from the south. These, plus 1 (RCAF) and 238 Sqns, intercepted the bombers during egress, shooting down seven more Heinkels and a ZG 2 Bf 110C. From 1620 to 1630hrs, the rest of the bombs and incendiaries fell upon and around Paddington Station and across five districts to the east-south-east.[25]

The day's strikes caused Dowding and Park to realize that 'the Germans had [begun] attempting to hit railway communications as well as docks'. Kesselring's planning staff had discovered that although the British railway network was centred on London, there was no through passage across the city and, on the east side of the capital, there was no way around the city by rail. British Army units responding to *Seelöwe* landings along the south-east coast would have to travel by train to a north London railway station, disembark, march through the city to a south London railway station, and then board troop trains headed south and south-east to the threatened landing zones. These attacks on railway installations were lines of communication interdiction strikes supporting the anticipated invasion operation.

The loss of ten bombers, more than ten per cent of the attacking force, seven Zerstörers and five 'Emils' certainly demonstrated that Fighter Command, despite severe losses being reported, remained a viable opponent. On this date, JaFü 2 claimed that another 34 Spitfires and 22 Hurricanes had been destroyed, but the strength and ferocity of Dowding's defence had obviously not diminished.

Even more disappointing for Hitler was the official response that Weißauer received from Mallet that evening: 'His Majesty's Government did not enter this war for selfish aims, but for large and general purposes affecting the freedom and independence of many States in Europe... The intention of all the peoples of the British Empire to prosecute the war has been strengthened by the many horrible crimes committed by the rulers of Nazi Germany against the small States on her borders, and by the indiscriminate bombing of London without the lightest relation to military objectives.'[26]

Whether he wanted to or not, to settle his 'English problem' Hitler would now have to invade Great Britain. As if to underscore the British perception of indiscriminate German bombing, that night Sperrle and Kesselring dispatched 180 bombers to drop 239 tons of bombs and 148 incendiaries on London. 'Existing fires [were] spread and augmented – particularly in the eastern and northern districts of the city – by further fires.'[27]

Additionally, Deichmann's planners went to work designing another maximum effort Fliegerkorps-size strike against the British capital. Planning for another major attack on London's East End docks was completed on the 12th; it was set for the next day at 1800hrs.

While Luftflotte 2 and I. and II. Fliegerkorps mission planners worked out the details of the two-phase assault, intermittent rain and low cloud blanketing south-east England and north-east France precluded normal operations and, when the inclement conditions persisted the following day, Deichmann's new 'Valhalla' attack was postponed to the 14th. That day, blaming the weather for preventing the Luftwaffe attaining its goal, Hitler postponed making the invasion decision until 17 September.

While weather prevented normal operations, that is formations of bombers concentrating on specifically selected targets, on 12 September, individual armed reconnaissance missions were flown by single aircraft, of which only four reported raiding London; three dropped a total of 2.4 tons of bombs and eight incendiary canisters on St Catherine's Dock, West Ham and 'south London'. The fourth bomber, most likely a Ju 88A, attacked the Air Ministry HQ at Harrogate, delivering three SC500s in a glide-bombing attack down to 650ft, its crew reporting: 'A hit was observed on the W[est] wing of the building'.

That night, 76 bombers were dispatched but only 43 reported reaching the target, 'of which 30 were obliged to drop their bombs by means of dead reckoning navigation [heading and timing] owing to unbroken cloud'. Some 60 tons of bombs and 61 incendiary canisters were dropped into the clouds over London.[28]

The next day, while still awaiting better weather for the 'Valhalla' operation, Luftflotte 2 continued individual aircraft raids, launching 53 bombers between 0825 and 1600hrs, to scatter 55 tons of bombs and 116 incendiary canisters across London. Most effective were 13 Ju 88As from LG 1, which made glide-bombing attacks. Hits were reported on Charing Cross, St Pancras and Marylebone stations, a railway station near Erith (along the south bank of the Thames, east of London), gasworks at Fulham and Waterloo, a fuel storage depot near Buckingham Palace, the 'West India Docks and large warehouses and blocks of houses directly to the east', and, in a continuation of the targeting of higher military HQs, the Admiralty and War Office. Some bombs came close: 'Buckingham Palace, the Admiralty [building], and War Office were slightly damaged'.[29]

Hydraulically operated bomb trolleys were rarely available to Luftwaffe ground crew during the Battle of Britain, muscle power often being used to load bombs. Here a 1,000kg SC1000 bomb, nicknamed 'Hermann' after the rotund Luftwaffe commander, is loaded on to an external rack. Painted sky blue, it was filled with one of two different types of explosive dependent upon whether the target was on land or maritime. (AHB)

Elsewhere, Hornchurch was bombed by an He 111 and five other airfields were raided by other individual aircraft. Park made little effort to stop the ineffectual nuisance raiders and 'only a few interceptions were affected [no daytime losses were incurred], but Fighter Command was compensated by two of its easiest days since the beginning of July'.[30]

On 14 September, 'weather conditions were rather better than on two previous days, although there was still a good deal of cloud between 5,000 and 10,000 feet'. Because the 'Valhalla' was slated for the 14th, with bombers loaded according to the operations orders and aircrews briefed for the mission, few daylight 'armed reconnaissance' sorties were flown. Instead, Kesselring substituted the Bf 109E-7 Jabos of Major Otto Weiss's II.(Schl)/LG 2, launching 49 fighter-bombers in two waves at 1530 and 1900hrs). They flew to London at 16,400ft to drop a total of 13.25 tons of bombs. 'Bomb strikes could not be observed owing to cloud.'

In the first raid, the Jabo strike force was one of six 'Emil' formations, altogether including150 Bf 109Es from JG 26, 27, 51, and 54, crossing the coast and arriving over London at 1600–1605hrs. They dropped bombs on Battersea, hitting the power station and gasworks, and a rail line near Clapham Junction, as well as Camberwell and Chelsea. Park responded by launching 20 squadrons but, since there were no bombers present, only four engaged some of the accompanying fighter sweeps, with rather inconclusive results.

Similarly, the second Jabo raid was accompanied by four other 'Emil' formations and was not intercepted. Park launched eight squadrons this time, but more fighter-versus-fighter combats resulted. Jagdfliegerführer 2 reported losing four Bf 109Es in exchange for shooting down 15 Spitfires and ten Hurricanes, but six and four were actually lost, with three pilots killed and five wounded.[31]

In the week-long intermission between the two major daylight strikes on London, RAF interceptors and AA fire brought down 28 bombers, while 61 Hurricanes and Spitfires were lost to Bf 109s and Zerstörers, which lost 22 and 11, respectively. The revised operational strategy was working, but just barely. The Jagdwaffe's actual kill ratio averaged approximately 2.2:1, but as with any attrition strategy, it would take time and time was what Hitler, Göring and 'his Luftwaffe' were running out of.

GÖRING'S DEFEAT OVER LONDON – 15 SEPTEMBER

Dawn broke on 15 September with clear skies and fine visibility over England as, in France and Belgium, Luftflotte aircrews reviewed their mission instructions while waiting for the 'Wekusta' (Wettererkundungsstaffel: weather findings squadron) reports and commanders' decisions to launch Deichmann's planned assault on London.

His plan followed the pattern of many previous raids: an initial attack by heavily escorted smaller bomber forces, in this case a Gruppe-strength raid by

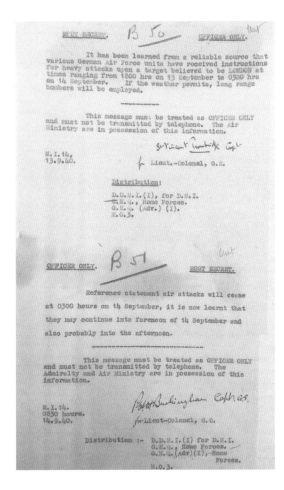

MOST SECRET.   *B 50*   OFFICER ONLY.

It has been learned from a reliable source that various German Air Force units have received instructions for heavy attacks upon a target believed to be LONDON at times ranging from 1800 hrs on 13 September to 0300 hrs on 14 September. If the weather permits, long range bombers will be employed.

This message must be treated as OFFICER ONLY and must not be transmitted by telephone. The Air Ministry are in possession of this information.

M.I.14,
13.9.40.

Distribution:

D.D.M.I.(I), for D.M.I.
G.H.Q., Home Forces.
G.H.Q. (Adv.) (I).
M.O.5.

OFFICER ONLY.   *B 51*   MOST SECRET.

Reference statement air attacks will cease at 0300 hours on 14 September, it is now learnt that they may continue into forenoon of 14 September and also probably into the afternoon.

This message must be treated as OFFICER ONLY and must not be transmitted by telephone. The Admiralty and Air Ministry are in possession of this information.

M.I.14.
0830 hours.
14.9.40.

Distribution :- D.D.M.I.(I) for D.M.I.
G.H.Q., Home Forces.
G.H.Q.(Adv)(I), Home
Forces.
M.O.5.

Hut 6 at Bletchley Park deciphered two Enigma messages that enabled Hut 3 to warn those in receipt of ULTRA intelligence of a proposed raid on London. In the event, weather conditions forced Deichmann to postpone his 'Valhalla' attack on the capital until 15 September. Despite rigorous research, a third ULTRA signal for the 15th has yet to be uncovered. Indeed, to date, no ULTRA intelligence signals sent to AI have been uncovered, despite the fact that it was clearly a recipient. (The National Archives)

I. Fliegerkorps' III./KG 76, followed by the main strike on the primary target, a maximum effort by KG 2, 3, and 53 (augmented by KG 26) from II. Fliegerkorps. The initial attack was intended to stir up Park's defences and weary his fighter squadrons, thus enabling the main strike to proceed with less opposition. The target was the tangle of railways passing through Battersea district north-east of Clapham Junction, the destruction of which would block troop trains departing southbound from Victoria and Waterloo stations; it was another *Seelöwe* lines of communication interdiction target.

Taking off from Cormeilles-en-Vexin airfield northwest of Paris at 1010hrs, Obstlt Alois Lindmayr led 19 III./KG 76 Do 17Zs northwards and, near Amiens, eight I./KG 76 Dorniers from Beauvais joined them. Climbing to ingress altitude, Lindmayr's formation encountered a cloud deck that proved thicker than expected and the Dornier pilots spread out to avoid mid-air collisions. Breaking out into clear air at 11,000ft, the 'Dorniers [were] spread out over a large area in ones, twos, and threes. Our attack formation had been shattered.'[32]

Lindmayr flew a wide circle to allow the flight leaders to reform their Staffeln and, minus two bombers that failed to find the formation, continued to the fighter rendezvous point ten minutes behind schedule. Approaching the rendezvous point south of Boulogne, Lindmayr's aircrews were pleased to see approximately 90 Bf 109s from JG 3 and 53 joining them, while about 60 more, from JG 27 and 52, were already well ahead, sweeping the direct route from Cap Gris-Nez to London.

At 1104hrs the Rye CH station reported its first contact, quickly followed by several more as the fighter escorts climbed into the wide radar swath. Park immediately scrambled his two Biggin Hill Spitfire squadrons (72 and 92) to patrol Canterbury at 25,000ft, ordered nine other squadrons airborne (take-offs between 1115 and 1120hrs) and requested additional coverage from the two flanking Groups.

Ten days prior, in his *Instruction to Controllers No 10*, Park had directed: 'The enemy's main attack must be met in maximum strength between the coast and our line of Sector aerodromes. Whenever time permits, Squadrons are to be put into the battle in pairs. Some Spitfire Squadrons are to be detailed to engage the enemy fighter screen at 20,000 or more feet. The Hurricanes, because of their inferior performance, should normally be put in against the enemy bombers, which are rarely above 16,000 feet by day.'[33]

Park's revised tactics – he had recognized that intercepting with individual squadrons of 9–12 fighters usually resulted in the unit being overwhelmed by the opposing escorts and few bombers being downed – had been attempted on 7 September and subsequently, but with very little success owing primarily to the fact that there was little time for the two units to join into a single combat formation. Consequently, squadrons continued to intercept individually and suffered accordingly, with little attrition of, or disruption to the inbound bomber formations.

Operationally, Park's new instructions overcame the restrictions imposed by the HF/DF's technical limitations – a maximum of four units operating Pip-Squeak at any one time – by coupling squadrons in pairs (later, in threes) as 'wings', with the leading squadron's formation commander activating Pip-Squeak for both units. This doubled the number of squadrons each sector controller could vector, thus ending the numerical disadvantage previously experienced.

On the 15th, the *RAF Narrative* records, Willoughby de Broke 'not only had sufficient time to couple ten squadrons into [five] wings, he was able also to bring in reinforcements from adjacent Groups before the first German force crossed the coast'. He ordered the 'Kenley Wing' of 253 and 501 Sqns to patrol Maidstone, sent the 'Northolt Wing' of 229 and 303 (Polish) Sqns to patrol over Biggin Hill, and joined 257 and 504 Squadrons, from Martlesham and Hendon, respectively, overhead North Weald before sending them to reinforce Kenley's squadrons over Maidstone. To guard the sector stations north of the Thames he placed the 'Debden Wing' of 17 and 73 Sqns over Chelmsford at 15,000ft. Finally, he dispatched 603 Squadron's 12 Spitfires to reinforce the 20 Spitfires of the 'Biggin Hill Wing' over Canterbury.

At 1120hrs, Brand sent 609 Squadron from Middle Wallop to protect Windsor and the factories at Brooklands. Leigh-Mallory, it seems, had to do Park one better. Reinforcing the 'Duxford Wing' of 19, 242 and 310 (Czech) Sqns with 302 (Polish) Sqn from Leconfield and 611 Sqn from Digby, he now called 'his formation' the '12 Group Wing'; it totalled 56 Spitfires and Hurricanes, and he sent it off at 1125hrs. 'Lorag Leader', Sqn Ldr Bader, was directed to patrol Hornchurch at 25,000ft.

Between 1135 and 1142hrs, Park launched six more squadrons, while holding his last four in reserve at readiness. The 'North Weald Wing', 46 and 249 Sqns, was ordered towards South London and 1 (RCAF) Sqn (from Northolt) and 605 Sqn (from Croydon) were directed to join over Kenley to patrol. Number 41 Squadron was launched from Hornchurch to overfly Gravesend and, once it arrived, 66 Squadron was scrambled to join it. This pair was vectored to the south-west to engage but, because of the great altitude disparity and distance between them, they did not see each other or operate together.

Due to the delay caused by having to orbit and re-form his Kampfgruppe, by the time Lindmayr's Dorniers crossed the coast near Folkestone at 16,000ft at 1137hrs, they were six minutes behind the 'freie Jagd' missions which, in the next

He 111H-3 '1H+CB' of 1./KG 26 was shot down on 11 September by AA and fighters, having attacked the London docks. The aircraft crashed at Burmarsh, Kent, and the crew managed to set fire to it prior to their capture. (Andy Saunders)

10–12 minutes, completed their sweeps without engaging any defenders and exited to the east. Meanwhile, passing behind the sweeping 'Emils' of JG 27 and 52, 'Tophat Control' had vectored 'Tennis Leader', Flt Lt John W. 'Pancho' Villa, leading the 'Biggin Hill Wing', from over Canterbury to intercept the raiders, instructing the Spitfire pilots 'to clear the way for later attacks by Hurricane squadrons upon the German bombers'.

At 1145hrs Villa spotted the bomber formation over Ashford at 16,000ft and its high-flying escorts at 22,000ft, and ordered his squadron into line astern before leading a swooping attack on I./JG 53. Number 92 Squadron followed and 603 Squadron joined the melee a few minutes later. Six 'Emils' were shot down, for three pilots killed in action, two POW, one wounded, without loss, but 'not all the escorting fighters were diverted by these attacks'.

Five minutes later, over Maidstone, the 'Kenley Wing' made a head-on attack against Lindmayr's bombers and was quickly engaged by the close escorts from JG 3. One 501 Squadron Hurricane was shot down, its Belgian pilot killed. Numbers 41 and 66 Squadrons arrived shortly afterwards, the latter attacking the bombers while 41 Squadron battled the escorts, losing one Spitfire, pilot killed, for one 'Emil' shot down, pilot captured.

Finally, approaching south-east London, Lindmayr's formation was spotted by 257 and 504 Sqns sent from over North Weald. They reported: 'A square formation of 25 Do 17s and 215s [sic] in five lines of five aircraft line abreast, all at 18,000ft with escorting yellow-nose Me 109s at 23,000ft… Both squadrons attacked the bombers from the starboard quarter and experienced little interference from enemy fighters.' The Canadians (1 (RCAF) Sqn) and 605 Sqn also attacked about this time, from the port quarter, but were quickly engaged by the escorts. Four Hurricanes were shot down and one Canadian pilot killed.

At about 1210hrs, the '12 Group Wing' arrived. 'The leader of this wing [Bader] was forced to delay his attack until the No. 11 Group fighters had cleared away. Then as arranged, he led his three Hurricane squadrons against the bombers while his two Spitfire squadrons went for the enemy fighters.'

During these last attacks Lindmayr's 25 Dorniers approached their target and, sighting it through the breaks in the cloud layer that had begun gathering at 4,000 to 6,000ft, he announced that the target lay ahead. Seconds later, peering through his Lotfe 3 bombsight, Lindmayr called 'Bombs away!' and his formation released 425 SC50 HE bombs, devastating an area approximately 500 yards long and 25 yards wide.

Amazingly accurate from that altitude, the attack cut railway tracks north-east of Clapham Junction in several places. The Pouparts Viaduct also collapsed onto the tracks beneath it in two places, the Battersea electricity station was damaged and four unexploded bombs lay in the rubble, delaying repairs. Some 24 civilians were killed and another 30 injured. The tactical objective had been achieved – there was no rail traffic through the area for two days.[34]

One Do 17Z, 'F1+FH' from 1./KG 76, was famously shot down over the target, the largest part of it crashing in the railyard at Victoria Station. Three crewmen were killed and two others captured. Five more Dorniers were shot down during the egress when four fresh 11 Group squadrons joined the '12 Group Wing' in chasing the retiring bombers back to the coast and two more crash-landed back in France, where they were deemed damaged beyond repair.

Altogether, No. 11 Group squadrons claimed to have shot down seven bombers and the '12 Group Wing' claimed to have destroyed 19 – 'F1+FH' was claimed nine times – as well as seven fighters. This wildly exaggerated success cost 11 Hurricanes and two Spitfires; the Jagdwaffe lost nine 'Emils' with a tenth mysteriously crashing into the sea during the return flight.[35]

THE REASON FOR 'BATTLE OF BRITAIN DAY'

As intended, the noon raid elicited a maximum response from 11 Group and all 21 of Park's squadrons were launched.

Deichmann hoped this disruption would result in Park having fewer interceptors ready to meet the larger follow-up strike. The II. Fliegerkorps mission targeted three large commercial dockyards in London's East End, the Surrey Commercial Docks south of the Thames and the Royal Victoria and West India Docks north of the river. Stahl's KG 53 would lead the 'Valhalla' with 24 He 111Hs, with the 43 Do 17s of Fink's II. and III./KG 2 in column on the left,

Pilot Fw Heinz Friedrich
(left) and another
crewmember walk into
captivity after their Heinkel,
'1H+CB', crashed. All five
crew survived. (Clive Ellis)

and Wechmar's 28 KG 26 He 111Hs following Hptm Otto Pilger's 19 II./ KG
3 Do 17Zs on the right.

Deichmann planned for an escort of 400 fighters, but several of the units had
flown in the initial attack and refuelling and rearming the returning Bf 109Es took
longer than anticipated. This resulted in an hour's delay and only half the required
number of 'Emils' actually accompanying the bombers. As the 'Valhalla' formed
up over the Pas-de-Calais, III./JG 54 joined to provide close escort on the left
flank while 20 I./ZG 26 Zerstörers took up station on the right. Five Jagdgruppen,
I.[J]/LG 2, I./JG 26, I./JG 3, III./JG 53 and I./JG 77, climbed above the bomber
formations to fly top cover.[36]

Appearing as three returns, the raid was first 'seen' by the Rye radar at 1345hrs
as three large contacts, estimated as '50+', '60+', and '30+', a low 'guesstimate' for
the 114 medium and light bombers, and 200 fighters. Trailing them, the radar
observers also saw five smaller contacts estimated to total a strength of '90+'. These
were the supporting 'freie Jagd' mission, flown by five Jagdgruppen (approximately
150 Bf 109Es) of Galland's JG 26 and Trautloft's JG 54. Rather than the usual
pre-strike sweep, in this case the fighters took off as the bombers passed overhead
and followed, climbing through the strike package's altitude as it crossed the
Channel westbound from Cap Gris-Nez to Dungeness. The intention was for the
faster fighters to pass above Stahl's formations as they turned inland and, moving
out in front, sweep ahead, but not so far ahead that the interceptors could come in
behind them.

Initially, the three bomber formations flew westbound in right echelon, with

Fink's Dorniers leading on the left, followed by Stahl's Heinkels offset to the right, then the combined KG 3/KG 26 column trailing on the far right. At Dungeness, all three simultaneously executed a 50-degree 'in place' turn to the right to point at Gravesend and the Tilbury Docks, crossing the coastline in a 6.5-mile-wide (10km) phalanx at 1410hrs. By this time Park had launched 15 squadrons and one flight. The Hurricanes and Spitfires, of course, had a much shorter and less difficult time 'turning' to the next mission because they were fighting over their home turf and wasted little time getting back to their bases.

Willoughby de Broke placed 501 and 605 Sqns over Kenley; 66 and 72 Sqns over Biggin Hill; two pairs 41 and 92 Sqns with Spitfires, and 249 and 504 Sqns with Hurricanes over Hornchurch; the 'Hornchurch Wing' to cover Sheerness (although 222 and 603 Sqns failed to join into their wing formation); the 'Debden Wing' of 17 and 257 Sqns over Chelmsford; and held the 'Northolt Wing' of 1 (RCAF) and 229 Sqns over their station as his airborne reserve. Number 46 Squadron from Stapleford Tawney was directed to patrol over the East End docks and 'B' Flight of 73 Squadron, just six fighters, was curiously sent to patrol over Maidstone, over which the raiders were almost certain to fly on their way to London. Five minutes later, 253 Squadron scrambled from Kenley to patrol over the station and the 'Tangmere Wing', comprising 213 and 607 Sqns, was launched to patrol Kenley–Biggin Hill.

Park had 183 Spitfires and Hurricanes airborne, and requested reinforcements from Nos 10 and 12 Groups. At 1415hrs, Brand launched 12 Hurricanes from 238 Squadron to patrol over Brooklands. Leigh-Mallory launched his '12 Group Wing' (now of 47 fighters) and Bader was directed to patrol over Hornchurch.

'Tophat Control' joined 41, 92 and 222 Squadrons' Spitfires into a 27-fighter wing and vectored them to intercept the high escorts over Romney Marsh at 1415hrs. Hauptmann Fritz Losigkeit, Staka 2./JG 26, recorded: 'After we crossed the coast the British fighters came in from a great height, going very fast. During their dive some of the Spitfires became detached from the others. Using full throttle, my Staffel was able to catch up with them and I got into an attacking position. I fired a long burst and pieces broke away from the Spitfire's wing and fuselage. The pilot [Plt Off Bob Holland, 92 Sqn] slid back the canopy and jumped from the cockpit. Overtaking rapidly, I pulled to the left of the Spitfire and saw his parachute open.'[37]

When 'Mitor Leader', Sqn Ldr Donald O. Finlay, OC 41 Squadron, called 'Tally-ho!' on the escorts, 'Tophat Control' began vectoring two pairs of Hurricane squadrons (213 and 607 and 501 and 605 Sqns, for a total of 37 fighters) to intercept the bombers, the first attacking at 1420hrs over Tenterden. Ignoring the escorts, Sqn Ldr James Vick led 607 Squadron in a bold frontal attack that resulted in a head-on collision with a 5./KG 3 Dornier – the Hurricane pilot baled out but the German crew were all killed. Four minutes later, the second pair engaged Pilger's column in a sweeping right-hand turn to attack their right-rear quarter, one of the 605 pilots lost control of his damaged fighter and collided with another

On 15 September, Do 17Z 'F1+FS' of 8./KG 76 was in a left turn having dropped its bombs on a target in London, when it was shot down at 1210hrs near Sevenoaks by Fg Off J.C. Dundas and Plt Off E. Tobin of 609 Squadron. The Dornier's pilot, Fw R. Heitsch and his three crew were captured, one later dying of his wounds. (Clive Ellis)

5. Staffel Do 17Z, causing both to crash. A third Hurricane was shot down by I./ZG 26 Zerstörers in the flank escort.

As Stahl's formation approached the Thames near Gravesend, the clouds below thickened appreciably, closing in to form 6/10th coverage with bases at 3,000ft and columns of cumulous towering to 12,000ft. Seeing the river through breaks between the clouds, the three mission leaders turned their columns left to fly up the waterway, but the clouds ahead closed to 9/10th coverage making further navigation difficult.

And navigation was not their only problem.

Vectored by 'Lumba Control' from overhead Hornchurch, 249 and 504 Squadrons attacked Pilger's column as II./KG 3 turned towards the Royal Victoria and KG 26 the West India Docks. Soon the 'Debden Wing' and 46 and 603 Squadrons, making a total of 50 Hurricanes and 13 Spitfires, joined them. The 5./KG 3 Staka's Do 17Z was shot down and his two wingmen were so badly damaged they abandoned the mission, escaping by diving into the clouds below. Return fire and escorts shot down two Hurricanes and two Spitfires; one pilot was killed.

Unable to find their targets due to weather, Pilger's depleted formation slid into line behind Stahl's Heinkels while Wechmar's KG 26 angled to the right, flying past the cloud-covered West India Docks to drop 33 tons of bombs, including five SC1000s, and about 36 incendiary canisters on West Ham, causing the Bromley-by-Bow gas works to erupt into flames, damaging railway lines near Upton Park Station, wrecking an electricity generating station and transformer substation, and severely damaging nearby residential areas. Seventeen civilians were killed and 92 seriously injured.

Stahl led his KG 53 Heinkels towards the Royal Victoria Docks. En route, from Dartford to London they were constantly attacked by the 20 Spitfires of 66 and 72 Squadrons and the 'Northolt Wing's' 21 Hurricanes. A Stab/KG 53

He 111H was shot down and crashed near a pier at Woolwich Arsenal; three more aborted the mission due to battle damage. The remaining 20 found the target obscured by cloud and about half dropped some 16.5 tons of bombs rather randomly on the city area north of the Thames.

Fink's left-hand column, now of 42 Do 17Zs, was confronted by 23 Hurricanes from 73, 253 and 303 (Polish) Sqns, but III./JG 53 successfully kept them away from the bombers. Arriving over the Surrey Commercial Docks, KG 2 found them obscured by cloud and turned back to the left without bombing. As the gaps in the clouds increased to the east, the bomb aimers scattered 30.4 tons of bombs and 20 incendiary canisters on Penge, damaging the railway station and blocking a tunnel, Erith, Bexley, Drayford and Dartford.[38]

As bombs began raining from the bellies of Heinkels and Dorniers, Bader's '12 Group Wing' approached from the north, eager to engage the bombers. Blaming Leigh-Mallory's late order to scramble 30 minutes earlier, the 27 Hurricanes and 20 Spitfires were still climbing southbound when Bf 109s attacked them from above. They were from Galland's JG 26. The approaching swarm of 47 RAF fighters could not be missed and the 30 or so 'Emil' pilots of Stab and II. Gruppe turned to engage.

According to Price's *Battle of Britain Day*, Bader quickly 'ordered his three Hurricane squadrons to split up and engage the enemy fighters while, in a reversal of their usual role, the Spitfires were to try to get through to the bombers.' Bader himself was very soon in serious trouble. His combat report reads: 'On being attacked from behind by Me 109 I ordered "Break up" and pulled up and round violently. Coming off my back partially blacked out, nearly collided with Yellow 2 [Plt Off Crowley-Milling]. Spun off his slipstream and straightened out 5,000 feet below without firing a shot.'[39]

Donald Caldwell's *JG 26: Top Guns of the Luftwaffe* includes Galland's report that he had been engaged in 'an unsuccessful ten-minute dogfight with about eight Hurricanes, during which much altitude was lost', when below him he spotted 310 (Czech) Squadron flying by in close formation.

With the Stabsschwarm I dove from about 800m above them, approached at high speed, and fired at the far left aircraft in the rear flight, continuing fire until point-blank range. Finally, large pieces of metal flew off the Hurricane. As I shot past this aircraft, I found myself in the middle of the enemy squadron, which was flying in stepped [sections line astern] formation. I immediately attacked the right-hand aircraft of the leading flight of three. Again, metal panels broke off; the aircraft nosed over and dove earthward, ablaze. The remaining English [*sic*] pilots were so startled that none as much as attempted to get on my tail; rather the entire formation scattered and dove away.[40]

Galland shot down Sgt Josef Hubacek. His wingman, Oltn Walter Horten, shot down Sqn Ldr Alexander Hess. Both pilots parachuted to safety. Meanwhile II./JG

RIGHT INSET
The crew of this Do 17 from
KG 3 managed to nurse
their battle-damaged aircraft
back to France, before
crash-landing, following
their attack on London on
15 September. (Chris Goss)

RIGHT
The final daylight raid of
15 September came at
1530hrs, and was not the
coup de grâce that Park
and Churchill had feared.
The fighter controllers of
10 Group assessed the raid
approaching the Dorset
coast at just '6+'. As a
result, the 27 He 111s of
III./KG 55 bombed Portland
unmolested. They were
intercepted by six Spitfires
from 'B' Flight, 152
Squadron as they egressed.
The RAF pilots destroyed
one bomber and damaged
a second. The attack
inflicted only minor
damage. (AHB donated by
Ken Wakefield)

26 engaged 19 Squadron and shot down two Spitfires; both crash-landed and one was written off. JG 26 suffered no losses.

Following this climactic dogfight, the Messerschmitts began heading home low on fuel, and the egressing bombers became particularly vulnerable to the host of pursuing Hurricanes and Spitfires. These were joined by 238, 602 and 609 Sqns, adding 12 Hurricanes and 25 Spitfires to the pursuers' ranks, and Fink's formation suffered grievously, losing eight Do 17Zs shot down. Mölders' JG 51 flew part of the post-strike egress coverage but could not stop the massacre. Stahl and Fink lost another six Heinkels, including one on a luckless weather reconnaissance sortie over Kent, and Pilger lost three more Do 17Zs, from 4./KG 3. Attempting to catch the pursuing interceptors low on fuel, a V.[Z]/LG 1 Bf 110 'freie Jagd' sweep engaged two Hurricane squadrons at 1550hrs and lost three Zerstörers.

The raiders had dropped more than 110 tons of bombs and 108 incendiary canisters on various locations in east and south-east London. Damage to civilian installations and residential areas was extensive, but nothing of strategic value or military significance was harmed. A total of 14 Do 17Zs and six He 111Hs was lost on the raid[41], amounting to 17.5 per cent of the force dispatched. Coupled with the noon raid's losses (eight of 25 Do 17Zs), the day's loss rate topped 20 per cent, exceeding the loss rates during the opening stage of *Adlerangriff*.

Fighter Command was clearly far from beaten.[42]

To quote KG 26 He 111 pilot Lt Roderich Cescotti from Price's *Battle of Britain Day*: 'I regarded 15 September as the fiercest battle. None of the other battles in which I was involved made such a profound impression. We were shaken by the numbers of fighters the Royal Air Force was able to put up that day, and by the determination of the pilots. It was becoming clear that we were likely to break before the enemy.'

Feldwebel Horst Schulz, a KG 3 Do 17Z pilot, writing on a more personal level, confirmed: 'When we got back, we all agreed it had been a terrible day, but there was not much discussion. Initially we were grateful for having survived; we were too shaken to think any further than that. Not until the following day did the significance of the one-third losses [KG 3 lost six of 18 Do 17Zs] we had suffered sink in fully. We came to realise that if there were any more missions like that, our chances of survival would be almost nil.'[43]

Despite claiming to have destroyed 51 Spitfires and 26 Hurricanes, even the usually upbeat, positive, and optimistic ObdL daily situation report was written in sombre, almost defeatist tones, noting: '[Enemy] Fighters appeared over the target in formations in some strength (up to 80 aircraft). The fighters attacked sharply either singly or in pairs – regardless of AA fire – and pursued German bombers from the target to the middle of the Channel and, in some cases, even as far as the French coast.'[44]

Obviously, air superiority for the invasion could not be assured. The following day, Schmid briefed Göring on the disappointing and demoralizing experience and, before 'departing for the front', the Luftwaffe Commander-in-Chief took the information to his Führer.

The following day, after receiving the Luftwaffe Wetterdienst's (Weather Service's) particularly discouraging forecasts for the next week, Hitler indefinitely postponed Unternehmen *Seelöwe*.[45] Extensive, heavy cloud with low ceilings and limited visibility underneath were anticipated across southern England and the Channel. The overcasts would completely prevent using the moon for illumination and navigation across the broad waters, making the massive undertaking extremely risky. Reduced illumination and limited night-time visibility meant the host of vessels making up the four transport streams risked losing sight of one another and becoming badly disorganized. Without the moon to navigate by, the transport group leaders would have to cross the Channel by dead reckoning, making landfall at precise locations doubtful. Thus, even without the Royal Navy's interference the chances of actually arriving in an organized fashion, at the planned invasion beaches, were slim at best.

The forecast weather would also preclude Stuka and Ju 88A anti-ship operations. The Luftwaffe's proven maritime capabilities would be neutralized and could not be expected to provide the counter needed to the Royal Navy's anti-invasion surface forces. Likewise, the typically effective He 111 lines of communication interdiction missions – bombing railway stations, marshalling yards, and other choke points – would be throttled, permitting the relatively free movement of British Army forces to counter the amphibious assault on England's south-eastern shores, while Do 17Z battlefield interdiction and army support missions would be restricted by the low ceilings and limited visibility.

This Ju 88A-1 is believed to be '3Z+BP' of 6./KG 77, damaged by RAF fighters during a raid on London on 24 September. Suffering no casualties, the crew successfully crossed the Channel before crash-landing near St Omer. (Chris Goss)

In the preceding five weeks of combat, Kesselring had effectively rolled back Park's active fighter defence to inland patrol lines, on a Maidstone–Canterbury line rather than the Hawkinge–Manston line as they had patrolled in mid-August; driven Fighter Command squadrons from Hawkinge, Manston and Lympne; and secured air supremacy over the Channel ever since Park had discontinued overwater interception missions on 19 August. Despite not having destroyed Fighter Command, the Jagdwaffe's continued favourable exchange ratio meant that the Bf 109E would continue to dominate the battlespace if the weather allowed. But, the Jagdwaffe could not be expected to provide fighter coverage, guarding against RAF Battle and Blenheim attacks such as those mounted against the Maastricht and Meuse bridges four months before, over the beaches in such dismal weather conditions.

Hitler's conclusion therefore resulted from the consideration of multiple factors, rather than just the Luftwaffe's failure to destroy RAF Fighter Command. Once the decision was made, from the Luftwaffe's perspective, as an offensive counter-air campaign, the Battle of Britain was over.[46]

On the wet and foggy morning following the last great battle of the campaign, *The Times* reported: '175 RAIDERS SHOT DOWN [in] Sunday Air Battles Over London and the S.E.' The next day an RAF press release amended the number to 185 – 178 by fighters and seven to AA guns. In reality, the Luftwaffe had lost 56 aircraft during a day that had not equalled its largest effort of the campaign and which had not been the most intense of the Battle of Britain for Fighter Command either, yet is was for ever cemented into the canon of Battle of Britain mythology thanks to this misinformation.[47]

While a much-needed tonic for flagging RAF morale and somewhat alleviating the increasing frustration, dissatisfaction and worry of the British public, and reinforced by the subsequent cancellation of the anticipated invasion, this propaganda ploy proved eminently successful and resulted in the annual celebration of 'Battle of Britain Day' on 15 September.[48]

In actuality, to the chronically fatigued RAF fighter pilots and acutely frustrated Luftwaffe aircrew alike, it was only another bitter day in an exhausting series of daily battles – the campaign continued, but took yet another turn.

Firefighters tackle a blaze following a raid on London. (NARA)

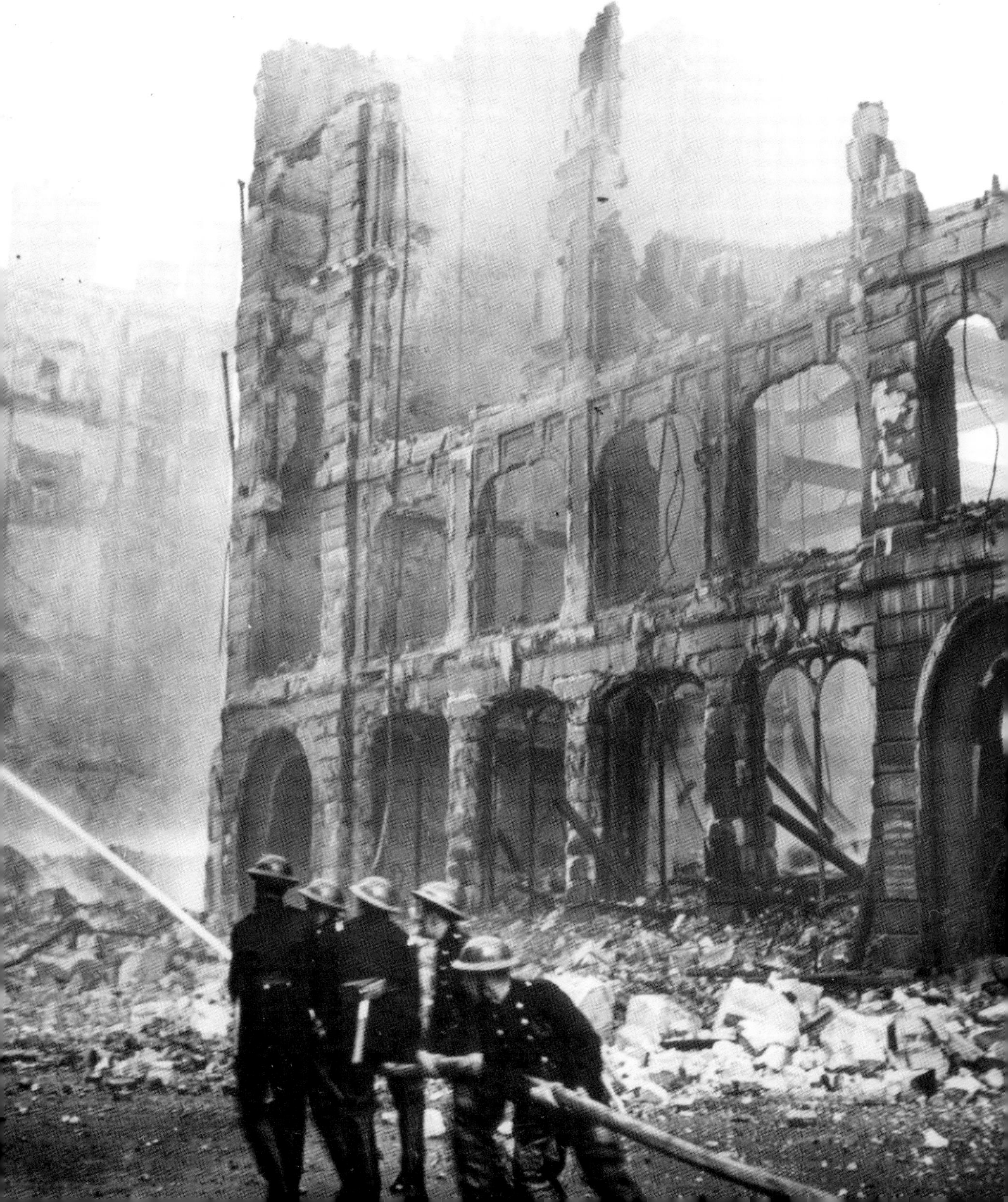

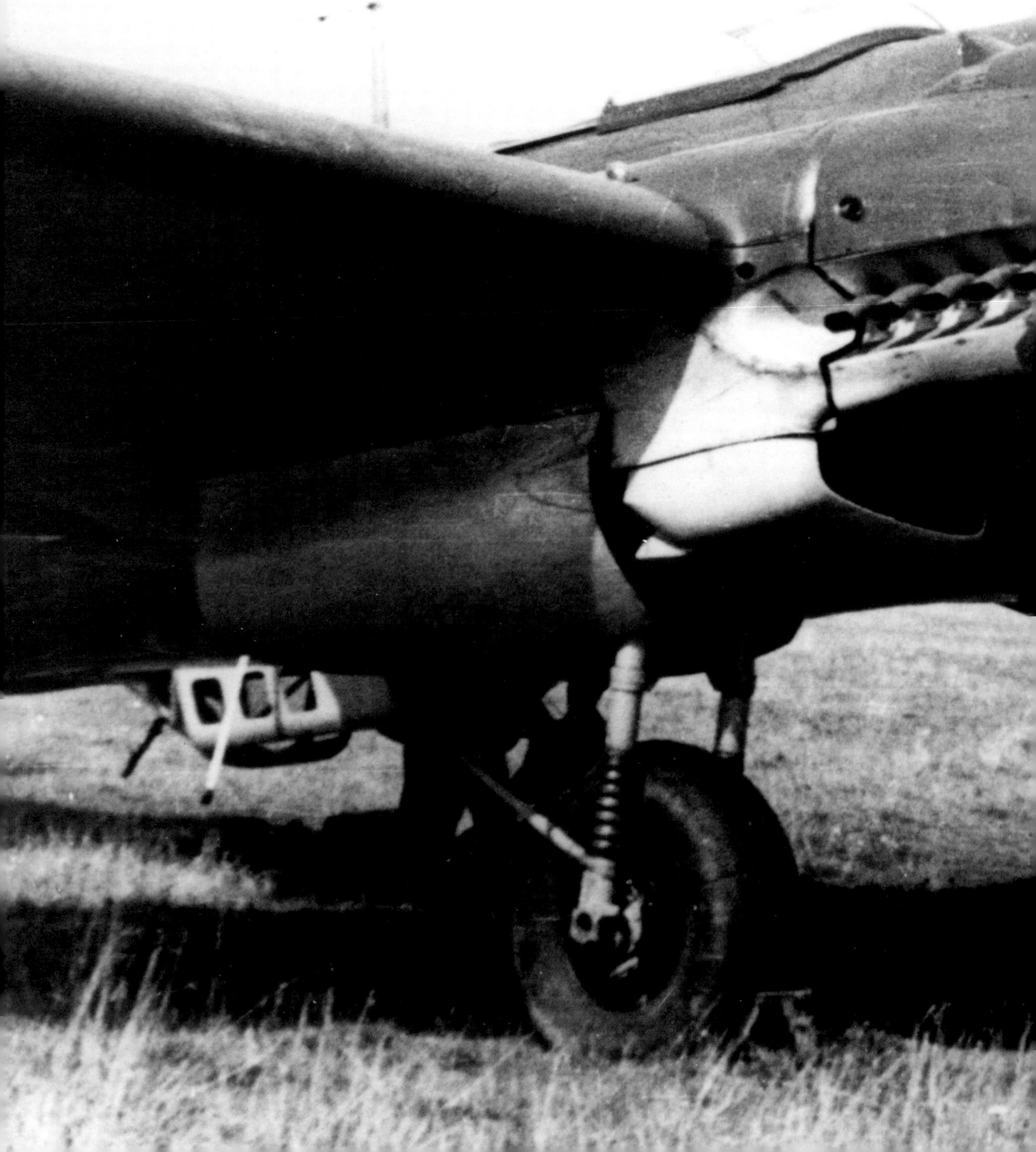

CHAPTER XIII

DEFEAT DIES SLOWLY
17 September through 31 October 1940

The enemy air force is still by no means defeated; on the contrary, it shows increasing activity. The weather situation as a whole does not permit us to expect a period of calm. The Führer, therefore, decided to postpone Unternehmen Seelöwe indefinitely.

Kriegsmarine Seekriegsleitung (Navy War Staff) Diary, 17 September, 1940[1]

THE END OF *ADLERANGRIFF*

'Robinson', Göring's ObdL mobile HQ, steamed into Boulogne railway station on 16 September and, the following day, the Reichsmarschall hosted his last *Adlerangriff* Besprechung. Dismayed by the results of the 15 September operation, he predicted: 'With four or five days of heavy losses he [the RAF] ought to be finished off…'[2]

Grauert, Loerzer and their Kampfgeschwader commanders were discouraged by the fact that all of the 15th's bomber formations had been met by large forces of interceptors. Losses were extremely high for the meagre results achieved.

In the ensuing discussion, JaFü 1's Osterkamp shared his Jagdwaffe pilots' report of encountering Park's paired squadrons and Leigh-Mallory's '12 Group Wing': 'The English have adopted new tactics. They are now using powerful fighter formations to attack in force… Yesterday these new tactics took us by surprise.'[3]

Unwilling to entertain what he considered Osterkamp's dissent, in urging his commanders to continue pressing their attacks on London Göring insistently – and stupidly – responded: 'That's just what we want! If they come at us in droves, we can shoot them down in droves!'[4]

Defeated, but not willing to admit it, Göring directed his commanders to continue their bombing of London (by Luftflotte 2) and British aviation industry targets (Luftflotte 3). The latter was due to his realization that: 'The British have used the breathing space [because of bad weather] to strengthen their fighter force with pilots from flight schools and new material [equipment] from their factories, including aircraft that have not yet even been painted. Thus, the enemy air force has been greatly reinforced.'[5] From the ObdL list of aviation industry targets sent to the Luftflotten HQs on 1 September, the Supermarine Spitfire, Bristol aircraft and aeroengine, and Westland Aircraft factories in Sperrle's AOR were picked as priority targets.

Meanwhile, Kesselring was to continue attacking militarily significant targets – railways, power stations, gasworks and so on – within London. Göring's forlorn hope was: 'to bring England to terms by the Luftwaffe's independent impact on morale and economy'. While not harbouring such sanguine expectations, Hitler

PREVIOUS PAGES
Bordmechaniker Uffz Karl Gerdsmeier with 'his' Heinkel He 111H, 'G1+DN' of 5./KG 55, at Chartres. This aircraft was the first bomber shot down on the raid against the Bristol factory at Filton on 25 September. (AHB donated by Ken Wakefield)

He 111s of 3./KG 55 taxi out at Villacoublay. The aircraft in the foreground is 'G1+CT' from the 9 Staffel. (AHB donated by Ken Wakefield)

did not want to relieve the pressure on the British government or its populace, for fear that *Seelöwe*'s cancellation might be discerned, so he ordered Göring to continue 'his Luftwaffe's' attacks on Britain.

The ObdL situation report notes that the increasingly adverse weather that had spoiled Stahl's 'Valhalla' attack on the East End docks on 15 September permitted only 'isolated nuisance raids' and 'all bombing had to be carried out on the basis of dead-reckoning navigation' for the two days that followed.[6] With the clouds dispersing the next day, Deichmann organized attacks against Chatham Royal Dockyards, 12 He 111s from I./KG 53 dropping 16.5 tons of bombs at 1250hrs; Port Victoria fuel storage depot, where 34 II.(Schl)/LG 2 Jabos dropped six tons of bombs at 1610hrs; and Tilbury Docks, 18 Ju 88As from III./KG 77 dropping 25 tons of bombs at 1640hrs.[7]

This series of small raids failed to do significant damage to any of the three targeted naval/maritime facilities – 'one Admiralty tank [at Port Victoria] was hit but the fire was soon under control', the Chatham naval yards were missed entirely, with bombs falling on or near Gillingham, and at Tilbury 'all [bombs hit] near the centre of town, not one striking the docks'.[8]

According to the ObdL situation report: 'Strong fighter defence was encountered. [Enemy fighter] Attacks were carried out in tight formations (comprising 10 aircraft in some cases) and pressed home to close quarters.' The intense fighter battles resulted in Jagdwaffe pilots shooting down five Spitfires and seven Hurricanes, with three pilots killed and three more wounded, for the loss of seven 'Emils'. More significant was that, due to weather at higher altitudes, the JG 54 escorts 'lost the [KG 77] bombers in the clouds'. Major Max Kless's III./KG 77 was on its first combat mission after converting to the Ju 88A and, unescorted, was attacked by eight RAF squadrons, losing nine bombers, fully half of the formation. Thirty-six aircrew were casualties, among them Gruppenkommandeur Kless, who was killed.[9]

TOP RIGHT
Bf 109Es from 4./JG 53,
based on Nazi-occupied
Guernsey, provided part of
the initial escort to KG 55
during the Filton raid. (AHB
donated by Ken Wakefield)

BELOW RIGHT
He 111Ps of 9./KG 55
from Villacoublay at Staffel
strength. The photograph is
believed to have been taken
on the day of the Filton
attack. (AHB donated by
Ken Wakefield)

The grey, soggy autumn weather closed in again for the next week, the period during which *Seelöwe*'s great Channel crossing was to have occurred, thus proving the *Wetterfrösche* (weather frogs, Luftwaffe slang for meteorologists) discouraging forecast correct. Kesselring's daylight attacks on London were limited to high-altitude Jabo raids by II.(Schl)/LG 2 Bf 109E-7s (flown in 22 sorties) and 'nuisance raids by single aircraft' (32 individual bomber sorties) over 19 to 26 September.[10]

Göring finally got the opportunity he had been looking for during the 17 September conference, for 'four or five days' of heavy attacks, during the final week of September.

THE FILTON RAID[11] – 25 SEPTEMBER

Covering two-and-a-half million square feet and employing 37,000 workers, the Bristol aircraft and aeroengine factories at Filton, near Bristol, were among the largest manufacturing sites of the type in the world. With ObdL shifting emphasis from the *Handelskrieg* strategy to attacking aviation industry targets, the Bristol factory was at the top of Sperrle's list of priority targets.

Despite several attacks over the previous three months, photo-reconnaissance by a 3.(F)/123 Ju 88A on 21 September revealed that there were only 13 bomb craters within the vicinity of the plant. 'The bomb-hits on the aero-engine works at Filton reported in Situation Report Nr. 382 on 22 September have not been confirmed. A subsequent examination by Luftflotte 3 HQ Photographic Section has shown that an error was made in the initial evaluation… It must be assumed that no appreciable damage has been done to the Filton aero-engine works.'[12]

Sperrle's chief of staff, Oberst Günther Korten, directed the meticulous planning of a bold Geschwader-strength daylight attack well beyond the range of the Bf 109E and mapped out an ingress route designed to outmanoeuvre Brand's fighter defences. The circuitous routing would be aided by large Gruppe-strength feints, 23 KG 51 Ju 88As threatening to attack Plymouth to the west of the main force, and 20 KG 54 Ju 88As flying against Portsmouth to the east. The main strike package initially consisted of 64 He 111H/Ps from Obstlt Korte's KG 55, following a 'freie Jagd' sweep by about 50 Bf 109s from I./JG 2, II./JG 2 and II./JG 53 – JG 2 elements of JG 53 having been transferred back to Sperrle's command mid-month – and escorted by a similar number of Bf 110s from ZG 26.

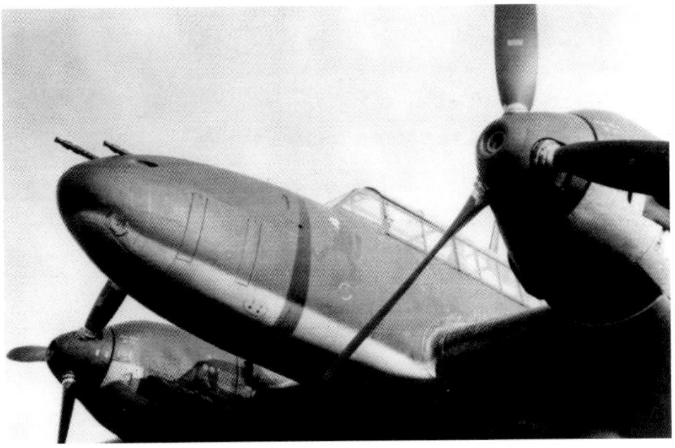

Bf 110C-4 '3U+GS' of 8./ZG 26 was the mount of Fw W. Scherer and his Bordfunker. Gefr H. Schumacher. They were shot down during a simultaneous attack by a Spitfire of 152 Squadron and a Hurricane of 601 Squadron. (AHB donated by Ken Wakefield)

Korten's staff planned the strike's ingress route to make landfall near Portland and then fly north-west across Dorset and Somerset – aiming at Cardiff, Wales – before turning right and flying up the Bristol Channel, hoping to keep Brand's controllers guessing as to the actual target until the last moment. The whole operation would also provide cover for another low-level 'snap attack' by ErprGr 210, with 11 Bf 110 Jabos raiding Portland naval base.

Taking off from their bases south-west of Paris between 0916 and 0924hrs, KG 55's three Kampfgruppen rendezvoused over Évreux, forming a *Geschwaderkeil* (wing wedge) with Major Friedrich Kless's II. Gruppe leading in the centre, I. Gruppe on the left flank and III. Gruppe to the right. Kless[13] led the entire Geschwader in the attack, flying as navigator and bomb aimer in the lead Heinkel. Korte also flew on the mission, leading his Stabskette on Kless's right wing, at the head of III. Gruppe. Within each Gruppe, the three Staffeln formed themselves into large 'vics', so that the whole formation appeared as a broad arrowhead as it continued climbing to 16,000ft.

Overhead Cherbourg at 1100hrs Kless's formation turned north towards Portland and was joined by its escorting fighters. Obstlt Huth's Zerstörers arrived as about a dozen four-aeroplane sections, climbing to 19,000ft and taking station above and behind the three Kampfgruppen, weaving gently to maintain their assigned positions with their slower charges. Appearing to be additional escorts, Boltenstern's Jabos, each armed with two SC500 bombs, joined below and behind the Heinkels and followed them across the broad expanse of water. Ahead

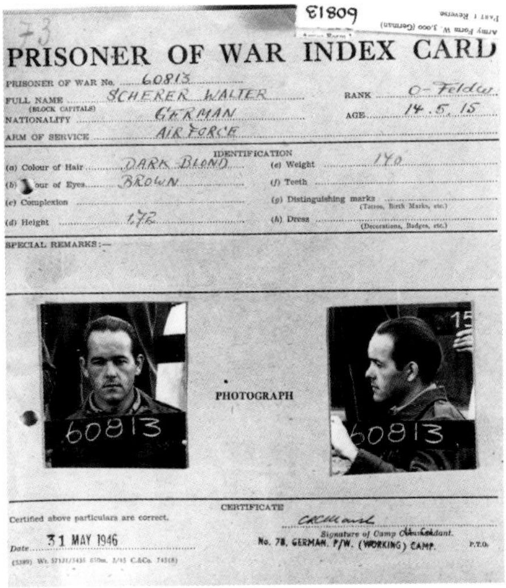

60813

Army Form W. 3,000 (German)

PRISONER OF WAR INDEX CARD

PRISONER OF WAR No. 60813
FULL NAME (BLOCK CAPITALS) SCHERER WALTER   RANK O-Feldw.
NATIONALITY GERMAN   AGE 14.5.15
ARM OF SERVICE AIR FORCE

IDENTIFICATION
(a) Colour of Hair DARK BLOND   (e) Weight 170
(b) Colour of Eyes BROWN   (f) Teeth
(c) Complexion   (g) Distinguishing marks (Tattoo, Birth Marks, etc.)
(d) Height 172   (h) Dress (Decorations, Badges, etc.)

SPECIAL REMARKS:—

PHOTOGRAPH

CERTIFICATE
Certified above particulars are correct.
Date 31 MAY 1946
Signature of Camp Commandant.
No. 78, GERMAN. P/W. (WORKING) CAMP.   P.T.O.

Schumacher was killed and Scherer wounded when '3U+GS' was attacked. Scherer was taken prisoner after the crash-landing near Boyton, Wiltshire – this is his Prisoner of War Index Card. (AHB donated by Ken Wakefield)

and out of sight of the main formation, the three Jagdgruppen of 'Emils' swept across the Channel hoping to prevent Brand's interceptors from interfering with the advance of the large *Geschwaderkeil* and its two flanking feints.

Going 'feet wet' northbound, Kless led 58 heavily laden Heinkels (six had returned to base with various faults) directly across the Channel towards Portland Bill; the Worth Matravers radar station detected them at 1104hrs. Within the next five minutes the large primary return, with smaller returns on each flank, advanced to 30 miles (50km) north of Cherbourg and for the first time in 31 days, No. 10 Group had to respond to the approach of a major daylight bombing raid. It appeared that the three Luftwaffe formations were approaching on a wide front to attack Plymouth, Portland and Portsmouth simultaneously. Brand immediately ordered 609 Squadron scrambled from Middle Wallop to patrol Swanage at 20,000ft and, two minutes later, launched 152 Squadron to patrol over Portland, also at 20,000ft.

However, the weeks of inactivity resulted in rather lazy responses and it took nine minutes for 'Sorbo Leader', Sqn Ldr H.S. 'George' (or 'Dampers') Darley to get 609 Sqn's 14 Spitfires airborne. By then, Kless's large formation, now accurately estimated at a strength of '60+', was just five miles east of Portland Bill, so 'Starlight Control' (Wg Cdr David Roberts, W Sector Fighter Controller) changed Darley's instruction and vectored the squadron towards Portland. Squadron Leader Peter Devitt's 152 Squadron already had one pair of Spitfires (Red Section) patrolling at 20,000ft off the Isle of Wight and they were ordered back to Warmwell to rejoin their unit while 'the rest of the squadron took off in sections and pairs of sections, each of which flew and fought independently'.

As Kless's formation approached the shoreline, at 1120hrs Boltenstern's 11 Jabos peeled off to the left and accelerated to high speed in their dives to low level. They attacked the Portland naval base fuel oil depot at 1120hrs and, opposed by only light, inaccurate AA fire, dropped 12 tons of bombs, although 'little damage was done except for fracturing the water main from the mainland to the naval base. This would have had serious effects if fires had been started by further attacks, but none were made'.

While this attack was in progress, two Sections of 601 Squadron Hurricanes were ordered off from Exeter and sent to Portland. Brand also scrambled 238 Squadron from Middle Wallop, with Roberts ordering Sqn Ldr H.A. 'Jimmy' Fenton to patrol 10 miles (15km) south of Yeovil at 15,000ft.

As Kless's formation crossed the coast at 1123hrs, it was ineffectively engaged by Portland's AA batteries and, having sufficiently confused No. 10 Group's initial radar picture, the Ju 88A decoys approaching Plymouth and Portsmouth all turned for home. Shortly thereafter, near the limits of their combat radius, the three Jagdgruppen also withdrew, having seen no enemy interceptors.

As the large formation of Heinkels and Zerstörers winged north-west across Dorset, at Middle Wallop it appeared to Roberts that Kless's force was probably headed inland to attack the Westland Aircraft factory at Yeovil and he directed all his airborne interceptors to rendezvous south of the city. The *RAF Narrative* reports: 'The four British squadrons [152, 238, 601, and 609 Sqns] were all ordered towards that area, only to find that the Germans had passed it and were forging ahead towards the Bristol Channel.'

Kless's *Geschwaderkeil* continued past the assumed target, apparently heading towards Cardiff, so at 1128hrs Brand scrambled 79 Squadron at nearby Pembrey, with orders to climb to 15,000ft and patrol five miles south of Cardiff. This squadron, too, was tardy, also taking nine minutes to get airborne. When 'Pansy Leader' got his three Sections of Hurricanes airborne, Roberts directed him to fly to Weston-super-Mare as quickly as possible, but 79 Squadron missed the raiders entirely.

During its flight across Somerset, the right flank of Kless's broad formation was attacked head on by the five Spitfires of Yellow and White Sections, 152 Squadron, damaging a 7.Staffel Heinkel. Reaching the Bristol Channel at 1138hrs, Kless crossed the shoreline at Weston and turned his large formation to the right, maintaining a course paralleling the coastline. It now appeared that Bristol was the intended target.

Simultaneously, Brand scrambled 'A' Flight of 56 Squadron from Boscombe Down and Roberts ordered every airborne fighter to 'buster' (proceed at full throttle) to the Bristol area. As the attackers passed Portbury, four army 3.7-inch

ABOVE LEFT
'G1+LR's' Bordfunker, Uffz Kurt Schraps, was recorded on gun-camera film, swinging beneath his parachute just off the coast of Poole, Dorset. (AHB donated by Ken Wakefield)

ABOVE
Schraps was the sole survivor of 'G1+LR'. (AHB donated by Ken Wakefield)

ABOVE
The Bristol Filton works under attack. (AHB donated by Ken Wakefield)

ABOVE RIGHT
The fourth and final Heinkel brought down during the Filton raid was 'G1+BH', flown by Fw Fritz Juerges of 1./KG 55. The aircraft crashed at Studland at 1210hrs, having been damaged in a previous attack and finished off by Plt Off Wigglesworth, flying a Hurricane of 238 Squadron. (Clive Ellis)

AA guns opened fire, hitting a 5. Staffel Heinkel; all five crewmembers parachuted safely before their aircraft crashed near Flax Bourton at 1145hrs.

Kless's bombing run took the remaining 57 Heinkels directly over all three main groups of buildings making up Bristol's Filton complex and, despite the enemy's extensive use of camouflage paint, he had no difficulty in aligning his large formation for a perfect run-in. At 1148hrs, some 350 bombs (96.5 tons) were delivered in a particularly effective attack that obliterated the target in an area measuring about one mile wide and three-quarters of a mile deep. 'Damage was severe, especially at the Rodney works, where complete aircraft were assembled and tested prior to delivery; and it was not until the middle of October that [production] output was normal again… Nearby railways were blocked in three places; and there were numerous craters and unexploded bombs on Filton airfield… [and] communications with No. 10 Group Headquarters were destroyed.'[14]

Following the Luftwaffe's highly successful raid on the Bristol aircraft and aeroengine plants, 504 Squadron was ordered to relocate from Hendon to Filton the next day, strengthening the plant's defences. (AHB donated by Ken Wakefield)

TOP LEFT
Bf 110C-2 'L1+LL' of
15./LG1 was one of 19
Zerstörers shot down on
27 September, which
marked the death knell for
the Bf 110 operating as a
day fighter over Britain. This
aircraft was attacked by
seven or eight fighters and
the Bordfunker wounded,
before the pilot crash-
landed at 0945hrs near
Oxted, Surrey. (Clive Ellis)

ABOVE
The pilot of 'L1+LL', Oblt
Otto Weckeisser, and his
Bordfunker, Gefr Horst
Brugow (pictured), both
survived the aircraft's forced
landing and were captured.
(Clive Ellis)

ABOVE LEFT
The crew of Bf 110C-2
'L1+XB' of V./LG1 were not
so fortunate as Weckeisser
and Brugow. Both were
killed when they were
brought down by a mid-air
collision on 27 September.
Note the four RAF kill
markings on the severed tail
unit. (Andy Saunders,
colourized by Richard
Molloy)

Clearing the target area, Kless wheeled his broad *Geschwaderkeil* to starboard to withdraw via Colerne and Frome. Fenton's 12 Hurricanes slashed through the bombers, diving from 22,000ft in a line-astern attack, firing as they went. Zooming away in climbing turns, they continued to harry their quarry with individual attacks throughout their egress. They were quickly joined by Darley's 14 Spitfires.

A section of 601 Squadron attacked Huth's retiring Zerstörers, now flying ahead of the bombers to sweep their egress route, shooting down one Bf 110C and damaging a second so badly it ditched in the Channel; a third crashed on landing in France. All three were from III./ZG 26. The three Spitfires suffered no losses.

Devitt's four Spitfires joined the running battle just short of Bath and the 30 interceptors began thinning the retreating bombers, shooting down two He 111Ps, from 6. and 7./KG 55, for the loss of two Spitfires and one pilot killed in action, and one Hurricane, pilot unhurt, to the bombers' defensive fire.[15]

Approaching Swanage, Fenton's Hurricanes scored the day's final kill, bringing down Feldwebel Fritz Jürges's 1./KG 55 He 111H.

In Kenneth Wakefield's *Luftwaffe Encore: A Study of Two Attacks in September 1940*, Beobachter Hptm Karl Köthke recalled:

As bad luck would have it we passed over an airfield from which we could see fighters taking off, leaving clouds of dust behind them, and we knew the end must come for us soon. We tried in the end to dive for cloud cover, but the clouds were insufficient for our purpose and at a height of about 6,000ft we were attacked again by fighters. With our few machine guns we stood no chance. Josef Altrichter, our flight mechanic, was badly wounded in his right leg and as he wore flying overalls, we were unable to apply a tourniquet. We knew we could not save him.

We were then hit in our left engine, which stopped as we crossed the English coast. All hopes of reaching mid-Channel now disappeared. We turned in over the coast at a height of about 1,000ft to attempt a landing and although the fighters were still following us they did not shoot any more. They knew we could not escape. We lost height very quickly now, heading straight for a quarry, but at the very last moment we managed to gain a little height and found ourselves over fields heading towards a small wood. We touched down and after sliding a short distance came to a standstill, a tree stopped us short.[16]

The Filton Raid was arguably the Luftwaffe's most successful strike against an aircraft factory during the entire Battle of Britain. When the 'All Clear' sounded at 1216hrs, the stunned survivors emerged from their shelters to view a level of destruction difficult to comprehend. In all, 168 bombs and 24 incendiaries had fallen within the factory area. Ninety-one employees had been killed and another 166 injured. Outside the factory compound, 58 people had been killed and more than 270 injured. At the cost of eight bombers and three escorts, eight newly constructed Blenheims and Beaufighters were destroyed and 24 more damaged. The main assembly halls were hit and severely damaged, effectively halting Beaufighter production for four weeks.

Next day Dowding transferred 504 (County of Nottingham) Squadron from Hendon to defend the Bristol factories. At 1030hrs on 26 September, 17 Hurricanes took up residence at Filton airfield after communications with Brand's HQ were restored.

THE LAST MAJOR RAIDS ON LONDON – 27 AND 30 SEPTEMBER

On 26 September, 49 KG 55 Heinkels and ten ErprGr 210 Jabos, with a strong fighter escort, dropped 74.4 tons of bombs on the Supermarine factory at Woolston, causing 89 casualties, destroying three Spitfires and damaging 20 more. The raid also temporarily stopped production. The *RAF Narrative* admits: 'The Germans had struck as severe a blow at the British aircraft industry as on the previous day at Filton. The northern part of the Supermarine works was extensively damaged; two workshops received direct hits and production was completely stopped.'

Unsure of the intended target, Brand's four scrambled squadrons were initially withheld as base CAPs and late vectors to intercept resulted in the raid striking unopposed. Engaged during egress, only one bomber and two Zerstörers were shot down for the loss of two 152 Sqn Spitfires and three Hurricanes from 238 and 607 Sqns; one intercepting pilot was killed.[17]

Hauptmann Horst Liensberger (Gruppenkommandeur, pictured) and his Bordfunker, Uffz Kopge, crewed 'L1+XB'. (Andy Saunders, colourized by Richard Molloy)

Meanwhile, on the eastern side of the battlespace, for the seventh consecutive day unfavourable weather conditions precluded Kesselring's attacks against his primary target. The next day, however, the clouds cleared sufficiently for Luftflotte 2 to dispatch three waves against London. Some 15 Ju 88As from I./KG 77 in late morning (1100–1215), 30 II./KG 53 He 111s at midday (1115–1230) and 55 I. and II./KG 77 Junkers mid-afternoon (1445–1600).

The Heinkel raid, escorted by 170 'Emils', was largely weather-aborted, dropping 19.3 tons of bombs ineffectively on Chatham and its dockyards, but releasing another four tons of HE at Maidstone, where, the *RAF Narrative* says, 'the railway station was hit; some sidings were damaged; and one bomb hit the high level bridge'. Others managed to scatter 'a small number of bombs in London south of the Thames shortly after noon… but important damage was caused to communications. All lines on the south-east section of the Southern Railway out of Victoria Station were blocked.'

Park's response was prompt and Willoughby de Broke's direction of the defence was timely and effectively employed three-squadron wings from Debden and Tangmere to reinforce intercepts by the two-squadron Biggin Hill, Kenley, Northolt and North Weald wings. The four-squadron 'No. 12 Group Wing' was scrambled 'but by the time it reached its patrol height, the enemy had retired'.

The interceptors were so numerous that for once the escorting units could not prevent heavy losses during their ingress – the afternoon raid fared no better. During the day, of the 70 Ju 88As dispatched, 'only 29 bombers with single-engined fighter escort [got through to the target], 26 tons of bombs being dropped', although they further damaged the Southern Railway near Brixton and Loughborough Junction.[18]

Altogether, Luftflotte 2 flew 100 bombing sorties with 909 escorting fighters. Discounting the aborted midday raid, the cost in aircraft and aircrew losses was both shocking and prohibitive: a dozen of KG 77's Ju 88As (a severe 17 per cent loss rate) were shot down, as were 17 Bf 109Es, while another crash-landed in France. Despite all the cautions and constraints

Flight Lieutenant Percy R.-F. Burton was killed flying Hurricane V6683 of 249 Squadron, after chasing Liensberger's Zerstörer at low level for 40 miles (65km). The Hurricane's wing severed the Bf 110's tail and both aircraft crashed near Hailsham. (Andy Saunders, colourized by Richard Molloy)

Bf 110 C4 'U8+CL' of 3./ZG 26 was flown by Lt Joachim Koepsell and his Bordfunker, Uffz Joachim Schmitt. They were shot down on 27 September by a Hurricane flown by Sgt H.B.D. Jones of 504 Squadron, while providing an escort to ErprGr 210, tasked with bombing the Frazer Nash gun turret manufacturer at Yate. Koepsell parachuted safely from the aircraft, but Schmitt had been killed during the engagement. (AHB donated by Ken Wakefield)

regarding Zerstörer operations made during the preceding weeks, nine Bf 110s of the 23 launched by ZG 76 and V.(Z)/LG 1 were also lost, for a prohibitive 39 per cent loss rate. Altogether, these 39 downed aircraft accounted for 73 aircrew killed or captured.[19]

Park's controllers had vectored 513 interceptors to engage the raiders. Number 11 Group lost ten Spitfires and ten Hurricanes in combat, with 15 pilots killed and three wounded. The 'No. 12 Group Wing' lost two fighters of each type, with three pilots killed and one wounded. All told, the defenders lost two dozen interceptors and 18 pilots, plus four wounded, but destroyed 12 bombers and 27 escorts; the exchange rate was steadily improving.

As Bergström records in *The Battle of Britain: An Epic Conflict Revisited*, Winston Churchill stated: '27 September ranks with 15 September and 15 August as the third great and victorious day of the Fighter Command during the Battle of Britain.'

Even to the Luftwaffe, it was becoming clear, especially now that Park was employing three-squadron wings, that Dowding's forces were getting stronger, not weaker. As the official RAF history concludes: 'It is not, therefore, surprising that, except for a somewhat half-hearted effort on 30 September, henceforth their attacks chiefly took the form of high-altitude fighter and fighter-bomber sweeps.'

Over the next two days Luftflotte 2 flew 49 Jabo sorties, scattering 57 SC250 bombs (16.7 tons) indiscriminately upon London. 'Owing to unbroken cloud, bombs were dropped by dead-reckoning navigation and it was therefore not possible to observe the exact location of hits.'[20]

Nevertheless, Kesselring made one last major effort against London on 30 September.

Following a morning 'freie Jagd' sweep by III./JG 26 and II./JG 27, in the early afternoon 150 'Emils', comprising one Gruppe each from JG 27, 51, 52, 53 and 54, escorted a small III./KG 3 Do 17Z raid headed for Hawker's Hurricane production facility at Kingston-on-Thames. The *RAF Narrative* says that owing to 'a good deal of cloud at 6,000ft', Hptm Erich Rathmann's dozen Dorniers flew past their intended target to unload 'approximately 100 bombs' on Greenford, a suburb of London close to RAF Northolt (the probable alternative target). 'No military damage was caused.'

Park countered by launching 14 squadrons, of which ten intercepted, shooting down 12 'Emils' and an 8./KG 3 Dornier (a second crash-landed in France) at the cost of only one Hurricane and Spitfire lost (one pilot was killed in action, the other wounded). It was a rare resounding victory for the defenders.

Later in the afternoon, a I./KG 77 Ju 88A strike went badly awry. Navigation over the unbroken cloud deck was faulty. Making landfall too far west, Hptm Joachim Poetter led his formation north but, before reaching London, turned west, reversing course near Reading to approach from that direction. Observer Corps tracking was precluded by the extensive overcast and Poetter's constant changes in direction prevented effective intercepts. Weather foiled the raid, the Observer Corps' estimated 18 Junkers dumping around 70 bombs near Marlow, 'most of them falling in marshy ground and doing no damage'.

The day's ObdL situation report records: '58 aircraft employed against London dropped approximately 25 tons of bombs and five incendiary canisters. Owing to weather conditions targets could not be clearly identified and observation of effect was

At 1405hrs on 30 September, Fw Walter Scholz, of 3./JG 53, crash-landed Bf 109E-4 'Yellow 13' near Eastbourne. Scholz was on a bomber escort sortie when the aircraft's engine cooling system was hit. (Andy Saunders, colourized by Richard Molloy)

TOP RIGHT
Ju 88A-1 '3Z+DK' of 2./KG
77 was flown by Oblt Fritz
Oeser on 30 September.
Twenty miles from London,
prior to reaching the target,
the aircraft was badly
damaged by RAF fighters
and the crew was forced to
jettison the bombs. '3Z+DK'
was finished off by Sgt P.
Farnes, 'Yellow 3', from 'A'
Flight, 501 Squadron. It
crash-landed on Gatwick
Race Course at 1645hrs.
(Clive Ellis)

RIGHT
Hauptmann Walter Kienzie,
of Stab JG 26, was flying
from Audembert in a
Stabschwarm with Galland,
Horton and another pilot
on 30 September. They
were bounced by RAF
interceptors and, in a later
interview, he recalled:
'Galland told me
afterwards that he saw my
Messerschmitt fall like a fire
ball and a parachute open.
I myself have no
recollection of the event...'
Kienzie was treated for
burns and his right leg was
amputated after being
smashed during bale-out.
(Chris Goss)

also not possible. Further aircraft which were dispatched against London attacked alternative targets owing to unbroken cloud. Intensive patrolling by enemy fighters was observed over the target area.'[21]

One 2./KG 77 Ju 88A was crippled by AA fire and, straggling behind the egressing formation, was shot down by a lone 501 Squadron Hurricane. Nine other squadrons had also been launched and they intercepted various roving formations of Messerschmitts. Two Hurricanes and two Spitfires were shot down, but eight Bf 109Es were lost, including five from Galland's JG 26, while another ditched in the Channel, out of fuel. Six more RAF squadrons were scrambled later, but never engaged.

In the west, Sperrle attempted to follow up his successful strikes against the Bristol and Supermarine aircraft factories with an attack against the Westland Aircraft works at Yeovil, using I. and II./KG 55, with a diversionary raid on Portland by 11 I./KG 51 Ju 88As. Korte's 43 Heinkels were escorted by 40 ZG 26 Zerstörers and 52 'Emils' from JG 2 and 53. Some 47.4 tons of bombs were dropped 'on the Westland factory [but] owing to dense cloud (9/10–10/10), bombs were dropped by dead-reckoning navigation and the effect could not be observed,' the ObdL situation report notes.

In fact, 'all their [KG 55's] bombs fell to the east of the target, mostly on the small town of Sherborne.' The only result of military value was that, 'the main line of the Great Western Railway was blocked between Yeovil and Sherborne'.[22] Brand engaged effectively with nine squadrons, which shot down five bombers and three

A ground crewmember warms the engines of an He 111 prior to start for a night-bombing sortie against Britain during the winter of 1940. (AHB donated by J.F. Rowling)

BELOW LEFT
Invasion was impossible after the Luftwaffe failed to smash Britain's integrated air defence system and bring Fighter Command to its knees. The only viable alternatives left to Hitler were blockade and night-bombing, the former a long-term strategy, the other a punishment, used as much to disguise plans increasingly centred on 'opportunities in the East'. Here, ground crew, or 'Black Men', so called because of the colour of their denim overalls, prepare to load one of two SC500 general-purpose bombs onto the wing hardpoints of a KG 51 'Edelweiss' Ju 88 night-bomber. (NMUSAF)

Bf 109Es, while a Bf 110D returned damaged beyond repair, for the loss of six Hurricanes from 56 and 504 Sqns, and a 152 Sqn Spitfire; two pilots were killed and two wounded.

For first time in the long, drawn-out Battle of Britain, the Hurricane and Spitfire pilots had significantly outperformed their opponents in both Luftflotten, shooting down eight bombers (another returned damaged beyond repair) and 27 Bf 109s for the loss of only 17 of their own.[23]

Even more significantly, the increasingly adverse weather over southern England prevented further successful daytime bombing missions. Only a few, small-scale bomber raids were therefore attempted the following month. The Luftwaffe's final daylight bombing mission against Britain occurred on 29 October, when a dozen I./LG 1 Ju 88As raided Portland naval base.[24]

JABOS, A POOR SUBSTITUTE FOR 'STRATEGIC' BOMBING

Considering the continuing, unrelenting attrition of Luftwaffe bomber forces and with no victory in sight, but encouraged by ErprGr 210's impressive string of dramatic successes, ObdL decided to substitute dive-bombing Bf 109E-4s and E-7s for more traditional high-level medium bomber attacks.

Major Weiss's II.(Schl)/LG 2 had been actively involved in *Adlerangriff*'s Stage 3 attacks on sector stations and raided London six times in September. During the month, the unit flew 19 missions, usually employing 20–25 Jabos on each raid, totalling 428 sorties, 264 of them against London. Four Bf 109E-7s were lost, three to AA fire and the fourth to a 72 Sqn Spitfire over Ashford during the unit's initial, 14 September raid on London.

Meanwhile, Sperrle's last effective daylight attack on aircraft industry targets, the 'Yates Raid' of 27 September, spelled the end of ErprGr 210's aggressive use of the Bf 110. On this mission, targeting the Parnall Aircraft factory (which manufactured Frazer Nash gun turrets for RAF bombers) just north of Bristol, ten bomb-carrying Bf 110Ds were escorted by 42 Zerstörers from ZG 26.

Air Vice-Marshal Trafford Leigh-Mallory

Born on 11 July 1892, in Mobberley, Cheshire, as the son of a cleric, Trafford Leigh-Mallory was educated at Haileybury and Magdalene College, Cambridge. Completing his Bachelor at Law degree, he applied to the Inner Temple in London to become a barrister. When World War I broke out, he volunteered to join the Territorial Army in the King's Liverpool Regiment and was commissioned as a second lieutenant on 3 October 1914. In the spring of 1915 he deployed to the Western Front with the South Lancashire Regiment and was wounded during an attack at the Second Battle of Ypres.

After recovering from his wounds, Leigh-Mallory transferred to the RFC in January 1916 and was accepted for pilot training. Upon completing his training, he was posted to No. 7 Squadron on 7 July 1916, where he flew B.E.2s during the Battle of the Somme. In November 1917 he became commander of No. 8 Squadron, which was heavily involved in army co-operation, directly supporting tank attacks in the battle of Cambrai in 1917. By the time of the Armistice, Leigh-Mallory had been mentioned in dispatches and awarded the Distinguished Service Order.

On 1 January 1925 he was promoted to wing commander and passed through the RAF Staff College; he received command of the School of Army Cooperation in 1927. Five years later he was promoted to group captain and posted to the Air Ministry, then commanded No. 2 Flying Training School. A posting to RAF Iraq followed and, having been promoted to air commodore, he returned to England in 1936. Appointed Air Officer Commanding No. 12 Group Fighter Command in December 1937, he became one of the RAF's youngest air vice-marshals when he was promoted in November 1938.

Fussy, hot-headed and argumentative, Leigh-Mallory was unscrupulously ambitious and acquired a reputation as an accomplished service politician and 'dagger man'. He was also intensely jealous that Park, who was not promoted to AVM until July 1940, was made commander of the premier, frontline No. 11 Group, and championed Sqn Ldr Douglas Bader's 'Big Wing' (embodied in the 'No. 12 Group Wing') concept as a means to discredit Park. He eventually took Park's job.[25]

AVM Trafford Leigh-Mallory, in 1944. (Photo by Popperfoto via Getty Images/ Getty Images)

Brand scrambled 56, 152, 238, 504 and 609 Sqns, but only Filton-based 504 Squadron was able to intercept the fast raiders before they reached the target. Its determined attacks caused the Jabos to jettison their bombs into open countryside south of Bristol (killing four civilians) and abort the mission. The Hurricanes shot down four Jabos, including the unit's latest Gruppenkommandeur, Hptm Martin Lutz, who was killed, and six escorts.[26]

With the loss of 17 Bf 110 Jabos and three group commanders in six weeks of combat, it was finally realized that 'the Messerschmitt 110 was too slow and cumbersome, its early successes [were] achieved mainly through the skill of its more experienced and aggressive pilots... It was apparent that, of the two aircraft being [evaluated], the Messerschmitt 109 was the better fighter-bomber and far better able to defend itself after delivering its load.'[27]

To reduce losses of his precious medium bombers, on 2 September Göring had directed the formation of additional Bf 109E Jabo units, ordering each Jagdgeschwaderkommodore to form three squadrons, one in each Jagdgruppe, of fighter-bombers. Substituting bomb-carrying fighters for medium bombers, especially on London raids, Göring hoped that their high-altitude, high-speed ingress would negate interception and allow his Luftwaffe to bomb London both with impunity and without continuing the horrendous losses of his bombers.

Commanding JG 26, Galland saw it for what it was: 'The [Bf 109E] fighter was made into a fighter-bomber as a stop-gap and a scapegoat. We started from the premise that the fighter was apparently unable to give sufficient protection to the bombers. This was true. If the Jagdwaffe is unable to protect the bombers, it must deliver the bombs to England on its own. The raids on England had become

TOP RIGHT
A KG 4 crew board their
He 111H-5 for a night
sortie. Note that the two
pale blue SC1000
'Hermann' bombs have
been given a hastily applied
coat of black 'paint' – it
was actually a mixture of
grease and soot. (AHB
donated by J.F. Rowling)

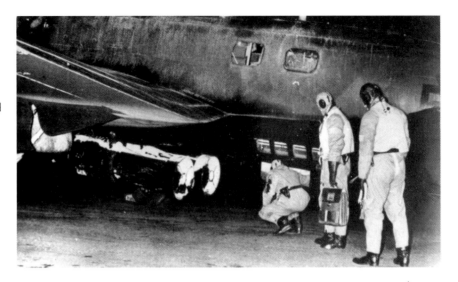

BELOW RIGHT
Flight at high altitude
provided some measure of
insurance against
interception, but it came at
the expense of bombing
accuracy. It also required
the crew to wear oxygen
masks, donned here by a
Heinkel crew. (AHB donated
by Ken Wakefield)

The forward, offset mast on
this He 111H-5 is for
Y-Gerät, a precision
bombing system. Flown
exclusively by III.KG/26,
this highly classified unit
received its orders via
Enigma, a cypher system so
complex that the Nazis
considered it unbreakable.
This particular aircraft was
from the E-Stelle at Rechlin.
(AHB donated by Ken
Wakefield)

Pilots of JG 53 chat idly while ground crews prepare their aircraft for another sortie over Britain. Bf 109E 'Yellow 4' is in the foreground. (Clive Ellis)

a matter of prestige, and as day-bombing could not be continued and night raids were only in preparation, this gap was to be filled by fighters transformed into fighter-bombers. Not military expedience but a momentary political demand…'[28]

With the field modification of 364 Bf 109E-4s and delivery of 186 factory-fresh E-7s, the rapid expansion of the 'Jabo-waffe' occurred in October. During the month, 140 missions were flown, totalling 2,633 sorties, of which 60 per cent reached London, 37 per cent dropped bombs on alternative targets, primarily due to weather, and 3 per cent were aborted. The RAF official history concedes: 'A fairly high proportion of small bomb-carrying formations reached their targets without interference.'

Losses were, indeed, minimal and only 29 Jabos failed to return from these missions. However, the lack of accuracy when releasing SC250s at medium altitudes (3,000–10,000ft) from a 45-degree dive resulted in the scattering of bombs in random places around the assigned targets. Galland's assessment was: 'Apart from their nuisance value, [they] achieved very little of any military value.'

THE NIGHT BLITZ BEGINS

Meanwhile, the night-bombing campaign, which was coincidental but never really part of *Adlerangriff* proper, increased from late August into September and continued through the approaching winter and following spring. Complying with Hitler's Directives Nr. 9 and 13, as part of the *Handelskrieg* campaign, Luftwaffe's night-bombing began on 2/3 June using single aircraft, sometimes several of them flying individually, from various bomber units as they became available for operations against Britain. They attempted to hit British industrial areas and airfield locations and, over the next ten weeks (until mid-August) 16 industrial plants, 14 ports and 13 airfields were targeted. 'Most of the bombs fell on [nearby] residential areas or harmlessly in open countryside. A few factories were damaged and there was some disruption to the country's rail and road transport systems.'[29]

ABOVE
Oblt Heinz Ebeling led 9./JG 26 through its conversion to the fighter-bomber role. From 15 October he led the Staffel on many fighter-bomber missions over England. (Clive Ellis)

TOP RIGHT
A Bf 109E Jabo of JG 53. Note the SC250 bomb on the centreline rack. (Clive Ellis)

For *Adlerangriff*, Göring decided that a more systematic night-bombing programme was needed and initially reserved General der Flieger Robert Ritter von Greim's V. Fliegerkorps (KG 51, 54 and 55) for nocturnal operations. At this time, Luftwaffe night-bombing was far more accurate than the RAF's nocturnal operations because of its use of the 30.0–33.3MHz Knickebein (literally 'crooked leg', but selected because it was the name of a raven in Germanic folklore) radio-beam, long-range VHF navigation system.

An adaptation of the Lorenz 'electronic beam' runway approach system developed for blind landings in low visibility conditions, the system used a powerful transmitter coupled with an aerial array to project a 0.33-degree wide beam some 250 miles to aircraft above 20,000ft altitude (this altitude restriction a result of the earth's curvature). The intersection of two Knickebein beams could be used to designate the location of a desired target. Because it used the bomber's on-board electronic landing aid system and pilots and navigator/bomb-aimer were trained in its use, it was no great challenge to convert it for use as an electronic bombing aid.

During the summer, however, the RAF quickly discovered that several such beams criss-crossed the airspace above Britain and, since the system was so simple, crude and well known, it was quickly exploited to render it far less effective by scattering replicate transmitters around England to 'cut' the Knickebein main beam at positions well short of anticipated targets. Among the first electronic countermeasures (ECM) systems, it was known as 'meaconing' (because it 'mimicked' the German 'beacons') and codenamed 'Aspirin' while Knickebein, poetically enough, was codenamed 'Headache'.

British ECM proved very effective when, following Göring's decision to concentrate day-bombing against No. 11 Group airfields with Kesselring's Luftflotte 2, Sperrle's Luftflotte 3 was re-roled to operate almost exclusively on night-bombing missions, resurrecting the *Handelskrieg* campaign. Second only to London, the ports of Liverpool and Birkenhead, together known as Merseyside, were the largest and busiest in Britain and naturally became the primary target for the renewed blockade strategy.

In a sustained four-night bombardment beginning on 28/29 August, 629 sorties dropped 496 tons of bombs and 1,029 BSK 36 canisters for the loss of only seven bombers. However, Wakefield reports, in *Pfadfinder: Luftwaffe Pathfinder Operations over Britain*, 'Only on the last night did Liverpool suffer badly, with 160 fires in the city centre and Birkenhead. However, only a few bombs hit the docks and, as on previous nights, many bombs again fell widely between the Rivers Severn and Dee.'

The raids ended on the morning of 1 September, but photographic reconnaissance did not discover the lack of destruction until days later. 'This revealed that the docks at both Liverpool and Birkenhead were virtually unscathed. Some damage could be seen in the city centres, but the photos also revealed numerous bomb craters in nearby open countryside, with many in the vicinity of devices that were eventually identified as decoy fire installations.'[30]

By then it was too late to go back; on 3 September Göring changed the Luftflotten's priority to bombing London day and night.

Following the massive daylight bombing of the city's East End docks four days later, London was bombed on 57 consecutive nights, destroying and damaging more than one million homes and killing more than 40,000 civilians. During the next 34 weeks, London was bombed 48 times, with multiple major attacks also hitting Birmingham, Liverpool, Plymouth, Bristol, Glasgow, Southampton, Portsmouth and Hull, while eight other cities were bombed once, killing another 20,000 British citizens.[31]

The Night Blitz lasted until 21 May 1941 when the Luftwaffe had to reorganize and deploy eastwards for Unternehmen *Barbarossa* (Operation *Barbarossa*), the Nazi invasion of Soviet Russia, slated to commence one month later.

On 25 October, this Bf 109E-4 of 5./JG 54 was being flown by Oblt Joachim Schypek, tasked to escort Bf 109 Jabos attacking London. Flying at 26,000ft and prior to reaching their target in the vicinity of Biggin Hill, they were intercepted by Spitfires of 41 Squadron. It is believed that Schypek, who was told that morning by the unit medical officer not to fly that day, was attacked by Fg Off Peter Brown. The 'Emil' pilot was forced to crash-land at Broom Hill, near Lydd, where he was taken prisoner. (Clive Ellis)

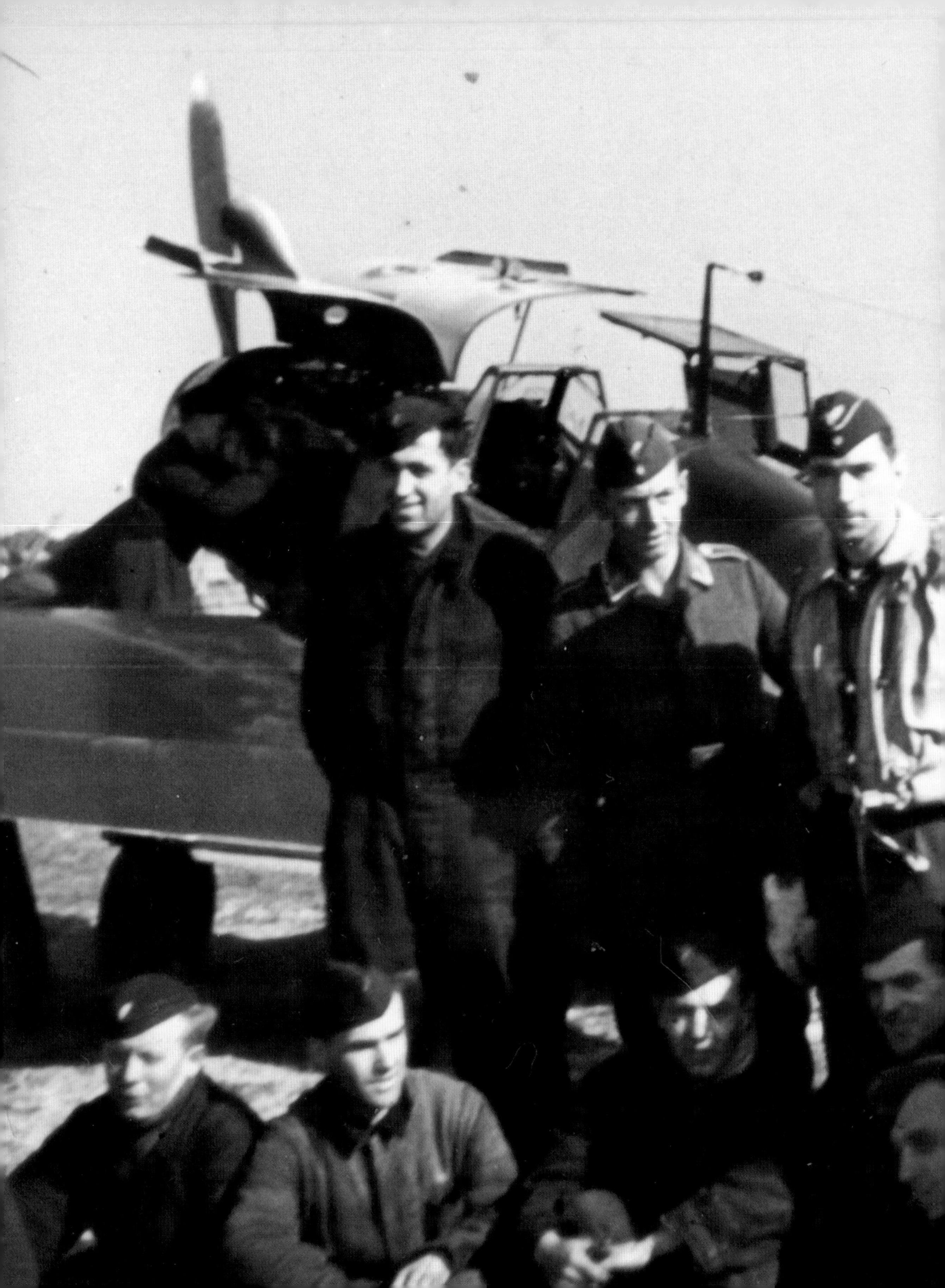

CHAPTER XIV

ANALYSIS

Assessing the Battle of Britain from
the Luftwaffe's perspective

It is commonly supposed that a heavily outnumbered Royal Air Force, by sheer gallantry and skill, achieved a well-nigh miraculous victory.

Telford Taylor, *The Breaking Wave: The German Defeat in the Summer of 1940*[1]

The traditional history – some might say legend – of the Battle of Britain, presents the campaign from the defensive perspective as an epic, titanic struggle for air superiority over southern England that climaxed in the defeat of the Luftwaffe's second major attack on London, on 15 September 1940. The cause for the Luftwaffe's defeat is typically ascribed to the 'efficacy of the Dowding System' and the courage, determination, and sacrifice of 'The Few', with comic relief provided by liberally seasoning the account with perceived German blunders.

The German historical accounts attribute the Luftwaffe's defeat to the progressively increasing adverse weather and the unwillingness of RAF interceptor squadrons to engage in fighter-versus-fighter combat, effectively neutralizing the advantage in combat capability enjoyed by the well-trained and highly-experienced Jagdwaffe pilots flying [they believed] the superior Messerschmitt Bf 109E and the exceedingly favourable exchange ratio they claimed to have whenever British defenders accepted battle.

Neither of these is completely correct.

Unlike ground campaigns, the success of an air campaign cannot be assessed by cities captured, territory occupied, or enemy armies defeated, routed, or destroyed. Likewise, an air campaign cannot be graded by comparing opposing sides' victory

PREVIOUS PAGES
Oberstleutnant Werner Mölders, Kommodore of JG 51, with ground crew. (Clive Ellis)

I.KG/40 operated Fw 200 Condors from June 1940. Based at Bordeaux-Mérignac, it began systematic anti-shipping operations in August, typically flying out over the Bay of Biscay, around Ireland and up to Norway. Some 90,000 tons of shipping was claimed sunk in the first two months, and 363,000 tons by February 1941 – claims that are vastly inflated. Churchill nevertheless called the aircraft the 'Scourge of the Atlantic'. It certainly played an important role in locating and tracking Allied convoys while transmitting their position to enable U-boats to co-ordinate attacks. (AHB)

claims. Kill claims are only an indication of the intensity of aerial combat, not the actual numbers of opposing aircraft destroyed. They fuel wartime propaganda and are frequently sensationalized by amateur historians and aviation enthusiasts, but they are valueless to professional military historians because they are always, and usually grossly, inflated. In this campaign, Luftwaffe victory claims were three times more than RAF losses. Fighter Command claims were similarly exaggerated. On two of the heaviest days of fighting (15 and 18 August), the RAF claimed 336 Luftwaffe aircraft shot down, when actually 143 were lost, an over-claim rate of 238 per cent. On 'Battle of Britain Day', the RAF over-claimed by 325 per cent.

In actuality, the Luftwaffe won the numbers game in combat. The Jagdwaffe's overall exchange ratio was 1.77:1 from 12 August through to 15 September, accounting for slightly more than three RAF fighters for every two Bf 109Es lost. However, every month (July–September) British factories were producing three times more replacements than Messerschmitt so that the Jagdwaffe's marginal superiority in air-to-air combat was insufficient to overcome the British production advantage and could not have destroyed Fighter Command.

The resulting maths reveals that at the strategic level, as a 'fighter battle' or 'battle of attrition', the Battle of Britain was never a winnable contest for the Luftwaffe.

That said, the fundamental error that cost the Germans victory in *Adlerangriff* was Göring's decision to shift operations from the Luftwaffe's previously successful offensive counter-air campaign formula of destroying the enemy air force (aircraft and ground facilities) on its bases, to attempting to win an airborne battle of attrition. Initially, this stratagem included striking six of the seven No. 11 Group sector stations to bring up RAF squadrons in defence.

During the last days of August, the Luftwaffe began winning the campaign by causing severe damage to two of them: Biggin Hill and, less so, Kenley. Additionally, Park's Spitfire and Hurricane squadrons were suffering heavy losses while trying to defend these vital airfields. Damage to the airfields and losses defending them were sufficient enough to cause Dowding to begin considering whether he should 'withdraw 11 Group from south-east England altogether'.

OPPOSITE
Although hopelessly out-performed as a day fighter, the Defiant proved a useful stop-gap in the night-fighter role. Pilot Officers James Benson and Leonard Blain from 141 Squadron were credited with the type's first confirmed nocturnal kill on the night of 22/23 December, against an He 111 from 3./KG 55, flown by Uffz Bruno Zimmermann. The aircraft crashed at 1805hrs near Etchingham, with Beobachter OFw Walter Richter the sole survivor. The Defiant pictured was from 264 Squadron, based at West Malling. (AHB)

However, had it occurred, this tactical withdrawal north of the Thames, excepting Eastchurch and Gravesend, would not have necessarily given Göring the victory. Dowding was talking about withdrawing the six squadrons stationed at Kenley and Biggin Hill. Rolling back No. 11 Group to the Thames would have had a significant operational impact, forcing Park's squadrons to have much longer flight times from Hornchurch, North Weald, Northolt and Debden (and their six FOLs), limiting their on station time over the invasion beaches and thereby permitting the Luftwaffe to have temporary air superiority as it had over Dunkirk in May.

But, even though the fighter squadrons may have been withdrawn, the command and control functions of Dowding's integrated air defence system would have remained in place and operating. 'Tophat Control', the Biggin Hill/C Sector Ops Room, was moved from its emergency location in the Pantiles to 'Towerfield', a rundown, empty Victorian mansion two miles (3km) from the airfield, near Keston crossroads. Set up in the mansion's spacious lounge, C Sector Operations Room was a reasonable facsimile of the original in the Operations Block destroyed by a Dornier's bomb on 31 August. It did not return to full control of its sector until 12 September, when 92 Squadron arrived from Pembrey, reinforced the next day by the return of 72 Squadron from Croydon.[2] Still recovering, 'Tophat Control' had played almost no role in defending against the devastating attack on London on 7 September.

Additionally, on 3 September, 'Sapper Control' (Kenley/B Sector) relocated its Sector Ops Room to a disused butcher's shop in Caterham village where it was set up to take over control without a break in operations. Park admitted that using these makeshift Ops Rooms had 'a serious effect on the fighting efficiency of the fighter squadrons,'[3] yet after 12 September it did not prevent the control of four, eight if they were paired, airborne squadrons arriving into B and C Sectors (with radios tuned appropriately) from Northolt, Hornchurch and other, more northern bases should the sectors' own units be withdrawn. This is evidenced by the success 'Tophat Control' had in helping defeat Luftflotte 2's attack on London three days later.

Considering the reduced efficiency imposed by the Luftwaffe's offensive counter-air campaign, at the operational level it is debatable whether Kesselring's Luftflotte 2 could ever have achieved the level of air superiority Raeder required for Hitler to launch Operation *Sealion*. However, the dual-effect approach, bombing sector stations and inflicting losses on the RAF squadrons defending them, was the only way it could have been won. This opportunity was lost when Göring shifted the target set from the crucial sector stations to London because, in doing so, he effectively cancelled one critical element of this dual-effect approach. As the more experienced air campaigner, Sperrle recognized that this was a mistake and argued against turning from the tried-and-true approach. Göring, the egocentric, bullying, power-hungry politician with the veneer credibility of a military aviator's war record, but with no concept of modern combat or air campaigning – refused to accept or adopt the advice of his most experienced air campaigner, the career air force leader.

Kesselring, the former army artillery and administrative officer, embraced the simpler, seemingly expedient, solution. He was avidly supported by Deichmann, his chief of staff, who wanted most of all to preserve his precious bomber aircrew, and the Fliegerkorps commanders, especially Loerzer, who were either World War I fighter pilots and therefore believed that the airborne battle of attrition was the answer, or were like Kesselring, former army officers who didn't know any better.

But Park had no intention of allowing his command to be drawn into a battle of attrition. One of his two most decisive directives was to instruct Willoughby de Broke and his Group sector controllers to refuse to have their interceptor squadrons engage in fighter-versus-fighter combat. Fighter Command's most critical asset – 'the Few' and the aeroplanes they flew – was to be preserved to fight instead against the anticipated invasion forces.

It is a military axiom that the success of any combat operation cannot depend upon a specific response by the enemy. In this case, to be successful the Luftwaffe's stratagem depended upon Fighter Command engaging Jagdwaffe units in aerial combat.

An He 111 H-6 of KG 26 on a mission to Britain on 25 February 1941. (AHB)

Flt Lt Eric Lock completed his pilot training in May 1940 and was posted to 41 Squadron, flying Spitfires from Catterick. On 15 August he shot down a Bf 110 (possibly from ZG 76) and a Ju 88. He moved with his squadron to Hornchurch on 3 September and two days later shot down two He 111s and two Bf 109s. By 31 October, he had taken his score to 21, in the process becoming the RAF's highest-scoring Battle of Britain ace. (Clive Ellis)

Park was not about to let that happen.

This was confirmed by Kesselring himself, in his autobiography: 'Although we gained air superiority within a restricted area for a short time at the beginning of September, we failed to keep it consistently after we began to raid the London zone… Air supremacy in an absolute sense, in other words mastery of the air, could only be won if the enemy air force accepted a trial of strength. This was not the case.'[4]

Additionally – and even more vital – his second decisive instruction overcame the technical limitation imposed by the HF/DF 'fighter locator' equipment, where only four units could operate simultaneously on the system, by pairing squadrons into wings, doubling the number of Hurricane and Spitfire squadrons that could be vectored to intercept the incoming raids.

The first successful use of this operational innovation was on 15 September – 'Battle of Britain Day'. Up until that time Fighter Command had fought the Luftwaffe to a draw, but starting on this day, 'the Few' began winning the Battle. The aerial combats that day marked a notable victory for the defenders – the heavy losses and psychological impact of the 15 September London raid on the enemy dramatically illustrated that Dowding's forces were attaining dominance through Park's effective use of larger two-squadron wings and Leigh-Mallory's four- or five-squadron 'No. 12 Group Wing'.

This point was not lost on the Luftwaffe participants or their commanders.

Five days afterwards, Göring issued his final directive of the daylight bombing campaign: There would be no more 'Valhallas'. From this point on bomber formations were to be limited to Gruppe-size, or smaller. Additionally, he ordered increased 'individual bomber… nuisance raids using clouds as protection from fighter attack' and that, 'The bomber war on England is to be mainly shifted to the hours of darkness.' Daylight attacks by Heinkels, Dorniers and Junkers bombers would be supplanted by Bf 109E Jabo raids. All of these decisions were intended to stanch the bloodletting experienced by 'his' bomber forces at the hands of Dowding's increasingly powerful RAF Fighter Command.

This ObdL Directive is an undeniable, though tacit acknowledgement of the Luftwaffe's defeat.

Despite subsequent tactical successes, especially by Luftflotte 3 (the Filton and Woolston raids on 25 and 26 September), the mauling that Kesselring's forces experienced on 15 and 27 September provide convincing proof of the continuing trend in Fighter Command's latent ascendancy. The extraordinary losses suffered by the Jagdwaffe on 30 September, highlighted by the RAF's unprecedented favourable fighter exchange rate, signalled that the Luftwaffe had truly and finally been defeated.

After losing 508 bombers and 668 fighters (Bf 109s and 110s), it was crushingly disheartening for the Luftwaffe's commanders to learn that RAF Fighter Command remained a strong and viable opponent, and was getting stronger with each new day's battles. In his autobiography, Galland wrote: 'Göring was shattered. He simply could not understand how the increasingly painful loss of bombers came about.'[5] By 7 October, the two Luftflotten were reduced to about 800 bombers from 1,131, and approximately 600 fighters, from 813. Of these, only 52 per cent of the bombers and 68 per cent of the fighters remained operational.

It was a defeat from which the Luftwaffe never recovered.

Dowding's 'Few' – and Park, as the operational commander; Willoughby de Broke, as the tactical co-ordinator; and the vital sector controllers who vectored 'the Few' to intercept the attacking bomber formations – through tireless, dauntless, persistent and determined resistance, eventually prevailed. But not on 'Battle of Britain Day'. They won the Battle nevertheless, the victory being attained during the fortnight that followed.

'To the victor belong the spoils' and as history has subsequently proven, that Britain avoided invasion, provided 'spoils' enough. However, it came at an awful cost. Some 510 of 2,332 RAF Fighter Command pilots lost their lives during the Battle and it is reasonable to ask if, even without the benefit of hindsight, cost could have been lessened.

Certainly, for an island/maritime nation, it is incredible that a co-ordinated, expansive air-sea rescue service wasn't available to pilots forced to bale out or ditch in the sea. Quoting Dr Richard North in *The Many Not the Few: The Stolen History of the Battle of Britain*: 'This was one of the most shameful and disgraceful episodes in the entire war. For an RAF airman to be shot down over the sea was an almost certain death sentence if the German rescue services were not close at hand. Many a good fighter pilot was lost who would have been invaluable in the days that followed.'[6]

But of far greater impact would have been the early adoption of air fighting tactics that were appropriate for the type of figher-versus-fighter combat that the RAF first encountered in France. Another military axiom is: 'Train like you're going to fight, because you will fight like you've been trained'. It's readily apparent from the narrative that those units which stuck rigorously to the methods taught in the training units, sustained alarming and avoidable casualties in combat compared to those units that ripped up the training manual early and adopted the more fluid tactics employed by the Jagdwaffe.

Some months after his departure, Dowding was requested to submit a comprehensive review of the Battle. The resultant *Battle of Britain Despatch by ACM Sir Hugh Dowding* wasn't therefore available until 20 August 1941, by which time many of Fighter Command's shortcomings had been or were in the process of being rectified. Notwithstanding, a summary report based upon Dowding's recommendations highlighting Lessons/Recommendations and Action Taken, was produced.

Top-scoring Battle of Britain Luftwaffe ace Major Helmut Wick was assigned to JG 2, where he remained throughout his flying career. In October 1940 he was appointed as the unit's commander, becoming the youngest man to hold such a position. He was shot down in the vicinity of the Isle of Wight on 28 November 1940, most likely by the British ace John Dundas, who was himself shot down by Wick's wingman. Wick was posted missing in action presumed dead, at which time he was credited with the destruction of 56 enemy aircraft. (Author Collection)

It began: 'The outstanding feature of Sir Hugh Dowding's Despatch is that it constitutes a testimonial to the efficiency of the Air Defence Systems of Great Britain… This system must surely be the most highly developed form of air defence ever organized and it is clear that it was a decisive factor in the Battle of Britain.' Paragraph two ends, 'It was this system, under the unified command of Sir Hugh Dowding himself, which brought about the defeat of the G.A.F. [German Air Force] and thus prevented the enemy from undertaking an invasion of this country in 1940'.[7]

Recognition, if any were needed, of the vital importance and success of 'the Dowding System', Fighter Command's integrated air defence system.

In closing, it is important to recall why the Battle of Britain was fought in the first place. It was the culmination of Hitler's *Westfeldzug*, launched with *Fall Gelb* on 10 May 1940. Hitler's strategic aim was the elimination of Britain and France from the war so that he could turn on his 'true enemy', the Soviet Union, without having to fight a two-front war. This campaign stormed across France and drove the BEF from the European Continent.

But a military campaign cannot be won if the last battle is lost.

By failing to defeat 'the Few', the Luftwaffe lost the last battle of the campaign. This means that, strategically, the entire campaign was a failure. So, by defeating the Luftwaffe's *Adlerangriff*, 'the Few', which includes all of Fighter Command, including its leadership and its sophisticated and complicated integrated air defence system, did much more than save Britain from invasion; they caused Hitler's *Westfeldzug* to end in defeat, with decisive catastrophic consequences for his Third Reich.

As Hitler said in his Führer's Directive Nr. 16, the aim of Operation *Seelöwe* was to 'Eliminate the English homeland as a base for the prosecution of the war against Germany'. By preventing this invasion, 'the Few' ensured Great Britain survived to continue the war and, with that, Western civilization benefited from the eventual destruction of Nazi Germany.

Länge(westl.Greenw.): 1°29'50", Breite 52°26' (Mitte Luftbild)
Mißweisung-11°45'(Mitte 1938)

Nachtrag
8.6.39

Aufnahme
017

500   0   500   1000
m

Maßstab etwa 1 : 16 200   1 cm = 162 m

GB 803 Morris Eng. Factory Autofabrik

2 Fabrikationshallen	etwa	85 000 qm
1 Kesselhaus	etwa	800 qm
7 Nebengebäude	etwa	6 200 qm
bebaute Fläche	etwa	92 000 qm
gesamte Fläche	etwa	220 000 qm

(B) GB 7312 Rover Werke, Flugmotoren

1) Fabrikationshallen	etwa	120 000 qm
2) Kesselhaus	etwa	1 500 qm
3) Nebengebäude	etwa	15 000 qm
4) Wohngebäude	etwa	9 000 qm
bebaute Fläche	etwa	145 500 qm

APPENDIX I

EQUIVALENT RANKS

Royal Air Force	Luftwaffe	USAF
Marshal of the Royal Air Force	Generalfeldmarschall	General of the Air Force
Air Chief Marshal (ACM)	Generaloberst	General
Air Marshal (AM)	General	Lieutenant General
Air Vice-Marshal (AVM)	Generalleutnant	Major General
Air Commodore (Air Cmdre)	Generalmajor	Brigadier General
Group Captain (Gp Capt)	Oberst (Obst)	Colonel
Wing Commander (Wg Cdr)	Oberstleutnant (Obstlt)	Lieutenant Colonel
Squadron Leader (Sqn Ldr)	Major (Maj)	Major
Flight Lieutenant (Flt Lt)	Hauptmann (Hptm)	Captain
Flying Officer (Fg Off)	Oberleutnant (Oblt)	First Lieutenant
Pilot Officer (Plt Off)	Leutnant (Lt)	Second Lieutenant
Warrant Officer (WO)	Stabsfeldwebel	Chief Master Sergeant
Flight Sergeant (Flt Sgt)	Oberfeldwebel (OFw)	Senior Master Sergeant
Sergeant (Sgt)	Feldwebel (Fw)	Master Sergeant
Corporal (Cpl)	Unteroffizier (Uffz)	Staff/Tech Sergeant
Leading Aircraftman	Obergefreiter	Senior Airman
Aircraftman First Class	Gefreiter	(Gefr) Airman First Class
Aircraftman Second Class	Flieger	Airman

EQUIVALENT CREW STATIONS

Pilot	Flugzeugführer (literally 'aircraft guider')
Observer	Beobachter ('observer', combining the navigation and bomb-aiming tasks)
Wireless Operator	Bordfunker ('on-board radio [operator]')
Flight Engineer	Bordmechaniker ('on-board mechanic')
Gunner	Bordschütze ('on-board shooter')

APPENDIX II

LUFTWAFFE ORDER OF BATTLE, *ADLERANGRIFF*, 12 AUGUST 1940

Oberkommando der Luftwaffe – Reichsmarschall des Grossdeutschen Reiches Herman Göring (Note: numbers represent available/serviceable aircraft strength on 13 August 1940)

Aufklärungsgruppe/ObdL (-) 47/28 various types

Luftflotte 2 – Generalfeldmarschall Albrecht Kesselring
HQ: Brussels, Belgium

2.(F)/Aufklärungsgruppe 122   10/8 Ju 88/He 111
4.(F)/Aufklärungsgruppe 122   10/8 Ju 88/He 111

I. Fliegerkorps – Generaloberst Ulrich Grauert
HQ: Compiègne, France

KG 1	I. Gruppe	27/23 He 111H
	II. Gruppe	35/33 He 111H
	III. Gruppe	32/15 He 111H
KG 76	I. Gruppe	29/29 Do 17Z
	II. Gruppe	36/28 Ju 88A
	III. Gruppe	37/24 Do 17Z

5.(F)/Aufklärungsgruppe 122 9/7 Ju 88/He 111/Do 17

II. Fliegerkorps – General der Flieger Bruno Loerzer
HQ: Ghent, Belgium

KG 2	I. Gruppe	43/27 Do 17Z
	II. Gruppe	42/35 Do 17Z
	III. Gruppe	34/32 Do 17Z
KG 3	I. Gruppe	43/31 Do 17Z
	II. Gruppe	35/32 Do 17Z
	III. Gruppe	30/25 Do 17Z
KG 53	I. Gruppe	28/27 He 111H
	II. Gruppe	33/16 He 111H
	III. Gruppe	33/24 He 111H
II./StG 1	38/30 Ju 87B	
III./StG 2	39/31 Ju 87B	
IV.(St)/LG 1	36/28 Ju 87B	

Erprobungsgruppe 210 (fighter-bomber trials unit)   36/30 Bf 109/Bf 110 Jabos
1.(F)/Aufklärungsgruppe 122 (as of 5 September)   9/6 Ju 88/He 111

9. Fliegerdivision – Generalmajor Joachim Coeler
HQ: Amsterdam, Netherlands

KG 4	I. Gruppe	36/17 He 111H
	II. Gruppe	31/25 He 111P
	III. Gruppe	35/23 Ju 88A

Kampfgruppe 100 (night pathfinders)   41/19 He 111H-3
Kampfgruppe 126 (naval support)   34/8 He 111H
I./KG 40 (naval support)   9/3 FW 200C
Küstenfliegergruppe 106 (naval support)   30/23 He 115/Do 18
3.(F)/Aufklärungsgruppe 122   11/9 Ju 88/He 111

Jagdfliegerführer 2 – Generalmajor Kurt-Bertram von Döring
HQ: Wissant, France

JG 3	I. Gruppe	33/32 Bf 109E
	II. Gruppe	32/25 Bf 109E
	III. Gruppe	29/29 Bf 109E
JG 26	I. Gruppe	42/38 Bf 109E
	II. Gruppe	39/35 Bf 109E
	III. Gruppe	40/38 Bf 109E
JG 51	I. Gruppe	32/32 Bf 109E
	II. Gruppe (I./JG 71)	33/33 Bf 109E
	III. Gruppe (I./JG 20)	36/34 Bf 109E
JG 52	I. Gruppe	42/34 Bf 109E
	II. Gruppe	39/32 Bf 109E
	I.(J)/LG 2	36/33 Bf 109E
JG 54	I. Gruppe (I./JG 70)	38/26 Bf 109E
	II. Gruppe (I./JG 76)	36/32 Bf 109E
	III. Gruppe (I./JG 21)	42/40 Bf 109E
ZG 26	I. Gruppe	39/33 Bf 110C
	II. Gruppe	37/32 Bf 110C
	III. Gruppe	38/27 Bf 110C
ZG 76	II. Gruppe	24/6 Bf 110C
	III. Gruppe	14/11 Bf 110C

Luftflotte 3 – Generalfeldmarschall Hugo Sperrle
HQ: Saint-Cloud (Paris), France

1.(F)/Aufklärungsgruppe 123   12/8 Ju 88/He 111
3.(F)/Aufklärungsgruppe 123   11/8 Ju 88/He 111

IV. Fliegerkorps – General der Flieger Kurt Pflugbeil
HQ: Dinard, France

LG 1	I. Gruppe	35/24 Ju 88A
	II. Gruppe	34/24 Ju 88A
	III. Gruppe	34/23 Ju 88A
KG 27	I. Gruppe	38/23 He 111P/H
	II. Gruppe	34/21 He 111P/H
	III. Gruppe	31/23 He 111P
StG 3	I. Gruppe	29/16 Ju 87B

Kampfgruppe 806 (naval support)   33/22 Ju 88A

3.(F)/Aufklärungsgruppe 31 (army cooperation)   Bf 110/Do 17/Hs 126

V. Fliegerkorps – General der Flieger Robert Ritter von Greim
HQ: Villacoublay, France

KG 51	I. Gruppe	31/22 Ju 88A
	II. Gruppe	34/24 Ju 88A
	III. Gruppe	35/25 Ju 88A
KG 54	I. Gruppe	35/29 Ju 88A
	II. Gruppe	31/23 Ju 88A
KG 55	I. Gruppe	39/35 He 111P/H
	II. Gruppe	38/28 He 111P
	III. Gruppe	42/34 He 111P

4.(F)/Aufklärungsgruppe 14 (army cooperation)   12/10 Bf 110/Do 17

4.(F)/Aufklärungsgruppe 121   8/5 Do 17/Ju 88

VIII. Fliegerkorps – Generalmajor Wolfram Freiherr von Richthofen
HQ: Deauville, France

Transferred to Luftflotte 2 on 29 August

StG 1	I. Gruppe	39/27 Ju 87R
	III. Gruppe	41/28 Ju 87B
StG 2	I. Gruppe	39/32 Ju 87B
	II. Gruppe	37/31 Ju 87R
StG 77	I. Gruppe	36/33 Ju 87B
	II. Gruppe	41/28 Ju 87R
	III. Gruppe	38/37 Ju 87B
V.(Z)/LG 1	43/29 Bf 110C	

2.(F)/Aufklärungsgruppe 123   9/8 Ju 88/Do 17

2.(F)/Aufklärungsgruppe 11 (army cooperation)   10/8 Bf 110/Do 17

Jagdfliegerführer 3 – Oberst Werner Junck
HQ: Cherbourg, France

JG 2	I. Gruppe	34/32 Bf 109E
	II. Gruppe	39/31 Bf 109E
	III. Gruppe	32/28 Bf 109E
JG 27	I. Gruppe	37/32 Bf 109E
	II. Gruppe	45/36 Bf 109E
	III. Gruppe	39/32 Bf 109E
JG 53	I. Gruppe	39/37 Bf 109E
	II. Gruppe	44/40 Bf 109E
	III. Gruppe	38/35 Bf 109E
ZG 2	I. Gruppe	41/35 Bf 110C
	II. Gruppe	45/37 Bf 110C

Luftflotte 5 – Generaloberst Hans-Jürgen Stumpff
HQ: Stavanger, Norway

X. Fliegerkorps – Generalleutnant Hans Geisler
HQ: Stavanger, Norway

KG 26	I. Gruppe	30/29 He 111H
	II. Gruppe (stand-down for R&R)	29/21 He 111H
	III. Gruppe	32/32 He 111H
KG 30	I. Gruppe	40/34 Ju 88A
	III. Gruppe	36/28 Ju 88A/C
JG 77	II. Gruppe	39/35 Bf 109E
ZG 76	I. Gruppe	34/32 Bf 110C/D

Küstenfliegergruppe 506 (naval support)   24/22 He 115
1.(F)/Aufklärungsgruppe 120   4/4 Ju 88/He 111
1.(F)/Aufklärungsgruppe 121   7/5 Ju 88/He 111
2. and 3.(F)/Aufklärungsgruppe 22 (army cooperation)   12/6 Do 17M/P

APPENDIX III

FIGHTER COMMAND ORDER OF BATTLE, 12 AUGUST 1940 – *ADLERANGRIFF*

RAF Fighter Command – Air Chief Marshal Sir Hugh C.T. Dowding.
HQ: Bentley Priory (Note: numbers represent available/serviceable aircraft strength at 1800hrs, 1 August 1940)

No. 10 Group – Air Vice-Marshal Sir Quintin Brand
HQ: RAF Box, Wiltshire

SECTOR Y **Middle Wallop**

Station Commander and Sector Controller: Wg Cdr David Roberts
'Starlight Control'

Middle Wallop	238 Squadron	15/12 Hurricane
	609 Squadron	16/10 Spitfire
	604 Squadron	16/11 Blenheim IF
Warmwell	152 Squadron	15/10 Spitfire

SECTOR W **Filton Station**

Commander and Sector Controller: Gp Capt Robert Hammer

Exeter	87 Squadron	18/13 Hurricane
	213 Squadron	17/12 Hurricane
Pembrey, Wales	92 Squadron	16/12 Spitfire
St Eval	234 Squadron	16/10 Spitfire
Roborough	Plymouth Air Defence Flight (247 Squadron)	
	12/10 Gladiator	

No. 11 Group – Air Vice-Marshal Keith Park
HQ: RAF Uxbridge, NW London

Senior Fighter Controller: Wg Cdr John Verney, Baron Willoughby de Broke

SECTOR A **Tangmere**

Station Commander: Wg Cdr Jack Boret
Sector Controller: Sqn Ldr David Lloyd
'Shortjack Control'

Tangmere	43 Squadron	19/18 Hurricane	
	266 Squadron	18/13 Spitfire	(to 11 Grp/Eastchurch on 13 August; then to Hornchurch on 14 August; to 12 Grp/ Wittering on 21 August)
	601 Squadron	18/14 Hurricane	(to Debden on 19 August)

Fighter Interception Unit   4/7 Blenheim IF   To Shoreham on 19 August
Westhampnett   145 Squadron   16/9 Hurricane   (to 13 Grp/Drem
                                                                on 17 August)

SECTOR B **Kenley**
Station Commander: Wg Cdr Thomas Prickman
Sector Controller: Sqn Ldr Anthony Norman
'Sapper Control'
Kenley   64 Squadron   16/12 Spitfire   (to 12 Grp/
                                                                Leconfield on 19 August)

                        615 Squadron   16/14 Hurricane   (to 13 Grp/
                                                                Prestwick 29 Aug)

Croydon   111 Squadron   12/10 Hurricane

SECTOR C **Biggin Hill**
Station Commander and Sector Controller: Wg Cdr Richard Grice
'Tophat Control'
Biggin Hill   32 Squadron   15/11 Hurricane   (to 13 Grp/
                                                                Acklington on 27 August)

                        610 Squadron   15/12 Spitfire
Gravesend   501 Squadron   16/11 Hurricane

SECTOR D **Hornchurch**
Station Commander and Sector Controller: Wg Cdr Cecil Bouchier
'Lumba Control'
Hornchurch   41 Squadron   16/10 Spitfire
                        65 Squadron   16/11 Spitfire
                        74 Squadron   15/12 Spitfire
Manston   600 Squadron   15/9 Blenheim IF

SECTOR E **North Weald**
Station Commander: Wg Cdr Victor Beamish
Sector Controller: Sqn Ldr John Cherry
'Cowslip Control'
North Weald   56 Squadron   17/15 Hurricane
                        151 Squadron   18/13 Hurricane
Martlesham   25 Squadron   14/7 Blenheim IF

SECTOR F **Debden**
Station Commander and Sector Controller: Wg Cdr Laurence Fuller-Good
'Garter Control'
Debden   17 Squadron   19/14 Hurricane
                        85 Squadron   18/12 Hurricane   (TDY to
                                                                Martlesham Heath)

SECTOR Z **Northolt**
Station Commander and Sector Controller: Gp Capt Stanley Vincent

Northolt	1 RCAF Squadron	22 Hurricane	(NONOP: under training, not operational until 18 August)
	1 Squadron	16/13 Hurricane	
	257 Squadron	15/10 Hurricane	

No. 12 Group – Air Vice-Marshal Trafford Leigh-Mallory
HQ: RAF Watnall, Nottingham

Senior Fighter Controller: Unknown

SECTOR G **Duxford**
Station Commander and Sector Controller: Wg Cdr A. B. Woodhall

Duxford	310 (Cz) Squadron	20 Hurricane	(NONOP: under training, not operational until 17 August)
Fowlmere	19 Squadron	15/9 Spitfire	

SECTOR J **Coltishall**
Station Commander and Sector Controller: Wg Cdr W.K. Beisiegel

Coltishall	66 Squadron	16/12 Spitfire
	242 Squadron	16/11 Hurricane

SECTOR K **Wittering**
Station Commander and Sector Controller: Wg Cdr Harry Broadhurst

Wittering	229 Squadron	18/14 Hurricane
Collyweston	23 Squadron	14/9 Blenheim IF

SECTOR L **Digby**
Station Commander and Sector Controller: Wg Cdr Ian Parker

Digby	46 Squadron	17/12 Hurricane
	611 Squadron	13/6 Spitfire
	29 Squadron	12/8 Blenheim IF

SECTOR M **Kirton-in-Lindsey**
Station Commander and Sector Controller: Wg Cdr S.H. Hardy

Kirton-in-Lindsey	222 Squadron	17/14 Spitfire	(to 11 Grp/ Hornchurch on 27 August)
	264 Squadron	16/12 Defiant	(to 11 Grp/ Hornchurch on 22 August)

No. 13 Group – Air Vice-Marshal Richard Saul   HQ: RAF
Blakelaw, Newcastle upon Tyne

Senior Fighter Controller: Unknown

SECTOR N Church Fenton
Station Commander and Sector Controller: Gp Capt C.F. Hardy

Church Fenton	73 Squadron	16/11 Hurricane	
	249 Squadron	16/11 Hurricane	(to 10 Grp/ Boscombe Down on 14 August)
Leconfield	616 Squadron	16/12 Spitfire	(to 11 Grp/ Kenley 19 August)

Sector Airfield: Usworth
Station Commander and Sector Controller: Wg Cdr Brian Thynne

Usworth	607 Squadron	16/12 Hurricane	(to 11 Grp/ Tangmere 1 September)
Acklington	72 Squadron	15/10 Spitfire	(to 11 Grp/ Biggin Hill 31 August)
	79 Squadron	12/10 Spitfire	(to 11 Grp/ Biggin Hill 28 August)
Catterick	54 Squadron	14/11 Spitfire	
	219 Squadron	15/10 Blenheim IF	

Sector Airfield: RAF Turnhouse
Station Commander: Wg Cdr Duke of Hamilton and Brandon

Turnhouse	253 Squadron	16/12 Hurricane	
	603 Squadron	15/11 Spitfire	(to 11 Grp/ Hornchurch 28 August)
Drem	602 Squadron	15/11 Spitfire	(to 10 Grp/ Westhampnett on 17 August)
	605 Squadron	18/14 Hurricane	
Prestwick	141 Squadron	12/8 Defiant	

Coastal Cmd Airfield: RAF Wick
Fighter Section Commander and Sector Controller: Wg Cdr Geoffrey Ambler

Wick	3 Squadron	12/10 Hurricane	
Sumburgh	232 Squadron	10/6 Hurricane	(One flight only)
Aldergrove, N.I.	245 Squadron	10/8 Hurricane	
Castletown	504 Squadron	17/13 Hurricane	
Dyce/Grangemouth	263 Squadron (one flight)	6/4 Hurricane	

GLOSSARY

AA	Anti-aircraft
AASF	Advanced Air Strike Force
AdA	Armée de l'Air, the French air force
ADGB	Air Defence of Great Britain, the RAF air defence command from 1925 to 1936
AéM	Aéronautique Militaire, the Belgian Army's air arm
AI	Air Intelligence, a branch of the Air Ministry
A.M.	Air Ministry
AMES	Air Ministry Experimental Station at Bawdsey where RAF Fighter Command radar was developed
Angels	RAF codeword for 'altitude', given in thousands of feet: 'Angels 10' is 10,000ft
AOB	Air order of battle
AK	German Armeekorps or army corps
AOC	Air Officer Commanding
AOK	German Armeeoberkommando or 'numbered army' command
AOR	Area of Responsibility, a geographical region for a specific command's or unit's operations
ATC	Air Traffic Control
Aufklärungsgruppe	Luftwaffe Reconnaissance group, designated either (F) for Fern (long-range) reconnaissance or (H) for Heer (army) co-operation and battlefield observation
Bandits	RAF codeword for 'enemy aircraft'
BAFF	British Air Forces in France, comprising AASF and BEF(AC)
BEF	British Expeditionary Force
BEF(AC)	British Expeditionary Force Air Component
Besprechung	German for 'conference'
CAP	Combat Air Patrol, a defensive fighter patrol area
CH	Chain Home coastal long-range early-warning radar network
CHL	Chain Home Low coastal short-range 'gap filler' radar network
CinC	Commander-in-Chief
CIS	Y-Service Central Intercept Station at RAF Cheadle
CONOPS	Concept of Operations, a general proposal describing the aims and means of conducting a military campaign
DF	Direction Finding, for determining the location of a radio transmitter
Enigma	German radio transmission teletype encrypting device
Fall Gelb	*Case Yellow*, the Wehrmacht plan for invading France and the Low Countries
Fall Weiß	*Case White*, the Wehrmacht plan for invading Poland, September 1939
FAA	Fleet Air Arm
FFA	Feldflieger Abteilung, German World War I observation/reconnaissance squadron
Flak	German contraction for 'Flugabwehrkanone' or 'aircraft defence cannon', AA artillery
Fliegerkorps	Luftwaffe 'Flying Corps', a component command of a Luftflotte
Fliegertruppe	'Flying Troops', short for Die Fliegertruppen des deutschen Kaiserreiches ('Imperial German Flying Corps') as Germany's World War I army air arm was known before October 1916.
FOL	Forward Operating Location, RAF 'satellite airfield', German 'Feldflugplatz', 'campaign airfields' in other European nations
Freie Jagd	Free hunting, or 'fighter sweep'
GC&CS	Government Code and Cypher School
Geschwader	Luftwaffe 'Wing', a component of a Fliegerkorps, specified by role
GHQ	General Headquarters
Gruppe	Luftwaffe 'Group', the component of a Geschwader, usually consisting of three Staffeln
Handelskrieg	Economic warfare, a blockade or siege strategy
HE	High Explosive, a type of bomb
Heer	German army
Heeresgruppe	Army Group
HF	High-frequency radio emissions
HF/DF	HF Direction Finding, called 'Huff Duff', a radio system for locating RAF fighter aircraft
HQ	Headquarters
IADS	Integrated Air Defence System
Indianer	'Indians' – Luftwaffe code word for 'enemy fighters'
Interdiction	Air operations intended to cut enemy lines of communication and prevent reinforcements and supplies from reaching the battle front
Jagdwaffe	Fighter Force, the generic term for Luftwaffe single-engined fighter pilots and units
Jagdschutz	Fighter Protection, or 'close escort'
JG	Jagdgeschwader – Luftwaffe single-engined fighter wing, typically comprising three fighter groups flying Bf 109Es
JGr	Jagdgruppe – Luftwaffe single-engined fighter group, typically comprising three fighter squadrons flying Bf 109Es
JaFü	Jagdfliegerführer – Luftwaffe fighter

	command for a Luftflotte or air defence region
Jasta	Jagdstaffel – Fighter squadron, used primarily during World War I
Kette	German three-aeroplane bomber/ dive-bomber formation
KG	Kampfgeschwader – Luftwaffe bomber wing, typically comprising three bomber groups
KGr	Kampfgruppe – Luftwaffe bomber group, typically comprising three bomber squadrons
KIA	Killed in action
Kirchturm	'Church tower' (or 'steeple') – Luftwaffe code word for 'altitude', given in hundreds of metres
Kriegsmarine	German navy
Küstenfliegergruppe	Coastal Aviation Flying Groups
Lockvögel	'Decoy' – Luftwaffe bombers used to lure RAF fighters to battle
LG	Lehrgeschwader (Instructional Wing) – Luftwaffe units used to develop employment doctrine and tactics for each type of combat aircraft. By May 1940, these had become standard combat units but retained this legacy designation
Luftflotte	Air Fleet, highest operational command within the Luftwaffe
Luftstreitkräfte	'Air Service', formal title for Germany's World War I army air arm as it was known after October 1916, before which it was the 'Fliegertruppe'
Luftüberlegenheit	Air superiority
Luftwaffe	German air force
LZ	Landing zone for airborne or amphibious assaults
MF	Medium-frequency radio emissions
MIA	Missing in action
MP	Member of Parliament
ObdL	Oberkommando der Luftwaffe – 'High Command of the Air Force'; Göring's personal staff HQ
OCA	Offensive Counter Air campaign, air operations intended to destroy the enemy air force
OKH	Oberkommando des Heeres – 'High Command of the Army', the army's General Staff
OKM	Oberkommando der Marine – 'High Command of the Navy', Kriegsmarine High Command
OKW	Oberkommando der Wehrmacht – 'High Command of the Armed Forces', Hitler's personal military staff
POW	Prisoner of war
RAF	Royal Air Force, the British air force
RDF	Radio Direction Finding, the original British designation for 'radar'
Reichstag	German parliament
Reichswehr	German military service of the Weimar Republic from 1919 to 1935, when it became the Wehrmacht
RFC	Royal Flying Corps, Britain's World War I army air arm
RLM	Reichsluftfahrtministerium or Reich Aviation Ministry
RN	Royal Navy
Rotte	German two-aeroplane fighter formation
ROE	Rules of engagement
R/T	Radio-telephony – voice radio communications on HF or VHF frequencies
RTB	Return to base
SASO	Senior Air Staff Officer, the COS at an RAF Command
Satellite Airfield	RAF name for an FOL, at least one per sector
Schwarm	German four-aeroplane fighter formation
SEAD	Suppression of enemy air defences
SKL	Seekriegsleitung (Maritime Warfare Directorate), the Kriegsmarine's 'Naval War Staff'
Stab	Staff, also used to designate combat unit HQ flights, such as Stabsschwarm (fighters) and Stabskette (bombers)
Staffel	Luftwaffe flying squadron
Staka	German contraction for Staffelkapitän or squadron commander
Stuka	German contraction for Sturzkampfflugzeug or 'diving battle aircraft' (dive-bomber)
StG	Stukageschwader – Luftwaffe dive-bomber wing, typically comprising three dive-bomber groups
StGr	Stukagruppe – Luftwaffe dive-bomber group, typically comprising three dive-bomber squadrons
ULTRA	Highly classified British signals intelligence programme used to decrypt Enigma transmissions
Unternehmen	Undertaking – used to designate German military operations, such as Unternehmen *Seelöwe* (Operation *Sealion*)
Wehrmacht	German armed forces – the army and Luftwaffe, did not include the Kriegsmarine
W/T	Wireless telegraphy, HF radio communications using Morse code
Zerstörer	Destroyer, referring to the Luftwaffe's Bf 110 twin-engined bomber escort 'heavy fighter' and the Kriegsmarine's small torpedo-carrying (usually escort) warships
ZG	Zerstörergeschwader – Luftwaffe twin-engined fighter wing, typically comprising three fighter groups

BIBLIOGRAPHY

PRIMARY SOURCES

British Sources

NOTE: PRO stands for UK National Archives Public Records Office, Kew, England, UK, now known as The National Archives or TNA. Records researched there include AIR 16, Air Ministry, Fighter Command Files; AIR 19, Air Ministry, Private Office Papers; AIR 20, Air Ministry, Unregistered Papers; AIR 25, Operation Record Books, Groups; 28 Operation Record Books, Royal Air Force Stations; AIR 41, RAF Narratives ADGB and Battle of Britain; CAB 65/7 and 13 War Cabinet Meetings and Conclusions, CAB 79/4 Chiefs of Staff Meeting Minutes, and WO 199/911A 'ULTRA Messages 29 June – 15 September 1940'.

AIR. UK National Archives records pertaining to RAF histories:

AIR 16. Air Ministry: Fighter Command: Registered Files. AIR 16/78 Fighter Command Battle Orders (1940); AIR 16/285 Sector Operations Standing Orders (1938).

AIR 19. Air Ministry: Private Office Papers. AIR 16/90 AVM Park's Report to Fighter Command HQ, 12 September 1940, and ACM Dowding's Letter to Air Ministry, 22 September 1940.

AIR 20. Air Ministry, Unregistered Papers. AIR 20/5202, Dowding's 'Despatch on the Battle of Britain', 20 August 1941, and Air Ministry 'Note On Despatch By Air Chief Marshal, Sir Hugh C.T. Dowding', October 1941.

AIR 25. Operation Record Books, Groups. AIR 28/197 No. 11 Group Operations Record Book, September 1939–September 1940: Group Controllers Instructions

AIR 28. Operation Record Books, Royal Air Force Stations. ORBs researched for this work were: AIR 28/32 Andover ORB, AIR 28/64 Biggin Hill ORB, AIR 28/178 Croydon ORB, AIR 28/187 Debden ORB, AIR 28/192 Detling ORB, AIR 28/225 Driffield ORB, AIR 28/234 Duxford ORB, AIR 28/243 Eastchurch ORB; AIR 28/282 Filton ORB, AIR 28/315 Gosport ORB, AIR 28/345 Hawkinge ORB, AIR 28/384 Hornchurch ORB, AIR 28/419 Kenley ORB, AIR 28/509 Lympne ORB, AIR 28/512 Manston ORB, AIR 28/526 Martlesham Heath ORB, AIR 28/545 Middle Wallop ORB, AIR 28/603 North Weald ORB, AIR 28/622 Odiham ORB, AIR 28/815 Tangmere ORB, AIR 28/838 Thorney Island ORB, AIR 28/888 Warmwell ORB, and AIR 28/907 West Malling. There are no ORBs for the Battle of Britain Period for Gravesend, Boscombe Down, Brize Norton, or Rochford.

AIR 41. R.A.F. Narrative, The Air Defence of Great Britain (First Draft): AIR 41–14, Volume I, The Growth of Fighter Command, July 1936–June 1940, and AIR 41–15, Volume II, The Battle of Britain, by Air Historical Branch (1). Written by T.C.G. James beginning in 1942 these two volumes were first published by Frank Cass Publishers in 2000 and have most recently been published in 2012 by Routledge. With Editorial Introduction written by AHB Chief Sebastian Cox, the published versions are exceedingly faithful to the First Drafts to

be found at AIR 41–14 and –15.

CAB. War Cabinet and Cabinet Records: CAB 65 – Second World War Conclusions, and CAB 79 – Chiefs of Staff Committee Minutes.

HW. German Military Communications: HW 2/73 'A.A.S.F. "Y" Section, France – Sept 1939 – June 1940', HW 5/1-5, German Military Communications: Secret Decrypts of German Armed Forces Signals and Italian Intelligence Service Signals from 1940, 3.

German Sources

Helmuth Greiner, *Kriegstagebuch des Oberkommandos der Wehrmacht* (War Diary of OKW) Volume I, ed. Hans-Adolf Jacobsen (Frankfurt-am-Main: Bernard & Graefe Verlag, 1965).

Luftwaffe *Führungsstab Ic Lageberichten* (ObdL Command Staff Situation Reports) Nrs 309 (11 July 1940) through 391 (1 October 1940). Original German texts are in authors' collection. English translations were published by A.M. AHB 6 as 'Part II 14th July – 31st July, 1940' and 'Part 3 [sic] 1st August – 15th August, 1940' on file at Air Historical Branch, RAF Northolt.

Paul Deichmann, General der Flieger GAF (Ret.), 'German Air Force Operations in Support of the Army', USAF Historical Study No. 163, edited by Dr Littleton B. Atkinson (Karlsruhe, Germany, 1962) published as *Spearhead for Blitzkrieg: Luftwaffe Operations in Support of the Amy 1939–1945* (London: Greenhill Books/Lionel Leventhal Ltd, 1996) original manuscript on file at USAF Historical Research Agency, Maxwell AFB, AL, as K113.107–163, IRIS #468159.

Paul Deichmann, General der Flieger GAF (Ret.), 'The System of Target Selection Applied by the German Air Force in World War II', Vol I, unpublished USAF Historical Study No. 186 (Karlsruhe, Germany, 1956) on file at USAF Historical Research Agency, Maxwell AFB, AL, as K113.107–186, IRIS #468189.

Kurt Gottschling, Colonel GAF (Ret.), 'The Radio Intercept Service of the German Air Force', Vol. 2, unpublished USAF Historical Study No. 191 (Berlin, Germany, 1955) on file at USAF Historical Research Agency, Maxwell AFB, AL, as K113.107–191, IRIS #468197.

Carl Hess, Lieutenant Colonel GAF (Ret.), 'The Air-Sea Service of the Luftwaffe', unpublished USAF Historical Study No. 168 (Karlsruhe, Germany, 1955) on file at USAF Historical Research Agency, Maxwell AFB, AL, as K113.107–168, IRIS #468177.

Karl Klee, 1st Lieutenant GAF (Ret.), 'Operation "Sea Lion" and the Role Planned for the Luftwaffe', Vol. 1, unpublished USAF Historical Study No. 157 (Hamburg, Germany, 1955) on file at USAF Historical Research Agency, Maxwell AFB, AL, as K113.107–157, IRIS #468154.

Bruno Maass, Generalleutnant GAF (Ret.), 'Organization of the German Air Force High Command and Higher Headquarters within the German Air Force', translated by Patricia Klammerth, unpublished USAF Historical Study No. 190 (Karlsruhe, Germany, 1955) on file at USAF Historical Research Agency, Maxwell AFB, AL, as K113.107–190, IRIS #468195.

Andreas Nielsen, Generalleutnant GAF (Ret.), 'The Collection and Evaluation of Intelligence for the German Air Force High Command', USAF Historical Study No. 171 (Karlsruhe, Germany, 1955), original manuscript on file at USAF Historical Research Agency, Maxwell AFB, AL, as K113.107–171, IRIS #468180.

Andreas Nielsen, Generalleutnant GAF (Ret.), 'The German Air Force General Staff', USAF Historical Study No. 173, published on behalf of the USAF Historical Division (NY: Arno Press, 1959), original manuscript on file at USAF Historical Research Agency, Maxwell AFB, AL, as K113.107–173, IRIS #468175.

Wilhelm Speidel, General der Flieger GAF (Ret.), 'The Campaign in Western Europe 1939–1940', translated by Patricia Klammerth, unpublished USAF Historical Study No. 152 (Karlsruhe, Germany, 1958) on file at USAF Historical Research Agency, Maxwell AFB, AL, as K113.107–1552, IRIS #468151.

Professor Richard Suchenwirth, 'Command and Leadership in the German Air Force', edited by Harry R. Fletcher, USAF Historical Study No. 174 (Maxwell AFB, AL: USAF Historical Division, 1969), original manuscript on file at USAF Historical Research Agency, Maxwell AFB, AL, as K113.107–174, IRIS #468176.

SECONDARY SOURCES

Air Ministry, Air Historical Branch, *The Rise and Fall of the German Air Force: 1933–1945*, ed. Wg Cdr Cyril March (NY: St Martin's Press, 1983).

Air Ministry, Air Historical Branch, *The Second World War 1939–1940, Royal Air Force Signals, Vol IV Radar in Raid Reporting* (London: HMSO, 1950).

Walter Ansel, *Hitler Confronts England* (Durham, NC: Duke University Press, 1960).

Ulf Balke, *Der Luftkrieg in Europa 1939–1945* [Air War in Europe 1939–1945] (Augsburg, Germany: Bechtermünz Verlag, 1997).

Pier Paolo Battistelli, *Osprey Command 27: Albert Kesselring* (Oxford, UK: Osprey Publishing, 2012).

Werner Baumbach, *The Life and Death of the Luftwaffe*, trans. Frederick Holt (NY: Ballantine Books, 1960).

Hans-Dieter Berenbrok (writing as Cajus Bekker), *Hitler's Naval War: The German Navy in World War II* (NY: Kensington Publishing Corp., 1977).

Hans-Dieter Berenbrok (writing as Cajus Bekker), *The Luftwaffe War Diaries: The German Air Force in World War II* (NY: Doubleday & Company, 1968).

Christer Bergström, *The Battle of Britain: An Epic Conflict Revisited* (Oxford, UK: Casemate UK, 2015).

Mark M. Boatner, III, *The Biographical Dictionary of World War II* (Novato, CA: Presidio Press, 1996).

Horst Boog, 'German Air Intelligence in the Second World War,' in Michael I. Handel (ed.), *Intelligence and Military Operations* (London: Frank Cass, 1990).

Horst Boog, 'The Luftwaffe's Assault,' *The Burning Blue: A New History of the Battle of Britain*, Paul Addison and Jeremy A. Crang (ed.), (London: Frank Cass, 1990).

Kurt Braatz, *Gott oder ein Flugzeug – Leben und Sterben des Jagdfliegers Günther Lützow* [God or an Airplane – Life and Death of Fighter Pilot Günther Lützow] (Moosburg, Germany: Neunundzwanzig Sechs Verlag, 2005).

Michael Bragg, *RDF1: The Location of Aircraft by Radio Methods* (Paisley, UK: Hawkhead Publishing, 2002).

Robin J. Brooks, *Aerodromes of Fighter Command Then and Now, Mark V* (Old Harlow, Essex, UK: Battle of Britain International Ltd., 2014).

Bungay, Stephan, *The Most Dangerous Enemy: A History of the Battle of Britain* (London: Aurum Press Ltd, 2015).

Donald Caldwell, *JG 26: Top Guns of the Luftwaffe* (NY: Ballantine Books, 1991).

Donald Caldwell, *The JG 26 War Diary, Volume One 1939–1942* (London: Grub Street, 1996).

Charles Christienne and Pierre Lissarrague, *A History of French Military Aviation*, trans. Frances Kianka (Washington, DC: Smithsonian Institution Press, 1986).

Winston S. Churchill, , *The Second World War, Volume II Their Finest Hour* (London: Cassell & Co. Ltd., 1949).

Aileen Clayton, *The Enemy is Listening The Story of the Y Service* (London: Crécy Books Ltd. 1993).

Richard Collier, *The Sands of Dunkirk* (NY: E. P. Dutton & Co., Ltd., 1961).

Matthew Cooper, *The German Air Force 1933–1945: An Anatomy of Failure* (NY: Jane's Publishing Incorporated, 1981).

Peter D. Cornwell, 'The Aircraft Losses', *The Battle of Britain Then and Now, Mark V*, ed. Winston G. Ramsey (Old Harlow, Essex, UK: Battle of Britain International Ltd., 1989).

Peter D. Cornwell, *The Battle of France Then and Now: Six Nations Locked in Aerial Combat September 1939 to June 1940* (Old Harlow, Essex, UK: Battle of Britain International Ltd., 2007).

Corum, James S., *The Luftwaffe: Creating the Operational Air War, 1918–1940*, (Lawrence, KS: University Press of Kansas, 1997).

Brian Cull, *Battle for the Channel* (London: Grub Street, 1995).

Brian Cull, *First of the Few: 5 June—9 July 1940* (London: Fonthill Media Limited, 2013).

Brian Cull and Bruce Lander, with Heinrich Weiss, *Twelve Days in May: The Air Battle for Northern France and the Low Countries, 10–21 May 1940, as Seen through the Eyes of the Fighter Pilots Involved* (London: Grub Street, 1995).

Len Deighton, *Fighter: The True Story of the Battle of Britain* (NY: Alfred A. Knopf, Inc. 1978).

David Divine, *The Nine Days of Dunkirk* (NY: W. W. Norton & Company, Inc., 1959).

Tom Docherty, *Swift to Battle: No 72 Fighter Squadron RAF in Action, Volume I 1937–1942* (Barnsley, UK: Pen & Sword Books Ltd, 2009).

Giulio Douhet, *Command of the Air*, ed. Richard H. Kohn and Joseph P. Harahan (Washington, DC: Office of Air Force History, 1983).

L. F. Ellis, Major, CVO CBE DSO MC, *The War in France and Flanders* (London: HMSO, 1953).

The Evacuation from Dunkirk: 'Operation Dynamo', 26 May–4 June 1940, ed. W.J.R. Gardner, Naval Historical Branch, Ministry of Defence (London: Frank Cass Publishers, 2000).

Robert Forczyk, *Fw200 Condor vs Atlantic Convoy: 1941–43* (Oxford: Osprey Publishing, 2010).

Robert Forczyk, *We March Against England: Operation Sea Lion,*

1940–41 (Oxford: Osprey Publishing, 2016).

Norman L. R. Franks, *Air Battle Dunkirk, 26 May–3 June 1940* (London: Grub Street, 2000).

Adolf Galland, *The First and The Last: The Rise and Fall of the Luftwaffe, 1939–45*, trans. Mervyn Savill (NY: Henry Holt and Company, Inc., 1954).

Chris Goss, *Luftwaffe Fighters & Bombers: The Battle of Britain*, (Mechanicsburg, VA: Stackpole Books, 2000).

Chris Goss, with Peter Cornwell and Bernd Rauchbach, *Luftwaffe Fighter-Bombers over Britain: The Tip-and-Run Campaign, 1942–43* (Mechanicsburg, VA: Stackpole Books, 2010).

Geoff Hewitt, *Hitler's Armada: The Royal Navy & the Defence of Great Britain April – October 1940* (Barnsley, UK: Pen & Sword Maritime, 2008).

F. H. Hinsley, *British Intelligence in the Second World War, Volume 1* (London: HMSO, 1979).

E. R. Hooten, *Phoenix Triumphant: The Rise and Rise of the Luftwaffe* (London: Arms & Armour Press, 1994).

E. R. Hooten, *Eagle in Flames: The Fall of the Luftwaffe* (London: Brockhampton Press, 1999).

Alister Horne, *To Lose a Battle: France 1940* (Boston, MA: Little, Brown and Company, 1969).

Robert Jackson, *Dunkirk: the British Evacuation, 1940* (London: Cassell & Co., 1976).

Hans-Adolf Jacobsen, 'Dunkirk 1940', *Decisive Battles of World War II: The German View*, ed. H.A. Jacobsen and J. Rohwer (London: André Deutsch Limited, 1965).

J. E. ('Johnnie') Johnson, *Full Circle: The Story of Air Fighting* (London: Cassell & Co., 2001).

Field-Marshal Albert Kesselring, *The Memoirs of Field-Marshal Kesselring*, translation of *Soldat bis zum letzten Tag* by William Kimber Ltd. (Novato, CA: Presido Press, 1989).

Karl Klee, 'The Battle of Britain', *Decisive Battles of World War II: The German View*, ed. H.A. Jacobsen and J. Rohwer (London: André Deutsch Limited, 1965).

H. T. Lenton, *German Warships of the Second World War* (NY: Arco Publishing Company, Inc., 1976).

Walter Lord, *The Miracle of Dunkirk* (NY: Viking Press, 1982).

Earle Lund, Lt Col, USAF, 'The Battle of Britain: A German Perspective', Campaign Analysis Study for Joint Doctrine Air Campaign Course (Maxwell AFB, AL: Air War College, 24 January 1996).

Helmut Mahlke, *Memoirs of a Stuka Pilot*, trans. John Weal (London: Frontline Books, 2013).

Francis K. Mason, *Battle over Britain* (Bourne End, UK: Aston Publications Ltd., 1990).

Eric Mombeek, with J. Richard Smith and Eddie J. Creek, *Luftwaffe Colours Volume One, Section 4: Jagd*waffe – *Blitzkrieg* (Crowborough, UK: Classic Publications Limited, 2000).

Eric Mombeek with David Wadman and Martin Pegg, *Luftwaffe Colours Volume Two, Battle of Britain* (Crowborough, UK: Classic Publications Limited, 2001).

Richard North, *The Many Not the Few: The Stolen History of the Battle of Britain* (London: Continuum Publishing, 2012).

Theo Osterkamp, *Durch Höhen und Tiefen jagt ein Herz* ('Through Ups and Downs Hunts a Heart') (Heidelberg, GE: Kurt Vowinckel, 1952).

Dr Alfred Price, *Battle of Britain: The Hardest Day, 18 August 1940* (New York: Charles Scribner's Sons, 1979).

Dr Alfred Price, *Battle of Britain Day: 15 September 1940* (London: Sidgwick & Jackson, 1990).

Dr Alfred Price, *The Luftwaffe Data Book*, (Mechanicsburg, PA: Stackpole Books, 1997).

Dr Alfred Price, *Osprey Elite 104: Britain's Air Defences, 1939–45* (Oxford, UK: Osprey Publishing Limited, 2004).

Paul Richey, *Fighter Pilot: A Personal Record of the Campaign in France 1939–1940* (Stroud, Gloucestershire, UK: The History Press, 2016).

Andy Saunders, *Battle of Britain, July to October 1940, RAF Operations Manual*, (Yeovil, UK: Haynes Publishing, 2015).

Andy Saunders, *Convoy Peewit: Blitzkrieg from the Air and Sea 8 August 1940* (London: Grub Street, 2010).

Ryan Shaughnessy, First Lieutenant, USAF, *No Sense in Dwelling on the Past: The Fate of the US Air Force's German Air Force Monograph Project, 1952–69* (Maxwell AFB, AL: Air University Press, 2011).

Christopher Shores with John Foreman, Christian-Jacques Ehrengardt, Heinrich Weiss, and Bjorn Olsen, *Fledgling Eagles: The Complete Account of Air Operations During the 'Phoney War' and Norwegian Campaign, 1940* (London: Grub Street, 1991).

J. Richard Smith and Eddie J. Creek, *Kampfflieger Volume One: Bombers of the Luftwaffe 1933–1940* and *Volume Two: Bombers of the Luftwaffe July 1940–December 1941* (Hersham, UK: Ian Allan Printing Ltd., 2004).

Peter C. Smith, *Stuka: Luftwaffe Dive-Bomber Units 1939–1941*, Hersham, UK: Ian Allan Printing Ltd., 2006.

Telford Taylor, *The Breaking Wave: The German defeat in the summer of 1940*, (London: Weidenfeld and Nicolson, 1967).

Telford Taylor, *March of Conquest: The German Victories in Western Europe, 1940* (originally published New York: Simon and Schuster, 1958, reprinted Baltimore: The Nautical & Aviation Publishing Company of America, 1991).

John Terraine, 'The Dowding System', *Battle of Britain, (Part 1), The Daily Telegraph Editorial Supplement*, 16 June 1990.

John Toland, *Adolf Hitler, Volume II* (Garden City, NY: Doubleday & Company, Inc., 1976).

Hugh Trevor-Roper, *Hitler's War Directives: 1939–1945* (originally published London: Sidgwick & Jackson, Ltd, 1964, reprinted Edinburgh: Birlinn Limited, 2004).

John J. Vasco and Peter D. Cornwell, *Zerstörer: The Messerschmitt 110 and its Units in 1940*, (Drayton, UK: JAC Publications, 1995).

Kenneth Wakefield, *Luftwaffe Encore: A Study of Two Attacks in September 1940* (London: William Kimber, 1979).

Ken Wakefield, *Pfadfinder: Luftwaffe Pathfinder Operations over Britain, 1940–44* (Stroud, UK: Tempus Publishing Ltd, 1999).

John Weal, *Osprey Aviation Elite Units 25: Jagdgeschwader 53 'Pik As'* (Oxford: Osprey Publishing, 2007).

Derek Wood and Derek Dempster, *The Narrow Margin*, Third Edition (Washington, D.C.: Smithsonian Institute Press, 1990).

Henry L. de Zeng, IV, and Douglas G. Stankey, *Bomber Units of the Luftwaffe 1933–1945: A Reference Source, Volumes 1 and 2* and *Dive-Bomber and Ground-Attack Units of the Luftwaffe 1933–1945: A Reference Source, Volumes 1 and 2* (Hinkley, UK: Midland Publishing, 2007 through 2010, respectively).

ENDNOTES

All source citations appear in abbreviated form. For full details, see appropriate entry in the Bibliography.

CHAPTER I

1 For example, German historian Karl Klee and Swiss historian Theo Weber – based on a post-war study by Gen d.F. Josef Kammhuber – regard the airfield attacks as a 'tactical phase' in preparation for *Seelöwe* while the attacks against the London East End Docks are considered a 'strategic phase', beginning with Sperrle's first night-bombing of this target on 6/7 September. See Klee, pg 85.

2 Begun in 1943, AHB's original official history of 'The Battle of Britain' – initially classified 'SECRET' – can be found at the UK National Archives under AIR 41, entitled *R.A.F. Narrative, The Air Defence of Great Britain (First Draft)*. AIR 41–14, is Volume I, *The Growth of Fighter Command, July 1936–June 1940*, and AIR 41–15, Volume II is *The Battle of Britain*, written by T.C.G. James, RAF Air Historical Branch (1). Referred to hereafter as *RAF Narrative*.

3 Trevor-Roper, 50.

4 Richey, 35–37.

5 Ansel, 23.

6 Boatner, 222–225.

7 Ansel, 11.

8 *Ibid.*, 9, 12, 13, 36. Note: Britain entered this agreement with Hitler without consulting the other Allied signatories to the Versailles Treaty or the signatories to the London Naval Treaty of 1930.

9 *Ibid.*, 13–14. As evidence of the end of Hitler's imaginary 'courtship', at this time (October 1938) he told Grand Admiral Raeder, CinC of the Kriegsmarine, to 'expand the Navy's building program without regard for the London Agreement.' Ansel, 13.

10 Trevor-Roper, 50.

11 For a full description of how Hitler established the OKW as his personal military staff, see Maass, 110. See also Ansel, 36.

12 These were air defence, tactical support of the army, and strategic air attack.

13 Klee, 3, 9, 10.

14 *Ibid.*, 10, 11.

15 Jacobsen, 31.

16 Ellis, 15.

17 These were No. 1 Sqn from No. 11 Group at Tangmere, 73 Sqn from No. 12 Group at Digby, 85 and 87 Sqns from No. 12 Group at Debden. At this time Fighter Command had 30 16-aeroplane single-engine fighter squadrons and seven 12-aeroplane twin-engine fighter squadrons, a total of 37 against the official Air Ministry requirement for 52. Of the 30 operational single-engined fighter squadrons, three were flying obsolete Gloster Gladiator biplanes and three others were converting to the new, modern Spitfire.

18 Shores, et al, 24, 26, 28, 45–47.

19 'A.A.S.F. 'Y' Section, France – Sept 1939 – June 1940', 1–4.

20 Cornwell, *Battle of France*, 202–204.

21 Klee, 9.

22 The 109 was initially referred to as the 'Bf 109' because it was produced by the Bayerische Flugzeugwerke A.G. (BFW – Bavarian Aircraft Works), an aircraft design and manufacturing company which was joined by Messerschmitt, as chief designer and engineer, in 1927. BFW was reconstituted as 'Messerschmitt AG' on July 11, 1938, with 'Willy' as chairman and managing director. The renaming of BFW resulted in the company's RLM designation prefix changing from 'Bf' to 'Me' for all newer designs and for all variants of earlier designs that were accepted by the RLM after the acquisition date. Bf 109E was called the 'Emil' after the name associated with its suffix letter in the German 'phonetic alphabet'.

23 Hooten, *Phoenix*, 197–201.

24 Shores, 147.

25 Cull and Lander, 8.

26 Johnson, 106.

CHAPTER II

1 Trevor-Roper, 57.

2 Baumbach, 72, 73.

3 Cornwell, *Battle of France*, 190–194.

4 Titled 'Panzer Corps' for ease of reading in this work, the proper name for the Wehrmacht's armoured corps was 'Armee Korps (motorisiert)' or 'Army Corps (motorized)', abbreviated as 'AK(mot)'.

5 Cornwell, *Battle of France*, 195–196, 198, and 236–238.

6 Cull and Lander, 35, 36.

7 Christienne and Lissarrague, 345.

8 'Panzergruppe Kleist' – named after its commander, General der Kavallerie Ewald von Kleist – was composed of the 1., 2. and 10. PzDivs that made up Guderian's XIX. Panzer Corps and the 6. and 8. PzDivs comprising Reinhardt's XLI. Panzer Corps, as well as Wietersheim's XIV. Motorized Corps of two truck-mounted infantry divisions. Covering Kleist's northern flank and advancing, in parallel, to Dinant, Belgium, was Hoth's XV. Panzer Corps, made up of the 5. and 7. PzDivs.

9 Cornwell, *Battle of France*, 180–242; Cull and Lander, 20–82.

10 Cornwell, *Battle of France*, 244–253.

11 Galland, 2, 3.

12 Cull and Lander, 84, 85.

13 Galland, 3.

14 Cull and Lander, 93, 110, 306.

15 Cornwell, *Battle of France*, 266–275.

16 Boatner, 93, 94.

17 Horne, 374. Churchill briefed the contents of the cable to the Cabinet at 1900hrs and sent a vaguely worded message of support back to Reynaud that night.

18 *Ibid*, 376. In addition to himself, Churchill's War Cabinet consisted of Lord Halifax (Foreign Secretary), Neville Chamberlain (former Prime Minister and still Leader of the Conservative Party), Clement Attlee (Leader of the Labour

Party), and Arthur Greenwood (Deputy Leader of the Labour Party).

19 The National Archives, CAB 79/4/33, 4.
20 The National Archives, CAB 65/7/18, 131–133; CAB 65/13/9, 2, 4, 8; and CAB 65/13/10, 3.
21 The National Archives, CAB 79/4/34, 2, 3; and CAB 65/13/10, 1–5. On this date Fighter Command had 46 single-engined fighter squadrons (of 52 total), 12 of which were already deployed.
22 Churchill, 45, 46.
23 Cull and Lander, 306.
24 *Ibid*, 307.
25 Not included in the departure of the BEF(AC) were the three Hurricane squadrons assigned to the AASF.

CHAPTER III

1 Trevor-Roper, 67.
2 Franks, 22.
3 Cornwell, 349, 350, 353.
4 Bushell was one of the 50 escaped POWs that were murdered by the Gestapo following the 'Great Escape' from Stalag Luft III in March 1944.
5 *Ibid.*, 349, 353, 356; Franks, 21–24, 29.
6 Franks, 15, 16, 33, 86, 94.
7 Ellis, 150.
8 Berenbrok, *Luftwaffe War Diaries*, 123. For full discussion of Hitler's controversial 'stop order', see Taylor, *March of Conquest*, 255–263.
9 Van Wyngarden, 97–98.
10 Suchenwirth, 113–148.
11 Berenbrok, *Luftwaffe War Diaries*, 122; Hooten, *Phoenix*, 255–257.
12 Kesselring, 59.
13 Berenbrok, *Luftwaffe War Diaries*, 122, 124, 126; Smith, *Stuka Units*, 41.
14 Berenbrok, *Luftwaffe War Diaries*, 125, 126.
15 Devine, 64; Lord, 55.
16 Berenbrok, *Luftwaffe War Diaries*, 122; Hooten, *Phoenix*, 259. On 26 May, Dunkirk was attacked by small formations from I. and IV. Fliegerkorps.
17 Berenbrok, *Luftwaffe War Diaries*, 127; Collier, 43, 165; Devine, 69; Hooten, *Phoenix*, 259; 260.
18 Toland, 704.
19 Cornwell, 377, 379, 380–383.
20 Franks, 115.
21 *Ibid.*, 157.
22 *Ibid.*, 155.
23 Berenbrok, *Luftwaffe War Diaries*, 128; Cornwell, 386, 388; Hooten, *Phoenix*, 260.
24 Berenbrok, *Luftwaffe War Diaries*, 128, 129; Cornwell, 390–393; Devine, 129–133, 149; Ellis, 220–221; *Evacuation from Dunkirk*, 38–46; Hooten, *Phoenix*, 260.
25 Berenbrok, *Luftwaffe War Diaries*, 129; Cornwell, 394, 396; Hooten, *Phoenix*, 260.
26 Franks, 111.
27 Taylor, *March of Conquest*, 269, quoting from General Franz Halder (OKH COS) Diary, 31 May 1940.
28 Berenbrok, *Luftwaffe War Diaries*, 129; Cornwell, 397–399,

29 Hooten, *Phoenix*, 259.
30 Berenbrok, *Luftwaffe War Diaries*, 129; *Evacuation from Dunkirk*, 88–95; Cornwell, 404, 406, 408, 409; Ellis, 243, 244; Franks: 111–115, 122, 123, 129, 138; Hooten, *Phoenix*, 260.
31 Cornwell, 410; Franks, 130. Assuming Mahlke's aircraft identification is correct the attacking 'Spitfires' were possibly from 64 Sqn. However, based on RAF reports, it is more probable that his formation was actually attacked by Hurricanes from 229 or 242 Squadrons.
32 Mahlke, 99–102. On 1 June 1940, I.(St)/TrGr 186 were credited with sinking four troop transports and severely damaging two transports, one destroyer, and a sea-going tug. During the Dunkirk evacuation, this *Stukagruppe* sank or damaged more Allied ships than any other Luftwaffe unit.
33 Franks, 138.
34 From Halder's diary 4 June 1940, quoted in Berenbrok, *Luftwaffe War Diaries*, 129.
35 Cornwell, 411–414; Franks, 139–148.
36 From all causes, from 10 May through 3 June Fighter Command lost 432 fighters, reducing Dowding's front-line strength to only 331 serviceable Spitfires and Hurricanes with 36 in reserve. Jackson, *Dunkirk*, 130.
37 Franks, 101, 102.
38 Churchill, 102.

CHAPTER IV

1 Taylor, *Breaking Wave*, 46.
2 *Ibid.*, 201–204.
3 Ansel, 43–50.
4 Forczyk, *March Against England*, 46, 47.
5 Ansel, 121.
6 The Kriegsmarine desperately needed more warships after its crippling losses in Norway and, on 18 June, Raeder had petitioned Hitler to acquire the French fleet as 'war booty'. Hitler denied the request so that he could use that 'asset' as an 'olive branch' to the British. Ansel, 94.
7 *Ibid.*, 87, 88, 94, 95, 121, 123–126.
8 Taylor, *Breaking Wave*, 61, 62. Churchill did not even bother dignifying Hitler's 'appeal' with a response. Instead, he had Lord Halifax, in a BBC broadcast three days later, inform the Nazi regime that there was no interest in reaching a diplomatic solution – the war would go on until one side or the other was ultimately destroyed.
9 Ansel, 98; Taylor, *Breaking Wave*, 48, 49.
10 Berenbrok, *Hitler's Naval War*, 371; Forczyk, *March Against England*, 46; Lenton, 139–157; Taylor, *Breaking Wave*, 23.
11 Battistelli, 5–10, Nielsen, 'GAF General Staff', 30–32.
12 Trevor-Roper, 57, 69; Hooten, *Phoenix*, 216.
13 A third command, Führer der Luftstreikräfte (Commander of [Naval] Air Service, abbreviated FdLuft) West, was responsible for maritime reconnaissance over the North Sea with five squadrons of Do 18 flying boats and two of antiquated He 111Js (early models of limited utility), but had no offensive capabilities.
14 Hooten, *Phoenix*, 217.
15 Zeng, *Bomber Units Volume 1*, 49, 50, 54, 57.
16 Hooten, *Phoenix*, 269.

17 Forczyk, *FW 200 vs Atlantic Convoy*, 26–28. Upon mission change, on 2 August I./KG 40 and the newly established Stab/KG 40 transferred to Bordeaux-Mérignac for operations against Britain's Atlantic convoys.

18 Boog, 'German Air Intelligence', 358.

19 Taylor, *Breaking Wave*, 26–28. Hitler's military response was to order 15 divisions (18. AOK) transferred to Poland as a deterrent against further opportunist actions by Stalin. Taylor, *Breaking Wave*, 55.

20 *Ibid.*, 54. The OKM responded with '*Studie England*' authored by KAdm Kurt Fricke, chief of SKL Operations Staff. Taylor, *Breaking Wave*, 57.

21 *Ibid.*, 64; Ansel, 131, 140.

22 Trevor-Roper, 74, 75.

23 Taylor, *Breaking Wave*, 63–66; Ansel, 143.

24 Taylor, *Breaking Wave*, 50; Forczyk, *March Against England*, 51.

25 Taylor, *Breaking Wave*, 36, 37.

26 These were *The Probable Aspects of The War of the Future* (April 1928), *Recapitulation* (in Italian *Rivista Aeronautica*, November 1929), and *The War of 19—* (March 1930). All are contained in the USAF Office of Air Force History *Command of the Air* (1983).

27 Made in November 1932 (between terms as Prime Minister) in a speech before Parliament entitled 'A Fear for the Future'.

28 Ansel, 113; Forczyk, *March Against England*, 50; Taylor, *Breaking Wave*, 24.

29 Boog, 'German Air Intelligence', 357.

30 Trevor-Roper, 80.

31 Taylor, *Breaking Wave*, 68.

CHAPTER V

1 *Ibid.*, 130.

2 As described in the 1934 edition of LDv 16, the three main roles of the Luftwaffe were 1) air defence of important government and industrial sites, 2) support of army and navy operations, and 3) strategic attack of industrial targets in the enemy homeland's interior. Cooper, 140–144.

3 Cooper, 64, 67, 68; Hooten, *Phoenix*, 64, 65, 74, 78; Smith and Creek, *Kampfflieger*, 13, 17.

4 Cooper, 68; Corum, *Luftwaffe*, 124, 125; Hooten, *Phoenix*, 156. The day Wever was killed, he authorized the development of 'Bomber A', a project that eventually resulted in the over-engineered problem-plagued Heinkel He 177 heavy bomber. It was planned to be operational by mid–1942, with a force of 500 bombers available by 1 April the following year. Cooper, 77, 78, 82; Hooten, *Phoenix*, 107–109.

5 Jodl's 12 July 1940 OKW Memorandum '*Erste Überlegung über eine Landung in England*' ('First Consideration about a Landing in England'). Halder called it a '*grosse Flussübergang*' or 'large-scale river crossing'. Taylor, *Breaking Wave*, 216.

6 Maass, 102, 103; Nielsen, 'GAF General Staff', 59.

7 This information and the descriptions that follow are from Nielsen, 'GAF General Staff', 61, 78–80; Hooten, *Phoenix*, 146–149; Price, *Luftwaffe Data*, 13.

8 Boog, 'Luftwaffe's Assault', 40. These included 477 twin-engined bombers, 123 Stukas, 250 Bf 109s and 121 Bf 110s.

9 The others were Air Defence, Procurement and Equipment (Udet's '*Technisches Amt*'), and Training, which included 14 role-specific 'Inspectorates'. There were also two independent

branches that oversaw the administration and organization of the RLM. In the February 1939 reorganization the RLM's 'Attaché Group' was transferred to ObdL's Intelligence Branch to ensure air attaché reports went direct to the Command Staff. This organization remained largely unchanged until 1944. Cooper, 22, 23; Nielsen, 'GAF General Staff', 78, 79.

10 Schmid's position was also known as *Luftwaffe Führungsstab Ic* (air force command staff Ic), derived from being the third General Staff Officer (Ic) on Göring's command staff.

11 Deichmann, 49–52.

12 Nielsen, 'Intelligence', 61–64; Lund, 10, 32–34.

13 Nielsen, 'Intelligence', 9–11, 14, 16, 25–27, 32, 33.

14 *Ibid.*, 66, 75–77, 85. The 1 January 1940 '*Gliederung der Britischen Fliegertruppe (Heimat)*' is contained in the 'Karlsruhe Collection' microfilm of original German documents used to compile various USAF Historical Studies, found at K113.108, images 0101 through 0123.

15 *Ibid.*, 120–126.

16 *Ibid.*, 99. It is these daily ObdL situation reports that provide the basis for the Luftwaffe's side of the story in this narrative Chapters 9 through 13.

17 At the time, Martini's staff was part of RLM's *Luftkommandoamt*; it became *7. Abteilung* in June 1937.

18 Gottschling, 1, 2.

19 *Ibid.*, 4–6, 158, 159.

20 *Ibid.*, 214.

21 *Ibid.*, 232, 233.

22 Nielsen, 'Intelligence', 17, 20.

23 Deichmann, 95.

24 Boatner, 524.

CHAPTER VI

1 Terraine, XI.

2 Boatner, 141–143.

3 Except for the mention of Y-Service this overview description, and the detailed sections that follow describing the operations of Fighter Command IADS, is taken from 'Fighter Command Battle Orders (1940)', dated 1st May 1940 and signed by H.C.T. Dowding, ACM, AOCinC Fighter Command, located at The National Archives, AIR 16/78. Hereafter all references to this document are listed as 'FC Battle Orders'.

4 The term 'low grade' refers to the degree of security provided by the code or cypher and does not imply that the traffic was unimportant or easy to break and interpret.

5 AHB, *RAF Signals, Radar in Raid Reporting*, 48–49; Price, *Britain's Air Defences*, 5, 6; Saunders, *Operations Manual*, 12–18.

6 Price, *Britain's Air Defences*, 4; Saunders, *Operations Manual*, 12–18; 'FC Battle Orders' Sections B.1, and F.1.

7 'FC Battle Orders' Sections B.1, C.1, E.1 and E.2.

8 Saunders, *Operations Manual*, 20.

9 From September 1940 to January 1941, one of Dowding's Duty Air Commodores was Acting Air Commodore Thomas W. Elmhirst, formally Group Captain DDI3.

10 Saunders, *Operations Manual*, 67–72; 'FC Battle Orders' Sections C.1 through C.4, D.2 and D.4.

11 Price, *Battle of Britain Day*, 30.

12 Saunders, *Operations Manual*, 73–80; 'FC Battle Orders' Sections C.4 and D.2.

13 For Sector Intercept Procedures see 'FC Battle Orders' Sections

D.4 and D.5.

14 'FC Battle Orders' Sections C.4 and K.6.

15 Saunders, *Operations Manual*, 81.

16 'FC Battle Orders' Section D.2.

17 HW 5/1, 'Procedure in War Office for Dealing with J.Q. Information', 18 August 1940, 1–3.

18 Hinsley, 1.

19 Hinsley, 108.

CHAPTER VII

1 Trevor-Roper, 67.

2 Cull, *Battle for the Channel*, 25.

3 *Ibid.*, 18.

4 Cooper, 112; Hooten, *Phoenix*, 267.

5 Ansel, 114

6 *RAF Narrative*, Vol II, 32.

7 Saunders, *Peewit*, 19, 21–24.

8 Cull, *Battle for the Channel*, 26–30. Liensberger was KIA in the last great aerial engagement in the Battle of Britain, fought on 27 September 1940.

9 *Ibid.*, 28, Saunders, *Peewit*, 24.

10 Berenbrok, *Luftwaffe War Diaries*, 133.

11 *RAF Narrative*, Vol II, 32.

12 Cull, *Battle for the Channel*, 143.

13 Luftwaffe ObdL Lagebericht Nrs 309–316, 11–18 July 1940.

14 Cull, *Battle for the Channel*, 20, 21.

15 *Ibid.*, 24.

16 Berenbrok, *Luftwaffe War Diaries*, 130, 131.

17 *RAF Narrative*, Vol II, 44.

18 Boatner, 410–411.

19 Cull, *Battle for the Channel*, 39.

20 Cornwell, *Battle of Britain*, 320, 537, 538; Cull, *Battle for the Channel*, 39.

21 Cull, *Battle for the Channel*, 43, 44, 299. Also sunk that day was the 1,905grt Canadian cargo ship SS *Waterloo* returning from London in ballast.

22 *RAF Narrative*, Vol II, 3–6.

23 ErprGr 210 was established on 1 July 1940 to evaluate the Stuka's intended replacement, the twin-engine Messerschmitt Me 210, in the close-support role, but that type's terminal developmental problems resulted in the unit being equipped instead with bomb-carrying versions of the Luftwaffe's standard single- and twin-engine fighter types to prove the fighter-bomber concept and to develop equipment and tactics to make them more effective in the groundattack role. ErprGr 210 arrived at Denain (SE of Lille) on 13 July and was equipped with two squadrons of Bf 110C-6/D-0 and a third of Bf 109E-4/B Jabos. Zeng, *Ground-Attack Units*, 316.

24 Cull, *Battle for the Channel*, 107–110; *RAF Narrative, Vol II*, 35.

25 *RAF Narrative*, Vol II, 64, 65.

26 One of the damaged vessels was the Danish SS *Grønland* (1,264grt) which took refuge in Dover harbour where, on 29 July, it was sunk by air attack with the loss of 19 crewmen.

27 Cull, *Battle for the Channel*, 166–172; *RAF Narrative, Vol II*, 37–39.

28 CAB 101/240/2.

29 Cull, *Battle for the Channel*, 209.

30 Goss, *Fighter-Bombers*, 35. On 25 July, during another air raid,

31 *War Sepoy* was hit again, amidships, broke in two and burned out – the wreckage was used as anti-submarine blocks in the harbour entrance.

31 Cull, *Battle for the Channel*, 122, 137; *RAF Narrative*, Vol II, 42. On 21 July ErprGr 210 attacked a convoy off the Isle of Wight sinking the 2,318grt SS *Terlings*.

32 Cull, *Battle for the Channel*, 188, 189; Hewitt, 154–157.

33 *RAF Narrative*, Vol II, 74, 75.

34 The best source of detailed information about operations and combats pertaining to Convoy CW9 is Andy Saunders excellent *Convoy Peewit: Blitzkrieg from the Air and Sea 8 August 1940* (London: Grub Street, 2010). See pages 55–60.

35 *Ibid.*, 26, 31, 33–35.

36 *Ibid.*, 37–54; Cull, *Battle for the Channel*, 254.

37 Saunders, *Convoy Peewit*, 64–72.

38 *Ibid.*, 73, 74.

39 Mahlke, 120.

40 Saunders, *Peewit*, 66, 187; Cull, *Battle for the Channel*, 255.

41 Saunders, *Peewit*, 90, 91.

42 *Ibid.*, 77, 78.

43 *Ibid.*, 79, 80,113.

44 Cornwell, *Battle of Britain*, 339, 342, 344, 556, 557.

45 Saunders, *Peewit*, 205.

46 Cull, *Battle for the Channel*, 281, 282.

47 The Luftwaffe claimed 950,000 tons of shipping sunk during July. *Ibid.*, 281.

48 British sources state that a total of 67 merchant ships totalling 192,000grt were sunk 'in UK waters' during July 1940. *Ibid.*, 209.

CHAPTER VIII

1 Trevor-Roper, 75.

2 *Ibid.*, 75, 76. Ziegenberg Castle had been extensively renovated as Hitler's forward HQ for *Westfeldzug* with seven extensive underground concrete bunkers, above ground disguised as half-timbered cottages, built nearby at Wiesental and connected with each other and with the main castle by tunnels. Another local castle, Schloß Kransberg, was converted into a massive Luftwaffe 'operations' HQ for *Fall Gelb* and *Adlerangriff*.

3 *Ibid.*, 75, 78.

4 Taylor, *Breaking Wave*, 67–69, 210, 216, 219–221.

5 *Ibid.*, 70, 71, 212, 223, 224. Additionally, he ordered the postponement of the three service HQs' move to the Giessen area 'until immediately prior to the commencement of the operation'.

6 Trevor-Roper, 79, 80.

7 Also present were Milch, Udet, Grauert, Loerzer, Keller, Greim, Richthofen, Putzier, Coeler, Bodenschatz, Dessloch, Gritzbach, Kastner, Speidel, Weiss, and Witzig; and from the ObdL staff: Jeschonnek, Waldau, Seidel, Schmid, Kühl, and Martini.

8 Hooten, *Eagle*, 19–25.

9 Taylor, *Breaking Wave*, 127, 128.

10 *Ibid.*, 57, 93; Price, *Luftwaffe Data*, 13.

11 Taylor, *Breaking Wave*, 128, 129.

12 *Ibid.*, 129, 130. A copy of this message is located in the Maxwell AFB 'Karlsruhe Collection' file 'Westen-V-3g, Luftschlacht'.

13 There are references in at least one German archive document to

Kesselring and Sperrle disagreeing on some subject – most probably whether the RAF's destruction would result from bombing its airfields or in an airborne battle of attrition. However, this difference of opinion was set aside to address the fear of suffering heavy bomber losses in daylight attacks on RAF installations. Greiner, *OKW Kriegstagebuch*, 1 August 1940.

14 Osterkamp, 324–327.

15 Of the other Fliegerkorps commanders, Loerzer (II. Fliegerkorps) was a 44-victory World War I ace who had spent the inter-wars years in aviation-related businesses; Greim (V. Fliegerkorps) was a 28-victory World War I ace who had been a barnstormer, flight instructor in China, and was involved in German civil aviation before joining the new Luftwaffe, and Richthofen (VIII. Fliegerkorps) was an 8-victory ace who became an aeronautical engineer before joining the Reichswehr as a technical – rather than tactical – expert. Boatner, 194, 325, 455.

16 Deighton, 164.

17 Taylor, *Breaking Wave*, 71, 132, 340n65.

18 *Ibid.*, 132, 133.

19 *Ibid.*, 130, 133.

20 HW 5/1, 3.

21 Taylor, *Breaking Wave*, 225–230, 240–242.

22 These were for LZ B, XIII. AK's 17th and 35th Infantry Divisions and, for LZ C, VII. AK's 7th Infantry and 1st Mountain Divisions.

23 These were for LZ D, XXXVIII. AK's 26th and 34th Infantry Divisions and, for LZ E, VIII. AK's 28th Infantry and 6th Mountain Divisions and X. AK's 8th Infantry Division.

24 These would be facing, potentially, from Plymouth and Portsmouth the ancient battleship HMS *Revenge*, three cruisers, 27 destroyers, five French and Dutch torpedo boats, and 8 MTBs. Hewitt, 143, 144.

25 These would, potentially, be defending against – from Sheerness/Chatham, Harwich, and the Humber – five cruisers, 29 destroyers, one Norwegian torpedo boat, and 24 MTBs. *Ibid.*

26 Taylor, *Breaking Wave,* 238–244.

27 *Ibid.*, 264, 268.

28 Hooten, *Eagle in Flames*, 13.

29 Clayton, 39.

CHAPTER IX

1 Trevor-Roper, 79.

2 For all this day's actions, see Luftwaffe ObdL Lagebericht Nr 342, 13 August 1940. For this particular action, see *RAF Narrative*, 110–112; AIR 28/509 Lympne ORB, 12 August 1940.

3 The SEAD attacks on 12 August, as related in ObdL Lagebericht Nr 342, differ from the stylized account presented by Berenbrok, *Luftwaffe War Diaries*, pg 147. See also *RAF Narrative*, 113, 114. Additionally, at 1120hrs 22 Stukas (IV. (St)/LG 1), escorted by III./JG 26, attacked small convoys 'Agent' and 'Arena' off Margate, sinking two Admiralty trawlers.

4 *RAF Narrative*, 119–120; AIR 28/512 Manston ORB, 12 August 1940; Berenbrok, *Luftwaffe War Diaries*, 147.

5 *RAF Narrative*, 121–125; AIR 28/509 Hawkinge ORB, 12 August 1940;AIR 28/509 Lympne ORB, 12 August 1940;

6 All losses this date are from Cornwell, *Battle of Britain*, 352, 353, 561–563.

7 *RAF Narrative*, 116–118.

8 Bragg, 215–217.

9 Goss, *Fighters & Bombers*, 250–252.

10 Luftwaffe ObdL Lagebericht Nr 343, 14 August 1940; Berenbrok, *Luftwaffe War Diaries*, 151; *RAF Narrative*, 127–130; AIR 28/243 Eastchurch ORB, 13 August 1940. Two Do 17Zs attacked 'two small merchant ships' in Sheerness harbour, dropping 20 SC50s – no hits were scored.

11 All losses this date are from Cornwell, *Battle of Britain*, 354–356, 565–568.

12 Bungay, 208, 462; Vasco and Cornwell, *Zerstörer*, 79, 105, 106. While the information regarding Luftflotte 3's *Adlertag* operations is available in the surviving Luftflotte 3 records, traditional BoB histories typically fail to include it.

13 Boscombe Down was a former light bomber base (88, 150, and 218 Sqns with Fairey Battles) and home to the RAF's Aeroplane and Armament Experimental Establishment (A&AEE), Worthy Down was a former RAF station transferred to the Navy's FAA in 1939 and in mid-August it was home to NAS 806 Squadron equipped with Fairey Fulmar two-seat maritime reconnaissance fighters; Andover airfield was a pre-war light bomber base (12 Sqn with Fairey Battles) and home of HQ RAF Maintenance Command.

14 Vasco and Cornwell, *Zerstörer*, 109.

15 Berenbrok, *Luftwaffe War Diaries*, 152–154; Bungay, 208, 210; *RAF Narrative*, 131–137; AIR 28/32 Andover ORB, 13 August 1940.

16 *RAF Narrative*, 138–140; AIR 28/192 Detling ORB.

17 Berenbrok, *Luftwaffe War Diaries*, 154, 155.

18 Luftwaffe ObdL Lagebericht Nr 344, 15 August 1940; *RAF Narrative*, 144–150; Cornwell, *Battle of Britain*, 356, 357, 568–570; Vasco and Cornwell, *Zerstörer*, 113. Although reported in Lagebericht Nr 344, *RAF Narrative*, and other sources as occurring on 14 August, AIR 28/512 Manston ORB, which appears to have been retyped, mistakenly attributes this day's attack to 15 August.

19 Cornwell, *Battle of Britain*, 334–354; Mason, 246. Additionally, in No 10 Group, 238 Sqn was withdrawn from Middle Wallop to St Eval, being replaced in Y Sector by 249 Sqn which brought 20 Hurricanes from Church Fenton (No. 12 Group) to Boscombe Down.

20 Franks, 101.

21 Berenbrok, *Luftwaffe War Diaries*, 155, 156. All this day's actions are from Luftwaffe ObdL Lagebericht Nr 345, 16 August 1940, supplemented as noted.

22 Brooks, 154, 180, 182; *RAF Narrative*, 152–154; AIR 28/345 Hawkinge, 15 August 1940; AIR 28/509 Lympne, 15 August 1940.

23 *RAF Narrative*, 154–163; AIR 28/225 Driffield, 15 August 1940.

24 *RAF Narrative*, 163–170; AIR 28/243 Eastchurch, 15 August 1940; AIR 28/526 Martlesham Heath, 15 August 1940; Mason, 257, 258.

25 *RAF Narrative*, 171–176; AIR 28/545 Middle Wallop, 15 August 1940; AIR 28/622 Odiham, 15 August 1940; Bungay, 216.

26 *RAF Narrative*, 177–180; AIR 28/178 Croydon, 15 August

1940; AIR 28/907 West Malling, 15 August 1940; Brooks, 130.

27 All losses this date are from Cornwell, *Battle of Britain*, 357–360, 571–575.

28 Brooks, 54, 55.

29 AIR 28/907 West Malling ORB, 16 August 1940. All this day's actions are from Luftwaffe ObdL Lagebericht Nr 346, 17 August 1940

30 *RAF Narrative*, 182–185; Berenbrok, *Luftwaffe War Diaries*, 164.

31 Bragg, 217.

32 *RAF Narrative*, 185–188; AIR 28/315 Gosport ORB, 16 August 1940; AIR 28/815 Tangmere ORB, 16 August 1940; Berenbrok, *Luftwaffe War Diaries*, 164; Brooks, 208; Bungay, 222; Deighton, 175; Mason, 213, 214, 216.

33 *RAF Narrative*, 188–195; AIR 28/315 Gosport ORB, 16 August 1940; Brooks, 108; Deighton, 175; Mason, 211, 214, 216–218.

CHAPTER X

1 As translated in *Moltke on the Art of War: Selected Writings* by Daniel J. Hughes (ed., trans.) and Harry Bell (trans.), (Novato, CA: Presidio Press, 1993) p. 92.

2 Cornwell, *Battle of Britain*, 366, 580; Luftwaffe ObdL Lagebericht Nr 347, 17 August 1940. The only combat loss over England/Channel this day/night was that of a Ju 88C night intruder from 4./NJG 1, which was not a part of Luftflotte 2 or 3. Erroneously the victim is frequently reported as an He 111 from II./KG 53.

3 Osterkamp, 325.

4 The best source of information about the combats of this day is the book by the same name. For further detail, descriptions and analysis, please read Dr Alfred Price's excellent *Battle of Britain The Hardest Day*, 18 August 1940 (London: Arms and Armour Press, 1988).

5 All this day's actions are from Luftwaffe ObdL Lagebericht Nr 348, 19 August 1940, supplemented as noted. *RAF Narrative*, 197, 198.

6 Caldwell, *JG 26 War Diary*, 59.

7 *RAF Narrative*, 197–203; AIR 28/64 Biggin Hill ORB, 18 August 1940; AIR 28/419 Kenley ORB, 18 August 1940; AIR 28/907 West Malling ORB, 18 August 1940.

8 NAS 829 was in the process of converting to new Fairey Albacore torpedo bombers. The attack destroyed five ancient Blackburn Sharks, five obsolete Fairey Swordfish, and two Albacores.

9 *RAF Narrative*, 197–203; AIR 28/315 Gosport ORB, 18 August 1940; AIR 28/838 Thorney Island ORB, 18 August 1940.

10 *RAF Narrative*, 208–214.

11 All losses this date are from Cornwell, *Battle of Britain*, 366–372, 581–591. Luftwaffe ObdL Lagebericht Nr 348, 19 August 1940.

12 The planning for the Warmwell raids probably began on 17 August (the 'stand–down day' between *Adlerangriff*'s Stage 1 and 2) because we know from preserved ULTRA reports that the Warmwell raid 'tasking order' was sent from Sperrle's Paris HQ to IV. and V. Fliegerkorps HQs in the early morning hours of 19 August.

13 According to Luftwaffe ObdL Lagebericht Nr 349, 19 August 1940, the only missions flown that day were seven insignificant – one bomber each – 'nuisance attacks' each dropping 1,000kg of bombs on a wide assortment of minor airfields from 1330–1815hrs with another seven one-plane raids on factories and nine others attempting to bomb various fuel and grain storage facilities, railway stations, military camps, and dockyards. Needless to say, accuracy was wanting and damage negligible.

14 The actual number of Hurricanes and Spitfires lost in combat from July 1 to August 16 was 214.

15 Anlage 5 zum (Attachment 5 to) Lagebericht Nr 345, 16 August 1940, pg 2.

16 With the resulting transfer and realignment of units, on 7 September, Kesselring's Luftflotte 2 totalled 398 twin-engined bombers, 669 Bf 109Es, 163 Stukas, and 184 Bf 110s. Battistelli, 21.

CHAPTER XI

1 Cooper, 142.

2 During the period 19–23 August, Luftflotten 2 and 3 flew 594 bomber and reconnaissance sorties, averaging only 119 per day. In addition to the bombing of convoys 'Topaz' and 'Totem' on 22 August, the only noteworthy missions were against Eastchurch airfield (20 August, KG 3 dropped 13.6 tons of bombs) and Manston (22 August by ErprGr 210). The only fighter missions flown were on these two days, totalling 540 sorties and claiming 19 Spitfires shot down. Actually, RAF Fighter Command lost eight Spitfires and one Hurricane during this 5-day period. Luftwaffe ObdL Lagebericht Nrs 349–353, 19–23 August 1940; AIR 28/512 Eastchurch ORB, 20 August 1940; AIR 28/512 Manston ORB, 22 August 1940.

3 JaFü 1 bears no relation to *Jagdfliegerführer Deutsche Bucht* (Fighter Command German Bight) at Jever, which is sometimes erroneously referred to as JaFü 1.

4 AIR 25/197, Group Controllers Instruction No 4, 19 August 1940.

5 Luftwaffe ObdL Lagebericht Nrs 354, 25 August 1940; *RAF Narrative*, 242–249; AIR 28/512 Manston ORB, 24 August 1940.

6 Ramsey, *Battle of Britain*, 147.

7 *RAF Narrative*, 249–253; AIR 28/384 Hornchurch ORB, 24 August 1940; AIR 28/603 North Weald ORB, 24 August 1940.

8 All losses this day are from Cornwell, *Battle of Britain*, 374–377, 593–597.

9 *RAF Narrative*, 253–255.

10 Luftwaffe ObdL Lagebericht Nr 355, 26 August 1940.

11 *RAF Narrative*, 272. Note that the use of Verey lights (flares) indicates that the Bf 110s and Bf 109Es were not on the same radio frequency/channel – a hindrance to effective co-operation between the two fighter formations.

12 Weal, *Jagdgeschwader 53*, 29, 30.

13 *RAF Narrative*, 270–272; AIR 28/888 Warmwell ORB, 25 August 1940.

14 All losses this day are from Cornwell, *Battle of Britain*, 379–382, 597, 598.

15 Luftwaffe ObdL Lagebericht Nr 356, 27 August 1940. Obstlt Hans Korte took command of KG 55 on 15 August, the day

after Oberst Stoeckl was KIA after attacking Middle Wallop.

16　There was no reaction from Warmwell, still recovering as it was from the previous day's pounding.

17　*RAF Narrative*, 283–286.

18　Deichmann, xvii

19　Given command of JG 3 the day before, Lützow was promoted to major on 30 August 1940.

20　Luftwaffe ObdL Lagebericht Nr 356, 27 August 1940; *RAF Narrative*, 275–277. All losses this day are from Cornwell, *Battle of Britain*, 383–385, 598–600.

21　Balke, 121.

22　AIR 28/187 Debden ORB, 26 August 1940.

23　*RAF Narrative*, 278–282.

24　Braatz, 227.

25　AIR 25/197, Group Controllers Instructions No 6 and 7, 26 and 27 August 1940.

26　Luftwaffe ObdL Lagebericht Nr 358, 29 August 1940; *RAF Narrative*, 288–293; AIR 28/243 Eastchurch ORB, 28 August 1940. Rochford has no ORB, see Ramsey, *Battle of Britain*, 156.

27　All losses this day are from Cornwell, *Battle of Britain*, 386–390, 603–604.

28　Kesselring, 70.

29　Luftwaffe ObdL Lagebericht Nr 359, 30 August 1940; *RAF Narrative*, 294; Cornwell, *Battle of Britain*, 390, 391, 605.

30　Mason, 508.

31　Taylor, *Breaking Wave*, 184.

32　Luftwaffe records for 30 August 1940 are lacking strength and unit information – all strengths given are from RAF reports that, since Luftflotte 2 flew only 80 bomber sorties this date, seem in all cases to be exaggerated.

33　Luftwaffe ObdL Lagebericht Nr 360, 31 August 1940; *RAF Narrative*, 296–306; AIR 28/64 Biggin Hill ORB, 30 August 1940; AIR 28/192 Detling ORB, 30 August 1940.

34　All losses this day are from Cornwell, *Battle of Britain*, 391–395, 607–609.

35　Luftwaffe ObdL Lagebericht Nr 361, 1 September 1940; *RAF Narrative*, 307–321; AIR 28/64 Biggin Hill ORB, 31 August 1940; AIR 28/178 Croydon ORB 31 August 1940; AIR 28/187 Debden ORB, 31 August 1940; AIR 28/234 Duxford ORB 31 August 1940; AIR 28/243 Eastchurch ORB, 31 August 1940; AIR 28/384 Hornchurch ORB 31 August 1940; Caldwell, 65. All losses this day are from Cornwell, *Battle of Britain*, 396–403, 609–613.

36　AIR 28/64 Biggin Hill ORB, 1 September 1940; *RAF Narrative*, 325–327.

37　Cornwell, *Battle of Britain*, 405.

38　Bungay, 283.

39　AIR 28/64 Biggin Hill ORB, 6 September 1940.

40　Luftwaffe ObdL Lagebericht Nrs 362–367, 2 through 6 September 1940; AIR 28/419 Kenley ORB, 1 September 1940.

41　AIR 19/60, Park's report to Fighter Command HQ, 12 September 1940, 6, 7.

42　Bungay, 290; Cooper, 144, 145–147; Taylor, *Breaking Wave*, 149.

CHAPTER XII

1　Cooper, 151.

2　Luftwaffe ObdL Lagebericht Nr 354, 25 August 1940; Irving, 115.

3　Luftwaffe ObdL Lagebericht Nrs 354–363, 25 August – 3 September 1940.

4　De Zeng, *Bomber Units*, 73–87, 115–122, 250–260.

5　Taylor, *Breaking Wave*, 152. This flawed information was passed direct to OKW staff by ObdL liaison officer Major Sigismund von Falkenstein on 3 September.

6　Hooten, *Eagle*, 24. Actually his revised estimate was not far off. On 1 September Dowding had 593 serviceable Hurricanes and Spitfires on strength (200 more were in squadron maintenance or under repair) with 127 in 'ready reserve' at depots and 160 'nearly finished' at the factories. Of the operational Hurricanes and Spitfires, 462 (344 serviceable) were stationed in No. 10 and 11 Groups. On 7 September, Luftflotte 2 had 623 operational Bf 109Es, of 787 total. Cooper, 151–153.

7　There is no contemporary account of this meeting extant. This description is from Berenbrok, 171, 172, Deichmann's discussion in USAF HRA Study No. 163, Klee's HRA Study No. 157. See also Taylor, *Breaking Wave*, 157, and Hooten, *Eagle*, 25, 26.

8　Berenbrok, *Luftwaffe War Diaries*, 171, 172. In this last opinion, as evidenced by Park's instructions to his Station Commanders, he was certainly correct – No. 11 Group command and control functions were not going to withdraw from its sector stations even if fighter squadrons had to be evacuated from non-operational airfields, the flying units would be returned as soon as the airfield could be repaired and rendered serviceable once again.

9　Luftwaffe ObdL Lagebericht Nr 367, 7 September 1940.

10　Cooper, 149, 151–153; Taylor, *Breaking Wave*, 158. During the morning Luftwaffe operations were limited to a 'freie Jagd' sweep by 50 Bf 109Es at 1100 followed 30 minutes later by another 'Jabo' strike by 12 Bf 109s against Hawkinge. *RAF Narrative*, 405.

11　Docherty, 118.

12　Vasco and Cornwell, 194–196.

13　*RAF Narrative*, 406–411.

14　*RAF Narrative*, 406.

15　Surviving documentation confirms that II. and III./KG 2 launched 51 Do 17Zs on this mission – I./KG 2's participation is not recorded. Chris Goss, email 11 July 2019.

16　Luftwaffe ObdL Lagebericht Nr 368, 7 September 1940; *RAF Narrative*, 411–415.

17　All losses this day are from Cornwell *Battle of Britain*, 424–437, 636–639.

18　These included KG 27 (35 ac), KG 51 (32ac), KG 54 (3 ac), KG 55 (42 ac), LG 1 (26 ac), KGr 100 (8ac) and KGr 606 (19 ac), plus one bomber each from KGr 806 and Stab/StG 3. Chris Goss, email 12 July 2019.

19　Luftwaffe ObdL Lagebericht Nr 368, 7 September 1940.

20　Graduating PhD from University of Munich in 1929, Weißauer became a lawyer, jurist, and legal counsel for the German Stage [Performers'] Union. Commissioned as an agent for the *Reichssicherheitshauptamt* (Reinhard Heydrich's 'Reich Security Head Bureau, an office under Heinrich Himmler's SS) ten years later, he travelled in Finland and Sweden attempting to advance Hitler's racial and foreign policy agendas.

21　The National Archives, CAB 65/15/3.

22　Luftwaffe ObdL Lagebericht Nr 369 and 370, 8 and 9 September 1940; *RAF Narrative*, 427–436.

23 Cooper, 154; Hooten, *Eagle*, 26.

24 Luftwaffe ObdL Lagebericht Nr 371, 10 September 1940; Cornwell, *Battle of Britain*, 636.

25 Luftwaffe ObdL Lagebericht Nr 372, 11 September 1940; *RAF Narrative*, 447–445.

26 The National Archives, CAB 65/15/3.

27 Luftwaffe ObdL Lagebericht Nr 372, 11 September 1940.

28 Luftwaffe ObdL Lagebericht Nr 373, 12 September 1940.

29 Luftwaffe ObdL Lagebericht Nr 374, 13 September 1940.

30 *RAF Narrative*, 449.

31 *Ibid.*, 450–453; Cornwell, *Battle of Britain*, 447, 448; Bergström, 211.

32 The best source of detailed information about operations and combats of this day is Dr Alfred Price's excellent *Battle of Britain Day 15 September 1940* (London: Sidgewick & Jackson, 1990). This quote is found on page 28.

33 The National Archives AIR 25/197, 11 Group ORB, September 1939–September 1940: Group Controllers Instruction No 10, 5 September 1940.

34 Accompanying this strike, II.(Schl)/LG 2 launched 21 Bf 109E-7 Jabos that overflew Lindmayr's bomber formation and scattered 5.8 tons of SC250s at various random locations in London. One aircraft was shot down over Ashford during ingress, pilot captured.

35 Luftwaffe ObdL Lagebericht Nr 376, 15 September 1940; *RAF Narrative*, 453–460; All losses this day are from *Battle of Britain*, 449–456, 640–647.

36 Berenbrok, *Luftwaffe War Diaries*, 174, 175. On 15 September, Luftflotte 2 possessed approximately 620 Bf 109E fighters that flew 769 sorties, resulting in 1.24 sorties per aircraft, so at least a quarter of the *Jagdwaffe* units flew two missions that day. Price, *Battle of Britain Day*, 135.

37 Price, *Battle of Britain Day*, 79.

38 *RAF Narrative*, 460–467.

39 *Ibid.*, 89.

40 Caldwell, *JG 26 Top Guns*, 60.

41 Of which '12 Group Wing' squadrons claimed a combined total of 17 bombers and 9 fighters destroyed.

42 RAF Fighter Command lost nine Hurricanes and three Spitfires shot down, half of them to Bf 109Es. The *Jagdwaffe* lost 16 'Emils' to defending fighters, with three more ditching or crashing in France due to fuel exhaustion. Another was shot down by British AA fire.

43 Both quotes are from Price, *Battle of Britain Day*, 129.

44 Luftwaffe ObdL Lagebericht Nr 376, 15 September 1940. With only two days remaining before initiating *Seelöwe*, Sperrle launched 27 He 111Ps (III./KG 55) to attack Portland naval base and fuel storage depot. Of 40 tons of bombs and 16 incendiary canisters dropped, only five bombs fell within the naval installations. Only six Spitfires (152 Sqn) intercepted and shot down one Heinkel. This was followed by 10 Bf 110 and three Bf 109E Jabos (ErprGr 210) making a surprise low-level attack on Vickers-Supermarine's Spitfire factory at Woolston – no hits were scored and no losses suffered. Additionally, the following night, Sperrle launched 181 effective bomber sorties, dropping 247 tons of bombs and 279 incendiary canisters on London.

45 Bergström, 222.

46 Cooper, 151–153; Taylor, *Breaking Wave*, 165, 166.

47 Price, *Battle of Britain Day*, 121–125. After the war, corrected the 'error' reducing the claim to 60 German aircraft destroyed on 15 September, a number very close to accurate, but by this time no one in the UK really cared for the truth in the matter.

48 Price, *Battle of Britain Day*, 18, 19. Balancing the British sense of – and penchant for – high drama, German historians do not share the opinion that 'Battle of Britain Day' represents some sort of decisive climax in the Luftwaffe's ongoing bombing campaign. To quote Horst Boog, for instance, '15 September, the turning of the Battle in the British view, does not occur as such in the German table of events.' *Burning Blue*, 39.

CHAPTER XIII

1 Cooper, 157.

2 Bergström, 221.

3 Osterkamp, 325.

4 Bergström, 221.

5 Balke, 176.

6 Luftwaffe ObdL Lagebericht Nrs 377 and 378, 17 and 18 September 1940.

7 Luftwaffe ObdL Lagebericht Nrs 379, 19 September 1940.

8 *RAF Narrative*, 473–478.

9 All losses this day are from Cornwell, *Battle of Britain*, 459, 461, 651, 652.

10 Luftwaffe ObdL Lagebericht Nrs 380–387, 20–27 September 1940.

11 The best source of detailed information about plans, operations, and combats on 'The Filton Raid' is Kenneth Wakefield's excellent *Luftwaffe Encore: A Study of Two Attacks in September 1940* (London: William Kimber, 1979).

12 Luftwaffe ObdL Lagebericht Nr 384, 24 September 1940.

13 Friedrich Kless was the brother of Max Kless, III./KG 77, KIA on 18 September 1940.

14 *RAF Narrative*, 483–486, and Luftwaffe ObdL Lagebericht Nr 386, 26 September 1940, which adds 'Owing to weather conditions it is generally impossible to carry out daylight attacks [on London]'; Luftflotte 2 reported 'One aircraft only dropped 1,000kgs of bombs by dead reckoning navigation, while the remainder either attacked alternative targets or broke off the operation'.

15 All losses this day are from Cornwell, *Battle of Britain*, 466, 467, 658, 659.

16 Wakefield, *Luftwaffe Encore*, 102.

17 Luftwaffe ObdL Lagebericht Nr 387, 27 September 1940, and *RAF Narrative*, 488–491. All losses this day are from Cornwell, *Battle of Britain*, 467, 468, 660.

18 Luftwaffe ObdL Lagebericht Nr 388, 28 September 1940 and *RAF Narrative*, 491–503.

19 All losses this day are from Cornwell, *Battle of Britain*, 468–479, 660–665. German losses included seven (of ten) Bf 110C/Ds and 15 aircrew – including Gruppenkommandeur Hptm Horst Liensberger – from V.(Z)/LG 1. The horrendous attrition suffered by this unit was so severe that it was disbanded and surviving personnel became the basis for I./NJG 3.

20 Luftwaffe ObdL Lagebericht Nrs 389 and 390, 29 and 30 September 1940. Luftflotte 3 fighter sweeps by 42 Bf 110s (ZG 26) and 53 Bf 109Es (JGs 2 and 53) on 28 September engaged three Hurricane squadrons (213, 238, and 607 Sqns) and shot

down six defenders (five pilots killed) for no losses.

21   Luftwaffe ObdL Lagebericht Nr 391, 1 October 1940.

22   *RAF Narrative*, 505–517.

23   All losses this day are from Cornwell, *Battle of Britain*, 486–490, 666–670.

24   Officially, for the RAF the Battle of Britain ended on 31 October 1940, although the Luftwaffe's 'night blitz' campaign against British cities continued until May 21, 1941 when the Luftwaffe transferred its remaining bomber units eastwards for Operation *Barbarossa*, the Nazi invasion of the Soviet Union.

25   Boatner, 315.

26   Wakefield, *Luftwaffe Encore*, 156–193.

27   Goss, *Fighter-Bombers*, 38–41; de Zeng, *Ground-Attack Units*, 175, 317, 318. ErprGr 210's Bf 109-equipped 3. Staffel was detached to II.(Schl)/LG 2 on 15 September and operated with Weiss's unit thereafter, eventually being incorporated into JG 51. It was replaced in December by a new 3./ErprGr 210 equipped with new, specially designed Bf 110E ground-attack aircraft. In April 1941, the group became I./ Schnellkampfgeschwader (SKG, Fast Bomber Wing) 210 and – with the newly formed II. Gruppe (from III./ZG 76) – was transferred to Radzyn, Poland, for Operation *Barbarossa*. De Zeng, *Ground-Attack Units*, 318, 331.

28   Goss, *Fighter-Bombers*, 43, 47–52.

29   The best source of detailed information about plans, operations, and combats on Luftwaffe electronic bombing aids, night-bombing operations and RAF ECM is Ken Wakefield's excellent *Pfadfinder: Luftwaffe Pathfinder Operations over Britain, 1940–44* (Stroud: Tempus Publishing, 1999). Wakefield, *Pathfinder*, 1.

30   *Ibid.*, 2.

31   Taylor, *Breaking Wave*, 158.

CHAPTER XIV

1   Taylor, *Breaking Wave*, 79.

2   AIR 28/64 Biggin Hill ORB, 12 September 1940.

3   AIR 19/60, AVM Park's report to Fighter Command HQ SASO, 12 September 1940, 6, 7.

4   Kesselring, 71.

5   Galland, 37.

6   North, 232.

7   AIR 20/5202, A.M. 'Note On Despatch By ACM Sir Hugh C.T. Dowding', October 1941.

INDEX

Page numbers in **bold** refer to illustrations.